U.S.-MEXICO RELATIONS: LABOR MARKET INTERDEPENDENCE

CONTRIBUTORS

Rafael Alarcón

Francisco Alba

Sandra O. Archibald

Jeffrey Avina

Jeffrey Bortz

Jorge A. Bustamante

Jorge Chapa

Leo R. Chávez

Wayne A. Cornelius

Manuel García y Griego

Bernardo González-Aréchiga

Peter Gregory

David E. Hayes-Bautista

Thomas Heller

Raúl A. Hinojosa Ojeda

Robert K. McCleery

Richard Mines

Rebecca Morales

Thomas Muller

Clark W. Reynolds

David Runsten

Saskia Sassen

Werner O. Schink

Robert C. Smith

Saul Trejo Reyes

Sponsored by the Project on
U.S.-Mexico Relations

U.S.-Mexico Relations

LABOR MARKET
INTERDEPENDENCE

Edited by
Jorge A. Bustamante, Clark W. Reynolds,
and Raúl A. Hinojosa Ojeda

STANFORD UNIVERSITY PRESS, STANFORD, CALIFORNIA

U.S.-Mexico Relations: Labor Market Interdependence is sponsored by the
Project on U.S.-Mexico Relations

The editors of this volume wish to acknowledge the work of Laura Elisa Pérez,
who translated all those chapters that were originally in Spanish

Stanford University Press, Stanford, California
© 1992 by the Board of Trustees of the
Leland Stanford Junior University
Printed in the United States of America

CIP data appear at the end of the book

Preface

This volume is one of a continuing series published under the auspices of the U.S.-Mexico Relations Project, which was founded in 1980 in order to coordinate the efforts of U.S. and Mexican experts in the areas of political development, economic growth and trade, energy resources, agriculture and rural development, and employment and labor markets. Administrative coordination of the project is located at the Americas Program, Stanford University, and the Center for Economic Studies, El Colegio de México. All workshops, conferences, sponsored research, publication, and outreach are organized and funded jointly by the coordinating institutions in each country, on the basis of full binational support, to ensure that the goals and perspectives of participants from each country are part of the research agenda, and to give each participant an opportunity to be fully critiqued by members from the other partner country.

The overwhelming success of the U.S.-Mexico Project, which as early as 1979 sponsored policy research on the benefits and costs of closer Mexico-U.S. economic integration, and with the active encouragement of scholars from the University of Toronto, caused the Americas Program to expand its focus to include Canada by the mid-1980s. This led to the establishment of a North American Project coordinated by Stanford's Americas Program, El Colegio de México, and the Centre for International Studies of the University of Toronto. This unique trinational effort led to a number of publications including the most recent volume, *The Dynamics of North American Trade and Investment: Canada, Mexico, and the United States* (Stanford, 1991).

The Americas Program is designed to cooperate with institutions and scholars from Europe, Asia, and other regions to explore the political economy of increased economic interdependence in the Americas in global perspective. Hemisphere-wide economic and technological integration, including freer economic exchange at the subregional level, are studied in the context of global economic liberalization. The first effort to go beyond the North American experience was a series of workshops and a major Stanford Centennial Conference on *Technology Policy in the Americas*, as a cooperative effort with the Institute of the Americas in La Jolla, Calif. The project involved academics, public, and private sector representatives from Europe, Asia, and the Americas at a watershed in North-South technology policy, with dramatic consequences for development in the next century.

The research in this volume, *U.S.-Mexico Relations: Labor Market Interdependence*, has been accumulating over a period of five years, from the conception of the project at a gathering of policymakers and researchers in Mexico City in September 1986. Some of the most important thinkers in economics, multinational investment, demographics, migration, Mexican and U.S. labor history, the *maquiladora* industries, and politics came together that autumn to discuss the effects of policies such as the (proposed) "Simpson-Rodino" legislation before the U.S. Congress, and to provide a conceptual framework on which further conferences and working groups could be built.

The organizers (and editors of this volume) argued on the basis of ongoing research and policy analysis that migration, trade, investment, and technology transfer between the U.S. and Mexico reflect increasing "labor market interdependence" between the two countries. Studies were designed to test the extent to which decision-making involving economic exchange between the two countries to be effective would have to deal with the underlying causes of exchange (including migration) rather than their symptoms.

A unique opportunity to test this hypothesis presented itself with the passing of the U.S. Immigration Reform and Control Act of 1986 (the amended "Simpson-Rodino" bill), only days after the September 1986 conference, entitled Labor Market Interdependence Between the United States and Mexico. Since that time labor market relations between the United States and Canada have evolved to reflect the peculiar contradictions between the interests of businesses in both countries (including *maquila* industries), organized labor, and the social and political forces underlying the migration policies espoused by each nation. For example, the more permanent settlement of Mexican migrants clashes with the increasingly xenophobic sentiment of U.S. white voters, yet U.S. service industries are seeking more migrants each year to work at low wages and for uncertain durations.

Some of the research in this volume deals with the underlying economic and social conditions of binational labor market interdependence, at the macro- and micro-economic level, as historical background. Other studies address experiences since 1986, which indicate that IRCA has made little impact on the volume of migration between Mexico and the United States, suggesting that approaches are needed that deal with the basic labor market conditions in both countries and their relationship to competitiveness and productivity growth, rather than their migratory symptoms. Such considerations underscore the decision by administrations in both the United States and Mexico (and Canada) to begin negotiations on a North American Free Trade Agreement that stresses liberalization of trade and investment rather than migration. But underlying both are the social conditions implicit in increased economic exchange among the three countries. This study is of fundamental importance to those interested in issues that relate to (and go beyond) the negotiation of a North American Free Trade Agreement, the process of which has begun at the time this volume goes to press (Fall, 1991).

The editors express strong appreciation to those institutions and individuals who have provided support for the U.S.-Mexico Project during the period of the Labor Market Interdependence activities, including in particular the William and Flora Hewlett Foundation, the Mellon Foundation, the Rockefeller Foundation, and the Tinker Foundation, as well as the Ministry of Industry and Commerce of Mexico, El Colegio de México, Stanford University, and the University of Toronto. Recent work on the employment impact of U.S.-Mexico integration has been supported by the Fraser Institute with funding from the Lilly Endowment, Inc. Appreciation is expressed to The MacArthur Foundation for support of Americas Program research on *The Political Economy of Interdependence in the Americas* and to the Ford Foundation for work on employment and migration aspects of agriculture and rural development.

Particular appreciation is expressed to Clint Smith for ideas and inspiration from the beginning of the project, to Julie Carlson for her exceptional editorial assistance on this manuscript, and to Denise Gilbert, Kevin Richardson, and other members of the Americas Program staff, including those who worked on early aspects of the project. Raúl Hinojosa, then an Americas Program research fellow, played an important role in the convening of workshops and conferences on labor market interdependence during the early years of this project. Tom Heller, an original co-coordinator of the project, has also been faithfully involved from its conception. We wish to express our feelings of respect, admiration, and collegiality in memorial to Matthew Edel, who worked with U.S. and Mexican colleagues from the earliest stages of this project until close to the end. His life and work symbolized a commitment to the spirit of inclusiveness and social justice essential to the stability of development with interdependence in the Americas.

J.A.B.
C.W.R.
R.A.H.O.

Contents

III. MIGRATION AND LOCAL COMMUNITIES IN THE UNITED STATES AND MEXICO

IV. SECTORAL DYNAMICS AND INTERDEPENDENCE

Contents

Contributors

RAFAEL ALARCÓN is a Mexican Research Investigator in Social Anthropology at El Colegio de Jalisco and a doctoral student at the University of California, Berkeley. He has written professional articles on Mexican migration to the United States and co-authored the volume *Return to Aztlán: The Social Process of International Migration from Western Mexico* (1987).

FRANCISCO ALBA, an economist and demographer, is Professor at El Colegio de México. His research interests include development economics, international migration, effects of demographic change, and labor markets. He has published on these issues in Mexican and international journals as well as in numerous collective books. His book *The Population of Mexico: Trends, Issues and Policies* (1982) has been translated from Spanish into English.

SANDRA O. ARCHIBALD is a Production and Resource Economist with the Food Research Institute at Stanford University. Her research focuses on the interaction of agricultural technology, natural resource use, and regulatory policy. She has served as Consultant to the National Academy of Sciences, the Environmental Protection Agency, the Department of the Interior, various state and federal agencies, and private industry on environmental and health policies for pesticides. She also has led a study for the University of California Agricultural Issues Center on chemicals in the human food chain.

JEFFREY M. AVINA is Consultant for the Inter-American Foundation, and leads a four-person team researching the problems faced by NGO's within the context of development work in the third world. He has a Law degree from Harvard University, a masters degree in Public Administration from the Kennedy School of Government, and a masters degree in International Development Education from Stanford University. His publications include "Maternity Rights in Turkey" (1988); "At the Frontier Beyond All Borders: Health Care in Czechoslovakia" (1986); and "Illegal Workers, Blight or Blessing?" (1984).

JEFFREY BORTZ is Associate Professor of History at Appalachian State University. He has published a number of books and articles on Mexican economic and labor history, including *Industrial Wages in Mexico City, 1939–1975* (1987) and *El Salario en México* (1986). He also co-authored *Schulden Krise, In Der Dritten Welt Tickt Eine Zeitbombe* (1987).

JORGE A. BUSTAMANTE is President of El Colegio de la Frontera Norte and holds the Eugene Conley Endowed Sociology Chair at the University of Notre Dame. He has published over one hundred scientific papers on Mexico-U.S. migration, and for the past ten years he has written a weekly column, "Frontera Norte" for the Mexican daily, *Excelsior*. His expertise in labor migration has led to several in-depth interviews on ABC Television, Nightline, and the MacNeil-Lehrer Report.

JORGE CHAPA is Assistant Professor at the Lyndon B. Johnson School of Public Affairs. He holds degrees in Biology, Sociology, and Demography, and is co-author of *The Burden of Support: Young Latinos in an Aging Society* (1988). His current research and publications focus on Hispanics' low rates of education and lack of occupational and economic mobility and emphasize the development of policies to improve these prospects.

LEO R. CHÁVEZ received his Ph.D. in 1982 from Stanford University. He joined the Center for U.S.-Mexican Studies in 1980, first as a staff member and then as a Research Associate. He has also served as Research Associate at El Colegio de la Frontera Norte. Currently Associate Professor of Anthropology at the University of California, Irvine, his publications include "Mexican Immigration and Health Care: A Political Economy Perspective," *Human Organization* (1986); and "Coresidence and Resistance: Strategies for Survival Among Undocumented Mexicans and Central Americans," *Urban Anthropology* (1990).

WAYNE A. CORNELIUS is the Gildred Professor of U.S.-Mexican Relations and founding Director of the Center for U.S.-Mexican Studies at the University of California, San Diego. A political scientist (Ph.D., Stanford University), he has conducted field research in Mexico since 1962, and has published extensively on Mexican migration to the United States, rural-to-urban migration in Mexico, and the Mexican political system. His most recent books are *Mexico's Alternative Political Futures* (co-editor, 1989) and *Mexican Migration to the United States: Process, Consequences, and Policy Options* (co-editor, 1990).

MANUEL GARCÍA Y GRIEGO is Researcher and Professor at the Center for International Studies, El Colegio de México, Mexico City. A historian and demographer, Professor García y Griego's work has focused on Mexican migration to the United States and U.S.-Mexican relations. His contribution to this volume was written while a visiting fellow at the Center for U.S.-Mexican Studies at the University of California, San Diego.

BERNARDO GONZÁLEZ-ARÉCHIGA is a member of the Department of Economics at El Colegio de la Frontera Norte. He is currently in his sabbatical year acting as Planning Director for the Bolsa Mexicana de Valores (the Mexican stock exchange). Some of his recent publications include *Subcontracion internacional y empresas trasnacionales* (1990), which he co-edited; "Maquiladoras e intercambio de servicios" (1991), a co-authored publication for the United Nations; and "La paradoja del crecimiento hacia afuera, 1960–1989" (1991).

PETER GREGORY is currently Professor of Economics at the University of New Mexico. He holds a Ph.D. from Harvard University, and his professional interests have centered on labor market operations and employment policy issues in developing countries. Among his publications are *The Myth of Market Failure: Employment and the Labor Market in Mexico* (1986); *Wages, Productivity, and Industrialization in Puerto Rico* (with L. G. Reynolds, 1986); and *Industrial Wages in Chile* (1967).

DAVID E. HAYES-BAUTISTA, Ph.D., is Professor in the Department of Medicine (Division of General Internal Medicine) and Director of the Chicano Research Center at the University of California, Los Angeles. He is the author of over fifty papers, books, and monographs on the topic of Latino health policy. He is the senior author of *The Burden of Support: Young Latinos in an Aging Society* (1988), which has been released recently in paperback.

THOMAS HELLER is Professor of Law at Stanford and is Deputy Director of the university's Institute for International Studies. Professor Heller's primary research in recent years has dealt with the political economy of information-intensive sectors and specifically with multinational investment, technology transfer, and the structure of international labor markets. He has taught at various institutions in Latin America and Western Europe.

RAÚL A. HINOJOSA OJEDA is Assistant Professor at the Graduate School of Urban Planning at the University of California, Los Angeles. He received his Ph.D. in Political Science at the University of Chicago in August 1989. He is coauthor of *Latinos in a Changing U.S. Economy: Comparative Perspectives on the U.S. Labor Market Since 1939* (1989) and author of various articles on debt, trade, and immigration relations between the United States, Mexico, and other Latin American countries. He is currently writing a book on the political economy of U.S.-Mexico relations, including the recent move toward a free trade agreement.

ROBERT K. MCCLEERY is a Research Associate with the Institute for Economic Development and Policy at the East-West Center in Honolulu, Hawaii. He has worked closely with Clark Reynolds, studying and writing about U.S.-Mexico economic interdependence over the past eleven years, both prior to and following his Ph.D. in Economics from Stanford University. He has worked on or headed a number of modeling projects on the implications of immigration control and trade restrictions on U.S.-Mexico interdependence.

RICHARD MINES began his career as a Peace Corps volunteer in Paraguay, and has served as a private consultant specializing in surveys of Mexican immigrants. He earned his Master's degree in Latin American History from Columbia University and his Ph.D. in Agricultural Economics from the University of California, Berkeley. He is presently on detail from the Department of Labor and is serving as Research Director of the Commission on Agricultural Workers. His publications include "Patterns of Migration to the United States from Two Sending Towns," *Latin American Research Review* (1985), and *A Profile of California Farmworkers* (1986).

REBECCA MORALES is Research Associate of the Lewis Center for Regional Studies, University of California, Los Angeles. She has written several articles on the U.S. and international automobile industries and is completing a book that examines patterns of industrialization evident in the worldwide automobile industry. She has also written extensively on Mexican immigrant workers in the United States.

THOMAS MULLER has a Ph.D. in Managerial Economics and is on the part-time faculty of George Mason University. He has written extensively on the economic effects of population changes at the local and national levels. His recent publications relating to immigration include *The Fourth Wave* (1985) and *Immigration Policy and Economic Growth* (1989).

CLARK W. REYNOLDS is Professor of Economics at the Food Research Institute at Stanford University and is the founding Director of the Americas Program, an interdisciplinary program that sponsors research on the social, economic, and political aspects of development, and regional and international exchange. He is currently writing the sequel to his 1970 volume, *The Mexican Economy: Twentieth Century Structure and Growth*, and he recently co-edited, with Leonard Waverman and Gerardo Bueno, *The Dynamics of North American Trade and Investment: Canada, Mexico, and the United States* (1991).

DAVID RUNSTEN is an Agricultural Economist and Director of Research at the California Institute for Rural Studies in Davis, California. He has participated in a variety of field surveys in Mexico and California focused on migration, agroindustry, agricultural technology, and farm labor.

SASKIA SASSEN has written extensively on international circulation of labor and capital and on large cities. She is the author of *The Mobility of Labor and Capital* (1988), and *The Global City: New York, London, Tokyo* (1991). She is a member of several boards and committees, among them the Social Science Research Council Committee on Hispanic Public Policy, sponsored by the Ford Foundation, and the U.S.-Japan Deindustrialization Project of the United Nations Centre on Regional Development (Nagoya, Japan). She is Professor of Urban Planning at Columbia University.

WERNER O. SCHINK is currently Chief of California's Job Training Partnership Program, where he oversees the administration of federal money for job training of economically disadvantaged and/or dislocated youth and adults. A graduate of the University of Nevada in Reno and the University of California at Davis, he has also served as Chief Economist for the California State Employment Development Department. A recent publication is *The Burden of Support: Young Latinos in an Aging Society* (1988), which he co-authored.

ROBERT C. SMITH is a Ph.D. candidate in the Political Science program at Columbia University. He has done research on migration and political economy on both U.S. coasts and in Mexico.

SAUL TREJO REYES is currently Special Adviser to the Secretary of Programming and Budget in Mexico. He received his Ph.D. from Yale University and has worked in the fields of industrial policy, employment, and international economics. He is the author of *Industrialization and Employment in Mexico* (1973), *The Future of Industrial Policy in Mexico* (1987), and *Employment for All: The Challenge and the Means* (1988). He has held a number of government positions and has been Senior Research Fellow at El Colegio de México.

U.S.-MEXICO RELATIONS: LABOR MARKET INTERDEPENDENCE

Introduction

WITH THE APPROACH of the twenty-first century, the United States and Mexico are finding their futures increasingly socially and politically interdependent. While their binational relationship is clearly asymmetrical in many areas, the United States and Mexico nevertheless share the most extensive and complex network of linkages of any countries on either side of the North/South divide; they conduct the most trade, exchange the greatest amount of currency, and share the longest contiguous border, over which the most border crossings and border commerce (both legal and illegal) occur. Since the Mexican debt crisis erupted in 1982, and especially after the inaugurations of the Salinas and Bush administrations, Mexico and the United States have begun to liberalize dramatically their trade and foreign investment policies, and have reintroduced the idea of a North American common market. Although official observers have often noted the importance of the U.S.-Mexico relationship for the national security of each country, their dialogue has come to the fore with the decline of the U.S.-Soviet antagonism and the rise of a multipolar world order.

Within this broad set of interrelations, the largest arena of binational linkage, both in terms of economic magnitude and sociopolitical ramifications, is the broadly defined area of labor market interdependence. At least 10 percent of the growth of U.S. labor supply in recent years has been composed of Mexican migrants, with Mexican workers playing a far greater role in the U.S economy than do U.S.-Mexico trade, direct foreign investment, or financial transactions. Native Mexicans working in the United States (many of whom are now naturalized) represent fully a fifth of the Mexican-born workforce, and immigrant remittances to Mexico are just as important as oil exports and net earnings from *maquiladoras*. One object of the current negotiations of a North American Free Trade Agreement is to shift the interdependence of labor markets from direct migratory flows to labor services embodied in binational trade, a goal pursued by both countries. It is becoming increasingly evident that for policy purposes, any analysis of trade and investment relations must take into consideration for policy purposes the tradeoffs and complementarities between such strategies and migration per se. How can continent-wide trade and investment policies serve the goals of the respective countries in terms of full employment, improved real wages, and better working conditions?

In this area of labor market linkages, Mexico and the United States are finding it increasingly difficult to make unilateral decisions. With a burgeoning population to the south and an aging society at home, the United States will no longer be able to approach issues of employment and growth in the spirit of the 1946 Full Employment Act, which addressed domestic goals with little attention to the international market. Even under the most optimistic scenarios of productivity growth, the United States will be facing a serious shortfall in labor supply as its native population ages and continues to decline numerically into the next century; Mexico, meanwhile, even under very optimistic scenarios of resumed growth, will be producing a dramatic labor force surplus. The gap in relative wages across countries will remain quite wide for the relevant time period regardless of the scenarios for convergence. And finally, deeply rooted social networks have now been established in which binational codependence has become a way of life for many communities on both sides of the border—forming a relationship that will continue as long as these networks provide a coherent option for workers in the midst of highly unequal labor markets.

The reality of demographic change and labor market conditions in North America have the potential for gains to both the United States and Mexico, if labor migration, trade, investment, and technology flows are managed in ways that take full advantage of competitive market forces fostering employment-enhancing investment and innovation on a binational basis. On the other hand, the same demographic trends and labor market conditions could lead to costly social and economic dislocation and widening inequalities in income and wealth, if present distortions in the areas of financial, trade, industrial, market and immigration regulatory policy are allowed to continue.

This volume illustrates the significance of labor market interdependence for the overall relationship between the United States and Mexico. Exploring flows of capital, goods, and services; interactions between political systems; and the struggles of economic agents in this network. These essays show that the pattern of relative wages and employment will be not only relevant for determining the level of labor migration, but also important for the future of sectorial restructuring, productivity growth, corporate profitability, investment spending, and international competitiveness. Throughout, we are made aware that labor migration determines to a large extent binational employment demand, wages, prices of consumer and investment goods, and profits. Any attempts to isolate, close off, or regulate these flows will only affect in a negative manner wages, cultural diversity, national sovereignty, and regional security.

One major goal of this book is to describe the underlying structures of labor markets across the United States and Mexico and frameworks of U.S. immigration policies, and how these markets and policies might evolve. To shed light on these issues, the authors have addressed the following questions:

- What is the nature of U.S.-Mexico labor market interdependence? What determines the pattern of labor supply and demand on both sides of the border? Where do migrants come from and where do they go, both regionally and sectorally? How is the evolution of labor market linkages tied to developments in other areas of the binational relationship, such as financial/debt relations or the evolution of industrial and trade restructuring?

- What are the effects of migration on specific sending and receiving communities, for given sectors and for each society as a whole? What groups bear the benefits and costs among capitalists, consumers, and workers from competition among the different labor markets? What is the political economy of potential class segmentation and of coalitional alliances resulting from closer relations between Mexico and U.S. labor markets as effected by migration, trade, investment, and other policies and the operation of market forces?

- How will changes in other areas of binational economic relations, including a North American Free Trade Agreement, affect labor market interdependence and vice versa?

The other major goal of this volume is to understand the relation of labor market interdependence to past and future immigration and immigration-related policies. In this area, we explore (1) reasons for past and present immigration policies from the perspective of both countries, leading up to the Immigration Reform and Control Act of 1986 (IRCA), in order to determine why it happened when it did; (2) whether the current IRCA policy is optimal from a overall welfare point of view, and if not, how the costs and benefits are distributed; (3) whether IRCA is an aberration that will soon be corrected or if it reflects a series of economic, sociopolitical, and institutional interests within a geopolitical context;

and (4) what alternative paths of future policy formulation and implementation we can reasonably expect. We explore ways in which changes in Mexican and U.S. economic relations eventually may well lead to new policies and institutions of a bilateral nature designed to address the separate labor market goals of each country through closer cooperation between them.

Despite considerable discussion and debate prior to the passing of IRCA five years ago, the legislation was enacted as an omnibus attempt to deal with the legal aspects of migration from all countries, without any comprehensive economic analysis of its potential effect on the United States or on its main source of undocumented immigration, Mexico. Despite the politically charged atmosphere surrounding the bill, there was a sense among many in Congress and the White House that "we need to regain control over our borders" and a determination by Mexico to stay out of what was regarded as a matter for U.S. legislators. The resulting lack of attention to basic economics in a bill so fundamental to the performance of both countries was surprising and disturbing.

This volume explores how the underlying structure of interdependence will likely persist and become more important. Handling interdependence well will undoubtedly imply a rethinking of immigration and labor market policy in the United States and Mexico, a rethinking that will include a variety of cost-benefit analyses including those begun by the U.S.-Mexico Project of the Americas Program at Stanford, El Colegio de México, and El Colegio de la Frontera Norte more than five years ago, in the context of the IRCA discussions. Much of this research has continued and expanded during the past year (1990/91) of debate on the employment impact of a possible North American Free Trade Agreement.

Given that the macroeconomic and social analyses in this book reflect the insights of the case studies and microanalysis from both sides of the border, what alternatives can we expect and what are the institutional impediments for the formation and implementation of a North American Free Trade Agreement? From this point onward we have to evaluate how this tension between labor market interdependence and existing policy might be resolved. Now is the time to review important work to date, much of which is collected and presented here as a contribution to a new policy dialogue, in order to develop a more comprehensive and equitable approach to North American productivity growth and employment.

Part I, which examines the conceptual frameworks of labor market interdependence and public policy, begins with an essay by Jorge A. Bustamante that profiles the dramatic disparity between political and scientific representations of migration. While scientific accounts view immigrants as simply part of a broad, bilateral dynamic between Mexico and the United States, U.S. politicians have made Mexican immigrants ideological scapegoats and have blamed them for unemployment, criminal activities, epidemics, communist and terrorist aggression, threats to national sovereignty, and, most recently, narcotics trade.

Bustamante takes this argument into the realm of social science. According to his paradigm, on a micro level each migrant and his employer form a social relationship; on a macro level markets for labor and goods interact. On both levels, the social relationship is fundamentally asymmetrical: individual social relationships are shaped by U.S. law, which renders undocumented immigrant labor vulnerable to employers; in addition, unequal power relations between the two countries constrain the trade of goods. Bustamante suggests that future research should investigate the relationship of Mexico's regional and national economic structures to out-migration; the relationship of the U.S. demand for labor to U.S. regional and economic structures; and the interaction between both processes. He calls for a new look at cooperation between the United States and Mexico in an approach to the achievement of complementarities from labor market interdependence through the joint consideration of migration policy.

Thomas Heller looks at immigration control as it influences, and is affected by, other regulatory programs of twentieth-century U.S. administrations. He treats immigration policy as one element that propels the development of the modern industrial state through "activist" and "neoliberal" phases, and directs particular attention to the symbolic aspects of immigration politics.

Heller's investigation corresponds to three phases of North American development. He argues that the first substantial immigration reforms were legislated during the period 1900 to 1937, when businessmen and intellectuals of the progressive movement, especially its corporatist wing, in the hope of stabilizing those distributional mechanisms they believed would lead to social and industrial peace, joined forces with the preexisting "nativists, racists, and organized labor." During and after World War II, national quota systems were delegitimized. In the wake of Nazism, images accompanying such policies were reconstructed to conform more closely to classical liberal discourse, in which social decisions are dealt with as abstract contractual choices.

Today, a realization that the job market in the primary advanced-industrial sector is no longer expanding has intensified efforts for restrictionist regulation and has caused comprehensive restructuring of the regulatory state. Viewed in this light, he suggests that a liberalization of immigration controls will require upsetting national and international institutions and exercising power against entrenched public and private coalitions.

Manual García y Griego focuses on the response of Mexico to Mexican in- and out-migration during the last fifty years by examining Mexico's general population laws of 1936, 1949, and 1974. The 1936 and 1949 laws emerged when Mexico was more sparsely populated than today and when strong incentives, such as economic development and national defense, existed to increase the national population. The laws thus encouraged in-migration while simultaneously protecting Mexican nationals in various economic sectors and professions; they restricted entrance to persons who did not fulfill certain health and moral requisites; and they ensured adequate cultural assimilation of the new entrants. In addition, both laws restricted out-migration of Mexicans and promoted repatriation and reintegration of Mexicans living abroad.

During the period 1949–1979, Mexico's population doubled, and its residents became alarmed at the evident demographic explosion. The objectives of population growth and access to in-migration especially from more developed countries gave way to an aim to assist the country's independent economic development. Thus the generally open in-migration policy was modified to invite only highly skilled foreigners, who were required to train Mexican nationals.

Since the 1960s, the people making Mexican migration policy decisions have been particularly concerned about the emigration of Mexican workers to the United States and the in-migration of South and Central American workers. According to García y Griego, Mexico has traditionally taken the position of opposing in principle the outflow of its workers to the United States; however, realizing that the emigration will continue (as a reflection of underlying economic and social conditions), the government has focused on protecting the human rights and labor conditions of Mexican workers abroad. Regarding South and Central American in-migration, Mexico has tried to maintain its status as a safe haven for political refugees while it seeks to restrict entry of economic migrants, who may compete with the many unemployed Mexican workers.

Part II takes a macro-global perspective on the supply and demand of migratory workers in Mexico and the United States. Raúl Hinojosa Ojeda and Robert McCleery present a binational computable general equilibrium model of Mexico and the United States, which is used to analyze the relationship between labor migration, the pattern of trade, and the flow of capital across the two countries. The model is used to analyze alternative scenarios of labor market interdependence in the context of different policy approaches to trade and financial relations. There is also a game theoretic component to the model that is used to analyze the impact of alternative policy scenarios on the strategic interactions between economic classes over distributional issues. The authors' central question concerns the ability of different policy regimes to allow for the establishment and maintenance of "social pacts" defined as broad political agreements on issues of income distribution and employment.

Three alternative scenarios are explored: a continuation along the current neo-liberal opening; a reversal toward neoprotectionism; or the adopting by both countries of a managed interdependence strategy. The model results point to a long-run and society-wide superiority of increased exchange while also revealing a short-run dilemma for workers' welfare that poses serious obstacles to the neo-liberal approach to greater exchange.

The neo-liberal scenario consists of a free trade agreement, continued debt-servicing, and restrictive immigration (at least in intent) à la IRCA. The authors show that changes in trade policies, as opposed to capital and labor policies, generally have smaller effects on production and welfare. A free trade agreement by itself is not capable of entirely reducing the trend toward increased illegal migration as some have claimed. Migration, in fact, will increase in the absence of significant capital inflows to increase employment and wages in Mexico. An attempt to close off either economy from exchange with the other, the protectionist alternative, emerges as the worst long-term welfare option for most workers' groups in both countries. The dilemma, however, is that in the short run this option is superior for those workers benefiting from direct protection. Of the three alternative scenarios, only managed interdependence can provide for continued growth, international exchange, and a basis for strategically agreed upon social pacts in both countries. The key to this approach is developing an optimal combination of debt, trade, and migration policies that maximize growth and welfare on both sides of the border.

Wayne Cornelius investigates the increasing heterogeneity of Mexican migrants—in terms of their settlement patterns, gender, legal status, and employment status—and discovers that four distinct causes can be identified: (1) increasing U.S. demand for Mexican workers, (2) the long-running economic crisis in Mexico, which reduced real wages for most Mexicans by 40 to 50 percent, (3) IRCA, and (4) the maturation of migrant-worker networks.

Cornelius' research shows that Mexican immigrants to the United States are coming from more diverse areas and family situations. In addition, they are staying longer, most frequently in California, and often send for family members after they arrive. He delves into the reasons why each of these phenomena are occurring and how fears by native U.S. residents seem to escalate as the Mexican population becomes an increasingly permanent part of U.S. society, predicting that unfortunately, "the level of anti-immigrant hostility is likely to rise, as the majority population confronts this new and unwelcome kind of challenge."

David Hayes-Bautista and his coauthors claim that the interdependence of the United States and Mexican populations is bound to grow over time, extending well beyond the current composition of the two labor markets. To substantiate this argument, the chapter projects likely changes in intergenerational and interethnic population characteristics over the next two generations, on the basis of recent historical trends, with implications for the future of the United States.

Intergenerational interdependence concerns the relationship between the three generations present in any society: youth, working-age parents, and the elderly. Working-age parents invest in the health and education of their children, in part so that their own future care is assured. In pre-industrial societies, the intergenerational compact operates within the family unit. With the rise of industrial society, the compact enters the political domain, with public programs created to provide for the youth and elderly generations which are sustained by the earnings of the working generation.

The authors developed a model to project changes in the composition of California's population and to speculate about the effects of these changes on the intergenerational compact. They forecast that for the period 1985–2030, the elderly will be largely Anglo, while the working-age generation will be mostly minority and generally Latino. Thus in the future, the intergenerational compact will increasingly take on the flavor of an *interethnic* interdependence. Under current U.S. social policy, however, the Latino population (37 percent of which were born in Mexico) does not participate fully in the economy, a fact that raises doubts about the ability of a future working-age population to support the large number of elderly. Hayes-Bautista and his associates suggest that fulfilling the intergenerational compact in the future may require developing an interethnic agreement today. Areas of policy concern for this agreement will include education, health, employment, income, and political participation.

Jeffrey Bortz concentrates on the evolving pattern of relative wages for the United States and Mexico during the period 1939–1985, because the disparity in wages between the two countries is one important cause of labor migration. From 1930 to 1952, Mexican wages declined as millions of campesinos flowed into the cities; willing to receive low wages, these workers fueled the industrial boom that supplied the expanding markets during World War II and the Korean War. The surge continued through 1976, but between 1976 and 1985 Mexico underwent a series of financial crises that caused real wages to decline.

Wage rates in the United States have been steadily declining since the 1960s, but have remained significantly higher than wages available in Mexico. This situation occurred, according to the author, because Mexico tended to lack the backward linkages that characterized industrialization in the more advanced countries, or because its most advanced areas of production were often the older industries of more advanced countries. Bortz concludes, through his analyses of geographically different communities in Mexico and of California, that significant net migration will continue as long as the disparity remains between the developed high-productivity economy of the United States and the Mexican economy, which is characterized by low productivity. Moreover, and unfortunately for both countries, Mexican and U.S. workers are likely to experience steadily eroding real income in the 1990s.

Peter Gregory critiques this analysis in his commentary following the Bortz paper, arguing against the choice of 1939 as a base year from which to study the path of real wages. He suggests that the Mexican economy demonstrated steadier gains in real earnings prior to the 1982 crisis than Bortz recognizes, by expanding the analysis to include more categories than those from which Bortz derived his (wage) data, and by observing such encouraging economic factors as increases in caloric intake and the number of people who own shoes.

Francisco Alba examines the demographic and economic factors affecting Mexican migrant supply and demand. Emphasizing the historical relationship between migration and development, he analyzes different policy positions on the issue in terms of present conditions and reasonable future scenarios. He shows that during the 1940s and 1950s, a relatively stable migration pattern was in place, with demand concentrated in southwestern U.S. agroindustries and supply originating in central Mexican rural communities as reflected in the "bracero program."

This historic rural/rural pattern of migration has undergone important changes in recent years. U.S. labor demand for Mexican workers has begun to shift away from agriculture, which was increasingly mechanized, and toward the expanding service and light manufacturing sectors in U.S. cities. Meanwhile, similar structural changes in the Mexican economy have created an increasingly urban source of labor supply which matches the changes in U.S. demand.

The apparent complementarity in the evolution of labor supply and demand between the two countries, however, masks important competition within U.S. labor markets. The growth of dualism in the wage and employment structure, with weakness at the low-skill end of the spectrum, has led to considerable friction along with political pressure to control immigration. In addition, Mexico's demographic profile is similar to that of the Caribbean and other Latin American countries, which are increasingly sending migrants to the United States. Given these conflicts, Alba argues that the most advantageous solution for both countries is to favor policies designed to alter the underlying conditions that give rise to present migration patterns, moving from protection of capital-intensive industries in Mexico and labor-intensive activities in the United States, toward liberalized trade in goods and services. This would lead to greater employment creation in Mexico and technological evolution in the United States, enhancing the competitiveness of both countries.

Saul Trejo Reyes discusses Mexican economic policies and U.S.-Mexico relations in the context of the labor force growth during the seventies and eighties. Although annual population growth has slowed from 3.4 percent during the 1970s to 2.7 percent in the 1980s, according to Trejo, the Mexican labor force appears to be growing at about 3.4 percent each year. Most of Mexico's population growth has occurred in urban areas with almost no rural growth expected for the future. An important component of labor force growth is an increase in the rates of participation of women, a trend that is certain to continue into the 1990s.

Since the 1982 debt crisis, there has been a shift in employment from large firms to the informal sector, with a large increase in open employment. Employment in the capital and intermediate goods sectors has been particularly hard hit. Using an input-output model of the Mexican economy, Trejo generates three alternative scenarios for employment growth from 1985 to 2000. Even with the optimistic projection of an annual 5 percent GNP growth rate (since growth was negligible through the end of the 1980s, this scenario would imply much more than 5 percent growth in the nineties), 8 million workers would be unemployed (except in the lowest productivity informal sector activities) by the end of the century.

Even Trejo's best-case scenarios anticipate the need for policies that favor increased urban growth, as well as greater pressure on undocumented workers to migrate to the United States. The natural complementarity between the United States and Mexican labor markets, and pressures on both countries to increase their competitiveness in global markets, as well as the need for greater investment and growth to service Mexico's debt and U.S. international borrowing help to explain why the administrations of both countries have sharply altered their policies in favor of closer economic relations over the past two years. The Trejo study supports the need for even closer links with the United States to achieve the objective of fuller employment in Mexico; it implies the need for complementary research in the United States, so that its employment and income goals can also be realized.

Part III highlights the case-study approach with comparisons of the migration patterns of different Mexican communities and investigations of the maturation of migrant networks in particular areas of the United States.

Leo Chávez explains how "anti-immigrant demagoguery and nativism" mask the legitimate concerns of the American public and U.S. policymakers about the impact of immigration, especially from Mexico, on their local communities. In order to respond to such concerns, the effects of the local community on immigration must also be analyzed. Chávez argues that Mexican immigrants, even the undocumented, cannot be viewed as a monolithic group. Rather, the process of integrating immigrants into U.S. labor markets produces both temporary and long-term migration patterns—patterns that result in two groups that respond to different local labor-market conditions and have dissimilar influences on society and integration.

Recent data suggest that an increasingly large proportion of Mexican migrants to this country, both documented and undocumented, are staying longer and appear to be settling here. This trend is a function of both the Mexican economic crisis and the rising demand for low-wage labor in the U.S. economy. Migrants to San Diego, Chávez reveals, base their decisions to enter the community and to settle there on the availability of employment; more jobs are available for longer-term immigrants. Furthermore, San Diego immigrants are overwhelmingly young and have young children, many of whom are born in the United States. Their households often contain members who are not a part of the immediate family, and the number of workers per household is higher than among documented immigrants.

For this young community, education and child and maternal health care are primary concerns, and the immigrants avail themselves of local resources—a fact not fully considered by those studying social services and social integration. According to Chávez, "The long-term impact of immigration on the local community will depend on the larger society's resolution [of] this question of social integration. The price the local community pays for paradise now could pale in comparison to future costs, should society fail to plan for the eventual integration of long-term undocumented residents and their families."

Rafael Alarcón explores the concept of *norteñizacíon*—the way in which Mexican migration to the United States has caused certain areas of Mexico to become dependent on U.S. labor markets. These dependent areas, usually socially cohesive rural communities, have in effect specialized in producing international migrant workers. This has led to profound transformations in the economic, political, familial, and cultural realms.

Alarcón examines the broad impact of this process on the town of Chavinda, Michoacán, which has a tradition of sending many of its workers to the United States. Over one-fourth of the adult males of Chavinda reported having worked in the United States sometime between 1980 and 1982, and over half had worked in the United States at some point in their lives. He found that from March to November each year, a significant proportion of the young adult male population leaves the town for the United States. As a result, older men and children have played an increasingly important role in the town's agricultural sector. Women, however, have not become further involved outside the home.

Chavindans use their U.S.-earned income primarily for subsistence as well as for home purchase and improvement. The strong demand for housing by returned migrants has sparked land speculation and rapidly rising housing prices as well as a tendency toward urban-type modernization. According to Alarcón, for many peasant families, migration to the north actually subsidizes their desire to remain tied to their land. However the savings accumulated from work in the United States are seldom sufficient to permit a peasant family to initiate empresarial agricultural production, especially given the poor quality of local resources; rather, maintaining their higher standard of living while retaining residences in the rural community requires a perpetuation of the migration process. The *norteñizacíon* of cultural life in Chavinda should not be confused with North Americanization. Migrants from Chavinda in the United States are influenced by Chicanos and other Mexicans, but have little direct contact with Anglo culture because of the social discrimination they experience here.

Bernardo González-Aréchiga argues that U.S. immigration policy has segregated borderland Mexicans according to their documented or undocumented status. The undocumented in the United States and Mexico have less mobility and employment opportunities than the documented, and they represent a captive market for commerce and services on the Mexican side of the border. The documented border population, in contrast, can choose between markets for the purchase of goods and services, may hold jobs on either side of the border, and are able to participate more freely in the border economy and society.

From data collected at El Colegio de la Frontera Norte, González-Aréchiga finds evidence for differential access to the United States. In his view, this differential access has had tremendous impact on immigrants' socioeconomic status and real-income distribution. Higher-income groups are more likely to have documents, to have access to U.S. jobs (which earn dollars), and to be able to purchase more of their consumer goods less expensively in the United States. While each border city has its own history and economic structure, the basic pattern is similar all along the border: socioeconomic inequality is perpetuated by U.S. authorities' tendency to grant border visas to members of high-status groups.

González-Aréchiga recommends that Mexico redress the current situation by redefining the duty-free character of the border so as to facilitate local residents' access goods and services on either side. He also calls for the United States to develop a more egalitarian way to process documents.

Thomas Muller points to the experience of labor shortages in many regions and economic sectors in the United States, despite the persistence of significant pockets of unemployment in those areas dominated by traditional manufacturing. The "labor shortages"—largely in the low-wage, low-skilled job areas—have curtailed economic growth in some sectors, especially in cases where employers face competition from low-wage international suppliers. Responding to this need, Hispanics have increased their rate of legal and illegal immigration to the United States.

Muller argues that greater employment of Hispanics has not decreased employment for non-Hispanic whites. Indeed, growth in the supply of native-born workers willing to engage in low productivity/low wage occupations is inadequate to meet present and projected employment needs: the baby-boom generation has already entered the labor market, growth in labor participation is decelerating, and rising educational achievement renders many native-born workers unwilling to accept low-wage, low-skilled jobs with little possibility for advancement.

He points out that the Black community has periodically expressed concern about potential or actual competition between Black and Hispanic workers. Though such fears may have been reasonable at one time, says Muller, there is presently less cause for concern. The two groups are concentrated largely in different sectors of the economy, with most Blacks occupying government, sales, and administrative jobs, and Hispanics in unskilled and semi-skilled blue-collar jobs. Moreover, considerably more Blacks than Hispanics hold professional or managerial jobs. (This paper was written in the late 1980s. Since then the U.S. recession has worsened employment conditions. Meanwhile recent pressures for greater Hispanic representation in government and related occupations have exacerbated the conflict.)

The potential for competition is most serious at the lower end of the occupational ladder, where immigrants and native-born workers are unable to advance. According to some projections, between today and 1995 approximately six million jobs will be added to the U.S. labor market in occupations where Hispanics, especially Mexicans, are heavily represented. (These occupations represent 38 percent of all jobs that will be created in the next decade.) Muller sees a danger that Hispanic immigrants will be concentrated in these low-wage, dead-end jobs because their real earnings are higher than their potential earnings elsewhere and because they are less able to choose welfare instead of low-wage employment, leading to what could become a permanent underclass.

Saskia Sassen and Robert C. Smith take a look at regions and labor markets in the United States that employ many Hispanics. They discover that even though family ties and residential discrimination help concentrate the Hispanic population, this effect is in many ways induced by the recruitment of Hispanics to the U.S. labor market. The U.S. economy is presently expanding its supply of both low-wage, low-skilled jobs and high-wage, high-skilled jobs, while primary-sector industrial jobs are becoming harder to find. This transformation is occurring because the United States is no longer dominated by a strong manufacturing sector but rather a dynamic service economy, and because the manufacturing jobs that remain are rapidly being downgraded. Major cities, New York and Los Angeles in particular, have experienced the concurrent effects of income and occupational polarization.

Sassen links the fact that more than 40 percent of Hispanics live in large urban areas with the recent data that suggest that certain jobs are "reserved" for Hispanic workers. Hispanics, Sassen deduces, are ensured access to those jobs that reproduce their low wages. Recruitment dynamics vary for different Hispanic nationalities: for Cubans in Miami, recruitment occurs in an enclave economy in which the labor market is contained within the immigrant community and the jobs cater largely to community-generated demand. Most Mexicans in Los Angeles, however, occupy a labor market that contains mostly low-wage jobs tied to non-Mexican firms. Although recruitment dynamics vary for different Hispanic nationalities, part of the variation stems from the different locations of these groups. In sum, the authors argue that while most Hispanics feed the low-wage, low-skilled labor pool, their insertion into these labor markets varies geographically and according to nationality.

Part IV, entitled Sectoral Dynamics and Interdependence, features essays on industry, agriculture, and services, and details the development, linkage, and interaction of sectors in which immigration plays an important role. Raúl A. Hinojosa Ojeda and Rebecca Morales analyze the historical transformations of the auto industry and consider these transformations in the larger contexts of industrialization and labor supply and demand across Mexico and the United States. The division between the parts and final assembly portions of the auto industry indicates that the primary labor market segments in both countries are similar and therefore competitive.

On both sides of the border, stages in the development of industrial structure have informed changes in the pattern of labor market interdependence. Hinojosa and Morales argue that analyzing trends in international industrial restructuring is central to effective migration and labor market policy-formation. They begin their investigation by tracing the historical evolution of employment in the auto industry and the use of different labor market segments in the United States and Mexico from 1890 to the present.

The authors allege that "import-substituting industrialization in both countries" during the middle of this century created a demand for industrial workers, with manufacturing replacing agriculture as the main source of employment. By the late 1960s and early 1970s, a crisis is shown to have occurred in the pattern of industrialization. In the United States, foreign competitive pressures forced the auto industry to find new strategies for survival, which included using more undocumented workers in the parts sectors and using high technology for final assembly.

In Mexico, the chronic balance-of-payments problems associated with import-substituting industrialization led the country to develop more export-oriented policies, both through labor-intensive parts *maquiladoras* and more capital-intensive plants for assembling and exporting "world cars."

In this context, two trends are occurring, each having different effects on labor markets: (1) the "world-car" trend, in which more final assembly production is being transferred to developing countries, and (2) the movement toward high-technology reconcentration, in which developed countries benefit from renewed production activity. Hinojosa and Morales conclude that both trends will hurt various labor markets in Mexico and the United States, and will pose unprecedented challenges to corporations, unions, and policymakers.

In their alternative scenario, the proposed pursuit of binational production and market-sharing would have potentially positive growth and

employment effects. More efficient distribution of production and a more
equitable distribution of value-added between the two countries would
stabilize employment and market growth on both sides of the border.
The success of this binational cooperative approach, however, calls for
a variety of new institutional arrangements between states, labor organizations, and corporations, the conditions for which remain to be
developed.

Richard Mines and Jeffrey Avina explore janitorial services as a growing service sector both nationally and in California, in terms of their employment practices including the growing importance of Mexican migrants. Given the increased demand for labor in these activities, they
expected to find conditions for janitors to be improving. However the
evidence collected through both on-site interviews and government surveys, indicate that conditions have deteriorated.

In the 1975–1985 period, two types of firms came into conflict in
California: mid-sized, nonunion firms, which hire recent immigrants;
and large unionized firms, which hire a more stable and settled labor
force. Similar changes in conditions confronted two janitorial locals, one
in Los Angeles and one in San Jose. A comparison of developments in the
two areas shows how increasing supplies of recent immigrants can lead
to different outcomes depending on the reaction of the participants involved and their ability to bargain for a share of the economic rents from
labor market penetration.

The managers of the nonunion firms in both Los Angeles and San Jose
learned how to tap into multiple networks of recent immigrants by using
Hispanic middlemen (usually settled Mexicans) to lower firms' labor payments through competition. In San Jose, the union local minimized the
damage done by the nonunion employers by aggressively organizing recent immigrants and harassing nonunion employees. In Los Angeles,
however, the janitorial union lost almost all of its power. In that case,
recent immigrants earning minimum wages have replaced the more
highly paid U.S.-born workers in most of the jobs and have contributed
to the low wages paid to veteran janitors.

David Runsten and Sandra Archibald analyze how agriculture and
food processing in the United States are increasingly subject to the internationalization of capital, trade, and labor flows. Although the United
States has grown dependent on exports of some crops, especially food
and feed grains and speciality crops suitable for temperate climates, import competition from Mexico and other countries is increasing for more
labor-intensive fruits and vegetables.

Changes in relative factor prices, such as the cost of farm technology and the wages of immigrant workers in the United States, therefore affect how the sector will develop within and between Mexico and the United States. The state of California has a comparative advantage over other regions because of its large landholdings, subsidized irrigation, and access to immigrant-hired farm labor. Its agricultural exports depend to a large extent on the opportunity cost of such labor, while rising incomes in Mexico will increase the demand for food and feed grains from the Midwest of the United States as well as the products of Western agriculture.

The authors show immigration to be a cumulative process; immigrant networks and contractors evolve and mature, changing the jobs, labor process, technology, and migration pattern itself. A recent tendency by immigrants to settle in the United States has affected the United States and Mexico in four ways. The possibility of migration from Mexico has increased because of greater contacts and job information, the spreading use of Hispanic intermediaries for recruitment, and a geographical broadening of labor markets. The maturation of settlement networks makes it possible for migrants to move into job sectors previously unavailable to them. Settlement creates new demands for local public services, which may not be counterbalanced by economic growth. And finally, settlement can reduce turnover rates in many jobs, allowing for unionization and increasing wages, while creating potential competition between more settled immigrants and new immigrants for these jobs.

Runsten and Archibald examine a number of alternative scenarios involving varying technologies, foreign investment, trade, and labor market policies. While trade protection and increased dependence on low-wage immigrants do not appear to be in California's interest, they argue that a sustainable pattern of agricultural production-sharing with Mexico is possible. Such a pattern would increase employment in Mexico and spur technological innovation in the United States.

With his final chapter, Clark Reynolds sums up some of the essential themes of the book, as well as the sense of urgency that has come to dominate the issue of labor migration in the 1990s. In the current economic environment, the importance of upward convergence in productivity and real wages cannot be overstated, since it is the only socially and politically acceptable outcome of a NAFTA. But how can we achieve upward convergence in recessionary times? A homogeneous labor pool will require rapid growth in investment, innovation, and productivity among all partners (including a rise in the rate of domestic savings and investment in the U.S.)—as well as increased skill levels for all workers. Ensuring broad social participation in resultant gains will be difficult as well. Yet certain aspects of this positive balance have been achieved in the European Community and must be attempted here. The North American countries, Reynolds maintains, can and should follow the European lead by creating a NAFTA that, through progressive liberalization of trade and investment policies and increased monetary cooperation, will increase the efficiency of production, competitiveness, output, and employment throughout the North American economy. Sooner rather than later a binational approach to migration in the context of an increasingly integrated labor market will be essential. The essays in this book take us beyond NAFTA toward an understanding of the ways in which the migration of peoples, cultures, and innovations between Mexico and the United States has linked irreversibly our economic and political futures.

Jorge A. Bustamante
Clark W. Reynolds
Raúl A. Hinojosa Ojeda

PART I
A Conceptual Framework

Interdependence, Undocumented Migration, and National Security

Jorge A. Bustamante

WALKING ALONG the U.S.-Mexico border, one soon realizes how many gaps exist in the fence between the neighboring countries. The passage of time and movement from one side of the border to the other only emphasizes the persistence of these openings; their evasive nature and the volatility they cause underscore their presence. The sealing of one hole merely seems to create others.

These openings along the border serve as conduits for more than people migrating north; undocumented migrants are only the most conspicuous users of these transboundary apertures. Undocumented capital fleeing Mexico also avails itself of many less-obvious openings along the border. Natural resources are escaping in unknown volumes underground and through aquatic routes. Undocumented contaminants originating on both sides of the border are polluting our international environment. And undocumented technology, values, ideas, and myths move back and forth through some of these apertures.

It is reasonable and desirable that everything that enters our respective countries be recognized, recorded, and pass through a controllable gate. The reality of border life, however, dictates something very different. The laws of interdependence, which are born of the free will of international neighbors but may not be symmetrical, decide the pattern of supply and demand for mutual satisfaction among labor force and capital, technology, services, and other resources.

In this paper, I will concentrate on some of the undocumented channels of transmission—in particular, those channels pertaining to undocumented migration and national security—in a legal, economic, and social context. First, I discuss the gap between the reality of labor market interdependence and the ideological perceptions of undocumented migration on both sides of the border. Next, I will present a framework for analyzing the economic interdependence, labor migration, and national-security relations between the United States and Mexico. Finally, this framework will be used to systematically analyze the possible effects on immigration and national security of different U.S.-Mexico political scenarios.

INTERNATIONAL MIGRATION AND NATIONAL IDEOLOGIES

A key obstacle to a mutual understanding between Mexico and the United States about undocumented immigration is their differing ideologies. Each nation has its own perception of U.S.-Mexico migration—a phenomenon that has been important to bilateral relations between the two countries for the past one hundred years. In addition, although undocumented immigration from Mexico is being viewed increasingly by social scientists as the result of a U.S. demand for cheap labor being matched by a complementary supply of inexpensive labor from Mexico,[1] the ideological gap remains wide between the U.S. and Mexican social scientific communities and U.S. public opinion.

The predominant view in the United States, according to the research of Celestino Fernandez, is that undocumented immigration from Mexico has negative effects for the American people.[2] It is either a "silent invasion," a "national threat," a cause of a variety of public calamities such as a "loss of control of U.S. borders," a burden for U.S. taxpayers because of "illegal aliens' " abuse of welfare and other public benefits, a cause of

[1] In my doctoral dissertation, I produced the concept of "commodity migrant" within a theoretical context of undocumented immigration as a result of an international labor market. See Jorge A. Bustamante, "Mexican Immigration to the United States and the Social Relations of Capitalism," Ph.D. diss., Dept. of Sociology, University of Notre Dame, 1975. Along the same line of thought see Clark W. Reynolds, "Labor Market Projections for the United States and Mexico and Their Relevance to Current Migration Controversies," *Food Research Institute Studies* no. 17 (Stanford, Calif., 1979). See also Jorge A. Bustamante, "Commodity Migration: Structural Analysis of Mexican Immigration," in Stanley Ross, ed., *Views Across the Border: The United States and Mexico* (Albuquerque, N.Mex., 1978), 133–203; Richard C. Jones, ed., *Patterns of Undocumented Migration* (Totawa, N.J., 1984); and Michael Greenwood and John M. McDowell, "Factor Market Consequences of U.S. Immigration," *Journal of Economic Literature* vol. 24 (Dec. 1986), 1638–1772.

[2] Among the various articles in which Celestino Fernandez of the University of Arizona, Tucson, has published the results of her extensive research on the formation of public opinion about the presence of undocumented migrants from Mexico, see *The Border Patrol and the New Media Coverage of Undocumented Immigration During the 1970s: A Quantitative Content Analysis in the Sociology of Knowledge* (Tucson, Ariz., 1981).

unemployment, or even a cause of drug traffic.[3] The absence of a scientific basis for this blame gives credence to the idea that an "ideology of immigration" is driving the U.S. public to perceive these effects on U.S. society, economy, culture, and national sovereignty to be caused by the "illegal alien." The contrast between U.S. public opinion and the economic realities of the undocumented immigration phenomenon is illustrated by the difference between a statement made by William Colby, former head of the CIA, saying that Mexican immigration could become a more serious national security threat to the United States than the Soviet Union,[4] and the conclusions of the *Economic Report to the President* (February 1986), which stated that undocumented immigrants produce more benefits than costs for the U.S. economy.[5]

IRCA

These contradictions between the ideology and the economy of undocumented migration from Mexico to the United States are reflected in the discrepancies between the objectives and the written text of the Immigration Reform and Control Act of 1986 (also called IRCA or the Simpson-Rodino Law), and the realities of the international labor market.

The most important reform introduced by the Simpson-Rodino Law is "sanctions to employers" who knowingly hire an undocumented immigrant. The predominant ideology of immigration indicates that the United States is interested in closing the door to the undocumented immigrants. Economic realities however, dictate something different. West Coast growers are complaining about labor shortages, and the written text of "sanctions to employers" has loopholes big enough to render the law's sanctions inapplicable. Perhaps the biggest loophole in the new Public Law 99–603 regarding sanctions to employers is in subsection (4) of Section 274A (b), which allows an employer to keep copies of the documents with which an alien job applicant, when he or she is hired, supposedly demonstrates eligibility to obtain employment in the United States:

Copying of Documentation Permitted. Notwithstanding any other provision of law, the person or entity may copy a document presented by an individual pur-

---

[3] See Jorge Bustamante, "Mexican Migration: The Political Dynamics of Perceptions," in Clark W. Reynolds and Carlos Tello, eds., *U.S.-Mexico Relations: Economy and Social Aspects* (Stanford, Calif., 1983).

[4] Fernandez, *The Border Patrol and the New Media Coverage of Undocumented Immigration During the 1970s.*

[5] See U.S. Council of Economic Advisors, *Economic Report to the President* (Washington, Feb. 1986), chap. 7.

suant to this subsection and may retain the copy, but only (except as otherwise permitted under law) for the purpose of complying with the requirements of this subsection.

In addition, an employer is considered to be found in full compliance with the new law if he or she signs an INS form I-9 stating that an alien who is applying for a job has produced a legal document demonstrating eligibility to work in the United States, regardless of the existence of such a document. Thus the employer's word determines whether or not he or she has complied with the law.

This is not to suggest that all U.S. employers are taking advantage of this loophole in the new immigration law. I assert, rather, that there is such a loophole in the new law and that a full use of it might render "sanctions to employers" inapplicable. In addition, the law as it stands today reflects an inherent contradiction between the negative perception of the presence of undocumented immigrants in the United States and the objective need for their labor. This contradiction creates an awkward situation in which the same undocumented immigrants are viewed simultaneously as a problem by those who believe that they are a cause of a series of calamities, and as a solution by those who need their labor.

Growers in northern California and Oregon blamed the Simpson-Rodino law for a labor shortage early in the summer of 1987.[6] According to the governor of Oregon, the acuteness of such a labor shortage was becoming a threat to the state economy to the point that he was ready to declare a state of emergency. Senator Pete Wilson of California demanded from Washington a relaxation of border enforcement in order to facilitate the entry of undocumented migrants, who could then apply for a Special Agricultural Workers visa (SAW).[7]

Simpson-Rodino was thus not yet fully enforced when several reforms were made. The first reform moved the deadline to apply for a SAW visa from May 1986 to July 26, 1987. INS officials had been saying since February 1987 that there was a decline in apprehensions, therefore indicating that the Simpson-Rodino Law was working.[8] The joy went sour when the self-financed offices that were opened to receive "amnesty" applicants received less than 10 percent of the expected numbers of undocumented migrants during their first two months of operation. The INS

[6]See *The Wall Street Journal*, 5 June 1987.

[7]A radio program sponsored by INS, broadcasted from Irvine, California, on 18 June 1987, included a telephone participation by Senator Pete Wilson from Washington, D.C., addressed to the INS and the U.S. Border Patrol, in which he asked them to relax border enforcement.

[8]Mr. Alan Nelson, Commissioner of INS, made this announcement at a press conference in Washington, D.C., on 22 June 1987.

amnesty program was saved from bankruptcy in early August 1987 with a partial budgetary increase of 33 percent, after conspicuous INS reports in June of the same year that the number of apprehensions was again on the rise.

One aspect of the Mexican ideology of emigration was sharply illustrated during the first quarter of 1987, when rumors swept all over Mexico that the United States was preparing a massive deportation operation that would begin on May 5. Public alarm in Mexico about the Simpson-Rodino Law was high as was ignorance of its text and the political history that formed it. In early May, a headline of one of Mexico City's major newspapers read: "Mexico-U.S. Border in State of Siege." Many other newspapers followed suit, all blaming the Simpson-Rodino Law but imputing different motives. The reason heard most often in the streets of Mexico City was that President Reagan had decided to teach Mexicans a lesson for their deviant behavior regarding U.S. foreign policy toward Central America.

Obscured by differing ideologies, the true picture of the Mexican migrant going north in search of a job was known only by the main actors: the U.S. employer, whose hiring practices were seemingly indifferent to any legislative changes on undocumented immigration; and the migrant worker, who was more ready to pay attention to the labor market laws of supply and demand than to the politics of immigration on either side.

MIGRATION AS ECONOMIC AND POLITICAL INTERDEPENDENCE

This part of the paper presents an analytic framework for a prognosis of relations between Mexico and the United States. This framework is rooted in a series of reasonably based presuppositions on which we can analytically relate two major themes: labor market interdependence (LMI) and national security.

Labor Market Interdependence

There is a growing consensus in the international academic community that international migration between Mexico and the United States is the product of an international labor market in which the pattern of labor demand in the United States is just as causally important as the pattern of labor supply in Mexico.[9] This perspective is shared by other authors

---

[9] Among those who sustain this perspective are Irving Sobel, "Human Capital and Institutional Fearing of the Labor Market: Rivals or Complements?" *Journal of Economic Issues* (Mar. 1982), 155–272; Reynolds, "Labor Market Projections"; and Greenwood and McDowell, "Factor Market Consequences of U.S. Immigration."

whose most recent investigations and field research with migratory workers have been conducted in both Mexico and the United States.[10] This view constrasts, however, with that of some authors whose research and analysis were conducted before the 1980s. Such is the case of Ray Marshall and Vernon Briggs.[11] In their time, these authors believed that the presence of undocumented workers in the United States was a phenomenon based on exogenous causes, in which the United States participated as an innocent victim. If in fact increasingly fewer authors now blame the U.S. economy's lack of responsibility for undocumented migration, this view still persists among some analysts with high credibility such as Barry R. Chiswick and Edwin P. Reubens (1979).[12]

For the purpose of this paper, I will refer to interactions as processes of social relations represented, at a micro level of analysis, by the interactions between the U.S. employer and the Mexican undocumented immigrant, and, at a macro level, by the interactions among the communities, regions, national economies, societies of origin, and destiny of the undocumented migrants. The common trait of these levels of analysis is given by the context of labor markets, in which most of the social relations of migrants take place. These labor market interactions should be understood solely in the context of the neo-classical concept of "market relations," in which market forces move toward equilibrium, rather than in the theoretical context that Max Weber used in referring to social relations "that conform to certain patterns of consensual repetition and to a structure in which actors occupy different positions of power and interact with others who understand the meaning of that behavior, and who thus behave within the cultural norm of expectations of those who initiate the relation."[13]

[10]Douglas S. Massey and Felipe Garcia-Espana, "The Social Process of International Migration," Science no. 237, 733–38; Wayne A. Cornelius, "Emigration from Rural Mexican Sending Communities," Population and Development Review vol. 15, no. 4 (Dec. 1989); Gilbert Cardenas, "Research on Mexican Immigration," in Armando Valdez et al., eds., The State of Chicano Research on Family, Labor, and Migration (Stanford, Calif., 1983).

[11]Ray Marshall, "Economic Factors Influencing the International Migration of Workers," in Stanley Ross, ed., Views Across the Border: The United States and Mexico (Albuquerque, N.Mex., 1978); Vernon M. Briggs, Jr., "Illegal Immigration and the American Labor Force," American Behavioral Scientist, vol. 19, no. 3.

[12]Barry R. Chiswick, "Illegal Aliens: A Preliminary Report on Employee-Employer Surveys," American Economic Review vol. 76, no. 2 (1986), 253–65; Edwin Reubens, Temporary Admission of Foreign Workers: Dimensions and Policies (Washington, 1979).

[13]I am referring here in particular to the notions of social relations, economic relations, and markets, analyzed by Max Weber in his book Economia y Sociedad (Mexico City, 1965), chaps. 1 and 2.

There is a belief, as popular as it is erroneous, that the Mexican economy, expressed in terms of poverty and unemployment, singlehandedly determines the exodus of migratory workers to the United States.[14] Various independent researchers have demonstrated that undocumented migrants do not come from the poorest regions nor from the poorest sectors of Mexico and that the majority of them have jobs in Mexico before they cross the U.S. border on their way to the United States.[15] Both countries explain the migratory labor phenomenon in terms of differences in salary:[16] the greater the wage difference, the greater the incentive to look for work in the United States.

The wage difference, however, is not the only or the most important factor in determining the volumes of migratory flows between the two countries. If that were the case, most workers would come from regions and sectors in Mexico with the lowest salaries. This has not been the case at least since 1977.[17] If there is a relation between poverty in Mexico and emigration to the United States, it can be found in the proximity of a migrant's residence to the United States and the predominance of border city and northern Mexico regions in the totals of migrants. The shorter the distance to the United States, the lower the cost of migration. Practically all the empirical investigations of this international migratory labor phenomenon in the last twenty years have found that most migrants come from the west-central area of Mexico.[18]

At a more detailed level, I refer to those relations that occur between a migratory worker and his or her U.S. employer as well as to the social, economic, political, and cultural conditions that have historically given rise to this relation. There is a congruence between the asymmetry of power that characterizes the U.S.-Mexico relation, and the asymmetry of

[14] Marshall, "Economic Factors Influencing the International Migration of Workers."

[15] This was a central result of the work of Julian Samora, *Los Mojados: The Wetback Story* (Notre Dame, N.C., 1971). See also Jorge A. Bustamante and Geronimo Martinez G., "Undocumented Immigration from Mexico: Beyond Borders but Within Systems," *Journal of International Affairs* vol. 33, no. 4 (Fall 1979), 265–84; and Rodolfo Corona Vasquez, et al., "Migrants internacionales con y sin antecedentes de migración interna: Algunas characteristicas socioeconomicas," Series ENEFNEU (Mexico City, 1980).

[16] Reynolds, "Labor Market Projections."

[17] This theory was refuted by the results of the ENEFNEU (Encuesta Nacional de Emigrantes a la Frontera Norte y a Estados Unidos) of Mexico's Secretary of Labor. See Secretaria de Trabajo y Previsión Social, Centro Nacional de Información y Estadisticas del Trabajo (CENIET), *Analisis de algunos resultados de la primera encuesta a trabajadores mexicanos no documentados devueltos de los Estados Unidos en 1977* (Mexico City, 1979).

[18] Since the time of Julian Samora's study in 1969 (*Los Mojados*) until the present there has not been one study to contradict this finding.

power that characterizes the relations between migratory workers and their U.S. employers. This asymmetry results from the inequality of power between two nations and from the way that U.S. nationals have historically exercised their greater power.

Between individuals, I have found the inequality to be most dramatically expressed in the vulnerability of undocumented migrants to their U.S. employers.[19] This vulnerability of worker to employee did not develop from the free play of supply and demand; rather, it was the result of a historical process that led the United States to be the only country in the world in which employers were expressly permitted to hire foreigners who had entered the country in violation of its own immigration laws. The undocumented migrant was therefore without power to exercise other options given the imposed conditions by the employer or risk being deported.[20] This legislative example of brutal asymmetry existed since the 1952 adoption of the famous "Texas proviso" until 1986, when this was explicitly overturned by IRCA.[21]

Demographic Interdependence

A second basic assumption of the framework is that the variations in the demand for foreign workers in the United States will depend principally on two factors: first, the pattern of economic growth in the United States, and particularly California, which contains 60 percent of all undocumented Mexican workers;[22] and second, the aging of the U.S. working population and the resulting growing scarcity of workers to fill lower-wage occupations.[23] As such, the future of the migratory phenomenon will depend more on these factors than on U.S. immigration policies or changes in Mexican economic growth.

The aging of the U.S. population. It is ironic that such a restrictive law as IRCA was approved the same year that the demand for foreign labor increased significantly due to changing demographic patterns in the

[19] For an analysis of the process within which this vulnerability is developed, see Jorge A. Bustamante, "The Wetback as Deviant: An Application of Labeling Theory," *American Journal of Sociology* vol. 77, no. 4 (Jan. 1972), 706–718.

[20] For a more detailed analysis, see Jorge A. Bustamante, "La migración de los indocumentados," in *El Cotidiano* no. 1 (Mexico City, 1987), 13–29.

[21] Jorge A. Bustamante, "La Migración Indocumentada de Mexico a Estados Unidos," in David Pinera, ed., *Vision Historica de la Frontera Norte de México* (Mexicali, 1987).

[22] Consejo Nacional de Población, *Encuesta en la Frontera Norte a Trabajadoes Indocumentados Devueltos por las Autoridades de Estados Unidos, Diciembre 1984,* (Mexico City, 1986).

[23] Howard N. Fullerton, Jr., "Labor Force Projections: 1986 to 2000," *Monthly Labor Review* vol. 110, no. 9, (1987), 19–21.

United States. This watershed year saw the first deficit of new young male entrants into the labor force. The U.S. Department of Labor calculated that by the year 2000 there would be a 6 percent decrease in the number of young males 16 to 24 years of age and a 15 percent drop in the 24 to 34 age group. The proportion of the labor market occupied by young males was 23 percent in 1972; by 1986 it had fallen to 20 percent. By the year 2000 it will fall to 16 percent, while the proportion of workers over 35 will increase to 61 percent from the 1986 ratio of 51 percent.[24]

If these data were not convincing enough, one could also add the latest projections concerning the composition of the U.S. labor force. Silverstri and Lukasiewics from the U.S. Department of Labor have found that the twelve occupations that will undergo the most growth between 1986 and 2000 will be the following: waiters, supermarket clerks, house and building cleaners, restaurant cooks and cook's helpers, bartenders, non-farm laborers, servants at private clubs, and private security personnel.[25] The authors add that the service sector will grow the fastest from now until the end of the century—from 17.5 million in 1986 to almost 30 million by the year 2000.

As can be readily inferred, these occupations are where one finds more than half of the undocumented population. Given the pattern of growth of those working-age groups from now until the end of the century, there is no way that the population disposed to work in the United States will satisfy the demand of more than 5 million vacancies that will open in those occupations where skills and salaries are the lowest. Unless in the next years robots are invented at a cost comparable to that of an undocumented worker, the economy of the United States will be threatened with a lower rate of growth, which is socially and politically unacceptable. The alternative is to "import" the foreign labor force that will cover the deficits produced by the aging of the U.S. working population.

The data point to a greater U.S. dependence on foreign labor, beginning precisely when the restrictive immigration legislation was passed in 1986. Nevertheless, this growing dependence can be dramatically altered by an economic recession and a critical increase in unemployment. If such a downturn occurs in the United States, IRCA will more likely be implemented to the full extent. This conjecture leads to two types of pos-

[24] Fullerton, "Labor Force Projections."

[25] George T. Silvestri and John M. Lukasiewics, "A Look at Occupational Employment Trends to the Year 2000," *Monthly Labor Review* vol. 110, no. 9 (1987), 46–63.

sible scenarios, which I will construct later in the paper: one based on conditions of economic stability and expansion; and another based on conditions of recession and economic instability.

THE QUESTION OF NATIONAL SECURITY

A third basic presupposition of the framework has to do with an operational definition of "national security." No definition for this concept has yet achieved consensus. For the purposes of this paper, I will assume that a problem of "national security" exists when the nation-state defines it explicitly or implicitly as such.

This definition of national security uses the theoretical elements of a definition of sovereignty. It has been universally accepted since the French Revolution that the sovereignty of a nation resides in the people, but that the legitimate representatives of the people, in an institutional form with a constitutional basis, exercise national sovereignty. This legitimate representation of the people is referred to as the "nation-state." The exercise of sovereignty by the nation-state constitutes the expression of the people's self-determination.

This explanation, however, still leaves open when and how a situation becomes defined as a national security problem. This problem can be resolved if we accept the elementary principle of the general theory of the State, which states that the latter is the only legitimate source for expressing the sovereignty of a nation. This is the same as saying that it is through the State that people express their self-determination, making the State the only legitimate organ to determine when there is a problem of national security.

I accept that the reason for a military establishment is to protect national sovereignty. Mobilization of the military by a state indicates that the state has decided to confront a problem of national security. The mobilization of the military in order to combat drug trafficking, then, may be given as evidence that the Mexican State defines drug trafficking as a national security problem. The extent to which a part or majority of the nation's population can object to such a definition is determined through the institutional mechanisms open to the electorate for correcting their representatives' decisions.

MEXICO'S POLITICAL STABILITY

Fourth, it is also assumed here that the highest priority for the national security of Mexico is its internal political stability. This assumption implies that political stability gives the State a greater capacity to respond to pressures or threats against national security, either from inside or from outside of the country, inasmuch as a situation of internal political instability weakens the state's capacity to define and respond to a foreign threat against national security.

I consider a threat to national security any event whose visible direction or concrete effects will impede the functioning of constitutional precepts. In this definition, the "functioning" of the constitution is understood in relative terms. It is evident that the Mexican Constitution is not respected in a pure fashion in the reality in which we live. It is probable that no constitution functions in absolute terms. Nevertheless, the constitution is not only the maximum normative ordering from which is derived the institutional notion of "public order." It has been said that there is also a "social contract" between a state and a society. On the basis of this operational definition, all problems of an internal nature defined by the State as "national security" problems have implications for the functioning of constitutional rights and the normative framework on which depends the legality of State actions and the institutional operation of the forces of public security, including the military. Based on these notions, it can be said that, in theory, the constitution legitimizes the defense of society and individuals against an arbitrary definition of "a national security threat" by the government. As such, the constitution is a reference point for any definition of "national security," be it legitimate or arbitrary.

It could be argued that Article 29 of the Mexican Constitution is too vague to define when there is a problem of "national security." This article identifies an "invasion" or a "grave disturbance to public peace" as conditions under which the president can partially or totally suspend the individual liberties contained in the constitution.

A BASIC SCHEME OF ALTERNATIVE SCENARIOS

Based on the above presuppositions, a scheme of analysis can be developed to try to organize them from the most abstract to the most concrete. Throughout this scheme, I suppose the interaction of two variables: (1) the state of the U.S. economy; and (2) the political situation of Mexico. To facilitate the analysis, I have divided the variables into two opposite categories: stability and instability. The four scenarios are derived from the intersection of these four variables.

Each scenario is derived from the contextual explanations that follow, which define what is understood by undocumented migration and by national security. Obviously, I am not attempting to predict with this scheme. I am only hypothesizing it in order to stimulate discussion concerning the possible future relation between the two countries from a perspective of national security and migration.

Given the bilateral nature of undocumented immigration, and given the importance of the U.S. economy in determining this phenomenon, the analytical model schematized above allows one to analyze the short- and medium-term future in terms of four hypothetical scenarios derived from a theoretical interaction of economic variables originating in the United States and political variables originating in Mexico.

The analysis for each scenario will be done through sequentially focusing on economic conditions in the United States; political conditions in Mexico; the effects on migration; and the implications for national security.

Case 1: U.S. Economic Expansion and Mexican Political Stability

In this case, we assume that the United States maintains a rate of economic growth of 3 percent annually (4 percent in California). Under these conditions, demographic tendencies (aging of the working-age population and a decline in young workers) would produce the maximum level of demand for foreign labor.[26] On this basis, we could expect a relaxing of the IRCA laws despite pressure from the INS and from restrictionist groups like the Federation for American Immigration Reform (FAIR) to enforce existing laws and implement new ones in order to deter new undocumented immigration flows. The demand for foreign labor should provoke the appearance of new legalization programs such as SAW and RAW. The contracting of undocumented migrants would be a progressively more open practice with the presentation of any type of document, regardless of its authenticity, deemed sufficient for employment. Given the labor demand generated by U.S. economic growth and the aging of the population, employers would pay more attention to the laws of market forces than to immigration laws. Under these conditions, IRCA would advance down the road of obsolescence.

Not everything would be rosy, however, despite the conditions of an expanding U.S. economy. It is likely that a situation would develop that is more a function of the bureaucracies than of individual wills. The Border Patrol in particular and the INS in general would see the importance of their daily work threatened in the eyes of public opinion as immigration laws are honored in the breach. It is safe to say that the bureaucracy could go through a phase of artificially provoking incidents in which they

[26] Reynolds, "Labor Market Projections."

would re-establish their image as the "guardians of the nation." This would not be the first time that the undocumented immigrant would have been used as a convenient scapegoat in the middle of quite autonomous political and bureaucratic battles about unemployment, social service troubles, and even environmental pollution.

This scenario assumes that President Salinas would be able to consolidate his presidential leadership with policies that generate broad support; political reform would be legislated despite some objections from opposition political parties; and the principal effect of the debt renegotiation would be a re-establishment of investor confidence, manifested through the repatriation of flight capital and new foreign investments.

As employment and real wages increase, strengthening government credibility, the ruling party would more than likely take the opportunity to change its name and restructure itself to formally include the middle classes and the private sector in addition to its traditional support bases in labor, peasantry, and popular organizations.

National economic growth of 6 to 8 percent would be uneven across regions. The oil-producing regions would benefit from renewed investment by PEMEX, drawing new, more highly skilled immigrants. The fastest economic growth would be concentrated in northwest Mexico, particularly Baja California. This area would benefit from foreign investment, which seeks to integrate production operations as close as possible to where new technologies in areas such as biotechnology and electronics are created, as well as near cheap labor supplies. New international service companies would be formed, with domestic cleaning workers, under contract to multinational corporations, living on the Mexican border and traveling daily to cities in the U.S. Southwest.

This regional growth would necessitate major investment in infrastructure, which in turn would create many jobs, and thus increase competition within the *maquiladora* industry for workers. The new national governing party might sweep the northern governorships as a result of this growth.

Implications for migration. Under a Case 1 scenario, the migration of Mexican workers to the United States would continue as it had during the late 1980s, when IRCA did not produce significant reductions in migration levels.[27] The principal tendencies of this migration will be a large proportion of women in the flow (Fig. 2); higher levels of urban migrants (Fig. 3); greater differences between mean national education and the

[27] Jorge A. Bustamante, "Research Findings and Policy Options," in Rordan Roett, ed., *Mexico and the United States: Managing the Relationship* (Boulder, Colo., 1988), 109–132.

education of those who migrate (Fig. 4); increasing costs of migration (Fig. 5); increases in political extortions in border cities (Fig. 6); a decrease in the number of immigrant workers (Fig. 7); and increases in the demand for immigrant workers in the United States.

In a scenario of economic growth and political stability in Mexico, conditions will be the best for a strong Mexican initiative for reaching a binational agreement on migrant workers. Nevertheless, given the high level of politicization that the issue of "illegal aliens" has reached in the United States, it will be very difficult to find general public support for a treaty between the two countries. The Mexican government will be buttressed in its support for such a treaty by the UN adoption of a multilateral convention on the rights of migrant workers after a decade of debate. While the United States will vote against this agreement, it would nevertheless be an opportunity for bilateral negotiations on this question.

The Mexican government could generate public support for negotiations by forwarding the following objectives: (1) to reduce the flight of human capital needed for national and regional development, asserting that in the long run labor emigration is against the national interest; and (2) given the impossibility of halting the escape of workers to the United States, to establish, with the United States, a means for defending the human rights and labor rights of migrant workers. Throughout, the Mexican government should include in all discussions authentic representation from migrant workers.

Given the low probabilities of reaching such an agreement on migrant workers, new mechanisms should be formed that can include migrant workers as part of an internationally traded service sector subject to a bilateral service trade agreement. In this type of agreement, Mexican workers would enter the United States under contract by a labor service company that would make itself responsible for their arrival and departure. The workers would remain only long enough to obtain certain service jobs contracted under a non-immigrant visa status. The advantage to the workers would be better salaries and benefits because of their affiliation to the Mexican social security system, which would be altered for this type of international work.

Even without this scenario, the conditions determined by a U.S. economic expansion, with the additional interaction of U.S. labor demand with Mexican labor supply, would result in a growing scarcity of labor in the United States and a greater demand for Mexican labor. On the other hand, the growing costs of migration to the United States from traditional sending regions in Mexico would tend to reduce the volume of undocumented migrants. Both conditions will facilitate the efforts of the Mexican government in negotiating a labor migration treaty.

Implications for national security. Under the assumptions of Case 1, the implications for U.S. or Mexican national security are minimal. From the Mexican perspective, the most serious implications would arise if there were continued extortion by Mexican police of Mexican and Central American undocumented migrants in northern Mexican cities, which would raise international concern for human rights along with strong criticism against the Mexican government. Nevertheless, under conditions of political stability, it is likely that this extortion would become more visible and the political costs to the government of not combating it would increase. In this scenario, the president himself would be pressured to implement measures to prevent extortion though a more thorough public review and evaluation of all police forces operating at the Mexican side of the border.

Case 2: U.S. Economic Recession and Mexican Political Stability

This scenario assumes that sometime in the early 1990s the United States will start showing signs of recession. Unemployment would begin to increase, interest rates would rise, and protectionist sentiments, targeted especially for low-wage countries like Mexico, would re-emerge.

Facing rapidly increasing unemployment, various political actors in the United States would once again use Mexican undocumented migration as a scapegoat for the problems of recession. There would be a resurgence of xenophobic rhetoric, particularly toward Mexicans, from INS officials and from politicians seeking election or re-election. Violence would increase along the border, and IRCA's provisions, including massive deportation of undocumented migrants, would be fully implemented.

On the Mexican side, a consolidation of electoral reform, with increased party competition, would begin. Under these conditions, there would be a very conspicuous reaction to the events in the United States, which, given the political rhetoric in the United States, would most likely be a nationalist response by all the political parties in Mexico. Energetic protests, particularly on the border, would be organized against INS violence. Various Mexican political parties would actively seek to organize Mexican workers in the United States as well as to invoke the solidarity of Hispanic organizations. Under this scenario, we should witness a surge of ethno-political activity in border cities in both countries that would link the interests of Mexican-origin organizations in the United States with political parties in Mexico.

Implications for migration. Despite the economic downturn in the United States, undocumented migration to the United States would continue. Immigrant workers would become the greatest conflict of the binational relationship. Mexico would gain international approval at international forums by attacking abuses of Mexicans' human rights in the United States. The tensions and violent incidents generated by the conditions of this scenario would result in committees along the Mexican border to help those deported return to their places of origin. The federal government would likely create an emergency plan in order to respond to the population crisis generated by the mass deportations on the border.

Implications for national security. There would be a significant increase of U.S. pressure on Mexico to negotiate an international agreement to close the border to undocumented migration and drug trafficking. From the United States would come suggestions that the Mexican army should patrol the border to impede the passage of undocumented migrants and of drug traffickers. Pressures would increase from conservative groups in the U.S. for a militarization of the border, perhaps including the building of a system of deep moats and guard houses on the U.S. side.

Case 3: U.S. Economic Expansion and Mexican Political Instability

In this scenario, in addition to the economic conditions listed in Case 1, circumstances in Mexico might cause the United States to try to take advantage of the political instability confronting the Mexican government by offering economic assistance in exchange for unprecedented concessions such as the acceptance of foreign investors in PEMEX operations. Pressures would increase for Mexico to accept the idea of a North American common market as well as to make ever more exceptions to Articles 27 and 123 of the Mexican Constitution, which favor foreign investors. The U.S. government would also take advantage of the situation to create conditions that would lower wages paid to Mexicans, both on the border as well as within the United States. Any loans accepted by the Mexican government under conditions of political instability would impel it to accept terms harmful to national sovereignty.

The political instability of Mexico would manifest itself most conspicuously in Mexico City, where protest demonstrations could well culminate in violent repression. Political instability would provoke capital flight, which would be accompanied by a human exodus, particularly from the middle and upper classes. An intensification of anti-Mexico City sentiment in northern Mexico would occur, and there would be calls for separatism supported by powerful groups in the United States.

Implications for migration. The disturbances in Mexico City would produce, among other effects, a massive exodus of people toward border cities and the United States. Having a major proportion of Mexico City residents participating in the migratory wave would immediately (1) increase the educational levels of migrants, (2) increase the proportion of women in the migrant flow, (3) heighten competition for the jobs most sought after by Mexico City migrants, (4) create an excess labor supply, which will tend to reduce the wages of immigrants in the United States, and (5) increase exponentially the number of people in the informal sectors on the border. We can also expect an increasing level of frustration resulting from U.S. expulsions; a depletion of funds before finding work in the United States; and/or an effect known as *relative deprivation* (when an immigrant can find work in border cities or the United States only in those occupations with much lower skill requirements than their former job). Combinations of these trends can lead to greater delinquency and violence in border cities—resembling the criminalization of some South American cities such as Bogota, Medellin, Rio de Janeiro, and Lima—and can increase the number and power of organized criminal "gangs." The massive exodus toward the United States would grow, along with the brutality of repression against those who attempt to cross the border. This violence would generate a strong reaction among Mexicans and Chicanos, with protest marches in large cities in the United States. A new wave of repression with racist overtones, like that against African American activists in the 1960s, would be inflicted on people from Mexico.

Implications for national security. Mexico's political instability and its increasing vulnerability with respect to the United States would have results that demonstrate the weakness of Mexico's government in confronting a crisis under those circumstances. For example, the government might give in to pressures from the Mexican right wing and reform some basic articles of the Mexican Constitution such as Article 3 (the separation of church and state in the field of education); Article 11 ("All persons have a right to enter the country, leave the country, travel through it, and change residences"); Article 14 ("No person can be deprived of their life, liberty, possessions or rights"); Article 27 ("The ownership of all land and water within the national territory, corresponds originally to the nation. . . . The nation will at all times have the right to impose onto private property modalities that are dictated by the public interest"); Article 123 ("All persons have the right to work that is dignified and socially useful"); and Article 130 ("The law does not formally recognize any religiously denominated churches").

Case 4: A Downturn of the U.S. Economy and Mexican Instability

This scenario comprises predictions of a large recession in the 1990s, such as those formulated by a number of economists including Ravi Ba-

tra, Alfred L. Malabre, Jr., and Lawrence Malkin.[28] In this scenario, the
long process of indebtedness since the 1970s by U.S. consumers, corporations, and the government would finally reach its limit and lead to a
sharp downturn in spending. Since corporations would have been investing more in the stock market than in the renovation of their plant and
equipment, growth in productivity would continue its 1980s' decelera-
tion. Because public spending in research and development would have
fallen drastically, the U.S. would lose the race with Japan and Europe for
advances in new technology.

In 1992, the European Community would emerge as a unified political and economic power, generating a commercial war in which the
United States would be at a disadvantage with manufacturing exports
that are not competitive in price or in quality. The U.S. economy would
stop growing and begin a new recession. To the extent that the revenues
and profits of corporations would begin to decline, the already huge deficit of the U.S. government would increase due to reductions in tax re-
ceipts. Because the U.S. Federal Reserve would decide to increase interest
rates—in order to stimulate more loans to the U.S. government to finance
its ballooning federal deficit (which surpasses $300 million)—high inter-
est rates would halt the growth of the economy by creating a vicious
cycle in which the government could not stimulate growth through further deficit spending. The U.S. government would be forced to maintain
high interest rates in order to obtain the funds necessary to service its
debts—an amount that would represent an increasingly greater share of
the federal deficit.

To the extent that the U.S. economy enters a recession, all the countries exporting to the United States would be affected by the reduction of
its import capacity. Those countries that depend the most on exports to
the United States would be affected most, and would consequently suffer
economic recession and increasing unemployment. As a result of the
growing practice of buying more imported rather than domestically produced goods (the inverse of export-oriented countries), the United States
would be inundated by dollars from countries to which it used to export
the most. The resistance to the flood of dollars from these countries
would provoke a fall in U.S. reserves. The high rates of interest that the
United States would have been maintaining would make the costs of

[28] Raveendra N. Batra, *The Great Depression of 1990* (New York, 1987); Alfred L.
Malabre, *Beyond Our Means: How America's Long Years of Debt, Deficits, and Reckless
Borrowing Now Threaten to Overwhelm Us* (New York, 1987); Lawrence Malkin, *The
National Debt* (New York, 1987); quoted by John Miller and Vince Valvano, "The Profits
of Doom," in *Dollars & Cents* (Oct. 1987), 39–42.

capital so high that investment would be prohibitive, thus deepening the recession.

Finally, all the accumulated debts would provoke a collapse in the economy. The foreign debt of the United States and the debt of consumers and corporations would be so large and interest rates so high that all these groups would stop paying their obligations. In a domino effect, the agricultural sector, with an older debt, would be the first to go bankrupt. The smaller banks that lent to the agricultural sector would fail next, followed by severe problems in the larger banks. Soon the most indebted countries, which would also cease to meet their obligations, would provoke the bankruptcies of the largest banks. A "crash" in the stock market more profound than in 1929 would occur.

As a result of the deepest depression in its history, the United States would resort to increasingly aggressive protectionist strategies. Xenophobic sentiments in the United States would be spurred on by those looking for foreign scapegoats to explain the crisis. This would not be the first time in the history of U.S. economic recessions when foreign immigrants, and Mexican undocumented migrants in particular, would become victims of this economic and sociological phenomenon. The xenophobic environment originating in the crisis would result in an organization such as FAIR finally succeeding in its proposal to construct a high wall and moat along the U.S.-Mexico border and to finance it through large fines on arrested undocumented workers and through a tax on Mexicans who want to enter the United States.

A border wall and moat would substantially change the nature of economic, social, and cultural relations characteristic of the U.S.-Mexico border region. There would be a rapid elimination of all transborder interactions, making it appear increasingly like the China-USSR border.

The depth of the economic recession in the United States would affect immediately the border region of Northern Mexico, provoking accelerated unemployment. This employment, in turn, would induce an exodus of Mexican workers to the United States so massive that the Border Patrol would institute a state of emergency—a situation that could involve deployment of paramilitary forces who would undertake a variety of well-publicized actions. This exodus of border residents would augment the already growing migrations from within Mexico. As the U.S. recession continues to penetrate Mexico, this flow would grow continuously. This phenomenon in Mexican border cities would reach a dramatic climax in a "sandwich syndrome" consisting of an accumulation of the locally disemployed, the migrant population deported to the border by the INS, and the migrant populations from the interior of Mexico who are frustrated in their attempt to cross into the United States. The coalescence of these three populations will be unprecedented, both in terms of numbers and in terms of their high levels of schooling. This increase could possibly reach the point of collective assaults on shopping centers similar to those witnessed recently in Caracas and in Brazilian cities.

The rest of the scenario described in Case 2 would be virtually mirrored within the United States.

In terms of Mexico's political instability, it would become difficult to distinguish when or where the violence and public disruptions in Mexico City and in other cities would correspond to increasing desperation, political militancy, or simple delinquency. Terrorist acts and kidnapping would increase. Mexican border cities would become powder kegs with sporadic outbreaks that would lead to repression, which in turn would lead to a proliferation of violence. In a maximum state of political instability, the constitutional government would fall and a military junta would take power and immediately suspend constitutional rights.

Implications for migration. Under these conditions, what was until recently only an exaggeration designed for domestic U.S. political consumption would come true: the United States would lose control over its southern border in the face of the largest human exodus in the history of the continent.

Implications for national security. Individual liberties would be suppressed under a military state of siege.

CONCLUSIONS

The hypothetical scenarios presented here are based on the assumption that, at a macrodimensional level, the interactions between Mexico and the United States have been of a very different nature for each country. Independent of the political intentions of U.S. officials toward Mexico, economic actions whose effects south of the border are determined by an asymmetry of power have dominated the formation of the bilateral relation.

From these premises, I derived a matrix that, to facilitate the analysis, dichotomizes the different dominate actions of one country and their effects on the other into (1) "stability-instability" of the Mexican state and (2) "expansion-recession" of the U.S. economy. In each case, a result from this matrix is used to study the immediate future of the bilateral relations between Mexico and the United States. Obviously my intent is not to make a single prediction. The purpose of this construction of scenarios is to analyze that which is remotely possible in order to plan and evaluate their possibility and avoid undesirable outcomes. Keeping all in perspective, this paper is an attempt to analyze to what extent we are prepared for those eventualities whose opportunity we see today as remote or for a disaster that we today see as improbable. The most certain aspect of this exercise is that the interactions between the U.S. economy and Mexican political stability will affect and be affected by the migration of Mexican workers to the North, which in turn will have implications for the national security of both countries.

[Eds. Note: Perhaps ironically, events that have occurred since this draft was written reflect a mixture of conditions among the scenarios presented here. First, Mexico has pressed for NAFTA, with argument by the United States and Canada in administration to negotiate in good faith, recognizing an inevitable linkage of the economies and societies and the growing challenge of external blocs. Second, a persistent weakness of the U.S. economy that is related is its international vulnerability. This leads to an apparent contradiction. NAFTA on the one hand raises fears mentioned in scenario four—of downward convergence. On the other hand, U.S. (and Canadian) competitiveness requires links with lower wage partners (such as Mexico, the ideal case). None of the scenarios addresses this.]

Immigration and Regulation: Historical Context and Legal Reform

Thomas Heller

T HE HISTORY OF American immigration policy has been discussed from a variety of perspectives. These alternative accounts have produced both positive and negative portrayals of immigration. The former emphasize its humanitarian and liberal economic effects; the latter, which have often relied on racist images that scapegoat immigrants as deviants, demand the exclusion of the foreign in order to preserve an American national identity. It may bring additional insight to the recent debates over immigration policy, which culminated in the passage of the Immigration Reform and Control Act of 1986 (IRCA), to consider them in the light of a less familiar historical perspective. This essay will focus upon the origins of American immigration controls within a wider movement to conceive and enact the comprehensive regulatory system that has defined the character of activist or neo-liberal American government in the twentieth century. Looking at immigration policy not as a separate domain of political life, but as one aspect of an integrated theory of the modern industrial state, allows particular features of its development and contemporary dynamics to be highlighted.

Pursuing this line of analysis, it is necessary to examine the relationship between immigration controls and the corporatist strain in Progressive thought in the early decades of this century, when the first comprehensive immigration laws were legislated.[1] It was the addition in the early 1920s

---

[1] *Corporatism* is a complex term that has generated an enormous literature seeking to define it. It continues to be plagued by debates over its relationship to organicism, fascism, and more broadly, authoritarianism, and has spawned a panoply of distinctions such as those between corporatism and neo-corporatism, and state and societal corporatism. Without entering this extensive argument, those principle features of corporatism as a post-liberal, industrial ideology that will be emphasized in this essay include (1) a commitment

of Progressive support to the previously insufficient strength of anti-immigration forces that ended the era of almost free entry to the United States. Consequently, the political motivations of these reformers—who were anxious for a fundamental restructuring of American institutions to make them better correspond to the needs of an advanced industrial society—provided the context that framed the economic and cultural understanding of immigration policy. However, after the first years of the New Deal when corporatist programs were openly embraced, the genesis of immigration control was forgotten or repressed. Hopeful of reestablishing the narrative continuity of American history by expurgating the memory of the socialist and corporatist currents that had emerged with the mass industrial economy, liberal authors of the postwar period reworked the prevailing images of the history and role of immigration in American life. It is these reconstructed cultural and economic images that persist and dominate current legal and political immigration debates, rather than the recollection of the circumstances in which immigration controls were embedded within the established, though increasingly contested, institutional regime in place since this period.

In a similar way, present-day problems of immigration policy can be seen as one aspect of a wider struggle over a second possible restructuring of advanced industrial societies. There is ongoing argument whether the existing immigration law should be strengthened against new demographic trends or abandoned because it is no longer necessary nor feasible to control the contemporary dual migratory flows of unskilled and superskilled workers to the United States. This reconsideration of immigration policy parallels the analysis of other institutional structures developed around the New Deal whose effectiveness has been made problematic by the changing place of the American economy and polity in the global system. The persistent effort to reinforce immigration controls, which are structurally associated with an earlier period when Europeans flowed into a stable mass-production economy, may be ever less appropriate in an era dominated by Latin and Asian movements to an economy confronting the need for flexibility, specialization, sustained innovation, and adjustment to a reformed international division of production. Although the history of immigration is more complex than this

---

to technocratic administration rather than politics in the ordering of social and economic affairs, (2) the creation of an ongoing institutional nexus of bargaining relationships between organized labor, advanced industrial capital, and the bureaucratic state, and (3) the sharing of the economic rents of modern production as a counterweight to the continuation of the class struggle. For a discussion of the different meanings and interpretations, as well as an extensive bibliography, see Peter S. Williamson, *Corporatism in Perspective* (London, 1989), 1–48.

schematic periodization permits, a sketch of the historical linkage between the origins of immigration and the formation of the American regulatory state suggests that the current politics of restriction are more a symbol of a generalized desire to protect the established elements of a broadly challenged and defended regime than an independent reevaluation of the evolution of the integration of international labor markets and multiculturalism.

THE ROOTS OF IMMIGRATION CONTROL: NATIVISM AND LABOR

In the first decades of the twentieth century, against the background of substantial technical change in the economy, there was increasing uncertainty and debate about the proper structure of social institutions. The prior period, from the end of the Civil War to the turn of the century, had been marked less by the existence of an explicit normative consensus than by the normalization of political and economic practices within a decentralized institutional nexus. This nexus would retrospectively be characterized by historians and ideologists as a laissez-faire regime. The predominance of industrial technologies based on small-scale production, regional networks of distribution, and a lack of institutional (public or associational) coordination of social life opened up a theoretical space in which a liberal culture of individualism would flourish and define a particularly American image of national identity.

On the whole, American immigration policy (or the lack thereof, since migration was largely uncontrolled) in the late nineteenth century was consistent with these cultural and economic developments. The formation of a restrictive immigration doctrine coincided with the recession of the small-batch, local, artisan-dominated manufacturing system. This recession was brought about by the rise of industries based on innovative technologies making use of relatively higher capital and energy intensivity, scientific management of coordinated job-specific tasks, and long runs of standardized products. There is no need to argue that these techniques were mandated by a teleology of modern history. Nor need we assert that technological change determined in any necessary sense the reform of the traditional institutions of capital, labor, or the state, including immigration.[2] Rather, the shift toward mass production should be seen as a beginning point for analyzing a complex dynamic of institutional change in modern society whose outcome was always contingent on local political conflict and led to alternative configurations of organizations in different historical settings.

[2] See Michael J. Piore and Charles F. Sabel, *The Second Industrial Divide* (New York, 1986), 19–48.

In the United States, this period of institutional redesign was experienced as a struggle between contending groups committed to one of the following strategies: (1) traditional non-interference in the economy, (2) expanded, though limited, governmental regulation of private markets and social behavior, accompanied by a restriction of large-scale producers' power, (3) centralized socialist planning with worker control of capital-intensive, integrated firms, or (4) the creation of new corporatist structures involving sectoral industrial policies formulated by cooperative boards with representatives from capital, labor, and public agencies. The openness, confusion, and indeterminate trajectory of this period—the context in which immigration controls were legislated—extended until the increasingly concentrated mass-production sector was convulsed by the Great Depression. The now familiar regulatory system, elaborated in the latter New Deal, during World War II, and in its immediate aftermath, appears as a necessary stage in the smooth and logical evolution of liberalism. Yet this image of liberalism's history suppresses the contingency that attended the resolution of the conflict among the alternative agendas for structural reforms and that enriches the narrative of American social development. Part of the price paid for the imagery of political continuity is a reduction in the understanding of how immigration policy fitted into these earlier conflicts before it was reimagined and integrated into the orthodox narrative of contemporary American history.

Given that immigration restrictions are the normal practice of modern nations, it is a less interesting problem to explain their existence than to account for their rather late appearance in America and the particular form that the law finally assumed. When the first general quantitative limits on entry, contained within a system of national quotas for admission, were passed in 1921, they marked a turning point that left behind more than a century of relatively free movement to the United States.[3] This political shift commands special attention because interest groups seeking immigration regulation on economic and cultural grounds had been continually active in the latter half of the nineteenth century. Demands for restrictive legislation from both racial nativists and trade unionists may be treated as a near constant in modern American life. Since the relative political power of these movements with respect to immigration did not seem to fluctuate substantially during the historical passage from unrestricted entry to statutory control, other elements must account for the marginal factors that produced the change in national policy.

[3] E. P. Hutchinson, *Legislative History of American Immigration Policy 1798–1965* (Philadelphia, 1981), 171–85.

This influence at the margin may be attributed to the rise of Progressivism, and especially of the corporatist elements within it, in the first decades of the twentieth century. It would be unfair to say that immigration was the major concern of those businessmen and intellectuals who experimented with corporatist solutions in order to deal with the functional problems of managing a mass-production economy and to create alternative social institutions necessary to support its stable evolution. Rather, immigration control was an instrument to fortify the distributional mechanisms Progressives felt would help ensure industrial and social peace. Moreover, the particular form given to the immigration law was consistent with and influenced by positivist philosophical commitments shared by early corporatists. These commitments suggested the utopian possibility of a technologically administered social order in which an objectively determinate theory of culture, built on a science of eugenics, could explain, predict, and control human behavior. The ultimate fate of Progressivism's corporatist wing was determined by both its ideological incompatibility with America's image of itself and the incorporation of residues of its institutional reforms within the neo-liberal system that emerged from the Great Depression and World War II.[4] An element of that corporatist residue was the insertion of immigration law into the structure of governmental controls that were later reproduced as the orthodox constitution of the American regulatory state.

Before the addition of Progressive elements to the coalition favoring immigration controls, the opponents of restriction had forestalled the passage of restrictive legislation with both cultural and economic arguments. The cultural definition of an American identity had been an arena of discord throughout the nineteenth century. On the one hand, the fundamental commitment to liberal principles implied that there should be open membership in the American community. Since liberal political philosophy imagined the individual to be the constitutive unit of social organization, there was a universalist norm of inclusion within the national

[4] Although American corporatists were vilified after the late 1930s for philosophical and institutional affinities to European fascism, in contradiction to the German, Italian, or the Argentine (Peronist) experience of corporatism, its American Progressive adherents did not advocate the totalitarian organization, or even the interinstitutional predominance, of the state apparatus. In fact, the theoretical uncertainty about the mobilizing and directive role of the American state led in the early New Deal to a set of bureaucratic practices that manifested a relative passivity of public agencies. This practice both reflected the classical American tradition of weak government and contributed to the delegitimating perception during its apogee in the early New Deal that corporatism was no more than a screen for the ongoing control of national policy by the industrial establishment of the East. See Ellis W. Hawley, *The New Deal and the Problem of Monopoly Power* (Princeton, N.J., 1966), 19–148, 283–382.

body politic. As opposed to the ascriptive linking of nationality with substantive cultural characteristics—a tendency that generally prevailed in Europe—liberal theory suggested that national identity turned upon a willed, personal commitment to shared political principles including liberty, equality, and government by consent. Membership through self-identification could be derived from liberalism's existential phenomenology, which stressed the subjective capacity to create one's own life history.[5] Early American accounts of immigration viewed the objective cultural element in American identity as recessive. They emphasized the individual act of leaving one's national origins behind—the American's abandonment of any prior cultural determination of character—and imagined the subsequent political transformation of personality to be perfectible in a single lifetime. To choose to migrate from Europe was itself evidence of a transformation of psychological nature homologous to the transformation of the social system from preexisting organic collectivities to modern liberalism. Open immigration and easy naturalization were the institutional reflections of this transfigured image of identity as an artifact of individual choice.

The idea of a liberal American culture was from the outset uncertain. First, there is a paradox inherent in basing a national identity upon universalist principles. The essence of culture has traditionally been understood as the collective reproduction of patterned social differentiation. However, American culture, in its insistence on individual self-determination, consistently denies its ability to define the substantive attributes of community membership. This tension between the particularity of nationhood and liberal subjectivism was never resolved completely in favor of a universalist logic. The legal exclusion of Asians from immigration and from citizenship after 1882 pointed to the tensions inherent in these contradictions. The wide consensus in favor of restriction made apparent that the belief in the limited ability of the members of some groups to assume the status of mature, willing subjects was embedded in a broader historical teleology of racial or cultural determinism, which demarcated the limits of liberal inclusiveness.

Moreover, there were rather deep philosophical problems in liberal individualism that led in post-Enlightenment Europe to a Romantic resurrection of organic theories of national identity. New World ideologists similarly imported the concept of Volksgeist elaborated in the anti-Kantian theories of Herder and Hegel.[6] American society in its formative

---

[5] Thomas C. Heller, "Structuralism and Critique," *Stanford Law Review* (Jan. 1984), 175–77.
[6] Heller, "Structuralism," 136–38.

years enjoyed the fortunate coincidence of a commitment to liberal individualism as a constitutional principle and the presence of substantial
homogeneity in cultural practices. When the mid-nineteenth-century
growth of Catholic and non-Anglo-Saxon immigration introduced to
American life a pluralism of cultural practices, important segments of the
political spectrum fell back on the Romantic analysis and identified
American national character with the predominant social institutions established in the Colonial period, rather than with personal commitment
to a set of procedural ideals.

Employing a variant of organicism as a theoretical discourse, an emergent American nativism argued that membership in the national community demanded subordination to a collectivity defined by traditional
Anglican practices in religion, politics, economics, and culture. The historical trajectory of subjectivity or spirit (Geist) was elevated from the
individual actor to a super-individual or nationalist level. Pluralism and
the capacity to express moral commitment through action became attributes of relations between cultures rather than of behavior within
them. This ill-worked-out world view was more a rationalizing mysticism
than a thoroughgoing scientific determinism of the characteristics of an
American national character. However, its pragmatic consequences were
overtly restrictionist.[7]

Nativism was always anti-radical in that foreign influences favoring
social change necessarily disrupted the conservation of American institutions. Nativism was originally focused especially on Catholic immigrants, who were seen as inextricably tied to a reactionary, anti-liberal
Europe. Their continued tie to the Church was taken as proof that their
cultural commitments to their society of origin had not been left behind.
Refusal to amalgamate in public schools and bloc voting in urban areas
were further evidence that immigrants were infiltrating agents of a different, antagonistic Volksgeist seeking to undercut American liberal institutions. In the latter half of the nineteenth century, xenophobes increasingly turned to a fundamentally anti-liberal rhetoric that identified
unassimilable peoples incapable of mature subjective choice in the name
of defending an American organicism whose attributes included a commitment to liberal imagery. The contradictory character of this discourse,
which categorized collectivities by their different capacities to socialize
individualists, did not impede the growth of an essentially anti-intellec-
tual nationalist nativism that has remained an abiding undercurrent of
American conservatism. However, except for its racist victory over the

[7] See John Higham, *Strangers in the Land* (New York, 1965), 35–97.

"exotic Oriental" in the Chinese Exclusion Act of 1882, nativism was not able, prior to the development of a theoretically more coherent determinism in Progressive ideology, to transpose its philosophy into comprehensive legal policy.

Organized labor constituted a second element of the pro-restrictionist coalition with a long history of anti-immigration politics. The dominant late-nineteenth-century view of international economics was in accord with classical principles of free trade, open factor markets, and stable rates of currency exchange. Business interests in particular, although they might still argue for sectorally limited high tariffs on developmental or infant industry grounds, were increasingly articulate about the stimulus to economic growth derivable from the unobstructed flow of capital and labor to the United States.[8] The politics of the formative organized labor movement were more complex. They reflected the evolving organization of trade unions within the industrial regime that preceded mass production, the contingencies associated with the transition to mass-production technologies in those sectors where they were initially established, and the residual features of an earlier production organization that persisted in the immature mass-production system.[9]

Before 1820, wage labor was unfamiliar in the United States. Slavery, independent farming, craft and artisan production, household manufacture and family work, and indentured servitude were the prevailing forms of petty commodity production. As the development of larger-scale production and the extension of markets fostered the emergence of wage labor, firms at once added workers and continued to rely on traditional arrangements of tools, craft skills, materials, and internal control processes. Most often, manufacturing in larger enterprises (textiles being a principal exception) was an agglomerated operation of small shops or work crews rather than an integrated line of production with subdivision of tasks. Factories were bigger but did not necessarily have higher productivity than traditional plants. As opposed to later periods in which economic growth resulted principally from a combination of technological change and the reorganization of production processes, this earlier period was characterized by a transfer of existing techniques into the

---

[8] As Lake points out, it is always expected that there will be some business lobbying for protection in particular industries, since the optimal position from the standpoint of any industrial sector is to free ride on free trade. This was equally true of late-nineteenth-century American industry. See David A. Lake, *Power, Protection, and Free Trade* (Ithaca, N.Y., 1988), 91–119.

[9] Piore and Sabel, *Second Industrial Divide*, 111–32; David M. Gordon, Richard Edwards, Michael Reich, *Segmented Work, Divided Workers* (Cambridge, Eng., 1982), 112–62.

capitalist sector. Development was extensive or derived from the expansion of employment rather than intensive or associated with qualitative production changes that lead to rising productivity per worker.

During the first part of the nineteenth century, the major institutional reforms that facilitated economic growth were aimed at removing feudal or mercantile legal barriers to the free flow of goods and production factors.[10] At the same time, within the expanding labor market, the existence of independent organizations of skilled artisans made it necessary to explore the industrial-relations problems presented by the incorporation of craft-production techniques into the wage system. Craft manufacture was characterized by workers with general skills acquired through limited-entry apprenticeships. These specialized workers produced a varied range of particular commodities and were capable of rapid, flexible response to shifts of demand. Multiple technologies were usually in evidence at any one time, and competition through product innovation predominated over wage or price competition, which was often internally constrained. In accordance with earlier guild traditions, craft workers often established local institutions. These included organizations to finance and support municipal projects as well as to develop a type of welfare capitalism in which networks of artisan shops, often grouped around core capital facilities, supplied social services to their members.[11]

The established forms of production control in small capitalist or family firms concentrated authority in entrepreneurs, foremen, or labor drivers. Craft workers, however, were usually self-paced and resistant to the external job definition and work timing implicit in the wage-control model. As employers struggled to break down the domination of the craft workers on whose technology they continued to depend, the workers transformed their collectivist impulses into local unions that resisted those changes in the production process that could diminish their control of the workplace. Labor activists had substantial difficulty forming comprehensive, generalized unions in fragmented markets among workers divided by both ethnic background and tensions between more- and less-skilled laborers. Nevertheless, as the nineteenth century matured, the organization of craft workers and their formation of associated labor federations became a principal source of resistance to employer-sponsored technological change.

The gradual increase in nationwide competition in the post–Civil War

[10] Thomas C. Heller, "Legal Theory and the Political Economy of American Federalism," in Mauro Cappelletti, Monica Seccombe, and Joseph Weiler, eds., *Integration Through Law: Europe and the American Federal Experience* (Berlin, 1986), 262–63.
[11] Piore and Sabel, *Second Industrial Divide*.

economy increased the intensity of problems created by the craft unions' resistance to those new forms of production that diminished craft workers' autonomy and importance. To reduce costs, more firms began to push to achieve greater managerial control of the labor process. Imposing a hierarchical internal organization allowed firms to follow new technological developments and to apply scientific management principles in pursuit of higher productivity. The history of the first period of American trade unionism was characterized both by struggles between craft workers and capitalists within the traditional organization of production and, simultaneously, by labor's resistance to the growing pressure by firms to transform production in a way that would wholly dissipate craft control.

This dual conflict, in turn, led to a bifurcation in the politics of unions with respect to immigration. To the extent that importation of labor was associated with firms' attempts to shift production processes toward newer techniques, which emphasized the use of deskilled (non-craft) labor, craft unions opposed immigration as one aspect of a more general campaign against industrial system reform. This tradition of opposing the expansion of the unskilled labor force and the technologies that encouraged its employment was well established in the American Federation of Labor by the beginning of the twentieth century, even though most unskilled immigrants at the end of the nineteenth century were moving into industries with few craft precedents.

In addition, when organized labor began to alter its strategy in response to the loss of craft power and turned to unionizing the growing number of unskilled and semi-skilled workers in the emerging mass-production firms, the opposition to free labor flows became in part grounded on the more familiar desire to monopolize labor markets and capture for unionized workers some greater share of the growing economic rents yielded by those technological innovations associated with capital-intensive production. While the introduction of capital-intensive technologies undercut crafts by deskilling traditional production tasks, it opened more extensive work possibilities for untrained immigrants. As early as 1904, unionists in the steel industry reported that "the number of [craft] steelworkers had been greatly reduced on account of improved machinery. On the other hand, a large number of unskilled workers are foreigners, hardly able to speak or understand the English language, thereby complicating and retarding our efforts [to organize]."[12] For trade-union strategists who were readjusting their program in response to an evolving industrial structure whose core industries employed an increasingly semi-

[12] Stephen Thernstrom, ed., *Encyclopedia of American Ethnic Groups* (Cambridge, Mass., 1980), 615.

skilled labor force with task-specialized knowledge acquired on the assembly line, exclusion of a competitive labor supply was seen as a possible substitute for the market power previously exercised through the craft-apprenticeship system.

Consequently, a double crisis impeded the transition of the American unionized labor movement to twentieth-century conditions. At once, the movement had to restructure its internal organization as craft dominance receded and discover politically the means to close off entry to the labor markets of those enterprises transformed by new production processes. Added to the progressively less-viable campaign to prevent technological change, the attempts to accommodate labor strategy to the reorganization of the advanced industrial sectors led trade unionists to harden their position in favor of a consistently pro-restrictionist immigration policy. Labor found itself firmly locked into an uncomfortable alliance with nativist conservatives who were deeply opposed to nearly all other elements of labor's agenda. Still, by itself, this odd coalition proved insufficiently strong to alter legislatively the doctrine of open boundaries that had characterized the first century-and-a-half of American nationhood.

THE PROGRESSIVE IMPULSE TOWARD RESTRICTION

The politics of the Progressive movement, especially those of its corporatist wing, were generated from both economic and cultural practices and ideas. On the one hand, Progressivism was a response to the practical needs of reshaping the composition of the modern firm and of readjusting the institutional relationship between management, the industrial labor force, and the bureaucratic state. Systematic reforms were advocated by corporatists to facilitate development of new productive technologies and to forestall the industrial conflicts portended by the increasingly credible Marxist predictions of class warfare in advanced industrial societies. On the other hand, Progressive thought also reflected a more comprehensive, particularly American utopianism, which imagined that applying scientific principles to every facet of human activity would maximize social harmony and material well-being.

In joining a political alliance to restrict immigration to the United States, Progressives advanced both their desire to establish managerial autonomy and social peace in the industrial sector and their belief in an objective discourse of genetic determinism that set forth the technical principles for constructing an ordered polity. The coalition of Progressives with traditional nativists and organized labor interests permitted immigration legislation in the 1920s to pass—more than a decade before the enactment of other elements of the Progressive agenda. Those remaining programs for social insurance, macroeconomic stabilization, and the restructuring of both interfirm and labor-capital relations—programs far more central to corporatist thought than immigration control—could be institutionalized only after the shock of the Great Depression had more generally uprooted the established system. The ascent and decline of an acknowledged corporatist politics during the New Deal left a patchwork legacy of regulatory laws, administrative bureaucracies, and reorganized industrial enterprises that constitute the modern American political economy. Included in this legacy is the general acceptance of immigration control. At the same time, these politics left behind a complex history of severe ideological conflict that would be rewritten after World War II to trace a smoother and more continuous historical image of the evolution of the American social system.

The Institutional Economy of Capital-Intensive Production

Corporatist Progressivism was grounded on an analysis of the political and economic implications of basic changes that were being incorporated, with variable speed, in the production technologies of many industrial sectors around the beginning of the twentieth century. The introduction of large quantities of capital- and energy-intensive machinery and the subsequent growth of manufacturing that aimed at long runs of uniform products increased rapidly from 1900 to 1929. Both capital per worker and real-value-added per worker soared. Economic expansion replaced growth by market extension. This shift responded to increasing competition and profit pressures from 1873 to 1900, a period in which improved transport, communications, access to raw materials, and financial integration had encouraged firms to continually enlarge the scope of their operations, standardize output and costs, intrude on local market preserves, and discover economies of scale.[13] Where enterprises could raise capital investment and the volume of manufacturing, this turn to mass production privileged price competition and the ongoing quest for lower unit costs.

Reliance on new techniques of mass production, however, increased the ratio of fixed-to-variable expenses and thereby made necessary a reform of the internal organization and labor relations of the firm. The economics of production with high fixed costs and sharply declining unit costs entailed rigidities that required the firm to maintain production at optimal levels of capital use. Adjusting production volume to changes in market demand by adding or subtracting variable cost factors was rela-

[13] Piore and Sabel, *Second Industrial Divide*, 66–70, 101–103, 106–107, 128.

tively less feasible than before fixed capital became a larger component of value-added. To run such a modernized plant fully and efficiently, management had to have both technical competence and substantial autonomy in the control of supply factors and large pools of capital. Competition through increased concentration of capital pushed the firm to reorganize and stress the stability of production at high levels of utilization; the scientific decomposition of production into discrete and specialized operations; and the internal control of mass demand and labor markets.

The substitution of capital-intensive, long-run production techniques for skill-intensive, small-batch artisanry stimulated corporatist theorists to appreciate the benefits of replacing industrial politics with technical administration. The increased scale permitted by mechanizing and by subdividing tasks on integrated production lines implied a reversal of the traditional worker/tool relationship. The worker could increasingly be seen as an adjunct of the concentrated machinery that determined work location, pacing, and job specialization. The new technologies used specialized resources (machines) to produce generalized commodities. They supplanted production through generalized craft skills that yielded hand-tailored products and seemed to impose on industrialization an objective logic amenable to engineering expertise. This reversal of the worker/tool relationship—which could also be understood as the political/technical character of production—was attacked as the end of labor freedom by craft unionists in the Proudoniste tradition.

Progressives instead conceived of this phenomenon as the first step toward automation's liberating man from compulsory labor. In so doing they reaffirmed an older American tradition of technological utopianism that presaged the movement toward Taylorism and other quasi-scientific corporatist movements.[14] In this latter discourse, the mechanization of production could be absorbed into a teleological narrative of progress from feudalism to cybernetics through which craft production could be superseded. Radicalizing labor conflicts over control of the shop floor would be forgotten in the material growth promised by efficient production. The key to this corporatist vision of the triumph of technique over politics was managers' autonomy to implement the new science of capital-intensive production.

In the emerging advanced-industrial sector, the primary expertise of technical managers was the continuing refinement of integrated manufacturing technologies based on an extreme division of labor. The objective

[14] Howard P. Segal, *Technological Utopianism in American Culture* (Chicago, 1985), 74–128.

was pursued by systematically engineering all stages of production and by procuring full capital employment through reducing those instabilities arising from demand, supply, and labor participation. Prevalent trends included: (1) backward vertical integration to acquire inputs and energy supplies, (2) a preference for financing through decentralized equity markets and retained earnings, rather than through centralized governmental or investment banks, which were more likely to interfere with managerial control, (3) horizontal integration of firms through pooling arrangements and mergers that limited competition and reduced market volatility, and (4) the increased use of advertising, strategies of market differentiation, and long-term contracts to generate a steady demand for output. At the same time, it was deemed essential to reduce labor absenteeism, sabotage, strikes, conflict over production decisions, and the loss of plant-specific work skills needed to maintain and operate complex machinery. Internal firm authority had to be redistributed away from unionists in the craft tradition to ensure stable production and managerial coordination of technical processes. Corporatism represented the principal Progressive response to the specter of labor unrest that seriously threatened the successful institutionalization of a mass-production economy.

The administrative systems appropriate for larger enterprise units demanded the rationalization of labor control to replace the former small-scale reliance on personal supervision and motivation. Assembly lines with integrated task specialization represented management's ideal of scientific, impersonal legitimation of job definitions and work-pacing decisions. Increased coordination requirements of linked lines of machinery led to an expansion of the authority and number of supervisory personnel. Finally, the character of labor itself was transformed from the independent exercise of craft skills toward an interdependent network of semi-skilled, station-specific tasks. What was needed was no longer a generalized variety of artisan's techniques; familiarity with a particular plant's specialized equipment became the more valued asset. Detached from this job-specific knowledge, labor could be treated as homogeneous and unskilled.

The combination of casual labor and virtuosity in the engineering of specialized job operations constituted the Taylorist reverie of a plant that approximates mechanical performance in all areas. Although this apolitical vision of industrial relations was never realistic, it highlights the point that the reformist, anti-unionist impulse in incipient mass-production corporations was strategically more concerned with the ability of scientific expertise to dictate the structure of the shop floor and assembly line than with minimizing wages or lowering the quality of working conditions. Manufacturing efficiency that depended on the reintegration of decomposed production tasks was believed to demand autonomous technical coordination. The craft-based unions' assertion of their right to determine the logic of production generated a fear of the loss of management autonomy that paralleled the technicians' fear that, without financial-market reform, their need for larger capitalization would cause them to surrender organizational authority to investment bankers. The opposition of corporatist capital to unionization would moderate only when labor, in return for a commitment from management to share the economic rents arising from rapidly increasing productivity, later abdicated its demand to intrude on technical discretion over production control.

The problematic readjustment of the system of industrial relations resulted in substantial discord and experimentation during the early decades of the century. Small firms, organized as the National Association of Manufacturers, struggled both to resist unionization and to limit industrial concentration by advocating assertive antitrust enforcement. Alternatively, some large-scale capitalists sought to take advantage of the potential of advanced capital to deskill labor by substituting unskilled operatives for craft workers and imposing, in mechanized plants, strict hierarchical controls to discipline the unorganized labor force. In turn, the increasingly uniform, emergent semi-skilled working class—freed from both former craft divisions and personal loyalty to management—grew in militancy as it discovered a new source of union power: the vulnerability of capital-intensive production to disruption. As the possibility of generalized industrial conflict was heightened by homogenization of work, labor theoreticians began to fashion a program of socialist resistance that demanded both workplace democracy and nationalized controls over the advanced industrial sector.[15]

Against this background, corporatist Progressive economists and capitalists explored a variety of reforms designed to reinforce the economic superiority of the mass-production technologies by eliminating the strife-producing antagonism toward labor displayed by more orthodox businessmen. The Progressives increasingly advocated adopting a strategy for industrial peace that would guarantee labor in the capital-intensive sector relatively high wages and benefits, better working conditions, and job ladders for intrafirm mobility—improvements that would create a sense of a lifetime's progress, job security, and identification with the company. In return for a reformed regime of industrial politics that

[15] Gordon, Edwards, and Reich, *Segmented Work*, 153–62, 176–84.

would yield a segmented economy with a primary sphere of advanced industries offering a privileged core of psychologically and financially preferred employment, management asked for autonomy with respect to the technical control of that modernized plant. As semi-skilled workers became more predominant in the reorganized leading segment of manufacturing firms, Progressives argued that a reform of industrial relations in that sector required a cooperative labor-capital relationship in which workers cede the objective domain of production to the scientific expertise of bureaucratized control, but appropriate a rising percentage of the monetary benefits of stable production.[16] Rejecting the inevitability of capitalism's evolution toward class war and proletarian revolution, corporatist Progressives imagined their modernist utopia as a harmonious, ordered society where the conflicting interests of labor and capital, like those of other traditional oppositions, could be reconciled through material growth and systematic administrative planning.

The structural reforms in the advanced economic sector by which the promised Progressive alliance between capital and labor might be institutionalized assumed a wide variety of forms. Some firms moved to create an atmosphere of legitimized hierarchical control by establishing bureaucratic personnel and industrial-relations departments to administer impersonal internal systems of career advancement, compensation schedules, and work rules. During this period of experimentation, firms advocating welfare capitalism based on company-founded plans for employee ownership of stock, corporate-sponsored social programs, and profit-sharing wage systems coexisted with others setting up company unions.[17] At the same time, the managerial turn away from confrontation was complemented by currents within the American Federation of Labor that favored abandoning the craft tradition of resisting cooperative, wage-oriented labor tactics. Business unionism was successfully promoted in order to forestall both militant socialism and the spread of a corporate paternalism that sought to break up industry-wide organization with in-house unions.

As an aspect of the broader corporatist quest to eliminate the specter

[16] The predominant institution for industrial relations in the unionized core was the labor contract fortified by a legal regime that demanded union recognition and good-faith bargaining over wages and working conditions, but not over business (production) decisions. In secondary, competitive markets, which were only unionized sporadically, governmental legislation of wage, hour, safety, unemployment, and social-security minima substituted for the absence of contractual terms. In all instances, these public floors were below the levels of wages, benefits, and pension packages that became the contractual norms in advanced sectors.

[17] Daniel Nelson, "The Company Union Movement, 1900–1937: A Reexamination," *Business History Review* (Autumn 1982), 335–57.

of working-class intransigence and to secure stable production through accommodating a privileged labor sector, Progressives were willing to agree to restrict access to the supply of high-quality, good-wage industrial jobs. The limitation of immigration, long a component of organized labor's program to close off markets to new labor flows, was a relatively easy political compromise for corporatist economic theoreticians. The effect of technological change on Progressive sentiment toward immigration was twofold. The changing labor/capital ratios in the modernized sectors meant that expanding labor supplies were no longer the key to industrial growth. Progressive commercial interests were therefore willing to give up the traditional business opposition to immigration legislation because (1) it was of declining importance to capital to depress wage levels by increasing the quantity of imported labor, and (2) there was a perceived need to negotiate an implicit social pact with potentially conflicting organizations of semi-skilled workers in order to eliminate the threat of disruption of capital-intensive production.

The political origins of immigration control were, in important part, not an independently conceived project. Rather, immigration restriction was for Progressives a side effect of their attempt to more thoroughly reorganize the institutional structure of advanced industrial society. This project aimed to create a stable and efficient core sector of mass-production firms, characterized by industrial peace and technical competence. Because the passage of immigration legislation helped assure the purchase of this reformed order, its meaning and utility may appropriately be evaluated in conjunction with the wider regime in which lay its roots.

Eugenics as Technology

The second impetus that led corporatist Progressives into an unlikely pro-restrictionist alliance with trade union and nativist forces was that these Progressives developed a conceptual representation of social life that was as discontinuous with the existing American cultural tradition as was their belief that the newly concentrated national economy was fundamentally different from its fragmented predecessor. The rise of corporatist ideology was one manifestation of a more comprehensive contest over the categories of discourse through which social organization should be understood. A successful displacement of the prevailing liberal political discourse would alter the terms through which legitimate claims to institutional reform could be put forward. The liberal representations that had constituted nineteenth-century American social imagery split the experienced world of events into ontologically and epistemologically distinct objective and subjective domains.[18] According to this division, the use of objective scientific or technical categories of analysis was appropriate in the realm of natural science and mathematical logic. In the description of economic, political, or cultural affairs, however, the predominance of subjective discourse, built up from the intentionalist grammar of existential phenomenology, accorded a semiotic priority to the voluntary actions of autonomous individual actors.

Classical liberal theory permitted no objective method, independent of the technical aggregation of the articulated expressions of its individual citizens, through which a legitimate philosophical definition of the collective good could be established. Social policy that was normatively valid had to be derived strictly from the diverse subjective choices of community members. This liberal separation of experience into the natural and the spiritual led to a *prima facie* case for the superiority of limited and decentralized political and economic institutions, which were constitutionally inhibited from imposing any external conception of substantive value. Markets and voting processes were the exclusive procedures for public choice because they pretended only to register and implement the revealed preferences of sovereign individuals.

In contrast, corporatist Progressives shared with a number of other groups critical of classical liberalism a desire to extend the objective discourse of technique into the sphere of social interaction. The analysis of human behavior was to be reimagined in organic or mechanical terms, with consciousness and subjective choice reduced to epiphenomena determined by biological or teleological laws of collective order. Informed by the understanding of the scientifically defined principles of optimal social organization, coordinated administration of the political economic body would supplant the anarchic liberal search to discover the desires of a chimerical, pre-social constituency.

In this movement toward a more widely deployed objective discourse, Progressives found themselves allied, at least in the language through which they represented social organization, with positivists, Darwinists, Marxists, and nineteenth-century American Romantic conservatives who traced their nationalist heritage to Herder and Hegel. The occasional coincidence, as in the case of immigration policy, of the practical interests of these diffuse anti-liberal groups was politically embarrassing and intellectually confusing. Both Romantic nativists and Progressive theorists dissolved the epistemological bifurcation of liberal discourse. However, they chose to move in opposite directions when they imagined

[18] Heller, "Structuralism," 179–81.

which set of analytical categories should constitute their anti-dualist cognitive order. The conservative nationalists subsumed the natural or objective domain in the higher development of a national or world spirit. The corporatists reduced individual spirit to an artifact produced by the mechanisms of scientifically accessible evolutionary processes.

In nineteenth-century Europe, an encompassing positivist critique had been already turned on Romantic metaphysics by figures as diverse as Comte, Saint-Simon, Darwin, and Marx. Marx combined a strict scientific analysis (dialectical materialism) of the recent history and the immediate future of contemporary capitalism with a prophetic, if vague, vision of a cybernetic industrial utopia (production systems as "the administration of things") that promised a restoration of man's lost subjective autonomy only in post-revolutionary society. Socialism combined the rhetorical power of a determinist discourse that objectively explained past and present with the legitimating appeal of a humanist image of the qualitatively transformed future—a complex, time-sequenced ideology that at once derided and embraced Enlightenment values by postponing their actual institutionalization until another era.[19]

The corporatist opponents of socialism were less vacillating than orthodox Marxists in their globalization of the science of society. They were also less committed to, or nostalgic for, a present or future political order based on the recognition of individual subjectivity. Rather, they believed the misunderstood phenomenon of autonomous consciousness could be exposed as an illusion that appeared in conjunction with immature liberal capitalism. Like European positivists, they argued for a new post-industrial institutional order in which the administration of technology and engineering would be substituted for liberalism's representative processes to solve both physical and cultural problems. The bureaucratic supervision of the continuing dialogue that adjusted relationships within the network of functional corporate associations would be founded on a scientific understanding of the logic of historical development from superstition to materialism and from need to abundance. However, unlike the pre-Enlightenment non-liberal regimes, the new managerial hierarchies would be established not with reference to social origins, but on the basis of social utility and meritocratic talent. The perspective was overtly undemocratic, anti-egalitarian, and anti-political.

The fundamental corporatist metaphor of society advanced from the Comtiste machine to a Darwinian organism that progressed through stages of genetic or teleological maturation. In contrast to the liberal re-

[19] *Ibid.*, 165–70.

duction of the normative realm to the aggregation of individual preferences, the organic representation of social order was one of a perfectible
integrated system involving internal differentiation, specialization, hierarchy, complexity, organization, and the immunization of its own evolutionary course. Order, community, and cooperative institutional adjustment were societal attributes that, when properly managed, yielded a
non-conflicted, well-adjusted collective identity. In turn, a healthy personality was derived from a psychological association with the modern,
sectoral corporate organizations in which an individual's production and
consumption activities were ideally founded. Corporatism was distinguished from Romantic nationalism by its thoroughgoing materialism
and from Marxism by its ideology of reform through the order of bureaucratic hierarchy, rather than through the disorder of class-based
revolution. Nevertheless, corporatism was intellectually linked both to
reactionary nativism and to socialism, its major modernist theoretical
competitor, in its break with the liberal discourse that had throughout
the nineteenth century defined the special identity of American culture.

One source of insight into the intellectual touchstones of Progressive corporatist politics is the extensive outpouring during the period
1880–1930 of tracts describing technocratic utopias.[20] Utopian writers,
quite similar in their demographic and occupational profiles to less out-
spoken Progressives, expressed hyperbolic and often grotesque visions of
an America transformed by technical expertise into an ordered, cooperative, apolitical social system. Even moderate examples of the genre, such
as *The Engineers and the Price System,* polemicized for a voluntary ab-
dication of all absentee owners of big business and their replacement by
reform-minded engineers and workmen. Veblen suggested that a national
directorate of technicians be permitted to supervise the reallocation of all
goods and services and to eliminate the decentralized market-price mechanism in order to increase production.[21] This proposed conflation of the
public and the private domains typified the pure corporatist insistence on
redefining the relations between state and society.

The Marxist antagonism between state and society was derived from
the basic theoretical postulate that the state apparatus was no more than
an instrument of capital in waging class warfare.[22] The liberal distinction
between carefully demarcated civil and governmental realms reflected its

[20] Segal, *Utopianism,* 98–140.

[21] Thorstein Veblen, *The Engineers and the Price System* (New York, 1963), 17–27,
132–151; see also Thomas P. Hughes, *American Genesis* (New York, 1989), 184–294.

[22] How vulgar or sophisticated an instrument it was has been the subject of endless refinement in Marxist theory. See Nicos Poulantzas, *Political Power and Social Classes* (London, 1973), 37–56.

restricted constitution of the permissible role of the collective in an individualist society. Corporatism imagined the supercession of both these dichotomies through an adherence to objective principles of scientific administration. This desire translated to a Progressive political program aimed at "the transformation of a decentralized, non-technical, loosely organized society, where waste and inefficiency ran rampant, into a highly organized, technical, and centrally planned and directed social organization that could meet a complex world with efficiency and purpose." [23]

The adoption of a comprehensive objective discourse that substituted scientific explanation for the expression of subjective intention suggested that a reconceptualization had occurred concerning the premises on which the organization of economic and governmental institutions were based. In the nineteenth century, authority had been associated with resource ownership or election to political office. The correlation of power with technical expertise was, when it existed, accidental. In contrast, the ideal of scientific management collapsed into a single metric the qualifications and methods of selection for both private and public positions of responsibility. The unifying characteristics of modern organization were believed to be the rationalization and bureaucratization of all complex systems. Advanced-sector corporations were identified as prototypical hierarchical and specialized objects of administrative science and quantitative management techniques. These corporations were ideally reimagined as vertically integrated firms with functionally related production, marketing, and coordination divisions, increasingly reliant on internalized basic research and product development.

At the same time, Progressive politics sought to restructure the direction of governmental agencies according to the same principles. Limitations on the political corruption that had become especially widespread at state and local levels were advocated in reform measures such as the initiative or referendum. More important were the efforts to substitute expert bureaucrats like appointed city managers, municipal research bureaus, and national research centers for non-technically qualified, elected officeholders. It should be reemphasized that corporatism was neither simply an apology for capitalism in its emphasis on the enhanced institutional importance of the large industrial corporation nor only a naive forerunner of totalitarianism in its stress on centralized coordination of modern social life. Rather, it consistently applied a single encompassing scientific discourse to the analysis of a collection of administrative phenomena seen by both liberalism and socialism to lie within segregated institutional domains.

[23] Segal, *Utopianism*, 106.

It would be a vast overstatement of the historical coherence of the Progressive movement to insist on a homogeneous attachment to, or even a consciously elaborated understanding of, a programmatic corporatist ideology. Most Progressive political activists saw themselves as pragmatic reformers rather than cultural apostates committed to installing a social discourse that repudiated American tradition. Nevertheless, even among those pursuing relatively more incremental changes oriented toward nurturing neo-liberal regulatory agencies or enacting redistributive governmental programs, the displacement of pre-existing boundaries between scientific and phenomenological discourse was important. Progressives commonly relied on determinist accounts of those spheres of social life they made the target of reformist attention in order to justify their proposed paternalistic interventions in free-market institutions. The actual condition of women, children, workers, immigrants, and other dispossessed groups was described in causal or scientific terms that at once absolved members of the target group from responsibility for their situation and exposed them as objects for the resocialization projects proposed by Progressive theorists of scientific education. Reformist sociological analyses both demonstrated how the environment produced dysfunctional behavior or restricted social mobility and extended the realm of regulatory intervention and administrative expertise over a broader, though often still not total, range of human conduct.

In this context, the corporatist technologists of the early decades of this century tended to view the increasing population influx as a problem that warranted collective reconstruction. Because it was generally asserted that environmental influences could be reversed through institutional intervention, those cultural attributes of immigrants inconsistent with the American social order were rarely seen as an absolute bar to assimilation. However, the expanded influence of objective determinants like the culture of origin in explaining social behavior meant that a simple subjective disavowal of one's historical past was less likely to produce social coordination than earlier liberal individualists had imagined. As the number of immigrants and their cultural heterogeneity grew, the administrative expense and technical burden of a scientifically sound program of reacculturation appeared less and less manageable. Seeking to implement a planned social order in industrial America was a formidable task even without the challenges posed to Progressive educational expertise by burgeoning and more diverse migratory flows.

The less-compromising corporatist theorists within the Progressive movement rejected this early sociological positivism in favor of a purer biological determinism. The theories of Darwin and Mendel provided not only metaphors for organic social systems, but also an impetus to extend the technology of utopian planning into eugenics and social breeding. Genetically based accounts of optimal demographic patterns and derivative immigration policies proliferated in carefully documented studies of inherited ethnographic traits and characteristics. Analyses by respected Progressive academics flourished with theories of long-term geopolitical determinism, hierarchies of the relative maturity of diverse cultures, and fears of racial suicide among Anglo-Saxon peoples.[24] The representation of society as a biological organism and the development of legitimate sciences in eugenics and cultural anthropology converted the demand for immigration reform from reactionary nativism into a component of a Progressive program for proficiently administering an equilibrated social system.[25]

In the new technology of immigration, races were objectively categorized as assimilable and nonassimilable according to their presumed inherited capacity to participate in American political or cultural institutions. Even though many political reformers shared with Romantic nativists and organic nationalists a logically convoluted posture that asserted that the capacity of individuals to act as autonomous liberal subjects was objectively determined, Progressives in no way believed themselves intellectually committed to the existence of an American Volksgeist in need of insulation against corrupting foreign spirits. Implied in their use of eugenics and ethnographic mappings to determine preferred immigration policies was simply another application of the technological principles of advancing administrative capacity. An improving knowledge of materialist science would allow the selection of those potential immigrant pools whose racial traits could blend with those of the existing American population with minimum conflict and resocialization costs. Nevertheless, in spite of the origins of Progressive thought in modernist imagery, the politics of immigration restriction tied it practically to conservative (nativist) intellectual currents that otherwise would have led in completely opposite directions.

THE LEGISLATION OF IMMIGRATION CONTROLS AND THE INSTITUTIONALIZATION OF THE REGULATORY STATE

Prior to 1917, the efforts of nativists and trade unions to pass general legislation restricting immigration had been unsuccessful. Labor had won

[24] See John R. Commons, *Races and Immigrants in America* (New York, 1967), 1–31; Edward A. Ross, "The Causes of Race Superiority," *American Academy of Political and Social Science* (July 1901), 67–89.
[25] Segal, *Utopianism*, 103–108.

limited controls over imported contract laborers as early as 1885. Traditional nativist defenders of the anglophonic American spirit had an early triumph against the intrusion of what they imagined were the most alien cultures when they limited Chinese inflows by 1882 and the admission of other Asians by 1908. Qualitative controls against the entry of the ill, enfeebled, impoverished, or otherwise undesirable individuals from any source were enacted in the first decades of the century. These controls did little to stem the increasing numbers of generally unskilled immigrants from southern and eastern Europe who settled in the metropolitan centers of advanced industrial growth in the North and Midwest.

Although national investigatory bodies such as the Dillingham Commission, which were sympathetic to the pleas of American workers, had found "an oversupply of unskilled labor in basic industries and presumably in industries of the country as a whole," and that "the situation demands legislation restricting the further admission of such unskilled labor," the legal measures enacted before World War I that quadrupled the entry-head tax proved incapable of achieving organized labor's aims. Instead, more serious controls, including the passage of a general literacy requirement for immigrants in 1917 and of national quota legislation in 1921 and 1924, had to await the altered political configuration that arose during the war. Effective reform occurred when the increased political influence of Progressive forces, placed in power to restructure the industrial economy during the war crisis, and the emergent voices of post-war isolationist nationalism were added to the restrictionist coalition.

Although the Bull Moose Republicans, the party that represented most closely the incipient corporatist elements of the Progressive movement, were defeated in the election of 1912, the outbreak of World War I transformed corporatist theory into institutional practice.[26] The military's need to mobilize the advanced industrial sector brought to Washington the modern technology of centralized bureaucratic management to deal with the problems of excessive wartime profits, the threat of socialist labor disruption, and the rationalization of production. Although the antitrust movement—backed by small firms organized principally in the National Association of Manufacturers and by reformist or noncorporatist Progressives—had in part successfully obstructed the growth of industrial concentration in the 1900–1916 period, the program initiated by the War Industries Board in 1917 to impose a systematic order upon manufacturing and to set prices among large firms fostered a model of oligopolistic competition in the modern sector that proved quite stable in

[26] James Weinstein, *The Corporate Ideal in the Liberal State 1900–1918* (Boston, 1968), 3–39.

later years. Moreover, through the same public-planning bureaus that coordinated the volume and quality of production, the advocates of technocratic management worked to integrate the business-oriented, more politically conservative segments of the union movement into the process of regulating the war economy. In return for the American Federation of Labor's no-strike pledges and commitments to reduce absenteeism, the War Industries Board and the National War Labor Board protected labor organization, decreed union wage advances, and required improved conditions on the production floor.

Prior to the war, because of substantial ideological splits on each side, it would have been difficult to generalize about the attitudes of large firms and organized labor toward one another. Uncertainty was generated among capitalists by the experimentation in some mass-production enterprises with welfare capitalism and company unions. In the trade-union movement, internal conflicts occurred over the ambivalence toward traditions grounded in craft practices; the increasing commitment to incorporate the semi-skilled workers in the emergent modern sector; and the rising prominence of shop-floor leaders espousing radical socialism. The administered economy of World War I exposed business unionism's accommodation to a reformed design of cooperative industrial relations—an accommodation that was to be managed within a framework of state-sponsored corporatism that proffered both prosperity for important elements of labor and tolerance of ongoing oligopoly in the capital-intensive sector. Progressive technocrats seized the opportunity provided by the extraordinary politics of the wartime regime to experiment with a comprehensive institutional restructuring of the traditional liberal economy. Public support for corporatist reorganization, which during the war promised and delivered both efficient production and a curtailing of the class struggle, lapsed in the post-war longing for a return to normalcy. Nevertheless, technocracy's claim to be the appropriate regime for advanced industrial society would be remembered during the critical initial phase of the New Deal, when the practitioners of corporatism would be called on to reproduce their wartime accomplishments in a less temporary form.

The war administration's program not only reflected corporatist ideology, but included the first passage of comprehensive immigration controls as well. The legislative history of the 1917 act that imposed a literacy test upon all applicants for admission to the United States argued "that the immigrants who would be excluded . . . do not go out to the western and southern states, where immigration is needed, and become an agricultural population, but remain entirely in the Atlantic states and in the great centers of population, where the labor market is already over-crowded."[27] When it was perceived at the end of the war that the restrictive and selective measures of the literacy test had not been adequate to control this perceived problem, a quota system "directly devised to exercise a racial and ethnic selection" was enacted.

The legislated quotas introduced in 1921 and revised in 1924 discriminated against immigration from the areas of southern and eastern Europe, where the great majority of unskilled laborers then originated. They offered no count at all for aliens ineligible for citizenship (Asians), descendants of slaves (Africans), or descendants of Native Americans (sec. 11D of 1924 Act). Behind this restrictive legislation lay, in addition to the longstanding nativist and labor demands, the assumptions of the Progressive corporatist technicians and businessmen that (1) future economic growth depended on increasing capital investment in the mass-production sector, (2) full-capacity production required the supercession of interclass conflict, attainable with cooperative industrial relations in closed, semi-skilled labor markets in the core industries, (3) within this closed labor sector, labor accommodation and macroeconomic stability depended on rising wages that reflected the sharing of economic rents from technological productivity and oligopolistic competition in the advanced industrial core, (4) immigration restriction expressed one element of enlightened capital's commitment to this restructured order, and (5) biological science had demonstrated the differential suitability of varied races to fit into an administratively coordinated American social system without excessive disruption or cost.

The political strength of the coalition of Progressives, unionists, and xenophobes in favor of immigration reform was complemented by a broadly based sentiment of national sovereignty that had developed as a consequence of the centralization of government and virulent nationalism experienced during the war. This relatively nascent sense of the American nation-state as a unitary actor in a conflicted system of international relations was embodied in a new emphasis on legal articulations of sovereignty. After the cessation of military activities, these perceptions focused in part on the institutionalized control of national borders and the specification of membership criteria for the American polity. The growing prominence of centralized governmental organizations, including both the Progressive agencies that coordinated domestic policy and the offices that administered an expanding American activism in foreign affairs, symbolized a reformed image of nationality that contradicted the open

---

[27] See generally Hutchinson, *Legislative History*, 163–68.

and undefined community of nineteenth-century liberalism. At the political margin, the emergent nationalist and corporatist motivations both permitted the passage of long-stalled immigration controls and shaped the particular character that the legislation assumed.

The argument that the origin of generalized immigration restriction was an aspect of the institutional development of the American political economy as the United States became a more advanced industrial society may throw light on a variety of otherwise less-expected features relating to the content and timing with which the laws were enacted. This is not to deny the reality of nativism within this history, but to explain the late moment of the legislation's passage in comparison with the much earlier propagation of racialist doctrines in American culture. The economic roots of restrictive regulation in the Progressive quest for cooperative industrial relations are reflected in the special position given to the agricultural sector in the early immigration acts. No numerical limits were imposed on population flows from the Americas, because Latin migrants were employed overwhelmingly on southwestern farms. Within the national quotas of the 1924 legislation, preferences were to be accorded to those skilled in agriculture and their families. The object of severe limitation was the threat of the continuing flow of unskilled labor from Europe that could, with minimal training, become qualified for semi-skilled tasks in capital-intensive industrial enterprises.

This point is underscored by the treatment of skilled or craft workers under these same laws. Within the mass-production sector, important pockets of highly skilled tasks, such as machine-tool and repair jobs, were still structured on a craft basis. At the same time, the shift of focus within industrial unionism to organizing the semi-skilled reduced the political influence and symbolic centrality of the older craft traditions. The effect of the immigration law's national quota systems, which reproduced the demographic composition of nineteenth-century America, was to concentrate entry preferences on northwestern European countries from which the outflow of skilled laborers was far more likely. In addition, from 1917 on, most immigration acts provided that skilled labor might be excepted from enacted controls when the secretary of labor determined its scarcity in the United States. The effect of the quota system was to protect the semi-skilled labor market in the core mass-production industries while leaving substantially free the non-unionized agricultural sectors and the politically less influential, highly skilled labor sectors. It was the semi-skilled market that was the growing object of organization by those unions whose cooperation the corporatists imagined to be the bulwark against both socialism and the disruption of management autonomy in production administration. In the terminology of the theory of segmented labor markets that would be formulated a half-century later, the legislation was aimed to stabilize a dependent primary labor sector, leaving alone the labor markets of the then-dominant secondary (agricultural) sector and the independent primary (craft) sector.[28]

The cultural pretensions of the new immigration laws similarly represent the genre of technocratic tracts that extended biological and eugenic discourse into social analysis. Throughout a series of revised statutes in the 1920s, the national quota system was refined in a variety of schedules that consistently expressed the racial categorizations that then were the accepted practice in ethnography and genetics. The restriction of the inflow of all Africans and Asians, combined with selective discrimination against the entry of southern and eastern Europeans, demonstrated the hierarchical rankings of advanced and pre-liberal peoples whose assimilation was agreed to be impossible or expensive. The objective of Progressive theorists was not the total end of immigration sought by more traditional nativists. Rather, they looked forward to engineering a managed population structure.

The principal aberration from this scientifically determined regime was the admission, free from all but qualitative restrictions on entry imposed on all individual applicants, of Latin Americans. Although rated as more assimilable than Blacks or Asians, peoples of Indian and Mestizo heritage generally fared poorly in the assessment of their cultural potential for integration into modern societies. This odd failure to attend to the still small-scale American source immigration seems simply to reflect the geographical concentration and administrative concerns of Progressive politicians. Inasmuch as their attention was primarily focused on the Northeast, Midwest, and, to a lesser degree, California, the racial and economic problems caused by Europeans arriving in the industrial metropolis was at the forefront of their attention in the 1920s. The cultural situation of the Southwest, like the economic growth of the less developed areas of the United States, was never the concern of the strongly regional program of corporatist politics.[29]

Although immigration legislation provided an initial success for Progressives, labor-flow control was only a marginal element of their agenda to reshape the institutional order of advanced industrial society. They envisioned reforming distributional policies, including social security and unemployment coverage, the stabilization of macroeconomics demand, the coordination of prices and production, the homogenization of im-

[28] Gordon, Edwards, and Reich, *Segmented Work,* 189–204.
[29] Heller, "Federalism," 277–79.

proved workplace and environmental conditions, the administration of industrial relations in mass-production labor markets based upon the sharing of the rents from productivity gains, and the protection of broadly based securities markets (to increase the freedom of technically qualified managers from investor interference). In pursuit of these goals, Progressives could rely, alternatively, on strategies that emphasized private cartelization, the passage of laws at the level of state government, or the creation of federal, centralized controls. What pushed immigration law to the leading edge of the corporatist agenda was not as much its importance to their program as the particular characteristics of its regulation.

While it might have been feasible to have firms contract with unions to close off semi-skilled labor markets, neither the potential for reducing social costs nor the presumed benefits of the eugenic effects of immigration control would have been achievable through private action. Moreover, although much Progressive legislation was initially enacted by state governments in the industrial regions of America, the Constitution has rendered any non-federal restriction of internal population flows highly problematic. Simple comprehensive border controls that states might have passed to limit the entry of alien immigrants to their communities were felt, even without the need for a litigated test, to contravene a plenary federal power related to the conduct of foreign affairs.[30] Although some state restrictions of the rights of aliens to hold professional jobs have been upheld on grounds of the political sensitivity of the work, this logic would have been difficult to extend to general semi-skilled labor.

In the light of the weaknesses of both private and state action in this field, a political strategy requiring federal legislation was uniquely appropriate and available for immigration control. First, there was no threat that centralized immigration restrictions would be deemed unconstitutional as had other federal Progressive programs based on the national power to regulate interstate commerce. The recently proposed enactment of federal minimum-wage and child-labor laws had been held to violate the Tenth Amendment, which was then interpreted to reserve a certain vague authority to the states. This bar did not apply to statutes built on the foreign-affairs clause where federal power was explicit. Second, in the area of immigration, Progressives in Congress found themselves in league with unfamiliar allies like southern conservative nativists who would support restrictive legislation. This fragile coalition would dissolve when confronted with any other object of Progressive desire. Consequently,

[30] *Ibid.*, 271–74.

corporatist sympathizers could advance immigration control as a first step that would eventually lead toward a comprehensive restructuring of the traditional relations between labor, capital, and the state. This hoped-for creation of a stable and orderly industrial society, with an institutional infrastructure appropriate to the advancing state of technology, would be completed only after economic depression, a second world war, and the ideological repression of the corporatist visions of which immigration control had initially been an element.

POSTSCRIPT TO IMMIGRATION REFORM

The development of an American immigration policy during the first decades of this century constituted one element of a comprehensive political program to design a new system of public institutions. This restructuring was made necessary by the recognition of a growing potential for economic inefficiency and social conflict that attended the replacement of nineteenth-century small-scale production by more advanced industrial technologies. Along with the need to stabilize aggregate demand, establish income-transfer programs, and regulate labor markets and workplace conditions, the restriction of immigration represented a reimagination of the basic relationship between labor, large-scale capital, and the bureaucratic state under the shadow of technological change. The critical situation during World War I provided the initial justification to impose a radically transposed institutional order that broke with traditional liberalism and reflected the incipient principles of corporatist theory. As the occasion for abnormal responses to war's exigencies faded in the early 1920s and brought a return to earlier liberal orthodoxy, immigration control became the leading edge of the peacetime enactment of the corporatist agenda because Progressives and unionists formed a unique legislative majority in this arena through their perverse alliance with nativists. A crisis threatening enough to disrupt the established order on a scale sufficiently general to replace immigration law within its original framework of a broadly activist state arose only with the Great Depression.

The period from 1900 to 1937 was one of serious conflict between divergent views of social order. Only with hindsight was the triumph of a regulatory and centralizing liberalism assured over corporatism, socialist planning, or an enforced continuance of the predominance of fragmented, deconcentrated markets. In the later years of the New Deal, political divisiveness over the delegation of civic power to private corporatist institutions combined with a growing stigma concerning the links between American corporatism and European fascism to delegitimate open adherence to any nonliberal doctrine. A continuing struggle that lasted through World War II gradually disclosed a hybrid American pattern of public and private institutions that blended transfigured corporatist structures with neo-liberal ideology. An unacknowledged bifurcation of the economy into an oligopolized advanced industrial core and competitive, labor-intensive secondary markets was marked by distinct institutional interactions between labor, capital, and the state in the different sectors.

Industrial relations in the core were characterized by the rent sharing and cooperative business unionism that grew from Progressive corporatism. Although the legalized industry-wide cartels of the 1930s were formally dissolved, functional substitutes were developed, such as interfirm wage contours, pattern bargaining, and fixed productivity formulas in the post-war era.[31] The state did not seriously intervene in the affairs of the advanced sector, leaving production decisions to management and wage/benefit levels to contractual bargaining. Instead, the federal government concentrated on setting regulatory minima for wages, income transfers, and working conditions in secondary markets; improving the imperfect order of liberal civil rights; extending American military security; and developing an open international trading and investment system for industrial production. The symbiosis of state and private institutions was evidenced equally in the public dependence on taxes levied on primary-sector economic rents for military and welfare expenditures and the ineffectual public regulation of large corporations and organized labor.

While there had been several contending alternatives for the design of the modern American state, the reconstruction of American history in the post-war years ignored these contingencies. In a Whiggish fashion, orthodox imagery has insisted that the resultant institutional relationships were the product of an uninterrupted evolution of an earlier and simpler liberalism. In industrial relations, the prevalent revisionism implied that labor markets were not structurally segmented and operated in the integrated fashion postulated by neo-classical economic theory. Similarly, the understanding of immigration controls was altered by reconception. The genetic ties between immigration and the collective problem of sectoral labor supplies were deemphasized as historical and contemporary accounts of immigration were presented as heroic, individual journeys of escape from pre- or anti-liberal societies. Immigration administration was bureaucratized in an autonomous agency that exposed no apparent linkages to other regulatory bodies or other international economic poli-

[31] Harry C. Katz, *Shifting Gears* (Cambridge, Mass., 1987), 13–36.

cies. Within this isolated domain, the analysis of immigration questions mirrored the standard tropes of American post-war law as the application of equal protection norms led to the repeal of explicit national quotas in 1952 and the assurance of due process for individual entrants dominated legal debate.[32] As the isolated domain of immigration law was increasingly reified as a natural expression of national sovereignty unrelated to any origins in particular domestic political programs, immigration control became a generic defense against foreign disturbance of America's security, internal tranquility, or economic well-being.

The liberal narratives of an unbroken evolution of the traditional American constructions of society and economy have been effectively reproduced since World War II. They currently reappear in the majority political positions on numerous public issues, including immigration control. However, the technological conditions and the nature of the international economic system that prevailed at the time of the initial design of American regulatory institutions have become increasingly antiquated in the years since 1970. Shifts in the global division of production associated with the redevelopment of Western Europe and Japan, as well as the spread of technological knowledge into third-world nations, have reduced American competitive advantage in core primary-sector industries like automobiles and machinery. Declining economic rents became inconsistent with established wage-determination formulas as productivity lagged and could no longer support the military and welfare budgets that were essential elements of the post-war system. In addition, economies based on information technologies, which promised renewed growth, required an organization of capital and labor at odds with the social pact in force since the 1930s. Innovation-intensive firms were less interested in stable, long production runs relying on semi-skilled workers than in a bifurcated superskilled and unskilled labor force able to respond flexibly to specialized demand. Finally, as firms created distributed international networks of subsidiaries and joint ventures, labor, capital, and technology, trade flows became increasingly substitutable. The diminishing capacity of nation-states to coordinate the regulation of goods and factor movements in different markets has left previously privileged sectors vulnerable to sustained dislocations.

Immigration law, along with other components of the governmental structure created in the 1930s, is both less defensible and more defended as the consequences of a potentially large-scale reformation of social institutions and cultural images become more apparent. American immi-

---

[32] Peter H. Schuck, "The Transformation of Immigration Law," *Columbia Law Review* (Jan. 1984), 5–34.

gration law, characterized by the revisionist images of its own genealogy, serves as a double window on a modern political history. While immigration restrictions were initially enacted to build new public institutions adequate to ensure a stable advanced industrial sector, intensifying those restrictions will not rescue those same mass industries from the instabilities they presently suffer from global competition and technological change. Contemporary flows of high- and low-skill migrants do not affect the labor supplies of challenged core sectors, and IRCA will not inhibit the offshore movements of other factors of production. As in the Progressive period, immigration control in the 1980s has been the leading edge of a wider program aimed at maintaining an American institutional order that has yielded a half-century of economic wealth and political stability. Like corporatism, to be effective this program will require extending that protectionist agenda across more important regulatory fields.

Alternatively, the prospects of repositioning American immigration law within the context of a reworked representation of international political economy are not encouraging. The attempt to reform immigration policy now carries with it the heavy burden of upsetting bureaucratic and conceptual structures associated with the normal imagery of the modern public order. Immigration law would have to be removed from its autonomous domain of legal doctrine and administration in order to be reintegrated with a more comprehensive understanding of the regulation of interactive trade and factor markets. In addition to reimagining deeply ingrained past and present historical understandings, to restructure regulation would require a redrawing of the boundaries of competence between existing agencies and would likely demand binational or regional coordination of economic policy. The disruption of existing national and international institutions, whose current relations are the product of intense conflict and social bargaining, involves exercising power against entrenched public and private coalitions. The last restructuring and reimagination of the advanced industrial order came only with the twin crises of war and depression, which, for better and worse, are not now with us.

Policymaking at the Apex: International Migration, State Autonomy, and Societal Constraints

Manuel García y Griego

THIS PAPER EXPLORES how international migration policy is made at the apex of the political systems of Mexico and the United States. Obviously, not all international migration policies of these two governments are in the domain of this analysis. The focus is on policy choices made and directions taken by "central decisionmakers" (to borrow Stephen Krasner's phrase[1]), meaning the chief executive and a small group of advisers and public officials. My purpose is to explain the policy choices made by high government officials in terms of their public-policy objectives and the lesser or greater constraints imposed by the most powerful societal actors. I hope to demonstrate that a state-centered approach to explaining immigration policymaking in the United States and emigration policymaking in Mexico is useful, and offers some promise in the issue area of international migration.[2]

The author thanks David Ayón, Julie Carlson, Wayne A. Cornelius, Steve Dubb, Raúl A. Hinojosa Ojeda, Etel Solingen, Robert C. Smith, and Jeffrey Weldon for their comments and suggestions. This paper was written while the author was a visiting research fellow at the Center for U.S.-Mexican Studies, University of California, San Diego. It drew from early drafts of *Los norteños: Mexican Migrants in the U.S. and Rural Mexico* co-authored with Wayne A. Cornelius, forthcoming 1992. Archival research for this paper was supported by El Colegio de México and by a 1988 critical issues grant from UCMEXUS.

[1] Stephen D. Krasner, *Defending the National Interest: Raw Materials Investments and U.S. Foreign Policy* (Princeton, N.J., 1978); Stephen D. Krasner, "United States Commercial and Monetary Policy: Unravelling the Paradox of External Strength and Internal Weakness," in Peter J. Katzenstein, ed., *Between Power and Plenty: Foreign Economic Policies of Advanced Industrial States* (Madison, Wis., 1978).

[2] Much of the literature on state and society that has conceived of the state as an actor (as I do in this paper) is grounded in one or more issue areas within foreign economic policy.

I make three general claims based on an analysis of several cases of Mexican and U.S. policymaking. First, the state is important, both in Mexico and the United States. When we look at international migration policymaking at the apex of the political system, we find goal-oriented public officials making policy choices relatively free of societal pressure. Even when public officials make concessions in the face of resistance from societal actors the policy process follows what I term a logic of the state. Political leaders use state resources to make the behavior of societal actors consistent with particular state interests and collective societal goals.

Second, the relative importance that central decisionmakers attach to the policy problems and issues that arise also matters. The extent to which decisionmakers make choices suggestive of autonomous state behavior is in part a function of how much importance the issue has in the context of the political agenda of these decisionmakers. Third, the degree to which high government officials are able to pursue autonomous objectives effectively is less a function of the societal resistance than of the resources they possess to achieve their goals.

To advance these state-centered claims, this analysis attempts to address several loosely connected questions that turn on the autonomy of the state from particular (and relatively powerful) societal actors. To what extent and under what circumstances do U.S. and Mexican political leaders pursue goals and formulate policies free from the pressures and constraints of particular interest groups? To the extent that U.S. and Mexican political leaders encounter pressure or resistance from societal actors, how does this manifest itself and how does it affect policy? What kinds of resources do central decisionmakers possess in the making of international migration policy, and how do these affect outcomes? What is the logic of the state? How do we differentiate its pursuit of collective societal or particular state goals from its response to particular societal pressures?

In the next major section of this paper, I summarize my theoretical

---

See, for example, Krasner, *Defending the National Interest,* and "United States Commercial and Monetary Policy," which focus on trade, monetary and on raw materials investment policies; see also G. John Ikenberry, David A. Lake, and Michael Mastanduno, eds., *The State and American Foreign Economic Policy* (Ithaca, N.Y., 1988). Examples of state-centric approaches to international migration policy analysis can be found in Martin O. Heisler, "Transnational Migration as a Small Window on the Diminished Autonomy of the Modern Democratic State," in *The Annals, AAPSS* vol. 485 (May 1986), 153–66; and James F. Hollifield, "Immigration Policy in France and Germany: Outputs *versus* Outcomes," *The Annals, AAPSS* vol. 485 (May 1986), 113–28; James F. Hollifield, "Immigration Policy and the French State: Problems of Policy Implementation," *Comparative Political Studies* vol. 23, no. 1 (April 1990), 56–79.

argument. In the third, I explore briefly seven instances between 1917 and 1986 when Mexican and/or U.S. central decisionmakers made policy choices that confronted them with societal pressure and constraints. In the fourth section, I present a case study of a policy process, regarding a series of critical decisions during the *bracero* program (a Mexican temporary worker program under which about 4.6 million Mexican agricultural laborers were sent to the United States under joint government supervision between 1942 and 1964). This study of a policy process focuses on decisions made between early 1953 and mid-1954. As a result of these decisions, U.S. and Mexican political leaders eventually substituted undocumented Mexican workers (called "wetbacks" at that time) with legally contracted *braceros*. In the final section, I discuss the implications of this analysis.

THE ARGUMENT

My central argument is that when the policies we are concerned with are adopted by high-level officials at the apex of government, a state-centered approach can offer a more useful explanation of international migration policy outcomes than its society-centered alternatives. I attempt to demonstrate this claim by examining several instances of policymaking by high government officials in both Mexico and the United States with respect to Mexican international migration over a period of several decades. The point is not that societal explanations of the same outcomes are always wrong or are necessarily irrelevant, but that at times they distort our understanding of how policy is made and almost always they are incomplete. I will argue that societal explanations leave out significant factors, even when both state- and society-centric explanations would predict the same outcome. Here I sketch what the extant (and mostly society-centered) literature tells us about international migration policymaking in Mexico and the United States, and define the theoretical notions that I apply later in the paper.

Societal Interpretations of Policymaking at the Apex

Existing society-centered interpretations of international migration policy do not offer satisfactory explanations of decisions made in the executive branch of government.[3] Many explanations of U.S. immigra-

---

[3] In developing the analysis in this paper I have benefited greatly from recent work on state autonomy, especially that by Stephen Krasner. See Stephen D. Krasner, "Are Bureaucracies Important? (Or Allison Wonderland)," *Foreign Policy* no. 7 (Summer 1972), 159–79; Stephen D. Krasner, *Defending the National Interest*; Stephen D. Krasner, "United States Commercial and Monetary Policy: Unravelling the Paradox of External

tion policy adopt, explicitly or implicitly, interest-group or pluralist approaches.[4] This theoretical perspective accounts for political outcomes in terms of the interplay among competing interest groups and the formation of "winning coalitions" in the democratic political arena. According to this interpretation, governments do not have a significant, independent effect on policy. They merely translate, more or less faithfully, the resource-weighted preferences of societal groups into public policy.

Actually, these approaches describe how the legislative branch operates. They note that Congress has frequently led in the making of immigration policy, and that the legislative process "represented efforts to accommodate the wide range of competing domestic interests."[5] Explanations based on the interactions of pressure groups have been found wanting even in the legislative arena,[6] but its inadequacies are especially apparent in the upper reaches of the executive branch.[7] I shall refer to these as "society-centered" explanations of international migration policy.

Class-based or Marxist interpretations of immigration policy stress the weight of one set of societal actors: the bourgeoisie. These interpretations suggest a model in which government anticipates or responds principally to societal pressure from this set of actors.[8] There is an emerging Marxist

---

Strength and Internal Weakness"; and Stephen D. Krasner, "Approaches to the State: Alternative Conceptions and Historical Dynamics," *Comparative Politics* vol. 16, no. 2 (Jan. 1984), 223–46.

[4] A sample might include William S. Bernard, Carolyn Zeleny, and Henry Miller, eds., *American Immigration Policy—A Reappraisal* (New York, 1950); Lawrence H. Chamberlain, *The President, Congress, and Legislation* (New York, 1946); Richard B. Craig, *The Bracero Program: Interest Groups and Foreign Policy* (Austin, Tex., 1971); Robert A. Divine, *American Immigration Policy, 1924–1952* (New Haven, Conn., 1957); Milton D. Morris, *Immigration—The Beleaguered Bureaucracy* (Washington, 1985); Frederick Warren Riggs, *Pressures on Congress: A Study of the Repeal of Chinese Exclusion* (New York, 1950); Robert D. Tomasek, "The Migrant Problem and Pressure Group Politics," *Journal of Politics* vol. 23, no. 2 (May 1961), 295–319; Mónica Verea, *Entre México y Estados Unidos: Los indocumentados* (Mexico City, 1982).

[5] Morris, *Immigration—The Beleaguered Bureaucracy*, 35.

[6] See, for example, Raymond A. Bauer, Ithiel de Sola Pool, and Lewis Anthony Dexter, *American Business and Public Policy: The Politics of Foreign Trade* (New York, 1963); and Theodore J. Lowi's re-interpretation of this study, in "American Business, Public Policy, Case Studies, and Political Theory," *World Politics* vol. 16, no. 4 (July 1964), 677–715.

[7] David McKay, *Domestic Policy and Ideology: Presidents and the American State 1964–1987* (Cambridge, Eng., 1989). This inadequacy is also observed regarding the bureaucratic politics model. This model views government policy as a negotiated outcome among dissident bureaus, even when the issues are of central concern to the President. See Krasner, "Are Bureaucracies Important?"

[8] A range of interpretations generally consistent with this perspective can be found. Their focus, however, is usually considerably broader than explaining why governments make certain policy choices and only indirectly reflects on this analytical problem. See Robert L.

literature that emphasizes structural explanations and incorporates a relatively autonomous state.[9] Some of the Marxist literature can easily be characterized as offering society-centered explanations of international migration policy in that, like interest-group pluralism, it assumes that the state is not an independent actor. Structural Marxist explanations, like the state-centered analysis developed here, assume that the state acts relatively autonomously in the face of more or less important societal constraints. The nuances of Marxist literature, however, are beyond the scope of this paper.

In comparison to U.S. immigration policy, there is practically no literature on Mexican emigration policy that attempts to anchor policy outcomes to a theory of the state or of government behavior. There are several descriptions of Mexican emigration policy responses and attempts to associate these with Mexican elite opinion and ideology during and after the Mexican Revolution.[10] The bilateral agreements that sustained the

---

Bach, "Mexican Immigration and the American State," *International Migration Review* vol. 12, no. 4 (Winter 1978), 536–58; Jorge A. Bustamante, "Espaldas mojadas: Materia prima para la expansión del capital norteamericano," *Cuadernos de CES* 9 (Mexico City, 1975); Jorge A. Bustamante, "Commodity-Migrants: Structural Analysis of Mexican Immigration to the United States," in Stanley R. Ross, ed., *Views Across the Border: The United States and Mexico* (Albuquerque, N.Mex.), 183–203; James D. Cockcroft, *Outlaws in the Promised Land: Mexican Immigrant Workers and America's Future* (New York, 1986): Patricia Morales, *Indocumentados mexiconos: Causas y razones de la migración laboral,* 2d ed. (Mexico City, 1989), chap. 1; Alejandro Portes, "Of Borders and States: A Skeptical Note on the Legislative Control of Immigration," in Wayne A. Cornelius and Ricardo Anzaldúa Montoya, eds., *America's New Immigration Law: Origins, Rationales, and Potential Consequences,* 17–30. A 1982 issue of *Contemporary Marxism,* edited by Marlene Dixon and Susanne Jonas, features discussion of a number of themes related to immigration policy that emphasize the impact of society on the state.

[9] For a discussion of this, see Fred Block, "The Ruling Class Does Not Rule: Notes on the Marxist Theory of the State," *Socialist Revolution* vol. 7, no. 3 (May–June 1977), 6–28; David Braybrooke, "Contemporary Marxism on the Autonomy, Efficacy, and Legitimacy of the Capitalist State," in Roger Benjamin and Stephen L. Elkin, eds., *The Democratic State* (Lawrence, Kans., 1985), 59–86; David J. Sylvan, "The Newest Mercantilism," *International Organization* vol. 35, no. 2 (Spring 1981), 391. A fully elaborated application of structural Marxism to the problem of explaining U.S. immigration legislation in the nineteenth and early twentieth centuries can be found in Kitty Calavita, *U.S. Immigration Law and the Control of Labor: 1820–1924* (London, 1984).

[10] Lawrence A. Cardoso, "Labor Emigration to the Southwest, 1916 to 1920: Mexican Attitudes and Policy," in George C. Kiser and Martha Woody Kiser, eds., *Mexican Workers in the United States: Historical and Political Perspectives* (Albuquerque, N.Mex., 1979), 16–32; Lawrence A. Cardoso, *Mexican Emigration to the United States 1897–1931: Socioeconomic Patterns* (Tucson, Ariz., 1980); Arthur F. Corwin, "Mexican Policy and Ambivalence Toward Labor Emigration to the United States," in Arthur F. Corwin, ed., *Immigrants—and Immigrants: Perspectives on Mexican Labor Migration to the United States* (Westport, Conn., 1978), 176–224; Juan R. García, *Operation Wetback: The Mass Deportation of Mexican Undocumented Workers in 1954* (Westport, Conn., 1980), chap. 2;

bracero program between 1942 and 1964 provided the Mexican government with opportunities to adopt more sharply focused policies, to maximize the benefits of emigration and reduce its felt costs, and to exercise some control over the migratory process. Historical analyses of Mexican emigration policy since the unilateral termination of the *bracero* program by the United States in 1964 have stressed Mexican policies aimed at providing minimal consular protection to the large and growing number of undocumented migrants and underscored Mexico's grudging acceptance that emigration was inevitable.[11] Although this literature on Mexican emigration policy has not explicitly adopted a state-centered orientation, the relatively coherent pattern of Mexican government policy responses in this issue area has lent itself to analyses that implicitly center on the state. The theoretical task, then, is in reinterpreting U.S. immigration policy toward Mexicans in state-centric terms, and articulating an explicit state-centric analysis of Mexican emigration policy.

The prevailing interpretations of the principal changes in U.S. policy on Mexican immigration have stressed the role of groups and, especially, the impact of employers on the policy process. The seven cases I discuss in the next section, and the one case of a policymaking process that follows, were selected because they have been interpreted by the literature on immigration in more or less society-centric terms. I will have more to say about them below, but a few references to the extant literature substantiate this point. Mark Reisler suggests, for example, that the recruitment of Mexican workers during the temporary admissions program of

Juan R. García, "'The Sacred Obligation to Defend and Protect': Mexican Consuls and the Problems of Emigration and Immigration, 1907 to 1930," paper presented at the Eighth Conference of Mexican and North American Historians, San Diego, Calif., 18–20 Oct. 1990; David R. Maciel, "An Unwritten Alliance: Mexican Policy on Emigration to the United States," unpub. manuscript, 1986; Patricia Morales, *Indocumentados mexicanos*, chap. 9; David G. Pfeiffer, "The Bracero Program in Mexico," in Kiser and Kiser, eds., *Mexican Workers in the United States*.

[11] Manuel García y Griego, "The Importation of Mexican Contract Laborers to the United States, 1942–1964: Antecedents, Operation, and Legacy," in Peter G. Brown and Henry Shue, eds., *The Border That Joins: Mexican Migrants and U.S. Responsibility* (Totowa, N.J., 1983), 49–98; Manuel García y Griego and Mónica Verea Campos, *México y Estados Unidos frente a la migración de los indocumentados* (Mexico City, 1988), 105–115; David R. Maciel, "An Unwritten Alliance: Mexican Policy on Emigration to the United States"; Stephen P. Mumme, "Mexican Politics and the Prospect for Emigration Policy: A Policy Perspective," *Inter-American Economic Affairs* vol. 32, no. 1 (Summer 1978); Carlos Rico F., "The Immigration Reform and Control Act of 1986 and Mexican Perceptions of Bilateral Approaches to Immigration Issues," in Georges Vernez, ed., *Immigration and International Relations: Proceedings of a Conference on the International Effects of the 1986 Immigration Reform and Control Act (IRCA)* (Santa Monica, Calif., and Washington, 1990), 90–100.

World War I was a direct response to grower demands.[12] The actions of the Department of State in opposing immigration restriction for Mexicans in the late 1920s and in 1930 are explained by Rodolfo Acuña in similar terms: "The State Department, representing Anglo-American foreign investors and exporters, joined southwestern industrialists to kill restrictionist measures."[13] Alejandro Portes, though conceding that the U.S. state had an "autonomous interest . . . as a corporate entity" in connection with immigration law reform in the 1980s, has suggested that the initiation of *braceros* in 1942 "was no war expedient but the expression of long-standing labor demand."[14] Similar arguments can be made about many other instances where U.S. or Mexican chief executives or high-level officials have made policy regarding international migration.

Toward a State-Centric Approach

The central analytic task of this paper is to explain public-policy outcomes, by which is meant something somewhat broader than "authoritative actions" (which include the absence of actions as well).[15] A state-centric approach to this objective is distinctive in that it accounts for government activity "shaped by forces beyond those generated by popular control."[16] My approach is to consider the state as an actor (actually to treat central decisionmakers as a unitary rational actor) and to equate the state with the government. This narrow conception of the state has limitations. The most important of these probably is that the state is treated as an exogenous variable, and the effects of changing institutional structures on public policy are not taken into account.[17] Though narrow, this conception of the state is justified here because it is empirically operational, and the issues of state autonomy, the priority of issues in a state

---

[12] Mark Reisler, *By the Sweat of Their Brow: Mexican Immigrant Labor in the United States, 1900–1940* (Westport, Conn., 1976), 27.

[13] Rodolfo Acuña, *Occupied America: A History of Chicanos* (New York, 1988), 188.

[14] Portes, "Of Borders and States," 20, 24.

[15] Eric Nordlinger, *On the Autonomy of the Democratic State* (Cambridge, Mass., 1981), 13. I include official proposals by the executive branch, which, if adopted, would be binding on society.

[16] Stephen L. Elkin, "Between Liberalism and Capitalism: An Introduction to the Democratic State," in Roger Benjamin and Stephen L. Elkin, eds., *The Democratic State* (Lawrence, Kans., 1985), 4.

[17] On the difference between the state as an exogenous or an intervening variable, see Krasner, "Approaches to the State"; on the limitations of the conceptualization of the state as actor, see Roger Benjamin and Raymond Duvall," The Capitalist State in Context," in *The Democratic State*, 27; Theda Skocpol, "Bringing the State Back In: Strategies of Analysis in Current Research," in Peter B. Evans, Dietrich Rueschemeyer, and Theda Skocpol, eds., *Bringing the State Back In* (Cambridge, Eng., 1985), especially p. 21.

agenda, and the significance of state resources and societal constraints can be readily examined through historical research.

The ambitions of this approach are certainly modest, though they are somewhat higher than merely offering a redundant term for government. It is government I am concerned with here, since the objective is to explain public-policy choices and the process by which they are decided. I have truncated the government at the apex à la Krasner to focus on the decisions of central decisionmakers as they pursue collective societal goals or even particular state goals. The objectives pursued by the presidency and high-level officials, who are relatively insulated from interest-group pressures, are chosen as a proxy for state objectives. As John Gerard Ruggie has observed, this draws from the Machiavellian roots of statism.[18] Machiavelli's Prince may be a poor surrogate of the totality of institutionalized coercion in society, but arguably he is a first approximation of the centralized authority of the government, which makes decisions for a collectivity. It is government as a potentially *autonomous* actor that interests us here, and if it is not capable of autonomous action then of course it would be pointless to introduce the notion of the state.

How do we know when the state is acting autonomously? One test is to find cases that require what Nordlinger defines as "type I state autonomy explanations": "Those in which state-society preferences diverge, with public officials being neither successfully pressured into translating societal preferences into public policy nor dissuaded by the threat of societal sanctions from acting upon their own."[19] In a democratic state, cases like these are unusual, and their identification is beset with some methodological difficulties. In the cases examined for this paper, only one—the initiation of a deportation campaign in 1954 that interrupted agricultural employer access to undocumented workers—approximates the requirements for this type of autonomy, and as shall be noted, how one interprets this depends on how extended the period of analysis is. In many instances, then, the policy outcome by itself is not evidence of state autonomy or societally constrained policymaking.

In the cases of policymaking discussed in this paper, we already know the outcomes—they are recorded in history. I am not attempting here to suggest that this history is factually incorrect. My point is that if the policy outcome appears to coincide with the preferences of certain interest groups—which in our cases most frequently are farm employers of Mexican labor—the analytical problem of explaining the outcome is far

---

[18] This is suggested in his review of Krasner's *Defending the National Interest*, in *American Political Science Review* vol. 74 (Mar. 1980), 298.

[19] Nordlinger, *On the Autonomy of the Democratic State*, 29.

from resolved, empirically and theoretically. There are, in essence, two competing explanations that need to be tested: (1) that the state followed its own logic and its own conception of the public interest more or less independently of the interests of special interest groups, or (2) that the government's actions merely reflect the resource-weighted demands of societal actors.

Although my framework differs from Nordlinger's in that I identify state interests with the central objectives pursued by high-level government officials, his typology of explanations is useful to organize this discussion. Explanation (2), above, accounts for instances where the "anticipation, threat, or deployment of private resources and sanctions, dissuades [central decisionmakers] from acting on their own preferences or pressures them into translating private preferences into public policy."[20] Explanation (1)—a Nordlinger type III state autonomy explanation— accounts for instances where "state-society preferences are nondivergent and the state acts upon its preferences."[21] There is a world of difference between these explanations, even though both would appear to account for situations in which the policy outcome appears to be consistent with the interests of societal actors.[22] To distinguish between them we need to examine the policy process itself and the context in which decisions are made.

My point is that even when outcomes and societal preferences appear to coincide, the state has its own logic, pursues its own agenda, and seeks to maximize its own values. Even when central decisionmakers have to make concessions to societal actors, as they often must in a system like that in the United States, the decisionmaking process shows something different from what the bureaucratic politics or pluralist paradigms might lead one to expect. Societal resistance obliges political leaders to choose which objectives matter most and which are attainable with their resources; these choices reflect pragmatic attempts to achieve important collective societal goals and particular state interests within those constraints.[23] The failure of central decisionmakers to achieve such goals is more often a reflection of the limits of their resources or of institutional constraints than societal pressure. At lower levels of government we should indeed find governmental behavior that reflects the penetration of bureaus of societal interests and sometimes,

---

[20] *Ibid.*, 28.

[21] *Ibid.*, 29.

[22] In "The Ruling Class Does Not Rule," Fred Block makes the same point from a Marxist perspective.

[23] Krasner discusses a similar point in his chapter "Policymaking in a Weak State," in *Defending the National Interest.*

dissident bureaus following their own corporate interests. I expect to show that these patterns of government behavior hold not only when we examine different kinds of cases of immigration policymaking within a single state but also when we compare states.

CENTRAL DECISIONMAKERS AND INTERNATIONAL MIGRATION POLICY, 1917 – 1986

Mexican migration to the United States is generally ignored by the higher reaches of U.S. government, though occasionally issues have risen and policy choices made at this level. The executive branch of government in Mexico, in contrast, has not been able to ignore emigration matters for long.

I have selected seven instances, spanning the period from World War I to the Carter immigration plan of 1977, in which issues were confronted and policies adopted by central decisionmakers in Mexico or the United States or both (Table 1). This is by no means an exhaustive list of the significant executive decisions made between 1917 and 1986; however, the selection does serve to both illustrate the possibilities (and limitations) of a state-centered approach and describe a pattern of state-centered decisionmaking in both countries regarding Mexican migration to the United States.

Wartime Recruitment of Mexican Workers

The first and fourth cases—the start of the first and second *bracero* programs, respectively—can be discussed together. Both programs were initiated by the U.S. executive branch in wartime, and in both cases the policy that was adopted coincided with the preferences of the most powerful societal actors in this issue area—U.S. agricultural employers. Does the pressure of these actors explain the process or account for the outcome?

There is one central reason for believing that the U.S. state pursued its own objectives in recruiting Mexican workers in 1917 and 1942: the U.S. need to marshall all the resources required to conduct a war. We see this priority reflected in U.S. government actions at the beginning of both programs.[24] In the opinion of U.S. central decisionmakers, during May

---

[24] Kiser and Kiser, *Mexican Workers in the United States,* 9–12; Johnny Mac McCain, "Contract Labor as a Factor in United States-Mexican Relations, 1942–1947," Ph.D. diss., University of Texas, Austin, 1970, 1–10; Mark Reisler, *By the Sweat of Their Brow,* chap. 2. A mixture of the two sets of concerns—resolving the wartime labor shortage and responding to long-term interests of agricultural employers—can be found expressed in internal correspondence prepared one year after the program began. See Herbert Hoover (Food Administrator) to Felix Frankfurter (Department of Labor), 4 June 1918, reproduced in Kiser and Kiser, *Mexican Workers in the United States,* 13–14.

TABLE I

Seven Illustrative Cases of Executive Policies Adopted Regarding Mexican Migration to the United States, 1917–1986

No.	Description	U.S. action	Mexican action
1	1917 Start of first bracero program	U.S. exemption of Mexican workers from formal requirements and unilateral recruitment	Expression of opposition to U.S. policy; no concrete action
2	1921 Repatriation of destitute Mexican workers caught in U.S. depression	Inaction	Presidential initiative to facilitate repatriation of tens of thousands of migrants
3	1927–1930 U.S. Congress debates extending quota to Mexican immigrants	Administrative restriction of visas to Mexican applicants by State Dept.	Opposition expressed; hints of reprisals; Proposes bilateral program
4	1942 Start of second bracero program	Initiates negotiations for recruitment of Mexican temporary farm workers	Agrees to bilateral management of farm labor program on condition Mexican laws followed
5	Oct. 1948 "El Paso incident": local INS office unilaterally opens border to Mexican workers	State Dept. apologizes for incident but presses demands of agricultural employers	Abrogates agreement and reopens negotiations for new agreement
6	Jan. 1951–Mar. 1952 Attempts to get U.S. Congress to adopt employer penalties; Texas proviso	Truman seeks Mexican agreement to continue program while Congress debates sanctions on smuggling and harboring undocumented aliens	Alemán agrees to Truman plan; Sec. de Rel. Exteriores presses U.S. for penalties on U.S. employers of undocumented workers
7	1977–1986 Attempts to enact legislation to curb undocumented migration	Carter Plan of 1977 (only executive proposal for legislation discussed)	Refusal to express official opinion; veiled opposition

1917 and July 1942 war produced a significant farm-labor shortage. The recruitment of farm labor may or may not in fact have turned out to be indispensable for conducting the war, but clearly central decisionmakers did not want to risk the alternative.

Nor were the policies adopted without opposition. In 1917 resistance came from Congressman Burton, author of the comprehensive immigration law that had been passed over Wilson's veto months earlier. In 1942 opposition emerged from organized labor and other groups.

Although it is not known precisely how much weight was accorded by central decisionmakers to the pressures of U.S. agricultural employers in 1917 and again in 1942, it is significant that this type of policy was not actively considered except under these extraordinary circumstances. Clearly the outcomes of these policies were affected by war. In 1942 the initiation of the *bracero* program was a byproduct of a broader U.S. policy aimed at securing Mexico's wartime cooperation.[25]

The U.S. employers of Mexican contract workers were not entirely pleased with either program. Growers expressed their dissatisfaction by inviting Mexican workers to cross illegally into the United States and by hiring them without a contract. (The term "wetbacks" was first used during World War I to refer to these casual entrants.) During World War II, employers voiced their displeasure with the terms of the labor contract and with the bilateral agreement with Mexico, which provided *braceros* with some labor protections not afforded by U.S. legislation to domestic farmworkers. The dissatisfaction of some employers with the policies adopted ostensibly in response to their own demands is one indicator that the thrust of state action in both instances had different origins. In both cases, the U.S. policy to initiate recruitment of *braceros* fits Nordlinger's type III category better than a societal-constraint explanation.

The action of Mexican leaders during these two instances of U.S. recruitment can also be grasped more readily in terms of state logic. Venustiano Carranza, the head of the Mexican government in 1917, expressed his opposition to the U.S. policy, but was unable to take concerted action to prevent the departure of emigrants. Carranza's position reflected the revolutionary consensus that had been expressed months earlier in the adoption of the 1917 Constitution, and which prohibited the recruitment of Mexican workers from abroad except when local authorities reviewed the terms of labor contracts. The government's attempt to dissuade emigrants, however, had no discernible effect.[26]

[25] I discuss this at greater length in Manuel García y Griego, "El comienzo y el final: La interdependencia estructural y dos negociaciones sobre braceros," in Blanca Torres, ed., *Interdependencia: Un enfoque útil para el análisis de las relaciones México-Estados Unidos?* (Mexico City, 1990), 101–108.

[26] Fernando Saúl Alanís Enciso, "La primera gran repatriación: Los mexicanos en Estados Unidos y el gobierno de México (1918–1922)," licentiate thesis, Colegio de Historia, Facultad de Filosofía y Letras, UNAM (Mexico City, 1987); Lawrence A. Cardoso, "Labor Emigration to the Southwest, 1916 to 1920: Mexican Attitudes and Policy," in *Mexican Workers in the United States;* García, "'The Sacred Obligation to Defend and Protect.'"

Notwithstanding the extraordinary changes in Mexico after the revolution that had begun in 1910 and the consolidation of its government by 1942, the Mexican position changed little. The terms of the 1942 *bracero* agreement in effect incorporated the constitutional conditions on which Carranza had insisted in 1917 but could not achieve. Emigration could be considered acceptable—perhaps even desirable—from Mexico's official point of view if certain political objectives could be achieved. These objectives included some control by the Mexican state over the process (hence the insistence on the bilateral management of migration); a limit to the magnitude of the flow in order to reduce the risk that large numbers of workers abroad would suddenly return during moments of economic crisis (hence the number of contracts issued were kept under 120,000 per year during the war);[27] and protections for Mexican workers, as stipulated by Mexican legislation.[28] It is striking here how political objectives had priority over economic interests.

Repatriation of Mexican Workers During the 1921 Depression

Our second case is the mass repatriation of destitute Mexican workers during the sharp, though brief, U.S. depression of 1921. Several tens of thousands of Mexican repatriates effected their return with Mexican government transportation and other support, provided mainly because President Alvaro Obregón took a personal interest in the matter. The Mexican government had requested assistance earlier, from the U.S. government and from the employers who had recruited them during World War I, in order to return these workers, but was refused. Subsequently, President Obregón authorized about $2.5 million to conduct a mass return from the United States.[29]

Although the Obregón government did take note of appeals from individual emigrants who petitioned the Mexican consulates and even the president directly, it would not be accurate to characterize the govern-

[27] As I point out in my paper "The Importation of Mexican Contract Laborers," Mexican and U.S. sources on the number of contract workers employed differ significantly during the war years. My numbers above refer to the Mexican figures. The U.S. figures are even lower, indicating that no more than 65,000 workers were contracted in any given year during the war.

[28] McCain, "Contract Labor as a Factor in United States-Mexican Relations, 1942–1947"; Ernesto Galarza, *Merchants of Labor: The Mexican Bracero Story* (Charlotte, N.C., 1964); Otey M. Scruggs, *Braceros, "Wetbacks," and the Farm-Labor Problem: Mexican Agricultural Labor in the United States, 1942–1954* (New York, 1988), chaps. 6 and 7.

[29] Rodolfo Acuña, *Occupied America: A History of Chicanos*, 3d ed. (New York, 1988), 185; Alanís, "La primera gran repatriación"; Lawrence A. Cardoso, "La repatriación de braceros en epoca de Obregón, 1920–1923," *Historia Mexicana* vol. 26, no. 4 (Apr.–June 1977), 576–95.

ment's action as a response to pressure exerted by a weighty societal actor; rather, it was a legitimating act by a nascent revolutionary state.[30] Given that the initiative came from the state and that the dimension of this effort was extraordinary (it was both unprecedented and unequaled afterward), it constitutes a clear example of autonomous state action, though not of one adopted in the face of domestic opposition.

Immigration Quotas and Mexican Workers

Our third situation returns us to central decisionmakers in the United States. Starting in 1928 the U.S. Secretary of State, in consultation with the U.S. president, ordered U.S. consuls in Mexico to apply existing criteria rigidly so as to limit severely the number of visas granted to Mexicans. Although my focus here is executive policymaking, and administrative restriction constitutes a decision by central decisionmakers using their own resources, policymaking cannot be understood without considering the threat of legislative action by Congress against Mexican immigration. This consideration also requires that we step back from the specific goals of political leaders in order to examine them in the context of public opinion and the manner in which issues were framed and debated.

The "problem" was a byproduct of the ideology that had prevailed in the establishment of quotas in 1924, which held that the "Nordic race" was superior to all others. The National Origins Act of that year had restricted "undesirable" immigration from southern and eastern Europe, but had left the door open for all immigrants who applied from countries in the Western Hemisphere. Though legal immigration from Europe declined after 1924, Mexican immigration grew to unprecedented levels. The prevailing consensus held that Jews, Slavs, Russians, Hungarians, Italians and others from "inferior races" (as well as Asians and others who had been barred earlier) were not suitable for unlimited admission to the United States. Not surprisingly, it also held that Mexicans were undesirable immigrants.

Two U.S. groups opposed the extension of the quota to Mexicans. The most visible group, and the one that applied most of the organized pressure on Congress, comprised farm employers from the Southwest. It is noteworthy that in Congressional hearings these employers conceded the social undesirability of Mexicans, but argued that their labor was indispensable and that social contamination would be minimal because they tended to return to Mexico. The other group, whose influence has re-

---

[30] The Mexican government response needs to be seen, more than in terms of the appeals from migrants as such, in the context of the violent persecutions against unemployed and destitute Mexicans. See Acuña, *Occupied America*, 185.

ceived less attention, was composed of U.S. businesses that had investments in Mexico and which feared Mexican reprisals. A third actor that
opposed the quotas was the government of Mexico.[31]

U.S. central decisionmakers who opposed extending the quota to include Mexicans thus did face societal constraints. However, this was not
an instance in which political leaders pursued a broad societal goal in the
face of opposition by a powerful but narrow societal group. The substantive effect of administrative restrictions had the same adverse consequences on the farmers as did the bill that both farmers and public officials were protesting. The political effect of administrative restrictions
was to undercut an objective sought by a broad array of societal groups
who, unlike farmers, could legitimately claim to support a broad societal
goal on which there was some general agreement (limiting undesirable
immigration). The only group whose interests coincided both with the
substantive and political effects of administrative restrictions was foreign
investors, but there is no clear indication that the White House and State
Department were pressured by this group.

This instance presents features of both type I and type III state autonomy with respect to farm employers and the broader society actively
promoting Mexican restriction. It is often interpreted as a reflection of
societal constraints (pressure from investors in Mexico), but it is unclear
why central decisionmakers would respond to this group's narrow interests and not to those of farmers. Clearly, the problem here is not the
traditional one of central decisionmakers facing pressure from a narrow
societal group. This argument assumes too much sensitivity by the State
Department to domestic groups and not enough to long-term foreign-
policy goals.[32] Rather, the very definition of what was in the public interest was at stake.

Given the wide range of controversy in this issue, U.S. political leaders
were free to pursue state objectives that coincided and conflicted with a
range of actors. These objectives were to maintain good relations with
Mexico and to avoid the uncertainty for U.S. policy that would result
from reprisals on U.S. interests there. These goals coincide in large part
with investor preferences but are distinct from them. It is for these kinds
of reasons that the State Department had opposed the restriction of Chinese and Japanese immigration. Indeed, in 1904 the Chinese initiated a

---

[31] Acuña, *Occupied America,* 187–88; Robert A. Divine, *American Immigration Policy,*
1924–1952 (New Haven, Conn., 1957), 52–68.
[32] Acuña, *Occupied America,* 188; Corwin, "A Story of ad hoc Exemptions," 145–46.
It should be noted that although State opposed the quota, the Department of Labor (whose
jurisdiction the Bureau of Immigration was under) supported it.

boycott of U.S. goods due to insulting legislation, and in 1907 the Department had negotiated an agreement with Japan by which it voluntarily applied quotas on the emigration of nationals to the United States.[33] Administrative restriction thus constituted a pragmatic measure by central decisionmakers to produce a result that was inevitable (the reduction of Mexican immigration) without incurring the political costs to long-term foreign policy interests.

Administrative restriction was not sufficient to stop the Senate from passing a bill extending the quota to Mexico, but the executive branch intervened in the Rules Committee to prevent the bill from reaching the floor of the House of Representatives. It died in the 71st Congress. There were "strong indications" that President Hoover would have vetoed the bill had it passed the House.[34] However, the bill was not brought up again, perhaps because the Great Depression reduced sharply the demand for foreign labor and in fact produced a large repatriation to Mexico. The administrative restriction of Mexican immigrants, however, continued for many years thereafter.

Mexican political leaders, though unhappy at the prospect of punitive legislation in Congress, did not favor permanent emigration of nationals to the United States.[35] The Mexican government's alternative, suggested in 1929, foreshadowed the beginning of the *bracero* program by thirteen years. Its proposal, not acted upon, was to manage by bilateral agreement the temporary migration of Mexican workers.[36] In this, as in the instances previously mentioned, the Mexican government agreed with the opinion of its public but did not act in response to identifiable pressure groups.

The El Paso Incident

The fifth case listed in Table 1, the "El Paso incident," is one in which two local bureaus obeyed the dictates of local societal interests rather

[33] On the vetoes of the first attempts to exclude the Chinese on foreign-policy grounds, see Chamberlain, *The President, Congress, and Legislation*, 353–54; on strained relations with the Chinese, see Mary Roberts Coolidge, *Chinese Immigration* (Taipei, 1968), 193; George M. Stephenson, *A History of American Immigration, 1820–1924* (New York, 1964), 263; Japanese-U.S. relations (and negotiations) over migration are discussed in Stephenson, *A History of American Immigration*, chap. 21; Raymond Leslie Buell, "The Development of the Anti-Japanese Agitation in the United States: I," *Political Science Quarterly* vol. 37 (1922), 605–638; Raymond Leslie Buell, "The Development of the Anti-Japanese Agitation in the United States: II," *Political Science Quarterly* vol. 38 (1923), 57–81.

[34] Divine, *American Immigration Policy*, 66.

[35] Manuel Gamio, *Mexican Immigration to the United States: A Study of Human Migration and Adjustment* (Chicago, 1930), 177–78.

[36] Cardoso, *Mexican Emigration to the United States 1897–1931*, 117.

than leaders in Washington. This event occurred in October 1948, three years after the end of World War II, but was the first major conflict of the *bracero* program in the postwar period.

Several agricultural employer organizations expressed their dissatisfaction with the *bracero* program during 1948 and during the summer were successful in getting the government to reopen negotiations with Mexico. They were dissatisfied with several aspects of the program, but the immediate concern at that time was their demand that recruitment centers within Mexico be located further north, close to the border. In September, the two bureaucracies responsible for administrating the program, the Employment Service (a division of the Department of Labor) and the INS, transmitted the impatience of growers with the Mexican government and advocated unilateral contracting of Mexican workers. The State Department opposed this proposal because of the "international repercussions" that would arise.[37] When this interbureaucratic disagreement rose to the White House for resolution, it took the position that the United States would not "condone violation of the agreement, nor suggest abrogation," but instead would conclude pending negotiations with Mexico.[38] In October, however, in direct opposition to the resolution of the executive branch, the El Paso offices of the U.S. Border Patrol and the Employment Service opened the border unilaterally, and for a few days allowed the entry and employment of Mexican workers without a contract.

During the immediate postwar period, the Mexican government had continued the *bracero* program for national economic reasons. President Alemán's ambitious industrialization program meant that fewer resources would be directed to rural areas, where emigrants left from, and that the country would count on migrant worker remittances as a source of foreign exchange. The Mexican government responded to the violation of the bilateral agreement at El Paso in 1948 by abrogating the agreement. The State Department subsequently sent a note of apology.[39]

Negotiations for a new agreement dragged on for several months. During the interim, since growers could not obtain workers legally, the Bor-

[37] "Chapter IX: The Executive Agreement," in Papers of David H. Stowe, White House Assistant (Kansas City, Mo., Harry S. Truman Library), 10–11. This is part of a larger manuscript, whose authorship is unknown, which summarizes the history of the Mexican farm-labor program. Peter Kirstein, in his book *Anglo over Bracero: A History of the Mexican Worker in the United States from Roosevelt to Nixon* (San Francisco, 1977), 67, refers to it as the Secret Study.

[38] "Chapter IX: The Executive Agreement," 12.

[39] The text of the U.S. diplomatic note is reproduced in Kiser and Kiser, *Mexican Workers in the United States*, 153–54.

der Patrol from time to time stopped expelling migrants who had entered illegally as long as they were employed in agriculture.[40] A new bilateral agreement was finally reached in August 1949, with the Mexican government making concessions to growers, though without leaving them entirely satisfied.[41]

The state-centered approach I have developed here accounts for the outcome in this case. The action taken by the bureaus at El Paso reflects clearly the pressure exerted by growers; the decision made in Washington reflected broader foreign-policy concerns. A state-centered approach would lead one to expect that the State Department and White House would put foreign-policy priorities before the concerns of these local growers (and the agencies they had "captured"), as they did. Central decisionmakers are more insulated from narrow societal concerns and pressures. The policy adopted reflects this separation.

A state-centered perspective is not inconsistent with bureaucratic politics' explanations of policy implementation at lower levels of government. In his classic study of the Cuban missile crisis, Graham Allison shows that even in situations in which national security and avoiding a war are at stake, the president had difficulty getting some of his orders implemented faithfully.[42] In the El Paso incident, two bureaus countermanded an order derived from a policy at the top, in response to bureaucratic interests or local societal pressures.

The Mexican state was similarly strong in the policymaking realm but weak in its ability to enforce it. The Mexican government did not face significant political opposition to its abrogation of the agreement (that is, opposition expressed verbally or by pressure on the governmental apparatus). Migrants did not hesitate to leave, however, notwithstanding the government's stated opposition to their departure. Emigrants left during the incident and in the months afterward, when a new agreement was being negotiated.

U.S. Legislation Regarding Employer Sanctions, 1951–52

The sixth case directs us to the role of U.S. central decisionmakers in the legislative arena. When the Mexican government's hand was strengthened in *bracero* negotiations by U.S. entry into the Korean War, it re-

[40] Robert C. Hayes, "Mexican Migrant Labor in the United States; Historical Notes on the Bracero Problem," unpub. report of the Division of Historical Policy Research, Department of State, Dec. 1950, 126. This report was found in National Archives, Records of the Department of State, RG 59 Decimal File 811.06 (M).

[41] *Ibid.*, 131.

[42] Graham T. Allison, *Essence of Decision: Explaining the Cuban Missile Crisis* (Boston, Mass., 1971), 130–32. Cf. Krasner, "Are Bureacracies Important?"

quested U.S. Congressional legislation to create a formal legal framework for the *bracero* program and to penalize employers of undocumented workers. Congress approved the first request but balked at the second, and in July 1951, Presidents Truman and Alemán agreed to extend the agreement for six months in order to pressure Congress for legislation on employer penalties.[43] Soon thereafter, however, it became clear that Congress would not adopt employer sanctions and the White House found a less-attractive substitute—a bill that applied criminal penalties for smuggling, transporting, and "harboring" undocumented aliens. Congress passed the bill in March 1952. However, the force of the measure was weakened by the proviso that "the usual and normal practices incident to employment shall not be deemed to constitute harboring."[44]

The Texas Proviso—so named because the Texas Congressional delegation authored it—presents a clear instance in which central decision-makers were unable to get their way and societal actors (in the interest-group theory sense) overwhelmed state purpose. Truman and Alemán did get some legislation that discouraged the trafficking of migrants, but Congress met them considerably less than halfway. Willing to settle for marginal benefits, Truman signed the bill into law and Alemán accepted that the program would continue on this basis. Although the U.S. president can veto legislation, he does not have the institutional resources to pass legislation. In the legislative arena, growers were able to thwart the pursuit of a particular state objective—living up to the agreement with the Mexican government.

The Failure of the Carter Immigration Plan of 1977

Between 1971 and 1976, a debate had been simmering in the United States about what to do about undocumented immigration, much of it from Mexico. Carter's plan contained the two central provisions that would eventually be adopted nine years later in the Immigration Reform and Control Act—employer sanctions to deter further undocumented labor immigration, and a legalization of long-standing resident undocumented workers. The proposal, however, was attacked from all sides. Some characterized the "amnesty" provisions as too lenient; they rewarded lawbreakers. Others characterized the same provisions as insufficiently generous, and opposed employer sanctions on the grounds that these would have adverse collateral effects such as job discrimination

[43] The exchange of correspondence between Truman and Alemán is reproduced in Kiser and Kiser, *Mexican Workers in the United States*, 155–58.

[44] Text of the law quoted by Hutchinson, *Legislative History of American Immigration Policy 1798–1965*, 302.

against ethnic minorities, or would place a regulatory burden on business. The interest-group paradigm would have no difficulty accounting
for the defeat of the Carter Plan in Congress, but it does not account for
the president's decision to offer the plan in the first place.[45]

A state-centered approach would describe the outcome as symptomatic
of policymaking in a weak state, but that only suggests the problem without explaining it. The executive branch is able to pursue its notion of the
national interest more effectively when it controls the resources needed
to achieve the political outcome. Getting Congress to adopt legislation
when the legislative package is controversial may not be possible. Although public opinion may have been more favorably disposed toward
adoption of employer sanctions in 1977 than it had been in 1952, interest-group opposition was fatal in both instances. There is no indication
that Carter had profited from Truman's lesson.

All of this, of course, sounds familiar. In many areas other than immigration, the image of a weak chief executive emerges when the objective
is getting legislative action. The problem is not just the role of interest
groups; it is also a matter of Congress guarding jealously its prerogatives.
Perhaps immigration policy is only unique in the degree to which the
Congress and the president have traditionally had conflictual relations.
"Between 1882 and 1952," Milton Morris has written, "ten immigration
laws were vetoed by six presidents with widely differing styles, perceptions of executive-legislative authority, and attitudes about the use of the
veto power."[46]

Congress responded to Carter's proposal by creating the Select Commission on Immigration and Refugee Policy, whose mandate it was to
recommend to Congress and the president legislation to address illegal
immigration and other problems. The Select Commission's report, *U.S.
Immigration Policy and the National Interest,* was issued in March 1981
to a new Congress and the Reagan administration.[47] The major compo-

[45] Verea, *Entre México y Estados Unidos,* 127–33.
[46] Morris, *Immigration—The Beleaguered Bureacracy,* 33–34. Chamberlain studied the
relative influence of the presidency, interest groups, and Congress per se on the origin and
outcome of ninety major pieces of legislation adopted between the late nineteenth century
and the New Deal in ten broad categories of issues, including immigration. In three issue
areas (immigration, natural resources, and railroads), none of the sixteen major laws studied reflected a preponderant influence of the executive branch. Chamberlain, however,
tended to see Congress as more important than interest groups per se in the adoption of the
principal immigration bills. These nine immigration laws encompassed the Chinese Exclusion Acts of 1882 and 1892, and the general immigration acts of 1882, 1903, 1907, 1913,
1917, 1921, and 1924. Chamberlain, *The President, Congress, and Legislation,* 352–74,
450–52.
[47] U.S. Select Commission on Immigration and Refugee Policy, *U.S. Immigration Policy
and the National Interest: Final Report and Recommendations of the Select Commission
on Immigration and Refugee Policy* (Washington, 1981).

nents of the proposals to reduce undocumented immigration were strikingly similar to those of the Carter Plan. The task of the Commission, as the title of its report suggests, was to create a consensus around a view of the "national interest" in immigration policy. In other words, it sought to gain public acceptance of a particular manner in which the issue could be framed and to articulate a goal for the state that could be supported over the objections of interest groups.[48] President Reagan presented his own version of an immigration control plan, which included employer sanctions and legalization (though in different forms) and a pilot guest-worker program.

Thus, legislation promoted by the executive branch as early as 1977 was finally adopted as the Immigration Reform and Control Act of 1986 (IRCA). Its central features were sanctions on employers that knowingly hired unauthorized workers and legalization of long-term undocumented residents. The adoption of IRCA reflected the emergence of a consensus in Congress regarding the appropriate package of legislative measures to reduce undocumented immigration. The opposition to employer sanctions and legalization, evident in the frustration of the Carter Plan, was overcome by 1986.

However, Congress did have to make some concessions to narrow interest groups in order for the bill to be passed. Some claim that legalization was one such concession. The most obvious provisions that served no broad societal purpose and that were adopted to neutralize an opponent (again, agricultural employers) were the legalization of agricultural workers (SAW), authorization to recruit replacement agricultural workers (RAW) between 1990 and 1993,[49] and the requirement that the Border Patrol get a search warrant (or owner's permission) to search open fields. As in the removal of Mexican undocumented workers in 1954 (below), agricultural employers were bought off by making legally admitted workers accessible to them.

The response of the Mexican government to the Carter Plan, and to the legislative process that led to IRCA, was to avoid adopting an explicit position, though veiled opposition could be discerned by close observers. Once the United States had decided to deal with the problem through legislation, Carlos Rico has written, "not much could be done regarding

[48] Lawrence H. Fuchs, "The Search for a Sound Immigration Policy: A Personal View," in Nathan Glazer, ed., *Clamor at the Gates: The New American Immigration* (San Francisco, 1985), 17–48; Charles B. Keely, "Current Status of U.S. Immigration and Refugee Policy," in Mary M. Kritz, ed., *U.S. Immigration and Refugee Policy: Global and Domestic Issues* (Lexington, Mass., 1983), 339–59.

[49] Frank D. Bean, Georges Vernez, and Charles B. Keely, *Opening and Closing the Doors: Evaluating Immigration Reform and Control* (Santa Monica and Washington, 1989), 29–30.

Mexican input into such a process."[50] Mexican public opinion was hostile to U.S. pronouncements and policy proposals, and the prevalent fear was that whatever measure was adopted, Mexico would have to face the mass return of migrants at a time when its economy could scarcely cope with existing employment problems.

The Mexican refusal to take a position was justified officially on grounds of nonintervention, but Mexican leaders generally opposed the legislative proposals and the Mexican government may have feared their consequences. Notwithstanding this justification, whatever preferences Mexican central decisionmakers had regarding U.S. options (outside of a bilateral arrangement), once expressed, would have given a bilateral cast to a unilateral U.S. decision. This may account for Mexican inaction on this issue; had the government heeded the opinions of critics, it would have sought changes in the U.S. legislation that may have been unattainable.

"BRACEROS" SÍ, "WETBACKS" NO (1953 – 54)

In the first section below, I describe the policymaking process that led to a resolution of the problem of undocumented Mexican migration in 1954. In the section following, I discuss the problem of interpretation.

Policy Objectives, Events, and Outcomes

In the spring of 1953, the agricultural committees of both houses of the U.S. Congress opened hearings on the extension of the farm-labor program in an atmosphere of acrimony. The problem was that the number of Mexican illegal entrants apprehended by the INS had been rising sharply and steadily, which suggested that more Mexican agricultural workers were being employed as "wetbacks" rather than as contract *braceros*. Members of Congress sympathetic to farmer concerns were nervous about the future of the program. On the one hand, taxpayers subsidized the program to recruit contract laborers from Mexico for the benefit of a small segment of the nation's farmers. On the other hand, taxpayers paid for the return of illegal entrants—and many of their employers were the same farmers that the contract-labor program was designed to benefit. In addition, the "wetbacks" were blamed for a broad range of social ills: unemployment of domestic workers, a drain on tax-supported social services, crime, disease, and even the introduction of subversives into U.S. territory. Grower representatives insisted that many farmers were forced to hire illegal entrants because

[50] Rico, "The Immigration Reform and Control Act of 1986," 95.

of Mexican government "red tape" in the operation of the contract-labor program.[51]

Also in the spring of 1953, U.S. and Mexican negotiators met in Mexico City to iron out longstanding differences of interpretation in the agreement. Though many of these were settled after two weeks, in the end minor differences still separated them. When the negotiations broke down in April 1953, SRE threatened an embargo of contract laborers, but eventually backed off.[52] In the United States the idea of contracting Mexican workers unilaterally was given serious thought, but not adopted.[53] Significantly, no evidence exists of pressure by agricultural interests to respond to the Mexican threats or to recruit workers unilaterally.

The idea that the *bracero* program required a major policy change did not spring overnight within the U.S. government. Indeed, it resulted from the idea promoted by Attorney General Herbert Brownell—which suddenly gained impetus in August 1953—that something drastic had to be done about undocumented immigration from Mexico. The point bears underlining. The idea in favor of a program somewhat more amenable to growers' interests did not originate as such. Rather, central decisionmakers adopted it as a solution to undocumented migration, which they conceived of as a problem and which many growers, instead, saw as a solution.

In August 1953 Brownell toured the international boundary between California and Baja California and publicly announced "shocking" conditions that required a drastic governmental response. Shortly afterward, he conferred with President Eisenhower and made a public statement to the effect that additional law enforcement action was needed. In so doing, Brownell reinforced the public's fear of undocumented migration from Mexico,[54] a mood heightened by the sense that the migration was growing to massive proportions. In July 1953 alone, the INS expelled nearly 108,000 undocumented Mexicans; the number rose slightly in August, to 111,000.[55]

U.S. options were constrained by societal actors and by the Mexican government. Employer sanctions, it was recognized, would not fly in Congress. Eisenhower administration officials explicitly took into ac-

[51] U.S. House of Representatives, *Extension of Mexican Farm-Labor Program, Hearings 24–26 Mar. 1953* (Washington, 1953).

[52] Dispatch 2232 from Ailshie 10 Apr. 1953. National Archives, *Records of the Department of State,* RG 59, Decimal File 811.06, (M).

[53] William Belton (Office of Mexican Affairs, State Department) to Ambassador Francis White, 15 Dec. 1953. National Archives, *Records of the State Department,* RG 59, Decimal File 811.06, (M).

[54] *New York Times,* 16 Aug. 1953, 1, 27; *New York Times,* 18 Aug. 1953, 16.

[55] These data are contained in a manuscript table, National Records Center (Suitland, Md.) INS File "Contract Labor—Border Patrol," 56364/43.38, pt. 3.

count Truman's debacle, which had produced the Texas Proviso in 1952.
The possibility that the Mexican government might use force to prevent
the departure of nationals who were without contracts had been raised
several times during the Truman administration, but all that President
Alemán had acceded to was the patrolling of the Reynosa-McAllen border area by a few soldiers.[56] A proposal by the U.S. Embassy in January 1953 that the Mexican government use police to stop migrants at
transportation nodes a hundred miles or more from the border was po-
litely refused.[57]

The range of policy alternatives available to U.S. central decisionmakers late in the summer of 1953 seemed limited. In August, Brownell
floated briefly the idea of using National Guard troops to stop Mexicans
at the border. U.S. Ambassador Francis White protested the idea vigorously and Under Secretary of State Walter Beddel Smith, who had served
in close association with General Eisenhower during World War II,
squelched it.[58] A thorough understanding of the rejection of this proposal
and the other alternative—doing nothing—requires additional research.
But there can be no doubt that the persons with military experience in the
administration—the president, Under Secretary Smith, and another friend
of Eisenhower's who would later become Commissioner of Immigration,
Joseph Swing—were singularly unenthusiastic about the use of troops for
this purpose.[59] Their rationale for ruling out the use of troops was that it
was "too likely to upset our relations with Mexico to be worth trying."[60]

The strategy adopted by U.S. central decisionmakers was to renegoti-

[56] V. H. Blocker (U.S. Embassy in Mexico) to Belton, 4 Feb. 1953, and Belton to Blocker,
9 Feb. 1953, mimeo. National Archives, Records of the Department of State, RG 59, Decimal File 811.06, [M].

[57] The U.S. interpretation of Mexican legislation ostensibly giving the government authority to control emigration, SRE argued, was too broad. It "contradicts the principle
of Article 11 of the Political Constitution of the country, which consecrates the right and
guarantee that every Mexican has to travel and move freely throughout the whole circum-
ference of the national territory." Translation, diplomatic note 13809, SRE to U.S. Embassy
12 Feb. 1953. National Archives, Records of the Department of State, RG 59, Decimal File
811.06, (M).

[58] Ambassador White to Secretary of State, 14 Aug. 1953 and Assistant Secretary John
Cabot to Ambassador White, 18 Aug. 1953, reproduced in N. Stephen Kane and William F.
Sanford, Jr., eds., Foreign Relations of the United States 1952–1954: Volume IV The
American Republics (Washington, 1983), 1340–46.

[59] "Brownell had asked [Swing] in 1953 to prepare a plan to send American troops to
the Mexican border to stop the 'illegal invation of wetbacks.' . . . Swing said that the plan
was dropped after he told Brownell that it was 'a perfectly horrible' way to handle the
situation because any such move would 'destroy' relations with Mexico." García, Operation Wetback, 171.

[60] Memorandum, Belton to Cabot, 26 Aug. 1953. National Archives, Records of the
Department of State, RG 59, Decimal File 811.06, (M).

ate the bilateral agreement with Mexico in terms that would make it "workable" and then to push growers into giving up undocumented workers and substituting them with *braceros*. It is notable that this strategy was formulated within the executive branch and not "leaked" or otherwise submitted for public comment. The first step was to present the Mexican government with a forceful U.S. position and, eventually, an ultimatum. If the Mexicans refused, the U.S. would contract workers unilaterally. After the legal program was straightened out, the government would launch a mass-deportation campaign to interrupt the access of growers to undocumented workers and to persuade them to accept *braceros* in their place.

Several elements of this process within the U.S. government point toward state initiative and not societal (grower) pressure. The first is the involvement of the highest levels of the U.S. government. Obviously, this was not so important a matter that it required the President's day-to-day attention. But the chief architects of the strategy seem to have been Attorney General Brownell and Under Secretary Smith—high-level officials relatively insulated from societal pressures who had direct access to the president and authority to pursue collective societal goals (the reduction of undocumented immigration). The negotiations with the Mexican government were conducted by the ambassador himself.

A second element is that state purpose and private interests are distinguishable. To be sure, the U.S. position was formulated in terms thought to be acceptable to many growers and, although the Department of Labor did not lead the process, it was involved in suggesting (though not determining outright) the U.S. position in negotiations. An internal State Department memorandum discussing this policy shift in August 1953 sketched the rationale: "An incentive system which would make the employment of legal immigrants [*braceros*] more attractive to employers and legal entry much more attractive than wetbackism to laborers seems to hold the greatest promise for satisfactorily dealing with the problem." [61] This rationale indicates the recognition by central decisionmakers that incentives had to be employed to get growers on board. But in its conclusion this memorandum returns to the state purpose in pursuing this policy. The unilateral recruitment of Mexican workers "would be distasteful to the Mexicans, but not as unpleasant as troops on the border." [62] The trade-off makes clear that the government's objective was not modifying the program in response to grower complaints, but reducing undocumented immigration.

[61] *Ibid.*
[62] *Ibid.*

Other elements include the timing and nature of the actions taken by the U.S. executive branch. Although it is not often recognized, unilateral recruitment and "Operation Wetback" were each a part of a single process. That is, the central objective, from August 1953 to August 1954, was to reduce undocumented immigration, even at significant social and political costs. A unilateral program was contemplated, though not instituted, when the negotiations reached an impasse early in 1953, and when the Department of Labor had control over the U.S. position. The bargaining strategy was to address the broad social problem of reducing illegal entries. (There is another element that can be seen as a state concern rather than a broad societal interest: the need to maintain the appearance, if not the substance, of state control over international migration.[63])

The concessions obtained from Mexico for U.S. growers were real, of course, but it is notable that many growers did not consider them as such and had to be pressured with "Operation Wetback" to see the light. Rather than constituting demands of the state by this societal actor, modifications of the program were inducements offered by the state to get growers to go along with the policy.

The response of the Mexican government to U.S. pressure was to stonewall the U.S. ambassador during the fall of 1953. In January, when the United States announced a plan to contract workers unilaterally, the Mexican government announced a plan to prevent the departure of its nationals. Mexican police and troops attempted to prevent the unilateral hiring, but hundreds of Mexican workers were only too willing to step over the border to get a contract. Some arrests and incidents of violence were reported.

As a result of this pressure, within days of instituting an embargo on the departure of Mexican workers, President Ruiz Cortines did an about-face. Mexico's ambassador was received by President Eisenhower and it was agreed to continue bilateral negotiations. At the border, Mexican police and troops no longer attempted to detain departing nationals and, since the United States had announced it was open for contracting, thousands of workers jammed into the ports of entry. When the United States had to close the ports because more workers showed up than could be contracted, riots ensued.[64]

[63] Portes, in "Of Borders and States," 25, has also suggested this in connection with the evolution of what became IRCA.

[64] These events are described in Craig, The Bracero Program, 109–112; García, Operation Wetback, 82–84; García y Griego, "The Importation of Mexican Contract Laborers," 71–72; Robert Tomasek, "The Political and Economic Implications of Mexican Labor in the United States under the Non-Quota System, Contract-Labor Program, and Wetback Movement," Ph.D. diss., University of Michigan, 1957, 259–60.

In the context of these events, it is not surprising that the Mexican government eventually capitulated on virtually all U.S. demands regarding the bilateral program. It does seem unusual, however, that the terms of the contract employed during the unilateral phase were not altered much to meet grower demands.[65] The nature of the changes made in the March 1954 agreement did coincide with some of the grower's preferences, but the emphasis was on those changes thought by U.S. decision-makers to be most likely to reduce undocumented immigration. For example, the Mexicans only agreed to allow contract laborers to be recruited from its northern border communities after Under Secretary Smith called President Ruiz Cortines to suggest that if an agreement was not worked out "there might be some Congressional action that would be disadvantageous."[66] By contrast, the minimum period for contracts (six weeks) did not return to the four-week standard until the start of "Operation Wetback" in July.

In April and May the INS planned "Operation Wetback." Some writers have erroneously suggested that this campaign produced one million expulsions—the number actually expelled between mid-June and mid-August was somewhat over 165,000.[67] This apparently small number looms larger when one distinguishes between apprehensions of persons shortly after crossing the border (which is relatively easy and generates large numbers quickly) and the apprehension of persons residing and working in the country. Unlike previous efforts, "Operation Wetback" rounded up and expelled thousands of Mexican families (along with U.S.-born children) to Mexico.

Two other distinctive features of this operation stand out when compared to previous efforts to expel illegal entrants. One was the central

---

[65] One significant concession to grower interests was the four-week minimum contract. However, the unilateral program did not even faintly resemble the "white card" system advocated by growers, especially from the Lower Río Grande Valley. To the contrary, with the exception noted, the contract retained all of the protections ectant in the bilateral version. See *New York Times*, 16 Jan. 1954, p. 15.

[66] Memorandum for the President, 8 Mar. 1954. Dwight D. Eisenhower Library (Abilene, Kans.), Eisenhower Papers, Ann Whitman File, box 1, folder "ACW Diary March 54 (4)." The memorandum noted that "To Beetle's surprise, he thinks we are going to get the kind of agreement we want regarding 'wet Backs' [sic]."

[67] About 76,000 undocumented Mexicans were apprehended in California, and 89,000 in the Lower Río Grande Valley of Texas, according to a letter from INS Commissioner Joseph Swing to John F. Dulles, Secretary of State, 22 Oct. 1954. National Archives, *Records of the Department of State*, RG 59, Decimal File 811.06, (M); García, *Operation Wetback*, 228. Additional enforcement activity, sometimes considered part of "Operation Wetback," was conducted in urban areas outside of the Southwest in later months. About 20,000 Mexicans were removed from industrial jobs in midwestern and northwestern cities. Julián Samora, *Los mojados: The Wetback Story* (Notre Dame, Ind., 1971), 53.

role played by the Mexican government in providing transportation from the border to points farther south for more than a thousand persons a day. Transportation facilities were strained to the limit and railroad cattle cars were employed to transport many. Some people were transported by boat and taken to Veracruz.[68]

The other distinctive feature of the operation was the deliberate effort made to substitute undocumented workers, who were taken away, with contract *braceros,* who were brought back to growers. Not infrequently the same individuals were expelled one day and contracted the next. Slightly over one thousand legal *braceros* per day were given contracts and distributed among agricultural employers.[69]

Though deplorable on several grounds, this strategy of U.S. central decisionmakers was successful. Prior to 1954, the number of contracted *braceros* had leveled off at about 200,000 per year. During the 1954 calendar year, the *bracero* population shot up to 304,000 (even though the substitution began at mid-year). During 1955 the number reached 399,000, where it leveled off for the rest of the 1950s.[70] The number of apprehensions of illegal entrants dropped dramatically—from 1,075,000 to nearly 243,000 to 72,000, in fiscal years 1954, 1955, and 1956, respectively. The numbers continued to decline thereafter.[71] The mass substitution of undocumented workers with *braceros* in 1954 is clearly a major turning point during the entire evolution of the *bracero* program (see Fig. 1). In January 1955, after the policy had run its course, a report on the outcome of the process presented at an Eisenhower cabinet meeting concluded that the government had succeeded in reducing illegal entries and increasing the legal contracting of *braceros.*[72]

Autonomy, Constraints, and Intended Beneficiaries of Policymaking

The Mexican response in this case illustrates what Krasner has called "policymaking in a weak state."[73] U.S. central decisionmakers chose a

[68] Samora, *Los mojados,* 51–53.

[69] Copy, unnumbered diplomatic note, Woodward to Nieto (Mexican Chargé d'Affaires) 11 Sept. 1954. National Archives, *Records of the Department of State,* RG 59, Decimal File 811.06, (M).

[70] "Report on Operations of Mexican Farm-Labor Program Made Pursuant to Conference Report No. 1449, House of Representatives, 84th Cong., 1st sess., 1 Jan.–30 June 1956." National Records Center (Suitland, Md.), *Records of the Immigration and Naturalization Service,* File "Contract Labor—Border Patrol," 56364/43.38.

[71] The number reached a minimum of 29,651 in fiscal year 1960. Samora, *Los mojados,* 46.

[72] Cabinet Paper CI-12, "Report on the 'Wetback' and Bracero Programs," 26 Jan. 1955. Dwight D. Eisenhower Library (Abilene, Kans.), *Eisenhower Papers* (Ann Whitman File, Cabinet Series), box 3, folder "28 January 1955."

[73] Krasner, *Defending the National Interest,* chap. 3.

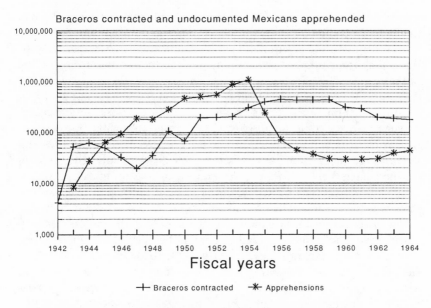

Fig.1. Substituting undocumented workers with contract *braceros* in 1954. SOURCE: U.S. Dept. of Labor data and INS reports.

broad societal objective: the substantial reduction of illegal entries. Subsequently, they calculated what costs they would have to assume and what costs would be imposed, and on whom, to achieve it. These calculations changed over time, but they are consistent with a pattern of state-centered decisionmaking in a weak state.

The objective was pursued in the face of resistance. Opposition was first voiced by the Mexican government, not to the objective as such but to the strategy, which entailed reducing substantially the administrative role of Mexican consuls; then by labor unions, Mexican-American groups, and private organizations during the unilateral recruitment phase; and finally, by growers during the implementation of the expulsion phase.

The history of this episode is striking because central decisionmakers took the initiative and largely prevailed in the face of significant external and internal opposition. If central decisionmakers were acting as a tool of the agricultural employers—the most powerful societal actor in this issue area—it is difficult to comprehend why the initiatives were opposed. Why was "Operation Wetback" necessary, if it was not intended to pressure growers into contracting *braceros*? In the design and execution of this strategy, central decisionmakers did consider what growers might accept, but there is no evidence that agricultural employers had any influence on the position of U.S. government officials responsible for this policy transition. At critical junctures, in fact, growers resisted the program.

Central decisionmakers pursued autonomous objectives in the face of certain constraints. The Texas Proviso ruled out the possibility that employer sanctions could be adopted. Mexican government opposition to the proposal that northbound migrants be intercepted within Mexican territory meant that the Mexicans were not going to solve the problem for the United States. More radical options, such as using troops to stop illegal entrants at the border, were seen as politically costly. The option, then, was to pursue a state objective at minimum cost to the state.

The Mexican case shows more clearly the need to distinguish between autonomous policymaking and strong policy implementation.[74] The Mexican labor embargo failed. It is difficult to see how it could have succeeded; the United States had been unable to prevent the same flow. The U.S. experience shows that it can be difficult to prevent the mass illegal entry of foreigners; the Mexican experience shows how much more difficult it is to prevent the mass departure of nationals. Although it might appear that Mexico's intention had been symbolic from the beginning since attempts to forcefully restrict immigration occurred at only a few points along the border and did not last long, accounts of what happened indicate that the Mexican government went far beyond making gestures: a miscalculation may be a better interpretation. A more thorough analysis of Mexico's options and calculus requires additional research in Mexican archives.

Notwithstanding the policy failure, however, I would underscore that the Mexican state was able to adopt a policy that would be unpopular and would be opposed by migrants, and was able to orchestrate mass popular support for it (at least in Mexico City and in the press). It was only after President Ruiz Cortines altered course that vehement opposition was voiced against a measure that violated the constitutional right of free transit. The authoritarian pattern of Mexican governance could account for this, of course, but it does not alter the observation that the state was able to pursue a broad societal objective (attempt to enforce a bilateral agreement affording labor protections to workers) at some political cost. It is striking that while in the United States unilateral recruitment was planned in secret (and the Eisenhower administration took the

---

[74] See Hollifield, "Immigration and the French State."

political heat after instituting it), the Mexican government announced its response and went to the public for support.

Before the president changed course, migrants were the most significant opponents of Mexican emigration policy. Yet although some workers did protest the attempt to enforce the labor embargo to the governor of Baja California, most did not attempt to pressure the government to change its policy. Most simply "voted with their feet" by going North, notwithstanding the presence of soldiers, the arrests by Mexican police, and the newspaper appeals for patriotism.[75]

The probability that political leaders will be able to get private actors to behave altruistically for the achievement of a public goal, or even for long-term self-interest, is smaller when these actors are many small units in a competitive market—an apt description for the mass of migrants.[76] One might add that if these actors are disorganized, they are not likely to express opposition by applying pressure on the policy process, but by silent noncompliance. This produces a strong/weak pattern of decision-making, in which policies adopted are initiatives, and policy outcomes reflect the strength of policy implementation.[77]

CONCLUSION

Policymakers at the apex of the political system pursue autonomous state goals within certain societal and institutional constraints. These translate into choices made by central decisionmakers in the pursuit of collective societal goals or particular state interests. The pressure of particular societal groups may be present, but it has little to do with the choices made at the apex. It does have a significant impact on lower-level officials and on the behavior of bureaus, and, of course, on the legislative process. What matters most in the pursuit of goals fixed by political leaders is the priority that has been assigned to the issue at hand (that is, whether the issue is addressed at the apex or left to the bureaucracy, and how it is addressed at the higher levels) and the resources that they possess to pursue those goals. The negotiation of bilateral agreements, the administrative restriction of visas, the launching of a deportation campaign—all these tasks can be accomplished with policy levers manipu-

[75] The costs of "voice" were evidently higher than those of "exit." See Albert O. Hirschman, *Exit, Voice, and Loyalty: Responses to Decline in Firms, Organizations, and States* (Cambridge, Mass., 1970).

[76] Krasner, *Defending the National Interest*, 81–82.

[77] Hollifield addresses a related problem when he notes the difficulty that the French state has had in controlling immigration (see "Immigration and the French State"). He attributes the failure of French policy to unexamined weakness of the supposedly strong French state and to the resilience of immigrants as "protorational" actors.

lated directly or indirectly by central decisionmakers. Getting Congress to adopt legislation is another matter, and when the legislative package is controversial it may be well-nigh impossible.

The image of a state so weak in immigration policymaking that it systematically yields to powerful societal groups and abandons its notions of the public interest is not an accurate characterization of the United States. To be sure, Congress is frequently stymied by special interests pressing their case, and bureaus can be penetrated by the very groups that they are supposed to regulate. None of this is new in the analysis of U.S. politics and policymaking. But, although there may be no "sense of the state" in the United States,[78] I argue that we find that the state is important for immigration policymaking, and we can see its significance clearly if we examine the choices made about Mexican immigration by high-level U.S. officials in the executive branch.

This study has examined instances in which central decisionmakers acted against a powerful societal actor—agricultural employers. Truman's employer sanctions in 1951–52 and the 1977 Carter Plan were frustrated in Congress. Interest-group analysis would account for what happened in Congress, true, but not for the executive initiatives. The consequences of "Operation Wetback" on *bracero* recruitment in 1954 and later years appear to be a prime candidate for a Nordlinger type I state autonomy explanation, since the government acted against grower interests, faced grower resistance, and restructured its behavior in the manner desired. As the history of this episode shows, however, there is more to the process and the outcome. It is clear that central decisionmakers were successful because the resources they required were within their control in the executive branch.

We can obtain a more complete understanding of the significance of policy outcomes if we examine the policymaking process and find a logic of the state in the policymakers' decisions. Wars, depressions, moments when issues rise to the top of the state agenda—these are circumstances that produce patterns of decisionmaking in which central decisionmakers are involved and for which state-centric perspectives offer a better explanation than society-centric orientations. The implementation of these decisions is apt to be more successful when the resources are within the control of decisionmakers.

Throughout the period of study, Mexican policy was remarkably consistent in stressing a state agenda that emphasized political over economic

---

[78] This observation was made by H. G. Wells in 1906. Quoted in Stephen Skowrenek, *Building a New American State: The Expansion of National Administrative Capacities 1877–1920* (Cambridge, Eng., 1982), 3.

goals. U.S. policy was less so. These differences in policy coherence are accounted for by the asymmetrical importance of the issue and by differences in state structure. To U.S. political leaders, the immigration of Mexicans was (and continues to be) largely a peripheral matter. Central decisionmakers only confronted issues in this area when these were part of a broader set of concerns: labor scarcities in time of war, broader foreign-policy goals, or recovering control of international migration across the nation's frontiers. To Mexican political leaders, emigration was always a sensitive domestic and foreign-policy issue. As is the case with other asymmetries, the same volume of migration from Mexico to the United States looms larger to Mexico than it does to the United States.

Let us recall briefly the outlines of Mexican policy coherence and consistency. The Mexican state supported the idea of the bilateral administration of Mexican migration to the United States for a remarkably long time—from 1929 to 1974. The reasons for doing so varied, but the central objective was to enhance the influence of the Mexican state over the terms of the movement and employment of Mexican workers. During the same period, the Mexican government promoted the conditional legal emigration of Mexican workers and opposed the undocumented flow. Emigration was fine as long as it served broader national purposes. During much of the *bracero* program, one of these was to bring in remittances at a time when the state promoted industrialization. Legal emigration was promoted as long as it was temporary; Mexican conceptions of national interest sustained that the country needed these workers at home.

The overarching themes of Mexican emigration policy responses were nationalism and the pursuit of national goals over particular societal objectives (such as those of migrants). In many instances in which the Mexican government had a choice, political objectives were placed above economic interests. In 1921 and again during the Great Depression, the Mexican government promoted repatriation out of a sense of sovereign obligation. During the *bracero* program, it consistently acted to keep the number of contracted *braceros* from growing too large or too quickly. The growth of undocumented migration during this period clearly indicates that many more migrants were willing to leave than the government wanted to send. And since migrants mostly "voted with their feet" instead of pressuring their government for a more liberal policy, Mexican policy remained relatively free from these and other potential societal constraints.

The lesser consistency and coherence of U.S. policy are in part related to differences in state structure (unlike in Mexico, the government, especially Congress and bureaus, faced societal pressure), but it is also the product of changing circumstances, which required re-ordering the state agenda. The decisions to recruit Mexican workers in 1917 and in 1942 would seem anomalous if the circumstances were not a major war involvement by the United States. Even the U.S. intervention in the Korean conflict in 1950 did not alter circumstances or the state agenda as radically as did World War I and World War II. Although the preferences of the most powerful societal actors, growers, did coincide in the decision to recruit workers, their unhappiness with the restrictions placed by the government on the terms of recruitment was also made clear. The context in which these decisions were made and their connection to broader goals suggest that a societal explanation distorts our comprehension of the matter.

Societal explanations may explain better why these recruitment programs were not stopped when the wars ended. But in the absence of a state imperative such as mobilizing the nation's resources for war, that is what I would expect. Ending these labor programs in peacetime might have served a collective societal goal, but this was not important at the apex of the political system.

In 1928 the U.S. chief executive sought to head off undesirable legislation by restricting administratively the legal immigration of Mexicans. The interpretation that the executive acted at the behest of employers or investors is facile. High-level officials ignored the entreaties (or protests) of farm employers on other occasions, and here they had good foreign-policy reasons to act as they did. But it is notable that, although administrative restriction helped the administration's position, by itself it was insufficient to prevent the bill from being passed in one house. Investors had little to gain directly from administrative restriction. It seems more sensible to examine government behavior in terms of the objectives of the state—objectives that had been articulated several times since the Chinese exclusion acts of the nineteenth century—and the limitations of central decisionmakers in terms of the kinds of resources available to them.

The Truman administration's push for employer sanctions (or a reasonable approximation thereof) in 1951–52, and the Carter administration's proposal to do the same in 1977 cannot be explained in terms of societal pressure. To be sure, there were some groups that advocated employer sanctions, especially in 1977. But central decisionmakers could have ignored these groups in both instances. Significant pressure on Truman did not come from U.S. societal actors, but from the Mexican president. Carter's choice of a labor secretary probably accounts for the prominence that was given to immigration reform—and especially employer sanctions—in 1977. Interest groups, of course, were very active in the process that led to the demise of employer sanctions under both presidents. U.S. presidents do not have the institutional resources to get legislation passed, and they can present the image of a helpless giant when controversial legislation is proposed but not defended as a matter of high priority. The approach I have taken here, then, accounts for initiatives proposed by the presidents themselves, not the product of pressure from particular societal actors, and for the high probability of failure in the legislative arena.

The actions by central decisionmakers in both Mexico and the United States during the "El Paso incident" of 1948 are consistent with a state-centric analysis. Leaders at the apex of the system acted on the basis of collective societal goals or particular state interests. In the U.S. case, they ignored societal pressures, including those that were translated into bureaucratic pressures from the Employment Service and the INS. In the Mexican case, the agreement was abrogated and a new one reached that sought to condition the flow of workers, even though these were not prevented from emigrating during the interim. The refusal of lower-level bureaus in the United States to obey a White House directive reminds us that it is more difficult for central decisionmakers to control policy implementation than the making of policy.

The events of 1953 and 1954 cannot easily by explained by society-centric explanations. No significant interest-group activity accounts for the strategy of negotiation with Mexico adopted by the United States in autumn 1953, the unilateral agreement by the United States and the Mexican attempt at an embargo in January 1954, nor for the deportation campaign later that summer. The initiatives for these actions came from within the state. Significantly, U.S. officials responsible for designing the strategy were relatively insulated from societal pressures. The objective pursued in this strategy—the reduction of illegal entries—was not only a broad societal concern, it was also a matter of particular interest to political leaders, who were interested in maintaining control, in fact as well as in appearance, over the entry of foreigners into national territory.

Certainly the administration of the program tilted markedly in favor of agricultural employers during and immediately after 1954. U.S. decisionmakers found that this was the price to pay for achieving a solution to what they conceived to be a broader problem. But the program was not handed over to the growers on a silver platter. Concessions were made over time in a sequence of events that suggests ad hoc bargaining between government officials and interest groups to achieve the outcome desired at the apex of the political system.

However, once the problem was "solved," central decisionmakers turned away from the issue. Control reverted to bureaucracies. This kind of change, by which a government agency at one point acts in a manner contrary to organized interests and in support of collective societal goals or in deference to instructions from political leaders, but over time succumbs to group pressures, is not uncommon in the experience of the United States.

PART II
Supply and Demand of Migratory Workers

U.S.-Mexico Interdependence, Social Pacts, and Policy Perspectives: A Computable General Equilibrium Approach

Raúl A. Hinojosa Ojeda and Robert K. McCleery

T HE LAST TWO decades have seen an explosive growth of transborder movements of goods and factors which have made the future welfare prospects of many socioeconomic groups highly interdependent across countries. Unlike the postwar era of relative national insulation, policy-making across countries has now become intricately linked through a wide array of unintended feedbacks and repercussion effects. In this changing environment, policymakers and social groups across countries can choose from a number of policy responses ranging from attempts to wall off their countries behind protectionist barriers, which often result in inefficient resource allocation; a unilateral liberal opening and the bearing of resultant adjustment costs; or attempts to internationally coordinate a variety of policy areas in a context of greater global exchange. The development of public policy that is both internationally efficient and can generate broad social agreement and support across countries, especially in the asymmetrical context of North-South relations, is one of the greatest challenges faced in this new era of interdependence.

The United States and Mexico are the two countries that share the highest level of exchange across the North-South divide, including the largest debt, trade, border commerce, and labor migration relations between a developed and developing country. Although U.S.-Mexico interdependence is highly uneven, feedbacks and tradeoffs are now a recognized feature of the relationship in many policy areas: U.S. monetary

Funding for this research was provided by the William and Flora Hewlett Foundation, the Rockefeller Foundation, and the Inter-University Program on Latino Research.

policy, for instance, affects Mexico's debt serving burden which, in turn, impacts real wages and migration pressures in Mexico, undocumented migration to the United States and the U.S. trade balance. United States political reactions against exchange with Mexico, such as trade or immigration restrictions, intensify Mexican employment pressures, while the political implications of Mexico's social inequality has long made Mexico a central U.S. national security concern. Further research on the political economy of interdependence is needed to determine how this wide range of linkages influences both countries' ability to maintain historic social pacts governing employment and income levels.

Since the outbreak of the debt crisis in 1982, the United States and Mexico have come to a crucial crossroad in their relationship, provoking debates on a broad variety of policy and political options. Calls for trade protection, a debt moratorium, and migration restriction have characterized most of the 1980s. In the midst of a severe external adjustment and facing growing political opposition, Mexican policymakers have moved to unilaterally reduce high tariffs and foreign investment controls. In a move sure to test further the political limits of increased interdependence, both governments have most recently declared their intent to negotiate a free trade agreement.

In this context, a number of essential questions need to be addressed. What is the capacity of alternative combinations of policy options to provide renewed long-term growth with broad sociopolitical support across both countries? What tradeoffs exist between different policy combinations, such as attempting to use trade liberalization to reduce migration or changing debt policies in order to affect trade and migration patterns?

The purpose of this paper is to contribute to a new generation of political-economy models of complex interdependence that are designed to aid social actors in evaluating the welfare and employment effects of a wide range of unilateral and bilateral policies. Such a complex analysis requires a multi-period computable general equilibrium model with endogenous social strategic interactions where interdependence both sets the basis for, and is affected by, distributional conflicts and bargaining between socioeconomic groups.

The paper is divided into five sections. Section 1 introduces the formal model after mention is made of several papers with which this work claims intellectual kinship. In section 2, the results of a counterfactual simulation of continued postwar growth and social pact maintenance in the two countries through the year 2000 are reported and discussed. Section 3 analyzes briefly growth and social pact implications of three alternative scenarios: protectionism; neo-liberal opening; and a managed interdependence approach. Section 4 offers some conclusions about the political and economic dynamics of continued interdependence.[1]

COMPUTER GENERATED EQUILIBRIUM MODELING OF INTERDEPENDENCE

The literature on U.S.-Mexican economic interdependence has developed through a series of tradeoffs. The models by Serra[2] and Reyes Heroles[3] have more domestic detail of the Mexican economy, but less international detail. Noyola[4] opts for more precise estimation of the actual migration parameters, but loses general equilibrium feedbacks in alternative scenarios. Hill and Mendez[5] similarly impose partial equilibrium migration coefficients on a general equilibrium model, but do so in a case where the coefficients are much less reliable—for U.S.-Mexico undocumented migration as opposed to Noyola's study of internal Mexican migration. Huffman[6] trades numerical results for comparative statistics. Reynolds and McCleery[7] concentrate primarily on migration policy dynamics without endogenizing strategic political interactions.

The model presented here is unique in a variety of ways. It is the only CGE model to combine all three critical areas of interaction between the United States and Mexico: trade, migration, and capital flows. The model is thus highly flexible and adaptable to a variety of policy concerns and combinations. The occasional deviations from standard neoclassical modeling techniques come in response to the stylized facts of the U.S.-Mexico

[1] Space constraints prohibit all but the barest sketch of the model and policy options, and the interested reader is directed to our theses for more comprehensive treatments of these issues. See Raúl Hinojosa Ojeda, "The Political Economy of North-South Interdependence: Debt, Trade, and Class Relations Across Mexico and the United States," Ph.D. diss., Univ. of Chicago, 1989; and Robert K. McCleery, "U.S.-Mexico Economic Linkages: A General Equilibrium Model of Migration, Trade, and Capital Flows," Ph.D. diss., Stanford Univ., 1988.

[2] Jaime Serra Puche, "A General Equilibrium Model for the Mexican Economy: An Analysis of Fiscal Policies," Ph.D. diss., Yale Univ., 1979.

[3] Jesus Reyes Heroles, G. G., *Politica Macroeconomica y Bienestar en Mexico* (Mexico City, 1983).

[4] Pedro Javier Noyola de Garagorri, "Urban Migration in Mexico: A General Equilibrium Analysis," Ph.D. diss., Stanford University, 1985.

[5] J. Hill and J. Mendez, "The Effect of Commercial Policy on International Migration Flows: The Case of the United States and Mexico," *Journal of International Economics* 17 (1984), 41–53.

[6] W. Huffman, "The U.S.-Mexican Labor Market," mimeo, Iowa State Univ., 1984.

[7] Clark W. Reynolds and Robert McCleery, "The Political Economy of Immigration Reform: The Impact of IRCA on the U.S. and Mexico," *Journal of Economic Perspectives*, 1988.

experience. It is designed to incorporate some of the international factors that affect equilibrium wages in each country but have not been previously featured in models of this type. It is the only CGE model in which the migration decision rests on firm microeconomic foundations and which also incorporates multi-period demographic projections. Finally the model explicitly endogenizes a strategic interaction between capitalist and workers over the setting of wages and savings behavior. In this way we can see whether a particular policy approach and resulting pattern of interdependence can provide for a compromise or "social pact" solution to distributional competition between economic classes.

Exposition of the Model

In this model, there are two countries with two goods being produced in each country. The heart of the economic model consists of a set of production functions by country and sector; a set of marginal conditions for each production function by factor of production; a set of demand functions for each sector's output by social group (factor owner); behavioral equations regulating movement of labor from the low wage sector to the high wage sector in each country and across countries; a (Stackelberg-type) bargaining "game" between unions and capitalists over the size of the wage bill in the high wage sector; and a set of equilibrium conditions and adding-up constraints. Each type of equation will be described, and the salient points and implications noted. The annotated equation list at the end of this paper contains all of the relevant equations, and data appendix 2, which follows the equations, lists the values and sources of the coefficients used.

Supply, Demand, and Sectoral Definitions

The CES (constant elasticity of substitution) production functions and marginal conditions for the United States are of the standard form (equations 1 and 2). The nature of the CES production function ensures that the Inada conditions hold on marginal productivities.[8] The production functions exhibit constant returns to scale and factor incomes are based on, if not always equal to, marginal productivities.

The high wage sector (sector 1) in the United States produces a tradeable good with labor and capital that is consumed in the United States but is used as an intermediate good in the production of Mexico's good 1.

[8] Marginal productivities are diminishing, approaching zero as the quantity of a factor approaches infinity, and all factors are necessary for production (in that marginal productivities approach infinity as the quantity of a factor approaches zero).

As is the case in Mexico, sector 1 is more technologically advanced and capital intensive. It comprises about 90 percent of the labor and 95 percent of the output of the U.S. economy.

Mexico's high wage sector (sector 1) produces output using labor, capital, and an imported intermediate good. Its output is sold as consumer goods both domestically and in the United States. Labor productivity is much higher in this sector, with one-third of the labor force combining with just under half of the country's capital stock to produce over half of GDP in the base year of 1982.

The low wage sector (sector 2) in the United States represents the areas in which Mexican migrants compete directly with U.S. citizens for employment. In sector 2 capital and labor combine to produce non-traded services. While it is true that many migrants still work in agriculture, and some now work in manufacturing, the emerging profile of the 1980s undocumented migrant is that of a construction worker, janitor, maid, gardener, or other service worker producing goods and services that cannot be traded internationally.[9]

In the low wage sector in Mexico (sector 2), labor and capital combine with a fixed factor we shall call *land* in a production function that exhibits decreasing returns to scale in the first two factors. Output of the sector, which will be called *subsistence agriculture and services,* is not traded internationally. While technically tradeable, rain-fed corn production on small plots in central and southern Mexico is largely for household consumption and cannot compete effectively in international markets with other major grain producers under any reasonable set of factor prices and exchange rates. The resemblance of this economic activity to the service sector in capital/output ratio and wage level justifies the grouping. Irrigated, mechanized agribusiness in the north, which produces fruits and winter vegetables for export to the United States, is grouped with the manufacturing sector.

The model allows for a perpetuation of a sectoral dualism in labor mobility within countries. Empirical evidence that wages are bimodal in Mexico and that an underclass of unskilled labor exists in the United States necessitates a departure from the neoclassical assumption that labor moves to equalize its marginal product. Two behavioral equations regulate the movement of labor from the low wage sector to the high wage sector over time. Equations 6 through 8A describe the movement of labor between sectors within a country, defining an incremental capi-

---

[9] See Wayne Cornelius's chapter in this book, "From Sojourners to Settlers: The Changing Profile of Mexican Migrants to the United States."

tal/labor ratio (IKL) that links labor growth in the high wage sector with the level of new investment and the savings behavior of capitalists.

The adding-up constraints (equation set 2) merely ensure that the total product is exhausted in the form of factor payments (Euler's theorem) and that production takes place on the production possibilities frontier. The demand specification used in the model (equation set 3) is the Stone-Geary linear expenditure system. An individual's demand for a good has two components: a constant or subsistence level of demand and a second term that is proportional to income. In addition to displaying proper relative price and income effects, the subsistence demand levels allow changes in the population of a country to have a significant impact on relative prices and production levels. The utility functions implied by the form of demands are log linear in non-subsistence or discretionary demand.[10]

The parameters of the CES production functions are drawn from other work by economic modelers in this area[11] and from data on the functional distributions of income. The former influenced the choice of rho, and thus the value of the (constant) elasticity of substitution in each production function and our use of constant returns to scale. The latter determined the values of the distributional parameters.

There was considerably less theoretical and empirical guidance for choosing the parameters of the demand functions, however. Work on demographic complementarities between the United States and Mexico stresses the growing demand for services such as health care, restaurants, domestic services, and care for the elderly, related to both continual income growth in the United States and demographic shifts in the U.S. population.[12] For that reason, sector 2 in the United States is modeled as having a slightly higher income elasticity of demand than sector 1. Sector 2 in Mexico consists in large part of rain-fed agriculture (more than one-third of Mexico's labor force is still employed in agriculture), whose output has a low income elasticity of demand. Thus sector 1 in Mexico is modeled as having a significantly larger

[10] Samuelson proves that ordinal utility must be of the form $U = F[B1^*\log x1 + \ldots + Bn^*\log xn]$, where the B's are the income shares in demand and F is any function with $F' > 0$. See P. Samuelson, "Some Implications of Linearity," *Review of Economic Studies* 15 (1947), 88–90. For linear expenditure systems for Mexico see Pascual Garcia Alba, *Estudios Economicos* (1987).

[11] Alan Manne and T. Rutherford, "LTM: A Long-Term Model of Mexico's Growth and Balance-of-Payments Constraints," presented to the Trade and Investment Working Group of the U.S.-Mexico Project at Stanford University, mimeo, 1983; Jaime Serra Puche, 1979.

[12] David E. Hayes-Bautista, Werner O. Schink, Jorge Chapa, *The Burden of Support: Young Latinos in an Aging Society* (Stanford, Calif., 1988).

income elasticity of demand, but sector 2 makes up the lion's share of the subsistence level of consumption.[13]

Internal Equilibrium Conditions

There are five types of equilibrium conditions. In the first (equation 28), the equality of the value of the marginal product of capital between the two sectors within each country is based on the microeconomic assumption that investment by profit maximizing capitalists drives the marginal return to capital to equality between sectors. Except in an extreme case (free migration, autarky in labor flows, or free capital mobility between countries), maintaining the equality between sectors does not require mobility of existing capital, just the freedom to allocate new investment by sector in accordance with rates of return.

In equations 29 and 30, prices work to equate supply and demand for each good in each country. By Walras's law, there is only one free relative price in Mexico and two in the United States that clear the product markets; good 2 in each country is the numeraire, with its price set equal to 1.

International Equilibrium Conditions: Modeling Labor Flows

The first international equilibrium condition to be discussed is one affecting the labor market. Obviously if the wage differential is critical to the migration decision, then modeling the wage determination process is a crucial intermediate step, with estimating demographic trends and their implications for labor force growth a necessary starting point.[14]

Projections of U.S. labor force growth for the years 1990 and 2000 are done every two or three years by the Bureau of Labor Statistics.[15] Their projected employment figures are used in the model, with minor modifications, and can be expected to approximate the year 2000 labor force to within a half of 1 percent, adjusting for business cycles.[16]

Labor force estimates for Mexico are less frequent and systematic.[17]

[13] See Nora Lustig, "Distribution of Income, Structure of Consumption, and Economic Growth: The Case of Mexico," Ph.D. diss., Univ. of California, Berkeley, 1979.

[14] See data app. 2 for the sources and assumptions used in creating the labor force series.

[15] H. Fullerton, "The 1995 Labor Force," *Monthly Labor Review* vol. 108, no. 11 (Nov. 1985), 15–25.

[16] *Ibid.*

[17] A flurry of demographic work followed on the heels of the publication of Mexico's 1980 census data in 1982–1984, following in the tradition of the work of Keesing and Urquidi in the 1970s. D. Keesing, "Employment and Lack of Employment in Mexico, 1900–1970," in *Quantitative Latin American Studies: Methods and Findings* (*Statistical Abstract of Latin America*, supp. 6), ed. J. W. Wilkie and K. Ruddle (Los Angeles, Calif., 1977), 3–22; V. Urquidi, "Empleo y Explosion Demografia," *Demografia y Economia* vol. 8, no. 2 (1974), 141–53.

Demographers have concluded from the 1980 census that Mexico has experienced a dramatic decline in the crude birth rate in the mid to late 1970s.[18] Since entrants into the labor force through 1992 had already been born in 1976, the drop in the birth rate will not be translated into a similar reduction in labor force growth from the recent peak of nearly 4 percent per year to 2.5 percent or less until between 1992 and 1996.[19]

These labor force projections feed into the wage determination process in each country. Wages for Mexicans in both economic sectors of Mexico and wages for U.S. citizens in the United States are determined in the standard neo-classical fashion; they are the value of the marginal product of labor for each group.[20] Yet the interpretation of the wage-setting procedure in the high wage sector of each country is not standard.

In both countries, all labor force entrants who are not accommodated in the high wage sector are crowded into the low wage sector. To the extent that those unable to find work in the U.S. high wage sector have the option in the real world of collecting unemployment or welfare benefits rather than accept unskilled work, the number of those willing and available for unskilled work is overstated in the model.[21] In Mexico, it is argued that self-employed farmers, vendors, and artisans function in a setting of truly competitive factor and product markets, more so than the larger import substituting industries.

The only individuals that do not receive the value of their marginal product are Mexican migrants working in the United States. Their marginal product is lower than their U.S. counterparts due to a language and skill differential. Additionally, discrimination on the part of employers and the government against these migrants based on superior legal and market power further reduces their earnings.[22]

If capitalists directly received the earnings differential referred to above

[18] D. Kirk, "Recent Demographic Trends and Present Population Prospects for Mexico," *Food Research Institute Studies* vol. 9, no. 1 (1983), 93–111.

[19] Francisco Alba and J. Potter, "Population and Development in Mexico Since 1940: An Interpretation," *Population and Development Review* vol. 12, no. 1 (Mar. 1986), 47–75.

[20] The marginal products are computed from the CES production function (eqs. 1, 2, 1a, and 2a of the equation list) by differentiating with respect to labor.

[21] The real minimum wage in the United States eroded during the Reagan years to the point that it is a binding constraint for only a few job categories and the prevailing unskilled wage is determined by market forces. Piecework in agriculture and construction is an example of tying earnings directly to the value of the marginal product of labor.

[22] Martin Carnoy, Hugh Daley, and Raúl Hinojosa Ojeda, *Latinos in a Changing Political Economy: Comparative Perspectives on Inequality in the U.S. Labor Market Since 1940* (New York, 1990). See also the note on discrimination in app. 2.

as discrimination, then they would prefer hiring migrants at a wage ratio equal to the ratio of the marginal products of labor. Under the assumptions of the Becker theorem, a wage differential not based on productivity differences is unsustainable in the type of competitive economy modeled here.[23] Thus all discrimination must take the form of taxes paid to the government for services the undocumented worker is not able to receive, such as social security, most state and federal income taxes, and unemployment and disability insurance.

The utility levels attainable by consumer utility-maximizing behavior are compared for migrants and non-migrants in equation 40 based on the comparative wage levels for unskilled labor in each country and the consumption levels these wages support. If one can move to a higher level of utility, migration will take place up to the point that the marginal potential migrant is indifferent between migrating and remaining in Mexico. In this comparison, one must subtract the cost of migration from the wage earned in the United States to make it comparable to income earned in Mexico. The cost of migration can be modeled as a rising function of the level of migration. In some models this increasing cost stems from an underlying distribution of potential migrants with regard to distance from the border, with those closest to the border migrating first. In the more complex context here, it is a proxy for the sum of several distributions: the distribution of cost, preferences, skill, and so forth, over individuals.[24] The Mexicans' preference for remaining in Mexico at a given level of consumption is also built into the utility comparison.

In equilibrium there remains a significant gap between unskilled wage levels in the two countries reflecting (1) differences in labor productivity, (2) transportation costs and U.S. migration policies, and (3) the intensity of the preference of migrants for living in Mexico. The way migration is modeled leads to a stable equilibrium. An inflow of migrants will raise wages in the sending sector and lower them in the re-

[23] G. Becker, "The Economics of Discrimination," in *Readings in Labor Economics and Labor Relations,* ed. L. G. Reynolds, S. H. Masters, and C. Moser (Englewood Cliffs, N.J., 1974), 181–85.

[24] In other words, any important heterogeneity in Mexico's low-wage labor force causes an ordering of potential migrants by their reservation wage differential. An interesting possibility is raised when one allows for differences between individual migrants. If migrants are the best and the brightest of those in the sending region, their relocation could actually decrease average productivity in the sending region, and perhaps increase the wage differential. But so-called brain-drain migration of this kind does not seem to be a large fraction of observed migration. See J. E. Taylor, "Undocumented Mexico-U.S. Migration and the Return to Households in Rural Mexico," *American Journal of Agricultural Economics* (Aug. 1987), 626–38.

ceiving sector, driving down the adjusted wage differential and reducing the closely related utility differential to zero.

Other International Equilibrium Conditions

In addition to labor migration, financial and trade dynamics are modeled, allowing for the estimation of tradeoffs between all three flows. Debt-service payments on Mexico's current foreign debt and imports of needed intermediate goods and capital goods are paid for through exports to the United States, migrant remittances, and flows of new finance to Mexico. Capital inflows to Mexico can be in the form of direct foreign investment or new loans with a concomitant flow to the United States of repatriated profits or additional interest payments. The dollar value of debt-service payments is a product of the endogenous level of the debt and the exogenous world interest rate. Mexico's balance of payments constraint, given in equation 32, ensures that dollar denominated obligations match dollar revenues exactly.

Equation 33 introduces a "shadow price of foreign exchange," which is defined as the value of the additional quantity of goods that could be produced given a one unit relaxation of the constraint of a non-oil export ceiling. The shadow price is related to both the marginal product of intermediate imports and the marginal product of capital, in the following way. Suppose one additional unit of good 1 (the manufacture) could be exported. Its sale to the United States would net dollars, which could be spent to import either intermediate goods or capital goods (subject to applicable tariffs). The additional quantity of each that could be purchased is multiplied by the value of the marginal product of that factor, and from this value (in pesos) is subtracted the return to selling the unit domestically to judge the profitability of the venture. Importing based on the relative profitability of the two goods drives the two shadow prices toward equality, and relaxing the export constraint would drive both to zero. Thus the value of the shadow price (the higher of the two, if they are different) reflects the tightness of the foreign exchange constraint on the Mexican economy.[25]

International transfers of goods feed into the domestic price determination process, leading to the establishment of an equilibrium purchasing power parity exchange rate at which this level of Mexican exports is an equilibrium. Thus the law of one price does hold for tradeable goods in

---

[25] The profits from increasing exports must be diminishing, because of the convexities involved. As exports increase along the demand curve, the price of exports declines. Increased demand for imports raises their price, and increased use of a factor in production given relatively fixed amounts of other factors will decrease its marginal product.

this model; a dollar buys the same quantity of the tradeable product on each side of the border when exchanged for pesos at this endogenously determined equilibrium rate. It must be pointed out that the process of exchange rate determination in the model is quite different from the workings of the actual market process. In the model, the exchange rate is determined solely by the interactions of real variables, whereas the monetary approach to the balance of payments holds that relative rates of monetary growth should be the dominant factor, especially when such rates are as disparate as in the U.S.-Mexico case.[26] Yet serious problems can arise from tacking a monetary "superstructure" on to a real CGE model.[27] Speculative demand for a currency is another potential factor excluded by the nature of this model but present in the real world. While capital flight has been an important feature of the U.S.-Mexico experience,[28] the model was not designed with the intent of explaining it. The model does, however, take into account the historical behavior of this variable and can deal with alternative assumptions about the path of capital flight in the future.

Dollar Transfers and the Government Clearinghouse

A simplified treatment of the government sectors portrays them primarily as clearinghouses, taking in revenues based on tax rates and levels of economic activity and making transfer payments to individuals (equation set 5). In the United States, the relationships are relatively simple. Tariff revenues on imports from Mexico and income taxes are collected. On the expenditure side, interest is paid on the existing debt and transfer payments are made to dependents, which can be thought of as social security payments to retirees. The difference between revenues and expenditures is the deficit.

The workings of the Mexican government are much more involved, even though goods and services are not directly consumed and the basic purpose of a government sector is the same as in the United States. The two primary reasons for the added complexity are the modeling of the oil sector and the special nature of dollar denominated obligations and incomes. Oil is treated as a resource endowment providing a constant stream of product for the government to export over the time horizon of

---

[26] M. Mussa, "A Monetary Approach to Balance of Payments Analysis," *Journal of Money, Credit, and Banking* vol. 6, no. 3 (Aug. 1974), 333–51.

[27] K. Dervis, J. de Melo, and S. Robinson, *General Equilibrium Models for Development Policy* (New York, 1982).

[28] Capital flight was an important part of the Mexican economic crisis, with the dollar exodus totaling approximately $25 billion between 1981 and 1986. Morgan Guaranty Trust Company, "LDC Capital Flight," *World Financial Markets* (Mar. 1986).

the model. In actuality, of course, the amount of oil to be exported is a policy decision, yet in practice the Mexican government has proven to be very reluctant to adjust the "export platform" even under emergency circumstances.[29]

Oil revenues are just one of a set of dollar denominated credits and debits that must balance for the Mexican economy as a whole. On the government's balance sheet, tariff revenues, oil revenues, new lending, and migrant remittances constitute dollar inflows, while debt service payments are the primary outflow. When the government's dollar balance is positive, it supplies dollars to the private sector at the purchasing power parity exchange rate for use in importing intermediate and capital goods (the private sector will always be willing to pay at least that many pesos per dollar). When the dollar balance is negative, due perhaps to high interest rates or low oil prices, the government must buy dollars from the private sector.[30]

Balancing the dollar accounts for the Mexican government results in a peso transfer to or from the private sector. The other peso inflow is the value-added tax, which is assumed to be paid by capitalists. Peso costs include interest on the domestic debt and peso payments to those who were sent remittances. The annual peso deficit is added to the domestic debt.

Class Strategic Bargaining

Expanding the scope of a largely neoclassical CGE framework to incorporate class conflict and bargaining outcomes is another important feature of this model. Following Przeworski and Wallerstein,[31] capitalist and workers each have an objective function which is expressed in equation 8. Workers choose a level of wage militancy (STAKMAX), which maximizes the current discounted value of their future wages where the expected path of wages depends on capitalist level of savings and the productivity of the economy. Capitalists, on the other hand, choose a level of savings out of profits which maximizes the current dis-

---

[29] The model is neither meant to nor able to track short-term economic fluctuations based on monetary policy or the two key exogenous variables: the world oil price and the world interest rate. The price of oil has followed a roller coaster path in the recent past, defying medium-range prediction even by models designed expressly for that purpose. Thus the results of the model presented in the following sections should be viewed as trends, which will, no doubt, be buffeted by various shocks affecting both economies.

[30] It is assumed that the same exchange rate holds on these transactions, despite the fact that the shadow price of foreign exchange may be higher. There are no efficiency implications of the dollar transfer price; production is the same as it would be were the government to expropriate the needed dollars without payment.

[31] Adam Przeworski, *Capitalism and Social Democracy* (Cambridge, Eng., 1985).

counted value of their future consumption which, in turn, is dependent on the level of wages. This approach assumes that classes act strategically with knowledge of their opponent's likely response to one's own choice of action.

A social pact, or "class compromise," can be reached if there exists a "Stackelberg[32] solution." Such a solution allows for the maximization of the material interests of both classes at rates higher than the rates at which they discount the future over a given time horizon.

In principle, high wage labor in each country uses its bargaining power and political influence to maximize some objective function. The objective function we postulated in our work was the wage bill in the unionized sector, reasoning that increases in the wage, holding employment constant, benefit both union members and leaders, and similarly raising membership (employment) at a given wage provides non-monetary benefits in terms of political power and prestige. The operation of this model reflects closely the historical record of the union/government coalition in Mexico,[33] subject to the constraints of the capitalists' reaction function (the endogenous savings propensity). In the United States, however, a hypothesis based on historical data must be restated to assert that U.S. unions act to maximize the wage bill within a constraint of maintaining a specific weighted balance between employment levels and wages. The 1960s and early 1970s in particular were a time of rising real wages but falling union membership as a fraction of total employment. By the 1980s, the calibration period for the model, a Stackelberg solution for the U.S. union workers given an unweighted wage-bill objective function would yield a much lower unionized wage, extremely high migration levels, and a very militant Stackelberg solution in Mexico. This solution is so far removed from the U.S. historical data that it was not used; instead, the Mexico Stackelberg was solved based on a point consistent with actual U.S. data and a weighted wage-bill objective, yielding a solution for Mexico that was likewise consistent with its historical data.

This modeling approach highlights an important point about interdependence and social pacts across countries. The solutions in the two countries are quite strongly related; in particular, the Stackelberg equilibrium for Mexico depends on the level of militancy in the United States, thus on wages in the United States, the incentive to migrate, and the size of the labor force in Mexico. A high level of militancy in the United States means that wages are high and employment low in the U.S. high wage sector, and that the reverse holds true in the low wage sector. This sur-

[32] H. von Stackelberg, *The Theory of the Market Economy* (London, 1952).
[33] Hinojosa (1989), chap. 4.

plus of low wage labor results in lower levels of migration, giving Mexican labor less opportunity and incentive for militancy while providing for potentially higher savings out of profits.

THE POSTWAR STATUS QUO SIMULATION

The previous section presented the basic structure of a general equilibrium model of the Mexican and U.S. economies, with special attention to how the two are linked through flows of labor, goods, and finance capital. While the model is complex in terms of linkages between countries and interactions and feedbacks between sectors and groups, it is kept simple by minimizing the number of factors, sectors, and social groups, having just those necessary to the stories being told.

In the 1980s, the United States and Mexico stood at a crossroads. The postwar era of rapid growth had reached its end along with the seeming complementarity in industrial, trade, financial, and migration relations. Also in serious trouble were the postwar social pacts in both countries wherein workers had grown to expect continued increases in real wages commensurate with continued capitalist investments and resultant productivity increases.

With the global recession of the early 1980s and the triggering of the debt crisis in 1982, a new era of conflict arose. A rapid expansion of U.S. imports and a public sense that undocumented immigration was "out of control" were seen as threats to the employment levels and incomes of U.S. labor, despite the continued growth of consumption. The U.S. political response to the perceived threats was twofold. Many pieces of protectionist legislation were introduced, particularly for the shoe, apparel, steel, automotive, and semiconductor industries. In 1986, after years of contentious debate, the U.S. government enacted the Immigration Reform and Control Act (IRCA).

This section explores a future that might have taken place in the absence of significant crisis and conflict in the 1980s. In actuality, the forces that undermined the postwar status quo were already in place before the 1980s, and while this scenario will serve as the backdrop against which the alternative options presented in section 4 can be evaluated, it cannot itself be viewed as a feasible alternative either then or now. Thus the following projections of U.S. and Mexican economic variables and interactions represents a counterfactual world in which IRCA was not adopted, voluntary lending to Latin America did not stop, and Mexico was not forced into a radical and rapid alteration in wage and trade policies. We assume that oil prices recover to 1982 levels ($29 per barrel) by 2000. Mexico receives $6 billion in net new loans per year. The world nominal interest rate is stable at 8 percent, with 4.5 percent inflation. The foremost implicit assumption is that the Mexican economy is efficient, overcoming its problems allocating investment efficiently, intermediating between domestic savings and domestic investment, and controlling the government sector.

In order to create a basis for comparing the policy options to be presented in section 4, we must answer the following counterfactual question: Under the postwar migration, trade, and capital market policies and the above assumptions, what would the pattern of output, employment, and undocumented migration to the United States be over the next fifteen years, as determined by the interaction of demographic trends, savings behavior, and technological progress and diffusion, in a setting of profit maximizing capitalists and utility maximizing consumers? In this context, what are the minimal components of a Stackelberg solution that would represent the continuation of the postwar social pacts?

Results and Their Implications

The following graphs are intended to give the reader a feel for the time paths of the important endogenous variables of the counterfactual simulation. The reasonableness of these time paths is a necessary but not sufficient indication of the reasonableness of the underlying model. Figures 1A and B record real output growth in Mexico and the United States, respectively. The volatility of growth over the past four years in Mexico stands in stark contrast to the smooth path of recovery and growth projected in Figure 1A. The caveat that this model is based on long-term trends and makes no claim to usefulness as a predictor of any given year's output level bears repeating in this light. Despite the linear nature of many of the assumptions and the observation that equilibrium (or constrained equilibrium) is reached each year, the path has some dynamic properties. Capital accumulation in each country is determined by augmenting a fixed net savings rate out of GDP of 7 percent in Mexico and 5.8 percent in the United States with a term raising the savings rate when the profitability of investment exceeds historical averages, and reducing savings when profit rates are depressed. Although the adjustment parameters are modest (0.3 for the United States and 0.4 for Mexico), this formulation is crucial to the convergence of the Stackelberg solution, because it represents the capitalist's reaction function. As workers demand higher wages, profitability declines, leading to a reduction in savings, investment, productivity growth, and future increases in earnings and investment.

Defining Mexico's long-term growth rate to be approaching 5 per-

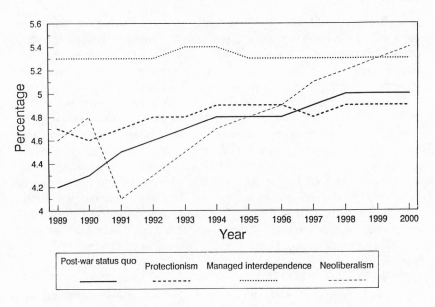

Fig. 1A. Mexico: Real GDP growth.

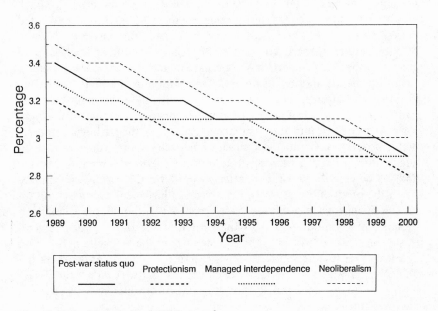

Fig. 1B. United States: Real GDP growth.

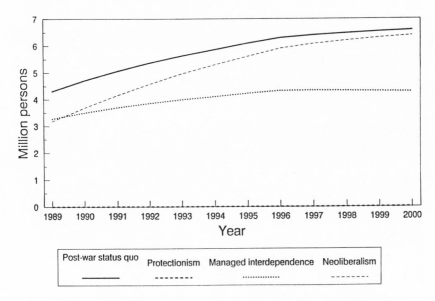

Fig. 2. Migration (stock).

cent, the recovery path shows the growth rate increasing at a decreasing rate, reaching 5 percent in 1999. The U.S. growth rate declines from 3.4 percent in 1989 to 2.9 percent in the year 2000. The United States would need a higher savings rate, more rapid technological progress, or an even larger influx of labor than in the status quo (see the projected migration path in Figure 2) to sustain 3 percent growth through the end of the century.

Figure 2 introduces the basic form of the migration path that will characterize many of the scenarios to come. The inverted U shape that will result from our model is very robust to alternative assumptions about the levels or time paths of the important exogenous variables. After rising at a decreasing rate to a peak of just over 6.65 million in 2000, the stock of migrants falls. This path would bring migration back down to the levels of recent experience shortly after 2010. At the risk of oversimplifying complex interactions, it can be said that the downturn is due to growth in Mexican demand for unskilled labor finally exceeding labor force growth. The demand for unskilled labor in the United States continues to grow throughout, but once real wages begin to rise significantly in the low wage sector in Mexico, migration levels decrease.

Even with an income elasticity of demand of about 2.5, the rapid

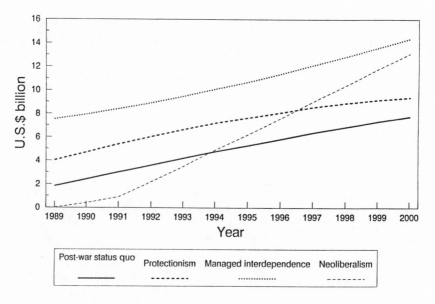

Fig. 3. U.S. capital goods exports.

growth of exports over the course of the scenario drives down their price. The real exchange rate (the ratio of the peso price to the dollar price of a unit of Mexico's traded good) increases (depreciates) by 25 percent over the course of the simulation. The terms of trade, defined as the price of exports divided by the price of imports, deteriorates by almost 22 percent.

Figure 3 displays time paths of Mexico's imports of capital goods. After a sharp drop in all imports following the fall in oil prices during 1985–86 (not shown), intermediate imports rise smoothly from $5.8 billion in 1988 to over $10 billion by the year 2000. Mexico's capitalists allocate scarce foreign exchange between intermediate good imports and capital imports to maximize output and profits, as explained in section 3. Early in the scenario, relative profitabilities are such that few capital goods are imported, but capital good imports rise rapidly thereafter, approaching $8 billion annually by the year 2000.

Mexican wage growth is balanced in absolute terms, but in relative terms favors the high wage sector. Figure 4A graphs wages in the high wage sector throughout the scenarios. The real annual wage in sector 1 grows 15 percent from 1987 through 2000, from $5,200 to $5,950. The non-union wage grows more rapidly (27 percent) as seen in Figure 4B, but absolute wage growth is less than in the high wage sector. The wage

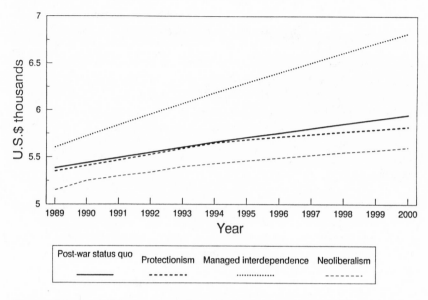

Fig. 4A. Mexico: High wage growth.

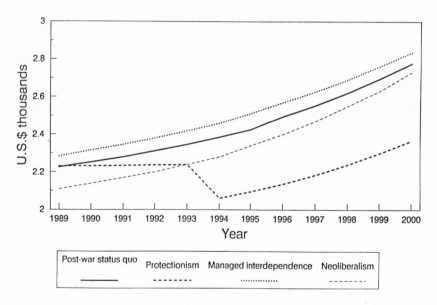

Fig. 4B. Mexico: Low wage growth.

gap increases despite the fact that high wage labor is an increasing fraction of total employment, rising from 35 percent to 41 percent.

Figures 5A and 5B indicate that U.S. earnings growth follows a similar path. Unionized wages in the year 2000 are 18 percent higher than in 1987, and low wage earnings growth is an impressive 50 percent, despite the increase in migration. The absolute magnitude of the difference remains very large, however, with the high wage ($33,000) dwarfing the low wage ($11,750) by over $21,000 in the year 2000. While wages in sector 2 are held down somewhat due to the migration linkage with sector 2 in Mexico, the effect of adverse shocks would be dampened as well.

The split of output between sectors changes in both countries during the course of the scenarios. In the United States the fraction of production represented by sector 2 falls slightly, from 6.3 percent to 5.4 percent, although its relative price rises some 20 percent. Additional labor inflows would be necessary to meet year 2000 demand at the 1982 relative price. In Mexico the relative rise in sector 1 production from 49 percent to 58 percent of total product is a normal part of the development process. The rise reflects both the pattern of demand growth and the distribution of technological gains. More rapid technological progress and output expansion have the net effect of lowering the relative price of good 1 in Mexico as well, by about 25 percent.

REVIEW OF ALTERNATIVE SCENARIOS

Three alternative scenarios were run with the intent of covering a stylized range of options each containing a different combination of policies concerning trade, capital, and migration flows. Their implications for growth, trade, migration, and wages are analyzed, particularly in terms of labor's willingness in both countries to agree to a social pact qua Stackelberg solution. The highlights of each scenario's assumptions and results are presented below, followed by a summary table. Welfare implications of the alternative scenarios will generally be based on the concept of Hicksian compensating variations (CVs), which represent the amount of money that would be required to compensate individuals for the change in utility between the status quo and the alternative scenario, measured at the status quo prices.

The neo-liberal scenario corresponds fairly closely to what has actually happened during the 1980s. Principal features of the scenario are a stoppage of non-concessionary lending to Mexico, necessitating balance of trade surpluses and a net transfer of resources from South to North; a more restrictive (at least in intent) migration policy; and a reduction

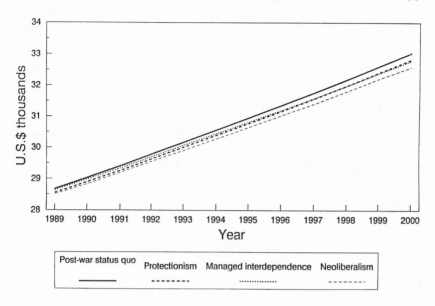

Fig. 5A. United States: High wage growth.

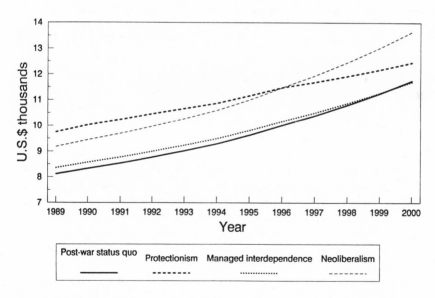

Fig. 5B. United States: Low wage growth.

(again, in principal) of trade barriers in both countries leading to the implementation of a Free Trade Agreement (FTA). In keeping with actual experience, Mexico chooses to pay its international debt, which cripples its industrial sector by depriving it of the capital goods it needs in order to grow, if not the intermediate goods necessary to sustain past production levels. In other words, the entire burden of adjustment is placed on trade flows, and trade is incapable of bearing the full adjustment load in the short run. Thus we have the debt crisis, which takes the form of a recession, a fall in real wages, and a collapse of the postwar class compromise. Given the imposed constraints, a Stackelberg solution to class bargaining is not possible because organized workers are unwilling to accept these conditions and their implications.

The scenario is very unstable for two reasons. First, the path of high wage earnings is unacceptable to the workers in the unionized sector, and their discontent would take the form of both raising their discount rate in an effort to move income and consumption forward in time, lobbying to change domestic policies, as well as strikes and other actions. Secondly, the unrest of unionized labor brings into question the stability of the economic and even political systems, reducing new loans, and raising interest rates, reflecting the rising risk premium on loans to Mexico. Workers would have the choice of either increasing their militancy, risking the economic and political consequences of their actions, or accepting a strategic defeat and settling for highly discounted lower wages.

Note that in the long run, a stable neo-liberal scenario could provide net benefits to both countries. With the decrease in militancy stemming from the collapse of social pacts in both countries, capitalists get a larger share of income. They use part of the larger share to invest, however, creating more high wage jobs and raising wages for the poorer workers. Wage growth is actually more rapid, after an initial wage fall, yet even this more rapid growth does little to improve worker's welfare, as it is offset by higher worker discount rates. By our computation, wages to the poor in Mexico are driven below the subsistence level by the workings of the enforced free market. Low wage workers need consumption subsidies from some source to maintain a minimum level of human needs, at a time when there is tremendous pressure on the government to reduce expenditures. Thus, while economic growth is more rapid, the discounted sums of wages are lower, and the long-term viability of the scenario must remain questionable.

Without correcting for the discount rate changes, all social groups except low wage U.S. labor and Mexican capitalists lose from the neo-liberal policy. U.S. low wage labor is protected somewhat by IRCA, while Mexican capitalists are protected from competition from the United States through capital controls and migration restriction, as well as aided by lower wages. U.S. capitalists gain from low wages but are net losers from lower migration and less direct interaction with Mexico. Capital goods exports to Mexico are nearly $10 billion less through 1994, although they recover in the second half of the simulation. At the country level, the United States is worse off by $30 billion through the year 2000 and non-capitalists in Mexico lose by $30 billion, while capitalists gain $55 billion. Thus Mexico gains slightly, but at the cost of a further deterioration in income distribution, and binational welfare declines. After taking into account the discount rate changes, all workers in both countries see themselves as losers in this scenario.

A second policy alternative, protectionism, can be conceived of as a response by organized labor to the long and painful adjustment problems of the neo-liberal scenario. Protectionism is modeled as default on Mexico's foreign debt, triggering a cessation of capital flows, trade retaliation, and a prohibitive immigration policy. We realize that no policy, including armed conflict at the border, could entirely halt migration, but the costs faced by migrants could be raised drastically.

In Mexico, GNP is higher due to the larger domestically employed labor force, but growth is slower. As a whole, Mexico gains in the short term from escaping the burden of the debt, but the gains accrue primarily to capitalists and land owners. Wages for the poor in Mexico are collapsed by a return of the deported migrants, again falling below subsistence levels, and the reduction in wages spills over into the high wage sector through a decline in militancy. By the year 2000, combined current dollar losses from the two countries are $85 billion, split proportionately according to their GDPs. Within Mexico, capitalists and landowners benefit from low wages, while workers lose. Despite its promising allure of offering protection for some social groups in some countries, a Stackelberg compromise along the lines of the postwar social pacts is not possible in either country. Small gains for the country as a whole through the year 2000 are erased when the present value of future losses are considered, leaving a net loss of $10 billion 1986 dollars.

The present value of U.S. losses is almost $200 billion, despite the fact that halting immigration does effectively protect low wage labor. U.S. GDP growth averages 0.2 percent less, with high wage labor bearing most of the loss.

The final scenario, called managed interdependence, is meant to address U.S. and Mexican concerns, without the displacement and upheavals in Mexico that the first two alternatives caused. Of particular importance is the impact of rising migration levels on U.S. low wage incomes. Also served are Mexico's interests in financing economic development while avoiding a debt trap, and in adjusting more gradually to pressures for a more open and efficient economy while improving its distribution of income.

All three major flows—trade, migration, and capital—are part of the adjustment process in the first years of the scenario. As a result, a gain in combined binational welfare relative to the postwar status quo can be achieved without the high migration levels of the neo-liberal and postwar scenarios and the substantial adjustment cost of either protectionism or neo-liberalism can be avoided. Additionally, the distribution of income can be improved in both countries, without slowing the wage growth of Mexico's influential unionized workers.

Assumptions of this scenario are as implied by the name; trade, capital market, and migration policies are coordinated between the United States and Mexico to improve both equity and efficiency. An open trade policy is modeled as in the neo-liberal case, although an FTA here could include, in a more desegregated model, temporary trade barriers to ease the costs of structural adjustment or promote emerging industries.

A co-investment scheme involving the cooperation of capital owners in both countries to their mutual benefit (in exploiting the difference in rates of return to capital) is simulated as part of the managed interdependence scenario. In this capital transfer scheme, five billion dollars of U.S. investment per year is matched with new Mexican investment, and the proceeds are shared such that each group benefits equally from the different values of the marginal product of capital in the two countries.

The other aspect of managed interdependence is a hybrid of immigration and capital market policies. Called a migration tax, it combines normalization of the undocumented migrant's status with taxation of the benefits of the normalization, leaving the migrant, for the moment, no better or worse off than before. It is reasonable to assume that the migrants, all else being equal, would prefer legal status subject to the tax over remaining undocumented. The money raised by the tax is divided between the two countries. The U.S. share is spent on income transfers intended to compensate those adversely affected by immigration. In Mexico, tax revenues ease the foreign exchange constraint and allow for increased capital imports and other development measures, which serve to create more high wage jobs and to raise wages for

TABLE 1

Summary of the Scenarios' Results

	Postwar status quo	Neo-liberal	Protectionism	Managed interdependence
Avg. migration level	5.48	4.55	0	3.89
United States				
Year 2000 GDP	$5,792.2	$5,830.7	$5,617.9	$5,719.0
Year 2000 CVs	$0.0	−$17.9	−$81.0	−$32.9
Discounted CV sums,				
1986–2000	$0.0	−$29.7	−$144.8	−$51.6
Upper class	$0.0	−$207.0	−$256.1	−$75.4
Lower class	$0.0	$177.3	$111.3	$23.8
Mexico				
Year 2000 GDP	$298.1	$301.1	$316.3	$334.3
Year 2000 CVs	$0.0	$11.0	−$4.3	$31.1
Discounted CV sums,				
1986–2000	$0.0	$24.9	$4.8	$109.8
Upper class	$0.0	$40.0	$22.1	$73.9
Lower class	$0.0	−$15.1	−$17.4	$35.9

SOURCE: Hinojosa Ojeda, "The Political Economy of North-South Interdependence: Debt, Trade, and Class Relations Across Mexico and the United States" (Ph.D. diss., Univ. of Chicago, 1989), Tables 6-1 through 6-10.
NOTES: Dollar figures in billions. CVs are Hicksian compensating variations. The U.S. upper class are high wage labor and capitalists and the lower class is low wage labor. In Mexico, the upper class is the aggregation of high wage labor, capitalists, and landowners, while the lower class consists of low wage labor and migrants.

Mexico's low wage workers, thus reducing the incentive to migrate from the sending side.

In this scenario, all social groups in Mexico gain relative to the postwar status quo. Capitalists and low wage labor (including migrants) gain about $36 billion each through the year 2000, while unionized labor gains some $32 billion. The infinite sum of the gains to the country as a whole, expressed in 1986 dollars, exceeds $200 billion. Average migration levels decrease, capital goods trade (indeed all trade) increases, workers in Mexico should be content relative to feasible alternatives, and income distribution is not worsened. The Stackelberg solution for Mexico is a relatively favorable one for labor, not only relative to neo-liberalism but also compared to the postwar status quo.

In the United States, low wage labor and capitalists gain $24 and $23 billion respectively through the year 2000. Unfortunately, this scenario is not Pareto improving in the sense that everyone wins. High wage labor in the United States is hurt by the capital transfers to Mexico and by the relative price shifts caused by lower migration and more consumption imports from Mexico. Notice in Table 1, however, that a fall in welfare for the U.S. high wage sector is a necessary result of the breakdown in the postwar status quo, and that the declines associated with the other two options are much larger. An application of the compensation principle directly, or an adjustment of the split of migration tax revenues or capital transfer profits, may be necessary to enlist U.S. participation, despite the apparent inevitability of the stagnation in U.S. unionized wages.

CONCLUSIONS: INTERDEPENDENCE WITH SOCIAL PACTS?

A computable general equilibrium model was developed that reflects the complexity of North-South economic interactions—migration, trade, and capital flows—that have linked the welfare of social groups and have made class strategic interaction and policy-making more complex. Calibrated to the uniqueness of the U.S.-Mexican situation, it can provide a means of analyzing some fundamental questions of North-South asymmetrical interdependence. Questions include: What are the tradeoffs between different policy combinations, such as using trade to reduce migration or a change in debt policy to affect trade and migration? What are the impacts of these strategies in terms of employment and income distribution and their ability to generate broad social support and sustain social pacts between organized agents in society?

We analyzed a series of alternative scenarios for U.S.-Mexico relations, ranging from protectionism to neo-liberal opening to managed interdependence. The results point to a long run and society wide superiority of increased exchange, while also revealing a short run dilemma for workers' welfare—a dilemma that poses serious obstacles to the neo-liberal approach to greater exchange.

An attempt to close off either economy from exchange with the other, the protectionist alternative, emerges as the worst long-term welfare option for most workers groups in both countries as well as for overall compensating variations. Yet for high wage workers in the United States and Mexico as well as low wage U.S. workers, protectionism provides higher welfare in the short run than the neo-liberal policy mix, although less than in managed interdependence.

While escaping the burden of debt produces short-term gains that accrue primarily to capitalists and land owners, this occurs at the cost of a sharp reduction in trade and subsequent growth. Wages for the poor in Mexico fall below subsistence levels with the return of the deported migrants, and this reduction in wages spills over into the high wage sector through a decline in militancy. The present value of U.S. losses is almost $200 billion, despite the fact that halting immigration effectively protects low wage labor in the short run (with high wage labor absorbing most of the loss). Despite its promise of short term protection for some social groups in some countries, a Stackelberg compromise along the lines of the postwar social pacts can still not be maintained in either country.

The protectionist scenario also demonstrates the way changes in migration levels affect low wage labor in both countries. The elimination of migration raises welfare for the U.S. lower classes and lowers the welfare of Mexico's lower classes. Yet the costs to other groups in the United States indicate that the reduction in migration and benefits to the poor in the United States are achieved at a huge cost in efficiency and growth.

While closing off from exchange is clearly the worst option in the long run, different combinations of policies through which open exchange occurs can generate very different levels of growth, employment, and income distribution. The ways in which the benefits to open exchange are distributed will have very important consequences for the pattern of development and the quality of social support for interdependence across countries.

The neo-liberal alternative, which is modeled on the current policy directions in the United States and Mexico, implies a free trade agreement, continued debt servicing, and restrictive immigration (at least in intent) à la IRCA. We show that changes in trade policies, as opposed to capital and labor policies, generally have smaller impacts on production and welfare. An FTA by itself is not capable of reducing migration as some have claimed. Migration, in fact, will increase substantially in the absence of significant capital inflows to increase employment and wages in Mexico.

While the burden of adjustment is placed principally on trade, a change in trade itself is also shown to be incapable of bearing the adjustment load in the short run, despite a fall in real wages. For high wage workers in Mexico and the United States, as well as low wage Mexican workers, neo-liberalism is the worst option in the short run. Given the continuation of imposed debt servicing constraints, a Stackelberg solution to class bargaining is not possible as organized workers remain unwilling to accept these conditions.

While a stable neo-liberal scenario in the long run could provide net benefits to both countries, this can only be achieved through lower wages and a decrease in wage militancy stemming from the collapse of social pacts in both countries and from capitalists getting a larger share of income. Eventual higher rates of growth, employment, and most wages can result from higher savings and investment rates, but only if social stability with lower wages can be maintained.

Of the three alternative scenarios, only managed interdependence can provide for continued growth, international exchange, and a basis for strategically agreed upon social pacts in both countries. The key to this approach is developing an optimal combination of debt, trade, and migration policies that maximizes growth and welfare on both sides of the border.

The migration tax was designed as a way to make a given level of migration more efficient in bringing about convergence in wage levels. When the gains to migration are maximized by minimizing costs, then split equally rather than accruing overwhelmingly to the United States, binational welfare can be increased even as migration levels fall. Mexico's use of migration tax revenues for capital and intermediate goods imports is beneficial to both countries, as about 70 percent of Mexico's imports come from the United States.

Moving capital from the United States to Mexico in order to exploit differences in factor returns is another main element of the managed interdependence scenario. Such a transfer can be modeled as resulting from a temporary postponement in debt servicing, a binational co-investment facility, and/or the funding of a regional development bank. Binational output under the capital transfer is about the same, however, as the capital inflow raises wages in Mexico, which reduces migration. Binational welfare rises, as the dead weight costs of migration are reduced and the gains from increased exchange are captured in goods markets as well.

The managed interdependence scenario also indicates that a trade-off between the welfare of the poor and workers in the two countries is not a necessary one. Instead, it stems from the perspective of attempting to use migration policy to alter the number of migrants, as opposed to using a wider range of migration, trade, and capital market policies to attack the cause of migration: depressed wages in the sending region. In the managed interdependence scenario, the average stock of migrants is actually 1.5 million lower with capitalists and low wage labor in the United States gaining along with Mexico's poor. The Stackelberg process by which wages are set in Mexico is also quite sensitive to the pattern of interdependence, and thus the U.S. equilibrium. For unionized wages to grow at or above the postwar pace would require more than just trade expansion. More access to the U.S. labor market and/or U.S. capital than the neo-liberal scenario provides would be necessary to just maintain the class compromise on which the United States and Mexico's postwar growth was based.

The relationship between interdependence and its impact on GDP and welfare has become more apparent through this modeling. Inter-country flows are inevitable and symptomatic of the differences in wages and rental rates between the two countries, and attempts to stem them in one area can provoke compensating changes in other areas that may be surprising and perverse from the perspective of the social actors and policymakers. The results of the model indicate that greater exchange yields more economic benefit, although the distribution of benefits between countries and social groups is subject to the precise form of the policy change. While protectionism results in sizable long-term losses across countries and social groups, freer trade without significant net capital inflows cannot be expected to increase employment and wages and reduce migration in the short run. While providing potentially long-term benefits, the current neo-liberal approach is producing severe hardship on groups that can be expected to block moves towards greater exchange. The managed interdependence scenario indicates, however, that there are significant gains to policy coordination that promote increased U.S.-Mexican economic interaction, through capital flows from North to South, labor flows from South to North, and increased trade flows in both directions. While solutions that can generate growth and broad social support across countries are possible, much more attention will have to be given to the institutional process of international policy coordination necessary for their implementation.

APPENDIX I: ANNOTATED EQUATION LIST

Note: All variables are implicitly time subscripted. The index i refers to sectors of the economy, the index j denotes the country, while k denotes social group within the country. Where equations are substantively different by country or sector, sector suffixes 1 or 2 or a prefix M for Mexico are used. In addition, equations for the United States were often given the same equation number as the corresponding equation for Mexico, with an "A" suffix. Alternative equations are noted with a prime (').

Section 1: Production Functions and Factor Allocations

1) $\text{MGDP1} = \text{MP}^*\text{MA1}^*(\text{Ma1}^*\text{ML1}^{-p1} + \text{Mb1}^*\text{MK1}^{-p1} + \text{Md1}^*\text{MIMP}^{-p1})^{-1/p1}$

1&2A) $\text{GDP}_i = \text{P}_i^*\text{A}_i^*(\text{a}_i^*\text{L}_i^{-pi} + \text{bi}^*\text{Ki}^{-pi})^{-1/pi}$

2) $\text{MGDP2} = \text{MA2}^*(\text{Ma2}^*\text{ML2}^{-P2} + \text{Mb2}^*\text{MK2}^{-p2} + \text{Md2}^*\text{MLAND}^{-p2})^{-1/p2}$

3) $\text{GDP} = \text{GDP}_{ij} + \text{GDP}_{ij}$

4) $\text{GDPRL}_{ij} = \text{GDP}_{ij}/\text{P}_{ij}$

5) $\text{ML1A} = \text{ML1}_{t-1} + (\text{MK1} - \text{MK1}_{t-1})/(\text{MIKL}*\text{MSTAKMAX})$

5A) $\text{ML1B} = \text{ML1}_{t-1}*\text{ML1GRO}$

6) $\text{ML1} = \text{MIN}(\text{ML1A},\text{ML1B})$

6A) $\text{L1} = \text{L1}_{t-1}*\text{LGRO}_t$

6A') $\text{L1A} = \text{L1}_{t-1} + (\text{K1} - \text{K1}_{t-1})/(\text{IKL}*\text{STAKMAX})$

7) $\text{ML2} = \text{MLINIT} - \text{ML1} - \text{MMIG}$

7A) $\text{L2} = \text{LUSINIT} - \text{ML1} + \text{MEXMIG}*\text{SKILL}$

8) $\max \text{M1WGBIL} = {}_{-t=0,h} (\text{ML1}*\text{MW1})*(\text{MDISRAT})^{t-1986}$

8A) $\text{SAVRT}_j = \text{SAVIN}_j + \text{IELAS}_j*(\text{RK}_j - \text{NORMPROF}_j)$

GDP = gross domestic product(bill 1982 $)
GDPRL = real GDP (at 1982 prices)
P = relative price of good1/good2
PIM = the price of Mexican exports in the U.S., in dollars
A = the production function constant, indicating the technological level
a = 'alpha', the labor share coefficient of the production function
L = the amount of labor, either in thousands of man-years or efficiency units (see eq. 9A)
b = 'beta', the capital share coefficient
K = the amount of capital, in billions of 1982 dollars
d = 'delta', the distribution parameter related to the third factor of production in Mexico
MIMP = the amount of the imported intermediate good, in billions of 1982 dollars
MLAND = the amount of land, in millions of hectares, assumed to be a constant
p = 'rho', the coefficient related to the elasticity of substitution (s) by the eq. $s = 1/(1 + p)$
SAVRT = the marginal propensity to save out of real production
MEXPORTS = Mexican exports to the U.S. of consumer goods
LINIT = the initial(pre-migration) labor force in millions of man-years
MMIG = undocumented Mexican migration to the U.S. in millions
SKILL = a constant adjustment factor to convert migrants into efficiency units of labor
MIKL = an incremental capital/labor ratio, which in turn, defines a time path of the mimimum wage

MLı GRO = the maximun rate of growth of the labor force in sector 1, based on the capacity of Mexico to educate and train new entrants for work in manufacturing

LGRO$_t$ = the growth rate of the U.S. labor force in time t

Mı WGBIL = wage bill

MDISRAT = discount rate

MSTAKMAX = index of wage militancy

MSAVIN = historical savings rate

MIELAS = interest elasticity of savings

MNORMPROF = profit rate consistent with historical savings rate

Section 2: Marginal Conditions

$$9)\ \mathrm{MRK1} = \mathrm{MP}^*\mathrm{MA1}^*\mathrm{Mb1}^*\mathrm{MK1}^{(-p1-1)*}[\mathrm{Ma1}^*\mathrm{ML1}^{-p1} + \mathrm{Mb1}^*\mathrm{MK1}^{-p1} + \mathrm{Md1}^*\mathrm{MIMP}^{-p1}]^{-(1/p1)-1}$$

$$10)\ \mathrm{MRK2} = \mathrm{MA2}^*\mathrm{Mb2}^*\mathrm{MK2}^{-p2-1*} \times [\mathrm{Ma2}^*\mathrm{ML2}^{-p2} + \mathrm{Mb2}^*\mathrm{MK2}^{-p2} + \mathrm{Md2}^*\mathrm{MLAND}^{-p2}]^{(1/p2)-1}$$

$$9\mathrm{A},10\mathrm{A})\ \mathrm{RKi} = \mathrm{Pi}^*\mathrm{Ai}^*\mathrm{bi}^*\mathrm{Ki}^{-pi-1*}[\mathrm{ai}^*\mathrm{Li}^{-pi} + \mathrm{bi}^*\mathrm{Ki}^{-pi}]^{-(1/pi)-1i} = 1,2$$
$$\mathrm{P2} = 1$$

$$11)\ \mathrm{MW1} = \mathrm{MP}^*\mathrm{MA1}^*\mathrm{Ma1}^*\mathrm{ML1}^{(-p1-1)*}[\mathrm{Ma1}^*\mathrm{ML1}^{-p1} + \mathrm{Mb1}^*\mathrm{MK1}^{-p1} + \mathrm{Md1}^*\mathrm{MIMP}^{-p1}]^{-(1/p1)-1}$$

$$12)\ \mathrm{MW2} = \mathrm{MA2}^*\mathrm{Ma2}^*\mathrm{ML2}^{-p2-1*}[\mathrm{Ma2}^*\mathrm{ML2}^{-p2} + \mathrm{Mb2}^*\mathrm{MK2}^{-p2} + \mathrm{Md2}^*\mathrm{MLAND}^{-p2}]^{-(1/p2)-1}$$

$$11\mathrm{A},12\mathrm{A})\mathrm{Wi} = \mathrm{Pi}^*\mathrm{Ai}^*\mathrm{ai}^*\mathrm{Li}^{-pi-1*}[\mathrm{ai}^*\mathrm{Li}^{-pi} + \mathrm{bi}^*\mathrm{Ki}^{-pi}]^{-(1/pi)-1i} = 1,2$$
$$\mathrm{P2} = 1$$

$$13)\ \mathrm{MPMIMP} = \mathrm{MP}^*\mathrm{MA1}^*\mathrm{Md1}^*\mathrm{MIMP}^{(-p1-1)*}[\mathrm{Ma1}^*\mathrm{ML1}^{-p1} + \mathrm{Mb1}^*\mathrm{MK1}^{-p1} + \mathrm{Md1}^*\mathrm{MIMP}^{-p1}]^{-(1/p1)-1}$$

$$14)\ \mathrm{MPMLAND} = \mathrm{MA2}^*\mathrm{Md2}^*\mathrm{MLAND2}^{-p2-1*}[\mathrm{Ma2}^*\mathrm{ML2}^{-p2} + \mathrm{Mb2}^*\mathrm{MK2}^{-p2} + \mathrm{Md2}^*\mathrm{MLAND}^{-p2}]^{-(1/p2)-1}$$

RKi = both the value of the marginal product of and return to capital in sector i i = 1,2

Wi = both the value of the marginal product of labor and the wage rate in sector i i = 1,2

MPMIMP = the value of the marginal product of the imported intermediate good

MPLAND = the value of the marginal product of land

Section 3: Aggregate Demands and Sectoral Incomes,
Demands, and Utilities

15) $MAD1 = MG1 + (MB1/MP)*(MGDPC - MP*MG1 - MG2)$
$+ MEXPORTSRL$

15A) $AD1 = G1 + (B1/P)*(GDPC - P*G1 - G2) + MIMPRL$
$+ 0.87*DSLV*DEPEND$

16) $MAD2 = MG2 + MB2*(MGDPC - MP*MG1 - MG2)$
$+ (MEXMIG + ML1*0.8 + ML2*0.6)*MDSLV$

16A) $AD2 = G2 + B2*(GDPC - P*G1 - G2) + 0.13*DSLV*DEPEND$

17A*) $AD3 = MEXPORTSRL = (B3/PIM)*(GDPC - P*G1 - G2)$

18) $MIGY = W2*SKILL - COST - DISC - REMIT$ note: $REMIT = $
$MDSLV/PPPE$, SKILL and DISC are constants, while cost is defined
immediately below

19) $COST = COST1982 + 0.1*(MEXMIG - 2.5)$

20*) $MIGDi = giMIG + (Bi/Pi)*(MIGY - P*g1MIG - g2MIG$
$- PIM*g3MIG)$ $i = 1,2$ $P2 = 1, P3 = PIM$

21) $UMIG = [_{-i=1,3} Bi*LOG(MIGDi - giMIG)] - PREF$

22) $ML2Y = MW2 - 0.6*MDSLV*ML2$

22A) $L2Y = W2$

23) $MD_{ik} = Mg_i + (MB_i/MP_i)*(MY_k - MP*Mg1 - Mg2)$ $i = 1,2$ and
$k = L2, L1, MK, LAND$

23A*) $D_{ik} = g_i + (B_i/P_i)*(Y_k - P*g1 - g2 - PIM*g3)$ $i = 1,3$ and
$k = L1, L2, K$

24) $UTIL_{jk} = _{-i=1,2}$ (and 3, for the U.S.) $B_{ij}*LOG(D_{ijk} - g_{ij})$

25) $ML1Y = MW1 - 0.8*MDSLV*ML1$

25A) $L1Y = W1*(1 - USINCOMETAX)$

26) $MKY = MRK*MK - MGDPRL*MSAVRT - MGDPRL*MTAX$
$+ MIMP*(MPMIMP*(PIM - P))$

26A) $KY = RK*K - GDPRL*SAVRT - NEWLOANS + KEXP$

27) $MLANDY = MPLAND*MLAND$

ADi = aggregate demand for sector i output

Gi = the aggregate 'subsistance' level of demand Gi>o implies an income
   elasticity<1 Gi = gi*Li
   note: G3 = o

Bi = the share of 'discretionary income' spent on good i

PIM = the dollar price of Mexican exports in the U.S.

MIGY = the amount of money migrants spend on goods which they
   consume

SKILL = the productivity of Mexican migrants in the U.S. relative to native unskilled labor (see section 1)

COST = all costs of migration, from bus tickets to lost wages and bribes

COST1982 = cost in the base year of 1982

DISC = discrimination against migrants due to their undocumented status

REMIT = remittances from migrants to dependents who remain in Mexico, in dollars

MDSLV = the subsistance level of the dependents of migrants who remain
   in Mexico

DSLV = the subsistance level of demand of U.S. dependents, at 1982
   prices. The elderly consume more services (health care, etc.) thus the
   fraction of demand representing good 2 is somewhat higher than B2,
   the 'marginal propensity to consume' good 2 of employed households

DEPEND = the number of dependents in the U.S. living outside the households of the employed; it can be thought of as the number of elderly
   receiving government transfers

PPPE = the peso/dollar exchange rate, converting target levels of Mexico
   good 2 consumption to dollar flows

MIGDi = consumption of good *i* in the U.S. by a representative migrant

gi = an individual's required consumption of good *i*
   note: B's are the same for all social groups within each country

UMIG = utility of the representative migrant

PREF = the preference of Mexicans for living and working in Mexico
   note: in starred equations, PIM includes the U.S. tariff

RK = average return in capital

K = total capital stock of the country

DEBT = Mexico's total foreign debt

RATE = the average interest rate on the debt (exogenous)

NEWLOANS = net inflow of lending in dollars

KEXP = the dollar price of capital exports to Mexico

MTAX = the Mexican tax rate, or average rate if rates differ between
   sectors

Section 4: Equilibrium Conditions

28) $RK1_j = RK2_j$

29) $0 = EXD_{ij} = [GDP_{ij}/P_{ij} * (1 - SAVRT_j)] - AD_{ij}$ $i = 1,2$

30) $0 = EXD3 = MEXPORTS - AD3$

31) $0 = UTILDIFF = UMIG - UML2$

32) $0 = GOVBP = MTAR*MIMP + OILREV + NEWLOANS$
    $+ MEXMIG*REMIT - DEBT*RATE - DOL\ TRANS$

33*) $0 = SPFOREX = MPMIMP*PIM/P - MP$
    $= MRK*PIM/PMKUS - MP$

34) $0 = PRIVBP = (PIM*MEXPORTS - P*MIMP - KEXP)$
    $+ DOLTRANS - CAPITALFLIGHT$

35) $CAPITALFLIGHT\ (1982-85) = (PIM*MEXPORTS$
    $- P*MIMP - KEXP) + DOLTRANS$

36) $CAPITALFLIGHT\ (1986-2000) = -(CAPITALFLIGHT\ (1982-85)/15)$

36') $CAPITALFLIGHT\ (1986-2000) = 0$

EXDi = excess demand for good *i*

SPFOREX = the shadow price of foreign exchange, i.e. the value of the additional product that could be made and sold given a one unit relaxation of the export ceiling constraint

GOVBP = the balance of payments of the public sector. DOLTRANS is the free parameter

PRIVBP = the balance of payments constraint of the private sector. Here, DOLTRANS and

CAPITALFLIGHT (after 1985) are the only true exogenous variables

MTAR = the tariff rate set by the Mexican government on imports

UTILDIFF = the utility differential between migrants and non-migrants
    note: in starred equation, P includes Mexican tariff

DOLTRANS = the Mexican government's dollar deficit (surplus), which is borrowed from (loaned to) the private sector

KEXP = capital exports from the U.S. to Mexico

PMKUS = the price of Mexican capital in the U.S., which can differ from the price of U.S. capital

CAPITALFLIGHT = the model estimates capital flight for the years 1982–

1985, then an assumption is made about the time path of the variable for future years

Section 5: The Government Sector

37) $MGOVREV = MTAX1*MGDP1 + MTAX2*MGDP2$

37A) $GOVREV = TAR*MEXPORTS + USINCOMETAX$

38) $MGOVEXP = PDEBTSRV + DOLTRANS + MTRANSFERS$

38A) $GOVEXP = DSLV*DEPEND + TRANSFERS + USDEBTSERV$

39) $DEFICIT_j = GOVREV_j - GOVEXP_j$

40) $GOVDEBT_j = GOVDEBT_{jt-1} + DEFICIT_j$

GOVREV = government revenue
TAR = tariff rate (percent)
GOVEXP = government expenditure
PDEBTSRV = payments on the government's internal (peso) debt
TRANSFERS = transfer payments to individuals
DEFICIT = the government deficit
GOVDEBT = internal government debt

Section 6: Updating Exogenous Variables

41) $LINIT_{jt} = LINIT_{j(t-1)}*LGRO_{jt}$

42) $K_{jt} = K_{j(t-1)} + SAVRT_j*GDPRL_{jt}$

43) $A_{ij\ t} = A_{ij\ (t-1)}*AGRO_{ij\ (t-1)}$ for 1983–1986, else
$= A_{ij\ (t-1)}*AGRO_{ij}$

44) $DEPEND_t = DEPEND_{(t-1)}*DEPENDGRO$

o
$LINIT_t$ = the initial (pre-migration) labor force
$LGRO_t$ = growth rate of the labor force in year $_t$
K_t = the capital stock
$AGRO_{i\ t}$ = the rate of technological progress in year $_t$
DEPENDGRO = growth of dependents

APPENDIX 2: BASE YEAR DATA AND SOURCE LIST

Subscripts refer to sectors within a country and prefixes US and M refer to the United States and Mexico respectively. Data are in millions of people or billions of 1982 dollars unless otherwise specified.

The 1982 values of:

The U.S. Labor Force—USL1 = 90 USL2 = 10 USLINIT = 98
Sources: National Income and Product Accounts (NIPA)—employment
by industry (note that only 8 of USL2 represent U.S. citizens).

The Mexican Labor Force—ML1 = 8.0 ML2 = 14.0 MLINIT = 24.5
Sources: Mexican census data—with corrections—assuming approximately six percent labor force growth from 1980–1982.

The U.S. Capital Stock—USK1 = $7054 USK2 = $546USK = $7600
Sources: Estimates drawn from Survey of Current Business (SCB).

The Mexican Capital Stock—MK1 = $170 MK2 = $180 MK = $350
Sources: Estimates computed by updating the 1975 capital stock estimate
of Reynolds—with net investment figures from "International Financial
Statistics" (IFS).—Capital allocation across sectors appears to be consis-
tent with available wage and productivity data for the U.S.—and for
Mexico from Anuario Estadistico (AE).

U.S. GDP data—USGDP1 = $3014 USGDP2 = $147 USGDP = $3161
Sources: U.S. GDP data is from SCB, with sector 2 consisting of parts of
the agriculture (20%), construction (10%), and services (25%) sectors.

Mexican GDP data—MGDP1 = $85 MGDP2 = $75 MGDP = $160
Sources: Mexican GDP data is from Banco de Mexico Informe Anual (IA)
1984, with sector 2 defined as Agriculture, Services, and Construction.

Undocumented migrants—MEXMIG = 2.5
Sources: Serious studies have estimated undocumented Mexican migration at anywhere from 1 to 6.5 million in this time frame. Studies whose
point of departure is the unexplained difference between 1980 census
data and predictions based on 1970 base data and crude birth and death
rates tend to place on the low end of the scale.

Studies based on border apprehensions and so-called "get away" ratios
tend to be on the high end.

The estimate used here, 2.5 million, is a reasonable compromise between the two camps, and closer to the mid-point than one might
think, since the high-range estimates include a considerable number
of non-working dependents, which do not formally exist in this model.
One could interpret the 80% factor used to convert migrants to efficiency units of labor as a participation ratio with no change in the
results.

SKILL = 80%   This factor represents the difference in productivity between migrants and native labor due to education, training, and language (see above comment).

COST1982 =   All costs of migrating from Mexico to the U.S. $1,200/person. Two-thirds of this figure represents unavoidable costs, like bus fares, wages lost in travel time, and job search costs, which are independent of the legality of migration. The other third consists of resources wasted avoiding the border patrol, time spent being detained or deported, and bribing officials or smugglers for crossing, all of which are a direct result of U.S. migration restrictions.

DISCRIMINATION =   This is the cost of being illegal, in terms of $1,200/person lower net pay. Overt discrimination, the paying of different gross wages to two people doing the same work because one is undocumented, exists but is not common. Covert discrimination, in terms of withholdings for social security, income taxes, and various other health or insurance programs for which the migrant is not eligible, is the important source of this difference.

PREFERENCE =   It is the preference of migrants for living and
1.7 Utility units   working in Mexico rather than the U.S., measured in utility units. This figure is arrived at by parameterizing the model to consider the estimated 1982 migration level in equilibrium. In dollar terms, this means that a potential migrant would require a wage about $3,000 higher than that available in Mexico in order to be better off if he migrates.

Constant elasticity of substitution production coefficients

Sector	Labor	Capital	Int. Good	Land
MS1	M alpha 1 = 0.498	M beta 1 = 0.404	Mdelta1 = 0.098	
MS2	M alpha 2 = 0.467	M beta 2 = 0.450		Mdelta2 = 0.083
USS1	US alpha 1 = 0.76	US beta 1 = 0.24		
USS2	US alpha 2 = 0.67	US beta 2 = 0.33		

These CES production function coefficients were chosen to be consistent with the 1982 functional income distribution for each country and reflect constant returns to scale production (the sum of the coefficients = 1). Mexican data on wages and income distribution is drawn from the 1980 census and from selected United Nations and Secretaria de Programacion y Presupuesto (SPP) publications.— Differences between sectors conform to observed wage differentials and technological differences where such data is available. The parameter p, related to the elasticity of substitutions s by the formula $s = 1/(1+p)$, was chosen such that $ms_1 = s_1 = 0.9$ and $ms_2 = s_2 = 0.93$. Thus the manufacturing sector has a lower elasticity of substitution, in keeping with the conventional wisdom.—

Technological efficiency coefficients for each sector were inferred from the other data by inverting the CES production functions in the base years. In 1982, the figures were:

$$MEXA_1 = 3.533 \quad MEXA_2 = 1.773 \quad USA_1 = 13.500 \quad USA_2 = 4.409$$

Class Strategic Bargaining Coefficients

$SAVIN = 0.058 \quad IELAS = 0.3 \quad NORMPROF = 0.09 \quad DISRAT = 0.84$
$MSAVIN = 0.07 \quad MIELAS = 0.4 \quad MNORMPROF = 0.19 \quad MDISRAT = 0.9$

Demand function coefficients

$MG_1 = .317$ $\quad$ $MB_1 = .7$

$MG_2 = 1.700$ $\quad$ $MB_2 = .3$

$G_1 = 5.568$ $\quad$ $B_1 = .934$

$G_2 = -.066$ $\quad$ $B_2 = .060$

$G_3 = -5/98$ $\quad$ $B_3 = .006$

$migG_2 = .035$

$migG_3 = .000$

These coefficients are not directly estimated, but are based on a variety of information, from estimates of the income elasticity of demand for key components of each sector to general $migG_1 = 3.714$ rules such as Engel's law.— See table 5-2 for the price = 1 demand expansion path consistant with the status quo income and population growth paths. Lluch, Powell, and Williams provide a source of estimates of budget shares, income elasticities, and Frisch parameters for linear expenditure systems based on various cross-country studies.[34] These provide checks on the reasonableness of the parameters used here.

[34] Constantino Lluch, Alan A. Powell, and Ross A. Williams, *Patterns in Household Demand and Saving* (New York, 1977).

Other 1982 Data

MIMP = $9.0

Intermediate good imports in 1982, from Comercio Exterior (CE), Banco de Mexico. As a simplifying assumption, all imports are treated as originating in the U.S. and all exports go to the U.S. In the past 10 years, some 70 percent of Mexican exports have gone to the U.S., while 65 percent of imports are bilateral. Alternatively, one can consider U.S. totals as underestimates of Latin American trade rather than overestimates of trade with Mexico.

MEXICAN NON-OIL

Mexican non-oil exports from CE, with an EXPORTS = $6.0 adjustment for underinvoicing made in order to reconcile Mexican and U.S. trade data. The adjustment factor is about 10%.

NEWLOANS = $8.2

New loans plus the fall in reserves for 1982, from IA.

DEBT = $85.0

Mexico's foreign debt in 1982, from IA, and IFS.

RATE = 9%

Average interest rate on Mexico's debt, from IA and IFS.

MDSLV = $0.125/migrant

Dependent's subsistence level for migrants. For Mexican labor, MDSLV is one of the demand parameters.

DSLV = $5.4/dependent

Dependent's subsistence level for the U.S. Each dependent consumes 4.7 units of good 1 and 0.7 units of good 2. As mentioned in the text, since 0.7/5.4 ($\sim$(difference) 0.13) exceeds B2 (0.06), increases in dependents relative to the labor force increases the demand for good 2 relative to good 1.

DEP = 37.9

Number of dependents in the U.S.

MIKL $= 24^* 1.0125^{(t-1)}$ Mexico's incremental capital/labor ratio, in thousands of dollars of capital per job created, inferred from recent Mexican government development plans. If Mexico reduces the capital intensity of growth further, this would have a significant effect on the results of the model. t is a time index, equal to 1 in 1982 and 19 in the year 2000.

"Simulating the Past": The Years 1983–1985

Growth rates of the labor force and savings rates are supplied for these years as described below, as well as observed values of production, imports and exports, and new loans. The split of capital and labor between sectors, migration, prices, factor rewards, etc., are endogenous. A's are solved for as described above.

	1983	1984	1985
MGDPRL =	$149.70	154.85	159.16
MGDP1/MP =	$77.42	81.01	83.08
MGDP2 =	$72.28	73.84	76.08
GDPRL =	$3279.84	3487.96	3562.47
GDP1/P =	$3121.58	3322.32	3394.62
GDP2 =	$158.26	165.63	167.85
MA1 =	3.287	3.237	3.219
MA2 =	2.696	2.709	2.702
A1 =	13.681	14.256	14.272
A2 =	4.420	4.441	4.357
NEWLOANS =	$7.5	2.8	5.0
MIMP =	$5.493	7.170	8.027
N-O EXPORTS =	$6.345	7.839	7.054

Growth Rates of Exogenous Variables for the Simulation

Labor force growth rates for the U.S. and Mexico are computed in a similar fashion to those reported in an earlier work,— but have been modified to take advantage of recent work based on 1980 Mexican census data.— On the U.S. side, estimates are updated to reflect recent BLS projections.— The first numbers below are the percentage increases in the labor force of Mexico and the U.S. from 1982 to 1983, and the eighteenth row is the growth from 1999 to 2000. Thus year 1982 + t labor force is $_{-i=1,t} (1 + LGRO_i)$.

MLGRO1 = 3.7 LGRO1 = 2.2   MLGRO10 = 3.25   LGRO10 = 1.7
MLGRO2 = 3.7 LGRO2 = 2.1   MLGRO11 = 3.1   LGRO11 = 1.65
MLGRO3 = 3.7 LGRO3 = 2.0   MLGRO12 = 2.95   LGRO12 = 1.6
MLGRO4 = 3.65 LGRO4 = 1.95 MLGRO13 = 2.7   LGRO13 = 1.55
MLGRO5 = 3.65 LGRO5 = 1.9   MLGRO14 = 2.5   LGRO14 = 1.55
MLGRO6 = 3.6 LGRO6 = 1.85   MLGRO15 = 2.35   LGRO15 = 1.5
MLGRO7 = 3.6 LGRO7 = 1.8   MLGRO16 = 2.2   LGRO16 = 1.5
MLGRO8 = 3.55 LGRO8 = 1.75 MLGRO17 = 2.1   LGRO17 = 1.45
MLGRO9 = 3.45 LGRO9 = 1.75 MLGRO18 = 2.05   LGRO18 = 1.4

ML1GRO = 5   The maximum labor absorption capacity of the high wage sector.

Productivity Growth:
Mex 1 = 1.8% Mex 2 = 0.8%
US 1 = 1.2% US 2 = 0.4%

Historical trends, 1970–1982 for the U.S., in ERP, 1983 "Increases in Output per hour," adjusted for capital increases. For Mexico, 1970–1980 trend based on shift-share update for change in output per worker, adjusted for changes in capital and labor.—

MDISRT = 0.91

Mexican and U.S. discount factors USDISRT = 0.93 (one minus the discount rates). Mexico discounts the future more heavily, an assumption consistant with consumers close to the subsistence level and a relatively high rate of return to capital.

DEPGRO = 3%

Growth of the "dependency burden" as the U.S. population ages.

NEWLOANS = $3.0
COST = $1.2 + $0.1*(MEXMIG-2.5)

Net new loans yearly for 1986–2000.
As the number of migrants rises in a given year, the cost of migration is assumed to increase slightly. Possible justifications include the effects of a distribution of migrants by distance

from the border, bidding up the scarce resources associated with border crossing, and the possibility that apprehension percentages and detention time increase with higher migration levels.

From Sojourners to Settlers: The Changing Profile of Mexican Immigration to the United States

Wayne A. Cornelius

THE OBJECTIVES of this paper are to highlight several important changes in the profile of Mexican migration to the United States since the 1970s, to offer some tentative explanations for these shifts, and to discuss briefly their implications for public policy, especially at the local level. The profile of the contemporary Mexican immigrant population that I present here is necessarily a composite, assembled from many different fragments. It draws heavily on data from a series of field studies conducted between 1982 and 1989 on both sides of the border by the Center for U.S.-Mexican Studies at the University of California at San Diego (UCSD). The research design, sampling methods, and data collection procedures for these studies are described more fully in the appendix to my paper. Our studies have included censuses, sample surveys, unstructured interviewing and ethnographic observation among U.S. employers, immigrant and U.S.-born workers employed in the same firms, recently arrived migrants who were seeking work as day-laborers in southern California's street-corner labor markets, and returned migrants and prospective first-time migrants living in three rural communities in west-central Mexico that traditionally export labor. These data are supplemented by findings from other sample surveys and ethnographic studies, Immigration and Naturalization Service (INS) apprehension statistics, samples of U.S. Border Patrol apprehension records, and evidence from El Colegio de la Frontera's ongoing studies of would-be unauthorized entrants, photographed and interviewed on the Mexican side of the border.

It must be emphasized at the outset that the available data, while suggestive of trends, are far from conclusive, and problems of comparability limit our ability to generalize from them. With very few exceptions, we lack historical time-series data, longitudinal studies of specific sending or receiving areas, and panel studies of samples of Mexican immigrants, which together would permit us to describe and explain changes in migration to the United States from Mexico (and other Latin American countries) with greater certainty and precision. Cross-sectional data, even when collected at various points in time using reasonably comparable sampling and interviewing techniques, are no substitute for systematic longitudinal evidence. Nevertheless, the available data provide a base from which certain plausible propositions about the changing character of Mexican immigration can be derived.

THE EROSION OF A STEREOTYPE

When the *bracero* program of contract labor importation ended in 1964, and for up to a decade thereafter, Mexican migration to the United States consisted mainly of a circular flow of mostly undocumented, mostly young adult males who left their immediate relatives behind in a rural Mexican community to work in seasonal U.S. agriculture for several months (normally six months or less) and then returned to their community of origin. Most came from a small subset of communities, located in seven or eight Mexican states that for many years had sent the bulk of Mexican migrants to the United States. Thus, the typical undocumented Mexican worker of the late 1960s and early 1970s strongly resembled his or her predecessors, who worked under legal contracts. In fact, in many cases the post-1964 illegal entrants had themselves worked in the United States as *braceros* up to 1984. This was the picture that emerged from data collected from apprehended "illegals" interviewed in the United States,[1] returned migrants interviewed in traditional "sending" communities,[2] and a national sample of 62,000 Mexican households interviewed in 1978 by Centro Nacional de Información y Estadisticas del Trabajo (CENIET), a Mexican government agency.[3]

[1] David S. North and Marion F. Houstoun, *The Characteristics and Role of Illegal Aliens in the U.S. Labor Market: An Exploratory Study* (Washington, 1976).

[2] Wayne A. Cornelius, "Outmigration from Rural Mexican Communities," in Interdisciplinary Communications Program, *The Dynamics of Migration: International Migration,* ICP Occasional Monograph Series, vol. 5, no. 2 (Washington, 1976); Wayne A. Cornelius, *Mexican Migration to the United States: Causes, Consequences, and U.S. Responses,* monograph C/78–9 (Cambridge, Mass., 1978); Raymond E. Wiest, "Wage-Labor Migration and the Household in a Mexican Town," *Journal of Anthropological Research* 29 (1973), 180–209; Raymond E. Wiest, "Implications of International Labor Migration for Mexican Rural Development," in Fernando Cámara and Robert Van Kemper, eds., *Migration Across Frontiers: Mexico and the United States* (Albany, N.Y., 1979), 85–97.

[3] Jorge A. Bustamante and Gerónimo Martínez, "Unauthorized Immigration from Mexico: Beyond Borders but Within Systems," *Journal of International Affairs* 33 (Fall–Winter

Because of their research designs and methods of data collection, these studies tended to understate the importance of permanent settlement in the United States by Mexican immigrant families. The 1980 U.S. Census, which some demographers believe counted a substantial portion of the illegal aliens in the United States at that time, found that most Mexicans were living with their immediate relatives.[4] To the extent that living with their families in the United States can be treated as a proxy for permanent settlement, the 1980 U.S. Census depicted a much more settled stock of Mexican immigrants than the stereotypic illegal alien population dominated by transient, mostly male, farmworkers living on their own or with unrelated persons. Of course, those enumerated in the U.S. Census were supposed to be settlers rather than sojourners, so Mexican migrants who stay for only a short time are virtually unrepresented in the census data. But evidence from more recent studies done on both sides of the border, using methodologies that enable us to differentiate with much greater precision among the various fractions of the stock and flow of migrants, have confirmed that Mexican migration to the United States has become much more heterogeneous, in terms of settlement patterns, gender, legal status, employment experience before and after migration to the United States, and in other ways—so much so that it increasingly defies generalization.

I hypothesize that the erosion of the stereotypic illegal alien population, which probably began in the late 1960s or early 1970s, has been intensified during the last ten years by four principal factors: (1) changes in the U.S. economy that have affected the nature and magnitude of the demand for Mexican immigrant labor, (2) the long-running economic crisis in Mexico, (3) the 1986 U.S. Immigration and Reform Act (IRCA), and (4) the maturation of transnational migrant networks, whose formation was initiated by earlier waves of migrants to the United States.

Origins in Mexico

In the last ten to fifteen years, Mexican migration to the United States has become increasingly diversified in terms of its points of origin in Mex-

---

1979), 265–84; Carlos H. Zazueta and Manuel García y Griego, *Los trabajadores mexicanos en Estados Unidos: Resultados de la encuesta nacional de emigración a la frontera norte del país y a los Estados Unidos* (Mexico City, 1982); Susan Ranney and Sherrie Kossoudji, "Profiles of Temporary Mexican Labor Migration to the United States," *Population and Development Review* 9 (1983), 475–93.

[4] Robert Warren and Jeffrey S. Passel, "A Count of the Uncountable: Estimates of Undocumented Aliens Counted in the 1980 United States Census," *Demography* 24 (Aug. 1987), 375–93; George J. Borjas, *Friends or Strangers: The Impact of Immigrants on the U.S. Economy* (New York, 1990).

ico. In 1973, 47.4 percent of the undocumented Mexicans apprehended in the San Diego area—which accounts for more than 40 percent of all apprehensions along the U.S.-Mexico border—originated in just two states: Jalisco and Michoacán. Other major sending states were Baja California Norte, Sinaloa, and Guerrero.[5] These data, from a sample of 3,204 "I-213" forms completed in the San Diego Border Patrol sector, reflect the high concentration within states like Jalisco and Michoacán of towns and rural communities that have built up their own multigenerational traditions of migration to California.

More recent data on Mexican migrants in southern California show greater diversity in states of origin within Mexico. In a random sample of 871 illegal Mexican entrants apprehended by the U.S. Border Patrol in the San Diego sector during 1987, only 28.7 percent had originated in Jalisco or Michoacán.[6] Among Mexicans (both legal immigrants and unauthorized migrants) employed in one hundred southern California nonagricultural firms in 1987–1988, 37.8 percent had resided in Jalisco or Michoacán just before their most recent migration to the United States (see Table 1). Twenty-seven out of Mexico's 32 states had sent migrants to these firms. An even more dispersed pattern is shown in our data collected from recently arrived, job-seeking, unauthorized migrants in southern California in 1987–1988 (Table 2, column 2). Jalisco and Michoacán accounted for just 21.9 percent of these post-IRCA migrants, while six nontraditional sending states (the Federal District, Puebla, Hidalgo, Estado de México, Morelos, and Oa-

[5] W. Tim Dagodag, "Illegal Mexican Immigration to California from Western Mexico," in Robert C. Jones, ed., *Patterns of Unauthorized Migration: Mexico and California* (Totowa, N.J., 1984), 61–73; Richard C. Jones, "Macro-Patterns of Unauthorized Migration Between Mexico and the U.S.," in Richard C. Jones, ed., *Patterns of Unauthorized Migration: Mexico and California* (Totowa, N.J., 1984), 45–49.

[6] Unpublished tabulation provided by the Statistics Division, U.S. Immigration and Naturalization Service, Washington, Apr. 1990. The data were drawn from a borderwide sample of 1,575 "I-213" forms filled out by Border Patrol agents on apprehended Mexicans (see John A. Bjerke and Karen K. Hess, "Selected Characteristics of Illegal Aliens Apprehended by the U.S. Border Patrol," paper presented at the Annual Meeting of the Population Association of America, May 1987). The sampling interval was one out of every 500 Mexican I-213 forms. The sampling error for migrants originating in Jalisco was plus or minus 2.3 percentage points, and 2.4 percent for those originating in Michoacán (95 percent confidence level). It must be kept in mind that this sample was designed to represent those clandestine entrants who were apprehended by the U.S. Border Patrol (about 97 percent of whom, in recent years, have been Mexican nationals); it is not necessarily representative of the overall flow of unauthorized aliens into California. Information on state-of-origin within Mexico is collected continuously by the U.S. Border Patrol, as part of the I-213 forms completed on each apprehended alien. However, this information is not keyed into the INS's computerized database on apprehensions, because of a shortage of data-entry personnel; hence the need to draw special samples of I-213 forms.

TABLE I

Points of Origin of Mexican Immigrants Employed in Southern California

State	Birthplace (N = 315)	Last place of residence before most recent migration to U.S. (N = 324)
Baja California Norte	8.6%	20.4%
Jalisco	24.8	18.8
Michoacán	13.0	11.1
Federal District (Mexico City)	6.7	9.9
Guerrero	9.8	7.1
Guanajuato	5.7	4.6
Oaxaca	4.1	3.4
Zacatecas	3.8	3.1
Nayarit	2.9	2.2
Chihuahua	1.6	1.9
Durango	2.5	1.9
Sinaloa	1.0	1.9
Puebla	1.6	1.5
Querétaro	1.3	1.5
Colima	1.6	1.2
Edo. de México (mostly Mexico City)	1.6	1.2
Sonora	1.9	1.2
Yucatán	1.0	1.2
Coahuila	1.0	0.9
Morelos	2.2	0.9
San Luis Potosí	1.6	0.9
Aguascalientes	0.6	0.3
Nuevo León	0.3	0.3
Tlaxcala	0.3	0.3
Veracruz	0.0	0.3
Hidalgo	0.3	0.0
Tamaulipas	0.3	0.0

SOURCE: Personal interviews with Mexican-born workers employed in 100 "immigrant-dependent" firms in San Diego, Orange, and Los Angeles counties, conducted in 1987–88 by the Center for U.S.-Mexican Studies.

xaca) accounted for 45.5 percent.[7] The state of Guerrero, while previously among the major sending states for Mexican migration to the

[7] For most of this century, about eight Mexican states have contributed the bulk of Mexican migrants to California (70 percent or more, according to most estimates). However, it has not always been the *same* eight states. For example, Sonora and Coahuila were important sending states in the 1920s, but are no longer important sources. The four entities that consistently have ranked among the top sending states are Jalisco, Michoacán, Guanajuato, and Zacatecas (see Jones, "Macro-Patterns of Unauthorized Migration Between Mexico and the U.S."). These, more than any others, merit the label "traditional sending states."

TABLE 2

Points of Origin of Recently Arrived Unauthorized Mexican Migrants
to Southern California

State	Birthplace (N = 184)	Last place of residence before migrating to U.S. (N = 187)
Federal District (Mexico City)	9.8%	17.7%
Guanajuato	11.4	11.2
Michoacán	12.5	10.7
Puebla	8.7	8.0
Guerrero	10.3	7.5
Hidalgo	7.1	7.0
Jalisco	5.4	5.9
Edo. de México (mostly Mexico City)	*6.0*	*5.4*
Baja California Norte	1.1	4.3
Morelos	3.8	3.7
Oaxaca	5.4	3.7
Chihuahua	2.2	2.7
Nayarit	2.2	2.1
Chiapas	1.6	1.6
Querétaro	1.6	1.6
Sinaloa	1.6	1.6
Sonora	2.7	1.6
Veracruz	1.6	1.1
Zacatecas	2.2	1.1
Aguascalientes	0.5	0.5
Colima	0.5	0.5
Nuevo León	0.5	0.5
Durango	1.1	0.0

SOURCE: Personal interviews with job-seeking, unauthorized migrants who arrived in San Diego, Orange, and Los Angeles counties in 1987 or 1988, conducted by the Center for U.S.-Mexican Studies.

United States, increased its relative contribution to the migrant flow in the 1980s.[8]

The increasing importance of the Mexico City metropolitan area (the Federal District and contiguous municipalities in the state of Mexico) as a source for unauthorized migration to the United States in recent years is particularly striking. Before the 1980s, the Federal District never

[8] This increase in contribution is reflected in data collected by El Colegio de la Frontera Norte, Tijuana, and Baja California (Jorge A. Bustamante, "Measuring the Flow of Unauthorized Immigrants: Research Findings from the Zapata Canyon Project," in Cornelius and Bustamante, eds., *Mexican Migration to the United States* [1990], 95–106), and two surveys conducted in southern California by the Center for U.S.-Mexican Studies, UCSD, in 1981–82. See Cornelius, Chávez, and Jones, *Mexican Immigrants and Access to Health Care*. Also, for 1987–88, see Wayne A. Cornelius, "The United States' Demand for Mexican Labor," in *Mexican Migration to the United States*, 25–47.

ranked among the top seven sending states. Several sample surveys conducted among apprehended Mexican illegal entrants during the 1970s found that *capitalinos* constituted from 0.6 to 3.0 percent of those interviewed.[9] The Mexico City metropolitan area accounted for only 3 percent of the unauthorized Mexican migrants apprehended in the San Diego sector in 1973;[10] in a 1987 sample of "illegals" apprehended in the same sector, it accounted for 8.2 percent.[11] Among 4,269 would-be illegal entrants interviewed from August 1987 through April 1989 as they prepared to cross the border in the Tijuana area, 11.7 percent came from the Mexico City metropolitan area.[12] The Federal District was the fourth most important sending state (after Michoacán, Jalisco, and Oaxaca) among migrants represented in this sample. Another study, based on interviews with 656 apprehended unauthorized immigrants interviewed in Laredo, Texas, in the first half of 1986, found that the Federal District was the third most important state of origin—accounting for 9.6 percent of the sample—behind Nuevo León and Guerrero.[13] As shown in Tables 1 and 2, among our 1987–1988 interviewees in southern California, the Mexico City metropolitan area was the top-ranking sending area for recently arrived unauthorized migrants (23.1 percent of the sample, combining those whose last place of residence was either the Federal District or the State of Mexico), and the fourth most important sending area for more settled, employed immigrants (11.1 percent of the sample). In sum, the available evidence indicates that at least one out of ten Mexican migrants entering the United States clandestinely in recent years has come from their country's largest city.

Such evidence suggests that while traditional source areas have by no means dropped out of the U.S.-bound migration flow, important new

[9] Jorge A. Bustamante, "Emigración indocumentada a los Estados Unidos," in Centro de Estudios Internacionales, *Indocumentados: mitos y realidades* (Mexico City, 1979), 33–35.

[10] Jones, "Macro-Patterns of Unauthorized Migration Between Mexico and the U.S.," 45.

[11] Data for this observation was obtained from the Statistics Division, U.S. Immigration and Naturalization Service, in particular, the above-referenced sample of I-213 forms completed in the San Diego sector during 1987. The sampling error for migrants originating in the Federal District was plus or minus 1.5 percentage points; for those originating in the state of Mexico, it was 1.1 percentage points.

[12] Unpublished data was provided by the Canyon Zapta Project, El Colegio de la Frontera Norte (COLEF), Tijuana, Baja California, March 1990. The figure for the Mexico City metropolitan area combines the shares of migrants from the Federal District (9.8 percent) and from the state of Mexico (1.9 percent). Each weekend since August 1987, COLEF's research project has interviewed 75 persons in Tijuana, selected at random from those gathered at the two points of entry most frequented by migrants attempting clandestine entry into California. See Jorge A. Bustamante, "Measuring the Flow of Unauthorized Immigrants," 95–106.

[13] Khosrow Fatemi, "The Unauthorized Immigrant: A Socioeconomic Profile," *Journal of Borderlands Studies* vol. 2, no. 2, (Fall 1987), 85–99.

ones have come "on stream" in recent years.[14] The economic crisis of the
1980s—which reduced real wages for most Mexicans by 40 to 50 percent—propelled into the migratory flow people from families, communities, and states without a long history of U.S.-bound migration. And
the 1986 U.S. immigration law has not prevented the formation of new
migrant networks originating in these nontraditional sending areas. To
the contrary, the extensive publicity surrounding IRCA's legalization and
Replenishment Agricultural Worker (RAW) programs seems to have attracted into the migratory flow persons from communities and states that
heretofore had not participated significantly.[15]

Mexican migrants to the United States in the 1980s included skilled,
urban-born workers from Mexico's principal cities, as well as destitute
campesinos from some of Mexico's most underdeveloped states, such as
Guerrero, Oaxaca, Hidalgo, and Puebla. These states all have large in-
digenous populations.[16] It is significant that several of the nontraditional

[14]Nor does the available evidence indicate that *within* principal sending states U.S.-
bound emigration has become less geographically concentrated than in previous decades.
On the contrary, a sample of U.S. Border Patrol apprehension records for the 1983–1986
period shows that the bulk of unauthorized migration from Mexico to the United States
continued to originate in a relatively small number of highly migration-prone municipios.
In this study, only 141 municipios of a total of 2,394 represented in the sample sent more
than five unauthorized migrants to the United States. See Richard C. Jones, "Micro Source
Regions of Mexican Undocumented Migration," *National Geographic Research* vol. 4,
no. 1 (1988), 11–22.

[15]The same effect was observed in connection with the *bracero* program of contract
labor importation, implemented beginning in 1942 (see Jorge Durand, "Los migradólares,"
Argumentos [Nov. 1988], 12). In 1989, the RAW program, which would provide short-
term visas to foreign agricultural workers, attracted some 650,000 applicants, virtually all
of them Mexican nationals. These applicants—the majority of whom are already working
in the United States, mostly in California—are now in a registry maintained by the INS,
awaiting the issuance of RAW visas. No such visas have been issued for 1990, and there is
substantial doubt whether any will be issued in the remaining three years of the RAW
program authorized by the U.S. Congress as part of IRCA, because the U.S. Departments
of Agriculture and Labor have determined through national sample surveys of farmworkers
and employers that there is an ample supply of legal resident farmworkers to meet anticipated demands for labor in perishable crop agriculture. The government surveys and determinations of the farm-labor demand and supply will be repeated annually through 1993,
at which time Congress will reassess the RAW program.

[16]On the "new" migration of Oaxacan Indians (esp. from the Mixteca region) to Cali-
fornia, Oregon, and Washington state, which actually began in the late 1960s, see Michael
Kearney, "Integration of the Mixteca and the Western U.S.-Mexican Border Region via
Migratory Wage Labor," in Ina Rosenthal-Urey, ed., *Regional Impacts of U.S.-Mexican
Relations*, Monograph no. 16 (La Jolla, Calif., 1986), 71–102; Carole Nagengast and
Michael Kearney, "Mixtec Ethnicity: Social Identity, Political Consciousness, and Political
Activism," *Latin American Research Review* vol. 25, no. 2 (1990), 61–91; Carol Zabin,
"New Migrants in California Agriculture: Farmworkers from Oaxaca," unpublished paper,
Center for U.S.-Mexican Studies, University of California, San Diego, 1990. For many Mix-

TABLE 3

Step-Wise Mexican Migration to Southern California via Large Cities in Mexico

	No. of step-wise migrants in	
Migration sequence	Sample of employed migrants (N = 320)	Sample of recently arrived migrants (N = 184)
Birthplace→Mexico City→S. Calif.	15 (4.7%)	18 (9.8%)
Birthplace→Guadalajara→S. Calif.	8 (2.5%)	3 (1.6%)
Birthplace→León, Gto.→S. Calif.	1 (0.3%)	3 (1.6%)
Birthplace→Baja Calif. N.*→S. Calif.	41 (12.8%)	6 (3.3%)
Total	65 (20.3%)	30 (16.3%)

SOURCE: Personal interviews with Mexican workers in San Diego, Orange, and Los Angeles counties, conducted by the Center for U.S.-Mexican Studies, 1987–1988.
* Includes cities of Tijuana, Mexicali, and Ensenada.

areas now sending migrants to the United States are among the Mexican states most adversely affected by the economic crisis of the 1980s (the Federal District, Morelos, Hidalgo, all of whose economies contracted by more than 2 percent during the 1980–1985 period; and Guerrero and Puebla, whose economies contracted by 0.1–2.0 percent in the same years).

Another indication that the economic crisis of the 1980s pushed more residents of Mexico's principal cities into the U.S.-bound migration stream is provided by a comparison of migrants' birthplaces with their last place of residence in Mexico before migration. As shown in Table 3, one of five migrants employed in our 1987–1988 sample of southern California firms were "step-migrants," who had moved initially to a major Mexican city and subsequently to California. Sixteen percent of our sample of recently-arrived, job-seeking, unauthorized migrants in southern California also came via one of these Mexican cities.[17] Rather than simply absorbing internal migrants from the countryside and provincial cities as they have done for many years, Mexico's large urban centers

tecos, the agricultural areas of Baja California and the city of Tijuana have become important way-stations. See Everardo Garduño, Efraín García, and Patricia Morán, *Mixtecos en Baja California: El caso de San Quintín* (Mexicali, Baja Calif., 1989).

[17] This pattern of stepwise migration to California was not common in the 1960s or 1970s. For example, in Dagodag's sample of apprehended unauthorized aliens, there was a very close (98 percent) correspondence between migrants' birthplace and their last place of residence in Mexico prior to migrating to the United States. See W. Tim Dagodag, "Illegal Mexican Immigration to California from Western Mexico," 64.

today are serving increasingly as platforms for migration to the United States. In the 1980s, internal migrants encountered saturated labor markets, skyrocketing living costs, dangerously high levels of air pollution, and rising crime in Mexico City and other large cities. Having failed to solve their economic problems there, many of them headed for cities in the United States.

As our data suggest, the native-born populations of large Mexican cities have also become increasingly important sources of migration to the United States. Further support for this contention comes from several surveys conducted among the population of Guadalajara during the 1980s by Agustín Escobar Latapí and Mercedes González de la Rocha. They found that in the 1982–1987 period, 23 percent of Guadalajara households were receiving regular cash remittances from household members living in the United States. Additional households had immediate kin in the United States who did not remit income to their Guadalajara relatives. In a separate 1982 sample of 1,223 Guadalajara workers in manufacturing, construction, and public-sector manual labor, 18.3 percent had worked in the United States. Another sample of Guadalajara manufacturing workers, interviewed in 1987, reported fewer sojourns in the United States. The researchers believe that this difference was not caused by fewer workers migrating to the United States, but occurred because more of them were staying there longer.[18]

This phenomenon is consistent with the widely held notion that, in relative terms, the economic crisis from which Mexico has suffered since 1982 has affected urban dwellers (especially residents of the largest cities) even more severely than the rural population. Prior to the economic crisis and the government austerity measures that it provoked, Mexico City and other large urban centers were heavily subsidized as places to live and work. Moreover, they were major centers of government employment, and the wages of government workers filtered back into the general urban economy. Therefore, crisis-induced austerity has disproportionately impacted Mexico's large cities.[19]

Even with a sustained economic recovery in the 1990s, we can anticipate that by the end of this decade the majority of new (first-time) Mexi-

[18] Unpublished tabulations provided by Agustín Escobar-Latapí and Mercedes González de la Rocha (Centro de Investigaciones y Estudios Superiores en Antropología Social-Occidente, Guadalajara).

[19] Agustín Escobar-Latapí Mercedes González de la Rocha, and Bryan Roberts, "Migration, Labor Markets, and the International Economy: Jalisco, Mexico, and the United States," in Jeremy Eades, ed., *Migrants, Workers, and the Social Order*, Monograph no. 26 (Washington, 1987), 42–64.

can migrants to the United States will come from urban Mexico. This trend reflects not only the emptying-out of traditional rural sending communities, as urbanization proceeds, but also the saturation of labor markets in Mexico's largest cities. Over half of the Mexican population now lives in large-scale urban areas (one out of every four in the Mexico City metropolitan area alone), and rates of labor force growth in these cities remain quite high despite declining fertility.

CALIFORNIA: THE PREFERRED DESTINATION

One of the constants in the profile of Mexican migration to the United States in recent decades is the leading role of California as a destination. The 1978 national survey of households in Mexico by CENIET found that California was the destination of 47.3 percent of Mexican migrants to the United States (49.2 percent of "long-stayers").[20] Although many parts of the United States attract Mexican labor—including the Pacific Northwest, Chicago and other midwestern cities, parts of the Southeast, eastern Pennsylvania, and even New York City—California now appears to be the preferred destination for the majority of Mexico's U.S.-bound workers and their dependents. This trend is reflected in national-level statistics on legal immigration and the unauthorized alien population, evidence gathered in Mexican sending communities, and applications for legalization under the two "amnesty" programs created by IRCA.

INS statistics show that since the 1970s California has absorbed about half of the total flow of legal immigrants from Mexico. In recent years, four of ten metropolitan areas receiving the most legal Mexican immigrants have been located in California (Los Angeles-Long Beach, San Diego, Anaheim-Santa Ana, and Riverside-San Bernardino); these and seven other California urban areas accounted for 50 percent of all Mexican legal immigrants admitted to the United States in fiscal year 1988.[21] The Los Angeles-Long Beach metropolitan area received 6.6 times more legal Mexican immigrants than any other metropolitan statistical area in the country.[22]

[20] "Long-stayers" (designated as "Population V" in the CENIET survey) were defined as Mexicans 15 years of age or older who were in the United States working or seeking work at the time of the December 1978 survey—a month when most short-term or seasonal Mexican migrants traditionally have returned to their home communities. See Zazueta and García y Griego, *Los trabajadores mexicanos en Estados Unidos.*

[21] The other seven principal receiving metropolitan statistical areas in California were San Jose, Oakland, Oxnard-Ventura, Fresno, San Francisco, Sacramento, and Stockton, in order of importance.

[22] INS, *1988 Statistical Yearbook of the Immigration and Naturalization Service* (Washington, 1989), Table 18, p. 38.

It is probable that the distribution of unauthorized Mexican migrants is roughly the same as previously, because most of these migrants are now part of extended-family networks anchored by long-staying legal immigrants in the United States. Jeffrey Passel and Karen Woodrow have estimated that 67 percent of Mexican undocumented aliens counted in the 1980 U.S. Census lived in California.[23] One-third of all censused, unauthorized immigrants in the United States (of all nationalities) were located in the Los Angeles metropolitan area alone.[24] Another study, based on a large, comprehensive sample of INS apprehension records covering the period from 1983 to 1986, found that among the thirty-five Mexican municipios having the highest density of unauthorized migrants to the United States per 1,000 residents, more than half sent workers principally to a California destination.[25]

Studies done at points of origin in Mexico have often found even higher proportions of California-bound migrants. In our study of three sending communities in the states of Jalisco, Michoacán, and Zacatecas, we found that among those residents who were considering a permanent or long-term move to the United States, more than 70 percent planned to go to California. California was even more dominant as a destination for short-term labor migrants from these communities. Among all residents aged 15 to 64 who had ever migrated to the United States, 81.7 percent had gone most recently to California, followed by Oklahoma (5.7 percent), Texas (5.0 percent), and Illinois (3.1 percent). Two of the three communities send virtually all of their migrants to California (95.5 percent and 99.0 percent, respectively); in the other community, 50.9 percent of those with U.S. migratory experience had chosen California as their most recent destination.

Another indicator of California's predominance in the Mexican migration stream is the distribution of applications for the general (pre-1982 arrival) and Special Agricultural Worker (SAW) legalization programs created by IRCA. California accounted for more than 54.4 percent of total applicants for the general amnesty program and 53 percent of the SAW applicants—far more than any other state.[26] The Los Angeles-Long

[23] Jeffrey S. Passel, and Karen A. Woodrow, "Geographic Distribution of Unauthorized Immigrants: Estimates of Unauthorized Aliens Counted in the 1980 U.S. Census by State," *International Migration Review* 18 (1984), 651.

[24] Unpublished data tabulations by Jeffrey S. Passel, U.S. Bureau of the Census, 1985.

[25] Richard C. Jones, "Micro Source Regions of Mexican Undocumented Migration," Table 2, p. 16.

[26] U.S. Immigration and Naturalization Service (INS), "Provisional Legalization Application Statistics," Statistics Division, Office of Plans and Analysis, U.S. Immigration and Naturalization Service (16 May 1990).

Beach metropolitan area alone generated 36 percent of the national total of applications for the general "amnesty" program, and 24 percent of the SAW applicants. Together, the general amnesty program and the SAW program may have legalized more than 1.5 million Mexican immigrants in California's work force.[27]

A substantial portion of the recent growth of California's Mexican immigrant population is the inevitable product of the maturation of immigrant networks that began to form in the early 1950s.[28] Data from sending-

[27] The final number of legalized aliens will not be known for some time. Those who secured temporary legal status under the general amnesty program—70 percent of whom were citizens of Mexico—had until sometime in 1989 or 1990 (depending on the date when their temporary *permiso* was issued) to apply for permanent legal residency. They must also meet English proficiency and requirements for knowledge of U.S. history during this period in order to retain their legal status. As of July 1990, more than 100,000 of the 900,000 persons who were legalized provisionally under the general amnesty program in California had not yet filed their "Phase II" (permanent residence) applications and were at risk of losing their legal status. Another complicating factor is the apparently high degree of fraud among applicants for the SAW legalization program. Only 250,000 to 350,000 SAW applicants were originally expected; 1,276,682 applications—82 percent from Mexican citizens—were actually filed nationwide by the November 30, 1988 deadline, leading some observers to argue that the SAW program had been "too successful." Researchers at the University of California, Davis have estimated that as many as two-thirds of the SAW applications from California could be fraudulent. See Philip L. Martin, "Harvest of Confusion: Immigration Reform and California Agriculture," *International Migration Review* vol. 24, no. 1 (Spring 1990), 69–95; Philip L. Martin and J. Edward Taylor, "California Farm Workers and the SAW Legalization Program," *California Agriculture* (Nov.–Dec. 1988), 4–6. My own research conducted in three Mexican sending communities in 1988–89 suggests that 76 percent of SAW applicants from those communities could actually have qualified, although the eligibility rate varied greatly from one community to another (the range was 42 percent to 92 percent). By May 1990, the INS has denied only 3.9 percent of total SAW applications, but 49 percent of the applications remained to be adjudicated (see INS, "Provisional Legalization Application Statistics").

[28] Roger C. Rouse, "Mexican Migration to the United States: Family Relations in the Development of a Transnational Migrant Circuit," Ph.D. diss., Stanford University, 1989; Richard Mines, *Developing a Community Tradition of Migration: A Field Study in Rural Zacatecas, Mexico, and California Settlement Areas*, Monograph no. 3 (La Jolla, Calif., 1981); Richard Mines, "Network Migration and Mexican Rural Development: A Case Study," in Robert C. Jones, ed., *Patterns of Unauthorized Migration: Mexico and the United States* (Totowa, N.J., 1984), 136–55; Joshua S. Reichert amd Douglas S. Massey, "Patterns of U.S. Migration from a Mexican Sending Community: A Comparison of Legal and Illegal Migrants," *International Migration Review* 13 (1979), 599–623; Douglas S. Massey, Rafael Alarcón, and Jorge Durand, *Return to Aztlán: The Social Process of International Migration from Western Mexico* (Berkeley, Calif., 1987); Omar Fonseca, "De Jaripo a Stockton, Calif.: Un caso de migración en Michoacán," in Thomas Calvo and Gustavo López, eds., *Movimientos de población en el Occidente de México* (Mexico City and Zamora, Mich., 1988), 359–72; Celestino Fernández, "Migración hacia los Estados Unidos: Caso Santa Inés, Michoacán," in Gustavo López Castro and Sergio Pardo Galván, eds., *Migración en el Occidente de México* (Zamora, Mich., 1988), 113–24; Gustavo López, *La casa dividida: Un estudio de caso sobre la migración a Estados Unidos en un pueblo michoacano* (Zamora, Mich., 1986).

community studies indicate that the social networks linking these communities to U.S. receiving areas have become the key factor affecting the choice of migration destinations. Among the interviewees in the three rural sending communities that we studied in 1988–89 who were considering permanent emigration, 45.1 percent explained their choice of destination by citing the presence of relatives and friends in that place, and an additional 14.6 percent mentioned job opportunities (in many cases, to be arranged by relatives) as the principal attraction. New migrants generally tend to follow their predecessors, settling in the same U.S. communities and often working in the same firms, where they will be more likely to have social support as well as assistance in finding jobs and housing.

Migration based on social networks does not necessarily tie a Mexican sending community to a single receiving area within the United States. While cases of "specialization"—migration to a single destination—can be found, the more common pattern entails multiple migration networks leading to a variety of U.S. communities, both urban and rural. For example, in a 1975–76 study of Unión de San Antonio, a town in the Los Altos region of Jalisco, I found that emigrants from that community were living in 110 different U.S. localities, 57 of which were in California.[29] Another community in the same municipio, studied in 1975–1976 and again in 1988–1989, had established immigrant networks linking it to the San Francisco Bay area, the Sacramento area, Watsonville, Los Angeles, Palm Springs, and other California cities; several cities in Texas and Illinois; Oklahoma City; Las Vegas, Nevada; and agricultural towns in the states of Oregon and Washington.[30] In the case of Las Animas, Zacatecas, Richard Mines found concentrations of *Animeños* working in four different agricultural towns in California and four urban areas in 1977.[31] Emigrants from this and other long-time, labor-exporting sending communities that we have studied in Mexico have dispersed geographically within California in the last two decades. Established migrant communities in the initial receiving areas have served as springboards for "settled-out" immigrants to move elsewhere in search of higher-paying, more stable (usually nonagricultural) employment opportunities.[32]

[29] Cornelius, "Outmigration from Rural Mexican Communities."

[30] Cornelius, "Outmigration from Rural Mexican Communities"; and field research in Jalisco by the Center for U.S.-Mexican Studies, 1988–89.

[31] Mines, *Developing a Community Tradition of Migration.*

[32] Mines, "Network Migration and Mexican Rural Development," 136–55; Wayne A. Cornelius, "Labor Migration to the United States: Development Outcomes and Alternatives in Mexican Sending Communities," final report to the Commission for the Study of International Migration and Cooperative Economic Development (Washington, Mar. 1990).

California's attractiveness to the most recent wave of Mexican migrants also reflects the more robust, more diversified employment growth in that state, relative to other potential destinations. Following the 1980–1982 recession, a boom occurred in most sectors of the highly diversified California economy. Since 1986, this boom has coincided with a sharp contraction in employment opportunities in "oil-bust" Texas, whose economy only recently has begun to revive. In the last two decades, employment growth in California has been far more robust than in the United States as a whole. During the 1970s, for example, blue-collar jobs increased in California at twice the national rate, and manufacturing employment expanded at nearly four times the national rate.[33] This pattern continued in the 1980s, and during the first half of the present decade, economists estimate that the California economy will generate about 300,000 to 350,000 new jobs each year. From 1988 to 2000, one of every six jobs created in the United States—an estimated 3.4 million jobs—will be located in California.[34] While new technologies continue to eliminate many blue-collar jobs in heavy industry, data for the 1984–1989 period indicate that "low-tech" light manufacturing continues to expand in California and other western states, more than offsetting job losses due to automation in higher-technology industries.[35]

In addition to its overall dynamism and diversity, there are certain structural features of the contemporary California economy that increase the demand for immigrant labor. For example, the system of contracting out labor-intensive tasks to small, largely nonunion, immigrant-dominated firms in such industries as garment, electronics, and construction appears to be advancing more rapidly in California than in other parts of the nation.[36] And while the demand for entry-level work-

[33] Thomas Muller and Thomas J. Espenshade, *The Fourth Wave: California's Newest Immigrants* (Washington, 1985).

[34] Estimates by the Bank of America and Wells Fargo Bank, reported in *The Los Angeles Times*, 6 May 1990; and by the Bureau of Economic Analysis, U.S. Department of Commerce (Washington, 10 June 1990).

[35] David Birch, "The Contribution of New, Locally-Owned Firms to Growth in the U.S. Western Economy," paper presented at the first annual Broadmoor Symposium "Beyond Decline: America's Resurgence in the New Century," sponsored by the Center for the New West, Colorado Springs, Col. (22–23 Jan. 1990).

[36] Edna Bonacich, "Asian and Latino Immigrants in the Los Angeles Garment Industry: An Exploration of the Relationship Between Capitalism and Racial Oppression," Institute for Social Science Research, UCLA, *Working Papers in the Social Sciences* vol. 5, no. 13 (1990), 4; Wayne A. Cornelius, "The United States Demand for Mexican Labor," 25–47; M. Patricia Fernández-Kelly and Anna M. Garciá, "Hispanic Women and Homework: Women in the Informal Economy of Miami and Los Angeles," in Eileen Boris and Cynthia R. Daniels, eds., *Homework: Historical and Contemporary Perspectives on Paid Labor at Home* (Urbana, Ill., 1989), 165–79.

ers in manufacturing and construction is likely to remain strong, the largest numbers of new jobs to be created in California during the next twenty years will be relatively low-paying, low-skill, low-status jobs in restaurants, hotels, and other parts of the urban service sector— precisely the kinds of jobs that are increasingly shunned by young, better-educated, native-born Californians. The need for personal services among the rapidly expanding business-financial-professional elite has been a significant source of jobs for female immigrants in Los Angeles in recent years.[37] Similarly, Roger Rouse has described the most recent emigrants from Aguililla, Michoacán to Redwood City, California (a bedroom suburb of northern California's high-tech "Silicon Valley") as that community's janitors, dishwashers, gardeners, hotel workers, and house cleaners—"proletarian servants in the paragon of 'post-industrial' society."[38]

As long as California's economy continues to outperform the national economy, the state will be a strong magnet for future waves of Mexican migrants. Jobs in both California agriculture and nonagricultural industries are likely to remain plentiful, quick to obtain, and high-paying, at least in comparison with those in other southwestern states.[39] A strong feedback effect also operates, in which consumer spending by Mexican immigrants and their availability as a large, young, flexible labor pool stimulates the creation of new, locally-owned small businesses (especially in the service sector), while helping to retain older labor-intensive industries like garment and shoe manufacturing. This feedback effect is strongest in the largest metropolitan areas, where California's immigrant population is increasingly concentrated. Los Angeles, for example, became the principal manufacturing center in the United States during the 1980s because of its combination of "a first-world infrastructure and a third-world work force."[40] In the Los Angeles

[37] Rebecca Morales and Paul Ong, "Immigrant Women in Los Angeles," Institute for Social Science Research, UCLA, *Working Papers in the Social Sciences* 5 (1990).

[38] Roger C. Rouse, "Mexican Migration to the United States: Family Relations in the Development of a Transnational Migrant Circuit," Ph.D. diss., Stanford University, 1989.

[39] Based on field interviews with illegal border crossers conducted by El Colegio de la Frontera Norte in Tijuana and other Mexican border cities since 1986, Jorge Bustamante concludes that "at any given time, close to 60 percent of the total of unauthorized immigrants from Mexico in the United States can be found in the state of California, where employer demand for Mexican unauthorized immigrants is higher and more diversified than in any other state, according to our survey data." See Jorge A. Bustamante, "Measuring the Flow of Unauthorized Immigrants," 98.

[40] Philip L. Martin, "Testimony Before the Immigration Task Force of the Committee on Education and Labor, and the Subcommittee on Immigration, Refugees, and International Law," Washington, 1 Mar. 1990, p. 2.

area, the number of manufacturing jobs increased between 1969 and 1987, from 880,000 to 906,000, even as manufacturing employment fell in Chicago, New York, and other major metropolitan areas.[41] In addition to favorable labor-market conditions and mature immigrant networks, California offers to prospective migrants from Mexico a variety of other inducements, including a superior climate and—for those who enter clandestinely—a relatively easy point of entry, the border city of Tijuana.

The reservoir of potential California-bound migrants in Mexico is likely to remain quite large in the foreseeable future. One indicator comes from a national sample of 1,835 Mexicans living in 42 randomly selected towns and cities throughout the country, who were interviewed in August 1989 for *The Los Angeles Times* poll. Thirteen percent of this national sample had already been to California at least once, and 23 percent expressed a desire to live in the state (14 percent in Los Angeles alone)—far more than any other potential destination.[42] While the gap between preferences and actual behavior undoubtedly will prove to be quite large, such data are suggestive of the powerful attraction that California exerts upon would-be migrants in Mexico today.

GENDER, FAMILY, AND DURATION OF STAY

The shift from a migrant population consisting mainly of highly mobile, seasonally employed "lone males" (unmarried or unaccompanied by dependents) toward a more socially heterogeneous, year-round, de facto permanent Mexican immigrant population in the United States accelerated in the 1980s. To be sure, the absolute number of young, temporary Mexican male farmworkers in the United States did not decline during the 1970s and 1980s, but it grew slowly in absolute terms and, in relative terms, this fraction of the Mexican immigrant population was overtaken and overwhelmed by migrants who remained in the United States for long periods, accompanied by their dependents. Ethnographic and survey studies of both sending and receiving communities, interviews with would-be illegal migrants at the border, and INS apprehension statistics all show that there is now considerably more migration

[41] Rebecca H. Morales, "Transitional Labor in the Los Angeles Automobile Industry," in Wayne A. Cornelius, ed., *The Changing Role of Mexican Labor in the U.S. Economy: Sectoral Perspectives* (La Jolla, Calif., forthcoming).

[42] Unpublished data provided by *The Los Angeles Times* poll. The margin of error in this survey (*The Los Angeles Times* poll #192) is plus or minus 3 percentage points. As in all "national" sample surveys conducted in Mexico, the population residing in the smallest rural localities is underrepresented to some unknown degree.

by whole family units (moving together), more family-reunification migration (women and children joining family heads already established in the United States), and more migration by single women than there was a decade ago.[43]

Increased Female Migration

There are many indications that the female component of the Mexican migratory stock and flow has expanded in recent years. An analysis of data from the U.S. Census Bureau's Current Population Survey of June 1988 suggests that females may now constitute a majority of the "settled" undocumented immigrant population from Mexico.[44] Our data from traditional sending communities in Mexico show that the probability of migration to the United States—especially temporary migration—is still much higher among males than among females. Nevertheless, we found substantial female participation in U.S.-bound migration in certain communities and age groups, especially women currently in their twenties.[45] A study of Mexican immigrants residing in rural and urban areas of San Diego County conducted in 1981–82 found that female immigrants are especially likely to originate in urban areas of Mexico; almost two-thirds declared their place of origin to be a city.[46]

Increased female migration to the United States reflects, in part, generational changes in the attitudes and expectations of Mexican women. González de la Rocha has summarized her findings from a high-migration town in Jalisco as follows: "During the last three years more women have left the town to be reunited with their husbands in the United States. . . . Upon getting married, the woman no longer stays in the town. . . . The young women do not want to repeat the loneliness that their mothers

[43] Frank D. Bean, Thomas J. Espenshade, Michael J. White, and Robert F. Dymowski, "Post-IRCA Changes in the Volume and Composition of Unauthorized Migration to the United States: An Assessment Based on Apprehensions Data," in Frank D. Bean, Barry Edmonston, and Jeffrey Passel, eds., *Unauthorized Migration to California: IRCA and the Experience of the 1980s* (Washington, 1990); Bustamante, "Measuring the Flow of Unauthorized Immigrants," 95–106; Wayne A. Cornelius, "Impacts of the 1986 U.S. Immigration Law on Emigration from Rural Mexican Sending Communities," *Population and Development Review* vol. 15, no. 4, (Dec. 1989), 689–705; Cornelius, "Labor Migration to the United States."

[44] Karen A. Woodrow and Jeffrey S. Passel, "Post-IRCA Unauthorized Immigration to the United States: An Assessment Based on the June 1988 CPS," in Bean, Edmonston, and Passel, eds., *Unauthorized Migration to the United States* (1990).

[45] Wayne A. Cornelius, "The United States Demand for Mexican Labor," 30–31.

[46] Rosalía Solórzano Torres, "Female Mexican Immigrants in San Diego County," in Ruiz and Tiano, eds., *Women on the U.S.-Mexico Border* (1987), 41–59.

experienced nor the hardships that they had to endure [while their husbands worked in the United States]."[47]

The higher propensity of females to migrate to the United States in recent years is also a consequence of Mexico's economic crisis, which has driven more wives, single women, and children into the work force. Especially among Mexico's urban poor, the male family head's income is not nearly sufficient now to meet the family's needs.[48] Among our 1988–89 southern California sample of recently arrived undocumented migrants who still had no regular employment and were found looking for work in street-corner labor markets and other public areas, 8 percent were women; and among the male interviewees who were married, 17 percent had brought their spouses with them to southern California.[49]

IRCA also gave new impetus to female migration, by encouraging whole-family migration and family reunification in the United States. Frank Bean and his colleagues found that by the third year after IRCA's enactment, there was a statistically significant increase in the number and proportion of females and children being apprehended by the INS.[50] Another indicator of IRCA-related migration for family reunification is the 82 percent increase in the appearance at the U.S. Consulate in Tijuana of Mexicans seeking non-immigrant visas during the last quarter of 1989, as compared with the same period in 1988. Most of these visa applicants were dependents of persons who were granted amnesty under IRCA. In 1986, the U.S. Border Patrol apprehended and expelled an average of three to five unaccompanied children (ages 5 to 17) each day from California at Tijuana; in the first quarter of 1990, an average of fifteen such minors were returned to Mexico each day.[51]

In the immediate post-IRCA period, there was widespread fear in Mexican sending communities that the "door was closing" because of employer sanctions and the deadlines attached to the legalization programs created

---

[47] Mercedes González de la Rocha, "El poder de la ausencia: Mujeres y migración en una comunidad de Los Altos de Jalisco," paper presented at the 11th Cologuio de Antropología e Historia Regionales, Zamora, Mich., 25–27 Oct. 1989.

[48] Field studies in Guadalajara by Agustín Escobar Latapí and Mercedes González de la Rocha (CIESAS-Occidente, Guadalajara, Jalisco), 1982–1987.

[49] Fieldwork in 1987–88 by the Center for U.S.-Mexican Studies, University of California, San Diego.

[50] Bean, Espenshade, White, and Dymowski, "Post-IRCA Changes in Unauthorized Migration to the United States"; also, compare with Bjerke and Hess, "Characteristics of Illegal Aliens Apprehended by the U.S. Border Patrol."

[51] Data from the U.S. Consulate, Tijuana, and Baja California; and from Jorge Bustamante, El Colegio de la Frontera Norte, Tijuana, Baja Calif.

by the 1986 law.[52] Especially in the first half of 1988, thousands of undocumented women and children left Mexican sending communities with their husbands, many for the first time, in hopes of gaining legal-immigrant status.[53] Many others were summoned to the United States by family heads who had secured amnesty for themselves or made application for it; they used "coyotes" to guide them across the border. Many of these dependents were disappointed, since they could not possibly meet the five-year, continuous-U.S.-residence requirement for the general amnesty program. More of them were able to secure legalization under the SAW program, since the eligibility criteria and documentation requirements for that program were much less stringent than for the general amnesty program.[54]

Female emigration to the United States also has been increasing because of the abundance of new employment opportunities for which women are the preferred labor source. For example, there is a booming market in California's largest urban areas for undocumented female Mexican labor to provide child care, clean houses and offices, and iron clothes.[55] In the San Diego area, recently arrived female Mexican migrants now find house-

[52] Interestingly, the abrupt shift toward restrictive immigration laws and policies in Germany and other West European countries in the last half of the 1970s had a similar effect—increasing family reunification immigration and speeding up the process of permanent settlement in the host country. See Judith-Maria Buechler, "A Review: Guest, Intruder, Settler, Ethnic Minority, or Citizen—The Sense and Nonsense of Borders," in Hans Christian Buechler and Judith-Maria Buechler, eds., *Migrants in Europe: The Role of Family, Labor, and Politics* (Westport, Conn., 1987), 283–304; and James F. Hollifield, "Immigration Policy in France and Germany: Outputs Versus Outcomes," *The Annals of the American Academy of Political and Social Science* 485 (May 1986), 113–28.

[53] Fieldwork by the Center for U.S.-Mexican Studies in three rural sending communities in Zacatecas, Jalisco, and Michoacán, 1988–89; and a sample survey by Germán Vega (El Colegio de la Frontera Norte, Tijuana) in the municipio of Jalostotitlán, Jalisco, conducted Jan.–Mar. 1990. See also Nancy Cleeland, "Many More Women Decide to Flee Mexico," *San Diego Union* 27 Aug. 1989; and Agustín Escobar-Latapí and Mercedes González de la Rocha, "The Impact of IRCA on the Migration Patterns of a Community in Los Altos, Jalisco, Mexico," working paper no. 41 (Washington, Commission for the Study of International Migration and Cooperative Economic Development, June 1990).

[54] Experienced observers of the migratory flow from the state of Oaxaca to California have reported that IRCA's legalization programs stimulated a great deal of first-time migration by women and children in 1988 and 1989. They observed that male heads of the family already employed in California encouraged their dependents to join them there almost immediately after the head of the family applied for legalization. Since the vast majority of these family members could not qualify for amnesty themselves, and had entered California illegally, they are now "stuck" there, unable to travel to and from their home community as easily as the head of the family. (Unpublished research reported at a workshop "Oaxacan Migration to California's Agricultural Sector," Center for U.S.-Mexican Studies, University of California, San Diego, and California, San Diego, and California Institute of Rural Studies, 15 Feb. 1990.)

[55] Fieldwork by Rafael Alarcón and Macrina Cárdenas (El Colegio de Jalisco and Center for U.S.-Mexican Studies, University of California, San Diego) in the San Francisco Bay area, 1988.

cleaning work by going door-to-door, as males have done (for gardening work) for many years. In San Diego and other U.S. border cities, such as El Paso, Texas, domestic work has become institutionalized as an occupation performed almost exclusively by unauthorized female immigrants.[56] And Mexican immigrant women are still the preferred work force for low-level production jobs in California's garment firms, Silicon Valley semiconductor manufacturing firms, fruit and vegetable canneries, and packing houses.[57] Moreover, the recent relaxation of federal laws restricting "homework" for the apparel industry enables increased employment of recently arrived undocumented women in their own homes.[58]

Sojourners vs. Settlers

The shift from a temporary to a long-staying or permanent Mexican immigrant population in the United States was well underway by the 1970s,[59] and it accelerated in the 1980s. Among Mexican workers employed in southern California non-agricultural firms whom we interviewed in 1983–84, 50 percent stated that they definitely intended to stay in the United States permanently; the proportion of "permanent settlers" among Mexicans working in the same firms in 1987–88 was 69 percent. Traditional temporary migrants—those working about six months in the United States during each sojourn, and returning regularly to their home community—certainly have not disappeared, especially in the agricultural sector.[60] Even in urban areas, Mexican migrants still pre-

[56] Solórzano Torres, "Female Mexican Immigrants in San Diego County," 55–56; Vicki L. Ruiz, "By the Day or the Week: Mexicana Domestic Workers in El Paso," in Vicki L. Ruiz and Susan Tiano, eds., *Women on the U.S.-Mexico Border* (Boston, 1987), 61–76.

[57] Karen J. Hossfeld, "'Small, Foreign, and Female': Immigrant Women Workers and Racial Hiring Dynamics in Silicon Valley," paper presented at the Annual Meeting of the American Sociological Association, San Francisco, Sept. 1989; Gail Mummert, "Mujeres de migrantes y mujeres migrantes de Michoacán: Nuevos papeles para las que se quedan y para las que se van," in Calvo and López, eds., *Movimientos de población*, 290.

[58] In both the garment and electronics industries of California, large numbers of immigrant women are now employed as "homeworkers." See M. Patricia Fernández-Kelly and Anna M. García, "Economic Restructuring in California: The Case of Hispanic Women in the Garment and Electronics Industries of Southern California," in Wayne A. Cornelius, ed., *The Changing Role of Mexican Labor in the U.S. Economy: Sectoral Perspectives* (La Jolla, Calif., 1990).

[59] Harley Browning and Néstor Rodríguez, "The Migration of Mexican Indocumentados as a Settlement Process: Implications for Work," in George Borjas and Marta Tienda, eds., *Hispanics in the U.S. Economy* (Orlando, 1985); Cornelius, Chávez, and Jones, *Mexican Immigrants and Access to Health Care;* Maria de Lourdes Villar, "From Sojourners to Settlers: The Experience of Mexican Undocumented Migrants in Chicago," Ph.D. diss., Indiana Unversity, 1989.

[60] For example, Massey and his associates found that two-thirds to three-quarters of the household heads, and 55 to 65 percent of all U.S.-bound migrants from four Mexican sending communities surveyed in 1982, adopted a temporary migration strategy.

fer to think of themselves as sojourners rather than permanent settlers.[61] But the reality is that most of these urban-based immigrants are settled more-or-less permanently in the United States.

The shift toward more "settled-out" Mexican migrants in the United States is directly related to the maturation of transnational migrant networks during the last fifteen years. Kinship/friendship networks reduce the costs and risks of long-term stays in the United States and facilitate integration into U.S. society, and they can offer extensive support systems for dependent family members. U.S.-born children and wives quickly become strong supporters of remaining permanently in the United States.[62] Teenagers are attracted to the lifestyle of U.S. young people, and housewives find that domestic chores are considerably easier in the United States, with all its modern conveniences, than in Mexico. Financial obligations—debts owed to friends and relatives in the United States, home mortgages, and so forth—accumulate. All these factors strongly increase the probability of permanent settlement. Indeed, many long-staying Mexican immigrants, irrespective of their legal status, feel trapped in the United States by these family and financial circumstances.

Greater "settling-out" is also very much related to changes in the U.S. economy that have increased the demand for year-round low-skilled labor.[63] Even in agriculture, recent changes in crop mix and technology have made it possible for many growers to engage in year-round production and have increased the labor-intensity of agricultural production.[64] Thus, year-round employment in the United States has become a realistic option for a growing segment of the Mexican migrant population. Many of the firms and industries in which Mexican migrants are now employed—including construction, landscaping, light manufacturing, restaurants, and hotels—are still subject to seasonal or cyclical fluctuations

[61] Leo R. Chávez, "Settlers and Sojourners: The Case of Mexicans in California," Human Organization 47 (Summer 1988), 95–108; Rouse, "Mexican Migration to the United States."

[62] In a 1986 study of unauthorized Mexican and Central American immigrants in San Diego and Dallas, over 80 percent of the respondents believed that their children did not want to return to the parents' country of origin. See Leo R. Chávez and Estévan T. Flores, "Unauthorized Mexicans and Central Americans and the Immigration Reform and Control Act of 1986," in Center for Migration Studies, In Defense of the Alien 10 (1988), 137–56.

[63] Wayne A. Cornelius, "The United States Demand for Mexican Labor," 25–47.

[64] Juan Vicente Palerm, "Transformation in California Agriculture," UC MEXUS News (University of California, Riverside), nos. 21–22 (1987), 1–3; Juan Vicente Palerm, "Latino Settlements in California," in University of California Task Force on Senate Concurring Resolution no. 43, The Challenge: Latinos in a Changing California, (Riverside, Calif., University of California Consortium on Mexico and California, 1989), 149–67; Juan Vicente Palerm, The Formation and Extension of Chicano-Mexican Enclaves in Rural California (Sacramento, Calif., 1990).

in demand for their product or service. Nevertheless, it is usually possible for migrants to ride out these slack periods. Thus migrants have a strong incentive to remain in the United States, and their employers prefer to have them continuously available—if not always on the payroll.

Accordingly, increasing numbers of Mexicans are being forced to choose, finally, between long-term residence in Mexico and long-term residence in the United States. With the option of more economically secure, year-round residence in the United States now open to them, more migrants from traditional sending communities view migration to the United States as a permanent change in their life situation, instead of just a short-term income-earning strategy. And high-emigration communities in central Mexico are being transformed increasingly into rest-and-recreation centers for families whose principal base is now in the United States.[65]

EMPLOYMENT PATTERNS IN MEXICO AND THE UNITED STATES

The Exodus from Agriculture

Since the late 1960s, the share of Mexican migrants working in the agricultural sector of the U.S. economy has declined sharply. According to recent estimates, agriculture currently employs no more than 10 to 15 percent of the Mexican immigrants (legals and illegals) in California, Texas, and Arizona, and a much smaller proportion of the Mexicans working in Illinois.[66] Among the males born in Mexico who do not have U.S. citizenship included in the 1980 U.S. Census, only 17.3 percent of those who had moved to the United States between 1975 and 1980 were employed in agriculture (or mining) at the time of the census; and an even smaller proportion—10.4 percent—of post-1975 female Mexican immigrants were working in these sectors.[67] This occupational distribution is not surprising, since any census or household survey conducted in the United States will record very few temporary migrants, who are more likely to be agriculturally employed than permanent settlers from Mexico. This does not necessarily mean, however, that most temporary Mexican migrants are still employed in agriculture. In fact, only about one-third of the "short-stay" migrants to the United States detected in the 1978 CENIET survey of households in Mexico were employed in agri-

[65] Cornelius, "Labor Migration to the United States"; Rouse, "Mexican Migration to the United States."

[66] Steven P. Wallace, "Central American and Mexican Immigrant Characteristics and Economic Incorporation in California," *International Migration Review* 22 (1988), 664–65.

[67] Frank D. Bean and Marta Tienda, *The Hispanic Population of the United States* (New York, Russell Sage Foundation, Census Monograph Series, 1987), Table 4.12, p. 132.

culture in the United States.[68] And as noted below, there is more recent evidence from Mexico-based research indicating that the majority of unauthorized, mostly temporary migrants to the United States are now working in nonagricultural occupations.

Especially since the enactment of IRCA, there has been much speculation about the rate of attrition of Mexican labor from U.S. agriculture. In our recent fieldwork, we found that Mexican migrants with extensive employment experience in the U.S. agricultural sector are not abandoning farm work in large numbers; but young workers migrating for the first time in the 1970s and 1980s were much more likely to choose less arduous, higher-paying jobs in nonagricultural enterprises as their point of entry into the U.S. labor market, and to remain in urban occupations for the duration of their U.S. migratory careers. Those most committed to working in U.S. agriculture tend to be older men who began their migratory careers as agricultural workers and have remained in that sector, acquiring permanent legal immigrant status along the way.

Those who legalized themselves through the Special Agricultural Workers (SAW) program created by the 1986 U.S. immigration law are not required to keep working in the agricultural sector, and many of those who obtained SAW status actually had little or no previous agricultural employment experience. Among a statewide sample of applicants for SAW visas in California, only 28 percent gave farm work as their premigration occupation.[69] Moreover, only about one-third reported usually working in agriculture during the twelve months preceding the interview, and among those who had been agriculturally employed, 60 percent said that they planned to seek employment outside of agriculture. In this survey, urban-based SAW applicants are overrepresented (indeed, almost 50 percent of the SAW visa holders in this sample were drawn from Los Angeles County). Other surveys of SAW applicants in California have found higher levels of continued commitment to farm work.[70] Local labor-market conditions appear to have a major impact on rates of exit from agriculture. A 1989 survey conducted in southern California (mainly the Santa Ana area) and the northern California community of Watsonville found that the overwhelming majority of SAW applicants in Watsonville remained employed in agriculture (85 percent), while only

[68] Zazueta and García y Griego, *Los trabajadores mexicanos en Estados Unidos.*

[69] Comprehensive Adult Student Assessment System (CASAS), *A Survey of Newly Legalized Persons in California: Prepared for the California Health and Welfare Agency* (San Diego, Calif., 1989).

[70] *Ibid.,* 5–9.

TABLE 4

Sector of Employment of Migrants to the U.S. from
Three Rural Mexican Communities, Before and During Their
Most Recent Trip to the U.S.

Sector	Sector of employment before most recent migration (N = 631)	Sector of employment during most recent stay in U.S. (N = 891)
Agriculture	75.8%	41.0%
Services	5.4	15.2
Retail commerce*a*	5.9	12.5
Manufacturing	4.0	13.4
Construction	9.0	18.1

S O U R C E : Center for U.S.-Mexican Studies survey of three rural communities in Mexico, 1988–89. The sample consists of all members of 586 households in the three research communities who have ever migrated to the United States (N = 1,126). Unemployed, retired, student, and other economically inactive persons are excluded from the tabulations.
*a*Including restaurants.

one-third of the SAW applicants in southern California still worked in agriculture.[71] Clearly, it is premature to reach any general conclusions about the effect of IRCA's legalization programs on the sectoral distribution of Mexican migrants in the U.S. economy.

The longer-term exodus from agriculture is reflected in the data from our recent field studies on both sides of the border. As shown in Table 4, more than three-quarters of the economically active population in the rural sending communities that we have studied who had U.S. migratory experience were employed primarily in agriculture in their home towns immediately before their most recent trip to the United States.[72] However, only 41 percent worked in agriculture once they got there during their most recent U.S. sojourn. The proportion of migrants agriculturally employed in the United States varied considerably among the three communities (14.9 percent, 21.3 percent, and 88.6 percent, respectively). Seventy percent of the migrants in the three-community sample who were employed most recently in agricultural jobs in the United States were residents of a community in Michoacán that has long specialized

[71] Susan Gabbard and Luin Goldring, "Occupational Mobility of Current and Former Farmworkers: A Comparative Analysis in Two California Labor Markets," unpublished report prepared for the California Employment Development Department, Apr. 1990.
[72] Among those agriculturally employed in Mexico, 44.1 percent were landless laborers; 25.2 percent were sharecroppers; 21.9 percent were small private landowners or employed on the family's small private landholding; and 8 percent were *ejidatarios* or employed on the family's *ejidal* plot.

TABLE 5

Sector of Employment of Migrants to the U.S. from
Three Rural Mexican Communities, During Their Most Recent Trip
to the U.S., by Immigration Status

Sector	Legal immigrants (N = 257)	"Rodinos" (N = 157)	Unauthorized migrants (N = 466)
Agriculture	51.8%	66.2%	26.4%
Services	15.2	7.0	17.6
Retail commerce[a]	10.5	9.6	14.6
Manufacturing	12.5	7.0	16.1
Construction	10.1	10.2	25.3

SOURCE: Same as for Table 4.
NOTE: Chi-square = 103.59; significance: p < .0000
[a] Including restaurants.

in exporting labor to the strawberry fields of Watsonville, California. Even among migrants from this community, however, there is attrition out of the U.S. agricultural sector, especially among the youngest, better-educated migrants, who prefer to work in urban services. The data reported in Table 5 show that, contrary to the popular stereotype, unauthorized migrants from our Mexican research communities were much less likely to be agriculturally employed in the United States than legal immigrants and those who were in process of legalizing themselves under the 1986 U.S. immigration law (popularly known as "Rodinos").

The migration profile of Tlacuitapa, Jalisco—a community with about 2,300 inhabitants located in the Los Altos region of Jalisco—is particularly instructive. This community, which I initially studied in 1976 and restudied in 1988–89, sends some migrants to work in the orchards and flower fields of Oregon; but these agriculturally employed migrants are now outnumbered by those who go to Oklahoma City to work in highway and bridge construction, those who go to Las Vegas and Palm Springs to work in the hotel and restaurant industries, and those who migrate to the San Francisco Bay area to work in light industry and services. In 1976, 55.3 percent of Tlacuitapa natives who had migrated to the United States had worked most recently in agriculture; in our 1988–89 survey of the same community, only 21.3 percent were employed in agriculture during their most recent trip to the United States. Between 1976 and 1988–89, the proportion of the community's U.S.-bound migrants employed in service activities more than tripled, and those in retail commerce and manufacturing nearly doubled (see Table 6). Similarly, in a 1982 sample of Guadalajara residents with U.S. migra-

TABLE 6

*Sector of Employment in U.S., Among Migrants from a
Rural Mexican Sending Community, During Most Recent
Trip to the United States, 1976 and 1988–89*

Sector	1976 sample (N = 76)	1988–89 sample (N = 300)
Agriculture	55.3%	21.3%
Services	6.6	21.0
Retail commerce[a]	10.5	20.7
Manufacturing	9.2	16.3
Construction	14.5	20.7

SOURCE: Author's sample surveys in the community of Tlacuitapa, Jalisco. Unemployed, retired, student, other economically inactive persons, and missing cases are excluded from the tabulations.
[a] Including restaurants.

tory experience, 91 percent of those who had last migrated to the United States before 1962 had worked in agriculture, while 48 percent of those who had been in the United States between 1962 and 1972 and only 33 percent of those who had migrated after 1972 were agriculturally employed there.[73]

Most Mexican migrants to the United States today—both legal and unauthorized—are being absorbed into the urban service, construction, light manufacturing, and retail commerce sectors. In the service sector, Mexicans work primarily as janitors, dishwashers and busboys, gardeners, hotel workers, maintenance and laundry workers in hospitals and convalescent homes, car washers, house cleaners, and child-care providers.[74] The Mexicans filling these types of jobs are increasingly likely to be persons whose previous work experience, if any, has been limited to nonagricultural employment.[75] Among our sample of Mexican immigrants employed in southern California nonagricultural firms in 1987–88, only 18.4 percent had been working in agriculture prior to their most recent trip to the United States (excluding those who had been economically inactive before migration). Nearly 14.6 percent had been factory workers in Mexico. Skilled craftsmen, small business owners, restaurant workers, white-collar workers, and other urban service workers were significantly represented. However, agricultural and horticultural enter-

[73] Escobar-Latapí, González de la Rocha, and Roberts, "Migration, Labor Markets, and the International Economy," 42–64.
[74] Wayne A. Cornelius, "The United States Demand for Mexican Labor," 25–47.
[75] Bilateral Commission on the Future of U.S.-Mexican Relations, *The Challenge of Interdependence: Mexico and the United States* (Lanham, Md., 1988), 91–93.

prises that require only seasonal labor continue to attract mainly migrants with rural, agricultural backgrounds.

Wages and Impacts on U.S. Wage Levels

Recent field studies have found that the majority of both legal and unauthorized Mexican immigrants in California are employed in jobs paying between $4.25 (the state's legal minimum wage, as of 1 July 1988) and $6.00 per hour. Among our sample of 146 regularly employed, unauthorized immigrant workers in southern California in 1987–88, most of whom were interviewed when the state's legal minimum wage was $3.35 per hour, the median hourly wage was $4.98. Among 154 "illegals" who had applied for amnesty, the median wage being earned was $5.16.[76] These wage levels may be upwardly biased because of our sample design, which excluded workers employed in very small, "underground economy" firms that are more likely to pay less than the minimum wage.

Wages in certain subsectors of the U.S. economy may have been depressed by the influx of Mexican labor in recent years. In the case of Los Angeles manufacturing industries, there is persuasive evidence that relative wage declines during the 1970s for low-skill jobs in these industries were related to the presence of large numbers of Mexican and Central American immigrants. In the apparel industry, for example, the wages of production workers grew considerably more slowly in Los Angeles than elsewhere in California between 1969 and 1977.[77] In southern California, for nonagricultural firms studied by the Center for U.S.-Mexican Studies in 1983–84 and again in 1987–88, the median hourly wage for unauthorized immigrants rose by only 19 cents per hour during the four-year interval between the surveys—a real wage decline, when inflation is factored in (see Table 7). Wages for legal immigrants in the two samples had risen by 85 cents per hour, and those of U.S.-citizen employees by $1.00 per hour.

Latino immigrant workers, especially unauthorized Mexicans, do tend to earn less than U.S.-born workers employed in similar job categories. But immigration status per se is not the most important determinant of

[76] Personal, in-home interviews conducted by the Center for U.S.-Mexican Studies, University of California, San Diego in San Diego, Los Angeles, and Orange counties in 1987 and 1988. Legal immigrant workers interviewed for the same study (N = 103) were receiving an average of $6.00 per hour.

[77] Muller and Espenshade, *The Fourth Wave*, 110; Borjas, *Friends or Strangers*; Marta Tienda, "Mexican Immigration: A Sociological Perspective," in *Mexican Migration to the United States*, 109–47.

TABLE 7

Median Hourly Wage Received by Workers in Southern California Non-Agricultural Firms, 1983–1984 and 1987–1988, by Immigration Status

| | Median wage in | | Increase: |
Immigration status	1983–84 sample	1987–88 sample	1983–84 to 1987–88
Undocumented immigrants	$4.79 (N = 235)	$4.98 (N = 144)	$0.19
"Rodinos" (legalization applicant)	—	5.16 (N = 154)	—
Legal immigrants	5.15 (N = 102)	6.00 (N = 98)	0.85
U.S. citizens	7.00 (N = 110)	8.00 (N = 93)	1.00

SOURCE: Personal interviews with two different samples of production workers employed in "immigrant-dependent" firms in San Diego, Orange, and Los Angeles counties, conducted by the Center for U.S.-Mexican Studies in 1983–84 (N = 447) and 1987–88 (N = 489). Missing cases are excluded.

these wage differentials.[78] Equally or more powerful predictors are labor union membership, gender, marital status, English language competence, and the particular region and sector of the economy in which the worker is employed. In our sample of immigrants employed in California nonagricultural firms in 1983–84, the wage penalty paid by an undocumented immigrant, purely by virtue of his immigration status, was $0.60 per hour. Being male added $0.63 per hour to a worker's wage, *ceteris paribus*, while labor union membership added $1.80. Workers employed in the San Francisco Bay area and San Diego County earned more than their counterparts in Los Angeles and Orange counties.[79]

Impacts of IRCA

The "employer sanctions" component of the 1986 U.S. immigration law was supposed to exert upward pressure on wage scales in immigrant-dominated industries, by reducing the supply of unauthorized job-seekers and inducing firms to raise wages in order to retain their newly legalized immigrant employees. Thus far, however, there is little evidence of such

[78] Results of an OLS regression analysis based on 590 observations. The sample includes workers from San Diego, Orange, and Los Angeles counties and the San Francisco Bay area. All results cited are statistically significant at the 95 percent level of confidence or higher.

[79] Among our sample of unauthorized Mexican immigrants employed in southern California nonagricultural firms in 1987–88, 17 percent were union members. This compares with 30 percent among legal immigrants, and 32 percent among U.S.-citizen workers in the same sample. Our 1983–84 study of Mexicans employed in immigrant-dependent firms, which included firms located in northern California where unionization levels traditionally have been much higher than in the south, found much higher proportions of union members, among both unauthorized and legal immigrants. See Wayne A. Cornelius, "The United States Demand for Mexican Labor," 34, 37.

an effect. Very few of the migrants who legalized themselves under IRCA have received pay increases as a result of their new immigration status, and surveys of both agricultural and nonagricultural employers in California show that only a small minority of them have any plans for wage raises, at least in response to any IRCA-related labor market changes.[80] In part, this is because IRCA thus far has failed to reduce the undocumented immigrant labor supply in most industries that have come to rely on such labor. But econometric studies suggest that even if the labor supply were to be reduced by IRCA, real wage rates in agriculture would not rise significantly because many growers would introduce labor-saving technology or switch to less labor-intensive crops to avoid paying higher wages.[81]

There is no evidence that IRCA has reduced the total pool of Mexican migrants employed or seeking work in U.S. labor markets. In fact, the 1986 law seems to have augmented that pool, by drawing into it thousands of first-time migrants who sought to take advantage of the SAW and general amnesty programs.[82] IRCA has also increased the segmentation of the Mexican immigrant labor force, by opening up interfirm and intersectoral mobility opportunities for the newly legalized segment (in theory, at least), and by adding a new layer of highly vulnerable, economically desperate workers at the bottom of the labor force. This new underclass consists mostly of recently arrived, unauthorized migrants, especially those coming from nontraditional sending areas in Mexico, who are not attached to well-consolidated family support networks in the United States. Even though they are being enforced cautiously and selectively,[83] employer sanctions have reduced the range of employment prospects available to these new arrivals, and have lengthened their job-search time. Unauthorized migrants without a pre-arranged job are still getting work in the United States, often using fraudulent or borrowed documents;[84] but it takes them longer to find steady, full-time employ-

[80] Wayne A. Cornelius, "The United States Demand for Mexican Labor," 44; Philip L. Martin and J. Edward Taylor, "Immigration Reform and California Agriculture a Year Later," *California Agriculture* vol. 44, no. 1 (Jan.–Feb. 1990), 24–27.

[81] James A. Duffield, "Estimating Farm Labor Elasticities to Analyze the Effects of Immigration Reform," Agriculture and Rural Economy Division, Economic Research Service, U.S. Department of Agriculture, Staff Report No. AGES 9013 (Feb. 1990).

[82] Cornelius, "Impacts of the 1986 U.S. Immigration Law," 689–705.

[83] Michael Fix and Paul T. Hill, "Enforcing Employer Sanctions: Challenges and Strategies," Program for Research on Immigration Policy, The Rand Corporation and The Urban Institute, Report JRI-04, May 1990.

[84] Cornelius, "Impacts of the 1986 U.S. Immigration Law," 689–705; Robert L. Bach and Howard Brill, "Shifting the Burden: The Impacts of IRCA on U.S. Labor Markets," Interim Report to the Division of Immigration Policy and Research (Washington, Feb. 1990).

ment. Many of them must devote several weeks or even months to poorly paid, highly irregular day-labor before finding steady employment.

One of IRCA's most conspicuous unintended consequences has been the proliferation of street-corner immigrant labor markets in major U.S. cities.[85] In Los Angeles County, for example, immigrant day-labor markets now operate at an estimated forty sites, and there are dozens of them in Orange and San Diego counties as well. These informal labor markets serve mostly nonagricultural employers—small building contractors, painters, roofers, landscape maintenance businesses, and individual homeowners who need help moving dirt, weeding yards, or moving furniture. The vast majority of workers who congregate in these markets are unauthorized, but some newly legalized workers can also be found there, reflecting a general oversupply of low-skilled immigrant labor in some areas. Four southern California cities, including Los Angeles, have opened their own "hiring halls" to give migrant workers a regulated alternative to the chaotic, often highly exploitative street-corner labor markets—and, not incidentally, to get the migrants off the streets and away from retail businesses.

IRCA has also contributed to the informalization of employment among the Mexican immigrant population by encouraging the growth of sweatshops and other "underground economy" firms, homework (especially linked to garment subcontractors), and self-employment (street-vending, participation in swap meets, and so forth). Such enterprises were by no means absent in the pre-IRCA period,[86] and it is difficult to estimate how much of their recent expansion is attributable only to IRCA. The proliferation of sweatshops, for example, is also associated with the intensification of competitive pressures within the garment industry resulting from the growth of imports and "offshore" production facilities.[87] It is clear, however, that such economic activities draw disproportionately on the pool of Mexican workers whose employment prospects have been most adversely affected by IRCA; that is, new "unattached" illegal arrivals and women who did not qualify for amnesty under the 1986 law.

CONCLUSION

Over the last 100 years, Mexican migration to the United States has never been a static phenomenon. The changes or intensifications of pre-

[85] Bach and Brill, "Shifting the Burden"; Bruce Kelley, "El Mosco," *Los Angeles Times Magazine* vol. 6, no. 11 (18 Mar. 1990), 11–20, 38, 42–43.

[86] See, for example, Merle L. Wolin, "Sweatshop: Undercover in the Garment Industry," *Los Angeles Herald-Examiner* (14 Jan.–1 Feb. 1981 [sixteen-part series]).

[87] Bonacich, "Asian and Latino Immigrants in the Los Angeles Garment Industry," 35.

existing trends that occurred during the 1980s, however, are particularly significant. The shift from short-term, shuttle migration to permanent settlement in the United States has accelerated considerably. Mexico's economic crisis has brought into the migration stream many rural communities as well as urban centers that had not been traditional labor-exporters to the United States. The crisis has also discouraged many Mexican migrants already here from returning to their places of origin, as they might otherwise have done.[88] The 1980s brought major changes in the social composition of the flow: many more women and children, and more whole-family units, are now participating in the migratory process. And the continuing dispersion of Mexican migrants outside of the agricultural sector is one of the most conspicuous features of the current wave of Mexican immigration to the United States.

Some of the patterns described above are not really new when viewed from a broader historical perspective. For example, there are important similarities between the profiles of Mexican migration to the United States in the 1920s and that which occurred in the 1980s. In both decades, points of origin within Mexico were relatively dispersed, and there was considerable employment of Mexican workers in nonagricultural sectors of the U.S. economy.[89] After the hiatus caused by the Great Depression, the *bracero* program of contract-labor importation greatly increased the proportion of short-stay, agriculturally employed migrants, and altered the migration flow in other enduring ways.[90] Thus in certain respects, the migratory profile of the 1980s represents a return to patterns established before the deformation of the migratory process caused by *bracerismo*.

In understanding the contemporary Mexican immigration phenomenon, we must also take care to distinguish analytically between absolute and relative changes. For example, while permanent emigrants may have

[88] Roger Rouse, who has studied migration to Redwood City, California, from the town of Aguililla, Michoacán, found that the economic crisis of the 1980s had stimulated inflation in land and livestock prices in the community of origin, thereby preventing migrants returning to Mexico from using their savings to good advantage. See Rouse, "Mexican Migration to the United States," 200–207.

[89] For example, a survey of Los Angeles manufacturing industries in 1928 found that 17 percent of all workers were Mexicans. The single largest concentration of Mexican industrial workers was in textiles, but substantial numbers were also employed in construction and railroad yards. See California Mexican Fact-Finding Committee, cited in Muller and Espenshade, *The Fourth Wave*, 57.

[90] Manuel García y Griego, "The Importation of Mexican Contract Laborers to the United States, 1942–1964: Antecedents, Operation, and Legacy," in Peter G. Brown and Henry Shue, eds., *The Border That Joins: Mexican Migrants and U.S. Responsibility* (Totowa, N.J., 1983), 49–98.

grown considerably as a proportion of the total flow of Mexican migrants to the United States in the 1980s, this does not necessarily mean that short-term migration has diminished in absolute terms. The same caveat applies to the decline in the proportion of Mexican migrants who are agriculturally employed in the United States. This does not mean that agriculture has ceased to be an important employer of Mexican migrants; indeed, a 1983 survey of California's farmworker population found that 73 percent were Mexican-born, and 44 percent of these farmworkers admitted that they were unauthorized immigrants.[91] In relative terms, however, Mexican migrants today are finding far more employment opportunities in the nonagricultural sectors of the U.S. economy.

The shift from a Mexican immigrant population dominated by transient, "lone male" agricultural workers to a much more socially heterogeneous, year-round, urban-dwelling immigrant community is unlikely to be reversed, barring an economic calamity in the United States that would severely reduce the demand by nonagricultural sectors for Mexican labor. This change has raised new questions about the social and economic effects of Mexican migration to the United States on both sending and receiving areas. For Mexico, the increase in permanent settlement in the United States and the higher incidence of emigration by better-educated, more occupationally skilled residents of Mexico City and other urban centers will inevitably increase the human resource costs of U.S.-bound emigration. This cost increase may lead Mexico to press the U.S. government for new bilateral accords on migratory labor—possibly including a "guestworker" program for Mexican nationals—aimed at encouraging shuttle migration and discouraging permanent emigration.

On the U.S. side, IRCA's legalization of a large part of the formerly unauthorized Mexican work force, combined with the steadily increasing proportion of women and children in the flow of migrants from Mexico, inevitably will increase the effects of the Mexican immigrant population on housing, schools, and health-care systems in localities that attract large numbers of migrants. In the foreseeable future, Mexican immigrants—both legals and unauthorized migrants—are likely to remain highly concentrated in a few states and localities, with California alone receiving well over half of the total. Transnational migrant networks are now anchored in those places, and the networks will continue to expand.

[91] Richard Mines and Philip Martin, *A Profile of California Farmworkers: Results of the UC-EDD Survey of 1983* (Berkeley, Calif., Giannini Foundation Report 86–1, 1986); J. Edward Taylor and Thomas J. Espenshade, "Foreign and Unauthorized Workers in California Agriculture," *Population Research and Policy Review* (forthcoming).

This high degree of spatial concentration will increase the perceived threat posed by Mexicans and other Spanish-speaking immigrants to the non-immigrant population.

It is important to recognize the *cultural* basis of that perceived threat. Polling data and anecdotal evidence show that most non-minority, native-born residents of the United States do not see themselves as being in competition with Mexican immigrants for jobs or social services.[92] They do see such people, however, as a very real threat to their quality of life. As a Los Angeles city councilman put it, "The immigrants are resented strongly because of their impact on livability."[93] They are accused of boosting local crime rates,[94] harassing school children and other passersby, littering, and creating public health hazards. Local merchants complain that their "regular" customers are being driven away by migrants loitering or seeking work on nearby streets. Owners of new industrial parks claim that the migrants' presence is intimidating to prospective tenants of the parks. For many members of the non-immigrant population, racism and fears of a bilingual society are additional sources of hostility toward Mexican and other Latino immigrants.

The shift to urban employment has greatly increased the day-to-day visibility of Mexican migrant workers, thereby intensifying the objection of the non-immigrant population to their presence. This phenomenon is illustrated by the "North County" area of San Diego County—home to more than 1.5 million largely middle- and upper-income people, the vast majority of whom have migrated from other parts of the United States. For over three years, several of the principal North County cities have been in an almost continuous uproar over the presence of Mexican and Central American day-laborers and the makeshift camps, built of cardboard, used lumber, and plastic sheeting, in which they live. IRCA has put more migrant day-laborers—the new underclass—on the streets of these communities, and high-priced housing developments, shopping centers, and industrial parks have encroached upon the vacant land where migrant farmworkers have traditionally sought shelter. The cultural clash implied by upscale housing developments in immediate prox-

[92] Wayne A. Cornelius, "America in the Era of Limits: Migrants, Nativists, and the Future of U.S.-Mexican Relations," in Carlos Vásquez and Manuel García y Griego, eds., *Mexican-U.S. Relations: Conflict and Convergence,* Anthology Series, no. 3 (Los Angeles, Calif.: UCLA Chicano Studies Research Center and Latin American Center, 1983), 371–96.

[93] Quoted in Joel Kotkin, "Fear and Reality in the Los Angeles Melting Pot," *Los Angeles Times Magazine* vol. 5, no. 45 (5 Nov. 1989), 8.

[94] Daniel Wolf, *Unauthorized Aliens and Crime: The Case of San Diego County,* Monograph no. 29 (La Jolla, Calif., 1988).

imity to third world-style squatter settlements could hardly be more dramatic.

On 24 April 1990, the North County community of Encinitas became the first city in California to declare a "state of emergency" because of its failure to resolve its perceived "migrant crisis" through local means. Encinitas, a community of about 55,000 residents, has a "crisis" consisting of an estimated 200 to 800 homeless Mexican and Guatemalan migrants, living and seeking day labor within its city limits. Authorities in Encinitas and other North County communities have spent the last three years raiding and bulldozing migrant encampments, hiring security guards to patrol vacant public land to stop migrants from camping there, passing ordinances to ban curbside hiring, and clamoring for more strenuous efforts by the U.S. Border Patrol and county sheriff's deputies to sweep the streets of migrant day laborers. They have demonstrated only that they can chase migrants from one vacant lot, canyon, or street corner to the next one; the migrants have not been induced to go back where they came from, nor to drop out of the U.S. labor market. Until quite recently, when Encinitas and another North County city reluctantly agreed to study the idea of establishing legal, city-maintained camps for migrant workers, no thought was given by local authorities to solving the fundamental problem afflicting both the migrants and irate non-immigrant homeowners: the almost total lack of low-income housing in their communities.[95]

The experience of San Diego's North County, together with abundant statewide polling data,[96] suggests that the majority of non-immigrant Californians are far from being prepared to accept the notion of a settled, highly visible Latino immigrant presence in their immediate living and working environments. If the futility of efforts to "stop them at the border" and other law-enforcement approaches comes to be widely recognized, the focus of public debate in California and other parts of the United States will gradually shift to how to deal more effectively with Mexican immigrants as a "settler" population, and to the problems of "assimilating" the second and third generations. Such a shift in the terms of the public debate over immigration occurred during the 1980s in West-

---

[95] This is clearly a statewide problem. A recent study by the California Coalition for Rural Housing found that no low-cost housing had been built in nearly one-fourth of all California communities during the 1985–1989 period, and most others had fallen far short of actual needs. In San Diego County, for example, only 4,281 low-cost housing units were built from 1985 through 1989, while an estimated 38,648 new low-cost units were needed during this period.

[96] For example, a poll by *The Los Angeles Times* conducted in January 1989 found that 57 percent of the respondents agreed that there are "too many" immigrants in California.

ern Europe, faced with the de facto permanent presence of millions of culturally distinct Algerian, Moroccan, and Turkish immigrants.[97] And as in Western Europe, the overall level of anti-immigrant hostility is likely to rise, as the majority population confronts this new and unwelcome kind of challenge.

METHODOLOGICAL APPENDIX

This paper makes frequent reference to data gathered through a long-term field study based in the Center for U.S.-Mexican Studies at the University of California, San Diego. The project began as an attempt to gauge the impact within California of a specific government intervention in immigrant-dominated labor markets—namely, "Operation Jobs," a well-coordinated, highly publicized national sweep by the INS of workplaces during the last week of April and the first week of May 1982. We were interested in how patterns of labor recruitment, hiring practices, and labor-force composition in immigrant-dominated or immigrant-dependent firms might have been altered by this government effort to reduce the utilization of unauthorized immigrant labor and, in the absence of any durable effects, explain the lack of change.

Our interests quickly broadened, however, beyond the realm of government attempts to regulate the use of immigrant labor. It became apparent that such a focus was too narrow; that there were some basic transformations underway in many sectors of the U.S. economy and society that were generating an increased demand for Mexican and other foreign-born labor; and that these processes of change and their consequences for the organization of production, labor/management relations, and the mobility of capital were of far greater significance in understanding the role being played by Mexican labor in the state's economy than anything that federal or state government agencies were doing (or might conceivably do in the future). We therefore began to focus more on the conditions within various industries and in different types of firms within these industries that affected the hiring of Mexican and other foreign-born workers, the terms of their employment, and, more generally, the ways in which labor was being utilized by businesses that heretofore have depended heavily on immigrant workers.

The original universe for the study was defined as all firms in California's three largest metropolitan areas (San Diego, Los Angeles-Orange County, and the San Francisco Bay area) with ten or more employees that make substantial use of Mexican and other foreign-born labor. "Substantial" users were defined as firms where at least 25 percent of the jobs in

[97] Buechler, "A Review," 283–304; and Zig Layton-Henry, ed., *The Political Rights of Migrant Workers in Europe* (London and Newbury Park, Calif., 1990).

production were filled by Mexicans. The actual average proportion of Mexicans in these jobs among our 177 firms, as revealed by our interviews with workers, was 65 percent as of 1983–84.

In each metropolitan area, we attempted to contact all firms that had been raided by the INS during "Operation Jobs" in 1982. Lists of these firms were compiled both from INS sources and from newspaper reports on "Operation Jobs." We then randomly sampled the more comprehensive lists of firms in each of the three metropolitan areas that the INS had already raided or had enlisted in its "voluntary" job applicant screening program, "Operation Cooperation." Access to these lists was provided by INS officials. About half of the 177 firms in our sample were chosen in this manner.

We wanted to document a wide range of dependence on Mexican labor, particularly unauthorized Mexican labor. Therefore it was important to expand our sample of firms beyond those that could be identified through INS enforcement activities, which were presumably targeted at the most intensive users of illegals. There are several other important biases in INS enforcement practices: concentration on larger, higher-wage, frequently unionized firms; on sites where substantial concentrations of illegals could be found and easily rounded up (factories, for example, rather than numerous office buildings being cleaned by unauthorized workers employed by a particular company); workplaces that could be raided between 9:00 A.M. and 5:00 P.M.; and so forth. In order to gain a more comprehensive view of the role played by Mexican labor in California economy, we took care to include in our sample representatives of certain types of firms that, by their very nature, are not cost-effective targets of the INS, and therefore were not represented well on the lists of firms that have been raided by the INS. Examples would be building maintenance firms, construction firms, and restaurants.

The one-half of our sample firms that had not been targeted by the INS were identified in various ways. During interviews with unionized employers, we asked them to name their principal non-union competitors, who were subsequently interviewed. Other firms were identified in our interviews with labor-union officials in each metropolitan area. Some firms were selected at random from industry and telephone directories. In San Diego, several employers who had been identified in a 1980–81 Center for U.S.-Mexican Studies survey of 2,100 Mexican immigrants in San Diego County were selected for inclusion in our new study. Several of our interviewers who had come originally from Mexico also used their personal contacts to tap into immigrant networks for assistance in identifying firms that might be appropriate for inclusion.

This eclectic set of sampling techniques limits the generalizability of our results in a strict statistical sense. However, considering the impossibility of sampling the universe of immigrant-dependent firms in California (no such sampling frame exists), and the limitations of a random sampling approach, which relies on populations that may have been significantly biased in various ways (for example, firms that have been raided by the INS, or apprehended illegals who identify their employers on INS forms), we opted for eclecticism. Our goal was to study a cross-section of immigrant-dependent firms that would be as representative as possible of the entire group, excluding only the smallest employers (businesses that were family owned and operated, household employers, and so forth). Agricultural employers were also underrepresented in our sample, because we limited our study to the state's three principal metropolitan areas.

The first stage of the study consisted of detailed interviews with employers and labor-union representatives (if they were present) in each firm. In the second stage, we selected for more intensive study those firms in seven nonagricultural industries that make heavy use of Mexican labor. They include construction (which encompasses roofing and construction-site clean-up), food processing, shoe manufacturing and tanning, high-tech electronics, building and landscape maintenance, hotels, and restaurants. We chose to concentrate on these nonagricultural sectors of the economy, because so much less is known about how they use Mexican labor than about agricultural employers, and because urban employers are considerably more important as sources of jobs for Mexicans and other immigrants in California today than are agricultural firms.

In this second stage of the project, we interviewed 834 workers employed in the 94 firms that fell into our seven "intensive-study" industries. So, for example, we interviewed no workers employed in agriculture, which had been excluded from the second stage of the study. We attempted to interview ten workers in each firm, chosen at random from the workers in all job categories in which Mexicans were employed. If non-Mexican workers (Anglos, Chicanos, Blacks, or Asians) were also found to be employed in those same job categories, we interviewed several of them in each firm as well. Interviewers were instructed to choose a cross-section of production workers in a given firm: some young, some older, some unauthorized immigrants, some legal immigrants, and (if present) some non-Mexican workers. One-fifth of the resulting worker sample consisted of U.S.-born workers, the majority of them second-generation Mexican-Americans (Chicanos). Our interviewers made initial contact with them at the workplace—sometimes inside the plant, sometimes outside the gates; sometimes with the knowledge of management, sometimes not. But all interviews with workers were conducted in the privacy of their homes, rather than at their workplace. Most of these interviews lasted from 90 to 120 minutes.

In the third stage of the project, from May 1987 to June 1988, we returned to a subsample of the original 177 firms, to conduct new interviews with management and with a new sample of workers employed in each firm. These employer interviews were done in 105 nonagricultural firms located in southern California (San Diego, Orange, and Los Angeles counties), 71 of which were included in the earlier stages of the project. These 71 firms represent all of the original-sample firms that were located in southern California and which were still in business by May 1987. Firms in the San Francisco Bay area could not be included in this last phase of the project, due to financial constraints. Thirty-two firms not represented in earlier stages of the project, but belonging to the same industries we have been studying, were selected for inclusion in the 1987–88 fieldwork. Detailed, in-person interviews were conducted with 105 employers or managers, 500 workers employed in their firms (an average of 5 workers per firm, interviewed, as before, in their homes), and 200 recently arrived unauthorized immigrants—interviewed mostly in street-corner labor markets and public parks—who were still seeking steady employment in southern California. In this phase of the project, particular attention was devoted to the impacts of IRCA on the behavior of U.S. employers and immigrant workers.

In the final stage of the project, 945 sample survey interviews were conducted in three rural communities located in west-central Mexico, a region with a 100-year tradition of sending workers to the United States. A binational field research team assembled by the Center for U.S.-Mexican Studies and several Mexican universities interviewed 586 randomly-selected household heads; 233 recent (after 1 January 1982) migrants to the United States; and 126 prospective first-time migrants—persons aged 14 or older who had no history of work in the United States, and who identified themselves as likely to migrate in the future. Our selection of the nonmigrant household member deemed most likely to migrate to the United States in the near future was based necessarily on the judgment of the interviewer. Nevertheless, the subsequent behavior of these interviewees suggests that we succeeded in tapping a highly migration-prone stratum of the nonmigrant population in these communities. In a follow-up study of residents of one of the three communities who had been interviewed in July or August 1988 as prospective first-time migrants to the United States, we found that about 15 percent had actually migrated between 1 August and 1 December 1988. This rate of emigration is particularly impressive, since these were first trips, occurring during a season when very few people normally leave for the United States; indeed, migration during the August-December period traditionally flows in the opposite direction.

In each community, a random sample of 200 households was drawn from a sampling frame assembled through a complete household census conducted by our research team. In May 1988, according to our census, the research communities contained 299, 400, and 691 households, respectively. Our interviews with recent migrants to the United States and prospective first-time migrants were done within the same set of households. Thus the number of interviews conducted per household ranged from one to three. Interviews with household heads averaged about two hours in duration; those with recent migrants to the United States averaged 1.5 hours; and interviews with prospective first-time migrants lasted about one hour.

The universe for our study of sending communities was defined as all households maintaining a residence in the three research communities. To be included in the sampling frame, a household need not occupy a dwelling in the community on a year-round basis. Indeed, in all three communities, numerous dwelling units are occupied for only a few weeks each year (usually in December, January, and early February, when migrant families traditionally return from the United States) or are occupied for most of the year by renters or housesitters (14.4 percent of the houses in the three communities, combined). We took several preventative measures to avoid underrepresenting residents who spend most of the year working in the United States. The field interviewing was divided into two principal periods: July-August 1988 and December-January 1988–89. The latter period was timed to coincide with the habitual return of migrants from the United States for the Christmas holidays and annual town fiestas. Some interviewing was also conducted in the interim months, as families returned from the United States. If an entire household was absent both in July-August 1988 and in December-January 1988–89, we substituted it with a household that was also absent in July-August 1988, but had returned to the community by December-January 1988–89. Finally, nine interviews with household heads (1.5 percent of the total) were conducted in various California cities, where they were located in the fall of 1988. The level of cooperation was quite high; the refusal rate among sampled household heads in the three communities ranged from 2.5 to 4.0 percent.

The research communities are located in the states of Jalisco, Michoacán, and Zacatecas. All three are predominantly agricultural (73 percent of the economically active adult males were principally employed in agriculture). U.S.-bound migration from all three communities began in the first decades of this century, was briefly interrupted in the 1930s by the Great Depression, and became a mass movement in the 1940s and 1950s, when many residents participated in the *bracero* program of contract labor importation. In numerous families having homes in these communities, members of three different generations have worked in the United States. All three communities had been studied in depth by members of our research team prior to the enactment of the 1986 U.S. immigration law.[98] Since these communities were selected purposively, we make no claim that our findings are statistically representative of the entire universe of Mexican communities—now including large cities as well as rural localities—that send migrants to the United States. Our research sites are, however, quite typical of the small rural communities of west-central Mexico that have contributed heavily to the U.S.-bound migratory flow since the 1920s.[99]

[98] The pre-IRCA fieldwork in these three communities has been reported in Gustavo López, *La casa dividida: Un estudio de caso sobre la migración a Estados Unidos en un pueblo Michoacano* (Zamora, Mich., 1986); Mines, *Developing a Community Tradition of Migration;* and Cornelius, "Outmigration from Rural Mexican Communities."

[99] See, for example, Massey, et al., *Return to Aztlán;* Thomas Calvo and Gustavo López, eds., *Movimientos de población en el occidente de México* (Mexico City and Zamora, Mich., 1988); Gustavo López and Sergio Pardo Galván, eds., *Migración en el occidente de México* (Zamora, Mich., 1988); González de la Rocha and Escobar Latapí, "Impact of IRCA on the Migration Patterns of a Community in Los Altos, Jalisco."

The Young Latino Population in an Aging American Society: Policy Issues Evoked by the Emergence of an Age-Race Stratified Society

David E. Hayes-Bautista, Werner O. Schink, and Jorge Chapa

THE AGING OF American society appears to be a well-documented and unavoidable phenomenon.[1] Much debate right now turns on the society-wide policy implications of such an unprecedented growth (perhaps as much as a doubling) of the elderly population in the next thirty to fifty years. Serious policy discussion about the minorities of this society has been set aside during this debate. Because of this lack of discussion, policymakers have not fully recognized that significant changes are occurring in the minority population—changes that pertain directly to the aging of American society.

The basic change is a rapid growth of minority populations, especially the Latino and Asian populations.[2] Due to the continued immigration and the high fertility rate of young Latinos in particular, some states, such as California, are rapidly acquiring an age-race stratified population, in which the older segment will be composed almost exclusively of whites, while the working-age segment will be increasingly made up of Latinos and other minorities.

[1] Dorothy Rice and Jacob Feldman, "Living Longer in the United States: Demographic Changes and Elderly Health Needs," *Health and Society* 61 (Summer 1983), 362–96.

[2] There is much confusion over the proper terminology to use when referring to the population of Latin American origin (See David E. Hayes, Bautista, "Identifying 'Hispanic Populations: The Influence of Research Methodology upon Public Policy," *American Journal of Public Health* vol. 70, no. 4 [1980], 353–56.) In the senior author's opinion, the term "Hispanic" is methodologically misleading. Data used in this study come from different sources, which not only use different terms for this ethnic group (for example, Mexican-American, Spanish surname, Chicano, Hispanic, Spanish origin), but to a certain extent different methodologies to determine who is included and excluded from the group in question. We use the term "Latino" to refer to those of Mexican, Central American, South American, and Spanish-speaking Caribbean descent. All data reported will use "Latino," even though the terminology used by the different sources might be different.

The data presented in this study are based on changes in the California population, but they have meaning for the rest of the country, which is experiencing the same age-race stratification at various rates.[3] We do not have sufficient data to make nationwide projections, but the findings for California are so compelling we feel it is appropriate to discuss this state and suggest implications for the rest of the country.

In examining California's age structure, it became apparent that segments of the population have different age structures, which change at different rates. The Latino population in particular is much younger than the rest of the population, and its fertility and immigration rates are substantially higher than those of the rest of the population. Immigrants are coming from populations whose age structures are significantly different from the California (and U.S.) age structures.

This trend can be appreciated in Table 1, which compares the ages of the populations of Mexico and California. In this table, it is immediately apparent that, much like the rest of the developed industrial world, California has an age structure that is the product of decreasing fertility rates. Mexico has an age structure typical of less developed countries—that is, high fertility and low life expectancy. The population moves from Mexico to California via immigration. Already an incipient stratification by age and race is being noticed in some segments of society such as the school systems, where the primary grades are increasingly filled with Latino children.

This paper looks inside the age pyramid of California to identify the dynamics that are creating an age-race stratified society. Projections for the state will be presented in some detail—projections that raise a number of policy questions, including support burden, current and future notions of equity, intergenerational income transfer, and interracial income transfer. We present a framework for analyzing future policy issues and choices and offer two possible scenarios to illustrate how different constellations of policy decisions could lead to different societal outcomes. Implications for other states will be mentioned. Our intention throughout is to raise the issue of the emergence of the age-race stratified society, rather than to provide definitive answers to the policy questions such a stratification will generate.

THE AGE SHIFT

By the year 2030, the median age of the U.S. population may easily rise from its current 30.2 years to 43.2 years (see Fig. 1). If one assumes a below-replacement fertility rate, which is the current rate, the number of

[3] Center for the Continuing Study of the California Economy, *Projections of Hispanic Population for the United States: 1985–2000* (Palo Alto, Calif., 1982).

TABLE I

1988 Population Pyramids for Mexico and California

(*In millions of persons*)

Ages (in years)	Mexico		California	
	Male	Female	Male	Female
0–5	5.7	5.7	1.0	1.0
6–10	5.2	5.2	0.95	0.95
11–15	4.4	4.4	1.0	1.0
16–20	3.9	3.9	1.3	1.3
21–25	3.1	3.1	1.6	1.6
26–30	2.3	2.3	1.3	1.3
31–35	1.9	1.9	1.1	1.1
36–40	1.7	1.7	0.5	0.5
41–45	1.6	1.6	0.5	0.5
46–50	1.4	1.4	0.4	0.4
51–55	1.0	1.0	0.4	0.4
56–60	0.7	0.7	0.4	0.4
61–65	0.6	0.6	0.3	0.3
66–70	0.5	0.5	0.3	0.3
71–75	0.5	0.5	0.3	0.3
76–80	0.3	0.3	0.2	0.2
81–85	0.1	0.1	0.2	0.2
86–90	0.1	0.1	0.1	0.1
Total population	70		23.7	

SOURCES: For Mexico: Consejo Nacional de Población, *México: Estimaciones y Proyecciones de Población, 1950–2000* (Mexico City, 1982), 44. For California: 1980 census data.

elderly as a ratio of the total population may well nearly double from our current 11.2 percent to as many as 22.1 percent by 2030. Our median age projections for California are also given in Figure 1, to compare with those of the United States. The California population will be slightly younger than the general U.S. population, a difference due in part to different methodologies, and in part to the growth of the younger Latino population.

In both the California and U.S. populations, a distortion of the age pyramid has occurred because of the many "baby boom" births between 1945 and 1960, and the sudden drop in births immediately thereafter. It is the aging of this baby boom generation that will increase greatly the numbers of elderly between the years 2010 and 2030.

THE RACE SHIFT

In 1980, minorities constituted 33.4 percent of the state's population, up from 20 percent in 1970 and 15 percent in 1960. Most of this growth has been due to increases in the Latino population, a factor that will

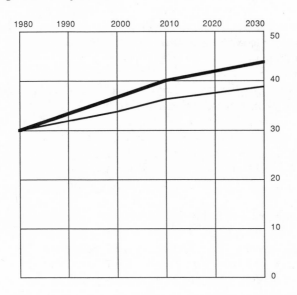

Fig. 1. Median age of the projected population for California (lower line) and the United States (upper line), 1980–2030. SOURCE: Government Printing Office, Current Population Reports, series P-65, no. 704 (Washington, 1980).

likely fuel much of the state's future population growth. The Latino population grows rapidly due to its high fertility and immigration rates.

Given that most of the sending areas, for example Mexico, have significantly younger populations than California and have a different demographic behavior, we wished to see the effects of a continued growth of the Latino and other minority populations on the state's population over the next fifty years. A model was developed that accommodates the problem of currently unknown immigration rates from Mexico and Latin America.

Assumptions in the California Population Projections

The population projections presented here were developed using a standard cohort-component procedure.[4] The number of people in each age group was projected taking into account the major components of change: fertility, mortality, and migration. The total population was initially divided into four groups: Anglos (that is, White non-Latinos); Blacks; Latinos; and Asians and Others. We will refer to this last group

[4]Henry S. Shryock and Jacob S. Siegel, *The Methods and Materials of Demography* (Washington, 1975).

simply as Asians. For baseline computations, the number in each group was taken from 1980 census data. Because of differential fertility patterns, the Latino population was divided further into native- and foreign-born Latinos.

Fertility rates for the state were calculated for the five major groups (Anglos, U.S.-born Blacks, Latinos, foreign-born Latinos, and Asians) using California Department of Health Services' vital statistics for 1980, and 1980 census data. The Anglo, Black, and Asian fertility rates are 1.31, 1.70, and 1.59, respectively: substantially lower than the 2.1 needed to maintain a stable population size. The native-born Latino fertility rate is significantly higher, at 2.06, and the foreign-born Latino is highest at 3.14 births.

The projections that follow are based on the assumption that the fertility of Anglos, Blacks, and Asians will remain constant until 2030. We also assumed that the fertility rates for the Latino population will drop, so that by 2030 the rate for native-born Latinos will equal that of Blacks in 1980, and the rate for foreign-born Latinos will decrease to the 1980 level for native-born Latinos.[5]

Mortality was assumed to decrease so that the life expectancy at birth would increase by five years for all groups. This decrease in mortality was further assumed to occur uniformly throughout the projection period.

Immigration is the wild card in all projections involving the Latino population.[6] There is no commonly accepted figure for Latino immigration; the presence of an unknown number of undocumented immigrants complicates any effort to identify such immigrants once they have arrived. The projections for this paper are based on a two-step calculation. The growth rate due to in-migration was determined by comparing 1970 and 1980 census figures for each age and sex cohort. These rates were then applied to an in-migration total of 250,000 per year. This gave us an annual immigration rate of 100,000 foreign-born Latinos.

These are the major assumptions used in calculating the projections. Certainly, any one of them is open to debate, and the collection of assumptions could be subject to even greater criticism. However, as the purpose of this paper is to draw attention to a trend that seems not to have been noticed by most projections of the aging of American society,

[5] The projections offered by Rice and Feldman assume a rise in the overall fertility rate to replacement level. We believe that if the nation's overall fertility were to rise, a corresponding rise (or perhaps more accurately, a slowdown in the decrease) in the Latino fertility rate would occur such that the proportions of each race in the population would remain about the same.

[6] Wayne Cornelius, Leo Chávez, and Jorge Castro, *Mexican Immigrants and Southern California: A Summary of Current Knowledge* (San Diego, 1982).

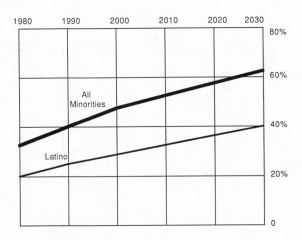

Fig 2. Projected composition of the California population, 1980–2030. SOURCE: Authors' data. For a discussion of these data, see David E. Hayes-Bautista et al., *The Burden of Support* (Stanford, Calif., 1988).

we felt it best to continue with known but debatable assumptions rather than wait for less-debatable assumptions to be developed.

The Growth of Latinos and Minorities

Using the model based on our assumptions, the change in Latino and minority populations may be seen in Figure 2. According to these projections, by the year 2010 about half the state's population will be minority, and almost 30 percent will be Latino. By 2030, more than 55 percent of the state's population will be minority, with slightly over 35 percent Latino. Clearly substantial growth in the minority population will occur over the next fifty years.

THE AGE-RACE STRATIFICATION

The importance to policymakers of this growth in the Latino and minority populations is made clear when one examines the age structure of these populations. Although they will make up an increasingly large percent of the total population, Latinos will not be equally represented in all age categories: rather, they will be overrepresented in the younger, working population and greatly underrepresented in the elderly, retired population. The generational age gap then is thus correlated with race.

Table 2 details the age pyramid of the state for 1980, broken down by Anglos, Blacks, Latinos, and Asians. The bulging baby boom population is noticeable in the 20- to 35-year-old cohorts. Latinos and other

TABLE 2

California Population
(In millions of persons)

Ages (yrs.)	1980 Asian	1980 Black	1980 Latino	1980 White	1990 Asian	1990 Black	1990 Latino	1990 White	2000 Asian	2000 Black	2000 Latino	2000 White	2010 Asian	2010 Black	2010 Latino	2010 White	2020 Asian	2020 Black	2020 Latino	2020 White	2030 Asian	2030 Black	2030 Latino	2030 White
0–10	1.6	1.4	1.4	0.8	2.0	1.6	1.6	0.8	2.2	1.8	1.6	0.8	2.4	2.0	1.8	0.8	2.4	2.0	1.8	0.6	2.4	2.0	1.8	0.6
11–20	2.0	1.6	1.6	1.0	2.0	1.6	1.4	1.0	2.2	1.8	1.8	1.0	2.4	2.0	1.8	1.0	2.4	2.2	2.0	0.8	2.6	2.2	2.0	0.8
21–30	2.4	2.2	2.0	1.2	2.6	2.2	2.0	1.4	2.4	2.0	1.8	1.4	2.8	2.4	2.2	1.2	2.8	2.6	2.4	1.0	3.0	2.6	2.4	1.0
31–40	1.8	1.6	1.6	1.2	2.8	2.2	2.2	1.6	2.8	2.6	2.4	1.6	2.8	2.4	2.2	1.4	3.2	2.8	2.4	1.2	3.2	2.6	2.4	1.0
41–50	1.4	1.4	1.4	0.8	1.6	1.4	1.4	1.0	2.4	2.2	2.0	1.0	2.6	2.4	2.2	1.4	2.4	2.2	2.0	1.4	2.8	2.6	2.4	1.2
51–60	1.4	1.4	1.2	1.2	1.2	1.2	1.0	0.8	1.6	1.4	1.4	0.8	2.2	2.0	1.8	1.0	2.4	2.0	2.0	1.2	2.2	1.8	1.6	1.0
61–70	1.0	1.0	1.0	0.8	1.0	1.0	1.0	0.8	1.0	1.0	1.0	0.8	1.4	1.2	1.2	0.6	2.0	1.8	1.6	1.0	2.0	1.8	1.6	1.0
71–80	0.6	0.6	0.6	0.5	0.6	0.6	0.6	0.5	0.6	0.6	0.6	0.5	0.6	0.6	0.6	0.5	0.8	0.8	0.8	0.7	1.4	1.0	1.0	1.2
81–90	0.4	0.4	0.4	0.3	0.2	0.2	0.2	0.3	0.2	0.2	0.2	0.4	0.2	0.2	0.2	0.4	0.2	0.2	0.2	0.4	0.4	0.4	0.4	0.4

SOURCE: Authors' data. For a discussion of these data, see David E. Hayes-Bautista et al., *The Burden of Support* (Stanford, Calif., 1988).

minorities make up nearly half the population in the cohorts aged five and under. As one looks at progressively older groups, fewer Latinos and other minorities and greater Anglo representation is noticeable. Beyond 65 years of age, there are very few minorities at all.

Table 2 also projects the age structure from 1990 to 2030 in ten-year intervals, using our population model. Marked changes by age and race are predicted to occur. The Anglo baby boom does not replace itself; rather, with each succeeding decade the young cohorts are increasingly composed of Latinos and other minorities.

In these projections, the age-race stratification is most pronounced from 2015 to about 2030. During this period, the large baby boom population that has been distorting the age pyramid will enter the retirement years, while Latinos and other minorities will increasingly constitute the younger, working-age population. With a marked increase in longevity (not assumed in our model), the age-race stratification would become even more pronounced.

Figure 3 provides another view of the age-race gap by looking at our projections of median age for the Anglo and Latino groups in the state. Due in large part to the aging baby boom generation, the median age of the Anglo population increases from its current 33 years to a possible

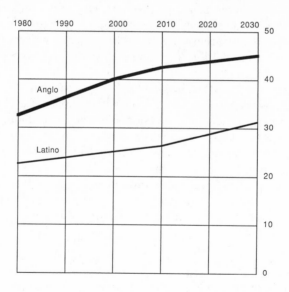

Fig. 3. Projected median age of California Anglos and Latinos, 1980–2030. SOURCE: Authors' data. For a discussion of these data, see David E. Hayes-Bautista et al., *The Burden of Support* (Stanford, Calif., 1988).

high of 45 years by 2030. The median age of the Latino population will be much lower, from its current 22 to only 31.3 years by 2030.

The Continuing Factor: Mexico and Latin America

These projections assume political and economic stability in Mexico and Central America. Currently, prospects are poor for economic and political stability there. Thus, there will likely be a sudden leap in the Latino population sometime in the near future. [Eds. Note: Circumstances in Mexico and Central America have since improved prospects for economic and political stability. However, the inflow of Latinos during the 1980s appears to have been considerably greater than the authors' projections.] In large part, therefore, the growth of the Latino population in California is linked to the growth and welfare of the populations of Mexico and Latin America. The median age in Mexico is 16.2 years, nearly half the median age of 33 of Anglo California.[7] As recently as 1960, the vast majority of California's Latinos came from Mexico. Gradually, the Latino population is beginning to include significant numbers of immigrants from other Latin American countries. Currently, about 80 percent of the Latino population is of Mexican origin.

The Support Burden and the Young Latino Population

As a number of authors have pointed out, some long-range projections concerning the financial future of elderly support programs depend on a certain number of retirees in relation to the number of workers.[8] We would like to add that in addition to absolute numbers of workers, one must also look at the ethnic composition of the work force, its present and future preparation, the distribution of incomes in the work force, and the ability of this work force to be taxed heavily to support the elderly.

Certainly an increase in the number of older persons will mean a larger need for support from the working-age population.[9] If there are proportionately fewer working-age people, they will have to carry a heavier burden than is currently the case with more workers per retiree.[10]

Currently, the Latino population in California is less educated than the overall population, as is shown in Table 3. Nearly 57 percent of all Latino adults have less than a high school education, while only 22 percent of

[7] Consejo National de Población, *Mexico Demografico: Brevario, 1978* (Mexico City, 1978).

[8] Peter Peterson, "No More Free Lunch for the Middle Class," *New York Times Magazine* (17 Jan. 1982); Peter Peterson, "The Coming Crash of Social Security," *New York Review of Books* vol. 29, no. 19 (1982), 34–38; Rice and Feldman, "Living Longer in the United States."

[9] Eric Kingson and Richard Scheffler, "Aging: Issues and Economic Trends for the 1980s," *Inquiry* 18 (1981), 197–213.

[10] Peterson, "The Coming Crash."

TABLE 3

*Years of School Completed by Persons 25 Years Old
or Older, California, 1980*

(*Percent of Latino and non-Latino population*)

	Latino	Non-Latino
Elementary	40.4%	9.8%
High School (1–3)	16.1	11.7
High School (4)	23.6	32.7
College (1–3)	13.5	24.0
College (4+)	6.4	21.8

SOURCE: 1980 U.S. Census data.

TABLE 4

Median Family Income, California, 1979

	Black	Latino	Anglo	Asian and other	Total
U.S. Dollars	$15,410	$16,140	$22,689	$22,721	$21,479

SOURCE: 1980 U.S. Census data.

non-Latinos have such a low educational attainment. At the upper end, nearly 22 percent of the non-Latino population has graduated from college, while only 6 percent of the Latino population has been able to do so. Moreover, educational attainment is directly related to earning power. In 1980, the median income for Latinos was $16,140, while for Anglos it was $22,689 (see Table 4).

Unless a major change is enacted in educational and job policies, the working-age population of the future, increasingly composed of Latinos and other minorities, will have a lower total wage base upon which to financially support the elderly. One analyst believes as well that maintaining current benefit levels would cause such high tax burdens that the Anglo work force, with greater education and income, might feel resentful—a resentment that could be much greater if the tax rate had to be further increased to offset the much lower earning capabilities of a largely Latino work force.

Clearly, a society under such pressures could become subject to serious strains and fractures. Policies for supporting and caring for the aged must be developed in conjunction with policies for preparing the Latino and minority work force to provide such care.

THE POLICY AREAS

The double division of age and race will be a fact of social life in the future. Can such a society, with great potential chasms separating one group from another, become single and unified? Will difficult policy decisions regarding the care of the elderly and the participation of the younger working-age population be made without having the reactions of one group tear society apart?

At least three policy areas need attention in order to achieve a smoothly functioning society, and within each policy area, different policy choices may be made. The constellation of decisions in all three of the policy areas will greatly determine the type of society that will emerge from the age-race shift.

Human Resources Investment

This paradigm conceptualizes the population of the state as a natural resource that has to be invested in and developed thoughtfully so as to create a maximized, sustained yield.[11] The yield can be defined as labor-force participation and productivity. As with any resource, short-range policies designed to extract maximum yield for the present may deplete the resource, making future yields much smaller. The growing minority population, which will make up the bulk of the labor force thirty to fifty years from now, may be seen as a human resource that will require some investment now for greater societal benefits tomorrow.

Education. This is a critical area, particularly as the California economy moves away from manufacturing and into the service industries. Brainpower, not manufactured products, may become the principal American export.[12] The population's level of education will be one of the principal determinants of success or failure in this movement from manufacturing to services. The educational level of different ethnic groups in California is given in Table 3. One might easily surmise that if current policies are followed, the general educational level in the work force will decline by 2030 as the proportion of Latinos increases; the baby boom generation, however, will continue to benefit from its very high level of educational achievement.

Health. A work force in poor health is less productive than one with good health. Although few reliable health statistics exist for Latino populations, the Hispanic Health and Nutrition Evaluation Survey does provide a nationwide database of the health status of Chicanos, Puerto Ricans, and Cubans. This information indicates that the Latino population

[11] Theodore Schultz, *Investing in People: The Economics of Population Equality* (Berkeley, Calif., 1981).
[12] Eugene Kelley, "Americas Economic Future: The Key Is Brains and Services," paper presented to the Commonwealth Club, San Francisco, 1982.

suffers from infectious diseases more than the general population. Such diseases are the ones most affected by public health programs, which are currently being cut back.

Social Cohesion

Social cohesion is the product of members of a society feeling that they have a stake in the outcome of events, and subsequently have some desire, urge, or obligation to participate in these events. When many members of society feel little or no desire to participate in society, low social cohesion results, and a possibility for social breakdown emerges. With high social cohesion, difficult policy choices may be made without certain groups feeling left out, even though the changes might entail decreasing the social benefits these groups might otherwise feel are theirs. Social cohesion can be measured and achieved in several dimensions. Three are mentioned here.

Economic participation. This is possibly the most important way to effect social cohesion. Social cohesion is maximized when the degree of economic participation is the same for all groups. If a large and growing part of the population maintains current low levels of economic participation, then we expect social cohesion to decrease. Full economic participation would occur in those situations where Latino and other minorities are fully integrated into all segments of the economy: research and development, administration, policy, and marketing; in the service industry; and in manufacturing and extraction. Low economic participation occurs when Latino and other minorities are confined to the assembly lines in manufacturing and the harvesting and processing lines in agriculture.

Political participation. In the public sector, political participation conditions the presence or absence of social cohesion. Currently, Latino and other minorities do not participate fully in the political process and often feel that decisions are being made at their expense. With full political participation, these feelings could be diminished because the decisions would belong to everyone, not just to a perceived few.

Immigration. Although in the federal province, immigration may affect statewide social cohesion. Certain immigration policy proposals would put at risk nearly all Latinos and Asians, who are racially distinct from the mainstream population, by forcing employers to require proof of citizenship before hiring. Rather than go through the trouble of verifying such status, employers might find it easier simply not to hire from those two groups. The need to carry identification, and the burden of being asked for it when others are not, could well create a feeling of separateness that could lead to low social cohesion.

Cultural Pluralism

Cultural pluralism is a situation in which various cultures are given equal importance and the contribution of each to the societal whole is acknowledged. Cultural pluralism recognizes the different histories, languages, and experiences that make up the cultural mosaic of the California and U.S. populations. Within state borders, a policy that emphasizes cultural pluralism will most likely help every group feel that it can retain its uniqueness and participate fully in economic and political life. All groups might then feel more attached to society and more willing to participate in some difficult decisions ahead.

Some cultural pluralistic considerations go beyond the borders of this country, however. In particular, the California economy stands poised at the brink of the larger Pacific Rim economy consisting of Mexico, Central and South America, the South Pacific, and Asia. In order to compete successfully, California legislators will have to understand and work with these other economies and cultures. Given that minorities descended from these areas will constitute most of the labor force, nurturing cultural pluralism could make working with other Pacific Rim economies easier.

In order for pluralism to occur, a policy of cultural homogenization must be reversed. Otherwise the advantage of having so many Latinos and other minorities in the work force will be lost: a totally assimilated minority would be as inept in the Pacific Rim markets as a culturally unaware non-minority.

The trick is to conceive of achieving social cohesion *through* cultural pluralism.

THE POTENTIAL COLLISION

The ingredients for projecting into the future are now in hand. The shift of age and race may be answered with different policies for human resources investment, social cohesion, and cultural pluralism. It is quite possible, however, that the shift will be responded to in a manner such that the policy needs of the largely Anglo elderly population and the largely Latino and minority working-age population will collide in the years 2010–2030.

Policy Area Responses Conducive to a Collision

The three policy areas mentioned above may be responded to in such a way as to yield an age-race collision. One projection, based on many current policy decisions, suggests the following scenarios for each category.

Human resources investment. The growing minority population is seen as a threat or drain rather than a resource, and policy decisions might be made so as not to invest in developing this resource. Because of the declining numbers of Anglo children in schools, education is given fewer resources: higher education in particular becomes more costly as fees are raised, and bilingual education is phased out as an extravagance. Health programs are cut back, and access to care is made quite difficult for the poor and working poor. The work force of 2030, in addition to being largely Latino and minority, has low educational achievement and is in poor health.

Social cohesion. Latinos and other minorities are relegated to the labor level in manufacturing and agriculture, rarely being able to pierce the important areas of research, administration, and policy. Professional positions in the high-technology and service industries are closed to them. Likewise, political participation can be quite low, so that government is seen as an intrusive agent that operates without the consent of the governed. The better jobs in industry, and the governmental decision-making process, are considered provinces of elderly whites.

Because of draconian measures adopted to try to stem immigration—especially from Mexico, Central America, and Asia—many people feel excluded physically and psychologically from the economic mainstream. In this situation, social cohesion will be quite low. Many in the population will feel that they have no stake in the outcome of social activities, and may increasingly refuse to participate in them.

Cultural pluralism. Cultural differentness is perceived as a threat to standard culture and values. Xenophobic measures limit the teaching of other languages, histories, and customs: cultural assimilation is society's goal.

A Collision Scenario

With such decisions in the policy areas mentioned above, it would be quite easy for California society to be set on a collision course at the age-race juncture between 2010 and 2030. While many scenarios are possible, we now offer a worst-case scenario for consideration.

The baby boom generation grows old and begins to enter retirement by 2010. The younger work force is largely Latino and minority. Possessing low educational levels, they occupy the lower end of the job market.[13] By virtue of having lower wages, the burden for sup-

[13] Richard Carlson, "Threats to the State's High-Technology Leadership," paper presented to the Commonwealth Club, San Francisco, 1982.

porting the elderly begins to fall disproportionately on this younger work force. Rather than paying a 45 percent Social Security payroll tax, the working-age population finds itself paying significantly more, perhaps 50 to 55 percent.[14]

The elderly are very active politically and sensitive to the inability of Social Security and other benefits to support them adequately. Thus, they use their disproportionate numbers and voting participation to vote themselves modest increases in benefits.[15] The burden of paying for these increases falls again on the lowered earnings of Latinos and other minorities.

Fearful of the large numbers of minorities, the elderly whites increasingly seclude themselves in security-patrolled retirement villages and physically separate themselves from the younger, darker population to which they can no longer relate on a cultural, linguistic, or historic basis.

Resentful for having to pay such high support burdens, shut out physically from the richer areas of the state, and frustrated at being relegated to the left-over menial tasks, the young Latino and other minority taxpayers become resentful. These taxpayers see much of their earnings being transferred to the elderly, leaving them with very little to spend on housing, education, and consumer goods. The decline in purchasing power may depress many markets, which causes companies to relocate to areas with greater purchasing power.

Capital investment has nearly ceased, with money that formerly had been used to construct and maintain streets, bridges, sewers, parks, schools, and other parts of the physical infrastructure transferred to the elderly. The physical plant falls into disrepair, further interrupting and decreasing economic activity in the state.

Social cohesion becomes threatened: the younger Latino and minority population begins to question its sacrifice to the elderly. After all, the elderly baby boom generation had free education, good health services, good roads and physical infrastructure, and job mobility, which are all denied the younger population.

A backlash develops among the younger Latino and minority taxpayers (and quite possibly among overburdened young Anglo taxpayers as well). The boundaries are sharply drawn: the Anglo elderly on one side, and the younger Latino and other minority generation on the other. Each group sees the other as a threat and a parasite. The scenario for social collapse is set.

[14] Peterson, "The Coming Crash."
[15] Robert Studer, "Charge of the Seniors Against the Power of PACs: Potential Army of Three Million Voters," *California Journal* vol. 13, no. 12 (1982), 457–58.

THE POTENTIAL OPPORTUNITY

Policy Responses to Develop Potential Opportunities

The same policy areas that can yield a collision between the generations and races could be handled so as to yield cooperation and greater growth, creating an entirely different scenario for each policy area.

Human resources investment. The educational levels of all minorities are brought up to norm. Latino and minority faculty teach in universities and research laboratories. Education continues to be subsidized, and language background is seen as an asset, not a liability. Health programs are continued, and health promotion efforts are expanded so that the threat of infectious diseases being imported from other areas of the world is lowered. The work force is basically healthy and fully educated.[16]

Social cohesion. Latinos and other minorities are employed at all levels in all sectors of the California economy: research and development, corporation boards, and administration; in high technology and service industries; and in advanced manufacturing, agriculture, and extractive industries. Latinos and minorities are fully represented at all levels of government, so that the difficult policy choices about elderly care are made without any group feeling left out.

Cultural pluralism. Throughout the educational years, and pervasive in everyday mass-media communications, the cultural diversity of the different ethnic groups is maintained. Building on this diverse base, the California economy serves as a place to translate and export goods, services, and knowledge to the various Pacific Rim markets. Feeling proud and secure in their respective ethnic identities, the different groups also feel part of a whole, made up *e pluribus unum.*

The Opportunity Scenario

Recognizing the growth in the Latino and other minority population, resources have been invested in education so that the average educational level is almost college graduation. This level is accomplished despite the constant immigration of people with lower educational achievement.

Links with cultures in Latin America and Asia are built into the economic life of the state, so that Latinos working at the research and decision levels in various industries can communicate and cooperate with their counterparts in Latin America. The Asian markets are handled by descendants of Asian immigrants, with international organizations spanning the gulfs that used to separate the American economic culture from

[16] Schultz, *Investing in People.*

those of other regions. The educated Black population, though small, begins to form links with rising African economies.

U.S. investment in Mexico, Latin America, and Asia grows, but policy decisions are made in cooperation with the governing structures rather than in spite of them. With economic growth, the economies of Mexico and Latin America begin to stabilize, as do their governments.

The overall growth in economic activity, and the close social cohesion that is a by-product of an active maintenance of cultural pluralism, make the policy decisions regarding support of the elderly much easier. The burden is not as onerous on this growing economic base as it would be on a shrinking economic base. The "we-they" feeling is limited, as all members of society recognize that they must look out for the welfare of all their members, not just a select few.

The cultural values from northern European countries, which formed the basis for California society in the nineteenth and early twentieth centuries, are expanded to include the values of Latin America and Asia.

CONCLUSIONS

These scenarios have been offered to draw attention to a demographic phenomenon that has not been yet fully investigated. They attempt to project a worst and best possible case. Neither situation is inevitable, nor are these the only two possibilities; many other scenarios can be inferred from the demograhic data. It is our intention only to place the problem in the public arena for consideration, research, and discussion. Certainly, at least for California, the age-race stratification has the potential for great societal effect. Whether the effect will be positive or negative depends on policy decisions made today.

Implications Beyond California

Although our defined policy areas and scenarios have been developed for California's population, the Latino population is growing across the country, albeit at different rates.[17] It is our feeling, without having done a close analysis, that the Southwest will experience similar age-race stratification at about the same time that California does. Other parts of the country will undergo somewhat similar stratification at slightly later dates. The influx of immigrants to the Eastern seaboard, especially New York, New Jersey, and Florida, will likely be composed of fewer Mexican Latinos, and more Latinos from other areas in Latin America. Again, a major collapse of an economy or government could speed this process.

[17] Center for the Continuing Study of the California Economy, *Projections of Hispanic Population*.

It is also quite likely that the small but important Asian population in California will not likely be replicated in many other areas; hence its effect will most likely be less outside the state, with the possible exception of New York. Again, these implications are very rough and need more careful analysis.

Tandem Policy Discussions

As policymakers have become aware of the aging of American society, they have begun to discuss the care and support of the elderly. Social Security, Medicare, pension plans, income maintenance, and other issues are in vogue, with an eye not only to the immediate future, but to the mid- and long-range effects as well. Yet it should be apparent from our projections that the policy future of the aging American society is intertwined with the policy future of Latinos and other minorities, for they are the ones, demographically speaking, who will be asked to shoulder the burden of the aged baby boom generation.

It will behoove American society to view its Latino and other minority populations as a resource to be thoughtfully developed not because it would be morally right or just. Rather, for the future of our aging society, we should view the Latino and other minorities as holding the key to the older population's ability to live their final years in some semblance of support and social tranquillity.

Our future societal cohesion could easily depend on choices made today, during the relatively short-lived "policy window" from the present to about 2000. It will be too late if we wait until the baby boom begins to retire in 2010 to become concerned about the education and earning capacity of the younger Latino and other minority populations. Certain negative social dynamics will have already been set in motion, the productive capacity of the work force will have already been lowered, and the age-race stratification will have solidified into a barrier against social cohesion.

Our projections are intended to bring attention to this area during the current concern about the plight of the elderly. Much more work needs to be done to understand the links between the policy areas of the elderly and those of minorities, but we hope that at least the need to engage in further work will now be appreciated.

The Effect of Mexico's Postwar Industrialization on the U.S.-Mexico Price and Wage Comparison

Jeffrey Bortz

ONE OF THE FUNCTIONS of labor markets, like other markets, is to assign scarce resources optimally through relative prices. In labor markets, relative prices are relative wages.

Minor regional differences characterize most national markets. Most products differ little from the national average. Important exceptions occur, however, when specific goods and services, such as land and labor, are not easily transportable.

Although constrained nationwide, the flow of factors of production—goods, capital, and labor—is restricted further by legal and other restraints in international markets. In the late twentieth century, none of these factors has been subject to more restrictions than labor. Throughout most of the world, workers can change their homes and jobs with relative ease within their own country, but with extreme difficulty between countries.

This general rule tends to hold even between neighboring countries. Mexico and the United States share more than a common border of 2,000 miles; both are sovereign nation-states with market economies characterized by relatively free movement of production factors within their borders. Additionally, both economies have a vigorous external sector in which the exchange of goods and services plays an important role. As sovereign states, both countries restrict severely the entrance of alien workers, so that strong legal barriers to the international exchange of labor exist.

On the other hand, Mexico is an underdeveloped yet industrialized country, which means that its national labor market is characterized by a relative labor surplus. The United States is an advanced industrial country that occasionally has high unemployment, but nonetheless has relatively and absolutely more jobs, more skilled positions, and higher wages than its underdeveloped neighbor to the south. As a result, significant labor flows occur from the low-wage to the high-wage economy.

Both societies are urban and industrial. By the 1980s, the United States was 74 percent urban and 32 percent industrial. Mexico in the same decade was 69 percent urban and 40 percent industrial.[1] However, U.S. per capita gross national product (GNP) was 15,390 dollars in 1984, 7.5 times the Mexican per capita GNP of 2,040.[2] Given the great disparity of wealth and accumulation between the two countries, it is not surprising to find that wage rates in Mexico are significantly lower than wage rates in the United States. While not the only causal factor, the wage difference has helped stimulate the legal and illegal migration of Mexican workers to the United States.

In the last fifty years, both countries have undergone deep structural transformations, although throughout that period the United States has been significantly wealthier than its neighbor. From 1932 to 1982, Mexican economic growth averaged almost 6 percent a year, which was higher than U.S. growth rates. In 1930, Mexico was primarily rural and agricultural. Today, urban industry produces steel, automobiles, tires, pharmaceuticals, electrical appliances, and other modern consumer durables and nondurables. Similarly, in the last fifty years the leading industries of the United States have shifted from automobiles and steel, to nuclear power and aerospace in the postwar period, to the current movement toward advanced electronics and information-related industries. As in Mexico, economic change has not always been painless. Since 1970, U.S. growth rates have slowed, recessions have become more frequent and more severe, unemployment has increased, and real wage rates have begun to decline. Mexico since 1970 has experienced slower growth rates, declining rates of productivity increases, a dramatic explosion of the external debt, severe devaluations of the peso, near hyperinflation, increasing pressures on the labor market, and severely contracting wages.

The U.S. and Mexican economies are linked through many markets, not the least of which is the labor market. In this sphere, however, the linkages take place under complex conditions. While differential wage rates, as well as industry-specific employment patterns, serve to assign

[1] World Bank, *World Development Report 1986* (New York, 1986), 185 and 241. *Urbanization* is defined as the percentage of urban population in the total population, and industry as percentage of GDP.
[2] *Ibid.*, 181.

workers to jobs, they do so under regional, national, and international constraints that the literature is only beginning to analyze.

I will look at only one element that plays a crucial role in the U.S.-Mexico labor market relationship: wage rates. Although throughout the economic changes in both countries since World War II the United States has had higher wage rates than Mexico, these changes have affected the wage-rate ratio between the two. I will therefore examine price evolution in both countries from 1939 to 1985, and its effect on real wages in both countries as well as on the peso-dollar exchange rate. After I explore the relationship between the long-run wage cycle in Mexico and United States, a brief glance at the U.S.-Mexican border will highlight the wage relationship. Finally, I will demonstrate that deepening industrialization in Mexico may have played a positive role for skilled workers in that country, but it did not raise Mexican wages in relation to U.S. wages. The kind of postwar industrialization that Mexico developed after World War II could not end the push effect on migration from Mexico to the United States.

PRICES IN MEXICO FROM 1939 TO 1985

Price movement in Mexico since 1939 has not been uniform. A period of high inflation was succeeded by one of low inflation, which was subsequently followed by a period of inflation even higher than that in the first period. From 1939 to 1955, average annual price increases were high, often in double figures. From 1956 to 1972, the country enjoyed moderate, single-digit inflation. The period from 1973 to date has seen a return to high inflation, with two phases. From 1973 to 1981, Mexico suffered from high inflation. From 1982 to date the economy has bordered on hyperinflation, with average annual price increases twice those of the 1973 to 1981 period. Table 1 traces the Mexico City consumer price index from 1939 to 1985.

From 1939 to 1955, the compound rate of growth of the price index was 13.3 percent. From 1955 to 1972, average inflation dropped dramatically to only 3.7 percent. From 1972 to 1981, annual growth of the consumer price index averaged 20.2 percent, a sharp return to double-digit inflation. Since 1982 the rise in the consumer price index has been quite sharp: 57.6 percent in 1982, 97.8 percent in 1983, 62.7 percent in 1984, and 57.4 percent in 1985. Current estimates of 1986 determine it to be close to 100 percent.

PRICES IN THE UNITED STATES FROM 1939 TO 1985

Table 2 contains the U.S. consumer price index from 1939 to 1985. The data indicate four phases of inflation. From 1939 to 1948, the com-

TABLE I

Mexico City Consumer Price Index, 1939–1985

(*1978* = *100*)

Year	Index	Annual variation	Year	Index	Annual variation
1939	2.67	—	1963	26.87	0.22
1940	2.95	10.50	1964	27.99	4.15
1941	3.21	8.66	1965	28.55	1.98
1942	3.98	24.15	1966	29.54	3.48
1943	5.06	27.12	1967	28.93	−2.05
1944	7.03	38.98	1968	30.20	4.37
1945	8.10	15.10	1969	31.30	3.64
1946	10.30	27.23	1970	33.00	5.43
1947	11.13	8.05	1971	34.90	5.76
1948	11.15	0.21	1972	36.60	4.87
1949	11.83	6.05	1973	40.80	11.48
1950	12.28	3.85	1974	49.90	22.30
1951	14.57	18.63	1975	58.30	16.83
1952	16.21	11.25	1976	67.70	16.12
1953	15.82	−2.44	1977	85.50	26.29
1954	18.01	13.83	1978	100.00	16.96
1955	19.64	9.09	1979	117.80	17.80
1956	20.62	4.99	1980	149.00	26.49
1957	21.61	4.77	1981	191.90	28.79
1958	23.23	7.54	1982	302.40	57.58
1959	24.59	5.82	1983	598.00	97.75
1960	25.71	4.58	1984	972.70	62.66
1961	25.96	0.98	1985	1530.50	57.35
1962	26.82	3.28			

SOURCES: From 1939 to 1968, Jeffrey Bortz, *Industrial Wages in Mexico City* (Garland Publishing, New York, 1987); from 1968 to 1985, Banco de Mexico, *Indicadores Economicos*, various issues.

pound annual growth rate of the price index is 6.3 percent. This drops 75 percent during the next phase, 1948–1967, to only 1.7 percent. From 1967 to 1982, the United States returned to high rates of inflation that averaged 7.3 percent. Finally, from 1982 to date inflation has moderated considerably, averaging only 3.7 percent.

It is interesting that periods of high and low inflation in Mexico and the United States coincide roughly. The early postwar period was inflationary for each country. From the mid-1950s to mid-1960s, the two countries enjoyed price-stable economies. In the late 1960s and early 1970s, both began to suffer from higher average price increases, which reached double-digit levels in the 1970s. Clearly the shared patterns of inflation are not accidental. Mexico imports most of its capital goods from the United States, so that U.S. price levels have an important effect on Mexican prices. In addition, some common factors—expanding

TABLE 2

United States Consumer Price Index, 1939–1985

(1967 = 100)

Year	Index	Annual variation	Year	Index	Annual variation
1939	41.6	−1.42	1963	91.7	1.21
1940	42.0	0.96	1964	92.9	1.31
1941	44.1	5.00	1965	94.5	1.72
1942	48.8	10.66	1966	97.2	2.86
1943	51.8	6.15	1967	100.0	2.88
1944	52.7	1.74	1968	104.2	4.20
1945	53.9	2.28	1969	109.8	5.37
1946	58.5	8.53	1970	116.3	5.92
1947	66.9	14.36	1971	121.3	4.30
1948	72.1	7.77	1972	125.3	3.30
1949	71.4	−0.97	1973	133.1	6.23
1950	72.1	0.98	1974	147.7	10.97
1951	77.8	7.91	1975	161.2	9.14
1952	79.5	2.19	1976	170.5	5.77
1953	80.1	0.75	1977	181.5	6.45
1954	80.5	0.50	1978	195.4	7.66
1955	80.2	−0.37	1979	217.4	11.26
1956	81.4	1.55	1980	246.8	13.52
1957	84.3	3.51	1981	272.4	10.37
1958	86.6	2.73	1982	289.1	6.13
1959	87.3	0.81	1983	298.4	3.22
1960	88.7	1.60	1984	311.1	4.26
1961	89.6	1.01	1985	322.2	3.57
1962	90.6	1.12			

SOURCES: *California Statistical Abstract 1970*; *Statistical Abstract of the United States 1986*; *Monthly Labor Review*, September 1986.

world trade, the postwar boom, the health of U.S. multinationals, developing technology—affected these two countries as well as others. Most important, however, is the international structure of the world economy, which tends to share expansive and recessive periods with the various national participants (most strongly with those participants that have market economies). In the United States and Mexico, the early postwar period drove inflation up and wages down, helping to finance the productivity surge of the following period, which in turn drove price increases to moderate levels. As productivity began to lag in the later postwar period in both countries, low inflation gave rise to high inflation.

Despite some shared patterns, Mexico and the United States have different levels of inflation. Average price increases in Mexico are almost always significantly higher than in the United States. In addition, shifts to new inflation patterns occur in different years for each country. Finally, while average price increases seem to be moderating considerably in the United States in the 1980s, Mexico has hovered dangerously near hyper-inflation in the same period.

The differences in inflation patterns are caused by differences in economic structure. While the United States was prospering as the world's leading economy after World War II, Mexico was trying to industrialize through import substitution. U.S. dollars, exports, and imports played a key role in international trade through the postwar period. Mexico continued to be vitally dependent on international trade to obtain capital goods and new technologies, but its own effect on the global market was relatively small. Today the United States still imports and exports a wide variety of goods and services. Mexico basically continues to import capital goods and export primary goods.

In other words, the United States is an industrialized, developed country, while Mexico is an industrialized, underdeveloped country. A basic difference between the two is overall productivity. Higher productivity levels in the advanced countries permit a greater range of industrial exports, whereas the underdeveloped countries are limited by lower productivity to geographically determined exports, or low-wage exports. Depending on social structure, this difference in productivity can generate an important employment problem in underdeveloped countries, although the employment problem can look like a land or a low-wage problem. If social pressures are strong, government will react by expanding employment beyond the level of productivity increases. Combined with the monopolistic structure of industry in countries like Mexico, this reaction generates strong inflationary pressures. During periods of rapidly increasing productivity, inflation may moderate, as it did in Mexico after 1956.

Nonetheless, as productivity growth slows, inflation easily escapes control. Industrializing, underdeveloped countries like Mexico tend to have permanently higher inflation than industrialized, developed countries like the United States. As a result, although the two countries sometimes coincide in low-inflation and high-inflation periods, in the long run, Mexico's currency has been consistently devalued with respect to the dollar, as shown in Table 3.

Since 1939 the Mexican peso has enjoyed two periods of stability with respect to the U.S. dollar. From 1949 to 1953 the ratio stayed constant at 8.65 pesos to the dollar, and from 1954 to 1976 the exchange rate did not move from 12.50 pesos to the dollar. From 1949 to 1953, however,

TABLE 3

U.S. Dollar–Mexican Peso Exchange Rate, 1948–1985

Year	Pesos per dollar	Year	Pesos per dollar	Year	Pesos per dollar
1948	4.855	1961	12.500	1974	12.500
1949	8.650	1962	12.500	1975	12.500
1950	8.650	1963	12.500	1976	15.426
1951	8.650	1964	12.500	1977	22.573
1952	8.650	1965	12.500	1978	22.767
1953	8.650	1966	12.500	1979	22.805
1954	12.500	1967	12.500	1980	22.951
1955	12.500	1968	12.500	1981	24.515
1956	12.500	1969	12.500	1982	56.402
1957	12.500	1970	12.500	1983	120.094
1958	12.500	1971	12.500	1984	167.828
1959	12.500	1972	12.500	1985	256.872
1960	12.500	1973	12.500		

SOURCES: 1950–1985, International Monetary Fund, *International Financial Statistics*; 1948–1950, Adam Perkal and James Wilkie, *Statistical Abstract of Latin America*.

the Mexican price index rose 34 percent, while the U.S. price index rose only 12 percent—a disparity that led to the 50 percent devaluation of Mexico's currency in 1954. The new rate then lasted twenty-two years, mostly because of Mexico's low inflation after 1956, but partly because of the policy of slowly allowing the currency to become overvalued.

From 1956 to 1970, the U.S. price index rose 43 percent, while the Mexico price index increased 60 percent. The disparity would pressure the peso, though not enough to force the devaluation that would have increased the peso price of Mexico's capital-goods imports. This devaluation would have had a negative effect on Mexican consumers and could have squeezed Mexico's industrial profits.

In the ensuing six years, inflation accelerated in both countries. From 1970 to 1976 the U.S. price index grew 47 percent while the Mexico price index more than doubled (105 percent). Despite rising U.S. inflation, ever-increasing levels of Mexican inflation finally forced the almost 100 percent peso devaluation of 1976. Table 3 shows only the average daily exchange rate throughout the year rather than the daily rates. In the latter part of 1976, however, the peso fell from 12.5 to the dollar to more than 22 to the dollar.

Noncompetitive industrial economies necessarily overvalue their currency. Generally industry sells at home rather than abroad because of lower productivity. Since industry sells to the domestic market yet must buy capital goods from foreign markets, an overvalued currency tends to buy more while keeping inflation low. Although this situation negatively affects industrial exports, in practice only labor-intensive products are at stake. Most industrial products cannot compete in foreign markets, and even need to be protected at home. These developing countries mainly export primary commodities. The prices of these commodities are strongly influenced by rents, so overvalued currencies generally do not affect them.

In such a case, the profits from commodity exports subsidize the currency rather than finance the industrialization of the export sector—that is, export-led development. This scenario was, in effect, the Mexican dilemma of the postwar period. Even though such policies eventually gave rise to a serious financial crisis in 1976, the Mexican government continued to overvalue the peso. From 1977 to 1981, the value of Mexico's money fell only slightly with respect to the dollar, despite the vast disparity between Mexican inflation (125 percent) and U.S. inflation (50 percent). Just as agricultural exports had in an earlier period, oil exports in the late 1970s subsidized the peso. In both periods, of course, external debt financing was also used to support the currency. In 1982 falling oil prices and rising interest rates ended the subsidies, and the peso began its current collapse. From 24.5 pesos to the dollar in 1981, average value reached 256.87 in 1985. The peso fell close to 1000 to the dollar at the beginning of 1987.

These elements—high inflation and devaluating currency—would affect wages in Mexico. As might be expected, periods of high inflation and strong devaluations would be accompanied by falling real wages and later wage rates that declined in relation to U.S. wages.

WAGES IN MEXICO FROM 1939 TO 1985

Table 4 contains an index of real industrial wages in Mexico City from 1939 to 1985. It shows the average weekly wage of blue-collar workers, without fringe benefits.

Since 1939 Mexico has undergone three real-wage phases. From 1939 to 1952 wages declined; the index fell from 100.0 to 54.0. From 1952 to 1976 real wages increased; the index jumped from 54.0 to 144.8. Finally, from 1976 to date real wages have fallen again. By 1985 the real-wage index stood at 86.6.

Movement is not continuous, however, throughout any given phase. During the 1940s' decline, the most negative period occurs prior to 1946. Over seven years, real wages dropped by half. During the current decline, wages have fallen only slightly in most years. The two exceptions are

TABLE 4

Index of Real Mean Industrial Wage, 1939–1985

(*1939 = 100*)

Year	Index	Year	Index	Year	Index
1939	100.0	1955	62.1	1971	100.4
1940	90.5	1956	65.4	1972	108.5
1941	86.0	1957	65.1	1973	117.7
1942	71.3	1958	69.0	1974	126.9
1943	72.6	1959	69.7	1975	118.7
1944	57.6	1960	70.3	1976	144.8
1945	54.6	1961	72.1	1977	126.8
1946	49.8	1962	77.1	1978	124.8
1947	50.5	1963	82.3	1979	123.9
1948	57.0	1964	80.7	1980	117.9
1949	56.7	1965	86.9	1981	120.9
1950	60.1	1966	91.9	1982	125.9
1951	55.3	1967	98.6	1983	99.4
1952	54.0	1968	99.3	1984	92.5
1953	58.0	1969	102.9	1985	86.6
1954	62.0	1970	97.8		

SOURCES: 1939–1968, Jeffrey Bortz, *Industrial Wages in Mexico City* (Garland Publishing, New York, 1987); 1969–1983, Secretaria de Programacion y Presupuesto, *Trabajo y Salarios Industriales*, various years; 1984–1985, estimated using Comision Nacional de los Salarios Minimos, *Salarios Minimos*, 1984, 1985; Banco de Mexico, *Indicadores Economicos*, various years.

1983 (-21 percent) and 1977 (-12 percent). Significantly, the two severe wage declines followed the two severe devaluations of the peso, after which stringent austerity programs held nominal wage increases to levels far below inflation. Overall real wages drop 40.2 percent between 1976 and 1985, somewhat less than the 1939–1946 fall.

While the real-wage index does not, and cannot, take into account structural changes in consumption patterns caused by qualitative shifts in the supply of goods and services, and does not measure transfer incomes, fringe benefits, or employment shifts, it can still indicate relative incomes to labor as well as changes in the living standards of Mexico's industrial workers. Each real-wage phase has been important for understanding recent Mexican economic history. The 1939 to 1952 decline helped finance the country's postwar industrialization. Falling wages increased industrial profits in a period in which labor productivity and gross domestic product (GDP) were increasing rapidly. The 1952 to 1976 increase helped distribute the fruits of the industrial boom to industrial workers, though not necessarily to agricultural workers. This distribution certainly played a role in cementing the state-labor alliance, which has been so crucial in maintaining political stability. In fact throughout the entire period, employment growth permitted increased social mobility and further cemented the social pact established after the revolution.

The current economic crisis has driven real wages to 1960s' levels, which in turn were below those of the late Cardenista period. While fringe benefits and transfer incomes have increased enormously since the 1930s, partially offsetting the wage decline, employment has not been growing since 1982, nor has GDP. One million Mexicans enter the labor market each year, so that frozen employment opportunities and falling incomes will no doubt strain a social pact that was based on increasing social mobility for Mexico's urban groups.

WAGES IN THE UNITED STATES FROM 1939 TO 1985

Table 5 shows the nominal and real minimum wage rates for the United States and for the state of California from 1939 to 1985. Two clearly marked phases can be observed. The real federal hourly minimum wage rose 125 percent between 1946 and 1968. It then fell 32 percent from 1968 to 1985. The California minimum wage generally parallels the federal rate to 1978; after 1978, state law tied the local figure to the federal one.[3]

Real-wage rates in Mexico and the United States have shown a remarkable tendency to move in similar directions in recent times. During World War II, wages fell rapidly in both countries, though this movement was more marked for the nation than for California. During the postwar boom, real wages increased sharply in both countries. The Mexican wage rate began to move upward later than its U.S. counterpart, and maintained that momentum after the U.S. wage began to decline. The last ten years in Mexico and the last twenty years in the United States have been marked by declining real wages, although the Mexican decrease has been greater.

In the United States, median family incomes continued to increase after 1968 despite falling wage rates because of increased family employment; women in particular were becoming more a part of the labor force. From the late 1970s, however, the employment effect has diminished, and now even median family incomes are declining in the United States. Similarly, at the beginning of the Mexican wage decline in the 1970s, the Lopez Portillo government argued that growing employment more than offset

---

[3] The legal minimum wage is not necessarily representative of actual wage rates in industry. The long-run movement of the minimum wage, however, is similar to the overall movement of private-sector, blue-collar wages in the United States. It is also true that a large number of workers from Mexico in the United States earn wages at or near the minimum.

TABLE 5

United States and California: The Hourly Minimum Wage Rate

Year	U.S. nominal	U.S. real	Calif. nominal	Calif. real
1939	0.30	0.72	0.33	0.79
1940	0.30	0.71	0.33	0.79
1941	0.30	0.68	0.33	0.75
1942	0.30	0.61	0.50	1.02
1943	0.30	0.57	0.50	0.97
1944	0.30	0.56	0.50	0.95
1945	0.40	0.74	0.50	0.93
1946	0.40	0.68	0.50	0.85
1947	0.40	0.59	0.65	0.97
1948	0.40	0.55	0.65	0.90
1949	0.40	0.56	0.65	0.91
1950	0.75	1.04	0.65	0.90
1951	0.75	0.96	0.65	0.84
1952	0.75	0.94	0.75	0.94
1953	0.75	0.93	0.75	0.94
1954	0.75	0.93	0.75	0.93
1955	0.75	0.93	0.75	0.94
1956	1.00	1.22	0.75	0.92
1957	1.00	1.18	1.00	1.19
1958	1.00	1.15	1.00	1.15
1959	1.00	1.14	1.00	1.15
1960	1.00	1.12	1.00	1.13
1961	1.15	1.28	1.00	1.12
1962	1.15	1.26	1.00	1.10
1963	1.25	1.36	1.25	1.36
1964	1.25	1.34	1.30	1.40
1965	1.25	1.32	1.30	1.38
1966	1.25	1.28	1.30	1.34
1967	1.40	1.40	1.30	1.30
1968	1.60	1.53	1.65	1.58
1969	1.60	1.45	1.65	1.50
1970	1.60	1.37	1.65	1.42
1971	1.60	1.31	1.65	1.36
1972	1.60	1.27	1.65	1.32
1973	1.60	1.20	1.65	1.24
1974	2.00	1.35	2.00	1.35
1975	2.10	1.30	2.00	1.24
1976	2.30	1.34	2.50	1.47
1977	2.30	1.26	2.50	1.38
1978	2.65	1.35	2.65	1.36
1979	2.90	1.33	2.90	1.33
1980	3.10	1.25	3.10	1.26
1981	3.35	1.23	3.35	1.23
1982	3.35	1.16	3.35	1.16
1983	3.35	1.13	3.35	1.13
1984	3.35	1.08	3.35	
1985	3.35	1.04	3.35	

SOURCES: State of California, Department of Industrial Relations; *Monthly Labor Review*, December 1986. The National CPI has been used to deflate both series.

the moderate wage declines. After 1982 that argument collapsed. There can be little doubt that both Mexican and U.S. workers confront steadily eroding income in the 1990s.

SOME ASPECTS OF PRICE AND WAGE CHANGE AT THE U.S.-
MEXICAN BORDER: TIJUANA / MEXICALI – SAN DIEGO

While regional price and wage trends within countries tend to be less important than those between countries, the U.S.-Mexico borderland represents a relatively unique area. After World War II, Mexico's northern border and the U.S. Southwest underwent more demographic and economic growth than did their respective national counterparts.[4] Though the proximity of the two countries has stimulated economic activity in the United States as well, Mexico's borderland developed during the late nineteenth century as a response to U.S. economic initiative. Since then, northern Mexico has been strongly oriented to its northern neighbor.

Existing studies, though not complete, indicate that northern Mexico may have higher wage levels than the central part of the country, whereas certain parts of the U.S. Southwest may have lower wage rates than other areas of the country.[5] These studies are far from complete, and deserve more attention. Nonetheless, in this section I will compare long-run price and wage trends on the border with long-run national price and wage trends.

Table 6 compares the consumer price index (CPI) of Mexico City with that of Mexicali, the capital of Baja California, a populous northern border state. From 1968 to 1982, the two cities move within 1 percent of each other. In the long run, regional prices within a given national market must move together if there is a relative free flow of the factors of production. In the short run, however, local differences can be quite significant. During periods of sharp devaluations of the peso, prices on the Mexican side of the border would be expected to surge since many consumer goods are purchased in the United States. The overvaluation of the peso would be expected to have the opposite effect. Table 6 shows that Mexicali prices increase most with respect to Mexico City prices following devaluations. In 1977, after the 1976 devaluation, the Mexicali CPI jumped 37.4 percent as opposed to 26.3 percent for Mexico City. With the 1982 devaluation, the CPI in Mexicali rose 76.3 percent in 1982 and

[4] Niles Hansen, *The Border Economy* (Austin, Tex., 1981), chap. 8.
[5] *Ibid.*, chap. 4. Also, Secretaria de Programación y Presupuesto, *Sistema de Cuentas Nacionales de Mexico, Producto Interno Bruto por Entidad Federativa* (Mexico City, 1982).

TABLE 6

Mexicali, B.C. and Mexico, D.F., Consumer Price Index, 1968–1985

(*1978 = 100*)

Year	Mexicali	Percent change	Mexico City	Percent change
1968	30.2	–	30.2	–
1969	31.0	2.6%	31.3	3.6%
1970	32.2	3.9%	33.0	5.4%
1971	33.9	5.3%	34.9	5.8%
1972	35.9	5.9%	36.6	4.9%
1973	39.3	9.5%	40.8	11.5%
1974	47.9	21.9%	49.9	22.3%
1975	53.8	12.3%	58.3	16.8%
1976	62.1	15.4%	67.7	16.1%
1977	85.3	37.4%	85.5	26.3%
1978	100.0	17.2%	100.0	17.0%
1979	114.7	14.7%	117.8	17.8%
1980	140.0	22.1%	149.0	26.5%
1981	172.7	23.4%	191.9	28.8%
1982	304.4	76.3%	302.4	57.6%
1983	665.0	118.5%	598.0	97.8%
1984	1076.2	61.8%	972.7	62.7%
1985	1693.4	57.3%	1530.5	57.3%

SOURCE: Banco de Mexico, *Indicadores Economicos*, Secretaria de Programacion y Presupuesto, *Boletin Mensual de Informacion Economica*.

118.5 percent in 1983, while the CPI in Mexico City rose 57.6 and 97.8 percent in 1982 and 1983, respectively. Conversely, during the long periods of peso overvaluation, the Mexico City price index often increased more than its border counterpart.

Table 7 contains the real minimum wage in two Mexican municipios, Naucalpan and Tijuana. Naucalpan is a central Mexican municipio in the state of Mexico that borders on Mexico City. It became one of the country's most industrialized zones during the long postwar boom. Industrialization and urbanization essentially merged it with Mexico City, and it now forms part of the greater metropolitan area. Tijuana is the populous municipio that borders San Diego, California. Like Naucalpan, it was quite small prior to World War II. After the war both cities mushroomed, and today Tijuana is the largest city on the U.S.-Mexican border. Unlike Naucalpan, however, the Tijuana economy is less industrial and more service and commercial oriented.

Real daily minimum wages in both municipios parallel the Mexico City industrial wage trend for the same period. From 1946 to 1974 real wages increased. From 1974 to 1985 they decreased. In Naucalpan, the

TABLE 7

Naucalpan and Tijuana Real Legal Minimum Wage, 1946–1985

(1978 pesos)

Year	Naucalpan wage	Tijuana wage	Year	Naucalpan wage	Tijuana wage
1946	27.92	60.50	1966	81.15	115.89
1947	25.64	56.00	1967	82.85	118.32
1948	25.79	85.97	1968	89.70	127.01
1949	24.32	81.07	1969	91.25	129.03
1950	29.27	78.06	1970	96.96	142.86
1951	24.67	65.80	1971	91.69	135.69
1952	28.80	88.72	1972	103.82	150.00
1953	29.52	90.94	1973	93.13	137.02
1954	27.96	91.87	1974	127.05	175.37
1955	25.63	84.22	1975	108.74	156.13
1956	37.20	93.00	1976	116.10	160.71
1957	35.50	88.76	1977	124.44	156.98
1958	41.27	94.92	1978	120.00	147.00
1959	39.00	89.70	1979	117.14	141.24
1960	48.48	93.23	1980	109.40	128.57
1961	48.01	92.33	1981	109.43	125.42
1962	60.79	103.70	1982	106.48	108.22
1963	60.66	103.48	1983	81.77	74.05
1964	73.66	109.63	1984	76.90	69.50
1965	72.22	107.50	1985	75.47	68.21

SOURCES: Comision Nacional de los Salarios Minimos, for wage data; Bortz, 1987, and Banco de Mexico, for price data. Mexico City price index used for Naucalpan, and a composite Mexico City/Mexicali/Tijuana (1968/1980/1985) price index used for Tijuana.

real legal minimum wage (in 1978 pesos) climbed from 27.92 per day in 1946 to 127.05 per day in 1974, an increase of 355 percent. In Tijuana, wages rose from 60.50 pesos per day in 1946 to 175.37 pesos per day in 1974, an increase of 190 percent. From 1974 to 1985, wage levels dropped 40.6 percent to 75.47 pesos in Naucalpan, and 61.1 percent to 68.21 pesos in Tijuana. By 1985, wages in Naucalpan had declined to their 1965–66 levels, and in Tijuana, to their 1951–52 levels.

In both municipios, real wages rose after 1946 and declined after 1974. While these changes mirror national trends, the Naucalpan wage increase is greater than that of Tijuana, and its later decline is less. From 1946 to 1985 real wages in Tijuana increased 12.5 percent, whereas in Naucalpan they jumped 170.3 percent. This occurred because Naucalpan was shifted into a legal minimum-wage zone—the Federal District—with higher wages, whereas Tijuana had always been a high-wage zone. Nonetheless, this legal change represents a real change.

After World War II, Naucalpan became one of the country's leading industrial zones. Multinational and local firms built many factories, which produced consumer goods for Mexico's growing urban market. While this type of dependent industrialization has often been criticized, in Naucalpan it generated employment, urbanization, and eventually better wages. Tijuana, on the other hand, has been consistently a commercial and service economy. It was placed in a higher minimum-wage zone because of its proximity to the United States. Urbanization there, however, was not accompanied by the industrialization that would provide skilled jobs with high wages for new workers.

For the United States, differences in price and wage movement at the California border seem less important than similar regional differences in Mexico. One similarity between the two countries, however, is the increasing homogenization of legal minimum-wage rates. Mexico has gradually reduced the number of minimum-wage zones that have their own rates, and Tijuana now has the same rate as the Federal District. Similarly, the California legal minimum wage has merged with the federal rate after long being higher. Actual wage rates in both countries, however, vary not only from the legal minimum, but greatly from region to region.

In two respects, however, the legal minimum wage is quite important in the border region. In Mexico, the minimum wage tends to be the unskilled rate in the *maquiladora* industry. In the United States, the minimum wage is similar to the unskilled rate paid to illegal migrants in rural and urban jobs.

MEXICO'S INDUSTRIALIZATION
AND THE U.S. WAGE COMPARISON

Mexico's postwar industrialization radically transformed the country. Fifty years ago Mexico was primarily rural and agricultural. Two-thirds of the population lived in the countryside, only one-third in the cities. Agricultural value-added was almost as great as industrial value-added, including mining. Three and a half million people labored in the fields, while only three quarters of a million worked in industry. Today the country is primarily urban and industrial. Two-thirds of the population lives in the cities, only one-third in the countryside. Industrial GDP represents close to 40 percent of the country's total, while agriculture is less than 10 percent.

The changes brought about by postwar industrialization urbanized the country. The industrialization process itself provided stable, skilled employment to millions of workers. It also generated, for thousands of national and multinational enterprises, enormous opportunities for growth and profit. Despite these gains, however, Mexico could not achieve two important goals. It did not attain a competitive industrial structure, nor solve the age-old employment problem. In other words, postwar industrialization modernized the country without lifting it from underdevelopment.

Starting in the 1930s, and at a faster pace after World War II, national and foreign investors created new industries in Mexico, including pharmaceuticals, automobiles, tires, electrical appliances, and synthetic fibers. Some of the new industries produced consumer nondurables. Others developed consumer durables that had not been manufactured in Mexico during the Porfirian industrial boom. Most of these new industries shared the following characteristics: they were protected by tariffs and regulations; they primarily sold to the domestic market; and they imported most of their capital goods and technological base.

Although many of these branches of production were new to Mexico, with significantly higher growth rates than the country's older industries (such as processed foods, tobacco, and textiles) they were not the newest, most advanced, or most competitive industries on a world scale. After World War II, the advanced industrial countries were developing nuclear and aerospace industries, computers, and other advanced branches of production. Mexico was developing industries that had been created in the more industrialized countries decades before.

Mexico, however, had often lagged behind other nations in industrial development. Railroads, for example, led Mexico's development after 1880; their great boom in the United States and Great Britain, however, occurred primarily before 1850. Significantly, the 1890s railroad expansion in Mexico consisted mostly of extending tracks. The United States and Great Britain not only laid track, but also produced railroad equipment itself, something Mexico continued to import into the post-World War II period. The U.S. automobile boom occurred before and after World War I, while Mexico's came after World War II. Although the United States developed the machine-tool industry that supplied capital-goods inputs to auto producers, Mexico's boom was mostly in assembly plants that imported parts from the United States. In other words, Mexico's advanced branches of production were often advanced industrial countries' older industries, while the latter's advanced branches of production were simply not to be found in Mexico or other underdeveloped nations. Additionally, Mexico's industrialization typically lacked the backward linkages that characterized industrialization in the more advanced countries.

Within Mexico, newer as well as older industries generally had to compete with processes that were technologically advanced and capital intensive for Mexico, but technologically backward and not the most capital intensive for the rest of the world. This disparity occurred because Mexican industrialists had to purchase capital goods abroad. They bought capital-intensive processes that were designed for labor markets in Europe and the United States, not necessarily for the low-wage Mexican labor market. On the other hand, because the industrialists lacked vertical integration in the industrial plant, they rarely had access to cutting-edge industrial processes, thus Mexico's industries never developed the same productivity levels as industries in more advanced countries. In turn, Mexico's underdevelopment limited industrial exports. A unique exception, of course, was labor-intensive industries.

Mexico developed an industrial base that had to import technology and capital goods but could not export enough to pay for those imports; therefore traditional mining and backward agriculture had to finance the industrial imports. The oldest sectors of the economy had to subsidize the foreign exchange demands of the newest. With industrial growth generally limited to the consumer-goods industry, which produced for an expanding but still restricted domestic market, the supply of new industrial jobs could not keep pace with the employment needs of Mexico's expanding population, in particular those needs of rural migrants to Mexican cities. As a result, millions of Mexicans continued to labor in the countryside in low-productivity activities, occupy marginal urban jobs, or even migrate to the United States. In 1900 little more than 30 percent of the total population was economically active; in 1987 the percentage remained about the same. Formal, permanent, skilled occupations never increased in proportion to the need for them. Worse, any attempt now to solve the employment problem through industrial expansion would lead to a foreign-exchange crisis.

The limits on industrial expansion created a permanently large labor surplus that in turn represented a serious downward pressure on wages. Rapidly expanding postwar industry needed a trained and docile labor force, however, and was willing to negotiate with unions that had already allied themselves with the postrevolutionary state. In addition, while there was always a surplus of unskilled labor, periodically shortages of skilled labor would occur because most Mexicans continued to labor at unskilled occupations. Both of these elements pushed wages upward.

This combination of factors eventually gave rise to the real-wage cycle that we have observed in Mexico. Wages declined from the 1930s to the early 1950s as millions of *campesinos* poured into the cities. Low wages and the expanding markets of World War II and the Korean War combined to finance the country's industrial boom. From 1952 to 1976, industry flourished and real wages surged. From 1976 to 1985, Mexico reeled from successive "financial" crises, and real wages embarked upon another decline. More importantly, however, real wages never increased in proportion to productivity growth. From 1940 to 1970 labor productivity in industry exploded 200 percent, whereas industrial real wages increased only 8 percent.

In dollars not adjusted for inflation, Mexican minimum-wage rates increased in the postwar period. Nonetheless, their growth was limited by the above-mentioned factors, so that dollar wage rates in Mexico always remained significantly below U.S. wage rates. Table 8 shows that in 1948 the daily minimum wage in Nacualpan was only 61 cents. The devaluation dropped that wage to 34 cents the following year. The dollar rate then rose steadily to 5.07 in 1975. The steepest increase occurred from 1970 to 1975, when the dollar-equivalent real wage doubled.

From 1970 to 1975, however, the Mexican economy had reached the limits of noncompetitive industrialization. In order to grow, the industrial sector had to import more capital goods. Since the export sectors were not expanding in the same proportion, Mexico made increasing use of the foreign debt to pay for the imports. From 1970 to 1975, Mexico's external public-sector debt jumped from 3.245 billion to 11.540 billion dollars.[6]

A more fundamental problem, however, was the declining rate of productivity growth, which would eventually make increased real-wage rates unsustainable. The compound annual growth rate of productivity in Mexico declined to 1.26 percent from 1970 to 1979, and from 5.23 percent from 1960 to 1970.[7] Dollar-equivalent wage rates could not continue to rise if the economy continued to lose productivity growth while facing decreasing export earnings relative to the labor market's demands on industry.

The 1976 devaluation and subsequent wage-austerity program began to lower dollar wage rates, though not enough to restore balance to the Mexican economy. Future wage growth would have to be held to a level below that of the modest productivity increases. Sustaining this level would eventually allow labor-intensive manufactured goods to compete in the world market because of the low wages. The cost, of course, would be a decline in employment because declining demand would initially have a negative effect on domestic industry.

Under Lopez Portillo, the country was unwilling to face the social con-

[6] Committee on Latin American Studies, University of California at Los Angeles, *Statistical Abstract of Latin America* vol. 23 (Los Angeles, 1985).

[7] Nacional Financiera, *La economia mexicana en cifras* (Mexico City, 1981).

TABLE 8

Naucalpan and Tijuana Daily Minimum Wage Rates
in Pesos and Dollars, 1948–1985

Year	Naucalpan pesos	Naucalpan dollars	Tijuana pesos	Tijuana dollars
1948	3.00	0.61	10.00	2.05
1949	3.00	0.34	10.00	1.15
1950	3.75	0.43	10.00	1.15
1951	3.75	0.43	10.00	1.15
1952	4.87	0.56	15.00	1.73
1953	4.87	0.56	15.00	1.73
1954	5.25	0.42	17.25	1.38
1955	5.25	0.42	17.25	1.38
1956	8.00	0.64	20.00	1.60
1957	8.00	0.64	20.00	1.60
1958	10.00	0.80	23.00	1.84
1959	10.00	0.80	23.00	1.84
1960	13.00	1.04	25.00	2.00
1961	13.00	1.04	25.00	2.00
1962	17.00	1.36	29.00	2.32
1963	17.00	1.36	29.00	2.32
1964	21.50	1.72	32.00	2.56
1965	21.50	1.72	32.00	2.56
1966	25.00	2.00	35.70	2.85
1967	25.00	2.00	35.70	2.85
1968	28.25	2.26	40.00	3.20
1969	28.25	2.26	40.00	3.20
1970	32.00	2.56	46.00	3.68
1971	32.00	2.56	46.00	3.68
1972	38.00	3.04	53.85	4.30
1973	38.00	3.04	53.85	4.30
1974	63.40	5.07	84.00	6.72
1975	63.40	5.07	84.00	6.72
1976	78.60	3.93	99.80	5.00
1977	106.40	4.67	133.90	5.88
1978	120.00	5.27	147.00	6.46
1979	138.00	6.05	162.00	7.10
1980	163.00	7.01	180.00	7.74
1981	210.00	8.00	210.00	8.00
1982	322.00	2.16	322.00	2.16
1983	489.00	3.03	489.00	3.03
1984	748.00	4.46	748.00	4.46
1985	1155.00	4.50	1155.00	4.50

SOURCES: Tables 3 and 7.

sequences of an austerity program that combined falling wages, increasing unemployment, and negative industrial growth. As a result, oil and debt were used in their traditional fashion—that is, to subsidize internally-oriented industrial growth. Dollar wage rates began to creep upward after the 1976 devaluation, reaching eight dollars a day in 1981.

TABLE 9

Ratio of U.S. Daily Minimum Wage to Tijuana
Daily Minimum Wage

(*In dollars*)

Year	Ratio	Year	Ratio
1948	1.55	1967	3.92
1949	2.76	1968	4.00
1950	5.19	1969	4.00
1951	5.19	1970	3.47
1952	3.46	1971	3.47
1953	3.46	1972	2.97
1954	4.34	1973	2.97
1955	4.34	1974	2.38
1956	5.00	1975	2.50
1957	5.00	1976	3.87
1958	4.34	1977	3.12
1959	4.34	1978	3.27
1960	4.00	1979	3.26
1961	4.60	1980	3.80
1962	3.96	1981	3.34
1963	4.31	1982	12.36
1964	3.90	1983	8.84
1965	3.90	1984	6.01
1966	3.50	1985	5.96

SOURCES: Tables 5 and 8.

In 1982 rising interest rates and falling oil prices squeezed the Mexican treasury. When the government ran out of dollars to subsidize industrial growth and industrial employment, it could no longer continue to overvalue the peso; and without support, Mexico's currency virtually collapsed. A true austerity program was implemented. GDP growth halted, and neither industry nor employment continued to receive the subsidies that had nurtured them in the postwar boom. The minimum wage fell from eight dollars a day in 1981 to 2.16 in 1982, and was still only 4.50 in 1985, as shown in Table 8.

Since the late 1960s, U.S. wage rates have not been increasing. Through the entire postwar period, urbanization, modernization, and industrialization have been the most salient characteristics of Mexican society. Yet Mexican wage rates have not increased in relation to U.S. wage rates precisely because Mexico's postwar industrialization lifted GDP without developing a competitive industrial base. As a result, Mexican wage rates have not increased relative to U.S. wage rates even though the latter have been stagnant.

Table 9 compares the U.S. and Tijuana daily minimum wage rates from

1948 to 1985. In 1948 the U.S. minimum was only 1.55 times the Tijuana minimum. The wage differential increased until 1957, reaching 5:1. From 1957 to 1981, a slow and irregular process of decreasing wage differentials occurred between the two countries. By 1974 it was 2.38:1. Even in 1981 the U.S.-Mexico ratio was only 3.34:1. The 1982 devaluation dramatically reversed the narrowing trend, sending the wage ratio to 12.36:1. Subsequently, wage differentials have decreased somewhat. Nonetheless, by 1985 they stood at 5.96:1, about the same as 1950–51 differences.

CONCLUSIONS

Mexico and the United States are linked by many factors, not the least of which is the northward flow of labor across the Mexico-U.S. border. National sovereignty impedes creation of a single labor market engulfing both countries: free labor flows are simply not permitted. On the other hand, proximity, historical migration patterns, and wage differentials tie together intimately the two national labor markets.

Both symmetry and asymmetry characterize price and wage relationships across the border. Mexico and the United States exhibit remarkable parallels in price and wage movement. With respect to prices, each country experienced a period of high inflation during World War II, followed by a period of low inflation in the 1950s and 1960s, and later succeeded by high inflation in the 1970s. With respect to wages, each country experienced a postwar cycle of declining wages during the war, rising wages in the 1950s and 1960s, and falling wages thereafter.

Asymmetry has also been important. Inflation has almost always been higher in Mexico than in the United States, while wages have always been lower. Specific points of inflection for the price and wage curves have varied considerably.

Postwar industrialization in Mexico, however, created more symmetry. Prior to World War II, Mexico was rural and agrarian while the United States was urban and industrial. After World War II, both countries were urban and industrial.

Postwar industrialization nonetheless left intact the most important asymmetrical relationship: a developed, high-productivity economy versus an underdeveloped, low-productivity economy. As a result, Mexican wage rates have not improved in comparison to wage rates in the United States. While that fundamental imbalance remains uncorrected, labor flows across the border will continue.

"The Effect of Mexico's Postwar Industrialization on the U.S.-Mexico Price and Wage Comparison," by Jeffrey Bortz: A Comment

Peter Gregory

IN THIS COMMENT I propose to review some of the findings reported by Professor Bortz and to offer a contrasting perspective for their interpretation. It should cause no surprise to find contrasting views expressed on the actual course of wages in modern Mexico and their implications for the welfare of the labor force for at least two important reasons. First is the nature of the disciplines to which we adhere. As an economist, I resort to methods of analysis that derive from economic theory, while Professor Bortz applies the methodology of history. Second, any researcher on the theme of wages in Mexico faces formidable data problems. As a result, each scholar will confront these in his own way, with each solution giving rise to a different interpretation of events.

At the outset I wish to acknowledge the enormous effort and care that Professor Bortz has devoted to the preparation of the statistical measures reported in his paper. The reader of this short essay cannot begin to appreciate the archival research that underlies his effort to improve on the quality of the official wage and price statistics for the modern period of Mexico's economic development. A full appreciation of his work requires that the reader consult the book from which the quantitative data reported in his brief essay have been drawn.[1] Working with the original questionnaires received by the Mexican statistical agency, he reconstructs a manual worker's wage index for the manufacturing sector of Mexico City.[2] In addition, he derives a price index that is held to reflect working-

---

[1] Jeffrey Bortz, *Industrial Wages in Mexico City* (New York, 1987).
[2] Since 1939, the official results of the annual wage surveys have been published in *Trabajo y salarios industriales* (Mexico City, various years).

class consumption patterns better than do alternative official indices. For a full account of the sources and methodology employed in developing his statistical series, the reader is referred to Professor Bortz's book.

In this comment I do not intend to take issue with the wage and price series produced by Professor Bortz. Even though they diverge from those derivable from official publications in important respects during some years since 1939, in general, they evince a similar evolution over time. Thus, I do not propose to challenge the accuracy of the indices as reported. My reservations concern the conclusions to be drawn from them, particularly in light of other available information.

Professor Bortz's essay has two principal themes. One points to a varying but persistently wide differential between industrial earnings in Mexico and the United States, which is held to have provided an incentive for Mexican workers to migrate to the United States in search of employment. The fact that such large wage differences serve as an important explanatory variable for migration flows would find wide acceptance by students of the two countries and is not an issue here.

The second theme concerns the welfare implications of the course of real wages from 1939 to the early 1980s. Bortz observes that real industrial wages have fluctuated widely over time. Between 1939 and 1952, real earnings fell by almost half; this decline was followed by a sustained and steady increase that carried real wages to a peak in 1976. Thereafter, real earnings went into a decline that accelerated in the aftermath of the economic crisis of 1982. By 1985, real earnings were approximately 13 percent below those of 1939. Throughout the period 1940–1970, real earnings lagged far behind increases in industrial productivity, 8 to 200 percent respectively, so that the Mexican development process may appear to have failed to share the fruits of economic growth with the working classes.

Professor Bortz's conclusions follow inevitably from his choice of 1939 as a base year for his real wage series. The sharp fall of 50 percent in earnings between 1939 and 1946, the actual low point recorded, makes the prolonged subsequent increases in real earnings appear simply as a process of recovery to previously attained levels rather than as indicative of a broad improvement in the economic welfare of workers. The Bortz real-wage index does not record a restoration of earnings to their 1939 level until 1969! It is my conviction that his choice of 1939 as a base year gives rise to unduly pessimistic conclusions, which do not stand up well when subjected to closer scrutiny.

My first observation concerns the representativeness of the sample that serves as the database for the Bortz wage series. He acknowledges that it is a nonprobabilistic sample drawn from firms considered by the statistical agency to be among the most important in their industries. More precisely, for the earlier years covered by his study, 1939–1963, the sample is limited only to large firms drawn from the capital city and six other industrial centers; subsequently the sample was increased to include firms in twelve urban areas. Due to a varying reponse rate, the number of establishments surveyed nationally fluctuated widely. For example, in the brief interval between 1939 and 1946, the number of included establishments varies between 517 and 747 and employment between 37.6 to 61.7 thousand workers. If estimates of the size of the manufacturing sector labor force derived from the population census of 1940, at 524,000, are viewed as acceptable, the sample represents only about 10 percent of sector employment during the early years of the 1940s.[3] While a 10 percent sample might have been adequate for charting accurately the course of wages in the sector as a whole *if it had been randomly drawn from a stratified sample including all size categories of firms in the sector*, it certainly cannot be considered adequate for this purpose if it is limited only to large firms in the modern part of the sector.[4] Wages paid by such firms were shaped by institutional factors that were unique to them and that, therefore, rendered those wages nonrepresentative of labor market conditions in general.

The course of wages in the modern large-firm manufacturing sector was determined largely by government wage policy, as evinced in the course of legal minimum wages, and enforced by worker organizations that were strong there. Thus, an evaluation of the significance of the decline of reported wages for the sampled work force requires a brief review of the Mexican government's wage policy during the 1930s and 1940s. Minimum wages were first implemented in 1934 by the Cardenas government. In line with its strong pro-labor sympathies, that government established the initial minima at very high levels. I have estimated the (simple) average urban minimum wage to have been equal to approximately 74 percent of gross domestic product (GDP) per worker.[5] The

[3] The figure of 524,000 for manufacturing employment is attributed to the Banco de México by Clark W. Reynolds, *The Mexican Economy* (New Haven, Conn., 1970), 164.

[4] The sample firms averages approximately 100 employees each. The 1940 industrial census included 13,510 establishments with 389,965 employees, or 28.9 per establishment. This census, however, was not all-inclusive, for it posed minimum size requirements for inclusion. The relaxation of the size requirement resulted in a very large increase in the number of establishments and employees covered, so that the average employment per establishment declined to 18.4 in 1945 and further to 10.9 in 1950. Secretaría de Industria y Comercio, Dirección General de Estadistica, *Censo industrial 1956* (Mexico City, 1959), table 1.

[5] Peter Gregory, *The Myth of Market Failure* (Baltimore, Md., 1986), 224.

rural minimum was slightly lower but clearly exceeded the average output per worker in agriculture. One might question whether minima pegged at such elevated levels could endure. (Even when the real urban minimum wage reached its maximum level in 1977, it was equal to only 34 percent of output per worker.)

Since the share of wages and salaries in GDP in a proximate year, 1940, has been estimated to have stood at 29.7 percent, it is clear that the legal minimum wage must have stood far above the market price of labor. And indeed, no sooner than the minimum wage had been enacted, its real value began to be eroded by inflation. By the 1938–39 biennium, it had already lost 12 percent of its initial value. By 1940, the average minimum wage for urban workers had fallen to a level equal to approximately 43 percent of GDP per worker. It was to continue to fall in real terms until 1946, after which it began a gradual recovery. Although the low point in the minimum wage coincides with the lowest point in the real wage series recorded by the Bortz index, other scholars have observed that the real earnings of unskilled workers in the industrial sector of Mexico City actually stopped declining in 1944, even as the real legal minimum continued to fall, suggesting that actual wages paid had finally declined to a level approximating a market-determined wage.[6]

It is universally acknowledged that legal minimum wages in Mexico have been observed only in larger firms of the modern sector. It is therefore no surprise that the earnings of workers included in the survey followed the minimum wage as its real value declined. Since actual wages paid were so far above the market, there were no market pressures compelling employers to adjust nominal wages fully in line with inflation. Outside of that limited sector, wages were determined by market forces and therefore lay well below survey levels. But these lower levels are likely to have been representative of the actual earnings of the bulk of the urban manual work force. Thus, to judge the course of the welfare of the manual working class by a standard applying to a small minority of the work force that was patently unsustainable seems unreasonable to me.

It should be recalled that the decade of the 1940s was one of vigorous growth. It would be truly surprising to observe generally falling wages in such an expansionary environment. That the survey data of the decade did record a decline excited a great deal of scholarly activity seeking to

[6]S. Perrakis, "The Surplus Labor Model and Wage Behavior in Mexico," *Industrial Relations* vol. 11, no. 1 (1972), 80–85. See also J. Isbister, "Urban Employment and Wages in a Developing Economy: The Case of Mexico," *Economic Development and Cultural Change* vol. 20, no. 1 (1971), 24–26.

evaluate and explain the phenomenon.[7] Indeed, Adolph Sturmthal noted the anomaly posed by the recorded decline in earnings and the observed changes in the functional distribution of national income. The latter suggested that real wages, instead of falling during the 1940s, must have risen by at least 10 to 12 percent.[8]

Indeed, there are several bases for concluding that the economic welfare of the urban working class, excluding that minority effectively governed by the legal minimum wage, not only did not deteriorate during the 1940s but also probably improved significantly. It is an axiom of the economic development literature that the market price of urban labor is a function of its opportunity cost. That, in turn, is usually taken to be represented by the average returns to labor in the agricultural sector. Can anything be concluded about the returns to agricultural labor during this interval? It may be recalled that some 18 million hectares of land had been distributed during the Cardenas regime in the late 1930s. The process of land redistribution continued into the 1940s, though at a reduced pace; 8 million hectares were redistributed. The promise of redistribution might have been expected to deter migration of labor to urban areas. Indeed, there are reports of urban workers returning to their villages in order to exercise claims to land, even though net migration flows were urban-bound. The transfer of land might be viewed as resulting in a once-and-for-all increase in the incomes of rural labor or at least an anticipation of such an increase. Under such conditions, one would not expect the reservation price of labor to the urban sector to be declining.

Furthermore, the trend in the returns to agricultural labor during the decade is not consistent with a declining price of labor to the urban sector. Output per worker was increasing at an average rate of 3.6 percent per year, much faster than the 0.5 percent rate of increase in the rest of the economy. Indeed, the rate of increase attributed to the smallest farm units, which were typical of those distributed to the beneficiaries of the land reform, was even higher than the average for the agricultural sector as a whole.[9] Given such an environment, one would expect an upward pressure to be exerted on urban market-determined manual wages.

[7] An extensive review of the literature on this issue appears in Gregory, *The Myth of Market Failure*, 219–25.

[8] Adolph Sturmthal, "Economic Development, Income Distribution, and Capital Formation," *Journal of Political Economy* vol. 63, no. 3 (1955), 187–88.

[9] Sergio Reyes Osorio, et al. reported that output increases for plots of less than 5 hectares reached an average of 4 percent per year between 1940 and 1960, with most of the increase realized during the 1940s. See *Estructura agraria y desarrollo agricola en México* (Mexico City, 1974), 50.

Fragmentary data from a number of sources also point to buoyant labor-market conditions. Wages for unskilled labor in both urban and rural areas were reported to be above legal minimum wages during the mid-1940s. Apparently, market wages did not follow the downward course of the real legal minimum wage after about 1944.[10] Furthermore, consumption data for the period point to significant increases that are inconsistent with a sharp decline in the incomes of the urban working class as a whole. For example, per capita consumption of corn, beans, and sugar showed sharp and steady increases throughout the period 1935–1960 and beyond.[11] Reyes Osorio reports an average increase of 47 percent in per capita caloric intake between the late 1930s and 1960s.[12] The proportion of the population without shoes fell steadily from 27.6 percent in 1940 to 19.1 and 14.3 in subsequent census years. The apparent consumption of beer expanded from 83 million liters in 1935 to 180, 353, 572, and 745 million in 1940, 1945, 1953, and 1957, respectively.[13] The ratio of radios to population increased sharply from 1:52 in 1940 to 1:16 in 1960.[14] Finally, vital statistics record significant gains in life expectancy and declining infant mortality rates from debilitating diseases usually associated with extreme poverty. These improvements would not likely have been achievable had earnings of the urban working class generally been falling as precipitously as those earnings recorded by the Bortz index.

In my opinion, a more sustainable interpretation of the events of the 1940s would begin by distinguishing between the course of earnings in the modern urban sector in which legal minimum wages were effective, and the rest of the labor market. While a decline in earnings in the former until 1944 clearly did occur, this is not necessarily inconsistent with constant or even rising wages in the rest of the urban labor market. It is noteworthy that once real wages in the modern industrial sector reached their minimum (and perhaps their market-determined level) in 1944, they immediately began a gradual but steady recovery, which appears to have been matched generally by urban wage levels. If the rate of increase in real wages recorded by the Bortz index after 1950 is compared with that in productivity, a very different relationship emerges from that ascribed above to Professor Bortz for the 1940–1970 interval. While productivity in the secondary sector increased at a 2.6 percent annual rate between

[10] For a review of these data, see Gregory, *The Myth of Market Failure*, 229–31.
[11] Secretaría de Agricultura y Recursos Hydraulicos, Dirección General de Economía Agricola, *Consumos aparentes de productos agricolas, 1925–1978* (Mexico City, 1979).
[12] Reyes Osorio, *Estructura agraria y desarrollo agricola en México*, 90 and 101–102.
[13] Nacional Financiera, *50 años de revolución en México* (Mexico City, 1963), 83.
[14] World Bank unpublished sources.

1950 and 1970, the Bortz real wage index records an annual increase of
2.8 percent.[15] Throughout the 1950s and early 1960s, market wages appear to have exceeded legal minimum wage levels and to have been increasing independently of the recovery of the latter. Indeed, at least from
1960 through 1975, it is possible to document a narrowing of the wage
differential between earnings in the informal and formal sectors of the
Mexican economy.[16]

It should be recalled that the number of industrial workers that were
effectively covered by the legal minimum wage in 1940 was small relative
to the size of the urban work force. Even if all of the workers recorded as
employed in the industrial sector by the industrial census of 1940 actually
earned at least the legal minimum, a highly unlikely event, they represented less than 20 percent of a nonagricultural labor force that numbered over 2 million. The sample on which Professor Bortz's conclusions
are based accounted for less than 3 percent of this labor force. Since the
sample is obviously biased, its course cannot be taken to reflect accurately the changing welfare of the bulk of the urban work force.

It is also noteworthy that industrial-sector employment expanded at
an approximate rate of 5 percent per year between 1940 and 1970. Since
such employment involved a shift of workers from less-productive and
poorer-paying alternatives, this represented a further source of improvement in the welfare of the urban labor force. For workers entering modern sector employment after 1945, Bortz's series shows real wages increasing at an annual rate of 2.8 percent over the succeeding 25 years
(Table 4). This series, it seems to me, provides a more realistic ap-
praisal of the changing lot of the urban work force than one departing from
the inflated and unsustainable wage level accruing to a small minority
in 1939.

Between 1970 and 1982, substantial increases in real earnings were
recorded. Even though these fluctuated in response to varying rates of
inflation, which accelerated during the decade, they recorded increases
of between 20 and 25 percent overall according to Bortz's data. If wages
of domestic servants are any indication of the course of earnings in infor-

---

[15] For a detailed account of wage movements during the post-World War II period in
Mexico, see Gregory, *The Myth of Market Failure*, chap. 7.

[16] The increase in secondary sector productivity is that reported by Clark W. Reynolds
and Francisco Javier Alejo in their essay, "Labor Market Interdependence: Notes on the
Relationship Between Labor Shifts and Productivity Growth in the Case of Mexico and the
United States," Americas Program working paper 86–85 (Stanford, Calif., 1986), table 1A.
The secondary sector is defined to include, in addition to manufacturing activity, mining,
construction, petroleum, and electricity. The rate of increase in real wages represents the
change between two three-year averages, 1949–1951 and 1969–1971.

mal employments, earnings were rising even faster there. While earnings in the formal industrial sector have been recorded as stagnant or falling in the final years of the 1970s, this is a reflection of two factors. The first was a policy of wage restraint pursued by the government in order to contain inflationary pressures; such restraint could more effectively be exercised on formal industrial wages than any others in the economy (outside of the public sector). The restraint on wage rates was compensated for, in part, by increases in fringe benefits. Second, the average earnings of the sector may have been depressed by the increasing weight of new workers hired at entry-level wages in response to the dynamic growth of the Mexican economy in the euphoric years of the oil boom. In fact, if one examines the terms of employment embodied in collective bargaining agreements concluded between 1977 and 1980, these provided for stable real wages.[17]

There is, of course, no question that modern industrial-sector wages have fallen sharply since the crisis of 1982. Employment in that sector has also stagnated so it would appear that increases in the labor force since 1982 have been largely absorbed in other sectors at lower levels of productivity than those holding in the large-firm industrial sector. What has happened to real earnings in the former cannot be ascertained, though it may be presumed from the course of GDP and the growth in the labor force that they have fallen there as well. Whether they have fallen by more or less than the measurable decline in the available wage indices would have to be consigned to the realm of speculation. It is reasonable to assume that the decline in real incomes of Mexican urban workers has led to shifts in consumption patterns, particularly among lower-income families, away from modern industrial goods toward cheaper, lower-quality goods produced by the informal sector. If such a shift were significant in its size, it may have served to moderate a decline in real earnings in that sector. Whatever the true extent of the decline in real earnings of the urban labor force, it seems clear from the recent performance of the Mexican economy that a recovery to levels of a decade ago will be slow in coming. A resumption of a rising trend in wages will require an early return to higher and sustained rates of investment and a growth in national output.

[Eds. Note—Since the completion of the Bortz and Gregory essays, Mexico's successful stabilization program has reduced inflation of consumer prices from 132 percent in 1987 to 11.2 percent in the first two quarters of 1991. Since 1990, GDP has also grown and real wages have begun to recover.]

[17] Gregory, *The Myth of Market Failure*, 239–60.

Migrant Labor Supply and Demand in Mexico and the United States: A Global Perspective

Francisco Alba

IN MEXICO AND THE United States, people have grown accustomed to the migration of Mexican workers. On both sides of the border, we find a willingness to accept this phenomenon and to reap its benefits. This is particularly true of the migrants themselves, who, through their repeated decisions to undertake transnational migration, display a high degree of adaptability to the circumstances prevailing in their personal and family contexts.

How this migratory process affects both the sending and receiving countries is a much debated topic. An understanding of its aggregate effects, both positive and negative, must account for various elements specific to each society.

This essay views the migration of Mexican workers to the United States as the product of a series of factors that impinge both on the demand to which this migrant labor force responds and on the configuration of its supply. By addressing both sides of the migratory equation, we can identify the elements that shape this particular labor market. Although political and sociological influences obviously play an important role in determining the size, direction, and valuation of the flow of migrant workers, this essay emphasizes demographic and economic factors.

A discussion of the supply and demand aspects of the Mexican migrant labor force engenders a number of questions about the function this phenomenon serves in both Mexico and the United States: What policies and public action arenas are best suited to deal with this binational labor force? Can the two respective administrations ignore the evolution of the migratory process? Can migration offer something beyond the individual goal of benefits maximization? The answer to the final query is probably "yes," but designing and implementing policies that would move in this direction require first clarifying the relationship between migration and development.

MIGRATION AND DEVELOPMENT

The traits that today characterize Mexican migration to the United States were defined in the 1940s and 1950s. The seasonal demand for labor among U.S. agrobusinesses in the western and southwestern United States coincided with a supply of available peasants in the central, west-central, and north-central areas of Mexico. The link between these two groups was forged and strengthened over time.

Although generations of Mexican workers and U.S. employers have participated in this process, the corresponding labor market has changed little over the intervening four decades. A good deal of supporting evidence attests to the durability of the initial pattern. The most important sending and receiving areas remain the same, as do the rural origin of the migrant labor force, the predominance of young men in the migrating population, and the seasonal nature of the migratory cycle.[1]

The durability of this migratory pattern over time suggests that the demand for foreign temporary workers by certain sectors of the U.S. economy remains strong. However, the permanence of this markedly cyclical and rotational migratory pattern cannot be explained solely by the demand for a cheap and docile labor force. The proximity between workers and employers obviously facilitates the flow in both directions (to the workplace and back to the home community), but the fundamental element shaping this labor market is the persistence of a peasant economy in Mexico and, within it, the household as the unit where the various reproductive processes take place.

Numerous studies demonstrate that the cyclical and rotational nature of this migration is assisted by the organization of families and peasant units, which facilitate the departure and return of their members. Indeed, the existence, or survival, of these family units, despite the changing circumstances that modernization has introduced in Mexico, owes much to the additional employment and earning opportunities offered by transborder migration.[2]

[1] Among the works that have noted the permanence of certain characteristics of the labor flow are those by Jorge A. Bustamante, "Emigración indocumentada a los Estados Unidos," in *Indocumentados: Mitos y realidades* (Mexico City, 1979), 23–60; and Centro Nacional de Información y Estadística del Trabajo, *Los trabajadores Mexicanos en Estados Unidos* (Mexico City, June 1982).

[2] This view appears in Kenneth D. Roberts, "Agrarian Structure and Labor Mobility in Mexico," *Population and Development Review* vol. 8, no. 2 (June 1982), 299–322.

The migratory pattern that emerged in the 1940s and 1950s has not gone entirely unchanged.[3] Despite its overall continuity, the labor demand of the U.S. agricultural sector has fluctuated since World War II. In the agricultural sector, this demand has become less dynamic in general; the number of workers employed in U.S. agriculture has dropped steadily.[4] But the demand for imported seasonal workers has not undergone these changes. The changing labor demands may be due to the major transformations occurring in U.S. agriculture during this period. Mechanization and significant increases in the size of productive units have generally increased labor's productivity, and hence reduced the demand for labor. Nevertheless, this trend is not uniform over all areas of agriculture; there has been a continuing demand for migrant workers, especially since this demand has been satisfied relatively easily by an available labor supply.

In stark contrast to the tendencies observed in the United States, the population employed in agriculture in Mexico continues to increase, although at a slowed pace since 1950. According to census figures, the economically active population employed in agriculture rose from 3.8 million in 1940 to 4.8 million in 1950, and was estimated at approximately 5.6 million in 1980.

Other factors have affected the labor flow as well. Economic transformations in the United States have modified and intensified the demand for migrant labor. One such new demand originates from the services sector. Highly visible as of the 1970s, the predominance of services as a generator of employment contrasts with the few jobs created in manufacturing over the same period.[5]

Concurrent with these economic transformations came changes in the employment structure of the labor force. Domestic blue-collar jobs became more scarce, while highly skilled technical-administrative positions became more available. These sectoral and labor-force evolutionary trends in the United States overlap an increase in productive processes dependent on relatively unskilled labor, a demand that was met largely with imported labor. Migrant workers encountered or created openings

[3] For an analysis of the changes in the migratory pattern, see Francisco Alba, "Continuidad y cambio en la migración laboral entre México y los Estados Unidos," in *Memorias del Congreso Latinoamericano de Poblacion y Desarrollo* 2 (Mexico City, 1984), 771–90.

[4] Of the total number of employed workers, the proportion employed in agriculture fell from 6.7 percent (7.2 million workers) in 1950 to 2 percent (3.4 million) in 1980.

[5] Between 1970 and 1980, the employed population in the United States rose by nearly 21 million individuals, from 78.7 to 99.3 million. Manufacturing accounts for 1.2 million of these newly employed, mining for 400,000, and construction for 1.4 million. The remainder found employment in the services sector.

in the labor market in services and industry, job categories that hold a low socioeconomic rank or offer limited opportunities for advancement.[6]

Economic transformations in the United States presented new opportunities to Mexican migrant workers. New sources of demand opened, and Mexican workers responded. The Mexican migrants found increasing urban-industrial employment opportunities in the United States, including those in the service sector.

Mexican workers' insertion into the labor force assumed a novel migratory pattern in the early 1970s. During these years, only 13 percent of documented Mexican migrants—and a significantly greater number of undocumented migrants—were involved in agricultural activities, while 25 percent were employed in industry, 16 percent in construction, and nearly 28 percent in services.[7] Among documented Mexican migrants who had resided in the United States for four years or more before being legalized, 39 percent were employed in the manufacturing sector, 25 percent in personal services, 18 percent in construction, and only 9 percent in the agricultural sector.[8]

These figures identify the sectors of the U.S. economy that absorbed Mexican migrant workers.[9] Another factor contributing to the changes in this labor market was the increasing skill level and diversification within the Mexican labor force. After 1940, Mexico modernized at a rapid pace. Mexico's urban population in 1940 comprised less than 4 million people—about 20 percent of the total population. By 1970, this group accounted for 45 percent of the population and numbered 22 million individuals.

Along with urbanization came the increasing absorption of Mexico's workers into industrial and service activities. In 1940, only 34.6 percent of the economically active population found employment in nonagricultural activities; in 1970, nonagricultural activities accounted for 60.6 percent of the country's employed population. This percentage increase is substantial, but the increase is even more notable in terms of the absolute increase in the labor force engaged in industry and services. From 2 million in 1940, this group grew to 7.9 million in 1970. In this environment

---

[6] The niches occupied by the migrants are associated with secondary labor markets. See Michael J. Piore, *Birds of Passage: Migrant Labor and Industrial Societies* (New York, 1979).

[7] These data are derived from a survey conducted on the U.S.-Mexico border between 1973 and 1975 under the direction of Alejandro Portes. See Francisco Alba, "Exodo silencioso: La emigración de trabajadores mexicanos a Estados Unidos," *Foro Internacional* vol. 177, no. 2 (Oct.–Dec. 1976), 152–79.

[8] *Ibid.*

[9] For more on the incorporation of the cohort of legal migrants in the U.S. labor market, see Alejandro Portes and Robert L. Bach, *Latin Journey* (Berkeley, Calif., 1985), 240–68.

of rapid and sustained economic growth and accelerated social change (increasing levels of literacy and formal education are indicative of this process), the country's labor force acquired skill levels that enhanced its ability to respond to this more varied and specialized labor market.

The processes of transformation and development occurring on both sides of the U.S.-Mexico border provide a frame of reference for both the continuity and change that characterize the evolution of the binational labor market. This evolution appears headed toward a harmonic balance in which U.S. labor demands are complemented by an availability of Mexican workers. From this perspective of complementarity, the evolving international migration may prove a dependable mechanism for increasing labor market integration between the United States and Mexico.

Although the migratory pattern that has prevailed to date has served the needs of both countries, its future prospects are uncertain. Other factors that interact in the migratory equation hint at limitations and obstacles that may hinder the development of a growing, tension-free labor market integration between the two countries.

ARE THE U.S. LABOR MARKET AND THE MEXICAN LABOR POOL COMPLEMENTARY?

Although a demand for Mexican workers clearly exists in the agricultural, industrial, and service sectors of the U.S. economy, this demand is neither unlimited nor necessarily linked to Mexican workers alone. Mexican labor is capable of meeting these labor demands, but the flow of Mexican migrant workers encounters now and will continue to encounter strong competition in the U.S. labor market, especially as work opportunities diversify.

Various factors could constrict extended expansion of the current pattern of labor exchange between Mexico and the United States. On the demand side, these limitations are both economic and sociopolitical. The multidimensional integration occurring in the global economy—which comprises trade flows, capital movement, labor displacement, and technology transfer—formed part of the strong and sustained economic growth that followed World War II. This integration has slowed since 1970 due to a fall in the level of economic activity in center countries. One result of this slowing has been a drop in the importation of migrant workers to these countries. Moreover, linked to these economic trends were social and political opposition to labor importation and efforts to stem the flow of foreign workers.

New policies on migration in western Europe during the 1970s failed to eliminate these flows, but they were able to reduce their magnitude.

TABLE I

Immigrants to the United States by Region of Origin, 1950–1985

(thousands and percentages)

	1951–60		1961–70		1971–80		1981–85	
	No.	Pct.	No.	Pct.	No.	Pct.	No.	Pct.
Western Hemisphere	996.9	39.63%	1,575.4	47.55%	1,929.4	43.94%	1,069.7	37.34%
Latin America	559.3	23.23	1,299.9	38.90	1,863.9	40.37	1,013.9	35.40
The Caribbean	123.1	4.89	228.3	6.87	284.4	6.33	326.9	11.41
Central America	44.8	1.78	97.7	2.94	132.4	2.95	123.1	4.30
South America	91.7	3.65	228.3	6.87	284.4	6.33	184.0	6.42
Mexico	299.8	11.92	443.3	13.35	637.2	14.18	335.2	11.70
Europe	1,325.6	52.70	1,238.6	37.29	801.3	17.83	321.8	11.23
Asia	150.1	5.97	445.3	13.41	1,633.8	36.36	1,376.3	48.05
Others	42.4	1.69	58.4	1.76	75.4	1.68	96.6	3.37
Total	2,515.5	100.00%	3,321.7	100.00%	4,493.3	100.00%	2,864.4	100.00%

SOURCE: U.S. Department of Justice, Immigration and Naturalization Service, *Statistical Yearbook* (Washington: various years).

The conflict between forces demanding that migration be contained and those demanding that the labor flow continue has created an atmosphere that affects negatively the flow of migrant workers in general and, in the United States, Mexican workers in particular.

The demand for Mexican labor comes from multiple sources. Some of these specify Mexican labor; others do not. Demands for Mexican workers arise because the seasonal and rotational characteristics of the Mexican migrant flow are not matched by any other group of migrant workers. In areas of labor demand that are open to a broader group of workers, Mexican migrant workers must compete increasingly with other worker flows seeking to replace the Mexican labor pool. In effect, that portion of the U.S. labor market traditionally served by Mexican labor is increasingly shared with other nationalities and other sources of labor supply.[10] Within this competitive labor market, patterns of legal migration to the United States contrast markedly with the very different pattern of Mexican migration, which has tended to rely on nonlegal routes.

Table 1 indicates that the number of immigrants to the United States has increased by approximately one-third every decade since 1950, a pattern that, from the data on the first five years of this decade, seems to be repeating. Legal Mexican migration was a strong component in this immigration pattern until 1980: from representing 11.9 percent of the migrating population in 1950–1960, Mexican migrants accounted for 14.2 percent in the 1971–1980 period. The relative position of the Mexican migrating population, however, fell during the 1980s to 11.7 percent, compared with absolute and relative advances among immigrant populations from the Caribbean, Central America, the rest of Latin America, and especially Asia.

The migratory flows from the Caribbean and Central America have enjoyed significant relative gains, while migration from Asia has gained in both relative and absolute terms. Asian immigrants display a very dynamic pattern. Only 150,000 Asians migrated to the United States in the 1950s, accounting for 6 percent of the total number of immigrants; during the 1970s, however, their numbers rose to 1.6 million (36.4 percent), and in the first half of the 1980s, the 1.4 million Asian migrants represented nearly half (48 percent) of the total number of immigrants, allowing Asia to displace Latin America and Europe as the leading supplier of immigrant labor to the United States.

The figures on migration to the United States are not, of course, direct

[10] On the compartmentalization of undocumented migration, see Charles B. Keely, "Illegal Migration," *Scientific American* (Mar. 1982), 41–46.

equivalents of net increases in the U.S. labor market. (Family reunification, especially after the 1965 immigration law reform, was a preeminent factor in immigrant flows.) In broad terms, however, the changing composition of legal migratory flows undoubtedly was reflected in the labor arena.

Thus, the increasing number of migrants and the diversity of their countries of origin are linked to the extension and growth of labor markets, which are responding to the existence and availability of a labor supply found beyond the nation's borders. In a world that is becoming smaller due to closer relations among countries, the pool of available labor is becoming larger.

Those labor markets that have for decades met their U.S. labor demand with the Mexican labor force are now encompassed by this transnationalization or internationalization of labor.[11] The introduction of this factor into a company's economic calculations results in a heightened demand for foreign labor. But this tendency can also lead to saturation and surplus in the labor markets. The global labor supply can adversely affect the demand for Mexican labor, even though the labor requirements of a growing U.S. economy could accommodate a sizable population of foreign workers.[12]

One indicator of an increasingly competitive labor situation worldwide is the population that is of working age. The future size of the working-age population—those between 15 and 65 years of age—can be precisely estimated. United Nations data reveal that in 1960 there were 1.146 billion working-age individuals in the less-developed countries. This population had nearly doubled (to 2.155 billion) by 1985 and will reach approximately 3.010 billion by the year 2000.

In developed countries, the working-age populations tend to be smaller and to increase at slower rates. This group will expand by only 50 percent between 1960 and 2000, from 595 to 842 million individuals. The contrast between the developed and less-developed countries is even more noteworthy if we compare the patterns anticipated to occur over the next fifteen years. In the developed countries, the working-age population will increase by 60 million between 1985 and 2000, while the less-developed countries will add 855 million persons to their working-age populations over the same fifteen-year span.

[11] See Alejandro Portes and John Walton, *Labor, Class, and the International System* (New York, 1981).

[12] See Clark Reynolds, "Labor Market Projections for the United States and Mexico and Their Relevance to Current Migration Controversies," *Food Research Institute Studies* vol. 17, no. 2 (1979).

The possible ramifications of this demographic disparity are numerous. It will likely produce an imbalance between labor supply and demand in the advanced and less-advanced countries.[13]

Within this global demographic-labor scenario, future trends in the regional and global arenas suggest that an established flow of migrant workers—in this case, Mexican migrant workers—will encounter strong competition for a limited number of employment opportunities. Mexican workers will find that it is an employer's, not a worker's, market.

A comparison of demographic trends forecast for Mexico and the United States until the year 2000 initially indicates a harmony of interests. Looking at the working-age population as an indicator of the potential future labor supply, the data in Table 2 suggest that the net additions to this population between 1970 and 2000 in Mexico and the United States are complementary.

In the United States, the working-age population grew by approximately 11 million each five-year interval between 1970 and 1980. This rate of growth then began to slow, a trend anticipated to continue until the year 2000. The increase was 7.4 million between 1980 and 1985 and is projected to be 5.3 million between 1985 and 1990, 5.7 million between 1990 and 1995, and 8.6 million between 1995 and 2000.

In Mexico, the opposite trend is occurring—a sharp increase in the working-age population until 1990, to be followed by a more stable pattern: 4.7 million were added to the working-age population between 1970 and 1975, 5.7 million between 1975 and 1980, 7 million between 1980 and 1985, and 8 million projected for 1985 and 1990. Growth per five-year period is expected to stabilize at about 8.2 million over the final decade of this century.

These figures are very rough indicators of the availability of labor. The working-age population is not identical to labor supply, much less to the population of migrant workers. Migrant labor, a residue from the "trickle-down" effect within the labor pool, merely reflects the changing dimensions of the working-age population. We can anticipate that an overwhelming proportion of the absolute increases in working-age popu-

[13] These figures on the population between ages 15 and 64 conceal differentials that may be significant for the relative importance of labor force sectors. First, the figures do not specify the anticipated level of participation by men and women. (The former will probably decline, and the latter increase, at least in some areas.) Second, only limited sectors of the working-age population are relevant to a consideration of binational or multinational labor markets. The figures presented include populations generally inscribed within self-contained labor markets or those that do not maintain open channels of communication with the world economic system (China is the most obvious example). The debate over the supply and demand of migrant workers only takes place within open economies.

TABLE 2

Absolute and Projected Growth Figures of the Population Aged 15–64, 1970–2000

(*thousands*)

Population	1970–75	1975–80	1980–85	1985–90	1990–95	1995–2000
World	234,495	276,191	317,097	315,353	291,110	309,441
More-developed regions	39,129	37,377	37,075	23,613	15,701	20,723
Less-developed regions	195,356	239,814	280,021	291,741	275,409	287,718
Latin America	23,802	27,777	29,690	31,908	33,941	36,966
United States	11,907	11,824	7,368	5,259	5,694	6,606
Mexico	4,698	5,708	6,954	8,009	8,190	8,263
Mexico and Central America	6,128	7,412	8,966	10,403	11,017	11,533
Mexico, Central America, and the Caribbean	7,770	9,424	11,123	12,626	12,971	13,743

SOURCE: United Nations, *World Population Prospects: Estimates and Projections as Assessed in 1984* (New York: 1986).
NOTE: For the projected figures, the mean variant was adopted.

lation will be absorbed within the national borders of each respective country, as has been the pattern in recent years. Nevertheless, the structure of U.S.-Mexican labor markets is not immune to the impacts of markedly uneven demographic processes. The potential labor supply available to meet the demand of the U.S. market would soon largely exceed the current demographic and labor complementarity apparent in the U.S.-Mexican relationship.

Table 2 presents the absolute increases in population between the ages of 15 and 64 in developing countries. The five-year estimates projected for the remainder of the century total about 300 million (this includes Mexico's projected population growth), compared to an increase of about 5.3 to 6.6 million in the United States. Clearly this comparison exceeds the breadth of our focus. A strictly binational comparison, however, does not suffice.

Perhaps the long history of the flow of Mexican migrant workers to the United States and the dependence of certain U.S. economic sectors on Mexican labor will assure that the demand for migrant workers from Mexico will rise at levels commensurate with the increasing labor supply. However, trends in worldwide demographic patterns and the emergence of new migratory flows to the United States cast doubt on any supposition that the future structure of this labor market will replicate what we have seen in the past. Thanks to technological and cultural changes worldwide, the comparative advantage that Mexico's proximity could represent for the United States is eroding as physical, social, and economic distances are closing.

One implication for Mexico concerns the advisability of viewing the labor force as an export product. Mexico should develop policies to maintain its market share (perhaps even to penetrate new markets). But assuming that it is ill-advised to continue exporting labor indefinitely, Mexico should also develop a transitional strategy for replacing exported labor with some other, more advantageous products. These two related aspects should form part of the ongoing discussion about the advisability or inevitability of continuing for another ten to fifteen years those labor market ties that have prevailed between Mexico and the United States for the last three or four decades.

This binational labor market is based on the persistence of labor migration. However, the inevitability of this flow does not prevent it from carrying costs or adverse effects. The fact that this labor has been available over generations suggests the reproduction of unfavorable conditions within Mexico. A second consideration is that international migration cannot be viewed as a component of any Mexican administration's domestic policy. Third, demand factors determine the dynamic of international labor flows, a fact that reinforces the need for a dual strategy that would both protect markets and ensure vertical mobility within them.[14] For these reasons, successive Mexican administrations have tried to identify substitutes for this one-dimensional labor market as a means of dealing with their domestic labor force.

The search for more favorable options has displaced some of the labor links between the two countries, though without severing the underlying relationship. One alternate source of employment for migrating labor is the expansion of the *maquiladora* industry.[15] This redirection of labor follows the general rule that it is preferable to exchange goods than to exchange labor. Nevertheless, Mexico's *maquila* industry has been excessively dependent on the advantages it offers in terms of cheap labor. Given the absence of backward linkages (for inputs) between the *maquilas* and the rest of national industry and the *maquila* sector's orientation toward low skill levels among its work force, this substitution strategy contains the same dilemmas associated with the internationalization of labor markets.

The *maquila* industry was initially visualized as a strategy to develop complementary production processes in twin plants and to produce goods efficiently and cheaply. But unless it alters as it matures, this industry's future expansion will depend on reproducing the labor conditions—comparative advantages achieved through low wage levels—which characterize it today. This is especially likely given the elevated levels of competition implicit in the rapid growth of the international labor pool.

More and more countries in the less-developed world hope to gain entry to this new international division of labor, and their competition for a foothold has repercussions on their respective internal labor markets. In Mexico, the precipitous drops in wage levels—in both real and international nominal terms—that have resulted from recession and stagnation in the Mexican economy have occurred simultaneously with a dynamic expansion of *maquila* industry. In 1986, the *maquila* sector cre-

[14] See W. R. Böhning, "Elements of a Theory of International Economic Migration to Industrial Nation-States," in Mary Kritz, Charles Keely, and Silvano Tomasi, eds., *Global Trends in Migration: Theory and Research on International Population Movements* (New York, 1981), 28–43.
[15] The simultaneity of the initiation of Mexico's *maquila* program and the United States's termination of a series of agreements on seasonal hiring of Mexican workers is not coincidental.

ated a quarter of a million jobs and generated earnings of $1.3 billion dollars.

Pressures on the *maquiladora* industry, and on the labor market that services it, come from the developed countries as well. Early on, it was difficult to determine if the *maquila* industry would affect the labor markets of the highly advanced countries, either in terms of jobs or salary and wage levels, because of the existence of export-oriented enclaves that relied on wage differentials. Nevertheless, this productive scheme soon entered the realm of interdependency. Perhaps even more than the migration of workers, the entry of manufactures produced with low wage costs established links among previously separate or segmented labor markets.

The introduction of inexpensive labor-intensive products in the advanced countries produced two effects in their labor markets. The first was pressure to restrict wage gains in the developed countries and even to decrease wage levels. The second was a loss of jobs in industries now served by the *maquilas*.

Resistance to these impacts took the form of a wave of protectionism aimed at preserving the wage differentials between countries, differentials that are the very foundation of the whole process of subcontracting and relocating to offshore production.[16] The circle is closed and the dilemma remains: either reduce wage levels or move production offshore.

Economic, demographic, and labor trends can produce contradictory situations. Strengthening exchange networks can evoke reactions aimed at preventing a country from overcoming those obstacles it set out to overcome through this process. It is still necessary, however, to develop such networks and to continue the search for options to transform and transcend relations between the two countries.

The design of concrete policies depends on accepting (1) that international migration is one aspect of the substantive disparities present within a single economic system, and (2) that barriers to product entry hinder the relocation of productive processes (including services) to such a degree that they exacerbate the discrepancies between labor supply and demand within given markets.

Despite Mexico's best national instincts, I believe that it should adopt an aggressive policy to preserve and extend that share of the U.S. labor market traditionally dominated by Mexican labor. This implies that the United States must resist domestic protectionist pressures, even if it must surrender certain areas of industrial production in which other countries hold a comparative advantage.

---

[16] Note the attempts to introduce clauses in U.S. trade legislation concerning working conditions in countries that are important trading partners of the United States.

From the perspective of global interdependence, the developed world should be prepared to admit new members to its club, and the newly developing countries should prepare to join the "graduates." Advances in the international development process will depend on qualitative changes among all members of the system.

Mexican-American Employment Relations: The Mexican Context

Saul Trejo Reyes

"We are ruined by Chinese cheap labor."
—Brett Hart, 1880

O N THE LIST OF issues of permanent importance for relations between Mexico and the United States, labor flows certainly appears near the top. This issue is significant not simply because it is constantly in the news; it has long-term importance for Mexican-U.S. relations. In addition, labor relations cannot be viewed separately from the global or international context, which affects each country differently. The United States is at a stage in its economic development in which it views the world as its economic territory both for international trade and in terms of labor and capital flows. Mexico, however, is definitely provincial, and at best regional, in its economic outlook. The widely divergent character and nature of both societies pose serious problems for any approach that seeks simply to find "natural" complementarities in a vacuum; both countries have differing definitions of their long-run national interests. These definitions must be the starting point for any analysis of their future.

It is useful to first review briefly the changes in population and labor force that have taken place in Mexico after 1970—a turning point not only demographically, but also for economic policy and performance. Beginning in the early 1970s, Mexico began its first sustained effort to reduce the growth rate of its population. Although this rate remained at an all-time peak of 3.4 percent for the decade, by 1980 it had dropped to an annual 2.7 percent. The labor force, however, grew at a record high rate of between 3.7 and 4.0 percent during the decade, reaching between 19 and 20 million persons in 1980.[1] By 1985, the labor force was esti-

[1] The official census datum, 23.7 persons, implies an annual growth rate of 6.2 percent; however, this figure is generally considered to be too high.

TABLE I

Population Growth Projections: 1980–2010

(*Thousands*)

Year	Urban		Rural		Total
	No.	Pct.	No.	Pct.	
1980	46,148	66.2%	23,507	33.8%	69,655
1985	52,138	68.5	24,034	31.5	76,171
1990	59,443	71.0	24,282	20.0	83,726
1995	66,457	73.4	24,069	26.6	90,526
2000	74,168	75.8	23,644	24.2	97,812
2005	81,557	77.9	23,172	22.1	104,729
2010	88,247	79.5	22,754	20.5	111,001

SOURCE: Leopoldo Nuñez and Lorenzo Moreno, *México: Proyeccions de la población urbana y rural, 1980–2010* (Mexico City, 1986).

mated to be 22.5 to 23.5 million persons—that is, after 1970 the average growth rate of the labor force has been about 3.4 percent annually.

A second important characteristic of Mexico's demographic evolution over the last fifteen years has been the high rate of urbanization. By 1985, Mexico's urban population was of the order of 52.1 million, while its rural population was 24 million. This means that 69 percent of the population was classified as urban, compared to only 59 percent in 1970.[2] Thus, between 1970 and 1980, Mexico's urban population grew from 28.3 to 46.1 million persons, at an annual rate of just over 5 percent. This urban growth has been concentrated in a few cities, especially the largest three, which between 1970 and 1980 increased their populations at 5.6 percent annually. These cities' share of total population rose from 23.4 to 28.5 percent over the decade.

Meanwhile, Mexico's rural population grew from 19.9 million to 23.5 million, at an annual rate of only 1.7 percent. Between 1980 and 1985, it is estimated that Mexico's urban population grew by 6 million: 92 percent of the total population increase for the period. Tables 1 and 2 show some of the main features of projected future demographic changes. The trend toward urbanization must be considered when estimating future labor creation requirements in Mexico. In the foreseeable future, as has been the case since the 1960s, practically all of the population increase, and the consequent increase in the labor force, will have to be absorbed by new urban jobs.

[2]Data for 1970 are from the population census and define *rural population* as those persons living in locales with less than 2,500 inhabitants. Data for 1980 are from unpublished revisions of census data and population projections prepared by Leopoldo Nuñez and Lorenzo Moreno, *México: Proyeccions de la Población Urbana y Rural, 1980–2010* (Mexico City, 1986).

TABLE 2

Ages of the Mexican Population

(*Pct. of total population*)

Year	Age groups			
	0–14	15–24	25–64	65+
1980	44.8%	19.7%	30.5%	3.9%
1985	39.5	22.2	34.1	4.2
1990	34.8	23.8	36.9	4.5
1995	31.2	22.7	41.1	5.0
2000	29.9	18.9	45.5	5.7
2005	27.8	17.3	49.8	6.7
2010	26.5	17.0	49.8	6.7

SOURCE: Same as for Table 1.

Along with the urban population, the tertiary sector has experienced a rapid growth that at best reflects simply the inability of the rest of the economy to create enough jobs for the growing labor force.

Estimates of future rural and urban populations imply that Mexico's rural population, which in 1985 was estimated at 24.0 million, will remain at that level for the next ten years and then will start decreasing in absolute terms.[3] It is estimated that in the year 2000, the rural population will be 23.6 million persons. Such tendencies imply that Mexico's urban population will increase from 46.1 million in 1985 to 74.2 million in 2000, at an annual rate of 2.4 percent, while its total population grows at an average rate of 1.7 percent for the period. By 2000, the population of the 15–24 age group will be 18.2 million, compared to 16.9 million in 1985. In the United States, by contrast, the civilian labor force aged 16 to 24 will likely fall from 25 million in 1981 and 23.2 million in 1985 to just over 20 million in 1995 as a result of the fall in the birthrate.[4]

A fourth phenomenon that must be considered is the large growth in labor force participation that took place after 1970. Much of this increase was due simply to the changing age of the population and was relatively easy to predict. A new factor, however, had to be considered: the rise in women's rates of participation, which occurred during the boom years of the late 1970s and early 1980s. Although at first thought to be a temporary phenomenon, this increase has apparently influenced the "permanent" participation rates even after the collapse of the economy. It is difficult to estimate what the magnitude of this effect will be in

[3] *Ibid.*

[4] "HELP WANTED: A Shortage of Youths Brings Wide Changes to the Labor Market," *Wall Street Journal*, 2 Sept. 1986, sec. 1:1.

TABLE 3
Sectorial Output Value and Change, 1981–1985

	Output value (1970 prices)					Percent change				
	1981	1982	1983	1984	1985	81–82	82–83	83–84	84–85	81–85
Total value	908,765	903,850	856,177	887,647	911,544	−0.5%	−5.3%	3.7%	2.7%	0.3%
Agriculture, cattle, forestry	80,299	79,821	82,132	84,153	86,023	−0.6	2.9	2.5	2.2	7.1
Coal, oil	20,755	23,627	23,332	23,640	23,487	13.8	−1.2	1.3	−0.6	13.2
Iron and metal ores	6,314	6,357	6,252	6,297	6,445	0.7	−1.7	0.7	2.4	2.1
Nonmetallic minerals	4,524	4,513	3,973	4,232	4,562	−0.3	−12.0	6.5	7.8	0.8
Dairy, processed foods	36,652	38,469	38,674	39,335	40,923	5.0	0.5	1.7	4.0	11.7
Beverages, tobacco	15,216	15,604	14,897	15,134	16,032	2.5	−4.5	1.6	5.9	5.4
Textiles	27,602	26,014	24,569	24,792	26,027	−5.8	−5.6	0.9	5.0	−5.7
Wood products	18,460	18,569	16,655	17,426	18,155	0.6	−10.3	4.6	4.2	−1.7
Chemicals	22,832	22,992	24,558	26,211	26,987	0.7	6.8	6.7	3.0	18.2
Other chemical products	26,471	27,003	25,582	27,116	28,356	2.0	−5.3	6.0	4.6	7.1
Glass, cement	12,408	11,940	10,635	11,574	12,534	−3.8	−10.9	8.8	8.3	1.0
Basic iron and steel	12,240	11,166	10,438	11,830	11,513	−8.8	−6.5	13.3	−2.7	−5.9
Metal products	8,850	8,425	6,488	6,696	7,058	−4.8	−23.0	3.2	5.4	−20.2
Machinery	10,955	9,383	7,182	7,440	8,588	−14.3	−23.5	3.6	15.4	−21.6
Electrical, electronics	12,034	11,035	9,322	9,234	9,821	−8.3	−15.5	−0.9	6.4	−18.4
Transport equipment	17,323	14,138	9,877	11,878	14,812	−18.4	−30.1	20.3	24.7	−14.5
Other industries	3,283	3,127	2,850	3,016	3,184	−4.7	−8.9	5.8	5.6	−3.0
Construction	51,852	49,259	40,393	41,766	42,810	−5.0	−18.0	3.4	2.5	−17.4
Electricity	13,647	14,554	14,655	15,745	16,831	6.6	0.7	7.4	6.9	23.3
Commerce	234,491	230,032	207,034	213,218	217,153	−1.9	−10.0	3.0	1.8	−7.4
Transport, communications	69,710	67,086	63,860	67,940	69,764	−3.8	−4.8	6.4	2.7	0.1
Financial services	86,113	88,625	90,482	93,097	95,436	2.9	2.1	2.9	2.5	10.8
Personal services	60,907	64,561	64,844	68,086	68,377	6.0	0.4	5.0	0.4	12.3
Other services, government	68,041	70,083	69,252	71,399	70,437	3.0	−1.2	3.1	−1.3	3.5
Financial intermediation	(12,215)	(12,533)	(13,059)	(13,608)	(13,771)	2.6	4.2	4.2	1.2	12.7

SOURCE: Banco de Mexico, *Informe anual* (Mexico City, various years, 1982–1985). Prices in billion Mexican pesos.

future years. However, casual observation leads one to believe that women's entry into the workplace has been more than just a passing event; women's participation has increased significantly, especially in occupations not previously filled by women.

It should be noted that there is great uncertainty regarding the size of the labor force. Data from the 1970, 1980, and 1990 population censuses are difficult to compare, and large changes in the rate of participation (labor force against total population) from one census to the next make accurate measurement difficult.

It is against this background that the future growth of the Mexican labor force and employment, and their implications for national economic policy and U.S.-Mexico relations, must be set.

EMPLOYMENT AND THE CRISIS

It is particularly difficult to ascertain what has happened to total and sectorial employment since the crisis began in 1982. A few facts seem well established, however. First, employment in the largest firms, as reported in *Estadistica Industrial Mensual* and *Anual*, has fallen sharply during the last few years.[5] Second, employment has substantially increased in the traditional or informal sector of the economy, apparently in response to the fall in employment opportunities in more attractive, formal-sector jobs.[6] Third, despite the lack of reliable statistics, it is evident that unemployment is now at an all-time high, primarily in the central part of the country, and more so in large urban areas. Finally, the impact of the crisis has differed widely among different activities, regions, and types of firms.

As Table 3 shows, the change in the output structure between 1981 and 1985 has been rather large. In sectors such as metal furniture, value-added has dropped by almost 38 percent, while in fertilizers, it has grown by more than 51 percent. The size of the changes means that the employment structure must have changed drastically as well, although by less than output change. In 1985, 31 of 72 sectors were still operating at output levels lower than those reached in 1981. In general, those sectors that produced intermediate and capital goods were much more seriously affected than those producing nondurables for final consumption.

When thinking about the next fifteen or twenty years, then, it is im-

[5] INEGI-SPP, *Estadistica Industrial Annual* (Mexico City, various annual issues).

[6] The term "underground economy" is a rather unfortunate misnomer when applied to a developing country, where most of the labor force is involved in such employment. The terms "traditional sector" or "informal sector" describe more accurately prevailing employment conditions.

portant to consider what might happen to consumption and investment; at present, it appears unlikely that the economy will recover rapidly. At best, the recently announced Programa de Apoyo Crecimiento Economico aims for an output growth rate of 3 to 4 percent in 1987. However favorable that change might be, it would have a relatively slight effect on employment given the large excess capacity in the economy. The possibilities for long-run employment creation depend on structural factors.

In order to estimate the general evolution of Mexican employment, it is thus necessary to consider some alternative growth scenarios (assuming that soon it will be essential to resume economic growth at some reasonable rate). Such a rate would most likely be lower than the long-run average observed between 1950 and 1980, which was over 6.5 percent annually. Of course, given the general scarcity of information about the labor force and employment creation in different sectors, it was necessary to develop some estimates based on the long-run performance of the economy, and to apply these estimates to the period between now and the year 2000. For this purpose, the following assumptions were made:

- The growth elasticities of sectorial output with respect to gross national product (GNP) for the period between 1970 and 1985 apply to the growth of the economy in the next fifteen years. Such elasticities were estimated using constant 1970 prices for sectorial value-added. By taking the entire fifteen-year period, no excessive weight is given to the boom years, when the pattern of output was quite distorted both with regard to long-run trends and in comparison with the period after the boom years. Moreover, a number of sectors that achieved satisfactory growth rates even during the crisis years will most likely have developed certain advantages that might make it easier for them to grow in the future. Table 4 shows the sectors with the highest growth rates between 1970 and 1985.

- The growth pattern in the future will be proportional to the pattern observed in the past, and the average growth rate of the economy will not affect the long-term structure of growth within the range considered. This assumption is rather restrictive, but it provides a useful approximation in the absence of a more detailed analysis about the short-term response of sectorial output to changes in the GNP growth rate and in the absence of a solid hypothesis, linked to probable developments in the external sector, about the future growth of the economy.

- The growth of value-added per worker will be higher in proportion with the growth rate of a sector in the past, and in no case will output per worker grow faster than sectorial output.

TABLE 4

GDP Growth Elasticities, 1970–1985

Sector	Growth elasticity	Standard deviation
Agriculture, cattle, forestry	0.5941	0.0347
Coal, oil	2.4938	0.1396
Iron and metal ores	0.7808	0.0736
Nonmetallic minerals	0.7436	0.0612
Dairy, processed foods	0.8448	0.0319
Beverages, tobacco	1.0619	0.0366
Textiles	0.5738	0.1008
Wood products	1.0172	0.0313
Chemicals	1.5226	0.0556
Other chemical products	1.3219	0.0259
Glass, cement	0.9599	0.0372
Basic iron and steel	0.9880	0.0598
Metal products	0.6212	0.0914
Machinery	1.1681	0.1160
Electrical, electronics	1.3651	0.1055
Transport equipment	1.1751	0.1370
Other industries	0.7844	0.0408
Construction	0.9942	0.0661
Electricity	1.5221	0.0570
Commerce	0.9260	0.0250
Transport, communications	1.6396	0.0231
Financial services	0.8198	0.0301
Personal services	1.3845	0.0489
Other services, government	0.8199	0.0236

SOURCE: Banco de Mexico, *Informe anual* (Mexico City, various years, 1970–1985).

- Finally, the growth rate of value-added per worker does not depend on the growth rate of output. This assumption tends to overestimate the rate of employment creation at higher levels of growth, and perhaps underestimates it at lower growth rates. Most likely the growth rate of output per worker is a positive function of the growth rate of total output, at least up to a point.

With these assumptions and with rough estimates by sector about the structure of employment in 1985, it was possible to estimate three alternative paths for employment growth between now and 2000.[7] Table 4 shows the growth elasticities for the period 1970 to 1985. The actual estimates of employment levels for different sectors are shown in Tables 5 and 6, under alternative assumptions about employment in the base year.

[7] No reliable employment figures exist for 72 sectors of the economy. The estimates used here are based on sector estimates for 1980 published in *Escenarios Economicos de México: 1981–1985* (Mexico City, 1981) and on population census figures for 1980. For Tables 3 through 6, the data have been aggregated to twenty-four sectors.

TABLE 5

Sectorial Employment Growth, 1985–2000

(1970–1985 elasticities)

	Employment[a]			Percentage employment growth 1985–2000		
	1985	2000 (3%)	2000 (4%)	2000 (5%)	(3%)	(4%)	(5%)
Total employment	21,159,000	22,493,626	24,877,557	27,593,142	6.3	17.6	30.4
Agriculture, cattle, forestry	6,070,000	6,145,803	6,557,874	6,956,792	1.2	8.0	14.6
Coal, oil	220,000	226,830	322,990	456,844	3.1	46.8	107.7
Iron and metal ores	95,000	100,526	109,937	119,435	5.8	15.7	25.7
Nonmetallic minerals	200,000	212,168	225,794	240,018	6.1	12.9	20.0
Dairy, processed foods	698,000	618,045	670,234	725,350	−11.5	−4.0	3.9
Beverages, tobacco	146,000	151,461	175,456	202,020	3.7	20.2	38.4
Textiles	655,000	634,578	672,665	712,486	−3.1	2.7	8.8
Wood products	195,000	212,101	238,739	266,875	8.8	22.4	36.9
Chemicals	155,000	150,235	185,976	228,859	−3.1	20.0	47.7
Other chemical products	140,000	135,557	160,469	188,547	−3.2	14.6	34.7
Glass, cement	93,000	89,645	101,033	113,197	−3.6	8.6	21.7
Basic iron and steel	110,000	105,366	118,480	132,317	−4.2	7.7	20.3
Metal products	95,000	96,013	101,189	276,034	1.1	6.5	190.6
Machinery	90,000	89,944	104,445	120,374	−0.1	16.1	33.7
Electrical, electronics	62,000	69,662	83,667	99,890	12.4	34.9	61.1
Transport equipment	155,000	149,941	173,828	200,125	−3.3	12.1	29.1
Other industries	100,000	94,505	103,422	112,407	−5.5	3.4	12.4
Construction	1,250,000	1,635,137	1,843,521	2,063,774	30.8	47.5	65.1
Electricity	80,000	76,087	93,125	113,057	−4.9	16.4	41.3
Commerce	3,250,000	3,689,833	4,114,048	4,555,091	13.5	26.6	40.2
Transport, communications	250,000	325,444	416,469	531,629	30.2	66.6	112.7
Financial services	700,000	722,701	801,364	883,477	3.2	14.5	26.2
Personal services	850,000	1,025,373	1,210,111	1,417,790	20.6	42.4	66.8
Other services, govenment	5,500,000	5,736,671	6,292,721	6,876,754	4.3	14.4	25.0
Employment deficit	2,341,000	12,500,000	11,100,000	9,400,000			

SOURCE: Employment estimates for 1985 based on *Proyecciones de la poblacion de Mexico y de las entidades federativas: 1980–2000* (INEGI-CONAPO, Secretaria de Programacion y Presupuesto, Mexico, 1985).

[a]Projections for 2000 are based on three different percent rates of annual growth in GDP.

TABLE 6

Sectorial Employment Growth, 1985–2000: High Employment Alternative

(*1970–1985 elasticities*)

	Employment[a]			
	1985	2000 (3%)	2000 (4%)	2000 (5%)
Total employment	23,274,900	24,742,989	27,365,313	30,352,456
Agriculture, cattle, forestry	6,677,000	6,760,383	7,213,661	7,652,471
Coal, oil	242,000	249,513	355,289	502,528
Iron and metal ores	104,500	110,579	120,931	131,379
Nonmetallic minerals	220,000	233,385	248,373	264,020
Dairy, processed foods	767,800	679,850	737,257	797,885
Beverages, tobacco	160,600	166,607	193,002	222,222
Textiles	720,500	698,036	739,932	783,735
Wood products	214,500	233,311	262,613	293,563
Chemicals	170,500	165,259	204,574	251,745
Other chemical products	154,000	149,113	176,516	207,402
Glass, cement	102,300	98,610	111,136	124,517
Basic iron and steel	121,000	115,903	130,328	145,549
Metal products	104,500	105,614	111,308	303,637
Machinery	99,000	98,938	114,890	132,411
Electrical, electronics	68,200	76,628	92,034	109,879
Transport equipment	170,500	164,935	191,211	220,138
Other industries	110,000	103,956	113,764	123,648
Construction	1,375,000	1,798,651	2,027,873	2,270,151
Electricity	88,000	83,696	102,438	124,363
Commerce	3,575,000	4,058,816	4,525,453	5,010,600
Transport, communications	275,000	357,988	458,116	584,792
Financial services	770,000	794,971	881,500	971,825
Personal services	935,000	1,127,910	1,331,122	1,559,569
Other services, government	6,050,000	6,310,338	6,921,993	7,564,429
Employment deficit	0	10,200,000	8,600,000	6,400,000

SOURCE: Same as for Table 5.

[a]Projections for 2000 are based on three different percent rates of annual growth in GDP.

As may be seen from the column in Table 5 referring to the number of people employed in 1985, it is assumed that at present the employment deficit is about 2.3 million persons. This is a large unexplained number, but no satisfactory way exists to reduce it. This deficit is considerably less than the labor force that the 1980 Population Census labels "unspecified" in its sector of employment: about 4.8 million. The latter may also be interpreted as "equivalent unemployment,"[8] and is approximately 19 percent of the labor force.

[8]By "equivalent unemployment" I mean "redundant" workers, or the slack in the labor force if all workers had the same skills. The concept, by its very nature, is not very precise.

The alternative assumption (Table 6) is that the employment deficit in 1985 is roughly zero. This is a deliberately optimistic alternative.

The final three columns of Tables 5 and 6 show three different esti-mates of employment creation for the next fifteen years, assuming three growth rates of GNP: 3, 4, and 5 percent annually. In each case, the second column of the table shows the average rate of growth of value-added per worker. The three resulting levels of employment in 2000 are shown in Table 5: 22.5, 24.9, and 27.4 million persons, respectively. In Table 6, the figures for total employment are, respectively, 24.7, 27.4, and 30.2 million persons.

An additional assumption was made regarding the size of the labor force in 2000. If GNP grows at 3 percent annually, the labor force in 2000 is assumed to be 35 million persons; at 4 percent growth, 36 mil-lion; and at 5 percent growth, 37 million. These estimates are rather conservative; the highest would imply a labor-force growth rate of 3.2 percent annually for the period 1985 to 2000.

The size of the employment deficit in 2000 under the observed tenden-cies is rather large. In the most pessimistic case—3 percent annual growth of GNP in Table 5—the deficit would grow from 2.3 million jobs in 1985 to 12.5 million jobs in 2000. That is, only 1.4 million jobs would be created during the whole period, compared to 800,000, the number needed every year simply to keep the employment deficit constant in absolute terms. Even in the most optimistic case, the last column of Table 6, during the fifteen-year period only 7 million jobs would be cre-ated—that is, about 467,000 new jobs annually, or slightly more than half of the new jobs required simply to keep the employment deficit at its current absolute level. The resulting employment deficit in the three cases would be 12.2, 10.6, and 8.4 million jobs in the year 2000.

At a growth rate of GNP of 3 percent, employment would grow mini-mally at 0.43 percent per annum. At 4 percent GNP growth, employment would increase by 1.11 percent. In the best case—5 percent growth—employment would increase annually by 1.76 percent. Under the more optimistic assumptions reflected in Table 6, employment growth rates would be the same, although the starting level of employment is higher. Thus the resulting employment deficits would be, depending on the av-erage growth rate of GNP, 10.2, 8.6, and 6.4 million jobs. Total employ-ment creation during the period under the more optimistic assumptions reflected in Table 6 would be 1.5, 4.2, and 7 million jobs, depending on the average growth rate of output.

I want to emphasize that the sectorial composition of employment is subject to a large margin of error; however, the results would not be substantially affected at the aggregate level. For instance, at 5 percent growth of GNP, agricultural employment would increase by 700,000 to 815,000 persons between now and 2000 (last column, Tables 5 and 6), even though agriculture would probably not absorb such a large amount of employment in the absence of special policies to that effect.

IMPLICATIONS

Given that projecting past observed trends gives such pessimistic results, it is necessary to identify the implications of such a large and growing employment deficit. In the context of bilateral U.S.-Mexican relations, the deficit means that pressure on undocumented migration will increase continuously. It also means, of course, that internal pressures on urban growth will continue, and probably that pressures to create urban, rather than rural, jobs will be even stronger. Of course, as has been pointed out in the past, there may be a natural complementarity of Mexican and U.S. labor markets. However, it becomes clearer each day that the political will to develop the advantages that might accrue to both countries from closer cooperation in this area is simply not present; each country, but especially the United States, is unwilling to contemplate the implications of such cooperation.

Despite such unwillingness, the potential problem is of such evident magnitude that some actions will have to be taken on both sides of the border. I will now consider what kind of possible scenarios might be relevant.

Under the current debt burden, it is difficult for the economy to grow at even 4 percent annually; thus the employment scenarios developed simply represent the current situation and its development under positive, but marginal, changes. Any higher growth rates would clearly depend on some type of agreement being reached with the countries' creditors and their respective governments regarding terms for debt repayment. A number of alternative proposals exist for partial payment of interest on the foreign debt in domestic currency in order to increase investment, particularly in export industries.[9] Such a scheme would allow the Mexican economy to grow and pay simultaneously if creditor countries would be

[9] Victor Urquidi and Saul Trejo Reyes, "La Deuda Externa y la Reconstrucción Nacional," *Novedades*, 1 June 1986; Victor Urquidi, "Consecuencias a Largo Plazo del Problema Mundial del Endeudamiento Externo," in Migual S. Wionczek, ed., *La Crisis de la Deuda Externa en la América Latina*, 2 vols. (Mexico City, 1987); and Saul Trejo Reyes, "Deuda Externa: Una Alternativa de Solución," *Estudios Economicos* vol. 1, no. 2 (Mexico City, July–Dec. 1986).

willing to run trade deficits with debtors like Mexico. Such deficits would allow debtor countries to service their debt and increase exports, output, and employment.

A scheme such as this, aimed at creating conditions for resuming output growth and employment creation in Mexico, would have to be accompanied by a large increase in the country's international trade, particularly its export trade. Although in principle Mexico's entry into the General Agreement on Tariffs and Trade (GATT) will allow Mexico to gain better conditions for this purpose, it is difficult to imagine a large enough increase occurring without a change in the internal industrial policies of developed countries, especially the United States, toward Mexico's economic and employment prospects. Such changes would necessitate substantial modifications of those subsidy schemes currently applied by developed countries (and exempted from the GATT due to their local or state character or to their direct link to defense spending, as in the United States), but also changes to the commercial positions of Japan and other Far Eastern newly industrialized countries that have been allowed to run large trade surpluses. Permanent surpluses for some countries, of course, imply permanent deficits for others, and if debtors cannot generate such surpluses but others do, no long-term solutions will be found to the debt quandary. Under present conditions, growth sufficient for Mexico to absorb its employment deficit seems an objective totally outside the scope of national policy instruments.

Of course, domestic policy changes might go a long way toward increasing the employment creation possibilities of the economy. Decentralization, technological development, changes in relative prices, a greater emphasis on agriculture and small-scale industry, and so forth, are all important and have been amply discussed. An understanding of the magnitudes involved, however, should place the nature of the task in perspective.

PART III
Migration and Local Communities in the United States and Mexico

Paradise at a Cost: The Incorporation of Undocumented Mexican Immigrants into a Local-Level Labor Market

Leo R. Chávez

ONE OFTEN HEARS on the San Diego news that "it's another beautiful day in paradise." San Diegans tend to think of their city in such terms, and not just because of the weather. Once a sleepy Navy town, San Diego has developed into a prosperous economy based on light manufacturing, the aerospace industry, agriculture, and tourism.[1] The satisfaction of local residents is reflected in the often heard expression that San Diego is "America's Finest City."

But all is not rosy in paradise. Rarely a day passes without a story about immigration appearing in the newspaper, on radio, or on television. San Diego, it is said, is on the front line in the battle to stem the tide of "illegal aliens" entering the country. A more recent development has been the barrage of reports on the crime allegedly committed by undocumented migrants, everything from car theft, burglary, rape, assault, and murder.[2]

In addition to the new image of the undocumented as criminals is the old image of the undocumented as abusers of local social services, particularly health care and welfare. These images add up to a social environment ripe for political demagogues who portray the undocumented immigrants as a threat to San Diego's prosperity.[3]

[1] Niles Hansen, *The Border Economy* (Austin, Tex., 1981).

[2] As representatives of the San Diego Police Department were quoted as saying, "These new criminals are undocumented aliens from Mexico, some of whom live here but many of whom sleep in their native land and cross daily into the United States to commit their crimes. At the end of their workday, they go back into Mexico with a few dollars to show for their efforts" (Tom Gorman, *The Los Angeles Times,* 17 Feb. 1986, sec. 2:1).

[3] Comments by Clyde Romney, a candidate for the county board of supervisors, provide an example of unsubstantiated criminal activity attributed to undocumented immigrants:

The response to the multifaceted "problem" of immigration affecting San Diego has been a number of "solutions" that appeal to the public's most basic fears about immigrants in society. One county supervisor recently blamed undocumented criminals for the county's budgetary problems and has proposed a lawsuit against the federal government to reimburse monies spent by the county on undocumented immigrants.[4] San Diego's sheriff has called for the Marines to be stationed along the border, a proposal seconded by California Senator Pete Wilson.[5] If the Marine solution falters as politically unpalatable, then stationing the National Guard at the border has been suggested as the more politically acceptable alternative.[6] The urgency of such proposals leaves the impression that if action is not taken soon, San Diego will quickly become a paradise lost.

Beyond the demagoguery and nativism, such solutions reflect a concern on the part of the U.S. public and its policymakers about the impact of immigrants, particularly Mexican immigrants, on the local community. Academic researchers have focused on this problem as well. This paper begins by turning the question around: What is the effect of the local community on immigration?

The argument made here is that integrating Mexican migrants into the labor market leads to two distinct types of migration patterns: temporary and long-term. Only after understanding these migration patterns can we begin to explore the impact of immigration at the local level. Temporary migrants and long-term residents (of whom many are actually settlers) have different social and economic needs and therefore dif-

---

"Nowhere else in San Diego County do you find the huge gangs of illegal aliens that line our streets, shake down our schoolchildren, spread diseases like malaria and roam our neighborhoods, looking for work or homes to rob. We are under siege in North County [San Diego], and we have been deserted by those whose job it is to protect us from this flood of illegal aliens" (Daniel Weintraub, *The Los Angeles Times,* 15 Oct. 1986, sec. 2:1).

[4] San Diego County Supervisor Susan Golding has proposed that the county of San Diego sue the federal government for $23 million she claims the county has spent on jail costs, health care, and court costs for undocumented immigrants (H. G. Reza, *The Los Angeles Times,* 13 May 1986, sec. 2:1).

[5] San Diego's sheriff John F. Duffy proposed placing Marines, in camouflage fatigues, every 15 or 20 feet along the border, day and night, until the new comprehensive policy is enacted. Part of his rationale for such a proposal was that "illegal aliens are gradually affecting the quality of life as we know it. For example, now we have to admit legal aliens into our colleges, which means my grandchildren may not be granted entry because of an illegal alien and they'll probably require her to be bilingual" (J. Stryker Meyer, *San Diego Union,* 6 Apr. 1986, sec. A:3).

[6] The proposal to place the National Guard at the U.S.-Mexico border was made by Congressman Duncan Hunter, a Republican whose district includes the California border area (Patrick McDonnell, *Los Angeles Times,* 24 June 1986, sec. 2:3).

ferent effects on the local community. And although our focus is the local level, we cannot ignore federal and state policies aimed at undocumented migrants; these policies have important implications for local decisionmaking.

CONCEPTUAL DEVELOPMENTS CONCERNING THE IMPACT OF THE LOCAL LABOR MARKET ON MIGRATORY PATTERNS

In *Birds of Passage*, Michael Piore argues that the structure of job opportunities or the labor market in developed countries influences migration from underdeveloped regions.[7] The U.S. industrial economy, he argues, generates two distinct types of employment: primary-sector and secondary-sector jobs. The secondary sector of the labor market consists of jobs that pay minimum wage, are unstable and often seasonal (relative to jobs in the primary sector), and offer few benefits and little opportunity for upward mobility. U.S. citizens, he argues, often view such jobs as undesirable. According to Piore, citizens prefer primary-sector jobs, which offer relatively higher wages, upward mobility, job security, and a wide range of benefits.

A migrant who intends to earn some dollars and then return home, however, seeks jobs in the secondary sector. The temporary nature of such jobs fits quite well with the migrant's objectives and pattern of temporary migration. The prevalence of this pattern was substantiated (at least for Mexican migration) by a study conducted in the late 1970s that found that for every 100 entries of undocumented Mexicans to the United States there were 92 "exits," either voluntary or under orders from the Immigration and Naturalization Service (INS).[8] Such migrants are referred to as "cyclical migrants," "temporary migrants," and "target earners."[9]

Although temporary migration has been, and continues to be, the predominant pattern of international labor migration, recent empirical evidence suggests that a significant portion of temporary migrants settle at their original destination. Piore has recently reevaluated his own position and concluded that the various ways that a migrant is incorporated into

---

[7] Michael J. Piore, *Birds of Passage: Migrant Labor and Industrial Societies* (London, 1979).

[8] Manuel García y Griego, *El Volumen de la Migración de Mexicanos no Documentados a los Estados Unidos: Nuevas Hipotesis,* CENIET Studies (Mexico City, Centro Nacional de Información y Estadisticas del Trabajo, Secretaria de Trabajo y Previsión Social, 1980).

[9] Alejandro Portes and Robert L. Bach, *Latin Journey: Cuban and Mexican Immigrants in the United States* (Berkeley, Calif., 1985); García y Griego, *Migración de Mexicanos no Documentados.*

a labor market can lead to distinct outcomes, one of which is long-term residence:

The difficulty with temporary migrants as a solution to the problem of filling secondary jobs is that they do not remain temporary. While many, maybe even most, actually return home, a significant number end up staying longer than originally intended. They tend to bring their families from home or to form new families, and as a result many of their children grow up in the country of destination. . . . When a significant portion of a given migrant stream begins to settle in this way, it tends to create opportunities for more permanent migrants moving from the country of origin and planning to remain on a long-term basis with relatives at the destination.[10]

Piore points to work on ethnic enclaves as revealing a mode of incorporation into the U.S. labor market that is distinct from the model of a dual labor market.[11] As Portes has argued for the Cuban immigrant experience in Miami, Florida, incorporating recent immigrants into ethnic-enclave enterprises often leads to stable jobs that offer a degree of upward mobility.[12] In contrast, Mexican immigrants generally found few alternatives to jobs in the secondary or informal sector of the labor market.[13]

However, even Mexican migration patterns may be changing. Recent evidence suggests that a substantial number of undocumented Mexican workers are abandoning temporary migration. Many of these undocumented migrants are becoming "immigrants" or "settlers" despite their immigration status and their prevalence in the secondary and informal sectors of the U.S. labor market.[14] As with workers in ethnic-enclave enterprises, undocumented workers, as a result of changes in job opportunities, may be finding relatively stable employment even in the secondary sector. In order to explore this trend, we must first exam-

[10] Michael J. Piore, "The Shifting Grounds for Immigration," *The Annals of the American Academy of Political and Social Science* 485 (1986), 24.

[11] *Ibid.*, 26, 27.

[12] Alejandro Portes, "Modes of Incorporation and Theories of Labor Immigration," in Mary M. Kritz, Charles B. Keely, and Silvano M. Tomasi, eds., *Global Trends in Migration Theory: Theory and Research on International Population Movements* (New York, 1981), 279–97.

[13] Portes and Bach, *Latin Journey*.

[14] Leo R. Chávez, "Migrants and Settlers: The Case of Mexicans in the United States," *Human Organization* vol. 47, no. 2 (Summer 1988); Leo R. Chávez, "Households, Migration, and Labor Market Participation: The Adaptation of Mexicans to Life in the United States," *Urban Anthropology* vol. 14, no. 3 (1985); Douglas S. Massey, "The Settlement Process Among Mexican Migrants to the United States: New Methods and Findings," in Daniel B. Levine, et al., eds., *Immigration Statistics: A Story of Neglect* (Washington, 1985); Harley L. Browning and N. Rodriguez, "The Migration of Mexican Indocumentados as a Settlement Process: Implications for Work," Texas Population Research Center Papers, ser. 4, no. 4.008 (Austin, Tex., 1982).

ine changes in both Mexico and the United States that influence the migratory patterns of Mexican laborers.

THE NEW DEMAND FOR MEXICAN LABOR

A number of recent trends in both Mexico and the United States influence whether a migrant decides to extend his or her stay in the United States or return to Mexico. Since its economic crisis became public knowledge in 1982, Mexico has experienced continued devaluation of the peso, high interest rates, decreasing oil prices, and little economic growth.[15] Given that economic situation, migrants may find returning to Mexico less attractive than continuing their residence in the United States. Not only would returning migrants find it more difficult to subsist in their places of origin, but the economic climate inhibits investment of whatever capital they may have saved during their sojourn in the United States. Moreover, gathering the necessary resources to return to the United States is now more difficult than before the devaluation; in short, it takes more pesos to make the trip.

Two interrelated changes in U.S. society and economy increase demand for foreign, mostly Mexican, labor. First, Americans are having fewer children. Americans now average 1.9 children per woman, which is below the number required to meet demographic replacement.[16] In and of itself, this demographic trend would not necessarily create a demand for foreign labor. However, when combined with the demands for labor found in the U.S. economy, it is apparent that there will be increasing demand for imported labor. Basically, a growing U.S. economy requires a supply of unskilled and semi-skilled workers who are entering the labor force for the first time. Traditionally, entry-level workers have come from the population of males 16 to 21 years of age. Although women are currently entering the labor force in greater proportions, their numbers will not offset the demand created by the insufficient supply of entry-level workers.

Because of this disparity between demographic and economic trends, it has been suggested that only 40 percent of the jobs created in southern California by the year 1990 can be filled solely by local entrants into the labor force.[17] The resulting demand will draw workers from both other

[15] Donald L. Wyman, ed., *Mexico's Economic Crisis: Challenges and Opportunities*, Monograph Series 12 (La Jolla, Calif., Center for U.S.-Mexican Studies, 1983).

[16] Wayne A. Cornelius, Leo R. Chávez, and Jorge G. Castro, *Mexican Immigrants and Southern California: A Summary of Current Knowledge*, Research Report Series, no. 36 (La Jolla, Calif., 1982).

[17] Thomas Muller and Thomas Espenshade, *The Fourth Wave: California's Newest Immigrants* (Washington, 1985).

U.S. states and other countries to the southern California area. Nationally, one labor market projection predicted that as many as 33 million foreign workers will be needed by the year 2000 in order to sustain even a modest 3 percent growth rate in GNP.[18]

Changes in the U.S. economy also increase the demand for Mexican labor. Traditional "heavy" industries, such as steel and automobile production, are in a state of decline. The new rising industries are communications and information processing, particularly computer-related technology. The nation is rapidly becoming dominated by service-sector industries. Saskia Sassen-Koob refers to this change as the "restructuring" of the U.S. economy, which is part of the "recomposition" of world capital.[19]

These economic changes have many implications for Mexican migration. Various service industries, particularly hotels and restaurants, actively seek immigrant labor.[20] The electronic industry creates a demand for two general types of workers: highly educated, highly trained individuals to work as managers, programmers, and in research and design; and unskilled and semi-skilled assemblers trained at the workplace to perform a highly specialized function in the production chain. The latter type of electronics workers are increasingly Asian and Mexican immigrant women.[21]

It is clear that the trend toward Mexican undocumented immigrants entering urban-oriented work as opposed to agricultural labor coincides with changes in the economy.[22] Urban undocumented workers help sustain otherwise uncompetitive industries, such as the garment industry.[23]

[18] Clark W. Reynolds, "Labor Market Projections for the United States and Mexico and Their Relevance to Current Migration Controversies," in *Food Research Institute Studies* 17 (Stanford, Calif., 1980).

[19] Saskia Sassen-Koob, "Recomposition and Peripheralization at the Core," in M. Dixon and S. Jonas, eds., *The New Nomads* (San Francisco, 1982).

[20] Muller and Espenshade, *The Fourth Wave*; Sheldon L. Maram et al., *Hispanic Workers in the Garment and Restaurant Industries in Los Angeles County*, Research Report Series, no. 12 (La Jolla, Calif., Center for U.S.-Mexican Studies, 1980); David S. North and Marion F. Houstoun, "The Characteristics and Role of Illegal Aliens in the U.S. Labor Market: An Exploratory Study," report prepared for the Employment and Training Administration, U.S. Department of Labor, contract no. 20-11-74-21 (Washington, 1976).

[21] Patricia Fernandez-Kelly and Anna Garcia, "Advanced Technology, Regional Development, and Hispanic Women's Employment in Southern California," in R. Gordon, ed., *Micro Electronics in Transition* (San Francisco, 1986); Sassen-Koob, "Recomposition and Peripheralization"; Bernstein et al., "Silicon Valley: Paradise or Paradox?" in Magdelena Mora and Adelaida R. Del Castillo, eds., *Mexican Women in the United States* (Los Angeles, 1980).

[22] Estevan T. Flores, "Research on Undocumented Immigrants and Public Policy: A Study of the Texas School Case," *International Migration Review* 18 (1984), 505–523.

[23] Sassen-Koob, "Recomposition and Peripheralization"; Maram, *Hispanic Workers*.

Although jobs in declining sectors have been categorized as belonging to the secondary labor market, which is characterized by temporary employment, low pay, and no benefits, Mexican undocumented workers have also been used as a transitional labor force in the primary labor market.[24]

Rebecca Morales defines a *transitional labor force* as one that "performs a valuable function until their employers mechanize, move overseas, or take other measures to make themselves more competitive." [25] Undocumented immigrants are particularly suited to this role given their relative powerlessness in relation to their employers and their already tenuous residence in the United States. Morales has shown that Mexican undocumented workers in the Los Angeles automobile industry served as a transitional labor force during a period of economic downturn—the economic recession of the late 1970s and early 1980s. Thus the use of immigrant labor is beneficial not only during times of economic expansion, which is the conventional wisdom on the subject, but also during a period of economic contraction, when firms are forced into restructuring the productive process.

Wayne Cornelius has focused on another type of restructuring underway in the U.S. economy that also affects the level and distribution of employer demand for Mexican immigrant labor: the proliferation of subcontracting arrangements.[26] According to Cornelius, many larger firms reduce costs, maintain competitiveness, and increase flexibility by subcontracting much of their labor-intensive work to small, predominantly nonunion firms, which rely heavily on undocumented immigrant labor.[27] Unions, to a certain degree, have acquiesced to using nonunion subcontractors in order to preserve the higher-paying, unionized jobs in the primary firm. Cornelius writes, "In California this phenomenon seems most prevalent in the construction, food-processing, restaurant, and landscape maintenance industries, but it can be found in nearly every sector of the California economy today." [28] It is quite likely that the Immigration Re-

[24] Rebecca Morales, "Transitional Labor: Undocumented Workers in the Los Angeles Automobile Industry," *International Migration Review* 17 (1983), 570–76.

[25] *Ibid.*, 575–76.

[26] Wayne A. Cornelius, "The Role of Mexican Labor in the U.S. Economy: Two Generations of Research," paper presented at the annual director's meeting of PROFMEX, the Consortium of U.S. Research Programs for Mexico, Cozumel, Mexico, 27 July 1984; Wayne A. Cornelius, "Immigrant-Dominated Firms and Industries in the United States: New Research Findings and Implications for Public Policy," paper presented at a symposium on Mexican immigration, Institute of Latin American Studies, University of Texas, Austin, 12 Apr. 1985.

[27] Cornelius, "Role of Mexican Labor," 14.

[28] *Ibid.*

form and Control Act of 1986 (IRCA), with its employer-sanctions provisions, has exacerbated this trend toward subcontracting, as employers pass along the risk of hiring undocumented workers to smaller firms.

The consequences of the changing demand for Mexican labor are reflected in the migration patterns and characteristics of non-detained, undocumented migrants.[29] Undocumented immigrants are now more likely to seek urban-based than agricultural employment. Their labor histories reveal a wide range of occupations, mostly concentrated in the service sector, and less often, but increasingly, in light manufacturing and construction.[30] Undocumented Mexican women also participate in the labor market, particularly the service sector. And finally, a significant proportion of the undocumented population has been in the United States for an extended period of time: 9.6 percent of those in the San Diego study have been in the United States more than ten years, and 37.8 percent of those in a recent Texas study have been in the United States for five years or longer.[31]

The effect on migration of recent economic patterns in both the United States and Mexico has yet to be definitively determined through empirical research. It is clear, however, that the international political economy in which Mexican migration occurs is reforming, as evidenced by economic restructuring in the United States and Mexico's weakened economic position vis-à-vis the United States. Moreover, the coalescence and resulting influence of U.S. demographic trends and of a changing U.S. economy on the migration patterns and characteristics of Mexican immigrants were already observable in the aforementioned 1980 U.S. Census data (which predated Mexico's economic crisis). These data emphasized the growing numbers of Mexicans, including undocumented Mexicans, who appear to be settling in the United States.[32]

In sum, temporary migration or settlement by migrants and their families must be viewed in relation to their participation in the U.S. labor market. Many migrants spend only a short time in the United States and

[29] Cornelius, "Role of Mexican Labor"; Undocumented Workers Policy Research Project, *The Use of Public Services by Undocumented Aliens in Texas: A Study of State Costs and Revenues,* report no. 60 (Austin, Tex., 1984); Reynaldo Baca and Dexter Bryan, *Citizenship Aspirations and Residency Rights Preference: The Mexican Undocumented Worker in the Binational Community* (Compton, Calif., 1980).

[30] Muller and Espenshade, *The Fourth Wave.*

[31] Wayne A. Cornelius, et al., *Mexican Immigration and Access to Health Services,* Research Report Series, no. 36 (La Jolla, Calif., 1982); Weintraub and Cardenas, *Use of Public Services.*

[32] Jeffrey S. Passel and Karen A. Woodrow, "Geographic Distribution of Undocumented Aliens Counted in the 1980 Census by State," *International Migration Review* 18 (1984), 642–71.

TABLE I

San Diego and Its Population, 1980 Census

	White	Black	Asian	Spanish origin
Proportion of county population	73.8%	5.5%	5.0%	14.8%
Proportion foreign-born	8.0%	2.2%	61.4%	37.5%

SOURCE: Bureau of the Census 1983:6-1206.

participate in an international labor market.[33] Others have made the transition to, or are in the process of becoming, long-term workers and residents of the United States. As we shall observe, temporary migrants and long-term residents have different effects and raise distinct questions concerning their eventual social integration.

OVERVIEW OF SAN DIEGO AND ITS POPULATION

Many of the trends that influence the demand for Mexican immigrants and lead to long-term residence for some migrants can be observed in San Diego. However, before examining the role of Mexican immigrants in the San Diego labor market, a brief overview of San Diego and its population is needed.

San Diego's population is diversified and includes blacks, Asians, and Chicanos (Mexican Americans), as well as immigrants from a number of other countries. According to the 1980 U.S. Census, more than a quarter of the San Diego County's population is made up of minorities or non-whites (Table 1).[34] Hispanics, or individuals of Spanish-origin as designated by the U.S. Census, are the largest group (14.8 percent). Given San Diego's proximity to Mexico, it is not surprising that among Hispanics, persons of Mexican origin are the largest single group, accounting for 12 percent of San Diego County's population.

San Diego's mild climate and thriving economy attract both U.S. citizens from other states and immigrants from throughout the world. Individuals born in foreign countries account for 12.7 percent of San Diego's population. As Table 2 indicates, individuals born in Mexico, Asia, Europe, and Canada account for most of the foreign-born population.

Immigration affects San Diego's population groups differently (Table 1). Among Asians, over 60 percent were foreign-born, largely a result of the settlement of Southeast Asian refugees into San Diego and

[33] Jorge A. Bustamante, "The Mexicans Are Coming," *International Migration Review* 17 (1983), 323–41.
[34] Bureau of the Census, 1983.

TABLE 2

The Foreign-Born Population in San Diego
County, 1980 Census

	Percent of total population
All foreign-born	12.7%
Born in Mexico	4.7
Born in Asia	3.5
Born in Europe	2.3
Born in Canada	0.8
Born in South America	0.2
Born in West Indies	0.1
Other countries	0.3
Country not reported	0.6

SOURCE: Bureau of the Census 1980:6-1136.

the subsequent secondary migration of those who had settled in other states.[35] Among Hispanics, well over a third were born outside the United States. In comparison, 8 percent of whites and very few blacks were foreign-born.

As to the number of undocumented immigrants in San Diego County, about 50,000 were counted in the 1980 U.S. Census, of which about 34,000 (68 percent) were from Mexico.[36] According to one assessment of the data on undocumented Mexicans in San Diego County, enumerators for the 1980 U.S. Census did an exceptional job of seeking out undocumented immigrants, even farmworkers living without housing in remote and isolated canyons adjacent to farm properties.[37] Consequently, the Census Bureau's estimate reflects the most reasonable and accurate estimate to date of undocumented immigrants in San Diego.

Predictions for San Diego's future economic and population growth make it clear that San Diego and Mexico's interdependence will increase in importance. Between 1980 and the year 2000, San Diego's population is expected to increase by about 45 percent. Civilian employment is expected to increase by 50.5 percent, with most jobs continuing to be in

[35] Ruben G. Rumbaut et al., "The Politics of Migrant Health Care: A Comparative Study of Mexican Immigrants and Indochinese Refugees in San Diego," *Research in the Sociology of Medicine* 7 (1987).

[36] Jeffrey S. Passel, "Estimates of Undocumented Aliens in the 1980 Census for SMSAs," memorandum to Roger Herriot, chief of the population division, Bureau of the Census, 16 Aug. 1985.

[37] Joseph Nalven, *Impacts and Undocumented Persons: The Quest for Useable Data in San Diego County, 1974–1986* (San Diego, Calif., 1986).

the service and trade sectors of the economy.[38] Such predictions indicate that San Diego's economy will be creating jobs at a faster rate than the population will grow, leading to a continued in-migration of workers to fill those jobs. Many of those workers will come from the Midwest and East Coast of the United States, but if current trends continue many others will migrate from south of the border. In short, the demand for unskilled and semi-skilled labor in the local economy will continue to parallel the supply of such labor in Mexico.

MEXICAN IMMIGRANTS AND THE SAN DIEGO LABOR MARKET

The San Diego labor market, like the U.S. labor market, does not offer uniform employment. Some jobs are highly sought after and belong in the primary sector of the economy.[39] In contrast, secondary-sector jobs are less advantageous and are often considered dead-end jobs. Jobs in this sector typically include seasonal farmwork, dishwashing, busing tables, cooking, attending to gas stations, car wash work, and waitressing.

A third sector of the local labor market that must be considered is the informal sector. The urban informal sector provides an easily entered niche for Mexican immigrants, particularly undocumented immigrants. However, participation in the informal sector has distinct disadvantages.[40] Such jobs typically do not operate under a formal contractual relationship. Individuals generally offer their services as, for example, gardeners or maids, and are hired on a personal basis. Because of the informal nature of such jobs, regulations concerning fair labor standards and practices are rarely observed. There are no guarantees of overtime pay nor are job-related benefits provided. Most importantly, informal-sector employment is extremely tenuous.

As Alejandro Portes and Alex Stepick have argued, these characteristics of the informal sector make it attractive to employers. "Payment of sub-minimum wages and non-payment of taxes and benefits confer on these activities a distinct competitive advantage, reinforced in turn by the absence of covenants protecting employees from arbitrary dismissal."[41]

Immigrant entrepreneurs who offer their services on an individual basis would also perceive advantages in the informal sector's lack of regulation. Under such conditions, they can take advantage of opportunities for

[38] San Diego Association of Governments, "Regional Growth Forecasts," in *Comprehensive Plan for the San Diego Region* ser. 6, vol. 10 (San Diego, Calif., 1984).

[39] Piore, *Birds of Passage.*

[40] Joan M. Nelson, *Access to Power* (Princeton, N.J., 1979).

[41] Alejandro Portes and Alex Stepick, "Unwelcome Immigrants: The Labor Market Experiences of 1980 Cuban and Haitian Refugees in South Florida" (1985), mimeo.

TABLE 3

Current Occupational Sector in the United States,
by Immigration Status and Sex

| | Undocumented | | Documented | | Total |
| | Pct. male (N = 561) | Pct. female (N = 425) | Pct. male (N = 460) | Pct. female (N = 463) | Pct. |
Sector					
Agriculture	16.2%	4.5%	29.8%	11.0%	15.6%
Construction	5.9	0.7	8.7	0.4	4.1
Manufacturing	4.5	3.8	7.2	6.9	5.6
Commerce[a]	29.8	4.7	13.5	7.1	14.8
Services[b]	36.5	48.9	26.3	17.1	32.1
Public service	0.0	0.2	1.3	1.1	0.6
Professions	0.0	0.7	3.3	3.9	1.9
Not participating in labor market[c]	7.1	36.5	10.0	52.5	25.3
Totals	100.0%	100.0%	100.0%	100.0%	100.0%

NOTE: Significance (χ^2): undocumented-documented = .001 or less.
[a]E.g., restaurant work, car wash.
[b]E.g., gardener, hotel maid, domestic, janitor, driver.
[c]Unemployed or not seeking work.

self-employment with low overhead, typically relying on skills they have personally acquired. The ease of entry into informal-sector jobs is particularly appealing, especially given the obstacles to employment in the primary sector.

Table 3 presents occupational data on Mexican immigrants interviewed as part of a study conducted by the Center for U.S.-Mexican Studies.[42] The respondents generally worked in jobs in the urban secondary and informal sector of San Diego's economy. Undocumented men worked predominately in services (gardening—often self-employed, nursery work, maintenance), commerce (restaurant, gas station, and car wash work), and agriculture. Undocumented women were clustered primarily in the services (maids or hotel workers). Although legally immigrated informants also worked in such sectors of the economy, they were employed more often than undocumented informants in construction and manufacturing. Agricultural-related work continues to be an important source of employment for Mexican immigrants.

MEXICAN IMMIGRANTS:
THEIR SOCIODEMOGRAPHIC CHARACTERISTICS

The job opportunities in the San Diego labor market have an affect on who migrates and how long they stay. Descriptive data for the interview-

[42]Cornelius, Chavez, and Jones, Mexican Immigration and Access.

TABLE 4
Characteristics of Mexican Immigrants, by Immigration Status and Sex

Characteristics (medians or percentages)	Undocumented		Documented	
	Men (N = 588)	Women (N = 491)	Men (N = 487)	Women (N = 537)
Years in the U.S.	3	4	16	13
Age at interview	26.8	27.3	40.3	38.6
Years of education	5.6	5.6	5.6	5.8
Pct. illiterate	11.4	14.5	4.4	6.5
Pct. cannot speak English	49.6	60.0	32.9	40.3
Pct. cannot read English	68.0	68.8	40.8	43.9
Pct. homemakers	0.0	36.5	0.0	52.5
Pct. currently employed	92.9	63.5	90.0	47.5
Annual job income	$7,334	$6,243	$9,099	$7,026

Data by Household	Undocumented head	Documented head
Total annual family income	$9,359	$13,281
Pct. owns house	3.8	29.8
Household size	4.1	3.9

ees is presented in Table 4. In general, undocumented interviewees can be characterized as relatively recent arrivals who lack English language skills, have limited education, and work at jobs that pay about the minimum wage. It must be emphasized that not all undocumented respondents were recent arrivals; indeed, 9.6 percent had been in the United States ten years or longer.

In comparison, their legal counterparts had been in the United States for a much longer period, received about the same level of education, were more proficient in English, and earned slightly more money. Undocumented women were more likely to be employed than women who were legal immigrants, and overall, women earned less than men. If we consider that on average (based upon their median years in the United States) the legal interviewees arrived in the United States at age 24 or 25, then the legal interviewees' characteristics reflect, in many respects, an older, more experienced version of their undocumented counterparts.

Compared to San Diego's other major population groups, including other Hispanics, Mexican immigrants are less educated, earn less money, and live in households with more individuals (Table 5). Of course, there is some overlap in the Spanish-origin category due to undocumented Mexican immigrants appearing in that census category.

A telling feature of the secondary and tertiary labor markets is the lack

TABLE 5

Selected Socioeconomic Characteristics of San Diego
Population Groups, 1980 Census

(Medians or percentages)

	White	Black	Asian	Spanish-origin
Years of education	12.9	12.7	12.8	11.9
Persons per household	2.52	2.84	3.66	3.50

	Male	Female	Male	Female	Male	Female	Male	Female
Total job income in $	17,300	11,192	10,440	10,095	13,103	9,729	12,106	8,997

SOURCE: Bureau of the Census 1983:6-1206, 6-1298.

TABLE 6

Medical Insurance Coverage by Immigration Status

	Undocumented immigrants (N = 836)	Legal immigrants (N = 713)
Have insurance	18.8%	63.7%

NOTE: Significance (χ^2) = .001 or less.

of benefits provided to employees. Rarely are pensions, medical insurance, paid vacations, or other benefits provided. Focusing on one of these, medical insurance, we can get a sense of the extent to which Mexican immigrants receive inadequate benefits (Table 6).

Both documented and undocumented respondents tend to receive private medical insurance coverage of significantly lower quality than that given to the general U.S. population. The Survey of Income and Education estimated that in 1980, 70 percent of the U.S. population was insured under private health insurance plans, most obtained through the workplace.[43] Data from the 1979 and 1980 National Health Interview Survey identified Mexican-Americans as the group with the highest proportion of uninsured persons. Nearly 30 percent of the Mexican-American population was uninsured, compared to only 9 percent of the white population.[44] Lack of medical insurance is a major problem for

[43] President's Commission, 1983.
[44] Fernando M. Treviño and A. J. Moss, "Health Insurance Coverage and Physician Visits Among Hispanic and Non-Hispanic People," in Health United States, 1983 (Washington, 1983).

TABLE 7

Federal Income Tax Withheld and Submission of Tax Forms

	Pct. Undocumented		Pct. Legal	
	Males (N = 468)	Females (N = 254)	Males (N = 360)	Females (N = 211)
Federal and state withholding tax deducted year before interview	63.2%	36.6%	76.9%	68.2%
Social Security (FICA) withheld	69.8	41.3	90.7	79.2
Filed income tax forms preceding year	34.5	38.7	91.7	82.6

Hispanics, even more so for Mexican immigrants, and especially so for undocumented Mexican immigrants.

Another indicator of the labor-market sector in which an individual participates is provided by data on income-tax payments. Most primary-sector and even secondary-sector firms pay by check and note tax deductions. Casual employment in the informal sector, however, is typically paid in cash and thus tax deductions are rarely made.

As Table 7 indicates, most undocumented men have federal and state withholding taxes deducted from their income. Women, who are concentrated in the services, particularly in domestic work, were less likely to pay such taxes. However, considering that both spouses often work, as discussed below, a household will likely have at least one member contributing federal and state taxes. Also evident from Table 7 is that a significant majority of undocumented immigrants do not submit income tax forms and thereby forfeit the return of any tax overpayment they may have made.

LABOR-MARKET PARTICIPATION AND SOCIAL ORGANIZATION

The social organization and composition of Mexican immigrants' households are influenced by the immigrants' participation in the San Diego labor market and reflect strategies for maximizing that participation. The marital status of migrants, their age and sex (as well as that of other household members), and the number of workers per household are factors that must be considered.

Labor migration is selective according to marital status, age, and sex. As Table 8 indicates, about half of the interviewees were single (including widowed, divorced, separated, and abandoned) or if married were without their spouse.

The age-sex distribution of the Mexican immigrant population also

TABLE 8

Marital Status of Mexican Immigrants, by Immigration Status

	Pct. undocumented immigrants (N = 968)	Pct. legal immigrants (N = 821)
Single	30.0%	11.6%
Married		
Spouse in household	53.6	68.5
Spouse not in household	9.4	6.6
Widowed	1.7	5.1
Divorced	1.5	5.0
Separated	2.6	2.8
Abandoned	1.2	0.5
	100.0%	100.1%[a]

[a] Error due to rounding off.

reflects migratory patterns. Table 9 compares data collected in the 1980 U.S. Census on the age and sex structure of undocumented and legal Mexican immigrants, as well as the population that is of Mexican origin, with data collected in San Diego. According to this table, Immigrant Status I comprises primarily—perhaps two-thirds—undocumented immigrants.[45] Compared with undocumented immigrants interviewed in San Diego, both samples show high frequencies of individuals between 20 and 29 years of age, the age most prone to migration. Moreover, the two samples also show remarkable similarities at all age categories for both undocumented men and women.

The ratio of undocumented males to females is also similar. Sex ratios are highest in the following age groups: 157.5 men for each 100 women in the 20–24 age group in San Diego, compared to 143.0 in Immigrant Status I; and 181.3 in the 25–29 age category for San Diego, 135.6 in Immigrant Status I. Sex ratios would be expected to be skewed toward males in these age categories in an undocumented population. The higher male-to-female ratios in the San Diego sample compared to Immigrant Status I reflect the fact that the latter sample has legal as well as undocumented adults.[46]

[45] Frank D. Bean et al., "The Sociodemographic Characteristics of Mexican Immigrant Status Groups: Implications for Studying Undocumented Mexicans," *International Migration Review* 18 (1984), 672–91.

[46] Such similarities and predictable differences in the age-sex structure of household members in San Diego compared to data collected in the 1980 U.S. Census suggest that the sampling procedure employed in this study identified a population that is similar to that of undocumented immigrants in the country generally.

TABLE 9

Age Distribution by Immigrant Status and Sex, San Diego Immigrant Sample and Mexican Origin Population Described by the 1980 U.S. Census

| | Males | | | | | Females | | | | |
| | San Diego | | 1980 Census | | | San Diego | | 1980 Census | | |
Age group	Undocumented (N = 603)	Legal (N = 585)	I	II	III	Undocumented (N = 603)	Legal (N = 585)	I	II	III
0–14	29.7%	32.2%	26.3%	9.8%	44.4%	32.4%	31.8%	30.2%	10.0%	42.2%
15–19	10.4	12.8	15.8	7.9	11.4	11.3	12.7	14.7	7.7	11.4
20–24	20.7	10.9	23.3	11.2	9.3	17.4	8.5	19.9	10.2	9.7
25–29	17.7	8.3	14.5	15.6	8.0	12.9	8.0	13.1	13.7	8.2
30–34	7.6	6.6	7.7	13.7	6.4	9.7	7.1	7.7	12.8	6.5
35–39	5.1	4.8	4.6	10.2	4.3	4.6	6.6	4.7	10.1	4.6
40–49	5.3	9.3	4.7	13.8	6.8	6.7	9.3	4.9	14.6	7.2
50–59	2.9	9.9	2.0	8.6	5.6	3.1	9.5	2.8	9.1	5.9
60+	0.7	5.1	1.1	9.1	3.8	1.9	6.5	2.2	11.8	4.4
Total	100.1%	99.9%	100.0%	99.9%	100.0%	100.0%	100.0%	100.0%	100.0%	100.1%
Total N	1,376	1,070	17,470	24,469	155,368	1,041	1,140	14,313	23,756	157,767

SOURCE: For the 1980 Census data: Bean, Browning, and Frisbie, "The Sociodemographic Characteristics of Mexican Immigrant Status Groups: Implications for Studying Undocumented Mexicans." *International Migration Review* 18(1984): 676.

NOTE: Immigrant Status: I. Mexican-born non-citizens who immigrated to the U.S. in 1975 or afterwords; mostly undocumented. II. Mexican-born non-citizens who immigrated to the U.S. prior to 1975; mostly legal immigrants. III. Persons born in the United States who self-identify as of Mexican origin.

TABLE 10

Demographic Characteristics of Mexican Immigrants and
Other Populations of San Diego

Population group	Median age	Pct. under 15 years	Pct. 50 years and over	Dependency ratio[a]	Child-woman ratio[b]
Mexican immigrants					
Documented	22.0	32.0%	15.5%	0.56	370
Undocumented	21.1	30.9	4.2	0.41	510
General population					
White	30.4	18.9%	26.7%	0.42	246
Black	23.2	26.6	11.7	0.43	381
Asian, other	25.4	27.4	12.4	0.46	346
Spanish-origin	22.3	31.8	11.8	0.55	464

SOURCE: Data for San Diego County general population were calculated from the 1980 Census, Bureau of the Census 1980.
[a]Dependency ratio = ratio of dependent-age population to working-age population.
[b]Child-woman ratio = number of children under 5 years of age per 1,000 women of child-bearing age (15 to 44 years).

The age-sex structure of Mexican immigrants and the members of their households can also be compared with San Diego's Hispanic, black, white, and Asian populations. As the median ages in Table 10 show, whites are generally older than blacks, Hispanics, and Asians. Documented Mexican immigrants are similar in age to Hispanics generally, while their undocumented counterparts are typically younger. When considering the proportion of the populations under 15 years of age, Latinos are generally younger, with Mexican immigrants having the largest proportions in that age category. In contrast, Mexican immigrants, particularly the undocumented, have few members who are over 50 years of age.

These data indicate the selectivity of migration. Migrants tend to be relatively young individuals who are early in the family formation period of their lives, a fact also reflected in dependency ratios.[47]

The dependency ratio refers to the ratio of the dependent-age population (the young and old) to the working-age population, and is therefore a useful index of the social and economic effects of different age structures. The measure defines all children under 15 years old and all adults over 64 years old as "dependent-age" and all persons 15 to 64 years old as "working-age." The higher the ratio, the more peo-

[47]For comparable data on Indochinese refugees, who tend to be demographically younger than even Mexican immigrants, see Rumbaut et al., "Politics of Migrant Health Care."

ple are dependent on each working-age person. As Table 10 indicates, in San Diego legal Mexican immigrants exhibit about the same ratio as Hispanics generally, whereas the undocumented have the lowest ratio, one that reflects the large proportion of single migrants in that population.

The age and sex structures of these populations also reflect their level of fertility, which in turn may have major long-term social and economic consequences. The child-woman ratio refers to the ratio of all children under 5 years of age per 1000 women of child-bearing age (defined as 15 to 44 years of age). Turning once again to Table 6, Latinos and whites differ dramatically in their unadjusted child-woman ratios. Undocumented women have the highest ratio—indicating more young children per woman—than the other groups. This ratio reflects their young age and early stage in family formation.

A consequence of the age structure is that undocumented immigrants who form a family in the United States are highly likely to have a child born in the United States. Of the households interviewed in San Diego that were headed by undocumented immigrants, 42.1 percent contained at least one member who was a citizen of the United States. This proportion is confirmed with similar data collected in Texas, where 41.4 percent of such households contained U.S. citizens.[48]

I have referred elsewhere to households of mixed nationality and immigration status as "binational families."[49] The implications of binational families are apparent when examining policies aimed at the undocumented that also affect the members of an undocumented immigrant's family. These demographic indicators provide a profile of the undocumented interviewees and the members of their households. A few points about these indicators deserve to be emphasized. Women and children make up a large part of the total household population, a result of a sampling methodology that allowed the interviewing of undocumented immigrants who were in the "community" rather than detained by the INS. Samples of detained undocumented migrants have overwhelmingly consisted of males who are temporary migrants rather than settlers.[50] In contrast, many of these interviewees live with their families and reside on a long-term basis in the United States. Their social needs will be similar to other residents who fit their demographic

---

[48] Weintraub and Cardenas, *Use of Public Services.*

[49] Chávez, "Migrants and Settlers."

[50] Harry E. Cross and James A. Sandos, *Across the Border* (Berkeley, Calif., 1981); North and Houstoun, "Illegal Aliens in the U.S. Labor Market."

TABLE II

Proportion of Relatives and Non-Relatives in the Households of Mexican
Immigrants and Major Racial/Ethnic Groups in San Diego

	Pct. with other relatives in household[a]	Pct. with non-relatives in household	Pct. total
White	3.1%	5.3%	8.4%
Black	5.2	5.1	10.3
Asian	9.6	4.0	13.6
Spanish origin	6.5	4.4	10.9
Total San Diego	3.9	5.2	9.1
Mexican immigrants Undocumented (2,430 individuals in 574 households)	19.7	13.1	32.8
Legal immigrant (2,278 individuals in 570 households)	10.4	1.0	11.4

SOURCE: Data on San Diego populations calculated from 1980 Census data. Bureau of the Census 1983:6-1206.
[a]Includes *compadres*.

profile, and will be concentrated in the areas of maternal and child health care and education for their children.

HOUSEHOLD COMPOSITION AND THE PRESENCE OF OTHERS

Adapting to the constraints of the U.S. labor market and immigration status influences the characteristics of Mexican immigrant households. As Table II indicates, Mexican immigrants, particularly the undocumented, lived in larger households than did other San Diegans. However, a relatively large median household size does not mean that Mexican immigrants have larger families. Rather, it can be attributed, in part, to the large number of individuals who are not part of the household head's immediate or nuclear family. These others include brothers, sisters, parents, cousins, nephews, assorted in-laws, and compadres. A friend from the same community or region in Mexico might also be in the household.

There is a significant difference in household composition based on immigration status (Table II). Undocumented informants had many more others in their households compared to legal immigrants. Particularly noticeable is the presence of cousins, nephews, and brothers- and sisters-in-law in the households headed by undocumented immigrants. A major difference between the two subgroups is the extent to which friends are brought into the household. Legal immigrants rarely lived

TABLE 12

Characteristics of Mexican Households in Northern Mexico

No. of households	Total in household	Median size	Total other relatives	Total friends
4,140	20,756	4.7	4.2%	0.7%

SOURCE: El Colegio de la Frontera Norte, *Report on the Annual Socioeconomic Survey of the U.S.-Mexico Border*, No. II, 1984.

with friends; however, they accounted for over 13 percent of the household members among the undocumented.

Although legal Mexican immigrants had about the same proportion of other relatives in their households as Asians (the other group with a large immigrant component), they had proportionately fewer friends in their household than did other groups. Legal immigrants exhibited proportions of friends in the household that were similar to those found among households in Mexico. On the other hand, undocumented Mexican immigrants had much higher proportions of both other relatives and friends in their households than did all other groups.

Cultural preference alone does not explain such distinctive patterns for legal and undocumented immigrants. Data on household composition gathered in cities along the Mexican side of the U.S.-Mexico border indicate that the presence of others does not represent a large proportion of household members (Table 12). And rarely do households in Mexico contain non-relatives or friends. It appears that migration causes friends to become acceptable household members.

WORKERS PER HOUSEHOLD

A strategy for coping with low-wage employment is to increase the number of workers per household and thus the resources available. As Table 13 indicates, undocumented immigrants rarely lived in households without at least one member participating in the labor force. In these exceptional cases, the migrants were either recent migrants still looking for employment or, more rarely, female heads of households receiving Aid to Families with Dependent Children (AFDC) for U.S.-born children. Likewise, relatively few of the households in Mexico had no workers. A reason for this similarity may be that in both cases government-funded assistance is generally not available. Households headed by undocumented immigrants and households in Mexico must rely on the income of its members and other income-generating strategies for survival.

Undocumented households commonly have three or more workers; this typically occurs through extension of the family to include other mi-

TABLE 13

Number of Workers Per Household for Mexican Immigrants,
San Diego Populations and Residents of Baja California, Mexico

	Workers per household			
	0 (pct.)	1 (pct.)	2 (pct.)	3+ (pct.)
Mexican immigrants				
Undocumented (N = 603)	5.0%	28.5%	34.3%	32.2%
Legal (N = 585)	20.5	44.4	25.1	9.9
San Diego populations				
White	15.9	33.5	40.6	10.1
Black	13.4	36.4	40.3	9.9
Asian	9.8	29.2	44.5	16.5
Spanish origin	10.3	39.0	37.7	13.0
Northern Baja California, Mexico, urban households (N = 4,151)	4.4%	57.6%	24.5%	13.5%

SOURCES: Data on San Diego populations computed from 1980 Census data, Bureau of the Census 1983:6-1298. Mexican household data, El Colegio de la Frontera Norte, *Annual Socioeconomic Survey of the U.S.-Mexico Border*, 1984.

grants. The Spanish- and Mexican-origin households tended to have more workers per household than did those of whites or blacks in San Diego, but they were still much less likely to have three or more workers than undocumented immigrants.

Asians and Hispanics were more likely than whites, blacks, and legal immigrants to have three or more workers in the household. However, blacks, whites, Asians, and those of Spanish origin commonly lived in households with two workers.

It is interesting that many legal Mexican immigrants and Mexican residents of Mexico lived in households with only one worker. Perhaps the woman's traditional role of staying in the home remains strong for these two groups.

THE IMPACT OF IMMIGRATION ON THE LOCAL LEVEL

The local community and its labor market have observable effects on Mexican immigration. Adaptations in household size, composition, and the number of workers within the household reflect strategies for dealing with the constraints of both secondary and informal-sector employment and an undocumented immigration status. Participation in the local labor market also influences whether a migrant returns to Mexico or takes up long-term residence in the United States. Such adaptations affect the impact of immigration on the local community.

A number of recent case studies and reports have examined the effect of immigration on U.S. communities, giving special emphasis to Los Angeles and Southern California.[51] Government reports have also examined various issues related to immigration's effect, including displacement of U.S. workers and other labor-market issues and the immigrants' use of social services.[52]

Without restating entirely the substance of the case studies and reports, a summary of the findings on specific issues is in order.

Work

Migrants with family in Mexico will work on a temporary or seasonal basis. Immigrants with families in the United States will rotate from job to job, but prefer long-term, stable employment.[53]

Health and Education Needs

Temporary migrants, who tend to be young, healthy individuals seeking work rather than an education, make little use of the education and health systems. Health care is episodic, and emergency care is sought in the event of accidents. With longer residence, immigrants seek out classes that teach English as a second language. The children of undocumented immigrants require an education. Maternal and child health care are needed because the undocumented are demographically young.[54]

Contributions

A large proportion of both temporary migrants and long-term residents pay taxes and contribute through their labor to the general productivity of the economy. The studies that have attempted to compare the cost of social services provided for undocumented immigrants to these immigrants' contribution through taxes have overwhelmingly concluded that contributions outweigh costs.[55] One recent study on the Los Angeles area failed to arrive at this conclusion;[56] however, the authors note that

[51] Kevin F. McCarthy and R. Burciaga Valdez, *Current and Future Effects of Mexican Immigration in California* (Santa Monica, Calif., 1986); Muller and Espenshade, *The Fourth Wave*; Julian L. Simon, *How Do Immigrants Affect Us Economically?* (Washington, 1985); Weintraub and Cardenas, *Use of Public Services;* Cornelius, Chávez, and Castro, *Mexican Immigrants and Southern California.*

[52] General Accounting Office, *Illegal Aliens: Limited Research Suggests Illegal Aliens May Displace Native Workers* (Washington, 1986); Library of Congress, *Impact of Illegal Immigration and Background on Legalization* (Washington, 1985).

[53] Chávez, "Migrants and Settlers."

[54] Rumbaut, et al., "Politics of Migrant Health Care"; Cornelius, Chávez, and Jones, *Mexican Immigration and Access.*

[55] For a review of this debate, see McCarthy and Valdez, *Mexican Immigration in California;* Simon, *How Do Immigrants Affect Us?;* Weintraub and Cardenas, *Use of Public Services;* and Cornelius, Chávez, and Jones, *Mexican Immigration and Access.*

[56] Muller and Espenshade, *The Fourth Wave.*

federal tax contributions were not taken into consideration, nor were the contributions of temporary undocumented migrants.

The Displacement of Citizen and Legal Resident Workers

The evidence on this complicated issue is inconclusive.[57] Although some displacement of U.S. workers occurs, it has been suggested that the added productivity and job creation in an area as a result of the presence of undocumented workers offsets the loss of jobs. In short, there is a net increase in jobs for U.S. citizens.[58] McCarthy and Valdez, however, argue that the price of higher job creation in places such as Los Angeles, which also has a large number of undocumented workers, has been low growth of wages, especially for Hispanic workers (citizens, legal residents, and undocumented immigrants).[59]

The following section focuses on undocumented immigrants' use of health services in San Diego. Health care is one of many areas where the characteristics of the undocumented population must be taken into account when examining the effects of immigration.

HEALTH CARE

Health care needs and the use of health services are related to factors such as whether a migrant travels alone or with dependents, whether he or she is a recent arrival to the United States or a long-term resident, and the population's demographic profile. Young, single migrants make little use of medical services in Mexico or the United States. Among the undocumented Mexican immigrants sampled in San Diego, 17.7 percent had never sought medical care from a conventional practitioner.[60] In other cases, migrants prefer to endure a health problem, if possible, until returning to Mexico.

For those who do use local health services, there is a question concerning their use (or overuse) of hospital emergency rooms, which supposedly leads to large unreimbursed health costs. As Table 14 indicates, however, migrants' utilization of health services varies according to their immigration status and length of residence. It is significant that Mexican immigrants use a variety of health-care providers. Large hospitals and hospital emergency rooms are not the most frequently used source of care among the undocumented population. Indeed, even recently arrived undocu-

---

[57] General Accounting Office, *Illegal Aliens.*
[58] Simon, *How Do Immigrants Affect Us?*
[59] McCarthy and Valdez, *Mexican Immigration in California.*
[60] Chávez, Cornelius, and Jones, *Mexican Immigrants and the Utilization of Health Services.*

TABLE 14

Health Care Provider by Various Migrant Types

	Pct. recent undocumented migrants (N = 309)	Pct. recent legal migrants (N = 121)	Pct. long-term undocumented migrants (N = 389)	Pct. long-term legal migrants (N = 726)
U.S. hospitals	19.4%	17.4%	21.3%	24.0%
U.S. clinics	40.1	25.6	36.8	29.6
U.S. doctors	19.7	13.2	34.7	36.8
Mexico care	20.7	43.8	7.2	9.6
Totals	99.9%[a]	100.0%	100.0%	100.0%

NOTE: Significance (χ^2) = 0.01 or less. "Recent" refers to three years or less residence in the United States. "Long-term" refers to more than three years residence in the United States.
[a] Total does not equal 100 owing to rounding off.

TABLE 15

Hospital Services Used by Various Types of Migrants

	Pct. recent undocumented migrants (N = 135)	Pct. recent legal migrants (N = 73)	Pct. long-term undocumented migrants (N = 211)	Pct. long-term legal migrants (N = 470)
Emergency room	50.4%	23.3%	46.4%	34.5%
Outpatient clinic	24.4	35.6	17.1	29.4
Inpatient (admitted)	9.6	28.8	21.3	27.4
Maternity	14.8	12.3	13.7	7.4
Other	0.7	0.0	1.4	1.3
Total	99.9%[a]	100.0%	99.9%[a]	100.0%

NOTE: Significance (χ^2) = 0.01 or less. Four cells have N of 5 or less. "Recent" refers to three years or less residence in the United States. "Long-term" refers to more than three years residence in the United States.
[a] Totals do not equal 100 owing to rounding off.

mented migrants (in the United States three years or less) used U.S. clinics more than hospitals.

However, when hospitals are used, undocumented immigrants tended to use the emergency room to a greater degree than other services (Table 15). The frequency of maternity care presented in Table 15 also shows that maternal health is important to this demographically young population.

The general lack of private medical insurance and the regulations limiting an undocumented resident's use of Medicaid (Medi-Cal) results in the undocumented having few resources other than personal savings to pay for medical care. As Table 16 indicates, undocumented Mexican immigrants in San Diego most often paid, or were paying, their medical

TABLE 16

Method of Payment for Last Health Service Usage by
Mexican Immigrants in San Diego

	Pct. undocumented immigrants (N = 816)	Pct. legal immigrants (N = 801)	Pct. total (N = 1,617)
Private insurance	10.3%	34.8%	22.5%
Gov't sponsored program	3.2	24.1	13.5
Personal resources	84.4	39.8	62.3
Other	2.1	1.2	1.7
Totals	100.0%	99.9%[a]	100.0%

NOTE: Significance (χ^2) = .001 or less.
[a]Total does not equal 100 owing to rounding off.

bills with personal funds. In some cases, however, small payments on a large debt for emergency room care are viewed by hospital administrators as part of the nonreimbursed costs attributed to undocumented immigrants.[61]

As our research in San Diego found, though, an accurate assessment of costs incurred by undocumented patients was hampered by problems of identification. Immigration status was often determined on the basis of hospital personnel's ad hoc, subjective evaluation of a patient's cultural characteristics or on the patient's refusal to apply for Medi-Cal.[62] When patients suspected of being undocumented requested Medi-Cal (Medicaid), their applications were routinely sent to the INS for verification.

STATE AND FEDERAL POLICIES AND THE LOCAL LEVEL

State and federal policies affect Mexican immigrants and local governments. Although it is beyond the limits of this paper to examine every law and regulation, I can present some policies aimed at undocumented immigrants that do not take into account the population's demographic characteristics and patterns of household composition. Since we have already mentioned the practice of verifying the immigration status of Medi-Cal applicants in San Diego, let us explore the policy on which that practice is based.

Since 1981, California has required that all noncitizen applicants for Medicaid (Medi-Cal), Food Stamps, and AFDC benefits complete the form CA-6, which is routinely sent to the INS for verification of the applicant's immigration status. Illinois and Colorado, since 1982 and 1983, respectively, have used the form to screen applicants for unemployment

[61]Cornelius, Chávez, and Jones, *Mexican Immigration and Access.*
[62]*Ibid.*

insurance. Such practices are part of the INS's Project SAVE (Systematic Alien Verification for Entitlements) and are intended to prevent undocumented aliens from receiving entitlement benefits.[63]

Such a policy, however, has additional consequences. For example, children born in the United States are entitled to use government-sponsored health programs such as Medicaid (Medi-Cal), but an undocumented brother or sister born in Mexico is generally not so entitled. Without Medicaid, and most often without private medical insurance, undocumented children will find non-emergency health care difficult to obtain. In other words, hospitals and many clinics request guarantees that a third party will pay Medicaid or private medical insurance—and, in some cases, proof of residence before non-emergency health care will be provided.[64]

Moreover, notifying INS of an undocumented immigrant's use of a service such as Medicaid could hinder that individual's attempt to legalize his or her status in the United States, on the grounds that he or she is likely to become a public charge. As a result, undocumented parents often fear using Medicaid for their U.S.-born child, so even that child may go without necessary health care.[65]

Juan's case (a pseudonym) illustrates this point well. Juan has been in the U.S. 21 years, his wife and daughter for 8 years. When his U.S.-born infant daughter had an operation, he said:

The hospital worker told us to apply for Medi-Cal for her. We said we were trying to legalize our status and didn't want to jeopardize our chances. The hospital worker told us there would be no problem, since my daughter was born here. But when the papers came, the worker had applied for my wife, too. We took the papers to our lawyer who told us we could be denied permission to legally stay in this country if we filed the papers.

Juan closed the papers immediately. But with what he earned working on a flower farm and his wife as a maid, he said candidly that he could not afford additional health care for his daughter.

FOOD STAMPS AND NUTRITIONAL SUPPLEMENT PROGRAMS

In other cases of access to social service programs, policymakers have paid special attention to the policy's impact on the U.S.-born children of

---

[63] Mexican-American Legal Defense and Education Fund, "INS Establishes 1985 Enforcement Priorities," memo to MALDEF (Los Angeles, Calif., 1985).

[64] Cornelius, Chávez, and Jones, *Mexican Immigration and Access.*

[65] A study conducted in February 1978 for the U.S. Department of Health, Education, and Welfare in San Diego County reported that "99 percent of the undocumented parents of [U.S.] citizen children will not complete Medi-Cal applications for their children because they fear detection and deportation" (Health Research Services and Analysis, "Unpaid Medical Costs/Illegal Immigrants," final report submitted to the U.S. Department of Health, Education, and Welfare, 1978).

undocumented immigrants.[66] The U.S. Congress has taken steps on food stamp eligibility to ensure that citizen children in families headed by undocumented immigrants qualify for aid. Amendments to the Food Stamp Act in 1980 require caseworkers to report to the INS those household members who are ineligible for such benefits because of their illegal status in the United States. While intending to prevent ineligible aliens from receiving food stamps, Congress clearly stated that caseworkers are not to act as "outreach officers of the Immigration and Naturalization Service."[67]

Consequently, current federal regulations allow undocumented parents to apply for food stamps on behalf of citizen children, but many exclude themselves for aid consideration by simply refusing to supply information about their immigration status. The immigration status of the parents thus becomes irrelevant and the caseworker has no legal basis to probe further into the subject. However, the Illinois Department of Public Aid continued to require information on immigration status from each household member; any "illegal" aliens were to be reported to the INS. Only after a successful lawsuit against the state of Illinois were federal regulations properly enforced.[68]

Not all services requiring information on all household members have such well-defined safeguards built into them. The Omnibus Budget Reconciliation Act of 1981 requires that applicants to the summer food programs, Child Care Food Program, and school breakfast and lunch programs include the names and social security numbers of all adult household members.[69] But the law is unusual in that it lacks an explanation of what uses will be made of the social security numbers and imposes no restrictions on access to that information by state and other federal agencies. In short, there is no guidance to school districts concerning the protection of the applicant's privacy.

This liberal use of information has a chilling effect on undocumented immigrants and their families, who are particularly vulnerable to abuses of discretion. A survey of school districts in California found that some

[66] In a similar case, the Superior Court of California ruled in February 1985 that the state could no longer require all applicants to the California Children's Services program to also apply for Medi-Cal, a practice that inhibited children of undocumented immigrants from applying to the children's services program. (See Laurie Becklund, "Handicapped Children of Illegals Can Now Get Aid," *Los Angeles Times*, 8 Feb. 1985, sec. 1 : 1).

[67] House Committee on Agriculture, *Food Stamp Act Amendments of 1980 H.R. 788*, 96th Cong., 2d sess., 1980, 155–57.

[68] Mexican-American Legal Defense and Education Fund, "INS Establishes 1985 Enforcement Priorities," 11–12.

[69] National Center for Immigrants' Rights, "School Lunch Programs-Social Security Number Requirement," memo released 30 Sept. (San Francisco, 1982).

district administrators believed they had either the authority or the legal obligation to report to the INS alien households whose school meal applications cited income without social security numbers.[70] Nowhere in the law is this authority expressly conferred.

Families may thus fear participating in a school nutrition program, believing it will result in the detection of undocumented parents using fake social security cards. In some cases both parents may be legal residents, but an adult brother, sister, or cousin without immigration papers may be in the household. While the U.S.-born child in a binational family may be deterred from using such programs, their undocumented brother or sister, who may also need the benefits of a nutritional program, is even less likely to participate. The Food Research and Action Center reports:

Many households that are eligible to participate in the child nutrition programs are reluctant to apply. Some believe that disclosure of their participation could result in harassment and ridicule by their neighbors or coworkers. Others believe that there would be adverse consequences at work if their employers found out. Still others believe that merely providing the information will result in investigations by federal immigration authorities. As a consequence, children who urgently need the nutritional benefits of the child nutrition programs do not receive them.[71]

EDUCATION

Although the U.S. Supreme Court determined that access to primary and secondary education for undocumented children was in society's long-term interest, the question of higher education still surfaces.[72] In California, junior colleges, state universities, and more recently the University of California attempted to institute policies that consider immigration status a criterion for determining a student's residence status and thus the amount and type of fees they will pay. Thus children of undocumented immigrants would be subject to non-resident tuition, which is at least $3,500 above the fees paid by other California residents. Although targeted at undocumented students, this policy has in some cases deterred

---

[70] C. Wilkins, "Targeting Benefits to the Truly Needy? Implementation and Impact of Recent Eligibility Changes in the National School Lunch Programs," master's thesis for the School of Public Policy, University of California, Berkeley; Food Research and Action Center, "Privacy Considerations Raised by Verification in the Child Nutrition Programs," *Clearinghouse Review* (June 1984), 140–42.

[71] Food Research and Action Center, "Privacy Considerations," 142.

[72] Flores, "Undocumented Immigrants and Public Policy"; Alien Children Education Litigation, "Brief for the Appellants," prepared for Alien Children Education Litigation State of Texas and Texas Education Agency v. U.S. and Certain Named and Unnamed Undocumented Alien Children, U.S. Supreme Court cases 80–1538, 80–1934 (Washington, 1980).

even students who are U.S. citizens from applying to college, in order not to draw attention to their parents immigration status.[73] The additional cost given their parents' generally low incomes is of course another obstacle. The constitutionality of tuition- and residence-related policies that target the undocumented as a group has been successfully challenged in California's Superior Court.[74] On April 3, 1985, the judge of the superior court of California ruled in favor of Leticia A., Sonia V., and other undocumented students. The policy of classifying undocumented students as non-residents for tuition purposes was found to be too broad and therefore unconstitutional under the state's constitution. In his ruling, the judge noted that: "Even if the clear and convincing evidence of the values of post-secondary education had not been shown by plaintiffs, the public policy encouraging an improved and dynamic society is sufficient to find that higher education is an 'important' interest in California."[75]

HOUSING

The Department of Housing and Urban Development (HUD) recently put forth a policy on access to federally subsidized housing that would require all applicants to show proof of U.S. citizenship or legal residency. Although the policy was to go into effect on September 30, 1986, its implementation has been postponed indefinitely in order for Congress to consider various options.[76]

HUD's latest proposed housing regulations provide another example of a policy that considers the undocumented population in monolithic, homogeneous terms. Little consideration is given to the demographic profile and composition of households headed by undocumented immigrants. As we have seen, many family members of undocumented immigrants are U.S. citizens. By denying the undocumented immigrant access to public housing, such policies also can deny U.S. citizens, often children, access to housing to which they would otherwise be entitled.

CONCLUSIONS

The U.S. public is concerned about the impact of immigrants on local communities. However, possible solutions to the immigration "problem" (as it is perceived at the local level) must be based on an adequate understanding of Mexican immigrants' incorporation into local and even regional labor markets. Mexican immigrants, even the undocumented, are

[73] See Michael Scott-Blair, "Tuition Controversy Has Aliens in a Trap," *San Diego Union*, 1 Oct. 1984, sec. B:1.
[74] *Leticia A. v. Univ. of California Board of Regents*, 1985.
[75] *Ibid.*, 8.
[76] J. Cantlupe, "HUD to Delay for Two Months Curb on Alien Housing Aid," *San Diego Union*, 28 July 1986, sec. B:1.

not a homogeneous group. Some are temporary migrants and others are in the process of settling in the United States.

The age and sex characteristics and the composition of Mexican immigrant households reflect adaptations to the local labor market and society. Mexican immigrants are a young population. Their households often consist of members who are not part of the head's nuclear or immediate family. This trend is especially true for undocumented immigrants who also have the highest number of workers per household.

The socioeconomic and demographic features of the Mexican immigrants incorporated into the local labor market determines their effect on the local community. Among a demographically young population, maternal and child health care are of greater relative importance, as is education for their children. Length of time in the United States and the associated cultural knowledge associated with longer residence also influence use of services, as shown in the medical services example. Moreover, we must also take into account that the type of jobs Mexican immigrants find do not generally provide private medical insurance—a fact that also influences their use of preventive health services.

The impact of Mexican immigrants on the local community can only be understood within the context of their participation in the local labor market. If the local economy is luring undocumented Mexicans into becoming long-term workers and thus residents (in effect, responding to the demand for their labor), then family formation will inevitably follow. And as we have seen, settler families and temporary migrants have different needs, which lead to distinct patterns of social service usage.

Settlers, as distinct from temporary migrants, raise issues concerning the long-term impact on a society of more-or-less permanent undocumented residents. Should society plan for the integration of undocumented settlers and their families? Or should obstacles be placed to their integration? Households headed by undocumented immigrants that also contain U.S. citizens complicate the issue of social integration for the undocumented and their families. Policies aimed at undocumented immigrants often affect, or potentially affect, children of undocumented immigrants who are U.S. citizens. The long-term effects of immigration on the local community will depend on the larger society's resolution of this question of social integration. The price the local community pays for paradise now could pale in comparison to future costs should society fail to plan for the eventual integration of long-term undocumented residents and their families.

Norteñización: Self-Perpetuating Migration from a Mexican Town

Rafael Alarcón

IMPLEMENTATION IN THE United States of the 1986 Immigration Reform and Control Act makes it more important than ever before to understand the transformations taking place in areas of Mexico that send the most labor to the United States. Sponsors of this immigration reform sought to "regain control of the United States' borders" and to reduce or eliminate the influx of undocumented workers.

What are the ramifications of this reform? And how does it affect regions within Mexico that, over the years, have become heavily dependent on the U.S. labor market? This essay considers how the migration of Mexican workers affects their home communities—in this case Chavinda, a community in the state of Michoacán, Mexico. Describing and analyzing the impacts of international migration on a community like Chavinda can further our understanding of similar processes occurring throughout much of rural western Mexico.

THE EFFECTS OF INTERNATIONAL MIGRATION IN WESTERN MEXICO

The migration of Mexicans who seek work in U.S. labor markets was identifiable as an important social process as early as the beginning of the

An earlier version of this article appeared in Thomas Calvo and Gustavo Lopez, eds., *Movimientos de Población en el Occidente de México* (Zamora, Mich., 1988). This final version benefited from comments by Guillermo de la Peña, Macrina Cárdenas, Andrés Jimenez, Jesús Martinez, and Gustavo Verduzco. Many of the ideas and materials used in this paper emerged from the volume co-authored by Douglas Massey, Rafael Alarcón, Jorge Durand, and Humberto González, *Return to Aztlán: The Social Process of International Migration from Western Mexico* (Berkeley, Calif., 1987).

twentieth century. Since the migratory process began, western Mexico has been a principal sending area of migrating workers.[1]

International migration from both urban and rural western Mexico has produced significant changes in the home communities. These changes can be analyzed from several perspectives, including demography, social organization, economic development, and culture.

A brief review of research conducted in western Mexico reveals both the constant and the varying elements that investigators have uncovered in their analyses of the effects of international migration. Juan Díez-Canedo identifies two perspectives adopted in the literature regarding this subject.[2] He mentions that Manuel Gamio, for example, indicated in 1930 that permanent migration should be discouraged because Mexico was underpopulated. Temporary migration, on the other hand, was to be encouraged as a source of jobs for Mexicans in periods of recession. Moreover, international migration raised workers' skill levels and provided Mexico with important revenues.

In the same perspective, other researchers asserted that the losses in agricultural production that result from migration are greater than the benefits to be gained from the migratory process. According to this view, Mexico loses its best workers to the United States. The migrants' struggle to locate jobs and the high costs implicit in the migratory process are additional negative factors for the Mexican economy. Jorge Bustamante addresses the subject of the transfer of value from the economies where the migrants originate to the economies that receive them in the United States.[3]

The observations of these authors are countered, however, by others who emphasize the importance of international migration's role in Mexico's rural communities. Richard Mines notes that many benefit from the modern international migration process: Mexican migrants earn U.S. wages; the Mexican government gains an escape valve for its high numbers of unemployed; U.S. employers have access to an inexpensive labor

---

[1] Generally speaking, western Mexico comprises the states of Aguascalientes, Colima, Guanajuato, Jalisco, Michoacán, and Nayarit. Since the 1920s, this region has repeatedly emerged as the principal sending area of migrants to the United States. In his pioneering work, *Mexican Immigration to the United States* (Chicago, 1930), Manuel Gamio analyzed where migrants' money orders were sent in Mexico. For more on this topic, see Humberto Gonzales, "Las migraciones a los Estados Unidos en el Occidente de México," in Sergio Alcantara and Enrique Sanchez, eds. *Desarrollo Rural en Jalisco: Contradicciones y perspectivas* (Guadalajara, 1985); and Jorge Durand, "Circuitos Migratorios," in Thomas Calvo and Gustavo Lopez, eds., *Movimientos de población en el occidente de México* (Zamora, Mich., 1988).

[2] Juan Díez-Canedo, *La migración indocumentada de México a los Estados Unidos: Un nuevo enfoque* (Mexico City, 1984).

[3] Jorge A. Bustamante, "Las mercancias migratorias. Indocumentados y capitalismo: Un enfoque," *Nexos* 14 (1979).

force; U.S. workers whose jobs complement the efforts of undocumented migrants retain their jobs; and the U.S. consumer obtains goods and services at low cost.[4]

Mines's research in Las Animas, Zacatecas, led him to conclude that migratory flows had distorted the community's economy. Among the factors producing this distortion is the outflow of young men from the community. Once they have migrated north and worked in the United States, most of these men are unwilling to work in Mexico. The scarcity of economic opportunities, as well as the returning migrants' lack of interest in developing their community, have produced further declines in the local economy.

Joshua Reichert, who studied migration in a rural community in Michoacán, characterizes the impact of migration as a "syndrome."[5] He observed that the income from seasonal migration is not used for strengthening the local economy. Instead, this income encourages more people to migrate to the United States, increasing the community's dependence on this outside source of income.

Raymond Wiest demonstrated how migration from Acuitzio, Michoacán, creates a form of community dependence on the U.S. labor market and how this process is perpetuated.[6]

In a study of nine communities in Los Altos de Jalisco, Wayne Cornelius found that in most of these communities migrants' remittances were very important.[7] He found that some migrants purchased entertainment and nonessential consumer goods with their earnings; but most made some investment in houses or land and in the means of production. Successful migrants also began small businesses. Cornelius reviews the case of one community that achieved significant economic development with migrants' earnings from the United States.

In Gómez Farías, Michoacán, Gustavo López found that those dollars migrants sent to the home community were extremely important.[8] Nearly

[4] Richard Mines, "Developing a Community Tradition of Migration: A Field Study in Rural Zacatecas and California Settlement Areas," Monographs in U.S.-Mexican Studies 3 (San Diego, 1981).

[5] Joshua Reichert, "The Migrant Syndrome: Seasonal U.S. Wage Labor and Rural Development in Central Mexico," Human Organization 1 (1981).

[6] Raymond Wiest, "La dependencia externa y la perpetuacion de la migración temporal a los Estados Unidos," in Relaciones, vol. 17 of Estudios de Historia y Sociedad (Zamora, Mich., 1983).

[7] Wayne A. Cornelius, "Outmigration from Rural Mexican Communities," in The Dynamics of Migration: International Migration Occasional Monograph Series 5, vol. 2 (Washington, 1976).

[8] Gustavo Lopez, La casa dividida un estudio de caso sobre la migración a los Estados Unidos en un pueblo Michoacáno (Zamora, Mich., 1986).

half of migrant earnings are spent on consumer goods and services in nearby towns. The investment of earnings in housing improvements has seriously inflated land values.

Research conducted by Douglas Massey and his associates in two urban and two rural areas in the states of Jalisco and Michoacán indicates that international migration is part of a survival strategy that households rely on during periods of economic need or when efforts are underway to improve the household's economy.[9] Migrants' periodic remittances went primarily toward sustaining their families, with some savings going to housing improvements. Income derived from work in the United States supported the establishment of some businesses in urban settings. But the use of funds toward this end was less frequent in rural Mexico, where remittances were mostly directed toward modernizing agriculture.

These various research findings, although uncovered in different settings, share a number of important elements: (1) Levels of participation in international migration vary; hence, there are varying intensities in the impact of this phenomenon in the home communities, (2) International migration's effects are not limited to economic considerations, (3) Most of the resources obtained through migration are directed toward supporting the migrants' families in the home community and toward housing improvements, and (4) The productive investment of these monies is less notable.

Most studies of international migration indicate that regions in general, and localities in particular, that show high levels of migration to the United States are not always economically depressed. In this sense, international migration is not always explained by poverty or unemployment. This underlines the need for a more adequate methodology for analyzing labor migration between Mexico and the United States. Until now, this migratory flow has been addressed through the same theoretical frameworks applied to the study of internal migration.

Migration to the United States can be distinguished from internal migration in two fundamental aspects: (1) its temporary character, and (2) the sizable differential between wages paid in the domestic market and those paid in the portion of the U.S. labor market accessible to migrant workers.

The central hypothesis of this analysis is that, in its nearly one hundred years of evolution, international migration has generated a close relationship between specific areas in rural Mexico and U.S. labor markets. I call the impacts of this linkage in Mexico *norteñización*, from the popular

[9] Douglas Massey et al., *Return to Aztlan: The Social Process of International Migration from Western Mexico* (Berkeley, Calif., 1987).

use of the term *norteño* to refer to those who migrate to the United States. *Norteñización* here refers to the process by which these communities have specialized in producing and reproducing international migrant workers by adapting their economic and social structures.

THE PROCESS OF 'NORTEÑIZACIÓN' IN CHAVINDA

The Road North

The municipality of Chavinda falls within the region that Luis González has designated the Bajío Zamorano, in the northwestern corner of the state of Michoacán. The Zamoran Bajío comprises between ten and fifteen municipalities, which are interlinked by their economic center, the city of Zamora.[10] Since the colonial era, this region has been an important center for agricultural production. Its topography is characterized by flat lands, good soils, and the potential for irrigated agriculture over much of its surface.[11]

Chavinda is a town of *mestizos*. The 1980 census registered 12,354 inhabitants in the municipality, more than one-quarter of whom (28.3 percent) were engaged primarily in agricultural activities.

A survey conducted in the municipal capital in 1982 found that the largest group within the economically active population was agricultural day laborers.[12] Nearly half of the employed population fell within this group. Peasants formed the second largest group, comprised mostly of *ejidatarios*. Nearly three-quarters of the land (73.1 percent) in Chavinda is *ejido* land. Table 1 presents the distribution of occupations in Chavinda.

Chavinda's population has little formal education. Adults average 3.4 years of schooling, and 28 percent have had no formal education. It is a town in which families of the rural proletariat predominate and where many of the inhabitants find only occasional and poorly paid employment.

Chavinda's recent history can be divided into three discrete periods. During the *porfiriato,* when hacienda owners formed the dominant group, the first *norteños* left their community to seek work in U.S. cities.

[10] The municipalities of the Zamoran Bajio are Zamora, Jacona, Tangancicuaro, Chilchota, Purépero, Tlazazalca, Churintzio, Tinguindín, Santiago Tangamandapio, Chavinda, Villamar, Pajacuarán, and Ixtlan.

[11] Gustavo Verduzco, "Crecimiento urbano y desarrollo regional: El caso de Zamora, Michoacán," in *Relaciones,* vol. 17 of *Estudios de Historia y Sociedad* (Zamora, Mich., 1984), 10–11.

[12] The survey was applied randomly in 200 households, which constituted almost 10 percent of the total 1,925 households.

TABLE I

Occupations of the Employed Workers in Chavinda,
Michoacán, 1982

Occupation	Percent
Professionals and technicians	2.1%
Peasants (campesinos)	16.4
Day-laborers (jornaleros)	48.1
Others	1.8
Craftsmen and laborers	6.9
Office workers	0.9
Merchants	12.5
Service employees	4.5
Domestic help	3.6
Transport operators	3.3
Unknown	0.3
Total	100.0%

SOURCE: Chavinda survey, 1982.
NOTE: This table presents the employment categories adopted in the X Censo General de Población y Vivienda de 1980 (the 10th General Population and Housing Census, 1980). The number of persons surveyed was 337.

Later, following the agrarian reform, a group of lenders and stockpilers of agricultural goods became the new local bosses. This period witnessed massive migrations of *braceros* who went to the United States as seasonal agricultural workers.

The third period, beginning in the 1960s, was marked by the ascent of agricultural entrepreneurs from the Bajío Zamorano as the dominant actors in agriculture. From the early 1960s onward, migration to the United States became an institutionalized social process. Huge numbers of workers responded to the availability of urban and rural job opportunities, especially in California. Most of these migrants (67.8 percent) indicated in 1982 that they had migrated to the United States illegally on their last trip north. Migration from Chavinda increased significantly since the 1960s. According to Michael Piore, immigration to the United States since that time has been dominated by undocumented workers from Mexico and the Caribbean.[13]

Throughout this century, Chavinda has been the site of regional processes in conflict. The interaction among these conflicting processes produced important changes in the community. The agrarian reform under the Lázaro Cárdenas administration—besides displacing the old land-

[13] Michael Piore, *Birds of Passage: Migrant Labor and Industrial Societies* (Cambridge, Eng., 1979).

owning oligarchy—converted most of the municipality's agricultural land into *ejidos*. Former laborers and sharecroppers became *ejidatarios*. Improved communication links enhanced Chavinda's integration with the national market. And commercial activities and crafts decreased in importance locally, as they concentrated in the more important city of Zamora. The early 1960s brought a dynamic agricultural modernization effort to Chavinda. The extension of commercial crops, especially sorghum, displaced the traditional food staple triad of corn, wheat, and garbanzo beans—a substitution accompanied by an intensive use of agricultural machinery and industrial inputs and by a generalized use of wage labor.

In this context, the working population of Chavinda has created the social structures needed to move more of the community's people into the U.S. labor market; hence the significant increase in international migration and its predominance over internal migration. Between 1980 and 1982, 36 percent of Chavinda's households included at least one international migrant, while only 13 percent included an internal migrant. Concurrently, 25.4 percent of the 18-year-olds surveyed indicated that they had worked in the United States; only 6.4 percent of them had worked elsewhere in Mexico.

International migration is primarily temporary, while internal migration tends to be long-term. The cities in Mexico that attract most of Chavinda's internal migrants are, in order of importance, Mexico City, Guadalajara, and Zamora/Jacona.

The U.S. labor market to which migrants from Chavinda have easiest access is California farm work. During the better part of the year—from March to November—Chavinda's young men are absent from their homes. Those who remain in Chavinda to work in local agriculture are generally either too young or too old to migrate; those who have once experienced migration to the United States are no longer willing to work for Chavinda's low wages. Together, these trends reinforce early incorporation into the labor pool. Although children are increasingly employed, however, women tend not to take on work outside the home.

When looking at migration to the United States by occupation, we find that it appears across all groups, although day laborers were those most likely to migrate (see Table 2).

Chavinda is a community where *norteñización* is strong. Its tradition of migration to the United States has endured for most of this century. Three generations of Chavinda natives have responded to the pull of the U.S. labor market. Over three-quarters of the households surveyed during

TABLE 2

Migration Flows by Occupation of Men 18 Years or Older,
Chavinda, Michoacán, 1980–82

(*As percentage of all migrating workers*)

	Non-manual workers	Manual workers	Peasants (*campesinos*)	Day laborers (*jornaleros*)	Service workers
Migrants to U.S.	7	3	10	41	2
	(25%)	(9.7%)	(20%)	(31.5%)	(22.2%)
Internal migrants	6	3	0	7	0
	(21.4)	(9.7)	–	(5.4)	–
Migrants both to U.S.	1	0	2	3	0
& within Mexico	(3.6)	–	(4)	(2.4)	–
Non-migrants	14	25	38	79	7
	(50)	(80.6)	(76)	(60.7)	(77.8)
Total	28	31	50	130	9
	(100%)	(100%)	(100%)	(100%)	(100%)

SOURCE: Chavinda survey, 1982.
NOTE: The peasant category includes farmers. Day laborers include *ecureros*, rural workers who do not own land but who rent and work an *ecuaro* (a section of marginal land). N = 248.

this research contained at least one individual who had lived in the United States. This finding confirms our assertion that international migration has become institutionalized in Chavinda. This institutionalization has led, in turn, to the development of an economy dependent on work in the United States and a social organization and culture adapted to the requirements of the migration process.

Economic Dependency

International migrants' earnings have become an important element in Chavinda's economic development. Within the dynamic of regional change, these resources can simultaneously exacerbate some processes and soften the impact of others.

The principal end toward which most migrant earnings are directed is the economic maintenance of the family. Most of Chavinda's migrants come from the lowest economic sector. Ascertaining the total amount of dollars entering the community is complicated by the fact that these earnings arrive on an irregular schedule and through a variety of routes. One clue to the amount of U.S. currency entering Chavinda is that during February 1982, when most of the migrants were in Chavinda, the local telegraph office registered 900,000 pesos paid out in money orders originating in the United States.

The uses to which migrant earnings are put vary according to each

TABLE 3

Use of Savings from Last Trip to the United States,
Chavinda Migrants, 1982

Productive investments	8.9%
Buy agricultural land	2.5
Buy livestock	1.3
Buy tools	1.3
Buy or start a business	3.8
Current Consumption	86.1%
Support family	3.8
Build or repair house	25.3
Buy house or lot	22.8
Buy other consumer goods	32.9
Recreation	1.3
Other	5.1%
Buy vehicle	0.0
Pay off debts	1.3
Savings not spent	3.8

SOURCE: Chavinda survey, 1982.

NOTE: These data do not agree with the results of a similar survey in 1988 (Rafael Alarcón, "El proceso de 'norteñización' impacto de la migración internacional en Chavinda, Michoacán," in *Movimentos de población en el occidente de México* [El Colegio de Michoacán, 1988]). The earlier survey did not define the "other" category as precisely, and 28.8 percent of expenditures fell into this category. The N for the present survey of migrants returning with savings was 79.

family's circumstances, in turn a reflection of its economic status, the phase of its family life cycle, and the number of family members. As noted earlier, most migrant earnings cover basic family needs. Families of *norteños* typically invest in housing improvements. Table 3 outlines how the savings accumulated by migrants during their most recent trip to the United States were spent. Housing was clearly a high priority. A migrant typically sends remittances for family maintenance periodically during his sojourn in the United States; these sums do not appear in the table.

Nearly half of all migrant savings (48 percent) went toward housing. This agrees with the observation that in Chavinda nearly one-third (32.5 percent) of owner-occupied houses were purchased with monies earned through international migration.

The strong housing demand created by the *norteños* produced a chain of effects, including inflation of the cost of urban land. People from Chavinda note that local prices for houses and land are nearly on a par with those in the land markets of Zamora and Guadalajara. Another result is the growing demand for construction workers and the formation of several construction-related businesses in the community. A final phenomenon owing to the demand for housing is an intense process of urban modernization, which began in the early 1970s. The cost of this expansion of urban services has been borne primarily by the residents themselves.

When considering the impact of international migration on productive activities, we find that most peasant-owned agricultural land is held by families whose members include migrants to the United States. Overall, migrants have better access to land than do nonmigrants. This access is facilitated further by additional migratory experience.

Mass migration to the United States has not caused a drop in local agricultural production; quite the contrary, it appears to have intensified it. Most of the vehicles and machinery used in agriculture are owned either by families with migrants currently in the United States or by families whose migrants had accumulated savings from earlier migrations north. Peasant families with migrants also tend to use more industrial inputs and own large herds of livestock. They typically use their earnings from migration to purchase land or increase their holdings.

In peasant families with limited resources, migration north seems to function as a subsidy that permits the families to maintain their ties to the land. In only rare cases have migrant earnings allowed members of a peasant family to become agricultural entrepeneurs.

Turning to the relation between migrant earnings and establishing commercial or manufacturing enterprises, Chavinda has lost ground as a business and manufacturing site. Over half of Chavinda's businesses relate to the sale of foodstuffs. Most of these are corner grocery stores.

This absence of manufacturing activities is notable. In 1982 there were only six small workshops in Chavinda. One small shop produced pressed-board furniture; another, iron grillwork. Three were carpentry shops, and the other business made children's clothing. Sixteen percent of all of Chavinda's businesses were started with earnings accumulated in the United States. Most of these businesses are run by families.

Migrant dollars were a key factor in establishing and operating two savings institutions: the Caja Popular de Ahorro and a branch of a national bank. The Caja Popular, which was founded by Chavinda's parish priests during the 1960s, combines individual remittances entering Chavinda into a sum substantial enough to help drive the local economy. In its activities report for 1980, the Caja Popular stated: "During this year 1,161 loans were made for a variety of purposes: agricultural machinery, seed, pigs, and cattle; business expansion; home buying or remodeling; medical care; debt payment; medical instruments; business travel; and even school repairs. The membership of the Caja de Ahorros was reported as 6,662 members."[14]

Fixed-term investments, at least when banks were paying high rates of interest, played an important economic role in the community. The migrants' strategy was simple. They deposited their savings, and interest payments from the accounts provided their families with a steady income.

One last feature that emerged as a result of the *norteñización* of Chavinda's economy is a much improved standard of living among migrant families, thanks to the availability of monies for basic necessities and improved housing. Our observations indicate that migrants find it more difficult to invest in productive activities than in housing and other essentials. Only a few families have had some success with the former. Reichert's "migration syndrome" applies well to Chavinda: the improved standard of living itself generates a demand among the population for maintaining such a living standard.[15] To meet this demand, workers must turn once again to international migration, thus perpetuating the migratory pattern.

The Social Organization of Migration

Migration to the United States is a strategy for family reproduction. It is the family that makes the important adjustments needed for the migrants' lengthy and recurring absences from the household.

The situation in Chavinda mirrors what happens among the popular classes throughout Mexico. The cultural rules that govern society assign to the husband/father the role of economic provider, while the wife/mother, who remains at home, assumes responsibility for everything related to social reproduction. This is the pattern of migration as well. The man must leave the community to work, while the woman remains to direct the household.

Confirming the disproportionate number of men in the migratory flow, we found that nearly half (46.3 percent) of the men we surveyed had migrated at least once to the United States to work, while only 10 percent of the women surveyed had done so. Women's migration from Chavinda increased after the 1960s, primarily because many families were able to obtain papers after the *bracero* program.

Responding to the demands imposed by migration, a new, matrifocal form of family organization emerged in Chavinda. Women now assume total responsibility for their households and the care and education of their children. A family structured along these lines requires a strong

[14] From the weekly newspaper *Guia* (Zamora, Mich.), 8 Feb. 1981.
[15] Joshua Reichert, "The Migrant Syndrome."

kinship and friendship network that can guarantee the support of relatives, neighbors, and friends. Thus, the development of strong social networks is another result of international migration.

Macrina Cárdenas notes that although women assume new responsibilities, they continue in a subordinate position vis-à-vis the community's men.[16] Most of Chavinda's women aspire to marry a documented migrant. The men, meanwhile, prefer to marry women who have never left their community, women who are traditional and hardworking. There are even cases of *chavindeños*, U.S.-born sons of migrants from Chavinda, who, based on the advice of their parents, return to Chavinda to find a wife.

After a migrant marries in the home community, he remains for several months before resuming his migratory pattern. Upon returning north, he generally leaves his new wife in the care of his parents. Occasionally a couple migrates to the United States, but once the pair has one or two children, the wife returns to Chavinda and begins the solitary existence of a migrant's spouse.

A second element that Macrina Cárdenas noted in Chavinda was a double behavior standard. Migrants' wives are held to a very strict behavior code; their particular situation puts them under suspicion and the only remedy is to be above reproach. In the few cases where a migrant's wife failed to live up to the code of behavior expected of her, the community responded harshly, forcing her to move away from the town and leave her children behind. This principle does not apply to the migrants.

For most migrants, the family is basic. Besides its obvious importance for biological reproduction, the family also functions to channel economic resources. When a migrant wants to establish a family, he will prefer someone from the village over women he has met in the United States, even though the latter may be able to regularize his status in the United States. Furthermore, once married, most of the migrants do not want their families to accompany them to the United States. Many of them do not feel that the conditions of their lives in the United States provide an acceptable context for raising their children.

Another very important aspect of migration viewed as a reproductive strategy surfaces in the family life cycle. Husbands and fathers are most likely to migrate during the most critical period within the family life cycle: when the children are small and the proportion of family providers to family consumers is most disadvantageous. As the sons grow older,

[16] Macrina Cárdenas, "La mujer y la migración a los Estados Unidos en Chavinda, Michoacán: Ponencia en I Encuentro sobre problemas del campo en el noroeste de México y el suroeste de los Estados Unidos," (Sinaloa, 1987), mimeo.

they tend to take over their father's duty—that is, migrating to the labor markets of the north. This produces a kind of generational relay, as described by Lourdes Arizpe.[17]

From a broader perspective, migration to the United States is a social process, and its persistence depends on social networks. These networks, in turn, depend on links of kinship, friendship, and communal identity—links that permit the relocation of a community's working-age men to the labor markets of the United States.[18] Evidence of the efforts of three generations of *chavindeños* to build a social network emerges in the pattern of *chavindeños'* distribution within the United States. Migrants from Chavinda concentrate in four areas of California. These "daughter communities" have been formed because of the settlement of many families in those places.

By order of importance, these receiving areas are three towns—one each in the San Joaquín Valley, the Salinas Valley, and the San Francisco Bay area—and a barrio in central Los Angeles. These sites do not function solely as places of employment; thanks to the contacts and information accumulated over time, they also constitute social spaces in which the migrants can re-create the life of Chavinda. In this sense, Chavinda has become a "transnational community."[19] The process of settlement is growing as migrants find urban jobs.

The social organization that emerged as a side effect of migration makes it easier for a native of Chavinda to find employment in the United States than anywhere in Mexico. This is another essential element in Chavinda's *norteñización*.

The Culture of the "North"

This analysis of the process of *norteñización* taking place in Chavinda would be incomplete without considering the theme of culture. Given the prominent, ongoing discussions about Mexico's national culture, one may well wonder if the migrants, who are in frequent contact with U.S. cultural patterns, disrupt their native local, regional, and even national

---

[17] Lourdes Arizpe, *La migración por relevos y la reproducción social del campesinado,* Cuadernos del CES, no. 28 (Mexico City, 1980).

[18] Douglas Massey, Rafael Alarcón, Jorge Durand, and Humberto Gonzales, *Return to Aztlan: The Social Process of International Migration from Western Mexico* (Berkeley and Los Angeles, 1987); Mines, "Developing a Community Tradition of Migration."

[19] Roger Rouse, "Mexicano, Chicano, Pocho: La migración Mexicana y el espacio social del posmodernismo," in *Uno mas Uno* (31 Dec. 1988). Rouse, using the concept of social space of postmodernism, offers a provocative analysis of the relationships between Mexican towns or regions that send migrants and the receiving U.S. communities. The author utilizes the term *transnational communities.*

cultures. Guillermo Bonfil suggests that Mexican culture is becoming "North Americanized"—that is, that Mexico may follow the model of a consumer society to its extreme.[20]

Are Chavinda's international migrants unconsciously contributing to this North Americanization of Mexican culture? A process of cultural change is clearly underway in Chavinda as local culture absorbs elements derived from the migrants' experiences in the United States. Nevertheless, Chavinda's culture exhibits few elements of the mainstream U.S. culture, because migrants' contacts in the United States tend to be with other Latinos in contexts dominated by Latin American influences. Nevertheless, Chavinda's local vernacular has absorbed a number of English words, which are used with equal frequency by *chavideños* who have and have not migrated to the United States. Since Chavinda's vocabulary also contains many remnants of old Spanish, outsiders may have trouble interpreting the odd linguistic mix.

Migrants generally display a marked sense of nationalism and "matriotism," a concept which Luis González defines as an individual's love of *matria,* or "little motherland," something much smaller and sentimentalized than the broader fatherland.[21] Migrants express their *matriotismo* through their determination to return to their home communities.

Despite the migrants' awareness of certain advantages to living and working in the United States, many of them reject the idea of integrating permanently into U.S. society. This resistance may reflect the fact that the migrants' experiences in the north are limited to the most degrading and arduous labor. Their experiences differ radically from those of Mexicans from other social sectors, who come to the United States as tourists, consumers, and savings depositors. These Mexicans show a high degree of North Americanization.

Understanding *norteñización* in Chavinda also implies looking at the community's popular culture, that particular view of the world and of life Jorge González finds at the level of institutions, the subjective "habitus," and practices.[22] All aspects of popular culture feel the impacts of the international migratory process. Working in the United States has become a tradition, a way of life, that "compels" *chavindeños,* especially the male population, to migrate. Their female counterparts learn that marriage might be an experience of solitude. To go north is a rite of passage for Mexican men.

[20] Guillermo Bonfil, "La querella por la cultura," in *Nexos* 100 (1986).
[21] Luis Gonzáles, "Suave Matria: Patriotismo y matriotismo," in *Nexos* 108 (1986).
[22] Jorge González, *Sociologia de las culturas subalternas* (Mexico City, 1981).

The "north" has become a central element in Chavinda's popular culture, and is now intertwined with hegemonic catholicism, a patriarchal social organization, and a social existence dominated by the transition from a rural to an urban life-style.

CONCLUSION

The *norteñización* of Chavinda and of many rural towns in western Mexico may hinder the implementation of the Immigration Reform and Control Act of 1986. This reform may not succeed in reducing or eliminating the flow of undocumented workers for two basic reasons. In the first place, the demand for Mexican labor continues in the United States. Second, the same development of this process over one hundred years in certain areas in Mexico has created the economic dependence and the social institutions that make migration possible and necessary.

Research in Chavinda uncovered an underlying element essential in understanding international migration: the evolution of the process itself generates the conditions that perpetuate it. The access to the labor market in the United States that was initiated by direct recruitment in western Mexico enabled the populations of these rural towns to reach a better standard of living. Since neither the regional economy (no matter how dynamic) nor the urban labor markets in Mexico can provide equivalent incomes, the population of Chavinda continues working in the United States in order to maintain a better standard of living. The development of social networks, contacts with employers, and the formation of "daughter communities" in the United States have made a segment of the labor market in the United States accessible to all families in Chavinda. Ironically, many of these jobs that are rejected by workers in the United States have become indispensable to many Mexican communities.

The process of *norteñización* must be examined in terms of its interaction with structural determinants. The relationship between Mexico and the United States, both linked and separated by their shared border, is in effect an encounter between two national economies at different levels of development. This economic asymmetry is a precondition for the emergence of push-and-pull factors. The binational connection is also marked by differing demographic trends. The U.S. population is aging, while Mexico's population is predominantly young. In addition, the United States presents an open labor market for migrant workers. On the other hand, from its beginnings, the Agrarian Reform Project in Mexico was unable to create an economically viable peasantry throughout the country. Later, demographic growth augmented the number of the landless and decreased parcel size among small holders. Rural areas have also gone through an intense monetarization that has led to the destruction or undercutting of craft manufactures. The peasantry requires currency, and to obtain it, it must sell its labor; thus producing more for the market and less for consumption.[23]

Mexico's current economic crisis has exacerbated the crisis of rural Mexico since the early 1980s. Unemployment and a falling standard of living are now generalized among the working population.

The concept of *norteñización* fits within the analysis of social reproduction that seeks to identify the strategies by which popular sectors seek not only to survive, but to gain higher levels of well-being. The sectors achieve these goals by advantageously exploiting their domestic resources and by inserting these resources into local, regional, and international markets.

Norteñización, which presupposes various degrees of involvement in international migration, lends itself to a comparative analysis. From a national point of view, western Mexico is the region with the highest level of *norteñización.* In part this is true because the labor-recruiting efforts of U.S. railroad companies at the beginning of this century were directed primarily at this region.[24] This helps to explain why in California, apart from the large communities of migrants from the states of Jalisco, Michoacán, and Guanajuato, there are no important concentrations of migrants from states such as Tlaxcala, Hidalgo, Veracruz, or Chiapas. There are also differing degrees of migratory activity within western Mexico. For example, communities with similar socioeconomic profiles within traditional sending areas such as the Zamoran Bajío or Los Altos de Jalisco display very different migratory flows. This fact shows the need to pay attention to the particular regional and local histories of migration.

The sociological and anthropological literature offers several works about communities that are markedly experiencing processes which parallel those underway in Chavinda such as (1) a growing number of families whose well-being depends on work in the "north," (2) dynamic growth or stagnation in the local economy provoked by migrant remittances (the direction of the economic trend depends on the regional context), (3) predominance of international over internal migration, (4) social and cultural adaptations to make migration possible, (5) the transformation over time from a temporary and seasonal migration pattern to

[23] Guillermo De la Peña, "Cambio social y migración internacional de trabajadores: Aproximación al estudio de cuatro regiones agrarias de México" (La Comisión Bilateral para el Futuro de las Relaciones México-Estados Unidos, 1988), mimeo.

[24] Lawrence Cardoso, *Mexican Emigration to the United States, 1897–1931* (Tucson, Ariz., 1980).

a more permanent, longer-term settlement, and (6) the new identity challenges faced by the generations born and raised in the United States.[25]

An elder of Chavinda who spent much of his life working in the United States very eloquently summed up the *norteñización* of his village and its people when he said: "Our women used to cry when the menfolk would go 'north,' now they cry when they don't go."

[25] For a review of other communities experiencing the effects of *norteñización,* see Omar Fonseca and Lilia Moreno, *Jaripo pueblo de migrantes* (Michoacán, 1984).

Undocumented Mexicans on the Mexican Northern Border: Their Identity and Role in Regional Development

Bernardo González-Aréchiga

MEXICO'S NORTHERN border region has had a unique pattern of development, subject less to the general process of import substitution and linked more to the U.S. economy than to the rest of Mexico. This development pattern is demonstrated by the region's dependence on a supply of U.S. goods and by its establishment of productive activities and services oriented toward that country (such as export agriculture and industry; the *maquiladora*; and domestic, personal, tourist, health, and maintenance services).[1]

This pattern of border development is strongly conditioned by the migration policies of the United States, which segment residents of the northern border of Mexico into the documented and the undocumented.[2]

I would like to express my appreciation to Victor Barraza, Arturo Torres, Francisco Cardenas M., and Crecencio Gomez del Villar for their collaboration in the processing of data, as well as to Luz Vega and Ana Maria Rodriguez for their secretarial support, and to Rosina Conde for her editorial assistance.

[1] Interpretations concerning development of the Mexican border region can be found in Jesús Tamayo and José Luis Fernández, *Zonas fronterizas: México-Estados Unidos* Colección Estudios Politicos, no. 2 (Mexico City, 1983), 231; D. Barkin, "Crisis, tecnología y transformación industrial en la frontera norte," *Campo libre: Journal of Chicano Studies* vol. 2, nos. 1, 2 (Los Angeles, 1984), 97–106; and Sofía Méndez Villareal, "El desarrollo industrial de la frontera norte: Un punto de vista mexicano," *Campo libre: Journal of Chicano Studies* vol. 2, nos. 1, 2 (Los Angeles, 1984), 143–52.

[2] In previous works I have discussed some related issues: distribution among different groups of the social costs of the devaluations of 1982, in *Vinculación a Estados Unidos y su cambio con la crisis* (Tijuana, 1985); the distribution of visas as a structural element of transborder commerce, in "Aspectos estructurales del comercio fronterizo entre México y Estados Unidos," *Estudios Fronterizos* vol. 2, no. 6 (Mexicali, Mexico, 1985), 33–40; the economic subsidy that accompanies possession of a visa, in *Utilidad y medición de índices de costo de vida e inflación en una economía fronteriza* (Tijuana, 1986); and the social conse-

The undocumented border residents represent the captive market of Mexican commerce and services. Undocumented workers have less mobility and less opportunities than the documented, and are largely passive spectators of the intense international processes of the region; they are marginalized agents of the binational experience.

In contrast, the documented border residents can discriminate between markets, gaining substantial savings and access to goods of higher quality. They may, in many cases, work or conduct business in the United States; they may directly influence the binational economic agenda of the region; and they may act, to different degrees, in both Mexican and U.S. economies and cultures.

The discrimination against the undocumented gives economic power to the documented in their U.S. labor relations and is reproduced at the Mexican border in industry, commerce, and the service sector, conditioning the very marrow of the region's development.[3] Evaluation of the border cannot be made without first understanding the distribution of participation rights in the binational dynamic. Though foreign decisions involved in documenting border residents weigh enormously on development, Mexico has not attempted to counterbalance the economic power generated by these decisions, which were made even more stringent with the enactment of the Immigration Reform and Control Act of 1986. In fact, Mexico's present strategy of economic aperture toward the United States, including the Canada-U.S. Free Trade Agreement, builds upon this state of affairs. The implicit acceptance of unequal access to the United States reduces the relative power of the Mexican undocumented population and preserves the unequal status quo.[4]

My objectives for this paper are to establish the relationship between border economic structure and access to the United States, describe the legal dynamic that determines the distribution of access rights, and analyze primary data of El Colegio de la Frontera Norte in order to create a preliminary profile of the transborder links between the border population and the United States. I suggest that (1) The Mexican response to undocumented international migration should take into account how visa policies affect the development of the northern border region,

---

quences of external (U.S.) expenditure, in *Distribución y consecuencias sociales del gasto fronterizo en Estados Unidos* (Tijuana, El Colegio de la Frontera Norte, June 1986), mimeo.

[3] See Jorge A. Bustamante, *Espaldas mojadas: Materia prima para la expansión del capital norteamericano* (Mexico City, 1977).

[4] By *economic aperture*, I refer to substituting a more flexible tariff system for the old quota system, the adhesion of Mexico to the GATT, and Mexico's adoption of an export-promotion strategy as a means of paying its foreign debt and modernizing its productive structure. The next step in the process of economic aperture is a free trade agreement to be signed by the United States, Mexico, and perhaps Canada.

(2) Mexico's openness toward the United States is not neutral—the resulting differences in income distribution, economic power, and general well-being, and other consequences, will surely be more intense near the border than in the rest of the country—in addition, these factors may merit adjustments in migration policies, as well as in customs and tax policies of free trade zones and border areas, and (3) The two preceding observations are not independent; at least near the border, the ability of Mexico and the United States to maintain a relatively open border depends on their response to undocumented migration.

A complete analysis of these problems will involve more than mechanically associating these aspects of Mexico's border development or simply declaring (as in the case of the Border Industrialization Program) that the economic strategy resolves the regional problem of undocumented migration.[5] These issues should be discussed in the negotiation of a free trade agreement, because they have to do primarily with the exchange of final goods and services and are only indirectly related to migration or even the export of Mexican labor services. All are different issues and should be analyzed separately.

ECONOMIC STRUCTURE AND DIFFERENTIAL ACCESS

The ability to travel to the United States determines each population's patterns of participation in the U.S. economy and whether they participate fully in the benefits of Mexican development. Mobility also determines which groups among the border population can initiate policies that involve the resources of both countries and which groups are condemned to receiving initiatives from outside.

If U.S. citizens, for example, were not able to cross the border, *maquiladora* plants probably would not exist in Mexico, nor would they if Mexicans could cross freely and conduct business (with their labor more than with their capital) in the United States. It is the asymmetry of the rights to cross the border and participate in the other country's economy that generates the dynamic of *maquiladora* industrialization and many other processes of regional development.

In economic theory it is well known that power increases with the capacity to choose where to act, so that those who have the greatest flexibility of movement have power over the less mobile.[6] Consequently, the

---

[5] This problem goes back to 1965 and is interpreted as a response to the U.S. cancellation of the *bracero* program. For a discussion of the program, see Jesús Tamayo and José Luis Fernández, *Zonas fronterizas*, 71–80, or E. Mendoza Berrueto, "Historia de los programas federales para el desarrollo económico de la frontera norte," in Mario Ojeda, *Administración del desarrollo de la frontera norte* (Mexico City, 1982), 52–77.

[6] The classic example encompasses price determinations and production levels in a monopoly with two segmented markets. In this case, the firm fixes different prices and gains

economic agenda of a region is determined by its residents and by the external agents who can act in it. External influences are balanced not only by the greater importance of the local agenda, but also by the greater capacity of residents to participate in determining the agenda for other regions. From this perspective, it is relevant that initiatives for establishing *maquiladoras* do not proceed from the undocumented workers (potential employees), but from external groups (private elites or public institutions). Independently of rhetoric, the decision of what type of operations to accept does not account for workers' interests.

Further, undocumented border residents cannot protect themselves economically: they cannot reject Mexico's national banking policies by opening accounts in the United States; they cannot counteract the economic power of their national facilities for monetary exchange by resorting to external ones;[7] they cannot reject the quality or the price of national products, nor the system of sheltered domestic articles (*artículos gancho*) by resorting to the U.S. market;[8] they cannot escape underdevelopment and the national crisis by seeking educational, health, transportation, mail, and other services in the United States; less still can they legally escape unemployment and low salaries.

Ironically, the assumption that all Mexicans soliciting a visa will abuse their rights by remaining in the United States as "illegal aliens" leads to the slowing of all legal flows and relations.[9] It is also ironic that the selection process involved in documentation legitimizes a pattern of dependent development based on a nondemocratic and elitist agenda. While the undocumented seek de facto rules that allow for mitigation of migration laws, the documented make de facto international rules—in finance that divide productive labor, and in commerce that affect the entire community.[10]

---

more profits than those that could be obtained by adding up the individual market demands. The same phenomenon is observed in more complex regional models in which mobility is a basic element.

[7] See González-Aréchiga, "Aspectos estructurales del comercio fronterizo," 37, 38.

[8] See González-Aréchiga, *Utilidad y medición de vida e inflación,* 15–17.

[9] The Immigration and Nationality Act of the United States declares that all solicitors of documents and all possessors of visas who intend to cross the border must show, to the satisfaction of the U.S. agent, that they do not intend to abuse the rights conferred by the visa. See a previous discussion on this issue in González-Aréchiga, *Districión y consecuencias sociales del gasto fronterizo en Estados Unidos,* 5–13.

[10] The topic of legal and de facto rules was discussed during the 1983 Third Reunion of Mexican and U.S. Universities in Tijuana. See Mario Miranda Pacheco and James W. Wilkie, eds., *Regalas del juego y juego sin reglas en la vida fronteriza: Tercera reunion de Universidades México y Estados Unidos* (Mexico City, 1985). For more on how these rules allow for mitigation laws, see Jorge A. Bustamante, "La migración mexicana a Estados Unidos: Reglas de factos," in *Reglas del juego y juego sin reglas en la vida fronteriza,* 127–50; for interesting examples of documented residents international rules, see Dale Beck Furnish, "Border Laws and Artificial Constraints," and Milton H. Jamail, "De Facto

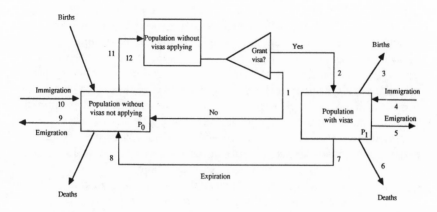

Fig. 1. Licenses and population flows that affect population composition (according to the disposition of visas).

In the binational sphere of daily economic activities, therefore, representation of all social sectors of the Mexican border population is not guaranteed. Consequently, laissez faire cannot rule on the border if an equitable distribution of the rights of access to the United States is not obtained first; in its absence, the effects of an unequal redistribution of general well-being distort both the possibilities for and the nature of development. Mexico cannot act in a neutral fashion with respect to differences in access to the United States without compromising the economic structure of the region, particularly the distribution of well-being.

POPULATION COMPOSITION IN RELATION TO LEGAL ACCESS TO THE UNITED STATES

Before analyzing concrete data on the transborder linkages between Mexico and the United States, it would be useful to examine how the population composition according to access to the U.S. market is determined. At any given moment, Mexico's border population is divided into three principal groups: the documented, the undocumented soliciting a visa, and the non-soliciting undocumented residents. These groups interrelate, as shown in Figure 1, through their own and institutional decision processes. A documented individual may cease being documented when his or her visa expires or is withdrawn (flow 7). Access to the United States is acquired if the undocumented solicits a visa (flow 12) and it is

---

Rules along the United States-Mexican Border," in *Reglas de juego y juego sin reglas en la vida fronteriza*, 111–26.

granted (flow 2), but if he or she is rejected, the non-soliciting undocumented state is reaffirmed (flow 1) and the person ceases to belong to the soliciting group. Figure 1 suggests a series of questions for understanding the Mexico-U.S. border linkage as a process. For example, what factors lead a person to solicit a visa? Why do some persons not solicit them? A consular representative of the United States in Tijuana stated that many people who do not seek visas could obtain them, while others present their documents repeatedly without any real possibility of success. This statement suggests that people are not adequately informed about the benefits of transborder access (since apparently some persons do not perceive these benefits) and that there is an ignorance of the necessary requirements for obtaining a visa (because some evidently underestimate and others overestimate these requirements).

With these antecedents, we may ask: What is the percentage of successful visa solicitations? That is, what is the value of flow 2 with respect to flow 1? What is the rotation of the undocumented population in the subcategories of solicitors and non-solicitors (by means of flows 12 and 1)? What process leads the undocumented to accept her/his exclusion in the binational sphere? What percentage of the undocumented are potential solicitors? How do those Mexican institutions that grant the necessary credentials affect the discrediting or detaining of solicitors?[11] That is, what is the relationship between the difficulties generated by Mexican institutions in moving through flow 12 and the external restrictions in obtaining documents (flow 2)? These questions underline the need to study the Mexico-U.S. migration process in more detail and specifically, to evaluate the global distribution of access to the United States.

Aside from visas (the most direct means), demographic events also affect the population's distribution. Although less frequently than before, many border residents are born in U.S. hospitals and therefore enjoy the right to double citizenship until the age of eighteen (flow 3). Many children are also born with mobility obtained through their parents' documentation (when these parents, for example, are U.S. citizens). Most chil-

[11] The principal limitation to obtaining documents is U.S. migration laws that disqualify illiterates, drug trafficants, and the mentally retarded; however, it is clear that the Mexican system slows the ability of, and on occasion makes it impossible for, potential solicitors to become actual solicitors. In this respect, Article 11 of the Mexican constitution states that "every Mexican has the right to enter the Republic, leave it, travel in her territory and change residency, without need of carta de seguridad, passport, safeconduct, or other requirements" ("todo mexicano tiene derecho para entrar a la Republica, salir de ella, viajar en su territorio y mudar de residencia, sin necesidad de carta de seguridad, pasaporte, salvoconducto u otros requisitos"). The exercise of that right is subordinate to the judicial, emigration, and health authorities who restrain it.

dren, however, are born undocumented (flow 11) and both their own mobility and their family's depend on their documentation.

Death does not preserve transborder mobility either: visas are not inherited and there is no guarantee that they will be transferred to new solicitors. At present, death (flow 6) takes proportionally more green cards and citizenship credentials than visas, like those that are granted now with greater ease to the border population (for example, B-1 and B-2 visas). Death, consequently, devalues the quality of the international rights of Mexicans, since the composition of rights lost by death (flow 6) is better than the rights received by the newly documented population (flow 2).[12]

Something similar happens to migration. In general terms, the border region "exports" the documented (flow 5), principally to the United States, and "imports" the undocumented to other regions of Mexico (flow 10). This process is accentuated by the present Mexican crisis, which has changed significantly the ability of Mexico's general population to influence the binational dynamic.[13]

The most immediate results of this reordering of access are structural changes in the determining factors: debits from border transactions; the use of U.S. medical, educational, recreational, and transportation services; the relative importance on the Mexican side of U.S. facilities for monetary exchange; and so on. Also, as a result of a general lack of mobility, only the United States and a Mexican border elite can actively participate in defining the de facto rules of the binational relationship, since, as mentioned previously, only the documented may autonomously initiate economic processes with U.S. counterparts.

The demographic phenomena suggest more specific questions with which to color the general observations. Which documented group has better visas in terms of economic rights: the one that emigrates from the region (flow 5), or the one that immigrates and integrates itself in the border community (flow 4)? What percentage of immigrants (sum of

[12] The term *quality of international rights* refers to the activities that may be realized (work, study, business); the distance into the United States that can be traveled without previous permission; the length of time that a document is valid (*vigencia*); power to participate in political activities, and so forth.

[13] Jésus Tamayo and J. Luis Fernández discuss the evolution of filtrations of border income to the U.S. economy in *Zonas fronterizas*, 100–111. Recent information about border transactions (today, these expenses include income and expenses of border travelers) appears on the balance-of-payments statistics collected by the method described by G. Vera Ferrer, *Transacciones fronterizas en el primer semestre de 1984* (Mexico City, 1984), mimeo. Recent and disaggregated information appears, for example, in *Informe anual 1985* (Mexico City, 1986), 205–207. Attempted in this paper, unlike the previous works cited, is identification of the socioeconomic origin of debits through border transactions, more than the amount and geographic distribution of these transactions.

flows 4 and 10) is documented (flow 4)? Has this percentage changed
through time? Or, inversely, what percentage of migrants (sum of flows 5
and 9) is documented (flow 5)? Has this relationship changed? How has
the composition of deaths (relative size of flows 8 and 6) and births (relative size of flows 11 and 3) varied in relation to the possession of documents? Finally, what is the relationship between the loss of documents
through expiration (flow 7) and the granting of new ones (flow 2), in
terms of numbers and the quality of rights?

Responses to the previous questions would constitute a complete description of the present power of Mexico's northern-border residents to
access the United States, and would explain the changes in potential and
in the mechanism through which this power is generated. At present,
partial information indicates that access to the United States is being reduced; the relative size of the documented population and the list of
rights conferred on it are decreasing. It is interesting that while Mexico
has decided to adopt a policy of aperture toward the United States, forces
apparently independent of this decision reduce the relative capacity of
the border population to link with the United States. This policy opens
the economy, while the potential of self-directed actions for linkage
on the part of the population declines. Direct free trade could become a
prerogative of a relatively small minority.

EMPIRICAL EVIDENCE OF DIFFERENTIAL ACCESS
TO THE UNITED STATES

Since complete information does not exist, we must study the U.S. access differential directly, through surveys that report the socioeconomic
characteristics of the documented and undocumented population, or indirectly, by means of observed patterns of Mexican linkages to the U.S.
economy.

Indirect Data

The indirect data are revealing. In cities like Tijuana or Tecate,
10 percent of the population in June 1984 was responsible for 87 percent
of direct food imports for domestic consumption, under article 40,
fraction 8 of the Mexican customs laws (*ley aduanera*); in Mexicali, the
same percentage imported 49 percent of the total.[14] In the upper sector of

---

[14] The information is derived from the *Encuesta de ingreso-gasto en Baja California* of
the Secretaria de Abasto (Department of Staple Supplies) of Baja California and El Colegio
de la Frontera Norte. For a description of the study and some results, see J. L. Contreras,
B. González-Aréchiga, J. J. Robles, and M. R. Valdez Cota, *Patrón de consumo de alimen-
tos básicos de la población urbana de Baja California* (Tijuana, 1985), mimeo.

Tijuana, 46 percent of the employed population speaks English; in the middle and lower sectors, these percentages are 27 and 15 percent, respectively. In contrast, in Matamoros, those percentages are 39, 13, and 9, respectively.[15]

In Tijuana, 37 percent of upper-sector families purchase some goods or services in the United States, an amount representing 28 percent of the total Mexican purchases there; among middle-sector families, 18 percent spend money in the United States, amounting to 10 percent of the total; in the lower sector, only 8 percent of families buy in the U.S. market, spending there 8 percent of the total. The percentages for Mexicali and Ciudad Juarez are similar to Tijuana's, but in Nogales the situation is very different: 79 percent of upper-sector families realized 62 percent of the total expenditure in the United States, while 39 and 15 percent of the middle- and lower-sector families realized 34 and 13 percent of this expenditure, respectively.[16]

Direct Data

The direct information from surveys also shows that access to the U.S. market differs according to each population's socioeconomic characteristics. In Ciudad Juarez, documented youth from 12 to 25 years of age who belonged to the upper socioeconomic sector (which represents 4.4 percent of the families) reported in September of 1984 crossing the border to Texas an average of 124 times per year, while those of the lower sector (52.2 percent of the families) crossed only 26 times per year. Further, while virtually all of the upper-sector youth possessed documents, not even one-third of those from the lower sector had them.[17]

In the principal border cities, 61 percent of the upper sector, 45.7 of the middle sector, and 22.2 percent of the lower sector reported having legal documents. Ciudad Juarez is an extreme case of concentration, since the percentage of documented that are employed is a large 69.8 percent

[15] The data are taken from the *Tercera Encuesta Socioeconomica Anual de la Frontera,* administered Oct. 1985 by El Colegio de la Frontera Norte. The upper sector of Tijuana comprises 14.7 percent of the population living in the highest residential sector; the lower sector resides in 38.9 percent of the marginalized urban spaces; and the middle sector accommodates the remaining 46.3 percent. The same definition applies to Matamoros, but the percentages are 11.3, 32.2, and 56.5 for each sector, respectively. A description of the objectives and the method of study (under the original name "Tensiones sociales en la frontera norte") can be found in Jorge A. Bustamante, "Tensiones sociales en la frontera norte y la Ciudad de México" (Tijuana, 1983), mimeo.

[16] The information proceeds from the *Tercera Encuesta Socioeconómica Anual de la Frontera.*

[17] Data from the *Segunda Encuesta Socioeconómica Anual de la Frontera del Colef.* In this study, the sectors were also defined as above.

in the upper sector and only 12.9 percent in the lower sector (the middle sector is similar to the border average).[18]

Another study showed that the percentages of women in Tijuana between 15 and 35 years old that reported not having legal documents to enter the United States constitute 9 percent of the upper sector, 31 percent of the middle sector, and 71 percent of the lower sector.[19]

In the remainder of this paper, information from two studies conducted by El Colegio de la Frontera Norte is analyzed in greater detail. The studies are complementary, since the first permits analysis of concentrations of food expenditure in the United States, and the second allows exploration of the distribution of legal documents and visits to the United States, as well as their effect on expenditure in the United States. Differences in the design of the surveys and sampling strategies do not permit me to simultaneously analyze the levels of concentration and the effect of legality on direct imports; the results, however, are consistent in both.

INDIRECT EVIDENCE: INCOME-EXPENDITURE SURVEY,
BAJA CALIFORNIA

In this section, distribution of food expenditure in the Mexican and U.S. markets is analyzed for the populations of the four major municipalities of Baja California. The data proceed from the income-expenditure survey of July 1984, which permits a minute examination of the factors that explain the expenditure, but does not report on household members' possession of migration documents or number of visits to the United States.

The section is divided into two parts: in the first, concentration indicators and hypotheses of U.S. expenditure are described, and in the second, these indicators and hypotheses are estimated with the available information and the results are analyzed.

Lorenz Curves for Distribution of Income and U.S. Expenditure

The study of concentration levels of direct expenditure in the United States uses the same indicators that measure income concentration: the Lorenz curve and the Gini coefficient.[20] The use of contiguous concepts of income distribution obeys the empirical observation (derived from En-

---

[18] Data from the *Tercera Encuesta Socioeconómica Anual de la Frontera.*

[19] See M. Jasis Silverg, "Perfil socioeconómica y de salud de las mujeres de Tijuana" (Tijuana, El Colegio de la Frontera Norte, 1985), mimeo.

[20] An excellent theoretical discussion of these concepts is found in A. B. Atkinson, *La economía de la desigualdad* (Barcelona, 1981), 20–43, or in Amartia Sen, *Poverty and Famines: An Essay on Entitlement and Deprivation* (New York, 1981), 1–38.

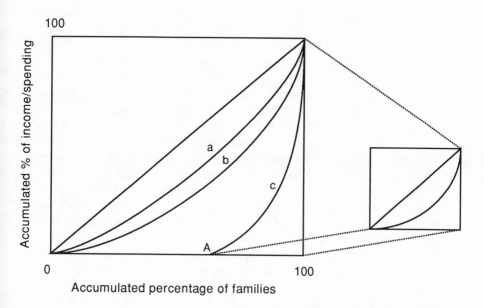

Fig. 2. Income distribution, expenditures on basic goods, and basic external expenditures. Lorenz curves or accumulated percentage frequency curves. Curve (a) is for total food expenditure; (b) is for income; (c) is for food expenditure in the U.S.

gel's Law) that expenditure on food and other basic goods is distributed in a more equal form than income[21] and the hypothesis that foreign expenditure, even if it is for basic goods, behaves like a luxury article in that it is distributed in a way that favors higher-income groups. Figure 2 summarizes these relationships. The figure arranges all families in ascending order of income, total food expenditure, or food expenditure in the United States, depending on which variable is studied. Taking as an example total food expenditure, the horizontal axis measures from left to right the accumulated percentage of cases, starting with those families that spend less on these goods and progressively adding those that spend more. The vertical axis registers the accumulated percentage of expenditure associated with each accumulated percentage of families.

Using both accumulated percentages, it can be established, for ex-

[21] In the case of basic goods, Engel's Law indicates that consumption grows less than proportionally with income; that is, it has a positive elasticity income, but it is less than one. Sumptuary or luxury goods, which are discussed shortly, have an elasticity income greater than one.

ample, that 10 percent of the families that consume the least contribute only 4 percent to the total food expenditure and that the less-favored half of the families spend 34 percent of the total.

The same method permits one to characterize the distribution of U.S. food and income expenditure and obtain the three distribution curves shown in Figure 2. It should be noted that, by design, the three Lorenz curves are necessarily contained within the inferior triangle of the diagram. If distribution of the attribute were perfect, the forty-five-degree straight line from the origin would define the Lorenz curve, since 10 percent of the poorest families would have exactly 10 percent of the attribute perfectly distributed, and so on successively. If, in an equally unlikely scenario, distribution is totally unequal and one family receives the entire bulk of goods, the Lorenz curve would be a horizontal line from the origin, which would break toward the top in a right angle until reaching the northeastern apex of the diagram.

The logic of extreme cases is applied to intermediaries, since the more remote curves from the forty-five-degree line describe more unequal distributions, whatever the nature of the described phenomenon. On this basis, it is understandable that income distribution in Figure 2 is more unequal than total food expenditure but less unequal than external expenditure distribution.

The Gini coefficient sums up the Lorenz curve by measuring the extension of the area between that curve and the line of perfect distribution (the forty-five-degree line) as a percentage of the total area of the smaller triangle in the diagram.[22] As inequality becomes greater, the distance between the two lines increases and the coefficient nears its maximum value of one, or 100 percent. If, on the contrary, the studied distribution nears perfection, the coefficient decreases and approximates its minimum value of zero.

I want to clarify that even if the lines of income and expenditure are superimposed in one diagram, groups ordered by either criterion should not be mechanically associated. It is possible that a family might be in the tenth income decentile (the highest), but in the sixth food-expenditure

[22] The following formula is used in this paper:

$$\text{GINI} = 1 - 2\,(0.10)\,(1/2 + 10 - i)\,\text{Pi}$$

where i is the increasing index of the ten income or expenditure groups (decentiles) and Pi is the income or expenditure percentage received by the decentile i. This formula approximates the area beneath the curve by means of rectangles and triangles. Derivation of the formula can be seen in Pan A. Yotopulos and J. B. Nugent, *Economics of Development: Empirical Investigations* (New York, 1976), 239–42.

decentile, or vice versa; this occurs because the number of members is very important for determining family food expenditure. Expenditure in the United States also has its own logic, to be examined later, which is not linked in a deterministic fashion to income or to total food expenditure. In fact, it is the differences between Mexican income distribution and food expenditure, on the one hand, and U.S. food expenditure, on the other, that reveal the most important structural aspects of the Mexico-U.S. transborder linkage.

The second important element of Figure 2 is that although all families have some income and food expenditure, not all obtain food in the United States. This fact is represented by a Lorenz curve that does not originate at zero, but rather from an intermediary point *A* along the horizontal axis, where the distance from zero to *A* represents the percentage of families that do not acquire foodstuffs directly from the U.S. market. This segmentation identifies the need to study separately the behavior of those who consume U.S. goods and those who do not. In fact, it is possible to consider levels of inequality for the total population (using the Lorenz curve from the central diagram in Figure 2) or exclusively for the "linked" population—that is, the portion of 1-*A* that imports only minute amounts (using the Lorenz curve of the diagram on the right in Figure 2). The first criterion emphasizes total inequality, while the second relativizes this inequality.

Unequal Access: The Case of Baja California

The concentration data of the counties of Baja California confirm that food expenditure is distributed more equitably than income and that external consumption is sumptuary. Table 1 shows three distinct indexes for income concentration (the Gini coefficient and the participation of the highest 10 and 20 percent), total food expenditure, and direct U.S. food imports. For the last variable, concentration levels are measured for the total and linked populations.

Table 1 permits derivation of the following conclusions: (1) The Gini coefficient, which measures the degree of concentration, is more than three times greater for consumption of imported foods than for total consumption of foods (comparing the second and third columns for each city)—this coefficient is also more than double the coefficient of income concentration (comparing the first and third columns), and (2) In all cities, the Gini coefficient is approximately 30 percent less for total consumption of foods than for income (comparing the first two columns). This result signifies that distribution of food consumption is more equi-

TABLE I

Indicators of Income Concentration and Expenditures on Food by the
Urban Population of Baja California

	Income	Exp. on food	Exp. on food bought in U.S.	Exp. on food bought in U.S. (bonded pop.)
MEXICALI				
Gini coefficient	.364	.238	.838	.545
Participation of the highest 10%	28.0	20.49	49.16	41.5
Participation of the highest 20%	43.6	34.46	88.81	60.9
TECATE				
Gini coefficient	.358	.236	.876	.609
Participation of the highest 10%	27.4	19.82	87.76	47.3
Participation of the highest 20%	43.2	33.91	100.0	65.2
TIJUANA				
Gini coefficient	.407	.272	.874	.584
Participation of the highest 10%	35.2	26.30	87.09	45.2
Participation of the highest 20%	46.3	38.32	100.0	63.8
TOTAL				
Gini coefficient	.376	.258	.900	.555
Participation of the highest 10%	29.0	21.02	100.0	47.5
Participation of the highest 20%	44.2	34.98	100.0	62.0

SOURCE: All figures except income from the government of the state of Baja California and El Colegio de la Frontera Norte, *Income Expenditure Survey* (July 1984). Income statistics from José Luis Contreras, *El ingreso familiar en Baja California: Su estructura y distribución*, El Colegio de la Frontera Norte, 1986 (mimeo).

table than income distribution, and both are more equitable than the distribution of the importation of foods.

The rest of the indices confirm the previous observations: the highest-income decentile (X) concentrates between 27 percent of income in Tecate and 35 in Tijuana; the highest decentile of food expenditure concentrates between 20 percent (in Mexicali and Tecate) and 26 percent (in Tijuana) of its expenditure for these goods; and for the variable U.S. expenditure, the highest decentile concentrates 100 percent in Ensenada, 87 percent in Tecate and Tijuana, and 49 percent in Mexicali. In all cases, concentration is greater for the consumption of imported goods than for any other variable.

The high level of concentration in the distribution of external expenditure is not resolved if we eliminate those families who consume only in Mexico. The Gini coefficient of the "linked" population (as seen in the fourth column of Table 1) is much greater than their income coefficient. Strong differences exist between those who buy in both countries and those who buy only in Mexico, but there are also large disparities within the group that can participate in and discriminate between both markets.

Tables 2 and 3 help explain the results of the concentration indexes. Parameter *A*—that is, the percentage of the population that does not import food products—is 98.1 percent in Ensenada, 65.8 percent in Mexicali, 82.7 percent in Tecate, and 80.8 percent in Tijuana (see the first column in Table 3). The same table reveals that few families assign more than 20 percent of their budget to foods that are minute imports and that this percentage of families decreases steadily as U.S. expenditure increases.

Table 2 shows that the wealthiest families avail themselves of their greater opportunities for supplying most of their needs in the United States. The column entitled "purchases" represents the percentage of food expenditure that the "linked" population realizes and the "participation" column registers the percentage of families in each stratum that are linked to the United States. In Mexicali, for example, 45.5 percent of the highest-income families imports foods at a value equivalent to 9 percent of their expenditures; in the poorest group, only 19.1 percent of families imports foods from the United States, allocating 2.5 percent of their budgets for those goods. The relationship between income and participation, as well as the relationship between income and percentage of purchases, steadily decreases in all cities, though with differing intensities; the only exception is Tecate's lowest stratum, whose percentages of purchase and participation are slightly higher than those of the low stratum.

The preceding arguments can be conveniently summarized through a series of parameters from regression equations, which permit measurement of the statistical association between socioeconomic factors and food expenditure according to the type of good and the place of purchase. The estimate measures the influence of each factor on the variable to be explained and indicates the statistical significance of both isolated and combined factors.

After a series of tests, the following explanatory variables were chosen: income; number of family members; location (in our case, a dummy variable for the cities of Ensenada, Mexicali, Tecate, or Tijuana); income in dollars; preference by the head of the household for U.S. goods (because of these goods' perceived higher quality); home ownership; and availability of savings or investment accounts. Income represents the purchasing capacity as a flow, and home ownership and possession of savings or investment accounts represent the accumulated purchasing capacity as wealth. Both are expected to contribute positively to food expenditure, but more toward U.S. expenditure. I included location of residence be-

TABLE 2

Indicators of Participation in the External Food Market

(*Percentages*)

| Stratum[a] | Mexicali | | Tecate | | Tijuana | | Total Urban | |
	Purchases	Participation	Purchases	Participation	Purchases	Participation	Purchases	Participation
Very high	9.0%	45.5%	24.8%	31.6%	36.3%	36.3%	8.9%	35.9%
High	6.7	43.0	11.8	20.2	18.7	18.7	3.9	23.5
Low	4.6	30.8	11.6	12.5	10.3	10.3	2.4	16.1
Very low	2.5	19.1	16.2	12.7	1.1	5.9	1.7	9.6

SOURCE: Government of the state of Baja California and El Colegio de la Frontera Norte, *Income Expenditure Survey* (July 1984).

[a]Each stratum constitutes 25 percent of the population of each city, divided according to family income.

TABLE 3

Distribution of Families According to the Percentage of Food
Expenditures Made in the United States, by City

(*Percentages*)

Range (%)	Ensenada	Mexicali	Tecate	Tijuana
0	98.1%	65.8%	82.7%	80.8%
1–20	1.3	25.0	12.8	12.5
21–40	0.6	7.4	3.6	4.0
41–60	0.0	1.4	0.8	2.0
61–80	0.0	0.2	0.0	0.4
81–100	0.0	0.2	0.0	0.2

SOURCE: Government of the state of Baja California and El Colegio de la Frontera Norte, *Income Expenditure Survey* (July 1984).

TABLE 4

Distribution of Baja California Families According to Form of
Work Compensation Received, Spending Habits, Ownership
and Type of Housing, and Financial Activities

(*Percentages of total*)

Percentage of pop. that:	Ensenada	Mexicali	Tecate	Tijuana
Earns dollars	0.6%	5.5%	3.4%	7.7%
Buys in the U.S. for quality	5.5	32.2	12.9	21.8
Lives in own concrete house	12.4	22.7	21.0	32.0
Has savings accts. or investments	35.9	31.4	31.7	31.1

SOURCE: Government of the state of Baja California and El Colegio de la Frontera Norte, *Income-Expenditure Survey* (July 1984).

cause the cost of food, access to the U.S. market, and quality of the commercial infrastructure on both sides of the border are different in the four cities studied, and all of these factors affect food expenditure. Finally, the variables income in dollars and reported preference for U.S. goods capture not the income level, but rather the currency in which income is received and how Mexican and U.S. goods are evaluated. Both variables are expected to relate positively to U.S. expenditure and negatively to local expenditure. Table 4 reports the basic parameters of the frequency distributions of the qualitative variables in each city.

Table 5 presents the regression coefficients in logarithmic terms (which are the elasticities in the demand function); "F" statistics (for the null hypothesis that the parameters are equal to zero); the adjusted multiple correlation coefficient (adjusted R^2); the aggregate "F" statistic (for the

TABLE 5

Explanatory Factors of Weekly Expenditures on Food Products, Expressed Logarithmically

(*Regression coefficients/"F" statistics*)

	Purchases of basic foodstuffs			Total purchases of food		
	In U.S.	In Mexico	Total	In U.S.	In Mexico	Total
Constant	4.230	5.197	5.028	3.670	5.825	5.686
Family income	0.169	0.212	0.221	0.246	0.228	0.244
	10.214	304.397	403.192	18.335	521.625	653.290
Number of persons in	0.126	0.449	0.428	0.101	0.397	0.382
family	2.478	801.260	797.997	1.239	—	—
Live in Ensenada	−0.179	−0.044	−0.050	−0.188	0.024	0.007
	1.244	3.535	4.998	0.271	1.385	0.130
Live in Mexicali	−0.093	−0.093	−0.072	−0.224	−0.082	−0.073
	1.426	28.285	18.946	7.122	30.218	26.033
Live in Tecate	0.185	0.018	0.025	−0.067	−0.005	−0.004
	1.507	0.415	0.888	0.178	0.041	0.036
Earn dollars	0.200	−0.077	0.009	0.505	−0.093	0.047
	4.419	5.384	0.085	23.592	10.497	2.929
Buy in U.S. for quality	0.170	0.035	0.116	0.506	0.041	0.128
	4.990	2.967	36.677	37.266	5.523	59.217
Live in own concrete	0.101	0.100	0.108	0.055	0.062	0.72
house	1.765	32.255	40.934	0.431	16.779	24.404
Have savings accts. or	−0.019	0.064	0.075	0.062	0.086	0.095
investments	0.073	15.038	22.575	0.627	36.391	48.791
R2 adjusted	0.053	0.303	0.347	0.512	0.357	.412
F	5.868	196.553	239.423	18.350	250.178	315.731
Number of cases	779	4043	4043	869	4044	4044

SOURCE: Author's data.

null hypothesis that all the parameters are simultaneously equal to zero); and the number of observations.

Before interpreting the results, it is useful to point out that in all cases it was easier to explain total food consumption and basic food consumption than consumption by place of purchase. Both the percentage of variations explained by the regression (R^2) and the intensity with which the hypothesis of non-regression ("F" aggregate) is rejected are greater for total consumption. The most difficult variable to explain is U.S. expenditure, since the regression explains fewer than half of the variations that it can explain for local consumption; however, the degree of global explanation reached and the significance of the parameters are sufficiently high to justify the following interpretations.

The regression parameters of the variables income and number of persons represent the income elasticity and the number-of-persons elasticity of food expenditure, respectively. The first indicates the percentage by

TABLE 5 (continued)

	Purchases of food by the bonded pop.			Pur. of basic foodstuffs by bonded pop.		
	In U.S.	In Mexico	Total	In U.S.	In Mexico	Total
Constant	3.67008	6.7096	6.692	4.3034	5.882	5.9079
Family income	0.2455	0.1363	0.1606	0.1612	0.1192	0.1450
	18.335	44.365	94.109	8.290	25.473	55.778
Number of persons in	0.1007	0.4478	0.3835	0.1387	0.5354	0.4575
family	1.239	192.361	215.619	2.516	206.601	223.189
Live in Ensenada	−0.1881	0.3153	0.2530	0.5324	0.2892	0.2104
	0.271	5.988	5.893	1.420	3.786	2.964
Live in Mexicali	−0.2239	−0.0325	−0.0696	−0.1269	−0.0579	−0.0866
	7.122	1.179	8.259	2.354	2.809	9.293
Live in Tecate	−0.0666	0.0501	0.0057	0.1675	0.0793	0.0735
	0.178	0.788	0.016	1.158	1.485	1.886
Earn dollars	0.5054	−0.1012	0.0567	0.2085	−0.0523	0.0111
	23.592	7.423	3.555	4.413	1.488	0.099
Buy in U.S. for quality	0.5055	0.0636	0.1236	0.1681	0.1092	0.1377
	37.266	4.628	26.739	4.196	10.257	24.124
Live in own concrete	0.0551	0.0749	0.0793	0.0748	0.1165	0.1111
house	0.431	6.251	10.717	0.836	11.365	15.295
Have savings accts. or	0.0625	0.0322	0.0455	0.0211	0.0160	0.0267
investments	0.627	1.308	3.987	0.075	0.243	0.998
R2 adjusted	.1525	.29636	0.413	0.0506	0.2903	0.368
F	18.350	41.620	68.860	5.123	40.458	57.159
Number of cases	859	859	859	687	859	859

which expenditures increase as income increases by 1 percent; the second measures the percentage by which the same expenditure increases as the number of persons per household increases by one in one hundred. A high income elasticity is associated with luxury goods, a low income elasticity (especially when it is negative) with inferior goods. In a similar fashion, a high number-of-persons elasticity indicates goods necessary to large families, and a low number-of-persons elasticity is associated with goods whose per capita consumption falls more than proportionally with family size.

Table 5 presents the values of these elasticities and lead to the conclusion that consuming U.S. imported goods is a luxury (it has a greater income elasticity than the consumption of necessary goods) that devalues national goods (since the income elasticity of national goods is less for the linked population than for the population average). These values also suggest that U.S.-imported foodstuffs cannot be considered a necessity in comparison to Mexican goods (since U.S. foodstuffs have a smaller number-of-persons elasticity expenditure for lesser foodstuffs), and that U.S. consumption intensifies the necessary nature of Mexican foodstuffs (the number-of-persons elasticity for national food expenditure is greater for those who consume imported goods).

The concrete results are the following:

- The general income elasticity for food consumption is greater for U.S.-imported goods (0.246) than for Mexican goods (0.228); however, for the linked population, the difference is much greater (the elasticities are 0.246 and 0.136, respectively). The sensitivity of expenditure to increments in the income of those who discriminate between the two markets (that is, the "linked" population) is almost double for U.S. goods than for Mexican ones—that is, for an additional income of one thousand pesos, 246 end up in U.S. supermarkets and 136 in Mexican stores. Consequently, the national component of the linked population's diet is reduced.

- Basic foodstuffs have a smaller income elasticity than foodstuffs as a whole. The general elasticity of the basic foodstuffs is 0.221; for total foodstuffs, 0.244. The consumption of basic U.S. foodstuffs also responds more slowly to income; it has an elasticity of 0.16, compared to 0.246 for the total of those goods. A linked household whose income increases by one thousand pesos would spend 161 for U.S.-imported basic foods and 119 for Mexican foods, while the average household would spend 212 pesos on national basics.

- The "linked" population reduces by one-half their additional food purchases as their income changes.

- Because of the special behavior in the consumption of basic foods, it can be expected that for those goods for which the Mexican market offers better prices, the percentage of the population linked to the U.S. market will fall and the income elasticity of the "linked" population's U.S. consumption will be reduced. Under these conditions, a devalued peso would reduce transborder linkage as it decreases the sensitivity of border transaction expenditures to changes in the Mexican product's value. The opposite would also hold in case of a revaluation.

In addition to the conclusions derived from the elasticity values, the signs of the regression equation parameters indicate that (1) In Ensenada, households spend more for Mexican foodstuffs than in Tijuana, but the "linked" population spends more on those foodstuffs that are directly imported, (2) Mexicali spends less than Tijuana on foodstuffs, regardless of their type and origin, (3) The case of Tecate is mixed; more is spent on basic goods than in Tijuana, but the linked population spends more on basic and non-basic Mexican foodstuffs (though less on U.S.-imported goods), (4) Households with dollar incomes spend more on foodstuffs, but less on Mexican foodstuffs, than the rest of the population, and (5) Mexicans who report to live in concrete homes of their own, buy in the United States because of quality, or have savings or investment accounts spend more on foodstuffs of all types and origin (the only exception is not statistically significant).

DIRECT EVIDENCE: SECOND ANNUAL SOCIOECONOMIC SURVEY OF THE NORTH MEXICAN BORDER

Direct information about the distribution of documents and visits to the United States is available from a survey administered in six cities on the Mexican border (Matamoros, Nuevo Laredo, Ciudad Juarez, Nogales, Mexicali, and Tijuana) and in the interior of the country (Mexico City).[23] Two hundred surveys were distributed to each of the three socioeconomic strata of each city. The upper stratum was defined as that residential sector that has all services at its disposal and owns ample, well-constructed homes; the lower stratum was selected from the marginalized areas that lack public services and the means available to the rest of the urban space.[24] This sampling strategy permits more information to be collected about the relatively small upper-socioeconomic stratum, which, as seen in the previous section, absorbs an important percentage of the total transborder transactions and is characterized by linkage patterns not observed elsewhere.

Factors Explaining Linkage to the United States

The survey's informants were youths between 12 and 25 years old who reported individual and familial characteristics and behaviors. Individual possession of visas, visits to the United States, and U.S. expenditure were analyzed; the results should therefore be regarded as provisional because they cannot be extended to all border residents. As dependent individuals, the youth enjoy or suffer their parents' socioeconomic status, and as independent persons, they are in the first stages of the life cycle. Nevertheless, the results not only show the situation of a group that represents 30 percent of the border population, but also reflects a generalized social problem.

Table 6 shows the percentage of youth who reported possessing legal documents to visit the United States. In the upper sector almost all youths

---

[23] Description of the survey appears in Bustamante, *Tensiones sociales en la frontera norte*, 4–30.

[24] Strata were identified using urban maps of each city, but were verified in the field.

TABLE 6

Youths and the United States: Cross-Border Patterns by
Place of Origin and Socioeconomic Status

(*Percentages*)

	Socioeconomic status		
	High stratum	Middle stratum	Low stratum
Hold U.S. visas			
Place of origin			
Tijuana	94.1%	72.9%	41.0%
Ciudad Juárez	93.1	58.1	27.8
Matamoros	90.4	70.8	37.0
Mexico City	92.7	23.0	3.3
Nogales	94.0	77.4	51.4
Nuevo Laredo	95.3	78.6	53.4
Mexicali	89.7	61.2	37.3
Have crossed to the U.S.			
Place of origin			
Tijuana	98.0%	79.7%	48.6%
Ciudad Juárez	97.7	73.9	43.0
Matamoros	93.4	78.2	50.9
Mexico City	95.3	20.2	2.6
Nogales	98.3	87.1	63.5
Nuevo Laredo	95.6	82.6	65.2
Mexicali	93.0	66.0	42.6
Have crossed to U.S. without documents[a]			
Place of origin			
Tijuana	3.9%	6.8%	7.6%
Ciudad Juárez	4.6	15.8	23.8
Matamoros	3.0	7.4	13.9
Nogales	4.3	9.7	12.1
Nuevo Laredo	0.3	4.0	11.8
Mexicali	3.3	4.8	5.3

SOURCE: El Colegio de la Frontera Norte, *Annual Socioeconomic Survey of the Border II*. Oct. 1984.
[a]Data for Mexico City have been excluded.

possess documents, in the middle sector the percentage oscillates between
65 and 75 percent, and in the lower sector, between 25 and 50 percent.
The differences between cities are also important. Nogales and Nuevo
Laredo show high percentages; Tijuana, Matamoros, and Mexicali median percentages; and Ciudad Juarez, low percentages. Mexico City reflects the lowest participation percentages because it is very far away
from the border.

Possession of legal documents does not necessarily determine access to
the United States, as is well known. Table 6 also presents the percentage
of youths who report crossing the northern border to the United States
whether or not they possess legal documents. The relationship between

socioeconomic stratum and access to the United States is maintained: without exception, the more fortunate have greater transborder access, even when the percentages of participation change.

The difference between having documents and crossing the border (as shown in Table 6) is approximately 3 percent for the upper sector, 8 percent for the middle, and 13 percent for the lower sector. The major discrepancy between the two linkage measures occurs in Ciudad Juarez, where the percentage of youths who report crossing exceeds documented youths' by 15.8 and 23.8 percent in the middle and lower strata, respectively. This difference is greater than 10 percent in the middle sector of Nogales and in the lower sectors of Matamoros, Nogales, and Nuevo Laredo. In the other cases, this difference is relatively small.

A combination of three factors explains these differences: (1) errors exist in the reporting of document possession or transborder crossings, (2) some youths between 12 and 14 years old are granted rights by their parents' documents, and (3) youth illegally cross the border (frequently by using visas belonging to their brothers or other relatives). Without a doubt, more investigation is necessary to explain the relative value of these three factors. For the present, however, it is sufficient to recognize that different variables exist that should be explained separately and can be used to help explain transborder linkages.

The characteristics shown in Table 6 permit us to suppose that undocumented crossing explains the discrepancies between the possession of visas and presence in the United States, since these discrepancies are greater for the less-documented sector and are smaller in border cities in which a greater probability of apprehension could be expected. This interpretation, however, does not affect the following analysis.

The number of annual visits to the United States is another indicator of the differences in access to that country. Table 7 records the average number of the young population's annual visits. The youth of the upper sector visit the United States an average of three to eight times more than the lower sector, and with the exception of Nogales, more than two times more than the middle sector. The high deviations occur because in all cases the probability distribution function of visits is asymmetric and extends toward the right (like an F distribution). The majority of cases are distributed around the most frequent value, which is less than the median; but there exist some cases which, though relatively few, greatly exceed the median. According to data from the survey, the lowest stratum disperses less toward the right.

In Tijuana, for example, upper-sector youths visit the United States an average of twice a week; those of the middle sector, once a week; and

TABLE 7

Adults and the United States: Cross-Border Patterns by
Place of Origin and Socioeconomic Status

(*No. of visits/standard deviation*)

	Socioeconomic status		
	High stratum	Middle stratum	Low stratum
Annual visits			
Place of origin			
Tijuana	103.8	43.0	12.2
	(91.8)	(64.7)	(41.6)
Ciudad Juárez	124.0	47.9	26.3
	(136.9)	(80.0)	(67.7)
Matamoros	101.1	52.4	38.5
	(117.5)	(104.4)	(149.9)
Nogales	141.8	99.0	51.9
	(147.1)	(172.7)	(150.1)
Nuevo Laredo	110.4	52.5	48.3
	(115.0)	(74.8)	(88.0)
Mexicali	75.7	33.4	25.2
	(76.7)	(46.0)	(69.2)
Monthly expenditures in U.S., in current pesos			
Place of origin			
Tijuana	29,751	14,649	2,288
	(75,998)	(30,173)	(6,380)
Ciudad Juárez	21,474	10,332	3,156
	(39,468)	(19,897)	(6,733)
Matamoros	16,745	10,742	3,938
	(24,403)	(13,592)	(7,604)
Nogales	22,262	10,761	6,713
	(39,772)	(11,218)	(8,557)
Nuevo Laredo	28,170	11,545	6,505
	(37,934)	(15,113)	(8,210)
Mexicali	11,283	9,294	4,965
	(10,370)	(13,155)	(10,742)

SOURCE: El Colegio de la Frontera Norte, *Annual Socioeconomic Survey of the Border II* (Oct., 1984).

lower-stratum youths, once a month. In Nogales, the average number of visits are 3, 2, and 1 times per month for the upper, middle, and lower sectors, respectively. The rest of the cities fall between these extremes, though the upper and middle sectors of Mexicali visit the United States less frequently than do Tijuana or similar sectors.

Calculation of monthly expenditure in the United States (reported in Table 7) also includes those who spend nothing in that market, so results have not been biased by the population that does not consume in the United States; even so, consumption in the upper sector is between three and fourteen times greater than the lower stratum's. Without exception, as socioeconomic position falls, U.S. expenditure and the standard deviation also decline.

In summary, Tables 6 and 7 show that the most fortunate youths (in terms of strata) are more likely to possess documents, visit the United States with greater frequency, and spend more in that market. The relationship between linkage to the United States and social position is positive, regardless of the indicator used to measure it. What remains to be analyzed is the relative importance of socioeconomic indicators to explain linkage levels. This analysis is accomplished through regression analysis, in which the dependent variable is the linkage probability (in the case of visa possession) or its intensity (in the case of visits per year to the United States and monthly U.S. expenditure). The independent variables are income (personal or at the disposal of the youth or relative), the border city, socioeconomic stratum, educational status, age, and whether the youth works or studies. For U.S. expenditure, instead of the four individual characteristics of the youths, possession of documents and transborder visits are measured. All regressions are estimated for the three alternative definitions of income (personal, available, and familial) in lineal and logarithmic terms; this explains the eighteen equations in Table 8.

The statistics in these tables indicate that it is easier to explain the number of visits to the United States than possession of documents, which in turn is easier to explain than distribution of U.S. expenditure according to the multiple-correlation coefficient adjusted by degrees of freedom. The general statistics also show that in most cases, logarithmic regressions explain a greater percentage of linkage patterns than do lineal regressions; further, logarithmic regressions have greater overall significance—that is, the multiple-correlation coefficients and the "F" statistics for the nonregression hypothesis are greater.

Without elaborating further, I can affirm that the most determining variable of visa possession is socioeconomic stratum. The probability that three youths from the same city and with the same income, schooling, age, residence, and status in the work force or school have visas is affected by the socioeconomic stratum to which they belong. If a youth belongs to the middle stratum, (s)he has an 18.3 percent greater probability of possessing documents than if (s)he belongs to the lower stratum; likewise, the youth has a 32.6 percent greater probability if (s)he belongs to the upper sector rather than the lower, according to the logarithmic regression (Table 8).

Income is also very determinant, irrespective of how it is defined. However, it is clear in all the tables that the greatest correlation occurs be-

TABLE 8

Determination of Visa Distribution Among the Youth Population with Various Definitions of Income

(Regression coefficients and "F" statistics)

	Family income		Avail. income for youth expenditures		Net income per youth	
	Coefficient	"F" statistic	Coefficient	"F" statistic	Coefficient	"F" statistic
Scenario 1						
Constant	-0.0501	—	-0.0020	—	0.0019	—
Income	7.190×10^{-8}	5.029	7.187×10^{-8}	1.221	1.6096×10^{-7}	0.429
Place of Origin						
Tijuana	0.0697	6.895	0.0581	6.131	0.0566	5.847
Ciudad Juarez	-0.0319	1.287	-0.0026	1.161	-0.0260	1.167
Matamoros	0.0499	3.304	0.0437	3.386	0.0428	3.244
Mexico City	-0.2464	74.251	-0.2573	120.978	-0.2598	123.535
Nogales	0.1481	28.211	0.1365	31.302	0.1362	31.145
Nuevo Laredo	0.1359	27.636	0.1258	28.716	0.1236	27.923
Socioeconomic status						
High stratum	0.4020	332.611	0.4378	627.740	0.4379	626.408
Middle stratum	0.2046	123.613	0.1903	139.769	0.1901	139.473
Schooling	0.0285	66.791	0.0286	87.177	0.0284	85.027
Presently employed	0.0045	4.064	0.0044	5.295	0.0047	5.687
Age	0.0042	1.956	0.0021	0.642	0.0021	0.651
Presently in school	0.1216	34.557	0.1230	47.041	0.1231	46.927
R^2 adjusted	0.2906		0.3242		0.324	
F	95.986		145.337		145.247	
Cases	3015		3912		3912	

TABLE 8 (continued)

	Family income		Avail. income for youth expenditures		Net income per youth	
	Coefficient	"F" statistic	Coefficient	"F" statistic	Coefficient	"F" statistic
Scenario 2						
Constant	7.6260	—	8.0728	—	10.4355	—
Income	4.4037×10^{-5}	21.681	3.7361×10^{-5}	3.687	1.221×10^{-4}	3.157
Place of Origin						
Tijuana	3.6361	0.236	8.0057	1.432	7.3615	1.213
Ciudad Juarez	15.7015	3.542	22.5350	9.961	22.5167	9.944
Matamoros	16.2246	4.247	16.3644	5.622	15.7871	5.225
Mexico City	−47.3779	32.656	−44.8081	43.176	−46.2224	45.970
Nogales	49.383	38.463	48.8933	48.266	48.7692	48.022
Nuevo Laredo	40.5515	30.526	41.1497	37.105	40.1262	35.498
Socioeconomic status						
High stratum	41.4162	42.417	52.4056	105.340	52.2927	104.672
Middle stratum	3.5245	0.433	5.0423	1.127	5.0201	1.117
Schooling	1.7716	2.972	1.5750	2.978	1.4015	2.342
Presently employed	0.0199	0.001	−0.1231	0.047	0.0043	0.000
Age	0.0226	0.001	0.0095	0.000	−0.0102	0.000
Presently in school	−1.3989	0.054	3.3117	0.389	3.6805	0.479
R^2 adjusted	10.099	—	0.112	—	0.1121	—
F	23.984	—	35.165	—	35.119	—
Cases	3522	—	3522	—	3522	—

TABLE 8 (*continued*)

	Family income		Avail. income for youth expenditures		Net income per youth	
	Coefficient	"F" statistic	Coefficient	"F" statistic	Coefficient	"F" statistic
Scenario 3						
Constant	-1417.925	—	-1773.709	—	-1526.755	—
Income	0.0266	142.581	7.7813×10^{-3}	1.613	0.0815	23.127
Place of Origin						
Tijuana	3904.495	4.970	7066.283	15.293	6806.718	14.316
Ciudad Juarez	2676.864	1.877	2770.825	1.990	2598.940	1.764
Matamoros	2428.906	1.701	2837.393	2.144	2265.246	1.379
Mexico City	-1543.502	0.622	1157.028	0.384	485.299	0.068
Nogales	3370.991	3.239	3497.503	3.240	3452.882	3.183
Nuevo Laredo	6089.001	12.857	6223.474	11.822	6032.351	11.259
Socioeconomic status						
High stratum	9911.052	44.547	13643.70	88.614	13277.26	84.220
Middle stratum	5022.636	16.137	5177.189	16.290	5176.843	16.395
Visits to the U.S.	15.580	12.837	23.157	26.690	22.437	25.192
Have legal visas	3050.925	6.072	3806.663	8.935	3602.995	8.052
R^2 adjusted	0.1302	—	0.073	—	0.0791	—
F	37.002	—	24.429	—	26.545	—
Cases	2647	—	3271	—	3271	—

TABLE 8 (*continued*)

	Family income		Avail. income for youth expenditures		Net income per youth	
	Coefficient	"F" statistic	Coefficient	"F" statistic	Coefficient	"F" statistic
Scenario 4						
Constant	−1.2062	—	−2.2868	—	−0.8566	—
Income (in log.)	0.1788	64.176	0.0472	7.348	0.0543	1.174
Place of Origin						
Tijuana	0.0563	4.542	0.0684	7.625	0.0143	0.042
Ciudad Juarez	−0.0197	0.478	−0.0088	0.115	0.0073	0.009
Matamoros	0.0475	3.009	0.0503	3.938	0.0893	1.483
Mexico City	−0.2535	80.391	−0.2310	87.751	−0.2268	11.842
Nogales	0.1615	33.025	0.1562	35.916	0.1289	3.144
Nuevo Laredo	0.1534	35.634	0.1360	30.727	0.0870	1.453
Socioeconomic status						
High stratum	0.3264	180.308	0.4310	489.074	0.4288	55.074
Middle stratum	0.1828	93.424	0.1958	128.819	0.1742	13.935
Schooling (logarithmic)	0.4709	41.370	0.5781	68.090	0.7169	20.536
Presently in school	0.1084	26.835	0.1121	33.094	0.6581	2.429
Presently working	−0.0380	3.404	−0.0360	3.509	−0.0819	0.542
Age in logarithms	0.2157	3.305	−0.0891	0.587	0.2715	0.761
R^2 adjusted	0.3070	—	0.3231	—	0.3542	—
F	100.410	—	128.10	—	21.462	—
Cases	2918	—	3462	—	486	—

TABLE 8 (continued)

	Family income		Avail. income for youth expenditures		Net income per youth	
	Coefficient	"F" statistic	Coefficient	"F" statistic	Coefficient	"F" statistic
Scenario 5						
Constant	−0.1766	—	0.7947	—	0.8352	—
Income (in log.)	0.2466	53.361	0.1869	48.419	0.2108	6.056
Place of Origin						
Tijuana	−0.1471	14.749	−0.0778	4.827	−0.1054	0.957
Ciudad Juarez	−0.0156	0.127	0.0757	3.796	−0.0562	0.242
Matamoros	−0.0073	0.031	0.0314	0.690	−0.2160	3.969
Mexico City	−1.650	806.176	−1.5075	1031.3	−1.660	186.834
Nogales	0.1745	19.357	0.2144	33.591	0.1923	3.102
Nuevo Laredo	0.0514	1.906	0.0856	5.814	0.0185	0.029
Socioeconomic status						
High stratum	0.3499	92.280	0.4269	188.103	0.3698	15.328
Middle stratum	0.1709	29.438	0.1973	43.517	0.1329	2.435
Schooling	0.3054	5.756	0.3091	6.524	0.1371	0.244
Presently at school	−0.0152	0.219	0.0279	0.835	−0.0382	0.344
Presently working	0.0367	1.324	0.0056	0.035	−0.0667	0.090
Age	0.0488	0.065	−0.4280	5.184	−0.234	0.192
R² adjusted	0.4029	—	0.4446	—	0.5061	—
F	94.134	—	135.58	—	23.077	—
Cases	1795	—	2186	—	281	—

TABLE 8 (continued)

	Family income		Avail. income for youth expenditures		Net income per youth	
	Coefficient	"F" statistic	Coefficient	"F" statistic	Coefficient	"F" statistic
Scenario 6						
Constant	1.9857	—	2.9025	—	3.1971	—
Income (in log.)	0.3783	126.521	0.2298	108.027	0.0894	1.119
Place of Origin						
Tijuana	-0.0280	0.595	-0.0018	0.003	-0.0626	0.364
Ciudad Juarez	0.0479	1.329	0.0364	0.877	0.0949	0.685
Matamoros	0.0285	0.563	0.0461	1.495	0.1027	0.953
Mexico City	-0.0233	0.188	0.1290	5.035	0.1558	0.966
Nogales	0.0175	0.235	-0.0005	0.000	0.0128	0.015
Nuevo Laredo	0.1484	19.605	0.1161	11.951	0.2239	4.446
Socioeconomic status						
High stratum	0.0551	2.468	0.177	31.331	0.2296	6.118
Middle stratum	0.545	3.101	0.1114	12.996	0.0319	0.142
Visits to U.S. (log.)	0.1629	46.599	0.1733	58.923	0.1977	9.704
Have legal visa	-0.2210	13.117	-0.2672	20.381	-0.0391	0.061
R^2 adjusted	0.1980		0.1708		0.1347	
F	33.084		32.322		4.313	
Cases	1431		1674		235	

tween linkage and familial income, rather than between linkage and a youth's own income. In fact, when familial income is doubled, the probability of having a visa increases 17.9 percent, visits to the United States increase by 24.7 percent, and U.S. expenditure increases by 37.8 percent.

In a similar fashion, upon doubling the schooling of a youth, the probability of possessing a visa and the number of annual visits increase by 47.1 and 30.5 percent each. The probability of possessing documents increases with age. If a youth's age is doubled, this possibility grows by 21.6 percent; it decreases with employment (youths that work, irrespective of other characteristics, have a 3.8 percent smaller probability of obtaining a visa), and increases if the youth is a student (10.8 percent).

Thus, the two most important variables for explaining the distribution of visas are income and socioeconomic stratum. The relative importance of each can be estimated using the regression coefficients. In order for two youths, identical in all factors except for residential sector, to have the same probability of possessing a visa in the logarithmic regression, the family of the youth of the lower sector would need to have a little over half of the income of the family of the youth from the middle sector and almost three times more than that of the higher sector. The same occurs for visits to the United States. To equalize the number of annual visits to the United States for lower-sector youth, his/her family would have to have an income 72.5 percent higher than that of an identical middle-sector family, and 141.9 percent greater than a twin family in the higher sector.

The results also show that U.S. expenditure is inelastic with respect to number of visits, because expenditure grows only 16.3 percent if twice as many visits occur. The results of the logarithmic regressions indicate that those who report visiting the United States without a visa spend more than those who visit with documents; however, this relationship is not observed in the lineal equations, since in this case the relationship between documents and U.S. expenditure is positive as expected.

When the effects of visits to the United States and possession of visas are isolated statistically, income is a much more powerful explanatory factor of U.S. expenditure than socioeconomic sector (in terms of the value of the coefficient and the "F" statistic). If two youths cross the border the same number of times per year, and both possess visas and have the same socioeconomic characteristics, they would spend the same amount on U.S. products if one was from the higher sector and the other from the lower, as long as the lower-sector family had an income 13.5 percent greater than the higher-sector family. Contrary to what occurs with visits, U.S. expenditure of the sampling responds to economic more than social factors.

Although not central to this discussion, the regressions also show that linkage to the United States has its own characteristics in each city. In the analysis of the effect of locale on linkage, Mexicali was used as a control; as a result, the coefficients of the rest of the cities reflect differences between behaviors of the youths interviewed and Mexicali's youths. The principal difference between border cities occurs in the distribution of visas, in which only Ciudad Juarez has a structure similar to that of the control locale. Tijuana and Nogales differ from Mexicali with regard to visits; more visits originate from Tijuana than Mexicali, but fewer originate from Nogales than either city. With regard to expenditure, only Nuevo Laredo exhibits a behavior different from that of the control city, since its youth spend considerably more in the United States. Mexico City obviously differs from the border (Mexicali) in visas and visits, but curiously does not differ significantly in terms of expenditure. It should be underscored that those differences only reflect what could not be explained through the socioeconomic variables included in the regression, so the coefficients of the locales can be attributed to the commercial, recreational, and transportation infrastructure on both sides of the border, or to specific tastes and preferences of youths in each place.

FINAL OBSERVATIONS

Clearly, the international mechanisms that transmit inequality and affect development in the Mexican border region correlate with the migration policies of the United States toward Mexico. I have stated that to thoroughly understand these processes, it is necessary not only to study in detail how economic power is transmitted to the documented in Mexico and the efficacy with which these transmission mechanisms operate, but that it is also necessary to understand the distribution of the population according to its access to the United States. Information is needed about the distribution of documents among the border population with respect to international rights and socioeconomic position, and even with respect to the politics of the beneficiaries.

Although evidence is scarce, I believe that document distribution favors the stronger socioeconomic groups and that differences exist in some important cases by age, locale, and gender. We still do not have a detailed account of what documented border residents do in the United States. Concrete studies, however, permit us to see their patterns of consumption and use of health, recreational, and other services.[25] All these studies

[25] Studies of linkage patterns by type of activity can be found in M. Jasís Silverg, *Perfil socioeconómica y de salud de las mujeres de Tijuana* (in the area of health); E. Pérez Santana, *Medición y usos del tiempo libre del trabajador en Tijuana* (Tijuana, 1986) for recreation; and my previously cited articles on consumption.

show tremendous disparities in access to the United States and in the exercise of the rights granted by documentation.

Most grave, the border population appears to be separating into two groups (documented and undocumented) that are increasingly defined in socioeconomic terms and by an increasingly limited mobility. This division gains greater importance under Mexico's new strategy of aperture toward the United States, and it will surely affect the development of the Mexican border region. The Mexican border appears to be immersed in a process of increased linkage to the United States, but the responsibility of such a linkage falls on a group that is increasingly smaller with respect to the rest of the border population.

Under these conditions, Mexico should attempt to make U.S. access more democratic for its border residents, and where this is not possible, should at least mitigate the negative effects of U.S. visa-granting policies. These issues should be discussed in the negotiation process of a free trade agreement between these two countries. First, however, it is necessary to evaluate and simplify the functioning of the official Mexican institutions that intervene and sometimes block the process of obtaining migration documents. It is also necessary for Mexico to recognize the relationship between regional border development (the base of an export platform) and U.S. migration policies in a manner that will affect the binational agenda.

Mitigation of the negative effects of U.S. immigration laws can be achieved by various means. One way would be to redefine the free zones and border areas to facilitate the undocumented population's indirect access to U.S. factor markets, goods, and services. This redefinition would require, at the least, changing customs legislation. Another way to mitigate these laws would be to adopt a social criterion for granting passports and other necessary documents for obtaining visas. The most adequate method would extend to the undocumented, by political means, the right to participate in the daily economic plebiscite in which the future of the border is defined.

The possibility for a bilateral negotiation cannot be closed. Just as the United States claims that a negative "externality" is transferred from the South to the North with undocumented migration, Mexicans can also maintain that a negative "externality" flows from the North to the South because of U.S. selective control of migration and border-crossing rights. A global vision should evaluate and contrast both perspectives; the challenge is to adopt international principles that internalize, in an equitable fashion, *both* foreign effects.

The Demand for Hispanic Workers in Urban Areas of the United States

Thomas Muller

S INCE ITS FOUNDING, the United States has depended on immigrant labor to sustain economic growth. Its level of dependence on European workers has been uneven, and ebbed during the Great Depression and World War II. Among Spanish-speaking entrants, Mexicans have been a substantial component of the urban labor force in California since the 1920s, and Puerto Ricans first came to the Northeast in large numbers during the 1950s.

Although Hispanic and other immigration accelerated significantly during the last two decades, the recent inflow has not prevented periodic labor shortages. In the mid-1980s, the media described such shortages in several regions and economic sectors. "Labor Shortages in Entry-Level Jobs Force Companies to Make Adjustments," reads a lead article in the *Wall Street Journal*, "Jobs Go Begging at the Bottom," decries *Fortune*.[1] These shortages have caused construction delays and forced wage increases in less-desirable occupations, and are generally curtailing the pace of economic growth in some sectors. For example, restaurant chains have slowed their plans to expand in several urban markets due to the unavailability of workers. In the New York region, housing projects are being delayed by six months, and wages for both skilled and unskilled persons in construction trades, already among the highest paid hourly wage workers in the nation, have risen further.[2]

Hotel and restaurant employers are becoming increasingly dependent on immigrants to meet their needs. Some hotels in the Washington, D.C.

---

[1] *Wall Street Journal*, 3 June 1986; *Fortune*, 17 March 1986.
[2] *New York Times*, 17 July 1986.

area, for example, utilize workers from thirty different nations.[3] In New York and Los Angeles, both legal and undocumented dependence on immigrant workers is even greater. Despite the absorption of close to one million immigrant workers since 1970 within the greater New York region, extremely low suburban unemployment is resulting in thousands of unfilled jobs. The two counties forming Long Island have alone added 350,000 workers since 1980, a level of expansion that may be slowed because of job vacancies. Most women seeking to find work in the region are already employed, and unless the area can attract additional migrants from within the United States or elsewhere, economic growth will likely be slowed.

Although substantial pockets of unemployment remain in areas dominated by traditional manufacturing, particularly the Great Lakes region, unemployment rates at the end of 1986 have fallen well below 5 percent in most suburban markets outside the Midwest. These low rates indicate that a labor shortage is already present in these areas. Public opinion, however, remains almost evenly divided on the relationship between undocumented (in the public perception, mostly Mexican) immigrant workers and employment opportunities for native-born labor. Despite known shortages in occupations that typically attract undocumented aliens, such as restaurant work, half of the public during a period of economic expansion continues to believe that alien workers reduce employment opportunities and cause unemployment for those born in the United States.[4] This perception appears insensitive to changes in the American economy: an earlier California survey during a period of high unemployment indicated a similar response.[5] A solid majority of survey respondents with below-average income or education continues to link immigrants with reduced job opportunities for those native-born.

Labor shortages have also developed in areas where the rate of legal, and no doubt undocumented, immigration to the United States has risen, such as Orange County, California. At the national level, legal immigration during the first half of this decade is about 48 percent above the level observed in the first half of the 1970s. Concurrently, the age structure of the Hispanic and black populations, both immigrant and native-born, and changes in the demographic profile of white native-born workers have increased the importance of immigrant labor. In particular, dependence on Hispanic workers, the majority of whom are Mexicans, has

[3] *Washington Post,* 29 August 1986.
[4] *Newsweek,* 25 June 1984.
[5] Thomas Muller, *The Fourth Wave: A Summary* (Washington, The Urban Institute, 1984). The survey was undertaken in 1982.

heightened in recent years. The objective of this paper is to briefly describe recent events that indicate the rising importance of these workers as one element in the growing labor market interdependence between the United States, Mexico, and other nations.

RECENT CHANGES IN THE U.S. LABOR FORCE

The United States experienced a level of unprecedented peacetime employment expansion between 1970 and early 1990. A total of 40.0 million jobs was added, a 52 percent increase in two decades. During this period, both the occupation profile and the ethnic composition of the labor force changed considerably.

The growth in the number of Hispanic workers is perhaps the most significant single shift in labor-force composition observed in recent years. During the 1970s, Hispanics accounted for under 10 percent of the total job growth in the nation. Between 1980 and 1990, however, one of five new workers, as shown in Table 1, was Hispanic.[6]

Mexican and other Central as well as South American residents, all groups composed largely of immigrants, account for over 80 percent of all persons identified as Hispanics, with Mexicans alone constituting over 60 percent of the total. These workers, as shown in Table 2, continue to have a somewhat higher labor-participation rate than non-Hispanics, primarily because only a small proportion are over fifty years old. These labor-participation rates are expected to rise further as more Hispanic women gain employment.

In addition to Hispanics, other minority and immigrant groups also show sharp employment gains, with the number of black workers (including black immigrants) rising about 30 percent since 1980. There is also substantial growth among "other non-white," mostly Asian, workers. This group shows a 71 percent rise during the first six years of the 1980s, only somewhat below the Hispanic growth rate. Unquestionably, the "other non-white" component, comprised primarily of Asian immigrants as well as Hispanics, is rapidly gaining a major foothold in the American economy. As shown in Table 1, non-Hispanic white employment increased by 1990 by only 13 percent, less than 1.4 percent annually; the Hispanic growth rate, meanwhile, was over 75 percent, approaching an annual rate of 7 percent. Non-Hispanic whites accounted for only somewhat more than one-half of the total employment gains in recent years (see Table 1). Because this group includes non-Hispanic white immigrants, the share of native-born, non-Hispanic whites gaining

[6] The statistics shown in this paper are based on sample tabulations that probably undercount undocumented Hispanic entrants.

TABLE I

Employment Growth by Ethnic Group, 1970–1990

(In thousands)

Group	1970	1980	1984	1990	Change 1970–1980	Change 1980–1990	Pct. growth 1980–1990	Pct. share 1970–1980	Pct. share 1980–1990
White	68,281	86,380	92,094	100,794	18,099	14,414	16.7%	85.5%	76.8%
Black[a]	7,361	9,098	10,119	11,858	1,737	2,760	30.3	8.2	14.7
Other[b]	910	2,242	2,792	3,827	1,332	1,585	70.7	6.3	8.5
Total	76,552	97,720	105,005	116,479	21,168	18,759	19.2%	100.0%	100.0%
Hispanic[b]	2,886	4,931	6,469	8,633	2,045	3,702	75.1%	9.7%	19.7%
White, non-Hispanic	65,395	81,449	86,143	92,161	16,054	10,712	13.2%	75.8%	57.1%

SOURCES: 1970 Census of Population and Bureau of Labor Statistics, *Employment and Earnings*, various issues. 1990 data for first quarter, 1990.

[a]First quarter, 1990.

[b]Estimated by author. Counts all Hispanics as white.

TABLE 2

Employment Status Among Hispanic Groups and Blacks in 1990

(*In thousands*)

	All Hispanics	Mexicans	Other South Americans[a]	Puerto Ricans	Cubans	Blacks	Total population
Population 16 years and over	14,234	8,768	3,079	1,479	912	21,289	187,977
Civilian labor force	9,649	6,066	2,169	821	593	13,652	126,367
Labor participation rate (%)	67.8%	69.2%	70.4%	55.5%	65.0%	64.1%	67.2%
Unemployment rate (%)	7.6%	7.7%	N/A	8.5%	5.6%	11.2%	5.3%

SOURCE: Bureau of Labor Statistics, *Employment and Earnings*, July 1990 (2nd quarter 1990 data).
[a]Including Central Americans.

jobs during the 1980s may represent only slightly more than half of the total expansion.

These statistics should not be interpreted to suggest that non-Hispanic whites have difficulties obtaining jobs; facts indicate the contrary is true. Unemployment among these workers is sharply below the level of other groups and labor-participation rates remain high. Indeed, suburban areas that have the highest concentrations of non-Hispanic white residents are experiencing the lowest unemployment rates. Two factors explain most of the disparity in growth rates among these groups. First, there are considerable differences in birthrates, and thus the number of young persons, between non-Hispanic whites and others, particularly Hispanics. Second, the vast majority of new immigrants is either Hispanic or Asian.

In the absence of immigration, employment growth would have been substantially lower in the 1970–1990 period. Even unemployment rates below 4 percent would not have provided sufficient additional unemployed native-born workers to meet the demand. Of course, a considerable share of the added demand is created by immigrants themselves, who are both workers and consumers of goods and services. But jobs appear to be expanding more rapidly than the native-born population can absorb.[7]

The concentration of Hispanics in young age groups is significant; it indicates the future share of the labor force Hispanics will likely hold. In 1986, only 7.4 percent of the civilian population over 19 years of age was Hispanic. However, 9.8 percent of all persons 16 to 19 years old was Hispanic in origin. This latter group accounted for 8.1 percent of all young persons employed and, as a result of above-average unemployment, an even higher percentage of those in the labor force. These demographic data demonstrate that young Hispanics are becoming an increasingly significant labor-force component, with the population of young Hispanics in urban areas of the United States exceeding one-eighth of the urban-area total.

The Hispanic unemployment rate (7.6 percent in mid-1990) continues to be well above the white average, although considerably below the black unemployment rate (11.2 percent in mid-1990). Most of the unemployment differences observed between Hispanics and whites can be explained by the occupational profiles of Hispanic workers and the industries where they are employed. Compared to the white population, blue-collar and semi-skilled occupations (where Hispanics are overrepresented) have consistently higher unemployment rates than professional or government jobs. But differences between black and Hispanic unemploy-

[7] This is an example of why the general thesis that immigrants cause massive displacement makes no sense at the aggregate level.

ment rates cannot be fully explained simply by these workers' concentration in particular occupations and industries. As for earnings, an examination of available data for full-time workers shows that black men and women continue to earn more than Hispanics. As shown in Table 3, the gap widened somewhat during the 1980s. Because a higher proportion of blacks than Hispanics hold white-collar and public-sector jobs (which tend to have low unemployment rates), one would have expected Hispanic unemployment rates to be no lower than rates among blacks.

Because definitions and data-gathering approaches have not been totally consistent, it is difficult to determine whether the relative wage gap between Hispanics and other groups has increased in recent years. Relative median earnings have fallen for both men and women. An examination of how displaced workers fared during the 1980–1983 recession suggests that the impact on Hispanics was somewhat more severe than on other workers. During the 1981–1983 economic decline, Hispanic employment fell, but recovered strongly as the economy expanded in 1984–85. Hispanics accounted for 5.5 percent of all those displaced who worked at their jobs three or more years. Only about half of those displaced found other jobs, a third remained unemployed, and 14 percent left the work force. In comparison, fewer than 23 percent of all displaced non-Hispanic white workers remained unemployed. The above-average unemployment rates among displaced Hispanics is mostly attributable to their industry concentration. Half of all displaced workers during the economic decline were in the manufacturing sector, including 200,000 in textile and apparel production, where a disproportionate share of Hispanics are employed.[8]

As one would expect, displaced workers who obtained new jobs typically earned less than their former pay. This was particularly true for workers initially working in high-wage primary metals and transportation sectors. However, those who lost jobs in the lower-wage textile and apparel sectors, which had a large Hispanic work force, had no loss in earnings as a result of job changes because their original pay was low. Thus, it is likely that Hispanics who obtained new employment accepted lower wages less frequently than other workers. More generally, Hispanic poverty rates are rising relative to other groups, suggesting that the concentration of such workers in low-paying jobs could be rising.

HISPANICS IN LARGE URBAN MARKETS

Aggregate statistics do not indicate the importance of the Hispanic work force in urban areas. During 1986, Hispanic workers made up

[8] P. O. Flaim and E. Seghal, *Displaced Workers of 1979–1983* (Washington, Bureau of Labor Statistics, 1984).

TABLE 3

Median Weekly Earnings of Full-Time Workers, 1980 and 1990

	White	Black	Hispanic	Total	Black as pct. of Hispanic	Black as pct. of total	Hispanic as pct. of total
1980							
Men	$342	$257	$241	$335	106.6%	76.7%	71.9%
Women	213	194	181	221	107.2	87.8	85.8
1990							
Men	$501	$364	$328	$488	111.0%	74.6%	67.2%
Women	354	309	283	346	109.1	89.3	81.8

SOURCE: Bureau of Labor Statistics, *Employment and Earnings*, April 1986, May 1990.

11.3 percent of all those employed in central cities and 8.5 percent of the suburban labor force, but only 2.6 percent of all nonagricultural workers outside metropolitan areas. Mexicans account for about 9 percent of all agricultural workers in the United States, but few other Hispanics are employed in agriculture.

This paper focuses on six large metropolitan labor-market areas that employ substantial numbers of Hispanic workers.[9] Five of the six, as shown in Table 4, also employ many black workers. The concentration of both Hispanics and blacks in central cities in large labor markets is even greater, with minorities constituting over half of the work force in New York, Houston, and Chicago. The sixth large Hispanic labor market, Orange County, California, has relatively few black workers but a growing number of Mexicans and Asians. The six areas in 1989 collectively employed 3.4 million Hispanics: 40 percent of all those working in the United States. Between 1980 and 1989, over 70 percent of all workers added in the six areas, 1,260,000 of the 1,744,000 increase, were Hispanics.[10]

Approximately 36 percent of the total job growth between 1980 and 1985 in the six standard metropolitan statistical areas (SMSAs) occurred in the higher-paying professional, managerial, and technical categories. By comparison, only 25 percent of new jobs nationally, a considerably lower share, was in these categories. Among Hispanics in the six areas, 14 percent of their total gain was in better-paying white-collar jobs, slightly better than the 13 percent national gain. This suggests that better-paying job opportunities for Hispanics were not reduced by their concentration in these labor markets.[11] However, these gains were no greater than the share of such jobs already held by Hispanics, indicating a lack of occupational mobility, perhaps attributable to the inflow of undocumented workers.

Semiskilled and unskilled blue-collar jobs fell by 1.4 million across the nation between 1980 and 1984, but stabilized somewhat in the subsequent two years. Nonetheless, a 1.7 million loss occurred in these predominantly factory jobs during the six years when the national economy was expanding and national income was rising. Although the share of all Hispanics working in blue-collar occupations also fell, the number of Hispanics holding such jobs actually rose. By the mid-1980s, one of three Hispanics in each SMSA held semi-skilled blue-collar jobs. In the five

---

[9] New York, Los Angeles, Chicago, Miami, Houston, and Orange County. Mexicans are dominant in four areas, Cubans in Miami, Puerto Ricans/South Americans in New York.

[10] Most of the statistics utilized are based on surveys of employees and workers, and thus probably underestimate the number of undocumented workers.

[11] To what extent Hispanics benefit from or are hurt by their labor market concentration remains in dispute. For a brief review of several studies, see *Hispanics and Jobs: Barriers to Progress* (Washington, National Commission for Employment Policy, Sept. 1982).

TABLE 4

Minority Share of Urban Employment, 1990

SMSA	Total employment (000)	Pct. Hispanic	Pct. Black	Pct. other non-White	Pct. total minority
HIGH PROPORTION OF HISPANICS AND BLACKS					
PMSA					
Miami	944	51.8%	21.5%	2.4%	75.7%
Los Angeles	4,418	33.3	10.7	10.0	54.0
New York LMA	3,990	19.0	22.9	6.7	48.6
Chicago	3,302	11.0	19.2	3.4	33.6
Houston	1,730	19.0	18.8	3.6	41.4
City					
New York	3,364	20.2	25.6	7.5	53.3
Houston	915	23.8	24.6	3.8	52.2
Dallas	755	14.2	29.1	1.0	44.3
Chicago	1,460	17.2	35.5	4.2	56.9
HIGH PROPORTION OF HISPANICS					
SMSA					
Riverside	1,096	23.2	6.2	4.6	34.0
Anaheim	1,274	23.9	N/A	N/A	N/A
San Jose	760	9.9	N/A	N/A	N/A
HIGH PROPORTION OF BLACKS					
SMSA					
Philadelphia	2,471	1.8	16.8	2.6	21.2
Newark	993	9.1	19.8	2.9	31.8
Detroit	2,162	1.3	16.6	2.0	19.9
St. Louis	1,236	N/A	15.6	1.2	N/A
Washington	2,145	3.9	22.9	3.8	30.6
Baltimore	1,226	N/A	25.4	2.2	N/A
City					
Philadelphia	732	N/A	41.7	1.6	N/A
Detroit	380	N/A	78.9	2.1	N/A
St. Louis	176	N/A	40.9	1.7	N/A
District of Col.	315	5.7	60.0	2.2	67.9
Baltimore City	353	N/A	59.4	1.4	N/A
HIGH PROPORTION OF ASIANS					
San Francisco PMSA	898	14.5	5.1	23.1	42.7
San Francisco City	404	15.8	N/A	33.4	N/A

SOURCE: Bureau of Labor Statistics data in *Geographic Profile of Employment and Unemployment*, 1989, May 1990.

urban areas with a large Hispanic work force, unskilled and semi-skilled blue-collar jobs fell from 2.0 million in 1980 to 1.9 million in 1985, but Hispanic employment in these occupations climbed in each SMSA with a total gain of 72,000 jobs.

The evidence is mounting that, primarily due to foreign imports, the United States and its large urban centers are unable to sustain a considerable part of their manufacturing sector.[12] This shift represents a serious long-term problem for Hispanic workers who are disproportionately concentrated in manufacturing industries. In 1989, 41 percent of all Hispanics in the Midwest, 32 percent in the Northeast, and close to a third in the West worked in durable and nondurable manufacturing goods industries, twice the rate of other ethnic groups. The continuing decline of the American manufacturing sector not only reduces the potential for jobs, but also means lower earnings for most new labor-market entrants, because wages in service industries, the major source for new jobs, are below those in other sectors. Indeed, there is growing, but not definitive, evidence that most new jobs pay relatively low wages.

The decline in manufacturing jobs does not necessarily suggest an overall future reduction in the number of Hispanics employed in manufacturing. More probable is that Hispanics will continue to replace others leaving lower-wage manufacturing jobs. Concurrently, opportunities in higher-paying unionized and nonproduction manufacturing jobs will remain limited for Hispanics, particularly immigrants. In several manufacturing industries, the share of all workers that are Hispanic will level off as their percentage reaches a saturation level, already evident in the apparel sector, where the vast majority of production workers in Los Angeles is Hispanic. Increased Hispanic employment opportunities in manufacturing industries will require an overall expansion in sector employment. But despite somewhat lower wages received by Hispanics compared to others in manufacturing jobs, such sector expansion is unlikely. Although wages in apparel are the lowest among manufacturing industries, they cannot match the wage structure in the third world and consequently the typically lower prices for such goods imported from these nations. Although the rapid decline of jobs in textiles and apparel stopped during 1986, the chances of expansion are limited.

HISPANIC AND BLACK WORKERS

Potential competition between Hispanics and black workers has been a concern to groups within the black community and has led to periodic

---

[12] The effect of the fall in value of the dollar compared to other currencies on import levels and the loss of jobs remains uncertain.

friction between the two groups. Recent California and national surveys (referenced earlier) indicate that considerably more blacks than other ethnic groups believe immigrants take jobs from native-born Americans. In part, these differences represent the higher-than-average concentration of both black and Hispanic workers in manufacturing and services.

The fears within the black community have deep historical roots. Since the 1850s, concerns have been expressed that immigrants—first the Irish, then Italians, and more recently, Mexicans and Asians—reduce black employment opportunities, causing ethnic friction and occasionally physical violence. The basis for black concerns is no doubt the substantial, if mostly anecdotal, evidence suggesting that blacks had difficulty competing with immigrants in large cities during the nineteenth and early twentieth century. One needs to recall, however, that fewer than 2 percent of all blacks held white-collar jobs during this period; most were concentrated in unskilled service jobs that immigrant women also found available. The vast majority of blacks until the 1920s resided in rural areas of the South and had no contact at all with immigrants, whether European, Asian, or Hispanic in origin. Since the occupational structure of blacks, particularly black women, has improved dramatically during the last several decades, historical concerns do not necessarily reflect current conditions.

As noted earlier, five of the six areas identified as having large numbers of Hispanic workers also have a substantial black labor force. There were 1,845,000 black workers in the five urban areas identified during 1980, nearly identical to the 1,861,000 Hispanics also employed during that year. By 1989, the number of Hispanic workers in these labor markets rose to 3,121,000, surpassing the number of blacks by nearly one million. In several other major labor market areas, however—particularly Baltimore, Detroit, Newark, Philadelphia, St. Louis, and Washington, D.C.—blacks continue to dominate Hispanics.[13]

How do the labor-force characteristics of the two minority groups compare in the five urban areas? Across the United States, considerably more blacks than Hispanics hold managerial/professional jobs (see Table 5). The occupational gap between the two groups that have a large proportion of Hispanics is somewhat greater than elsewhere. This difference may be attributable to the large inflow of unskilled and semi-skilled Hispanic immigrants to these large labor markets. But the somewhat above-average proportion of blacks in these jobs, compared to other areas, also suggests that these areas provide blacks (and other non-Hispanic groups

[13] Nationally, Hispanics and Asians, due to immigration, are outpacing black employment gains by considerable margins.

TABLE 5

*Characteristics of the Labor Force in Selected Large Labor Markets
with Substantial Minority Employment, 1986*

	Large Hispanic and Black labor force[a]	Primarily Hispanic[b]	Primarily Black[c]	U.S. average[d]
Percent Professional/Managerial/Technical of all Workers				
Blacks	20.6%	N/A	16.2%	20.2%
Hispanics	12.9	13.4	N/A	14.1
Asians & other non-Whites	33.6	N/A	N/A	N/A
Unemployment Rates				
Blacks	12.8%	—	14.7%	15.1%
Hispanics	9.4	9.7	7.8[e]	10.5
Whites[f]	6.0	5.4	4.1	6.2

SOURCE: Bureau of Labor Statistics, *Geographic Profile of Employed and Unemployed,* December 1986.
[a]Chicago, Houston, Miami, Los Angeles, New York.
[b]Anaheim (Orange County), San Jose, Riverside.
[c]Atlanta, Baltimore, Detroit, Newark, Philadelphia, St. Louis, Washington.
[d]All areas of nation.
[e]Includes only three areas.
[f]Including Hispanic.

such as Asians) additional opportunities in higher-paying, white-collar occupations, including those in the public sector. At a minimum, these data fail to indicate that blacks as a group have fewer opportunities to hold better-paying jobs in areas where Hispanics are a significant element of the labor force. Unemployment rates for blacks in urban markets with large numbers of both blacks and Hispanics, as shown in Table 6, are below average; yet whites are also shown to have low unemployment in areas with large minority working populations. Because intergroup comparisons do not hold other factors constant, these statistics must remain only suggestive; nonetheless, they are consistent with an earlier analysis of black unemployment that looked at Hispanic immigrant worker relationships in urban areas and controlled several factors based on 1980 U.S. Census data.[14] This analysis indicated that there was no negative (but, in fact a somewhat positive) correlation between Hispanic immigration and black employment. That is, the presence of immigrants may have marginally improved employment opportunities for blacks.

To what extent the Hispanic presence affects internal black migration patterns cannot be determined directly. However, black employment in the five areas with many black and Hispanic workers increased by only

[14]Muller, *The Fourth Wave.*

TABLE 6

Job Growth in Six Large Labor Markets by Ethnicity, 1980–1989

Area	Total job gain 1980–1989 (000)	Pct. Hispanic	Pct. Black	Pct. other	Pct. total minority[a]	Labor market ranking
Houston SMSA	294	45.7%	24.1%	14.6%	84.4%	7
Los Angeles County	813	75.4	10.9	23.6	*	1
New York SMSA	248	53.4	19.2	34.9	*	3
Miami/Dade County	203	97.5	15.3	4.9	*	N/A
Chicago SMSA[b]	186	34.9	12.4	11.8	59.1	2
Total	1,744	1,260	304	353	1,917	—

SOURCE: Bureau of Labor Statistics, *Geographic Profile of Employment and Unemployment*, 1980 and 1989.
[a] Includes black Hispanics. Thus, there is a small overcount.
[b] Chicago, 1980–1985, due to changes in metropolitan area boundaries in 1986.
* Indicates net reduction in employment among non-Hispanic whites.

304,000 (26 percent) between 1980 and 1989 (see Table 6). A considerable share of this increase (and most of the increase in New York) was attributable to black immigration rather than native-born growth. The black share of total employment in these areas increased from 15.7 percent in 1980 to 17.4 percent in 1989, consistent with their national share growth during this period. Asians, however, gained more jobs in the five areas than blacks.

In the six labor markets where blacks are the largest minorities, black employment during the 1980s increased to become greater than the non-black rate. But fewer blacks were working in the industrial cities of Detroit and St. Louis during 1989 than nine years earlier. Most growth in black employment within this group was attributable to gains in two areas: Atlanta and Washington, D.C.

Blacks, particularly women, remain concentrated in sales and administrative jobs within large urban centers, positions held by few Hispanics because Hispanic workers remain overrepresented in unskilled and semiskilled blue-collar jobs. Hispanics are twice as likely as blacks to work in the manufacturing sector. Government remains a major employment source for blacks, particularly black women, in large cities and probably contributes to relatively high earnings among these women. In New York, one of every four black workers is found in the public sector; in Chicago, one of five. But relatively few Hispanics (particularly outside New York and Washington) and even fewer Mexicans work for government agencies. In the service sectors, both Hispanics and blacks are overrepresented compared to other ethnic groups, but ethnic differences exist within this sector as well. The proportion of blacks working in health services exceeds Hispanics by a factor of three, with Hispanics concentrated in food services.

The pattern of concentration among minorities in particular sectors of the economy continues. Differences in the occupational profile between blacks and Hispanics may have actually grown during recent years. This does not, of course, demonstrate that no significant job competition exists, but the likelihood of head-on competition is reduced by these concentrations. (The one exception is at the lower end of the occupational ladder. In janitorial services there are instances where unionized blacks have been displaced by immigrants, and no doubt other examples may be found.) Immigrants and native-born workers unable to advance themselves continue to form part of the so-called urban "underclass" with all the economic and social burdens this term connotes. The least desirable jobs are typically the only legal route open to these workers. Fortunately, the "underclass" currently forms only a minority of the black population, comprised primarily of single males and females who are head of their respective households. Earnings of full-time black women approximate the average for the total female working population.

As employment data described earlier suggest, one probable impact of the growing Hispanic and black Carribean immigrant presence is the reduction of internal migration of native-born blacks to New York, Los Angeles, and Miami. Further analysis will be required to fully substantiate this relationship.

PROJECTED DEMAND FOR HISPANIC IMMIGRANTS

In the United States there is a common, but incorrect, perception that structural changes in the economy, expansion of high-tech industries, automation, and rising educational levels will result in future job concentrations in occupations that require advanced education and extensive formal training. Although opportunities for computer programmers, electronic engineers, and other highly technical personnel will grow at an above-average rate, a substantial share of all new jobs will remain in low-wage, low-skill categories. The projected total number of jobs to be added at the lower end of the earnings scale, namely service workers, operators, and laborers, will be 4.6 million over an eleven-year period.

An examination of the ten occupations projected to add the most jobs during the next ten years, shown in Table 7, indicates that only two will require a college degree. Most of these occupations require only modest language skills, a basic education and little, if any, formal training. Labor

TABLE 7

Fastest Growing Occupations in the United States, 1984–1995

Rank	Occupation	No. of jobs (000)	Percent growth, 1984–1995	Skill Requirement				Wage level
				English	Education	Formal training		
1	Cashiers	556	29.1%	Modest	Basic	Minimal		Low
2	Registered nurses	452	32.8	Excellent	College	Substantial		Average
3	Janitors & cleaners	443	15.1	Minimal	None	None		Low
4	Food preparation workers	434	19.5	Minimal	None	None		Low
5	Truck drivers	428	17.1	Modest	Basic	Basic		Average
6	Waiters, waitresses	424	26.1	Good	None	None		Low
7	Wholesale trade salespersons	369	29.6	Good-Excl.	Basic	Modest		Average
8	Nursing aides	348	28.9	Modest	Basic	Modest		Low
9	Salesperson, retail	343	12.6	Good	Basic	Minimal		Low
10	Accountants, auditors	307	34.8	Excellent	College	Substantial		High

SOURCE: Employment Projections for 1995: Data and Methods Bulletin 2253, Bureau of Labor Statistics, Washington, D.C., April 1986.

shortages have been developing in many of these expanding entry-level occupations. The ten occupations collectively represent 26 percent of the total job expansion projected to the year 1995. Of course, other jobs requiring limited skills will be growing over the next decades. No expansion is projected in much of the manufacturing sector because of continuing foreign competition and, to a lesser degree, rising productivity.

Hispanics currently represent well over 10 percent of workers in occupations ranked third and fourth in growth—namely, janitorial services and food preparation. These two occupations alone are expected to gain close to 900,000 jobs in the next decade. Approximately six million jobs are projected to be added in occupations where Hispanics in general, and Mexicans in particular, are overrepresented. These broad occupational categories represent 38 percent of all jobs anticipated to be added over the next ten years.[15] As Mexican immigrants improve their English language skills, many will obtain jobs in industry as salesclerks or in medical services as, for example, nursing aides. Many Hispanic entrants also bring specialized knowledge that will enable some to obtain higher-paying jobs. However, most recent arrivals, particularly Mexicans, will continue to depend on low-skill, low-wage jobs. Most of the economic and political concerns expressed in the United States involve these entrants with few skills rather than highly trained, professional immigrants.

The insufficient growth of native-born workers to meet projected employment needs can be attributed to a combination of factors. First, and most important, people of the so-called "baby bust" generation are now adults. Second, labor participation is expected to decline. During the last two decades, women made up a considerable share of workers new to the labor force. The most recent projections indicate that the percentage of white women in the work force will rise over the next decade to no more than 58.4 percent from the current 53.3 percent. Concurrently, male labor-participation rates will likely fall from 77.1 to 75.8 percent. Thus the net labor-participation rate increase for the white population over an eleven-year period will be limited to 2 percent.[16]

Third, the rise in educational achievement reduces the willingness of many young native-born adults, including minority youths, to accept entry-level jobs with limited opportunities for advancement. In part, the high youth unemployment, even in areas where adult unemployment is low and at least limited job opportunities for youth exist, may be attrib-

---

[15] Given the surge of job growth since projections were completed, forecasts shown may be conservative.

[16] *Employment Projection for 1995: Data and Methods* (Washington, Bureau of Labor Statistics, April 1986).

utable to this phenomenon. Immigrants, Hispanics, and others, including refugees, are typically willing to accept these "dead-end" jobs while attending school, gaining language skills, or merely surviving. These workers are well aware of the severe limitations of these jobs, but are willing to hold them because their real earnings are higher than they could achieve in their country of origin. Further, they expect that if they attend school part-time, improve their language skills, and gain experience, that opportunities for advancement will arise. Finally, undocumented immigrant workers do not have social-service benefits as alternatives to low-wage employment. Given a family to support, they have no other option.

The combination of demographic changes and the inability to substantially increase the number of native-born adults in the labor force will increase the demand for immigrants (particularly Hispanics), especially during periods of economic expansion. The likelihood of this phenomenon was anticipated by the National Commission on Employment Policy in its 1982 report on the status of the U.S. labor force. The report states that "despite current concern about the impact of undocumented workers on U.S. employment, recent research suggests that the projected major decline in new labor force entrants could raise the issue of encouraging immigration."[17] It is notable that this report was released in 1982, when unemployment rates in the United States were particularly high. Recent labor-market conditions substantiate this view, although the need to encourage immigrants is unlikely, as the supply is virtually without limit.

CONCLUSION

For the millions of unemployed or underemployed in Mexico and elsewhere, it is difficult to imagine that toward the northern horizon, jobs for unskilled and other workers remain unfilled. But there is little question that the United States will continue to face a shortage of entry-level workers despite periodic economic declines. Some economists would, of course, argue that the concept of labor shortages is a myth. Increase wages sufficiently, and someone will be found to fill any slot. At the individual level, of course, this view is correct. If McDonalds would pay $10 per hour, more workers would become available than could possibly be absorbed by this fast-food chain. However, most of these workers would already be employed elsewhere, causing shortages in other establishments. Further, such high wages would cause demand to fall and consumer prices to rise. The major pools of workers that have contributed to the growth of the urban economy—women and rural residents—have

[17] *The Work Revolution* (Washington, National Commission for Employment Policy, Dec. 1982).

been virtually exhausted. Some high-school students, unemployed youths, and those retired could be induced to work at higher wages, but these gains would not likely meet the projected demand for workers. The economy could also invest more in labor-saving capital. But as the fast-food industry found, it is difficult and very costly to automate some jobs. Growth in demand that exceeds supply obviously causes wages to increase. Such a rise may be a desirable social end, as higher wages for low-skilled workers would redistribute income that in recent years has become more concentrated at the upper end.

U.S. history suggests that a more likely response to the current labor problem will be to find workers elsewhere. To the extent that the domestic supply is exhausted, one can expect a continuing inflow of legal and even undocumented immigrants despite new legislation. Such a market response may be criticized by those who would argue that we are creating a generation of "cheap" labor that is being exploited to benefit primarily the U.S. middle class. I have difficulty accepting this position. In an economic sense, many immigrants including Mexicans are being exploited, but most prefer their status to returning home, where opportunities and earnings are even more limited. Of course, some elect to return, and there are no barriers to this option. But the majority benefit economically from their presence in the United States.

The federal and state governments need to vigorously enforce labor laws and ensure reasonable working conditions for all. No worker, regardless of his or her status, should be exempt from these basic regulations. But a greater concern partially linked to this is that Hispanic immigrants, concentrated in low-wage jobs, will form a permanent underclass. From the perspective of the United States and Mexico, this may be the most serious problem associated with the continuing Mexican inflow. A related problem is the continuing decline in manufacturing jobs, which have replaced agriculture as the mainstay of the Mexican immigrant.

Despite these concerns, all studies indicate that the Hispanic share of the U.S. labor force will continue to rise during the next two decades and beyond. Within a decade, the Hispanic labor force in a number of large metropolitan areas can be expected to represent the dominant share of all young new workers. These changes will have long-term economic, political, and social implications that are beyond the scope of this paper. But it is certain that Hispanic workers will play an increasingly crucial role in the U.S. economy.

Post-Industrial Growth and Economic Reorganization: Their Impact on Immigrant Employment

Saskia Sassen and Robert C. Smith

W E SEEK TO EXAMINE the interaction of three developments as they are taking place in the United States today: current changes in the labor market; continuing third-world immigration; and the 1986 immigration law. Our particular case for empirical analysis is New York City. There is now considerable evidence of pronounced changes in the demand for labor and in the conditions under which labor is employed, both in the country as a whole and in New York City in particular.[1] Strong evidence also exists that third-world immigration to New York City, including illegal immigration, continues.[2] Finally, there is growing proof that the new immigration law, the Immigration Reform and Con-

---

[1] For information on U.S. labor trends, consult T. M. Stanback and T. J. Noyelle, *Cities in Transition: Changing Job Structures in Atlanta, Denver, Buffalo, Phoenix, Columbus (Ohio), Nashville, Charlotte.* (Totowa, N.J., 1982); John D. Kasarda, "Urban Change and Minority Opportunities," in Paul E. Peterson, ed., *The New Urban Reality* (Washington, 1985); Robert G. Sheets, Stephen Nord, and John J. Phelps, *The Impact of Service Industries on Underemployment in Metropolitan Economies* (Lexington, Mass., 1987); Allen J. Scott, *Metropolis: From the Division of Labor to Urban Form* (Berkeley and Los Angeles, 1988); Bennett Harrison and Barry Bluestone, *The Great U-Turn* (New York, 1988). For descriptions of the situation in New York City, see Saskia Sassen-Koob, "New York City: Economic Restructuring and Immigration," *Development and Change* 17, 85–119.

[2] Immigration and Naturalization Service, *Annual Report* (Washington, 1988); Emanuel Tobier, "The 'New' Immigration in the New York Metropolitan Region: Characteristics and Consequences," unpublished paper presented at New York University, Graduate School of Public Administration, 1988; Demetrios G. Papademetriou and Nicholas DiMarzio, *Undocumented Aliens in the New York Metropolitan Area* (New York, 1986); Columbia University, *Immigration Research Project* (New York, 1989).

trol Act of 1986 (IRCA), is contributing to new forms of differentiation in the immigrant labor force.[3]

What conditions allow for continuing absorption of third-world immigration, notably a new Mexican influx, despite a restrictive law and a shift to an economy dominated by advanced services? This question seems particularly pertinent for New York City, where finance and business services account for a third of all employment and where half of all the new jobs since 1977 are in high-income managerial and professional occupations. The labor market locations for new immigrant arrivals, many of whom are poor and have little education (and in the case of Mexicans, are lacking a well-established, resource-rich immigrant community in New York), must also be addressed.

Our central argument is that there is a growing casualization of the labor market in the United States, especially in major cities such as New York, and that casualization is one set of processes that provides useful insights into the intersection of labor markets, immigration, and the new immigration law. This casualization assumes a range of specific forms, some of which have been documented, and it raises a number of questions about the plausibility of others that still need to be studied. The most extreme version of casualization in the labor market is the recent expansion of an informal economy in several major cities in the United States, particularly New York, Los Angeles, and Miami.[4] Other forms of casualized work include the growth of temporary and part-time employment and the increase in subcontracting.

Several general trends point to the growth of casualization: the decline in unionized production jobs along with the growth of small-batch, often craft-based manufacturing evident in central areas of large cities such as Los Angeles and New York (for example, apparel, furniture, and toys); the massive increase in low-wage, dead-end service jobs (such as fast-food sales and messenger work); and the Bureau of Labor Statistics' projections that these occupations, along with clerical work, will produce the largest number of new jobs over the next decade. Finally, a growing

[3] New York State Interagency Task Force on Immigration Affairs, "Workplace Discrimination under the Immigration Reform and Control Act of 1986: A Study of Impacts on New Yorkers" (New York, New York State Interagency Task Force on Immigration Affairs, 1988); Columbia University, *Immigration Research Project.*

[4] Patricia Fernandez-Kelly and Anna Garcia, "Informalization at the Core: Hispanic Women, Homework, and the Advanced Capitalist State," in Alejandro Portes, Manuel Castells, and Laura Benton, eds., *The Informal Economy: Studies in Advanced and Less-Developed Countries* (Baltimore, Md., and London, 1989); Alex Stepick, "Miami's Two Informal Sectors," in *The Informal Economy*; Saskia Sassen, "New York City's Informal Economy," in *The Informal Economy*.

body of research is being developed about the impact of labor market characteristics on employment outcomes; these studies have established direct links between loose labor markets and the declining economic position of urban minority groups.[5]

These developments raise the following questions for the purposes of our inquiry: Most generally, what is the impact of casualization in specific labor markets on employment outcomes for immigrants and, conversely, what is the impact of the availability of a casualized labor force on labor-market characteristics? More specifically, does the casualization of the labor market interact with, reflect, or respond to the availability of a large supply of immigrant workers, and if so, how does this happen? To what extent are immigrant workers an effective supply for many of these casualized jobs? And finally, how does the new immigration law affect the characteristics of the immigrant labor supply—specifically, how does it help casualize or decasualize this labor supply?

We will explore these questions by focusing on the informal economy and on the new Mexican immigration in New York City. A central question for theory and policy is whether the formation and expansion of the informal economy in advanced industrialized countries and in a city such as New York are the result of conditions created by advanced capitalism or simply have to do with the survival strategies of third-world immigrants. In order to identify systemic links between informalization and structural conditions in advanced capitalism, we examined how major growth trends shaped a vast array of types of jobs, types of firms, and subcontracting patterns that induce or are conducive to informalization. There is no precise measure of informalization and there is no exhaustive evidence to support our claims. Rather, juxtaposing these systemic trends with the available evidence permits us to make inferences about the patterns, scope, and conditions promoting informalization. We posit that the economic restructuring that has contributed to a decline of the post-World War II manufacturing-dominated industrial complex and to the rise of a new, service-dominated industrial complex provide the general

[5] George J. Borjas and Marta Tienda, "The Economic Consequences of Immigration," in *Science* 235 (6 Feb. 1987), 613–20; William J. Wilson, "The Urban Underclass in Advanced Industrial Societies," in *The New Urban Reality;* William J. Wilson, *The Truly Disadvantaged* (Chicago, 1987); Richard B. Freeman and Harry J. Holzer, "The Black Youth Employment Crisis: Summary of Findings," in Richard B. Freeman and Harry J. Holzer, eds., *The Black Youth Employment Crisis* (Chicago, 1986); Kasarda, "Urban Change and Minority Opportunities"; Saskia Sassen, *The Mobility of Labor and Capital* (Cambridge, Eng., 1988); Marta Tienda, "Puerto Ricans and the Underclass Debate," in William J. Wilson, ed., *The Ghetto Underclass: Social Science Perspectives, The Annals of the American Academy of Political and Social Science* 501 (Jan. 1989).

context within which we need to place informalization if we are to go beyond a mere description of instances of informal work.

This analysis is based on three research projects: a study of the informal economy in New York City;[6] a survey of electronics and garment factories in the New York area;[7] and a study of the impact of the 1986 immigration law on Mexican immigration to New York City.[8]

The first section examines major trends in New York City today in order to situate theoretically and empirically the emergence of casualization trends in the leading "post-industrial" city of a highly developed economy. A central question is whether the formation and expansion of casual labor markets in advanced economies are the result of conditions created by advance capitalism. In the second section, we detail our evidence on the informal economy. And in the third section, we discuss the evidence with particular attention to undocumented immigration to New York City after IRCA, and report on research regarding new Mexican immigration.

CHANGES IN THE JOB SUPPLY

In order to understand the trends toward casualization and the expansion of an informal economy, we must first explain several processes of economic and spatial organization. One such process is the labor market effect of the sectoral and occupational transformation in advanced economies over the last two decades. Another process, intricately connected to the first, is the decline of Fordism, which entails a change in the economic and political place of unions and mass production as well as the demise of a broader institutional framework sustained by that model of production—a framework with significant shadow effects for larger sectors of the economy. A third process is the transformation in the spatial organization of the economy, particularly the locational patterns of growth sectors and their impact on the land and housing markets, commerce, personal services, and other sectors of the economy with which they are linked.

[6] Saskia Sassen, "New York City's Informal Economy," in Alejandro Portes, Manuel Castells, and Laura Benton, eds., *The Informal Sector: Theoretical and Methodological Issues* (Baltimore, Md., 1989); Columbia University, *The Informal Economy in Low-Income Communities in New York City* (New York, 1987).

[7] Saskia Sassen-Koob and S. Grover, "Unregistered Work in the New York Metropolitan Area," working paper, Columbia University Graduate School of Architecture and Planning, 1986.

[8] Robert C. Smith, "The Immigration Labor Process, the Welfare State, and the Informal Economy: A Look into the Effects of the 1986 Immigration Reform and Control Act in New York and Pennsylvania," paper prepared for the Immigration Research Project, Cornell University, 1988.

The purpose of examining these trends is to understand whether there are forms of economic growth today that promote informalization. We assert that the historical forms assumed by economic growth in the post-World War II era, which contributed to the vast expansion of a middle class—notably, capital intensity, standardization of products, and sub-urbanization-led growth—deterred and reduced informalization. Furthermore, so did the cultural forms accompanying these processes, insofar as a large middle class contributes to mass consumption and thus to production standardization. These various trends are conducive to greater levels of unionization or other forms of workers' empowerment that can be derived from large-scale production, and from the centrality of mass production and mass consumption to national economic growth and profits. It was during that post-war period, extending into the late 1960s and early 1970s, that workers were most incorporated into formal labor market relations.

The shift away from mass production toward services as the leading economic sector contributed to the demise of a broader set of arrangements. In the post-war period, the economy functioned according to a dynamic that transmitted the benefits accruing to the core manufacturing industries to more peripheral sectors of the economy. The benefits of price and market stability and increases in productivity could be transferred to a secondary set of firms, including suppliers and subcontractors, but also to less directly related industries. Although a vast array of firms and workers still did not benefit from the shadow effect, their number was probably at a minimum in the post-war period.[9] By the early 1980s, the wage-setting power of leading industries and this shadow effect had eroded significantly—a transformation evident in the evolution of wages.[10] Average weekly wages, adjusted for inflation, peaked in 1973, stagnated over the next few years, and fell during the 1980s.[11] Furthermore, until 1963 there was growing equality in the distribution of earnings.

[9] Paul Blumberg, *Inequality in an Age of Decline* (New York, 1981).

[10] Although average production wages in New York City have never been among the highest in the country given the absence of such key industries as steel, auto, and aerospace, average wages had been increasing and had reached their highest level ever as recently as 1970 (101.2 percent of the national average hourly production wage). One indication of the extent of downgrading is the decline of this wage level, which fell to 87.6 percent of the national average in 1982—not including sweatshops and industrial homework. The decline can also be seen in an area like Los Angeles that has an economic base, unlike New York City's, dominated by aerospace and electronics; hourly production wages fell from 108 percent of the national average in 1970 to 100.7 percent in 1982.

[11] During the post-World War II period, the real inflation-adjusted average weekly wages of workers increased from $67 to almost $92 in 1965 and declined slightly to $89 in 1979.

Since 1975, the opposite has been occurring. Bennett Harrison and Barry Bluestone, using Current Population Survey data, showed that the inequality index grew 18 percent from 1975 to 1986, a finding confirmed by other studies.[12] The data show a clear increase in low-wage, full-time, year-round jobs since the late 1970s and a less-pronounced increase in high-income jobs (compared with the decade 1963 to 1973, when nine out of ten new jobs were in the middle-earnings group and high-paying jobs actually lost share). After 1973, only one of every two new jobs was in the middle-earnings category.

If one were to add the increase in the numbers of workers who are not employed full-time and year-round, then the inequality becomes even more pronounced. Part-time work increased from 15 percent in 1955 to 22 percent in 1977.[13] By 1986 part-time workers comprised a third of the labor force.[14] About 80 percent of these 50 million workers earn less than $11,000, the level used by Harrison and Bluestone to define low-wage jobs. And only 400,000 earn at or above the high-pay level. Over the past few years, the government has implemented a number of decisions that promote the growing use of part-time and temporary workers.[15]

Objective transformations have occurred. Production has been orga-

---

Bureau of Labor Statistics data show that from 1947 to 1957 real spendable earnings grew by over 20 percent; from 1957 to 1967 by 13 percent, and from 1967 to 1977 by 3 percent (Blumberg, *Inequality in an Age of Decline,* 71).

[12] Bennett Harrison and Barry Bluestone, *The Great U-Turn* (New York, 1988); Linda Bell and Richard Freeman, "The Facts About Rising Industrial Wage Dispersion in the U.S.," Industrial Relations Research Association, *Proceedings* (May 1987); Organization for Economic Cooperation and Development, *OECD Employment Outlook* (Paris, Sept. 1985), 90–91. Several analysts maintain that the increased inequality in the earnings distribution is a function of demographic shifts, notably the growing participation of women and young baby boomers, who traditionally earn less than white adult males. When Harrison and Bluestone (*The Great U-Turn,* chap. 5) analyzed the data controlling for various demographic factors as well as the shift to services (another generally low-wage category) they found that these demographic variables offered an incomplete explanation for the increased inequality in the earnings distribution. Rather, they found that the inequality has occurred within each labor group. Moreover, they discovered that the sectoral shift accounted for one-fifth of the increase in inequality, but most of the rest of this increase occurred within industries so that, as with labor groups, there is a growth in inequality in the earnings distribution within industries (see their appendix, Table A.2). The authors explain the increased inequality in the earnings distribution in terms of the restructuring of wages and work hours (chaps. 2 and 3).

[13] Blumberg, *Inequality in an Age of Decline,* 67, 79, 267; Harrison and Bluestone, *The Great U-Turn,* 102.

[14] W. V. Deutermann, Jr. and S. C. Brown, "Voluntary Part-Time Workers: A Growing Part of the Labor Force," *Monthly Labor Review* 101 (June 1978).

[15] U.S. Congressional Budget Office, 1987.

nized with more small-batch production, small scales, high product differentiation, and rapid changes in output.[16] These changes have promoted
subcontracting and the use of flexible ways of organizing production.
Flexible forms of production can range from highly sophisticated to very
primitive and can be found in advanced or backward industries. Such
ways of organizing production assume distinct forms in the labor market,
in the components of labor demand, and in the conditions under which
labor is employed. Indications of these changes are the decline of unions
in manufacturing, the loss of various contractual protections, and the
increase of involuntary part-time and temporary work or other forms of
contingent labor. An extreme indication of this downgrading is the
growth of sweatshops and industrial homework.[17] The expansion of a
downgraded manufacturing sector partly involves the same industries
that used to have largely organized plants and reasonably well-paid jobs
but have replaced these with different forms of production and organization of the work process, such as piecework and industrial homework.
This expansion also involves new kinds of activity associated with the
new major growth trends. The possibility for manufacturers to develop
alternatives to the organized factory becomes particularly significant in
growth sectors.[18] The consolidation of a downgraded manufacturing sec-

[16] Today many industrial branches need to accommodate rapid changes in output levels
and in product characteristics. There has been an overall decline in the production of basic
goods and consumer durables, the leading growth industries in manufacturing in the postwar period. The most rapidly growing sectors within manufacturing are high-technology
complex and craft-based production in traditional branches such as furniture, footwear,
and apparel.

[17] The growth of sweatshops and industrial homework is the result of several concrete
developments other than the more general processes of social and technical transformation
cited. First, labor-intensive industries were affected differentially by capital flight from the
city. In the garment industry, the largest employer in the city's manufacturing sector, the
biggest shops with mechanized production moved. The less-mechanized branches, specialized shops, and the industry's marketing and design operations have remained in the city.
Furthermore, the changing structure of consumption has also affected the garment industry;
the greater demand for specialty items and limited-edition garments has promoted the expansion of small shops and industrial homework for highly priced garments and accessories
in the city because small runs and a need to be close to design centers are important locational constraints (see Sassen, "Immigrant Women"). A parallel argument can be made for
other industries, notably furniture, furs, and footwear. Second, small-scale, immigrant-
owned plants have grown in number rapidly because of easy access to cheap labor and,
more important, a growing demand for their products in the immigrant communities and
in the city at large.

[18] In New York City, three kinds of activities, which are not always mutually exclusive,
occur; see Saskia Sassen-Koob, "The New Labor Demand in Global Cities," in Michael P.
Smith, ed., Cities in Transformation (Newbury Park, Calif., 1984). First, there is evidence of
a type of manufacturing that has a specific clientele: it might produce tools or furniture or
box gloves for particular firms. The second group includes small-scale production for re-

tor, whether through social or technical transformation, can be seen as a politico-economic response to a need for ongoing or expanded production in a situation of growing average wages and militancy (as was the case in the 1960s and early 1970s) and intense competition for land and markets in the late 1970s and 1980s.

The decline, if not demise, of the broader institutional framework has taken place in a context of rapid growth in several service industries. The growth industries of the 1980s—finance, insurance, and real estate; trade; and business services—show high shares of low-wage jobs, weak if any unions, and a higher incidence of part-time and female workers. The Bureau of Labor Statistics has actually reported declines in real earnings beginning in the 1970s in these industries.[19] Robert Sheets, Stephen Nord, and John Phelps found that the growth of producer services and retail in major metropolitan areas were particularly strong contributors to low-wage jobs.[20] Harrison and Bluestone, the OECD, and Linda Bell and Richard Freeman found growing wage dispersion within industries and a tendency for industries with low average wages to suffer additional declines in wages and for those with high average wages to experience

---

tailers selling to the growing high-income stratum, whose numbers have increased sufficiently to promote the creation of a whole array of small businesses catering to their tastes (such as gourmet restaurants and boutiques). Undoubtedly, the possibility of gaining access to cheap labor and achieving huge mark-ups on final products makes this production profitable, and subcontracting to small plants willing to manufacture a small number of items is a key strategy to ensure the viability of this type of limited-market production. Third is production for the newly expanded low-income mass market, much of it sold on the street, which has partly replaced production for the middle-class market. The locational constraints on plant production for middle-income markets are probably somewhat different than for other markets because they have access to mass distribution and often distribute nationwide, a factor that makes producing through large plants more attractive. The low-income mass market emerging in large cities like New York and Los Angeles is supplied to a large extent by local or overseas sweatshops (see Fernandez-Kelly and Garcia, "Informalization at the Core"). The existence of a very large immigrant work force facilitates sweatshop production close to the final market, a strategy particularly desirable for production of perishables and bulkier items like pillows. It is not possible to obtain measures of these three kinds of activities; this is merely a tentative organization of the fragmentary evidence available.

[19] Using Bureau of Labor Statistics and Census data, Blumberg (*Inequality in an Age of Decline*) estimated net spendable average weekly earnings of production or nonsupervisory workers with three dependents for several industries. Of the six major industry groups, all recorded increases from 1948 to 1968. From 1968 to 1978, all except FIRE and trade recorded gains though at much lower levels than in previous decades. FIRE recorded a decline of 5 percent and trade of 3.6 percent. Manufacturing, which had experienced increases of 20 percent from 1948 to 1958 and of 18 percent in the subsequent decade had an increase of only 7.4 percent from 1968 to 1978. FIRE and trade had had increases of about 20 percent in the first post-war decade and about 13 percent in the subsequent decade to arrive at negative rates in the 1970s.

[20] Sheets, Nord, and Phelps, *Impact of Service Industries on Underemployment.*

additional increases.[21] There is a growing body of research about the impact of labor-market characteristics on employment outcomes, which has established direct links between loose labor markets and the declining economic position of urban minority groups.[22]

The overall result is a tendency toward increased economic polarization. Our argument is that while the middle strata still constitute the majority, the conditions that contributed to their expansion and politico-economic power—the centrality of mass production and mass consumption in economic growth and profit realization—have been displaced by new sources of growth. This is not simply a quantitative transformation; we see here the elements for a new economic regime.[23] This tendency toward polarization assumes distinct forms in (1) its spatial organization, (2) the structures for social reproduction, and (3) the organization of the labor process. How do these trends play themselves out in a major city like New York?

The incidence of major service industries with growing earnings dispersion is far higher in New York than in the country as a whole. In 1985, over 26 percent of all private-sector employment in New York City, compared with 15 percent in the country as a whole, was in finance, insurance, and real estate; the communications group; business services; and legal services. The incidence of these industries in New York City is also higher than in other major cities, where it reached 17.8 percent in Los Angeles and 20.3 percent in Chicago. If we consider the producer-services category as it is usually defined, which includes membership organizations and miscellaneous business services, this group of industries accounted for 32 percent of all employment in the city (and 35 percent of the city's private-sector payroll) in 1985, up from 25 percent in 1970, for a total employment of almost 1 million workers. In Manhattan, these industries accounted for almost 40 percent of employment and

[21] Harrison and Bluestone, *The Great U-Turn;* OECD, *OECD Employment Outlook;* Bell and Freeman, "Rising Industrial Wage Dispersion." Using Census data and the 1976 survey on income and education, T. M. Stanback and Noyelle, in their book *Cities in Transition: Changing Job Structures in Atlanta, Denver, Buffalo, Phoenix, Columbus (Ohio), Nashville, Charlotte* (Totowa, N.J., 1982), showed that there is a high incidence of the next-to-lowest earning class in all services except distributive services and public administration. Almost half of all workers in the producer services are in the two highest earnings classes, but only 2.8 percent are in the middle earnings class compared with half of all construction and manufacturing workers.

[22] George J. Borjas and Marta Tienda, "The Economic Consequences of Immigration," in *Science* 235 (6 Feb. 1987), 613–20; Wilson, "Urban Underclass;" Wilson, *The Truly Disadvantaged;* Freeman and Holzer, "Black Youth Employment Crisis"; Tienda, "Puerto Ricans and the Underclass Debate"; Kasarda, "Urban Change and Minority Opportunities."

[23] Saskia Sassen, *The Global City: New York, London, Tokyo* (Princeton, N.J., 1991).

45 percent of payroll.[24] It is thus a significant factor in the city's economy, even more if we include its indirect effects through the housing market, commerce, and personal services. The available evidence for New York City confirms the trend toward dispersion of earnings within industries.

The rapid growth of industries with a strong concentration of high- and low-income jobs has assumed distinct forms in the consumption structure, which in turn has a feedback effect on the organization of work and the types of jobs created.[25] The expansion of the high-income work force in conjunction with the emergence of new cultural forms has led to a high-income gentrification that rests, in the last analysis, on the availability of a vast supply of low-wage workers. As I have argued at greater length elsewhere, high-income gentrification is labor intensive, in contrast to the typical middle-class suburb, which is capital intensive—the suburb features tract housing, road and highway construction, dependence on private automobile or commuter trains, reliance on appliances and household equipment, and large shopping malls with self-service operations.[26] High-income gentrification replaces much of this capital intensity with workers, directly and indirectly. Similarly, high-income residents in the city depend to a much larger extent on hired maintenance staff than do occupants of the middle-class suburban home with its concentrated input of family labor and machinery.

Behind the delicatessens and specialty boutiques that have replaced the self-service supermarket and department store lies a very different organization of work from that prevalent in large, standardized establishments. This difference in the organization of work is evident both in the retail and the production phases. High-income gentrification generates a demand for goods and services that are frequently not mass-produced or sold through mass outlets. Customized production, small runs, specialty items, and fine food dishes are generally produced through labor-intensive methods and sold through small, full-service outlets. Subcontracting part of this production to low-cost operations, and to sweatshops or households, is common. The overall outcome for the job supply and the range of firms involved in this production and delivery is rather different from that characterizing the large department stores and supermarkets where mass production is prevalent and hence large, standardized factories located outside the city or the region are the norm. Proximity to stores is of far greater importance with customized producers. Mass production and mass distribution outlets facilitate unionizing.

[24] U.S. Dept. of Commerce, various years.
[25] Sassen-Koob, "The New Labor Demand in Global Cities."
[26] Sassen, *Mobility of Labor and Capital.*

The expansion in the low-income population has also contributed to the proliferation of small operations and the move away from large-scale standardized factories and large chain stores for low-price goods. In good part the consumption needs of the low-income population are met by manufacturing and retail establishments that are small, rely on family labor, and often fall below minimum safety and health standards. Cheap, locally produced sweatshop garments, for example, can compete with low-cost Asian imports. A growing range of products and services, from low-cost furniture made in basements to "gypsy cabs" and family day care, is available to meet the demands of the growing low-income population.

In any large city, a proliferation of small, low-cost service operations, made possible by the massive concentration of people and the daily inflow of commuters and tourists, tends to occur. This proliferation will often create intense inducements to open up such operations as well as intense competition and very marginal returns. Under such conditions, the cost of labor is crucial and contributes to the likelihood of a high concentration of low-wage jobs. This tendency was confirmed by Sheets, Nord, and Phelps when they found that each 1 percent increase in retail jobs in 1980 resulted in a 0.88 percent average increase in below-poverty-level jobs in the 100 largest metropolitan areas.[27]

Numerous examples show how increased inequality in earnings reshapes the consumption structure and how this in turn affects the organization of work. Among the cases to be discussed in greater detail in the next section are the following: the creation of a special taxi line that only serves the financial district, and the increase of gypsy cabs in low-income neighborhoods not serviced by regular cabs; the increase in highly customized woodwork in gentrified areas, and low-cost rehabilitation in poor neighborhoods; the increase of homeworkers and sweatshops making either very expensive designer items for boutiques or very cheap products.

In brief, we found that there are inducements to informalization in the combination of several trends, particularly evident in major cities: (1) the increased demand for highly priced customized services and products by the expanding high-income population, (2) the increased demand for extremely low-cost services and products by the expanding low-income population, (3) the demand for customized services and goods, or limited runs from firms that are either final or intermediate buyers with a corresponding growth of subcontracting, (4) the increasing inequality in the bidding power of firms in a context of acute pressures on land—pressures caused by the rapid growth and strong agglomerative pattern of the lead-

[27] Sheets, Nord, and Phelps, *Impact of Service Industries on Underemployment.*

ing industries, and (5) the continuing demand by various firms and sectors of the population, including demand from leading industries and high-income workers, for a range of goods and services typically produced in low-profit firms, which find it increasingly difficult to survive given rising rents and production costs. The transformation of final and intermediate consumption and the growing inequality in the bidding power for space of firms and households invite informalization in a broad range of activities and spheres of the economy; the existence of an informal economy in turn emerges as a mechanism for reducing costs (even for firms and households that do not need it for survival) and for providing flexibility in instances where this is essential or advantageous.

THE INFORMAL ECONOMY

Our research involved secondary data analysis; ethnographic research in select communities and several kinds of workplaces; interviews with informed individuals, including local planning officials, union officials, community members, and inspectors from several government agencies; and data on occupational safety and health violators, along with violators of overtime or minimum-wage legislation. On the basis of these data, we targeted certain industries for more in-depth study of the informal component of their production chain. We conducted fieldwork in communities identified as having a large informal sector or having a high density of immigration population, knowing that these factors are good indicators of informal activity. We used interviews with community boards and local development corporation representatives to target specific sites with recorded violations.[28] Zoning maps and data from the Department of Buildings were used to obtain more detailed information on informal producers. We also did field visits in four of the five boroughs of New York City. These visits and interviews helped us to identify the extent and kinds of informal activities in these communities; assess how existing regulations influence informal producers; and determine if new modes of regulation are needed.[29]

On the basis of our secondary data analysis, fieldwork, and interviews, we found the following profile of the informal economy in the New York City area: (1) Informal work is present in a rather wide range of industrial sectors, though with varying incidence. These sectors include apparel, accessories, general construction contractors, special trade con-

[28] Complaints of businesses in violation of legally defined uses of building or zoning ordinances are normally registered with local development corporations and community boards before being referred to the Department of Buildings.

[29] Columbia University, "The Informal Economy."

tractors, footwear, toys and sporting goods, furniture and woodwork, electronic components, packaging, and transportation. (2) Such operations were also found in lesser measure in activities such as packaging notions; making lampshades, artificial flowers, or jewelry; distribution activities; photo engraving; and manufacturing of explosives. (3) A strong tendency exists for such operations to be located in densely populated areas with very high shares of immigrants. (4) There is an emergent tendency for "traditional" sweatshop activities (notably, garments) to be displaced from areas undergoing partial residential and commercial gentrification. (5) Finally, new forms of unregistered work catering to a new clientele tended to be located in gentrifying areas.[30]

Evidence points to several distinctions in the informalization process in New York City that have implications for theory and policy. One set of distinctions concerns the origin of the demand for informally produced or distributed goods and services. We can identify informal activities that result from the demand for goods and services in the larger economy, either from final consumers or firms. Most of the informal work in the garment, furniture, construction, packaging, and electronics industries is of this type. And we can identify informal activities that result from demand internal to the communities where such activities are performed. Immigrant communities are a leading example, and probably account for much of this second type of demand.

Second, an examination of the conditions that may be contributing directly to the demand for informal production and distribution indicates several sources. One of these is competitive pressures in certain industries, notably apparel, to reduce labor costs given massive competition from low-wage, third-world countries. Informal work in this instance represents an acute example of exploitation. Another source is a rapid increase in the volume of renovations, alterations, and small-scale new construction undertaken to transform many areas of the city from low-income, often dilapidated neighborhoods into higher-income commercial and residential areas. This process, which for many other cities in the United States would have involved a massive program of new construction, was for New York mostly a matter of rehabilitating old structures. The volume of work, its small scale, its labor intensity and high skill content, and the short-term nature of each project all encourage a large informal work industry. A third source for demand of informal production and distribution is the inadequate provision of services and goods by the formal sector. This inadequacy may consist of excessively high prices,

[30]Sassen, "New York City's Informal Economy"; Sassen and Grover, "Unregistered Work in New York."

inaccessible or difficult-to-reach locations of formal providers, or actual lack of provision. The inadequacy of formal provision involves mostly low-income individuals or areas; examples are gypsy cabs serving areas not served by regular cabs, informal neighborhood child-care centers, low-cost furniture manufacturing shops, informal auto repair, and other activities providing personal services and goods. The existence of a cluster of informal shops can eventually generate agglomeration economies that induce additional entrepeneurs to move in. This process is illustrated by the emergence of auto-repair districts, vendors' districts, or clusters of both regulated and informal shops in those few areas not zoned for manufacturing, but which are viable for such activity given the increased demand for space by high bidders. The existence of a diverse set of informal firms making use of a variety of labor supplies may lower entry costs for entrepreneurs and hence contribute to further expansion of the informal economy. This last source can be construed as a type of supply-side factor: it signals to employers the existence of an informal "hiring hall."

Third, we can distinguish different types of firms in the informal economy in terms of the locational constraints to which firms are subject. For some firms, access to cheap labor, though typically in combination with access to the city's final or intermediate markets, is the determining inducement for a New York City location because it allows these firms to compete with third-world factories or to compete in markets with rapid production turnover times. Indeed, the expansion of the Hispanic population in New Jersey has brought about rapid growth of garment sweatshops and homework in several New Jersey counties. In contrast, many of the shops that engage in customized production or operate on subcontracts evince a host of locational dependencies on New York City. These firms are bound to the city for some or all of the following reasons: demand is local and involves typically specific clients or customers; vicinity to design and specialized services is important; brief turnover time between completion of design and production is possible; demand is predicated on the existence of a highly dynamic overall economic situation that generates a critical volume of demand and spending capability on the part of buyers; and immigrant communities exist there that have some traits of enclave economies and hence contain specific types of markets. In other words, the market for these firms is right there in New York City; leaving the city for a lower-cost location is not an option. In this case, informalization functions to incorporate firms into an economic system with great inequality in the bidding power of firms for land and a sharp increase in the demand for space by high-bidding firms, both factors having contributed to reduce sharply the supply of low-cost space.

Fourth, we can distinguish differences in the types of jobs we found in the informal economy. Many of the jobs are unskilled, with no training opportunities, and involve repetitive tasks. On the other hand, the growth of informalization in the construction and furniture industries can be seen as having brought about a re-skilling of the labor force. Some jobs pay extremely low wages, others pay average wages, and still others were found to pay above-average rates. But typically employers or contractors save by entering the informal market.

Fifth, we can identify different types of locations in the spatial organization of the informal economy. Immigrant communities are a key location for informal activities meeting both internal and external demand for goods and services. Gentrifying areas are a second important location; these areas contain a large array of informal activities in renovation, alteration, small-scale new construction, woodwork, and installations. A third location is characterized by informal-manufacturing and industrial-service areas serving a citywide market.

In sum, important sources for the informalization of various activities are found in larger urban economies. Among these sources is the demand for those products and services that lend themselves to small-scale production, are associated with rapid transformations brought about by commercial and residential gentrification, or are not satisfactorily provided by the formal sector. This trend suggests that a good share of the informal sector is not simply the result of immigrant survival strategies, but is also an outcome of structural patterns or transformations in the larger economy of a city such as New York. Workers and firms respond to the opportunities contained in these patterns and transformations. However, in order to respond, workers and firms need to be positioned in distinct ways. Immigrant communities represent what could be described as a "favored" structural location to seize the opportunities for entrepreneurship as well as often undesirable jobs being generated by informalization.

While the Mexican immigration in New York City is relatively small, it offers an insight into how labor market conditions and the new immigration law interact to produce opportunities and barriers for the formation of a new, mostly undocumented immigration, and its incorporation into the New York City economy.

THE NEW MEXICAN IMMIGRATION

We can explain the increase in Mexican immigration to New York City as the result of changes in the demand for labor, the effects of IRCA, and of Mexico's deepening economic crisis in the 1980s. The confluence of

these factors has facilitated the emergence and rapid growth of new immigration networks from Mexico.[31] The formation of these new networks
is important because it is precisely what IRCA sought to discourage; because such networks constitute the primary mechanism by which a transnational labor market is established and reproduced between Mexico and
the United States; and because widespread emergence of these new networks signals the emergence of New York City as a major new receiver
of Mexican immigration.

The Mexican community in New York City is not new. Its earliest
history dates back to the 1920s, and the community has experienced a
steady influx of new immigrants since the early to mid-1960s. What is
new is the steep growth in the number of Mexicans over the last three
years, the apparent lack of integration of these new immigrants into the
established Mexican community, and the noticeable emergence of Mexicans as a preferred labor source in the low-wage sector of New York
City's economy. We posit that IRCA has been an important factor in
these developments. Recently arrived Mexican immigrants to New York
seem to be integrated into four different labor markets, largely determined by their membership in a kinship network. They are the low-wage
service sector, self-employment, the day labor market, and the more traditional "immigrant" industries, such as apparel. The existence of rather
developed informal economic networks provides a structure for these
forms of participation in the city's economy.

In the discussion of each of these forms of labor market participation,
we will distinguish between IRCA's identification effect and its facilita-
tion effect. The large number of newly legalized Mexicans in New York

[31] The rise in Mexican immigration to New York City has been noted by various sources.
Mexicans accounted for the second largest number of legalization applications in New York
City, surprising city and state officials. New York/Newsday has run stories on this emerging
ethnic group, and has even sent reporters to Mexican villages. Spanish language newspapers
have noted Mexicans as the fastest growing Spanish-speaking ethnic group in the city, and
estimated the numbers of Mexicans in New York City to range between 60,000 and
100,000. Researchers in California note that an increasing number of recently arrived
Mexican immigrants indicate they will move on to New York City. Finally, my research in
New York City suggests that the number of undocumented Mexicans here has increased
significantly—perhaps even doubling—since 1987. See Josh DeWind, "The Effects of Le-
galization Outreach on the Rates of Application in New York City," report to the New
York Community Trust (Fall 1988); Sylvia Moreno, "Between Two Worlds," *Sunday
Magazine, New York Newsday* (8 Dec. 1988); Robert C. Smith, "The Immigration Labor
Process, the Welfare State, and the Informal Economy: A Look into the Effects of the 1986
Immigration Reform and Control Act in New York and Pennsylvania," paper prepared for
the Immigration Research Project, Cornell University, Ithaca, N.Y., 1988; Robert C. Smith,
"A Comparative Study of Two Transnational Communities: U.S. and Mexico," a working
paper for Columbia University's Institute for Latin American and Iberian Studies,
forthcoming.

City now provide a nucleus around which new immigration networks are forming. IRCA has, ironically, facilitated undocumented immigration by lowering the cost and uncertainty of immigration. Yet even while the costs of migrating to New York City have decreased, the identification effect has limited the kinds of jobs for which these new immigrants can apply and has caused greater demand for Mexican labor in certain "labor-sensitive" industries, especially in the service sector. Newly legalized immigrants seem more willing to travel, and this may be widening the reach of immigration networks across the United States. "Labor-intensive" industries, as discussed by Adriana Marshall,[32] are those which expand their use of labor and their production as labor gets cheaper, and produce less or not at all when labor costs rise.[33]

The most important labor market for Mexicans is in labor-intensive service industries. These have grown sharply in the last several years, as discussed above. Mexican immigrants who have arrived within the last three years have found jobs working in restaurants, ethnic take-out places, as delivery and messenger boys, and in other such consumer industries. A prominent example is bicycle delivery boys in midtown.

Over the last three years, the geography of immigrant Mexican employment networks has expanded greatly in Manhattan. The networks have moved "down" from Washington Heights in northern Manhattan and "up" from downtown Manhattan, to cover most of the island. Other boroughs have also experienced an influx of Mexicans, especially Brooklyn and the Bronx. In the restaurant industry in particular, a front-house, back-house pattern has emerged: Mexicans wash the dishes and prepare the food, while the non-Mexican owners (frequently immigrants themselves) take orders and serve food. Similar patterns have been noted in California.[34]

Many recently arrived Mexicans find jobs as shelf-stockers in Dominican *bodegas* and Korean green groceries. These workers were paid $180.00 per week for 6 days, 12 or more hours per day, for a little over $2.00 per hour. Our inquiries found that in a section of Manhattan, more than a third of the Korean green groceries employed Mexicans in this way. In the Korean case, the oversupply of Mexicans appears to create

---

[32] See Adriana Marshall, *New Immigrants in New York* (Ithaca, N.Y., 1987).

[33] On the greater mobility of newly legalized immigrants, and the increased mobility of their undocumented relatives, see Robert Smith, "Report on the Effects of IRCA in the Pennsylvania Mushroom Industry," prepared for the Center for Immigration Studies and funded by the Ford Foundation (Washington, 1990).

[34] Rick Morales, "The Utilization of Mexican Immigrants in the Restaurant Industry: The Case of San Diego County," in Wayne Cornelius, ed., *The Changing Role of Mexican Labor in the U.S. Economy* (San Diego, forthcoming, 1992).

jobs, because Korean green grocers usually employ unpaid family labor in these positions; Mexicans in this case thus seem to serve as a cheap substitute for family labor. The employment of Mexicans in these *bodegas* and green grocers also seems to be repeated in some Greek-owned delis and diners. Some Mexican informants indicated that they were referred to their green grocery, *bodega,* or deli jobs by Mexican relatives who worked for a Korean, Dominican, or Greek relative of their boss. These hiring patterns suggest that parallel immigration networks between immigrant employers and immigrant employees are facilitating the formation of new Mexican immigration networks.

The second employment situation of these undocumented workers is in traditional "immigrant" industries, such as garment manufacturing, that have been declining nationally but show some signs of regional revitalization in a few sectors and growth of informal operations.[35] We have found well-developed kinship recruiting from Mexico in the garment industry, which has apparently increased in the post-IRCA period and most strongly over the past year. Women are the predominant work force in the garment industry, and many balance homework with more traditional household duties. The emergence in the last several years of Mexican entrepreneurs in the garment industry seems to have been important in increasing the number of Mexicans working there.

IRCA appears to have contributed to the increase in the demand for Mexican labor in the New York City garment industry and to the emergence of a new labor market in the informal economy. Dominican garment workers in New York City told us that there were certain garment shops where only Mexicans—or other newly arrived undocumented workers such as Salvadorans or Guatemalans—would take jobs because the pay was so low. Dominicans and other members of established immigrant groups would not take such jobs. Others reported incidents where newly hired undocumented workers were paid less than the minimum wage and less than other workers with documents. Finally, in the last two years signs have been seen posted in the garment industry announcing, "Mexicans Wanted."

The third labor market situation involves recently arrived, undocumented Mexican immigrants who have circumvented IRCA's employer-sanctions provisions by becoming, in effect, self-employed in the informal economy. A prominent example is that of flower vendors who sell from shopping carts on neighborhood streets. Others sell *churros* (Mexican

---

[35] See also the research on day labor markets in John Gaber, "The Informal Economy: Regulation and Reproduction," Ph.D. diss. in progress (Columbia University, Department of Urban Planning).

donuts). The economic and social organization of the flower vendors has increased dramatically over the last year, along with their knowledge of the New York City subway system. Whereas at first these vendors sold only along stops that could be reached via the #1 Broadway Local, which traverses Manhattan from south to north, they now sell in good locations in all four boroughs, primarily in low-income neighborhoods where the police will not bother them. There is an unofficial line in northern Manhattan: south of that line vendors sell, but must keep moving or the police may confiscate their flowers; north of that line, they can sell in the same place all day without being harassed by the police. Vending spots are respected alternatively by custom and on a first-come, first-served basis. Some of these vendors have organized themselves to buy flowers collectively, and have sponsored relatives who wish to come to New York to sell. Frequently, a relative will take over the vending while another goes home for a visit.

The fourth employment situation is the day labor market. The emergence of a day labor market of Mexicans in New York City is new and echoes patterns in Southern California and on Long Island for landscaping.[36] These workers typically are not members of well-connected immigration networks, and have trouble finding good jobs. Some wait outside grocery stores, especially on Sunday, to carry packages home in the Dominican neighborhoods of Washington Heights. Others who have relatives working in garment factories might help fill a specific order if the factory employer gets caught short.

The foregoing discussion focused on the creation of low-wage jobs and IRCA's impact on the increase in Mexican immigration to New York City. We posit that IRCA caused Mexicans to be identified as the newest source of plentiful, cheap labor in New York, with exploitation as a frequent result. While IRCA's legalization program lowers the cost of new immigration by forming new networks around relatives who received amnesty, the employer-sanctions provisions have limited both the kinds of jobs these recently arrived immigrants can apply for and the pay they receive. We noted that $180.00 per week for about 70 hours of work seemed to be the prevailing "undocumented" wage for Mexicans.

In the remainder of this section, we will range beyond the demand for Mexican labor in New York to discuss the "push" forces in Mexico and to explain how class formation becomes transnational when particular Mexican villages become the sources of labor supply that match a par-

[36] Sassen, "New York City's Informal Economy," in *The Informal Sector;* Sassen, "Immigrant Women in the Garment and Electronics Industries in New York," Third Research Report presented to the Revson Foundation, New York (May 1989).

ticular demand for labor in New York City.[37] Some of these dynamics are internal to the immigration process, while others seem to be caused by the increasing importance of the national and international economies for Mexico's poor (including the liberalization and internationalization of the economy in the 1980s).[38] We will also concentrate on the dynamics internal to the immigration process itself by examining how IRCA contributes to the formation of class transnationally: it has caused income to be determined according to the kind of immigration network into which one is incorporated.

The importance of the general economic crisis, in which wages in Mexico fell 50 percent during the 1980s, is shown by the emergence of Puebla, especially the southern part of the state, as an important sending district in the post-IRCA period. Wayne Cornelius's work in southern California indicates that although Puebla had not been an important sender before IRCA, it has been the fourth largest sender of recently arrived, job-seeking immigrants in the post-IRCA period.[39] Robert Smith's research in New York and in the Mizteca Sur region, which includes the area where the Puebla, Oaxaca, and Guerrero states meet, indicates that the region has been experiencing a steady out-migration that has accelerated during the last several years. Many of the immigrants Smith interviewed in New York are first-time immigrants coming directly from their villages to New York City.

In the summer of 1988, Smith researched a *municipio*, which we will call "Progreso," and the surrounding region. The causes of the outmigration in Progreso involve the creation of expectations and the formation of a transnational class of workers. Progreso has a twenty-five-year history as the "epicenter" of out-migration from the southern part of Puebla, and the president of the municipio estimated that about 40 percent of the 10,000 Progresistas are in the United States at any one time. The reasons for the out-migration from Progreso are similar to those Richard Mines found in his 1981 study of a rural community in

---

[37] For a more extended treatment of the same topic in a different case, see Robert C. Smith, "Social Structure of Accumulation, Immigration Pathways, and IRCA: The Construction of Labor Markets in the Pennsylvania Mushroom Industry, 1969–1989," in Wayne A. Cornelius, ed., *The Changing Roles of Mexican Immigration in the U.S. Economy: Sectoral Perspectives* (La Jolla, Calif., 1990).

[38] Merilee F. Grindeile, Searching for Rural Development: Labor Migration and Employment in Mexico (Ithaca, N.Y., 1988); Sassen, *The Mobility of Labor and Capital.*

[39] Puebla has not been listed as an important sender of immigrants in previous studies. Kearny has done work in the Mizteca Baja, in parts of Oaxaca farther south than the area being considered here. See Michael Kearny, "Integration of the Mixteca and the Western U.S. Border Region via Migratory Wage Labor," in Ina Rosental-Urey, ed., *Regional Impacts of U.S.-Mexican Relations* (San Diego, 1986.)

Zacatecas.[40] Mines found that out-migration widened differences in wealth and led to a concentration of land ownership in a few hands. Moreover, a "dollarization" of the economy occurs as migrants who reside in the United States remit money; local residents must compete with their neighbors, whose incomes are multiplied by the exchange rate. Out-migration is encouraged both by the negative effect of this dollarization and by the positive "demonstration effect," as potential migrants are lured north by the promise of stereos, cars, and a generally higher standard of living.

The class-widening dynamic seen in Mines' work is manifest even more strongly in the case of Progreso because of the incorporation of its labor force into New York's labor markets. In Mines' village, workers could be incorporated into networks that offered work in the agricultural or service economies in southern California. Workers who chose southern California (the "fortunate" group) were offered better pay and the possibility of eventually legalizing their status. The New York City labor market, however, into which Progreso's work force was integrated, offered greater opportunities than southern California for legalization and financial success. Some of the earliest migrants from Progreso now own restaurants and factories, and one even owns a hotel in Acapulco. The dollarization of Progreso's economy was correspondingly greater, and the push of migration to New York was stronger as well.

In addition to the divisions such as whether one's job network taps into union or non-union jobs, or whether one's relatives have management positions in a restaurant, IRCA has introduced a new division that may widen further the differences in the class structure of the sending communities. Lack of legal status for post-IRCA migrants, especially for those who lacked a migrant network established prior to IRCA, lowers their status relative to earlier migrants from the same *municipios*. These workers earn less and seem more likely to work in the informal economy than those workers in pre-IRCA networks. Moreover, because IRCA has increased the uncertainty of how long one will stay in the United States and of the prospects of finding a job after returning to Mexico, it has encouraged these more unfortunate immigrants to bring their families north, even though they would ordinarily remain "lone male" migrants at that stage of the migrant cycle. Bringing part or all of their families to New York City creates further disadvantages for these workers, because this city has a much higher standard of living than Puebla. Ultimately, the

[40] Richard Mines, "Developing a Community Tradition of Migration: A Field Study in Rural Zacatecas, Mexico, and California Settlement Areas" (San Diego, Center for U.S.-Mexican Studies, 1981).

class structure of the *municipios* of southern Puebla will be affected, as income and welfare are increasingly determined by structural factors such as access to labor markets based on kinship networks, legal status, and whether one has migrated before or after IRCA.

CONCLUSION

The decline in U.S. manufacturing, the shift to services, and the reorganization of work in both these sectors has entailed significant transformations in the conditions of employment. While the shift to services has resulted in the dominance of finance and advanced services, it has also contributed to the demand for low-wage workers—directly through the job supply, and indirectly through the sphere of social reproduction or consumption. In addition, the decline of manufacturing has brought about job losses and a downgrading of many of the remaining or newly created jobs—that is, the expansion of sweatshops and industrial homework. One overall outcome has been a growing casualization of employment. Casualization opens up the hiring process, lifts restrictions on employers, and typically lowers the direct and indirect costs of labor.

It is in this context that we have considered the new Mexican immigration to New York City and the incorporation of these migrants into what is a leading post-industrial city. Our argument is that recent developments have facilitated the formation of new migration flows and that the casualization of many labor markets has made it possible for new undocumented immigrants to find jobs or become self-employed. IRCA has had a dual effect on the condition of immigrants. On the one hand, it has strengthened the position of those immigrants who have become legalized and, on the other hand, it has raised the vulnerability of those ineligible for regularization. By creating a critical mass of legalized Mexicans in New York who can help newcomers, IRCA has facilitated new immigration inflows, while the worsening conditions in Mexico have induced out-migration. This process, together with the growth of casual labor markets, has contributed to the formation of a transnational labor market. In sum, the new Mexican migration illuminates the relationship between IRCA, class formation, and the labor market patterns that arise from post-industrial growth patterns.

PART IV

Sectoral Dynamics and Interdependence

International Restructuring and Labor Market Interdependence: The Automobile Industry in Mexico and the United States

Raúl A. Hinojosa Ojeda and Rebecca Morales

A S IN PREVIOUS periods of industrial transformation, automobile manufacturing is setting trends in international investment production, sourcing, and trade; development and use of technology; patterns of labor-management relations; and the formation and use of the labor force. Important changes in all of these areas are particularly evident across Mexico and the United States, the two countries with the most industrial and labor market interdependence across the North-South border. Since the early 1970s, the restructuring of the automobile industry has increased internationalization and production sharing, linking as never before the fate of many types of workers.

Much debate surrounds the future of this restructuring. Some suggest that a greater tendency toward offshore production in the South is taking place, while others stress that the introduction of new technologies is paving the way for reconcentrated production in the North. How this industrial restructuring evolves promises to affect the level and quality of employment and earnings within both countries, as well as the demand and supply of immigrant workers across countries. While policies of industrial restructuring and trade between Mexico and the United States

Research on this paper was supported by the Project on U.S.-Mexico Relations, Stanford University, the UCLA Program on Mexico, the UCLA Academic Senate, and the University of California Institute for Transportation Studies. This paper represents an equal effort on the part of both authors.

are most recently being developed with emphasis on balance of trade and debt repayment considerations, our intent is to refocus attention to the labor-market dimensions and possible alternative binational approaches to this policy discussion.

In the first of three parts, we analyze the patterns of production and employment in the Mexican and U.S. auto industries that emerged in the mid-1920s, were later consolidated in the postwar decades, and saw their demise in the late 1970s. In the United States, this period was characterized by the rise of so-called Fordist mass-production techniques, institutionalized labor-market regulations, and mass-consumption patterns. In Mexico, import substituting industrialization (ISI), which tried to reproduce some elements of the Fordist model, arose. This period of ISI comprised various crucial stages, which resulted from bargaining encounters between multinational corporations (MNCs) in the auto industry, labor organizations, and the Mexican and U.S. states as they developed trade and industrial policies. The resulting patterns of international investment, production, trade, and employment in the assembly and auto-parts segments of the industry proved conducive to high rates of growth and labor-management stability both within the auto industry and in other industrial sectors. However, these patterns were also cause to and accompanied by persistent problems in the Mexican economy, including (1) chronic trade and balance-of-payments deficits, and (2) a relative price regime biased against agriculture and exports and in favor of capital-intensive manufacturing. Both of these problems contributed to the migration of labor into U.S. labor markets.

In the second part of the paper, we explain the crisis and transition of this relatively stable pattern of auto production, trade, and labor use beginning in the 1970s. We show that the crisis of Fordism in the United States stemmed from an inability to match productivity increases and per-unit labor costs of international competitors who were gaining U.S. market share through imports. In Mexico, the balance-of-payments interests of the import-substituting industrialization pattern were simply no longer sustainable. This dual crisis set forth an intense restructuring of the industry across the United States and Mexico, the nature and direction of which is the subject of much debate. Some analysts say that in order to cut costs and increase economies of scale, the industry will develop in the direction of the "world car," where similar car models and auto parts will be produced in a standardized fashion in different parts of the world, particularly at lower-wage assembly sites, to serve a global market. Others say that a reconcentration of production will occur within advanced industrial countries as the increased use of automation and flexible technologies allow servicing of increasingly differentiated markets. A variety of data from the United States and Mexico show that neither postulate is accurate; rather, what characterizes the present restructuring is a continuum of strategies by firms that are adopting elements of both approaches.

In the final part of the paper, we present three scenarios of binational industrial restructuring and labor market evolution. We demonstrate that not only are the world-car and reconcentration patterns occurring simultaneously, but that each will have detrimental impacts on various labor markets in both countries, posing unprecedented challenges to corporations, worker organizations, and policymakers. In a third scenario, we examine the potentially positive growth and labor-market effects of a binational production-sharing and market-sharing approach to restructuring. The success of this international cooperative approach will necessitate a wide variety of new institutional arrangements between states, labor organizations, and corporations. The conditions for these arrangements must still be developed.

FORDIST AND IMPORT-SUBSTITUTING INDUSTRIALIZATION

The period from the mid-1920s until the late 1960s marked the rise of Fordist industrialization in the United States and of ISI in Mexico—a complementary international division of labor that was consolidated in the post–World War II decades. Fordism in northern countries was characterized by (1) high levels of productivity growth based on mass-production technology, which was complemented by the advent of mass-consumption markets sustained by rising real wages (assured through collective bargaining pacts), and (2) government commitments to policies for stimulating aggregate demand.[1] As long as wages generated demand for consumer goods and reinvested profits generated a demand for productivity-enhancing capital goods for mass production, the articulated industrial base of the United States enjoyed a virtuous growth cycle.

In developing countries like Mexico, industrialization involved setting tariffs on consumer goods and importing capital goods. Increased domestic production and employment were maintained through demand growth derived from rising incomes of urban middle classes and unionized workers. Urban/rural relative prices, set by the state, subsidized workers' food consumption at the expense of productivity-enhancing in-

---

[1] Michael Aglietta, *A Theory of Capitalist Regulation: The U.S. Experience* (London, 1976); Michael J. Piore and Charles F. Sabel, *The Second Industrial Divide* (New York, 1984).

vestment in the countryside, setting the stage for migrations to service and urban-manufacturing labor markets or to the United States. An overvalued exchange-rate regime reduced the relative price of imported capital goods, contributing to a bias favoring capital-intensive manufacturing at the expense of traditional primary exports.[2] Despite growing sectoral and distributional imbalances, this pattern of growth could be sustained as long as lucrative, protected markets continued to grow and attract domestic and multinational investors, and as long as traditional exports, net foreign investment, and loans could finance the importation of capital and intermediate goods.

The auto industry was a leading sector in this international development pattern, not only in setting trends in technology, consumption, and labor-management relations, but in its direct and indirect contributions to growth in industrial activity and employment. While U.S. auto production rose and stabilized, representing a smaller percentage of global production, the rapid growth of the auto industry in Mexico resulted in its increased importance in the economy. In addition, related growth in assembly and auto-parts employment occurred, with auto-related employment reaching 21.5 percent of total U.S. employment in 1977. Auto-related investment and trade also played an important role in the problematic relations concerning the balance of payment between both countries, with the Mexican automotive trade deficit reaching 57.7 percent of the total deficit in 1981.

The evolution of labor markets was an integral part of this international pattern of development. In the United States, union contracts explicitly linking wage increases to productivity—the landmark provision of the 1950 General Motors-United Auto Workers "peace of Detroit" pact—bifurcated labor markets between organized workers in large, dynamic manufactures and those in smaller, usually unorganized firms. Wages at multinational assemblers, particularly in the Detroit area, traditionally led those other industrial sectors, while wages at smaller auto-parts establishments lagged.[3] In the 1970s, this less-renumerated auto-parts sector of the industry began to employ immigrant undocumented workers from Mexico.[4]

[2] Clark W. Reynolds, *The Mexican Economy: Twentieth-Century Structure and Growth* (New Haven, Conn., 1970).

[3] Wage data for the years 1958 to 1976 were taken from U.S. Department of Labor, *Employment and Earnings: United States, 1909–1978* (Washington, 1979); those data for 1977 to the present were derived from U.S. Department of Labor, *Employment and Earnings, Supplement Revised Establishment Data* (Washington, Nov. 1989).

[4] Rebecca Morales, "Transitional Labor: Undocumented Workers in the Los Angeles Automotive Industry," *International Migration Review* 17, 570–96.

In Mexico, manufacturing wages have historically exceeded average wages in other sectors, with unionized workers in those final-assembly auto plants run by MNCs offering among the highest manufacturing wages.[5] Auto assembly was relatively capital-intensive; its contribution to employment represented a much lower percentage than its contribution to output. Auto parts, on the other hand, contributed more to employment than to its share of output.[6] Wages in assembly were far greater than those in auto parts, where firms were smaller and the organization of the work force weaker.[7] Thus, the auto-parts sector was more related to those labor markets in which the surplus labor derived from rural to urban migrations predominated.

At the height of the Fordist/ISI period, these different labor-market segments evolved rather independently. Trade competition was not an employment issue. As long as auto investments in the United States were sufficient to maintain employment and productivity growth, overseas investments by MNCs were not detrimental and in fact could benefit workers in globally powerful corporations. This relatively complementary situation, however, changed dramatically in the 1970s.

Periodization

The development of relations between the U.S. and Mexican automobile industries can be divided into two major periods, each containing a number of specific phases. The first phase, the rise of Fordism/ISI, includes the years leading up to 1925 and the important 1925–1969 period. The second phase, which involves crisis and tradition, encompasses the years 1969 to the present. These periods in the rise, crisis, and transition of the international industry and labor-market structures are distinguished by the development of specific relations between international and domestic firms, nation-states, and domestically organized and unorganized labor—interactions that took place within particular global environments of auto-industry competition and negotiations between developed and developing countries.

Pre-1925. European automobile producers, the builders of the first commercially viable automobiles in 1885, dominated global car production as late as the turn of the century. Although U.S. producers initially suffered from high costs and poor quality, the nation's industry was

[5] SPP (Secretaria de Programación y Presupuesto), *Sistema de Cuentas Nacionales de Mexico* (Mexico City, various years); Comision Nacional de Salarios Minimos, *Salarios Minimos* (Mexico City, various years).

[6] SPP, *Sistema de Cuentas Nacionales de Mexico, 1979–1981* vol. 1, no. 2.

[7] Secretaria de Industrai y Comercio, *Censo industrial de 1970* (Mexico City, 1975).

helped by the early imposition of a 45 percent ad valorem tariff, which was reduced to 25 percent in 1922.[8]

As their domestic market grew, U.S. automakers were better able to respond due to their early use of mass production for national markets (the European method involved low-volume, custom-built craft production). By 1907, U.S. auto exports exceeded imports, and with Ford's adoption of the moving assembly in 1914 and General Motors' annual model changes in the 1920s, mass producers quickly dominated several national markets. Production at Ford rose from 12,000 cars in 1909 to 2,000,000 in 1921. The Europeans responded by protecting their markets through high tariffs, a tactic that prompted Ford to lead the early internationalization of the U.S. industry by building plants in Canada in 1904 (behind a 35 percent tariff) and England in 1911.[9] In contrast, the Mexican market throughout this period consisted of automobiles manufactured abroad, either custom-built or assembled in the incipient mass-production lines of the United States.

1925–1961. With the 1924 Auto Decree, the Mexican state attempted to limit importation of completely assembled cars by imposing high tariffs while reducing tariffs on imported assembly components by 50 percent. The new situation was thus similar to that faced by U.S. auto producers in Europe. The strategic response of foreign carmakers was similar as well—they built local assembly plants for small production runs, using only parts imported in complete knockdown kits and assembling only with craft and primitive, mass-production techniques. Ford, the most powerful U.S. company at that time, was the first to open a Mexican assembly plant in 1925. It was followed by one U.S. firm after another before World War II and was joined after the war by European and Japanese producers. Between 1941 and 1945, four assemblers opened with Mexican equity participation, indicating the strength of local capital to become involved in the automotive sector (a phenomenon not found this early in other Latin American countries).[10] By 1961, twelve

[8] Mira Wilkins, "Multinational Automobile Enterprises and Regulation: An Historical Overview," in Douglas H. Ginsberg and William J. Abernathy, eds., *Government, Technology, and the Future of the Automobile* (New York, 1980), 221–58.

[9] Motor Vehicle Manufacturers Association, *Digest of Import Duties Levied by Selected Countries* (Detroit, 1974); Toyota Motor Sales Corporation, *The Motor Industry of Japan, 1981* (Tokyo, 1981); Daniel T. Jones, "Maturity and Crisis in the European Car Industry," research paper for the University of Sussex Science Policy Research Unit (Brighton, Eng., 1981); and tariff schedules in Alan Altshuler, et al., *The Future of the Automobile: The Report of MIT's International Automobile Program* (Cambridge, Mass., 1984), 17.

[10] Rhys Owen Jenkins, "Internationalization of Capital and the Semi-Industrialized Countries: The Case of the Motor Industry," *Review of Radical Political Economics* vol. 17, nos. 1 and 2 (1982), 59, 81.

firms were engaged in similar assembly operations and another seven firms imported assembled vehicles. Most of the early investments were made in the immediate vicinity of Mexico City, the major market during ISI.[11]

The first stages of ISI were thus initiated in lucrative protected markets where labor-intensive techniques could still be profitably employed. Assembly employment, however, remained relatively small, representing 1 percent of total employment and 3 percent of industrial production in 1940. Nevertheless, the census for that year already showed the beginnings of an employment multiplier effect with 115 repair shops employing 306 workers. During this period, no domestic auto parts were produced; 95 percent of primary assembly materials and 50 percent of repair materials were imported.[12]

The workers in these Mexican factories were primarily second-generation urban craft workers. The unionization structure was fractured from the outset as competing labor confederations each tried to gain a foothold in the industry. As a result, the level of strike activity in Mexico would rise only a generation later, during the postwar period.[13] In the United States, however, this period was characterized by intense labor strife. While there was some early strike activity among U.S. craft unions before World War I, broad union participation in the whole auto industry developed only in the mid-1930s. By 1941, with the signing of the Ford-United Auto Workers contract, all assembly workers in major firms in the United States and Canada were represented by a single bargaining agent. The uneven differences in union structure between the United States and Mexico have not changed up to the present time, severely complicating attempts at international union cooperation.[14]

1947–1961. The immediate post-war era saw a boom in Mexico auto consumption, with vehicle circulation increasing at a phenomenal rate through 1960 and domestic production still being regularly surpassed by imports.[15] In 1954, assembled auto imports constituted 14 percent of to-

---

[11] Douglas Bennett and Kenneth Sharpe, *Transnational Corporations versus the State: The Political Economy of the Mexican Automobile Industry* (Princeton, N.J., 1985).

[12] Secretaria de Comercio, *Census industrial de 1940* (Mexico City, 1945) and *Census industrial de 1945* (Mexico City, 1950).

[13] Ian Roxborough, "Labor in the Mexican Motor Vehicle Industry," in Rich Kronish and Kenneth Meride, eds., *The Political Economy of the Latin American Motor Vehicle Industry* (Cambridge, Mass., 1984); Kevin J. Middlebrook, "International Implications of Labor Change," in J. Dominquez, ed., *Mexico's Political Economy* (Beverly Hills, Calif., 1982).

[14] Middlebrook, "International Implications of Labor Change."

[15] Data are from Secretaria de Industria y Comercio-Dirección General de Estadisticas reported by NAFINSA in *Economia Mexicana en cifras* (Mexico City, 1974); Dirreción

tal imports. Road construction, meanwhile, was increasing more than 10 percent annually and truck production began to assume a larger role. From 1950 to 1960, the automobile industry began to play a much more important position in manufacturing production. At the same time, however, the participation of the auto industry in domestic intermediate demand lagged as the ratio of imported parts to total imported inputs continued to rise. Foreign inputs represented 80 percent of total value compared to 12 percent domestic from auto parts and 8 percent from oils, lubricants, and other primary inputs. Exports made up only 4 percent of imports, generating a growing balance-of-payments constraint on the national economy to which the state was forced to respond.[16]

In 1947, the Mexican government prohibited the importation of tires and wheels. Quotas on auto imports were imposed for the first time, lifted in 1950, and then replaced by quotas on auto parts and assembly materials in 1954. During this phase, employment in nonassembly aspects of auto production began to take off. Total auto employment rose from 4 percent to 6.5 percent of employment.

In terms of employment, however, large differences began to appear in the 1950 census between assemblers (462) and tire (644), chassis (23), and accessories (9) manufacturers. The assemblers accounted for 43 percent of employment and 77 percent of the value of output despite the fact that by 1960 there were 150 auto parts establishments, mostly for the aftermarket.[17]

1962–1969. In response to the chronic external problems of the auto industry, Mexico began to shift its strategy toward developing greater backward linkages (engines, drive trains, and other parts) through import substitution. The objectives of the state were thus to (1) directly confront the balance-of-payments problem, (2) capture more value-added in domestic production and thus increase the basis for national accumulation via domestic consumption, and (3) expand its political base by increasing both Mexican capital in the industry and employment for some of the most powerful unions in the country. The 1962 Auto Decree was an attempt to reach these goals by imposing local-content requirements of 60 percent over ten years on autos produced in Mexico, thus stimulating development of a domestic auto-parts industry that was to be 60 percent

---

General de Estadisticas reported by Industrialisation and Trade Project, *Introduction to the Mexican Automobile Industry* (Paris, OECD Development Centre, 1986).

[16] "Mexico, El Comercio Exterior de la Industria Automovilistics en Mexico," *Comercio Exterior* (Dec. 1982).

[17] Census industriales de 1940, 1945, 1960 [Industrial data for 1940, 1945, 1960] (Mexico City, various years).

nationally owned. Yet as of 1950, and especially after 1960, indirect taxes minus subsidies continued to fall in relation to the value of intermediate input demand, wages, and profits.[18]

This shift in state thinking coincided with a new outward-oriented vision by large multinationals toward the growing auto markets in Latin America.[19] Provided with a change in price and cost structures—due to higher tariffs on final automobiles and lower tariffs on imported capital goods, as well as lower net taxes—multinationals could take advantage of the growing markets and adopt the import-substitution strategy proposed by the government. This coincidence of interests set off a second wave of mass investment, characterized by new integrated plants (foundry, engines, and assembly) built on the perimeter of Mexico City, where wages were lower and union control less developed.

Several underlying conditions in the world automobile industry at this time were crucial for multinationals' decision to embark on these investments: (1) Fordism in northern countries allowed for production to be absorbed at sufficiently high economies of scale, making auto and auto-parts exports unnecessary for the profit realization,[20] (2) The operation of the product cycle allowed MNCs to obtain high rents on technology packets obsolete for use in the North but which could still be profitably transferred to the South,[21] (3) The existence of "easy" ISI levels meant that auto-parts production could be profitably transferred to Mexico, while other more capital- and technology-intensive auto-parts production could be maintained in the United States (automatic transmissions, and so forth), thus establishing a new international division of labor,[22] and (4) An intense struggle occurred among U.S. and European MNCs competing to establish themselves within new growing markets in the developing economies under threat of being left out of a relative share of global auto profits.[23]

For organized labor, this period corresponded to an increased fracturing of auto unions at the regional and confederation levels.[24] The Confederación de Trabajadores Mexicanos' (CTM) support of the policies of this phase of auto industrialization and union fracturing reflected a strat-

---

[18] Asociación Mexicana de Distribuidores de Automoviles, *Diez Anos del Sector Automotiviz en Mexico, 1973–1982* (Mexico City, 1983).

[19] Motor Vehicle Manufacturers Association, *World Motor Vehicle Data* (Detroit, 1986).

[20] Krish Bhaskar, *The Future of the World Motor Industry* (London, 1980).

[21] Jenkins, "Internationalization of Capital and the Semi-Industrialized Countries."

[22] Mark Bennett, *Public Policy and Industrial Development: The Case of the Mexican Auto Parts Industry* (Boulder, Colo., 1986).

[23] Bennett and Sharpe, *Transnational Corporations versus the State.*

[24] Roxborough, "Labor in the Mexican Motor Vehicle Industry."

TABLE I

Percentage Wage Increases in Mexican Automobile Terminal Industry, 1968–1976

Firm	1968	1969	1970	1971	1972	1973	1974	1975	1976	Period average
Diesel Nacional (DINA)	15.4%	–	15.1%	–	17.2%	–	10.0%*	–	15.0%*	14.5%
Nissan	17.3	–	16.1	–	17.1	–	22.0*	–	20.0*	18.5
Volkswagen	NA	–	16.0	–	20.0	–	24.0*	–	26.0*	21.5
General Motors	–	8.9	–	14.0	–	15.0	–	13.0	–	13.0
Ford	–	11.0	–	14.0	–	15.0	–	16.0*	–	14.0
Vehiculos Automotores Mexicanos (VAM)	14.7	–	16.7	–	14.1	–	NA	–	NA	15.2

SOURCE: With the exception of those values marked*, wage increases are calculated as the average increase over all wage categories, as reported in pay scales for each firm's collective contract for the year indicated. Nationwide "emergency" wage increases in 1973 (20%), 1974 (22%), and 1976 (23%) are not included in those percentage increases reported in this table. NA = Not Available. Values marked * are from Francisco Javier Aguilar García, "El movimiento obrero automotriz en Mexico, 1965–1976," Universidad Nacional Autonoma de Mexico, Facultad de Ciencias Politicas, tesis de licenciatura, May 1978: DINA, 1974 (p. 167), 1976 (p. 170); Nissan, 1974 (p. 195), 1976 (p. 200); Volkswagen, 1974 (p. 215), 1976 (p. 230); Ford, 1975 (p. 173).

egy to divide their competition from other unions in order to increase their own influence in the industry and in the state. The 1965 Confederación Revolucionaria Obrera y Campesina (CROC) strike against General Motors, where the principal demand was maintenance of a national union clause in the new Toluca contract under CROC, is a case in point. After the strike was broken, CTM eventually got the new contract, thus splitting the General Motors work force into two unions.

Both a quantitative and qualitative change also occurred in the work force in terms of class background and region of origin: the new type of worker employed in the plants outside Mexico City came from a more rural area. This new generation of workers coincided with the introduction of new productive processes—foundry work and mechanization with machine tools—as well as new technologies in final assembly. More unskilled workers were also needed for maintenance. The result was a segmentation between highly specialized machine workers and the assembly workers deskilled via Taylorism.

Table 1 shows the new differences in wages across plants. Workers in MNCs were paid more than those employed by state and private national-assembly firms and auto-parts producers. Overall, renumerations for wage workers in 1970 was 60 percent higher than the industrial average, whereas the productivity was 73 percent higher. Per-unit costs of labor were thus 12 percent lower, explaining the lower level of salaries to value-added.[25]

CRISIS AND TRANSITION

Beginning in the late 1960s and accelerating through the 1970s, the North-South reciprocity in growth, investment, and trade began eroding as part of a global economic crisis. The causes of this crisis can be traced to factors affecting the exhaustion of traditional sources of productivity growth across countries, the rise of newly competitive trading blocks, and increasing international monetary, financial, and price instability—all of which were compounded by the oil shocks of 1973 and 1979. Meanwhile, accelerating balance-of-payments deficits of ISI were increasingly financed through northern lending of dangerously large amounts of commercial bank resources. As productivity among U.S. firms dropped, the engine supporting continued wage increases slowed down, resulting in a drive for give-backs by organized labor. As policies of Keynesian demand management became less sustainable, this slow-down was used by the government to justify dismantling social programs. In a circular fashion,

[25] Motor Vehicle Manufacturers Association, *World Motor Vehicle Data.*

the breakdown of the engines of productivity growth led to the dissolu-
tion of institutions supporting traditional consumption market patterns
that supported the structure of production. With the slow-down of U.S.
economic activity, exacerbated by a monetary shock policy, traditional
patterns of growth, trade, and capital flows between North and South
ground to a halt.

Within the United States, the automobile industry suffered particularly
during this period. From a 75 percent share of world auto production in
1950, the portion attributed to U.S. firms dropped to 28 percent by 1970
and continued to fall to 20 percent by 1980.[26] U.S. manufacturers were
unable to match the productivity rates and per-unit labor costs of production of the increasingly more efficient Japanese and Germans. Though
U.S. firms realized an increase from 5.16 to 8.36 automobiles per thousand man-hours from 1953 to 1977, Japanese manufacturers underwent
a meteoric rise from 0.32 to 8.57 during the same period.[27] U.S. sales of
domestically made cars shrunk by one-third between 1978 and 1982.[28]
Assembly plants in the United States closed, in some cases to shift production to lower-cost, foreign sites, and in other cases to reorganize production more efficiently within the United States through new technology
or coproduction agreements. In two of the worst years, 1979 and 1980,
twenty plants closed or announced closure, which affected directly the
employment of over 50,000 workers, and indirectly an additional
350,000 to 650,000.[29] The number of employees working in auto assembly dropped from nearly 470,000 in 1978 to 317,500 in 1982, and unemployment among workers in motor vehicles and parts production rose
from 3.9 percent in 1977 to 20.4 percent in 1980.[30] Nonetheless, average
hourly wages increased from $10.52 in 1979 to $15.33 by 1984.[31]

The collapse of productivity growth and the rise in per-unit labor costs
in the North affected conditions for trade and investment in the South as
well. From a period of stable relations during the early 1960s, through
the breakdown of Fordism into the 1970s, North-South development
patterns grew increasingly linked. During the 1960s, technological ad-

[26] U.S. Department of Commerce, *Census of Manufactures* (Washington, various issues).
[27] Japanese Ministry of International Trade and Industry (Tokyo, various issues).
[28] Secretaria de Industria y Commercio, *Trabajo y Salarios Industriales* (various issues).
[29] Carol MacLennan and John O'Donnell, "The Effects of the Automotive Transition on
Employment: A Plant and Community Study," report to the Transportation System Center,
U.S. Department of Transportation, Dec. 1980.
[30] Bureau of Labor Statistics, *Employment and Earnings* (Washington, 1971–1986);
Motor Vehicle Manufacturers Association, "Economic Indicators: The Motor Vehicle's
Role in the U.S. Economy," *MUMA Bulletin* (31 July 1986), 10.
[31] *Ibid.*

vances in the North's consumer durable-goods industry were complemented by the transfer of older technology to the South for an extended life. Within Latin America, ISI policies progressively shifted the composition of imports from final goods toward capital goods and intermediate inputs. Though the trade relation generated national deficits, these were offset by the increasing inflows of foreign capital—first as direct foreign investment in manufacturing, and later as commercial bank loans. The U.S. share of total direct foreign investment in Latin America grew to 59 percent by 1969, with over 60 percent of that allocated to manufacturing in rapidly industrializing countries such as Mexico.[32] Despite a relatively stable North-South division of production, an apparent denationalization was also taking place. U.S. productive capacity was gradually shifting to developing nations, while domestic firms in these countries failed to realize significant growth due to direct takeovers and competition.

As a target of national industrial policy, the automobile industry in Mexico was greatly affected by these transformations. With the 1962 Auto Decree, Mexico pushed forward import-substitution strategies of stimulating backward linkages by establishing a 60 percent local-content requirement on the value of automobiles for final market, including the engine and other major parts of the drive train. Furthermore, Mexico insisted that parts suppliers could not be directly owned by the assemblers and had to have 60 percent Mexican participation. Local suppliers, even though many were subsidiaries of U.S. firms, proved unable to provide parts at internationally competitive prices and quality. Local-content requirements were thus not being met, a situation that exacerbated balance-of-payments deficits. This was to be expected; the Mexican auto-parts industry was still technically inexperienced and was operating from a weak financial base while it produced at low economies of scale for the many auto lines. Ultimately, a mere 36 percent local content was achieved by 1970. Consequently, in 1969 and 1972, while still sustaining its import-substitution goals, the Mexican government adopted an auto-parts export policy in an effort to address the balance-of-payments problem and increase the competitiveness of auto-parts producers.

The 1969 and 1972 Auto Decrees reiterated the 60 percent local-content requirement and declared that the industry had to balance imports with their exports of auto parts. Although the goals of the decrees were not

[32] Rhys Owen Jenkins, *Dependent Industrialization in Latin America: The Automotive Industry in Argentina, Chile, and Mexico* (New York, 1977).

TABLE 2

Value of Mexican Automobile Production

(Millions of pesos)

	Baja Calif.	Coahuila	Chihuahua	Nuevo Leon	Sonora	Tamaulipas	Total
1965							
Fabrication/assembly of vehicles	—	—	—	57,377	—	—	4,417,411
Fabrication of chassis	—	—	—	—	—	—	182,909
Fabrication of motors	—	103,589	—	118,367	—	—	363,419
Fabrication of access., parts	—	—	—	—	—	2,398	1,299,135
Repair of vehicles	23,202	12,795	15,996	40,229	22,556	20,389	684,147
1970							
Fabrication/assem. of veh. & truck cabs	—	—	—	370,125	—	—	8,966,717
Fab. of chassis	—	9,458	1,588	125,360	—	—	559,621
Fab./assem. of motors & motor parts	—	—	—	—	—	—	1,121,035
Fab. of access., parts	12,191	199,795	4,200	381,544	1,293	24,755	3,452,898
1975							
Fabrication/assembly of vehicles	5,527	—	1,281	294,187	—	3,704	25,447,195
Fab./assem. of chassis & drive trains	—	8,407	—	536,596	—	—	1,935,216
Fab./assem. of motors & motor parts	—	471,846	—	89,348	—	—	2,896,017
Fab. of transmission parts	133,056	—	—	—	—	—	2,930,846
Fab. of suspension parts	—	—	—	36,890	—	—	1,061,580
Fab. of brake system parts	—	—	—	35,396	—	—	782,336
Fab. of access., parts for elect. system	—	—	—	88,487	—	—	1,069,325
Fab. of other parts & access.	91,374	44,505	46,141	1,182,110	19,923	33,610	3,303,124

SOURCE: Secretaría de Comercio y Fomento Industrial, Mexico City.

fully met, trade in auto parts did begin to grow exponentially. While in 1965 the ratio of auto-parts exports to the export of passenger cars was 3:2, by 1970 it had increased to 4:1, and by 1980 had reached 50:1.[33] In addition, a geographical shift was taking place; northern Mexico was rising in prominence. Compared to national auto output, there was a significant increase in auto production in every northern state from 1970 to 1975. This was particularly true for Baja California, which saw an increase of SIC category 3815 (Fabrication of Parts for Auto Suspension System) from under 1 percent to 12.5 percent of national production; Coahuila, which realized an increase of SIC 3813 (Fabrication of Motors and Their Parts) from 0 to 16.3 percent of national production; and Nuevo Leon, where SIC 3812 (Fabrication and Assembly of Chassis and Drive Train) grew to 27.7 percent of the national total. Across all northern states, SIC 3819 (Fabrication of Other Parts and Accessories for Autos) rose to 35.8 percent of national production by 1975 (Table 2).

Being Mexico's primary foreign market, U.S. imports of auto parts from Mexico grew rapidly, increasing from $100,000 in trade during 1965 to $18 million in 1970, to $131 million by 1975, and again to $242 million by 1980. With the steady expansion of the auto sector in Mexico, exports from the United States also grew. From $126 million in 1970, auto parts exported to Mexico increased to $937 million by 1980.[34]

Fueling the move toward internationalization by U.S. automakers and the growth of the auto-parts industry in northern Mexico was the Border Industrialization Program. Begun in 1965, it established duty-free export processing and assembly zones within a twelve-mile strip along the U.S.-Mexican border—a designation that was later extended to include the entire country. The *maquiladoras* became significant contributors to industrial growth in the region. Initially dominated by garment and electronics assemblers, as of 1979 there were 38 plants nationwide involved in auto-parts production, largely located in the North, and in all, employing 5,035 persons.[35]

This was also a period of qualitative change in the composition of the work force within the Mexican automobile industry. On the one hand, there was the emergence of the largely nonunionized *maquiladora* labor force in those parts-producing plants oriented toward export. On the other, a relative homogenization was occurring among the autoworkers

[33] Bureau of Labor Statistics, *Employment and Earnings*; Motor Vehicle Manufacturers Association, "Economic Indicators: The Motor Vehicle's Role in the U.S. Economy," 10.
[34] *Ibid.*
[35] Secretariat of Programming and Budget, *Estadistica de la Industria Maquiladora de Exportación* (Mexico City, various issues).

situated in Mexico City's plants and those in the outlying areas in terms of wage demands and labor militancy. Thus, with the unfolding of the crisis surfaced a new international division of labor—a profile distinguished by the disassociation of the unionized work force of the automobile assemblies and major parts manufacturers operating within the U.S. or Mexican domestic markets from the disenfranchised, Taylorized workers of the export-processing zones.

As the intensity of international competition accelerated throughout the late 1970s and early 1980s, U.S. automakers picked up the pace of industrial restructuring and labor-market change. From the near bankruptcy of Chrysler in 1979 to the demise of auto and related production in branch plant locations such as Los Angeles, the impact was widely felt. Parts manufacturers at the branch-plant sites often could not hold on to the original equipment market, and many were forced to close, shift location or product, or redirect their product line to the replacement or aftermarket. In Los Angeles, which had been the second largest auto-producing region after Detroit during the 1950s with a wide-ranging though not fully developed parts industry, and which was a major point of destination for immigrants to the United States, some parts producers attempted to control production costs by employing undocumented workers. Employers gained by paying lower wages and benefits, undermining union organization and bargaining efforts, and by having access to an easily releasable work force at a time when the extent of labor demand seemed highly unpredictable. Though this strategy was initially developed by economic pressures of the time and the availability of a unique labor force, it became an enduring part of the regional industry. Immigrant workers provided an alternative to relocation or retooling. With undocumented workers' penetration into the auto industries of industrialized countries, the circuit of the new international division of labor appeared to close.

The complexity of the 1970s was further evident in the responses of organized labor in the United States and Mexico, of the governments of the respective countries, and of the automakers themselves. Watching its ranks shrink, United Auto Workers' employment in the five largest auto companies decreased by 26 percent from a peak in 1978 to January 1986.[36] The United Auto Workers' call for local-content legislation, which became the hallmark of organized labor, established a formula for imposing requirements, a phase-in period, and a ceiling of 90 percent

[36] United Automobile Workers of America, *Research Bulletin,* special convention issue (Detroit, 1986).

among high-volume sellers.[37] Wanting to retain free trade, yet needing to address the concerns of labor, the U.S. government turned instead to voluntary trade restrictions with the Japanese in 1981.

Within Mexico, the response to the economic pressures of the 1970s took the form of two successive auto decrees in 1977 and 1983 that firmly redirected national industrial policy away from import substitution and toward export promotion. The 1977 Auto Decree lowered the local-content requirement to 50 percent for the auto assembly, but extended the requirement to auto parts with the provision that exports could be included in parts manufacturers' calculations of local content. Mexico's intent was to combine export-led industrialization via parts (including engines) with backward linkages. Due to the consumer boom (precipitated by oil revenues) that made Mexico the fastest-growing market in the world, as well as the willingness of multinationals to shift production toward export to the United States, the auto industry was geared for growth. Investments in Mexico continued to decentralize, as investors realized that production was aimed at both the domestic and export markets.

This optimistic scenario, however, was clouded by other factors. Labor unrest continued in Mexico; in 1980, a 106-day strike by the CROC occurred, the longest ever in the auto industry, and organized labor was consistently unable to create a national union. From 1977 to 1981, while exports increased 14 percent, imports surged to 21 percent, making the deficit jump from 20 to 57.7 percent. In 1982, Mexico suffered its worst economic crisis since the 1930s. Collapse of the domestic market led to a 40 percent drop in auto production and a 41 percent drop in auto sales. In the face of mounting problems financing Mexico's international debt, the 1983 Auto Decree liberalized the backward linkage provisions of the 1977 Auto Decree by waiving local-content requirements on cars for export. It further allowed exceptions to requirements limiting the number of lines and models if exports balanced imports used in production.

Among the automakers, the options available for addressing the crisis were also far more mixed than initially realized. As firms began internationalizing production, it appeared that a strategy would be found that could simultaneously meet local-content requirements and respond to the need to restructure. This hope lay in the "world car" concept, an idea that consisted of a base car from which several models of similar specifications for different countries would be built using standardized produc-

[37] Douglas Fraser, "Domestic Content of U.S. Automobile Imports: A UAW Proposal," *Columbia Journal of World Business* (Winter 1981), 57–61.

tion processes and interchangeable parts. In contrast to Fordism-style manufacturing, in which production is characterized by mechanized assembly lines, local inventory sourcing, and vertical integration and is sustained by mass national markets, this world-car approach was characterized by vertical disintegration/global reintegration, multiple sourcing, parallel production, increased automation, and the capturing of economies of scale in global markets, with industrializing countries clearly integral to the process. Although the Ford Fiesta, introduced in 1976, was intended to illustrate this strategy, wholesale adoption of the idea was slow to materialize. Many observers suggested that it was never a viable concept, especially since the auto-parts industry did not seem to be taking off in industrializing nations that had adopted import-substitution policies.[38] In addition, the dedication to specific technology, which facilitated mass production, also lacked the ability to respond easily to rapid model changes, while the extensive decentralization of production required expensive inventories to guarantee a sufficient number of high-quality parts.[39]

Yet another alternative for automakers began to surface in the 1980s. With the United States still the most significant new-car market in the world, direct foreign investment in autos increased. As of 1982, Honda became the first Japanese firm to establish assembly operations in the United States, with Toyota and Nissan following its lead. The incentive to remain in the United States and produce for the domestic market was strong even though the market was becoming crowded and extremely fragmented. The heterogeneity in demand suggested a need for product variability; consequently, as advances in production technology lowered the cost of small production runs and model changes, another form of industrial organization emerged.

Described as "flexible specialization," this method employed flexible manufacturing technology, "just-in-time" inventory sourcing (or *kanban*), and Japanese methods of labor-management relations. To institute *kanban*, which required establishing close supplier ties, and to facilitate technological development, this strategy reconcentrated production in the United States, particularly in the Midwest. Furthermore, to capture what have been called "external economies of scope" (in reference to

[38] U.S. International Trade Commission, *The Internationalization of the Automobile Industry and Its Effects on the U.S. Automobile Industry*, USITC Pub. 1712 (Washington, 1985).
[39] Harry C. Katz and Charles F. Sabel, "Industrial Relations and Industrial Adjustment: The World Car Industry," paper presented at the Conference on the Future of Industrial Relations, 22–23 Feb. 1985, Berkeley, Calif.

flexibility in batch size and product variability), firms committed to this route also began a process of vertical disintegration with the intent of increasing versatility, not standardization. Examples of this move include the 1979 joint venture of Toyota and General Motors (NUMMI) and General Motors' 1990 Saturn project. When fully in place, the role of industrializing countries under this scheme was reduced to supplying only the most labor-intensive, minor products. Although the alternative between standardization/internationalization and industrial strategies using flexible specialization was more conceptual than absolute because the actual practice of automakers reflected a mixture of both approaches, these strategies became the subject of intense debate. Projected into the future, the way each strategy would affect labor markets within the United States and abroad and their implications for the future role of industrializing nations were quite distinct. Furthermore, because conditions in the U.S. auto industry changed considerably since 1979— through the closure of older plants, a reduction in work force, lower inventory costs, increased outsourcing, and improved efficiency and quality control—the breakeven point for each company dropped substantially. This made a U.S. location even more attractive and the flexible specialization strategy increasingly viable. For General Motors, the breakeven point dropped from 8.4 million units in 1980 to 5.6 million units in 1984, based on worldwide vehicle sales; among Ford's North American operations, the fall was from 3.6 million units to 2.1 million units in the same period; while for Chrysler, the reduction was from 2.3 million units to 1.1 million units.[40]

These developments seemed to support the flexible-specialization concept, and those who interpreted the trends this way were specific about what they saw as Mexico's future. One OECD report listed four reasons why developing countries would face an inherent bias: "Some of the theoretical advantages of low-cost production in newly industrialized countries have been offset by (1) much lower productivity, (2) a lower degree of system efficiency, (3) higher component costs resulting from local-content requirements, and (4) macroeconomic disturbances such as rapid exchange-rate changes."[41] Thus, with critical advancements occurring in the structure of production, developing countries seemed to have a very low-level niche. A recent study by the Massachusetts Institute of

[40] U.S. International Trade Commission, *The Internationalization of the Automobile Industry and Its Effects on the U.S. Automobile Industry.*

[41] Organization for Economic Cooperation and Development (OECD), *Long Term Outlook for the World Automobile Industry* (Paris, 1983).

Technology categorized auto parts into three types: major mechanicals (for example, engines and transmissions); finish parts (such as body stampings, trim, seats, and instrument panels); and minor mechanicals (for example, starters, radiators, springs, and wiring harnesses), each with production-specific requirements. Major mechanicals necessitate high initial capital investments for their highly automated production and technically skilled labor; finish parts are bulky to ship and must fit precisely, thereby requiring strict quality control; while minor mechanicals with their low technology, labor-intensive production methods are seen as best suited for low-wage sourcing.[42]

Despite this minimal area of relative advantage, a trend toward modular-component assembly, coupled with increasingly automated machining and manufacture and the projected introduction of new technology into critical product lines (for example, fiber optics replacing wire harness methodology), suggests that certain manufacturers of minor mechanical parts may soon find the United States a preferred site of production, and in the process, abandon their developing-nation sites.[43] Where extensive production is taking place in industrializing countries (such as Mexico), the MIT study states quite clearly,

The need to achieve scale economies in developing countries with high local-content requirements, coupled with the feasibility of building highly automated plants in those countries which can produce at an adequate standard of quality, means that [while] some OECD production is being transferred [there] . . . the main aim of such transfers is not to produce cost savings for multinational producers in the OECD markets; rather it is to gain access to developing and developed markets.[44]

Despite opinions that the world-car strategy never materialized and that the flexible-specialization approach offered few opportunities for significantly integrating industrializing countries into the international automobile industry, developments in Mexico suggested that the situation was actually more complex. In its sectors engaged in parts production and assembly of autos for export, Mexico displays trends that contradict and go beyond the predictions of recent studies. Seen in overview, these important export developments are immediately apparent.

In response to Mexico's auto decree stipulations, certain products such as engine manufacture have become well-developed. In addition, due to the Border Industrialization Program, other labor-intensive parts for ex-

[42] Altshuler, *The Future of the Automobile.*
[43] *Ibid.*
[44] *Ibid.,* 83.

port have similarly grown in importance. Although these policies were crucial in defining the possible range of the auto industry in Mexico, the strategies of individual firms created the broad diversity of automobile and auto-parts production now visible. With Ford essentially adopting a world-car strategy and General Motors largely committed to flexible specialization, with its reconcentration of production in the United States, the sourcing and assembly policies of these companies are both significantly different and suggestive of the viability, as well as distortions, of the two industrial strategies. Looking first at the parts profile, these points will be examined in detail.

Approximately 80 percent of Mexico's parts exports are for the U.S. market, and of all exports, only 20 percent go to the aftermarket.[45] While Mexican parts still constitute a small share of the parts imported into the United States, that number is growing and is expected to continue increasing in the near future.[46] Of these, the rise of engine exports is most clearly identified with the auto decrees. In the United States, the production of engines, along with transmissions and transaxles, reached their highest level in 1979 and then declined. A major trend has been for U.S. firms to import their engines from either wholly owned subsidiaries or foreign joint ventures. From 1980 to 1983, U.S. imports of engines grew by 300 percent, from 544,020 to 2,183,842 units.[47] Most of this increase was attributed to offshore purchasing from Mexico, Brazil, and France or joint-venture operations from Japan.[48] The contribution attributed to Mexico grew from $68,866 in gasoline engine exports to the United States in 1980 to $422,813 in 1983, and again to $531,932 in 1984.[49] In 1983, virtually all of the engines were imported under TSUS item 807.00.[50] When surveyed as to why firms were purchasing from Mexico and Brazil, the most important considerations were net price, local-content requirements, and product quality, while the least important con-

---

[45] Douglas C. Bennett, "Regional Consequences of Industrial Policy: Mexico and the United States in a Changing World Auto Industry," in Ina Rosenthal-Urey, ed., *Regional Impacts of U.S.-Mexican Relations,* monograph 16 (La Jolla, Calif., Center for U.S.-Mexican Studies, 1986).

[46] U.S. International Trade Commission, *Internationalization of the Automobile Industry.*

[47] U.S. International Trade Commission, *Internationalization of the Automobile Industry.*

[48] U.S. International Trade Commission, *Imports under Items 806.30 and 807.00 of Tariff Schedules of the United States, 1980–1983.*

[49] TSUS statistics of the U.S. Department of Commerce as contained in U.S. International Trade Commission, *Internationalization of the Automobile Industry.*

[50] Compiled from official statistics of the U.S. Department of Commerce, as contained in USITC Publication 1688, *Imports under Items 806.30 and 807.00 of the Tariff Schedules of the United States, 1980–1983* (Washington, Apr. 1985).

sideration was proximity of supplier.[51] Since the Massachusetts Institute of Technology study used data through 1980, they neglected to include Mexico as a significant supplier of engines and in turn, made an incorrect conclusion about the importance of Mexican major mechanicals.[52] As of 1982, the following plants in Mexico were making engines for export: Ford, with 400,000 units, Chrysler, making 220,000 units; General Motors, at 360,000; American Motors/Renault, with 300,000; Volkswagen, manufacturing 140,000; and Nissan, with 120,000 units.

Ford's state-of-the-art plant in Chihuahua demonstrates the direction in which engine production is going. This plant uses the most advanced technology available and as of 1984 used 600 robots, from small polishers to the most sophisticated pieces. In 1985, the relatively skilled work force consisted of 47 supervisors, 253 administrators, and 468 technicians and workers, of whom 350 were direct production workers. These workers received 40,000 pesos a month (approximately $1 per hour) in 1984 and produced 750 engines every eight-hour shift.[53] On average, the Chihuahua plant is expected to provide 1,500 direct, and 1,000 indirect, jobs. The four-cylinder 2.2 liter engines manufactured here had the same design as those manufactured at the Lima, Ohio, plant.

While engines provide significant insight into the growth of Mexican auto-parts exports to the United States—constituting between one-third and one-fourth of the value of auto-parts imports from Mexico in 1982 and between one-half and one-third of imports in 1983—other parts were also important. In order of significance, other prominent parts were radios; electrical starting and ignition equipment; motor-vehicle stampings; furniture designed for autos; brakes; springs; and glass products.[54] As this list demonstrates, finish parts (stampings) is another item that the MIT project did not attribute to Mexico. Altogether, the United States imported over $1.2 billion in auto parts from Mexico in 1983, creating a trade deficit of over $440 million.[55]

Growth of the *maquiladoras* explained much of the increase. From 1979 to 1985, the number of border *maquiladoras* involved in producing transport equipment grew from 38 to 49.[56] These products generally en-

[51] U.S. International Trade Commission, *Internationalization of the Automobile Industry.*

[52] Altshuler et al., *The Future of the Automobile,* 178.

[53] Graciela Martinez, "Sistemas Productivos en la Planta Ford de Chihuahua," paper prepared·at Colegio de la Frontera Norte (Tijuana, 1984).

[54] U.S. Department of Commerce, *Motor Vehicles, Motor Vehicle Parts, and Accessories: U.S. Trade with Mexico 1982 and 1983* (Washington, 1985).

[55] *Ibid.*

[56] Secretariat of Programming and Budget, *Estadistica de la Industria Maquiladora de Exportación.*

tered the United States under TSUS items 806.3 and 807.0. In 1983, $179,918,000 worth of motor-vehicle parts entered under 807.0, or nearly one-tenth of the total value of goods, while $11,807,000 entered through 806.3. (From 1980 to 1983, Mexico moved from third to first place as the largest importer of goods to the United States under item 807.0). The rise of the *maquiladoras* has resulted in a significant increase in employment. In 1979, the number of persons employed in transport equipment along the border was 5,035 and had grown to 34,484 by 1985. Given respective increases of value-added per million pesos from 859 to 20,215, this sector resulted in the highest value-added per employee. This finding confirms the relative capital intensity associated with auto-parts production compared to other *maquiladora* sectors, such as textiles at .29 in 1985, or electronic materials at .30 for the same year.[57] Geographically, most *maquiladoras* are concentrated around Cd. Juarez, which is largely geared toward the original equipment market (most of these plants assemble electrical parts), and Tijuana, which is oriented toward the minor-mechanical aftermarket. By far the largest employer among the *maquiladoras* is General Motors, which uses the *maquilas* mostly to manufacture wire harnesses. General Motors had ten in-bond plants by 1985, had grown to sixteen by 1986, and was expected to double by 1987.

Over the years, employment in auto parts for export became increasingly significant relative to employment in the terminal sector. In 1979, 107,874 people were employed in the automotive industry; 116,500 were employed by 1984. While 49,738 persons were employed in the terminal sector in 1979 and 48,200 by 1984, in auto parts the respective increases were 58,136 to 68,300.

These numbers, of course, do not illustrate how employment is divided between the two main strategies of industrial organization. Despite attempts to disassociate itself with the term "world car," Ford maintains a policy that any new car design be easily adapted for any market in the world.[58] At the same time, Ford's Alfa project seems to be moving toward greater efficiency faster than similar endeavors by General Motors or Chrysler—progress attributed more to changes in management and shop-floor practices (85 percent) than to new technologies (15 percent).

These policies suggest that Ford is moving to combine the world-car and flexible-specialization strategies.[59] When operations are fully underway in the Ford Hermosillo plant opened in 1988, it is expected that

[57] *Ibid.*
[58] *BusinessWeek*, 11 Feb. 1985.
[59] *Fortune*, Dec. 1985.

90 percent of the auto parts it needs will be imported from around the Pacific, and 90 percent of its output will be shipped to the United States. Mazda Motor Corp., which is 25 percent owned by Ford, will provide the basic design and major components. When the cars are coming off the line, 3,000 workers will be employed making 100,000 cars annually, and the product will replace the Mercury Lynx compact, now made in the United States.[60] Thus, by retaining a primary commitment to the basic world-car concept, Ford, at least in this plant, is not helping to build the supplier linkages in Mexico but is rather using Mexico as an export-processing zone, a strategy made all the more possible after the 1983 Auto Decree.

Alternatively, General Motors is applying its reconcentration/ flexible-specialization strategy in Mexico two ways. At the Ramos Arizpe plant near Saltillo, it has implemented just-in-time inventory sourcing, even though most of the parts come from the United States as temporary imports. In addition, it has shifted production of many of its low-value-added parts into Mexico for integration into modular pieces to be assembled in the United States. While many parts are manufactured in the *maquiladoras*, including electrical parts, control devices, solenoids, switches, trim, bumpers, and brake hoses, wire harnesses remain the main product. This fact is important, because many future car design improvements will come from electronic components. Thus, while a general trend toward vertical disintegration is taking place in the industry, General Motors remains the most vertically integrated, and by retaining capacity among electronics, it can better control the design and cost.[61] General Motors' dual strategy, then, is to couple vertical integration with a relocation of subsidiary facilities to low-wage areas, which would thereby define the outer boundaries of reconcentration. Over the long term, this strategy could have a similar outcome to the world-car strategy; while employment is lost in the United States, only minimal employment is gained in Mexico because supplier networks will not be strengthened.

Overall, the automobile industry in Mexico has undergone several unexpected developments. Traditional trade theory, which assumes a relative immobility of factors, argues that trade reflects each country's comparative advantage. The North would specialize in capital-intensive production, while the South would specialize in labor-intensive production. However, according to this theory, once capital became mobile, the parameters defining comparative advantage would change because the

[60] *Ibid.*; *BusinessWeek*, 14 Apr. 1986.
[61] OECD, *Long Term Outlook for the World Automobile Industry*.

cost of all factors would have to be taken into account. Thus, capital-intensive production could occur in locations like Mexico if the technology was standardized, and if savings in transportation and labor warranted the move. With the transformation from Fordism to post-Fordism, this process, in fact, began to take place.

In part, Mexico's ability to capture a variety of products reflected its relatively strong market potential for growth and its established experience with the industry. The stages through which a country goes as it proceeds from importing finished vehicles to manufacturing a complete car consists of (1) the supply of a few replacement parts, distribution, and services, (2) local assembly of semi-knocked-down and knocked-down cars, (3) development of backward linkages evolving out of the replacement market, and (4) further integration until even the most advanced parts are made domestically.[62] As the industry matures, the tendency for production to become technologically complex and capital intensive increases.[63] This tendency is clearly exemplified by Mexico, where capital intensity more than doubled from 1960 to 1965 when capital per-unit output grew from 440 to 1,101; the capital/output ratio rose from .17 to .33; and the capital/value-added ratio jumped from .38 to .86.[64]

This descriptive stage theory, however, can offer only a limited explanation of how the transitions actually occurred. Within Mexico, the 1969 Auto Decree specified local-engine sourcing as a term of production that, when coupled with recent trends toward internationalization by U.S. manufacturers, pushed production to greater capital intensity. While the various auto decrees guided Mexico's economic structure, trends in the industry determined which parts and technology would locate in Mexico for export abroad.

ALTERNATIVE SCENARIOS

In what direction can we expect international industrial, trade, and labor-market relations to evolve across the United States and Mexico? As shown in the last section, a variety of strategies are being attempted in response to the crisis of the previous international development pattern. What factors will determine which strategy will prevail? What are the implications of each strategy for labor groups on both sides of the border? Will either of these approaches address the fundamental problems

[62] Jenkins, *Dependent Industrialization in Latin America*, 91–98; George Mexcy, *The Multinational Automobile Industry* (New York, 1981).

[63] Jenkins, *Dependent Industrialization in Latin America*, 88; Jack Baranson, *Automotive Industries in Developing Countries* (Baltimore, Md., 1969), 14.

[64] Asociación Mexican de la Industria Automotriz, A.C., *La Industria Automotriz de Mexico en Cifras* (Mexico City, 1972).

now facing the United States and Mexico in their effort to construct a new pattern of international development that assures both productivity growth and increased social participation in these gains?

Each strategy has significantly different long-term consequences for industrial organization, as pointed out by the OECD.[65] The two strategies imply different approaches to productivity enhancement; the world-car strategy stressing greater standardization with plants of higher economies of scale (400,000 units), and the reconcentration strategy emphasizing technology that allows greater flexibility for changing design in plants with lower economies of scale (250,000 units).[66] For the United States and Mexico, both strategies also promise very difficult strains on the nature of employment and earnings across the two countries.

The implications of an expanded world-car strategy include increased model standardization, larger scales of production in key countries, global sourcing of auto parts, the favoring of replacement components over the trade-in of cars, and market concentration by large integrated producers at the expense of specialist producers. The labor-market effects in assembly include a tendency to transfer employment in final assembly of cheaper, more standard models away from the United States toward export platforms in Mexico, as in the Hermosillo case, while the United States assembles high-priced cars for specific regional markets. In both countries, these effects imply a move toward greater technological intensity in standardized production.

The net employment effect for U.S. final assembly would probably be negative, especially for lower-skilled assembly workers. The incremental effect on Mexican employment, however, would be small, as in the Hermosillo case. Global sourcing of auto-parts production would probably result in a net loss of employment in the United States, except for some sophisticated specialty parts specific to U.S. markets, which could be produced profitably in the United States with flexible technology. Mexico could increase production of some auto components like motors and other heavy parts for North American markets, in tandem with other sourcing countries, but would probably lose some of its market share for lighter low-tech auto parts to cheaper assembly sites in Asia or elsewhere.

Projected consequences of the technological divergence and specialization strategy include increased model differentiation with advanced flex-

---

[65] Organization for Economic Cooperation and Development, *Long-Term Outlook for the World Automobile Industry* (Paris, 1983).

[66] Organization for Economic Cooperation and Development, *Industrial Robots: Their Role in Manufacturing Industry* (Paris, 1983).

ible technology; reconcentration of production in major market countries; emphasis on model trade-in over component replacement; and market penetration by smaller "specialist" producers, which would entail a loss of market share by large integrated producers. The strategy would have different employment effects among assemblers and parts manufacturers. While the United States would retain a greater share of assembly production, employment levels would still suffer due to the greater use of automation, as the projected investment-per-employment levels of the high-tech Saturn project suggest. Since production would be for the local market, employment growth would be limited to the rate of the slowly growing U.S. market.[67] Growth in Mexican assembly employment would also be a function of the size of the local market rather than of export markets.

Parts production, on the other hand, is projected to evolve into a tiering system, with the flexible-technology production of more advanced parts being a first tier and those parts produced with more traditional technologies constituting a second tier. The first tier would be organized in just-in-time *kanbans* around final assemblers in the United States, and would require lower rates of employment per unit of investment. The second tier would face the choice of using offshore labor or competitive domestic labor markets, including the continued use of immigrants. Mexico would probably continue to attract second-tier offshore auto-parts assembly as long as these parts do not change substantially due to innovations in process or product technologies. The introduction of fiber optics, for instance, would reduce the production of wire harnesses in Mexico. If growth in exports slowed, the rate of Mexican auto-parts employment would be limited by the growth of demand from Mexico's final assembly.

Tradeoff Factors

Which of these tendencies will grow in prominence depends on global competitive trends, of which relative prices between the United States and Mexico will play an important part. A crucial factor for this process is the relative evolution of Mexican wage costs compared to U.S. technology costs. Available data from 1985 suggest that the amortization and operation cost of robots doing assembly work similar to that at the new General Motors plant in Ramos Arizpe is $4.80 an hour, compared to local wages of $.82 an hour (in Davila, Comercio Exterior). United Auto

[67] Instituto Mexicano de Comercio Exterior/Comision Economica para America Latina (INCE/CEPAL), based on figures from the Chase Manhattan Bank.

Workers estimates that every robot displaces an average of four workers and creates 0.3 jobs for maintenance and control.[68] Given these relative costs, it may be profitable to displace U.S. assembly workers with robots, but it appears to be more profitable to operate the assembly of some products offshore.

The recent decision by Ford to build an engine plant in Mexico for export to the United States illustrates the actual pattern of relative costs and the role of policy. When only production and freight costs are taken into account, the landed cost in Detroit of Mexican-produced engines is only marginally cheaper than the two alternatives considered: producing in the United States or purchasing Japanese engines. Despite lower wages in Mexico, this is not surprising, because engines made in Japan require only 3.5 hours of labor, at a cost of $40 (equivalent to less than 5 percent of total costs). Nevertheless, Ford estimated that because increased exports from Mexico allowed for additional imports, earnings were raised by 37 cents per dollar exported. This compares to a direct export subsidy, in the form of tax reductions, of only 8 cents per dollar exported.

In a recent study on the tradeoffs between production in the United States versus Mexico and Singapore, Walsh Sanderson concluded that there appears to be little incentive to make large investments in automated plant and equipment in Mexico.[69] The choice is more clearly between continued manual assembly in Mexico and automated assembly in the United States. Mexican wage rates are still low enough to attract U.S. firms, and the pressure toward a yet lower value of the peso could tend to support the status quo. Reductions in the capital cost of automating assembly processes, however, with other potential gains from increased quality and coordination, may entice firms to automate plants in the United States at the expense of Mexican manual assembly.[70]

The alternatives appear grim indeed. Mexico will have to maintain reduced wages to attract greater investment and increase productivity. The United States will face greater pressures to automate given its present wage and productivity structure. The potential for displacement of workers in the United States, either through automation or offshore assembly, will continue, because labor costs in the United States represent 35 percent of total costs and 32 percent of labor is employed in assembly.[71] OECD projects a 50 percent displacement of manual labor in the 1980s

[68] United Automobile Workers of America, *Research Bulletin.*
[69] Walsh Sanderson, *Impacts of Automated Manufacturing Technology on Offshore Assembly* (Pittsburgh, 1985).
[70] *Ibid.,* 97.
[71] Organization for Economic Cooperation and Development, *Industrial Robots,* 72.

in the auto industries of advanced countries, because workers on both sides of the border are, in effect, competing to reduce their contribution to costs.[72] The lack of international organizational capacity among workers allows different groups of workers to play off against one another.

Many problems also exist concerning the long-term macroeconomic viability of these two trends. Global markets make the wages in a particular nation appear merely as production costs. Resulting reductions in industrial employment and union givebacks tend to lower and distort the level of aggregate demand in the United States. The Mexican debt crisis exacerbates this reduction in global demand, because the capacity for domestic expansion and imports is limited by austerity policies designed to create a trade surplus for net capital outflow. As it stands, the austerity measures imposed due to the debt crisis are causing a larger drop in U.S. employment through lost export markets in auto parts than the employment displacement effects of the increased Mexican exports to the United States. From 1921 to 1984, the drop in U.S. exports in more labor-intensive auto-parts exports was $520 million compared to an increase in Mexican exports of $235 million—most of which was engines, which use less labor than U.S. exports.[73] It is ironic that the Mexican industrial policies in the 1970s are responsible for the recent surge in Mexican auto exports (auto exports represent 40 percent of the growth of non-oil manufactured exports), which have allowed Mexico to pay back foreign creditors in the 1980s.

As the old Fordist order degenerates, the emerging alternative patterns of restructuring do not appear to be able to fill the role of an international growth mechanism. To deal effectively with the crisis, a much more comprehensive policy and institutional approach is needed. The goals of such an approach would have to include reestablishing an international virtuous growth dynamic—a type of global Fordism capable of generating growth in productivity, output, employment, and markets across North and South. The new approach would have to include the following components:

- International production-sharing as a means of more efficiently distributing the production process and the growth of employment;
- Distribution of value-added-per-worker gains in both regions such that effective demand is allowed to expand internationally;

[72] Organization for Economic Cooperation and Development, *World Automobile Industry*, 100.
[73] TSUS statistics of the U.S. Department of Commerce as contained in U.S. International Trade Commission, *The Internationalization of the Automobile Industry*.

- Sharing of market growth across both regions;
- Movement toward balance trade equilibrium;
- New regime of capital flows that does not burden the South with net outward-resource transfers;
- New state/state and capital/labor institutional arrangements to regulate and assure the operation of this approach (such as the 1965 Auto Pact between Canada and the United States).

Such an approach would obviously have to be organized multisectorally. Nevertheless, important insights can be obtained from understanding how this approach could be implemented in the auto sector. For the U.S.-Mexico automobile sector, the important question is how to redirect and build on current trends in order to distribute employment and earnings gains, thus expanding markets while increasing productivity across North America. This growth will require a series of difficult institutional rearrangements, which will not occur without a concerted binational effort.

This approach would also imply a new international division of production whereby Mexico would concentrate on assembling smaller, medium-priced cars and trucks using more standardized technologies. The United States would concentrate on the flexible-technology assembly of more specialized, higher-priced markets. This international sharing of assembly production could induce sharing of auto-parts production according to a two-tiered specialization. The United States would develop *kanban* production systems for the more technologically advanced auto parts, while Mexico would concentrate on mass producing second-tier parts. Over the long term, Mexico may attempt to develop expertise in specific advanced product and process technologies.

In order to assure a broadening distribution of the gains from this new international division of production, the two basic strategies currently being experimented with would have to be restructured simultaneously in the following manner: (1) The world-car strategy would have to evolve so that production sharing in final assembly is maintained while North American local content and value-added are increased, particularly through auto-parts production, and where final assembly services both markets; and (2) The flexible-specialization and *kanban/maquila* approach would need to develop in a number of ways: the lower-tier *kanbans* that employ immigrant workers in the United States would have to be transferred to border production; meanwhile, this *maquila* production would need to graduate to sourcing inputs from Mexico as well as to selling their products within Mexico, integrating these operations with the Mexican economy and thus increasing domestic value-added and distributing efficiency gains within Mexico.

Labor Market Effects

The transfer of lower-tier auto-parts production to Mexico would result in an increase in employment demand in Mexico as well as a reduced demand for the competitive U.S. labor market. Both results would lessen the pressures for labor migration to the United States. In Mexico, the multiplier effects of value-added retention and employment creation would allow for increased domestic demand for both domestic production and imports from the United States, and thus for greater employment in both countries.

For the United States, this international division of production would create a dynamic source of auto parts that are globally competitive in terms of quality and costs, which would improve the international competitive position of U.S. auto manufacturing. The development of this competitive sourcing reserve would also make the United States more attractive for Japanese and European foreign investment. Production sharing could deter a large-scale departure of auto manufacturing as corporations opt for coproductive pacts with Mexico. U.S./Mexico market sharing in automobiles would also be potentially very important to global producers, given the predicted market saturation in the United States of 2 percent future growth, while much higher growth potentials exist in Mexico and developing countries.[74]

Operation of this new international division of labor would entail important new institutional arrangements with respect to both international public policy and international capital-labor relations. To some extent, this trade and industrial policy pact can be seen as a variation of the U.S.-Canadian Auto Pact, although the situation for the United States and Canada in 1965 was very different than for the United States and Mexico today. As recently as 1982–83, attempts to develop sectoral trade pacts between the United States and Mexico collapsed for lack of a cohesive position among producer groups in both countries and lack of priority in the binational agenda-setting process. The opportunity for such pacts is arising again, however, as the United States and Mexico prepare to develop a trade and investment agreement as a result of the August 1986 Presidential meetings. Recent discussion with Department of Commerce and USTR officials, however, indicate that for antiregula-

[74] Organization for Economic Cooperation and Development, *World Automobile Industry*, 100.

tionist reasons and because of problems in coordinating producer groups, the prospects are not promising. Yet as the interdependence between economies and the demands for increased participation in the gains from international industrial restructuring continue to grow, the viability of this approach should once again become the object of serious discussion.

Immigrants and Labor Standards: The Case of California Janitors

Richard Mines and Jeffrey Avina

IN THE UNITED STATES, there are over half a million janitors, and janitorial service firms clear over $8 billion in sales each year. Two-thirds of all janitors are part-time workers and earn little better than the minimum wage without benefits. In the major metropolitan centers, however, about half of the janitors are covered by union contracts and as a result enjoy better wages and benefits. The proportion of part-time to full-time janitors varies immensely from city to city; only 10 percent of San Francisco's janitors are part-time compared to 90 percent in Memphis.

The demand for janitors is increasing rapidly; the Bureau of Labor Statistics has predicted growth of half a million jobs during the 1980s. The Service Employees International Union (SEIU), the janitors' main representative, however, has not kept pace. Between 1977 and 1981, for example, the representation of SEIU workers in the major metropolitan areas of the United States fell from an average of 62 percent to 52 percent.[1] Our research suggests that the SEIU's downward slide in California has occurred at a substantially more rapid rate.

The SEIU's main problem in California has been spiraling competition from nonunion contractors, whose reliance on low-wage immigrant labor allows them to easily underbid unionized firms. Nonunion pressure has prompted unionized firms to adopt various strategies to try to reduce their own labor costs. They have asked for and have obtained two-tier and three-tier agreements with lower wages for suburban areas; some

---

[1] Bureau of Labor Statistics, *Industry Wage Survey: Contract Cleaning Services* (Washington, July 1981).

have set up nonunion sister companies (double-breasting) and others
have reduced workers' hours at the job and sped up the work pace.[2]

The deterioration of wages, working conditions, and union strength in
California's janitorial industry over the last decade reflects changing market conditions and nonunion contractors' timely adaptation to the large-
scale availability of recently arrived immigrants. The effects, however,
have not been uniform. In southern California, almost all union janitors
in the service firms have experienced drastic cutbacks in wages, benefits,
and working conditions. Northern California janitors, on the other hand,
despite real losses in many areas and a threatening future before them,
have suffered much less. We will examine the decline of the SEIU in California and analyze the distinct responses to similar conditions in different areas of the state.

CHANGING INDUSTRIAL STRUCTURE: CONCENTRATION AND FRAGMENTATION

There are three types of janitorial service firms—small mom-and-pop
operations (less than twenty workers), mid-sized firms (usually nonunion), and large unionized companies. During the 1970s and early
1980s, the percentage of small and very large firms declined in California
and the percentage of mid-sized, nonunion firms expanded (Table 1).
This trend is particularly noticeable in Los Angeles and Santa Clara
counties. The increase in the number of mid-sized firms represents an
unprecedented phase of market readjustment in the janitorial sector. But
this growth in importance of mid-sized firms in Los Angeles and Santa
Clara counties was unusual. American Building Maintenance (ABM), ISS
International, Service Master Industries, Servisco, and Temco Service Industries all have over $50 million in sales a year; Service Master has over
$700 million in sales. Mergers and buy-outs are common in the indus-
try. For example, ABM, the biggest California firm, continues to expand nationwide through acquisition. "We're real pros in the acquisition
business," says Sydney Rosenberg, company president. "We've acquired
some . . . 120 companies in the last fifteen years."[3] Considerable foreign
investment also occurs in the industry; the Pedus Group from Germany,
for example, has a large presence in Los Angeles.

Even as the last of the unionized giants battled for market dominance,
a small but growing number of mid-sized, nonunion firms were success-

[2] Service Employees International Union, "Report to the Building Services Division,"
paper delivered at the SEIU International Conference, Dearborn, Mich., May 1984.

[3] "Giant Firm Finds It Profitable to Mop Floors, Wash the Windows," *San Diego Union*,
17 Apr. 1983.

TABLE I

Employment for Building Maintenance Workers

(*All California*)

Year	Total no. of firms	Pct. 1–19	Pct. 20–49	Pct. 50–99	Pct. 100–249	Pct. 250–499	Pct. 500 or more	Total
1970	1,738	87.2%	7.2%	2.7%	1.9%	0.6%	0.3%	99.9%
1981	2,041	84.9	8.0	3.3	2.4	1.1	0.3	100.0
Los Angeles County								
1970	610	64.4	9.0	3.3	1.5	0.9	0.8	99.9
1981	525	79.6	9.7	5.7	2.7	1.9	0.4	100.0
Santa Clara County								
1970	143	93.0%	3.5%	0.7%	1.4	1.4	0	100.0
1981	130	88.2	4.5	3.8	4.6	0.8	0	100.0

SOURCE: County Business Patterns, 1970 and 1981

fully undermining the large firms' most fundamental premise—that only giant firms could provide the professional and diversified services high-rise office buildings required. The key to the mid-sized firms' success was their ability to organize a cheaper labor force at the precise moment when recessionary pressures mandated that building managers review all cost-cutting alternatives.

SKILL, WAGES, AND JOB MOBILITY

Until recently, the unionized janitorial trade in many parts of California offered high wages for unskilled, manual-labor positions. As late as 1983, for example, Los Angeles union janitors earned a wage and benefit package worth $12.53 per hour. According to Dave Stillwell, business agent for SEIU Local 399, while some janitors do perform skilled tasks such as window washing, easily 90 percent of union janitors spend their work time "pulling trash, emptying ash trays, vacuuming, mopping floors, and cleaning toilets."

Union militancy and favorable economic times—not natural skill barriers—were largely responsible for the wage and benefit gains by SEIU janitors in California. As the vice president of a janitorial firm in Foster City put it, "There is no definition of skill used in the maintenance industry." Union workers tend to agree. A SEIU shop steward in Los Angeles admitted, "Someone with no experience can easily replace someone with eight years experience."

NONUNION STRATEGIES: THE HISPANIC MIDDLEMAN

Immigrant-dominated labor markets can be differentiated both by wages paid and the turnover rate tolerated. When strong unions are present, a low turnover, high-wage environment normally prevails. Most nonunion janitorial firms willingly risk high turnover in exchange for the cost advantages of paying close to the minimum wage. This high turnover option is predicated on easy access to the many immigrant workers throughout California who have recently arrived. As the vice president of Mission Maintenance in San Jose said, "We could get 150 Mexican workers in 24 hours."

The nonunion companies have adapted to this ample reserve of available workers by delegating a great deal of decisionmaking power to Hispanic crew leaders, who typically recruit, hire, fire, and pay workers. These foremen are aware of different networks of potential workers including those that encompass newer, less-experienced workers. As one manager put it, "Recent arrivals take whatever they get and stay until they realize they can look around." Good crew leaders, because they must have recruitment and supervisory skills, are harder to find. They typically earn 50 to 70 percent more per hour than the janitors they supervise and are often convinced to move from one company to another by offers of higher pay.

The astute management of turnover and wage scales can be an effective cost-reducing strategy. Since most nonunion janitors are undocumented, they rarely use unemployment insurance or workers' compensation—a practice that keeps employers' premiums low. Some nonunion employers have apparently violated overtime provisions against newcomer immigrants. United Building Maintenance was ordered by the labor commissioner to return back pay because the company violated rules regarding overtime pay.[4] In one nonunion firm in Los Angeles, ten randomly selected employees all complained about unpaid work hours. None, however, intended to file a grievance for fear of losing his or her job.

Another cost-reducing tactic adopted by some janitorial firms has been to create a piece-rate payment scheme. This approach takes advantage of the targeted earning objectives of many recent immigrants, who prefer to work hard for a few months and save money for their return to their native area.

Nonunion janitorial firms also use turnover to defeat union drives. If the supervisors at a firm are well connected to various networks of potential immigrant workers, it may be very effective to replace the entire crew when union activity threatens. In 1982, Charles Perkel, president of Local 77 in San Jose, recalled employer responses to union drives in these words:

[4]"Undocumented Workers Win Claims Against San Jose Firms," *San Jose Mercury News*, 5 Dec. 1980.

This industry, like the restaurant industry, is difficult to organize because there is a high turnover rate, some of it forced by management to avoid unionization. Two years ago, [Service by] Medallion Company fired all fifty of its workers to halt a union drive. Many of the fired employees were undocumented and were afraid to testify. Medallion has since doubled its work force. The majority of new workers are undocumented. Another company, United Building Maintenance, periodically turns over its work force. Their feeling is that the older workers are the ones who are more prone to unionization and consequently they rarely hold onto their workers for more than two years. In a recent instance, the United Building Maintenance management fired all union activists, got ineligible voters on the voting list, and harassed remaining workers in an effort to sway an upcoming union vote.

Paradoxically, many nonunion janitorial firms prefer a low-turnover environment. The district operations manager for Doral, a booming nonunion firm in Los Angeles, maintains that "the key to this business is to get a good crew and hold them." Reliance on recently arrived immigrants, however, allows nonunion firms the best of both worlds. When low turnover is required, new immigrants are happy to remain with minimal wage incentives; yet when quick replacement of the labor force is necessary, other immigrants can be found. Doral boasts a turnover rate of under 15 percent annually, even though according to union sources the management has removed its entire crew when faced with union-organizing efforts.

U.S.-born janitors, on the other hand, strongly resent low wages and excessive managerial supervision. In 1984, Doral broke with past practices of hiring exclusively Hispanic immigrants in order to acquire a government contract requiring domestic workers. The firm complained of 75 percent monthly turnover and had difficulty fulfilling the contract.

Employer preferences for immigrant workers are often extreme. The vice president of Mission Maintenance stated, "If I could find another labor force as reliable . . . as Mexicans, I would use it. But I can't." The manager at a unionized firm in Los Angeles justified his hiring of nonunion immigrant janitors by saying, "There are plenty of people on the union benches, but they are rejects."

THE SWITCH TO NONUNION CONTRACTORS: AN OVERVIEW

Conditions for California's janitors improved in the 1960s and 1970s as demand for their services increased—in 1983, there were 52,000 California janitors compared to 30,000 in 1970. But by the end of the 1970s, the favorable tide had begun to recede.

A general antiunion atmosphere is partly responsible. National Labor

Relations Board (NLRB) rulings have not helped organizing efforts among janitors in recent years. For example, the NLRB now requires "wall-to-wall" organizing by unions at hotels (only one union is allowed to organize at a given job site), which has caused jurisdictional problems between janitorial and hotel unions. Also, the NLRB has not acted quickly in calling elections, and rulings are less frequently in favor of unions than in previous periods. As Lynda McClure, business representative at Local 18 in Oakland says, "It's a miracle when the NLRB issues a complaint today."

Without a skill barrier to back up high wage and benefit demands, the union's position has become less and less tenable. In addition, the rising immigrant presence in California SEIU locals has been a factor in the decline of union strength. According to Alfredo Tepete, a Local 399 shop steward, "The [immigrants] don't know how to defend themselves or use the union." He explains that most immigrants' "unwillingness to make the effort to participate actively in the union assures that they don't learn about their rights."

These inherent problems opened up the cost wedge for the mid-sized nonunion firm. These mid-sized companies, often run by the ex-managerial staff of large unionized firms, have combined professional experience in delivering quality service with a willingness to use Hispanic middlemen to tap into networks of recent immigrants. This combination has meant inexpensive, high-quality service, which has presented formidable competition for large unionized firms.

At most job sites, the unfavorable tide has meant changes for many, if not most, janitors. A return to more part-time work has occurred as hours for each employee have on average been reduced. Wages have fallen in most places and work loads have increased. At the same time, the percentage of immigrant janitors has increased and the number of U.S.-born janitors has dwindled. In Los Angeles, the number of employed black members of SEIU Local 399 has fallen from 2,500 in 1977 to 600 in 1985. The manager of the Commercial Maintenance Company reports that "whites have been totally filtered out of the market."

Adverse developments in the janitorial trade have not affected all California locals uniformly, despite the similar conditions that they face. The San Jose and East Bay area locals (77 and 18, respectively) have a smaller share of the growing labor market than before, but they have held onto their members. In San Francisco, Local 87 has continued to command almost complete control of the janitorial service trade. Although most union locals have had to accept a two-tier wage environment, the results also vary by area. In Los Angeles, almost all unionized janitors work under lower-rate contracts, while in Oakland and San Jose most do not. In San Francisco there is no two-tier system: the San Francisco employers asked for deep cutbacks in the negotiations of June and July 1985, but the janitors were able to retain wages at levels above $10 an hour.

A CLOSE LOOK AT LOS ANGELES JANITORS

SEIU Local 399's ability to protect Los Angeles janitors has suffered a rapid collapse. Even the nonunion firms are surprised how quickly the union lost ground. These events demonstrate the fragility of union strength in low-skill, relatively well-paid sectors, where a large pool of immigrant labor is available and where employers have learned how to gain access to this labor.

Rapid office-space expansion in recent decades has increased demand for Los Angeles County janitors. Accounts in small buildings have always been handled by mom-and-pop firms, while traditionally the suburban medium-sized contracts were taken by nonunion contractors and the large downtown and suburban accounts by the large unionized firms. In the 1970s, a small number of these large companies, competing vigorously against one another, came to dominate almost all the lucrative contacts in the Wilshire Corridor, Century City, and other high-rise areas. These firms had mostly U.S.-born black employees. At the same time, mid-sized firms were expanding in the suburbs, with nonunion work forces consisting mostly of Hispanic immigrants.

In the 1980s, the tables turned on the unionized firms. Due to mergers and a general decline of the large firms, only four unionized firms have survived—American Building Maintenance, Commercial Maintenance Company, Pedus, and Property Care, Inc. Ironically, these unionized firms have lost most of their downtown contracts and have had to take up suburban jobs with an immigrant labor force in order to survive in the area. Meanwhile, the lucrative downtown contracts have fallen to the mid-sized nonunion firms. Local 399, which estimates that one-third of all Los Angeles janitors were in the union in 1977, admits that they represented only 8 percent of the janitors in 1985. The rise and fall of SEIU's Local 399 deserves careful attention.

LOCAL 399 AND THE JANITORS: YEARS OF SUCCESS

The SEIU began organizing janitors in 1946 in Los Angeles under the supervision of San Francisco-based leaders. Organizers concentrated their efforts almost exclusively on the large-scale janitorial firms with large market shares because these firms were sufficiently capitalized to support union demands. The janitors of the larger firms, who by the

TABLE 2

Blacks and Hispanic Immigrant Membership in Local 399, 1977 to 1985

Year	Number standard agreement	Number maint. on-site	Number route suburb	Percent Black	Percent Hispanic immigrant	Number of Blacks
1977	2,500		2,500	50%	50%	2,500
1983	1,800		200	40%	60%	800
1985	100	700	1,200	30%	70%	600

SOURCE: Dave Stillwell, Local 399

1960s were a mostly black group, were extremely receptive to the union. United under the SEIU banner, Los Angeles janitors pressured building-maintenance companies for full-time jobs, instead of the part-time arrangement that characterized (and still characterizes) most of the industry. Once full-time jobs were obtained by union contract, the SEIU began to push for better wages and benefits.

The 1965–1975 period was the best decade for Local 399's janitors and unionized contractors. Strict SEIU surveillance kept nonunion firms at bay, and an aggressive, pro-strike posture forced unionized companies to accept rising wages and benefit demands. At the same time, unionized building-maintenance companies benefited from the increasing dedication and professionalism of its work force. Local 399's strength among janitors peaked during this period at about 5,000 members (Table 2). Nearly all of the large downtown building contracts were under union lock and key, and most of the large buildings in Pasadena, Santa Monica, Hollywood, and other high-rise satellite areas were policed by SEIU contracts.

Neither the union leadership nor its militant labor force, however, were entirely satisfied with the job conditions that prevailed in 1975. Wages had more than doubled from those available a decade before, but still were only $3.75 an hour. Members also felt that benefits were too low and an eight-hour day too long.

Bolstered by their previous successes and the credibility of their strike threat, Local 399 continued to push for better conditions. Between 1976 and 1983, union wages under the Standard Contract Agreement rose an average of fifty cents a year (Table 3). Moreover, unionized contractors acquiesced to an attractive benefit package that ultimately included eleven paid holidays and full medical, dental, vision, and prescription coverage. According to Dave Stillwell, head business agent for the janitors at Local 399, "We fought hard to make building maintenance a full-

TABLE 3

Wage Increases for Local #399 Janitors, 1976 to 1983

Year	Increase in cents	Year	Increase in cents
1976	50	1980	30
1977	40	1981	60
1978	50	1982	40
1979	40	1983	30

SOURCE: Dave Stillwell, Bus. Agent, SEIU Local 399.
NOTE: There were no increases after 1983.

time job and one that provided benefits and wages attractive enough for U.S. workers."

Each new victory achieved by SEIU negotiators made Local 399 less cautious. The more they pushed, however, the more vulnerable their position became. At their peak in 1982, contract gains had boosted total wages and benefits under the Standard Contract Agreement to over $12 an hour, compared to the approximately $4 being paid by nonunion firms. The mounting gap between union and nonunion labor costs exposed the unionized firms to attack. Individual building managers, hit hard by the recession of the late 1970s, willingly began to entertain nonunion contract bids.

THE DECLINE OF THE LOS ANGELES JANITORS' UNION

A small group of mid-sized, aggressive firms sensed the union's vulnerability and made their move. Some nonunion firms actually offered a month's free service and reportedly promised kickbacks to building managers. In most instances, however, additional incentives were unnecessary. At labor costs half those of unionized firms, the new contenders could easily take attractive offers, provided they could guarantee quality service. The vice president of one unionized firm in Los Angeles reflected in 1983, "Nonunion contractors are our biggest problem, and now more professional people are getting into it so it is harder to convince building managers that nonunion firms aren't as professional as [we are]."

Many managers of the successful nonunion, mid-sized contractors have had experience in the large unionized firms. For this reason, many know how to deliver the professional service expected by the customers. At least some firms seemed to have been formed with the knowledge, if not the outright assistance, of the management in certain unionized firms. Bradford Building Maintenance is headed by Larry Smith, an ex-president of industry giant ABM, and Flagship Building Maintenance is headed by an ex-vice president of ABM, Aaron Cohen. The union has tried to stop this activity, which it calls "double breasting," because it believes it violates antitrust laws. In 1980, the union won cases against the two largest unionized firms, ABM and Pedus. ABM was fined $2,000, and Pedus was held to be illegally running a sister firm called General Building Maintenance.

The union, however, is not actively trying to stop the creation of sister companies because it is relatively easy for the newly created firms to elude union lawyers. As Joyce Muscato, head of the building maintenance division of the SEIU research office in Washington, D.C., says, "The legal battles are long and expensive . . . the money is better spent organizing. Double breasting is the result of nonunion competition . . . we can't win the battle by holding the line and making union contractors pay through the nose."

In fact, not all nonunion firms have direct or indirect financial ties with the large unionized firms. Downtown Maintenance, probably the most successful, was formed in 1978, before the tide had turned against the union. Within two years, the firm had gained considerable notoriety for its ability to move in on once-unionized buildings in the Los Angeles periphery and stray buildings in the downtown area as well. By early 1983, the fledgling company had nearly fifty contracts, including the lucrative Bank of America contract and the contract for the new downtown Security Pacific Building. The district-operations manager for Downtown Maintenance, Jack Kowsky, noted in 1983 that the nonunion sector had 40 percent of the labor costs of the union sector and was able to deliver quality service to increasingly cost-conscious building managers.[5]

The union tried to fight the nonunion contractors both by organizing them directly and by making concessions to the union firms. The direct organization effort has not led to any signed contracts. Employers can easily evade the NLRB-run elections, and their only financial interests are their contacts to worker networks and goodwill with the building owners and managers. As a result, when the union moves in and wins an election (they won three between 1981 and 1985), the firm can just sell the accounts to another nonunion firm through various procedures. The same individuals responsible for organizing the nonunion crews then reappear in new or reorganized companies. It may take the NLRB as long as three

---

[5] Downtown Maintenance in 1983 had 400 workers. Almost all were earning $3.35 an hour, 95 percent were undocumented Central Americans, and the majority had been in the country for less than two years. For many, this was their first job in the United States. (Jack Kowsky, interview with author, 1983).

years to adjudicate an election, but only a year or less is needed for new corporate forms to emerge.

The inability to organize the growing nonunion firms has blunted the strike weapon for the union. As Dave Stillwell put it, "We used to walk out to settle our differences, but now if we go out, we don't get back in." In the summer of 1984, the union stopped striking with firms holding out for wage cutbacks. The result has been the union's accommodation to management. In 1982, Local 399 (in line with a national trend) acquiesced to management demands for separate suburban and route contracts at lower rates than the standard agreement. Starting wages were $3.50 and $4.00 respectively for the 1985 contracts, and the only benefit provided is a rarely used plan for vision care. In addition, in its downtown contracts, the union agreed to "maintenance on-site" agreements at wages from $5.75 to $6.40, which are well below the standard agreement. Dave Stillwell estimated in April 1985 that 1,200 workers were covered under the route and suburban contracts, 700 under the maintenance on-site contracts, and 100 under the high-wage standard agreement (Table 2). Moreover, the days of these last few standard agreements are numbered.

The nonunion sector has had for some time a work force comprised almost entirely of Hispanic immigrants. The Hispanic presence was growing even within the union, especially in suburban areas, before the crisis struck. The nonunion sector had also been made up of mostly part-time workers and had very rapid turnover, again especially in the suburban areas. When nonunion crews began competing with the unionized firms, it was an unequal economic battle. "They can put in two or three people for our every one in a building," Stillwell explains. The standard contract paid nearly $13 an hour, while the nonunion firms were paying $3.35. Contractors could bring large part-time crews and clean a building quickly, whereas union firms had to take more time to employ full-time janitors. For union firms to compete in the suburbs, they wrung from the union the right to hire part-time workers and pay $4 an hour or less. This has meant high turnover and few differences between the union and nonunion labor forces. It has allowed the janitors' union to stabilize its total membership during 1985 and 1986, but the makeup of that membership has changed from U.S.-born to Hispanic immigrant.

The decline of union membership and the shift within union firms to a new labor force as the firms moved to the suburbs has meant a massive layoff of black workers. The union estimates that 1,900 fewer unionized blacks are working in 1985 than in 1977 (Table 3). Moreover, if the

TABLE 4

Janitorial Wages in Non-Manufacturing (Service) Firms, Dollars per Hour,
1978–1986

Year	Los Angeles	San Jose	Year	Los Angeles	San Jose
1978	4.37	4.54	1983	6.58	6.35
1979	4.94	5.07	1984	5.95	6.55
1980	5.37	5.40	1985	5.63	6.33
1981	5.94	5.57	1986	n.a	6.31
1982	6.15	6.00			

SOURCE: "Area Wage Surveys," in Bureau of Labor Statistics, *Hourly Earnings of Material-Movement and Custodial Workers* (Washington, 1978–1986).

union firms lose the rest of their downtown contracts, the remaining blacks will face displacement as well. The growing nonunion firms and the suburban contracts acquired by the old unionized firms use almost exclusively recent immigrants from Latin America.

Government statistics corroborate the findings of wage depression discovered by our survey research. From 1983 to 1985, according to a Bureau of Labor Statistics survey, janitorial-service wages in Los Angeles fell by 15 percent (see Table 4).

The displaced blacks were themselves immigrants from the U.S. South, and many remain unemployed. Doris Boyd, a black business representative for Local 399 says, "A very small percentage of these worker[s] have found jobs. They are unskilled people; they don't know anything but janitorial. Most have had fifteen to twenty years experience. About 700 are out of work right now because of the changes."

LOCAL 399 SURVIVES AS A HOSPITABLE WORKERS' UNION

Not all SEIU Local 399 representatives feel that the decline of union strength in the Los Angeles janitorial industry was inevitable. One slighted union organizer claimed that the nonunion trend could have been reversed if union local organizers had put their minds to it. "The union wants to operate like a business," he charged. "They always pursue the easiest strategy to get new members."

Indeed, Local 399's leadership did choose to forgo the financial risk of mounting an all-out organizing drive against nonunion janitorial firms and instead set their sights on easier prey. In the past six years, union interest and resources have shifted steadily away from the janitorial sector and into more lucrative areas, especially hospitals. Local 399 has hammered out contracts with many of the major medical service providers in the Los Angeles area. Every time Kaiser builds a new facility, for example, the union automatically acquires at least six hundred new members—far more than the numbers provided by the largest building-maintenance contract.

By mid-1985, SEIU 399 had largely abandoned unionized janitors. Only janitor faithfuls Stillwell and Boyd remained to address the upward-spiraling number of grievances from the remaining janitorial membership. Defeatism has replaced the retaliatory tone that marked both business agents as late as May 1983. "People say we don't do anything now for the janitors because in comparison to before 1975, we don't," admitted Stillwell. Today, the most aggressive action the union musters in defense of union janitors is a feeble flier-distribution campaign. To reflect the changing priorities of SEIU's leadership, the local has reversed its name from "Service and Hospital Employees Union" to "Hospital and Service Employees Union."

A CLOSE LOOK AT SANTA CLARA VALLEY JANITORS

Conditions in the Santa Clara Valley are quite similar to Los Angeles, but events have taken a somewhat different course. Local 77 of the SEIU has lost ground if one evaluates its strength by the proportion of the labor market held by its members. The union has been able to maintain a constant membership in recent years, but the demand for janitors has jumped by leaps and bounds.

Familiar events have taken place. Mid-sized nonunion firms, which underbid large unionized companies for contracts, have become important in the valley. High turnover strategies are commonly used to avoid unionization and keep wages low. Supervisory tasks are routinely delegated to Hispanic middlemen who have extensive contacts to networks of recent immigrants. The pressure for give-backs by unionized firms, which claim that relatively high labor costs are driving them out of business, is as familiar in San Jose as in Los Angeles. Yet despite these surface similarities, there is as yet no sign of collapse at Local 77. One unionized firm, Mission Maintenance, continued to expand in the early 1980s despite paying union scales. Also, most of the large contracts are firmly in union hands. What accounts for Local 77's durability?

History of Local 77

The past thirty years have seen the Santa Clara Valley change from a predominantly fruit-growing area into the nation's leading center for high technology. The expansion of offices and "clean" industries has meant a fivefold growth in the demand for janitors in the last quarter century. Mexican, Filipino, and Portuguese immigrants have made up the bulk of the area's maintenance workers and during the most recent boom in janitorial employment the Mexican contingent in the work force become dominant. In the five firms interviewed, approximately 80 percent of the workers were from Mexico.

Although they control a declining share of the market, mom-and-pop operations, which normally employ twenty workers or less and cater to the sprawling commercial and residential markets, still do about half of the area's maintenance work. These small firms have been less affected by the labor-market changes of recent years. The other half of the maintenance market in the Santa Clara Valley consists of larger industrial and commercial projects—the private domain of the union firms until the late 1970s, when the nonunion shops, staffed by former managers of the largest union firms, began to make inroads into this expanding market. Differences in labor costs explain the growing appeal of the nonunion contractors. In 1985, the nonunion contractors were paying between minimum wage and $5 an hour while the union contracts mandated wages of $5.12 to $7.96 with ample benefits. The union was forced to accommodate nonunionized firms by agreeing to the "new member advancement program" instituted in 1981 through a union contract. According to this program, new employees are subject to a four-year apprenticeship period during which they are paid a percentage of journeymen's wages (70 percent the first year, 80 percent the second year, and so on).

The agreement is tantamount to the two-tier system, which has allowed unionized firms to lower their labor costs. The flexibility of the "advancement program" has allowed several foremen at unionized firms to tap into networks of recently arrived Mexican immigrants and institute high turnover in an effort to keep an ever-changing work force from achieving journeymen's wages.

The appearance of a viable nonunion element has also weakened the union's position in bargaining sessions for job security. In one case, the union could not prevent a client firm from replacing full-time workers with part-time workers. Though a bargaining session did take place in 1983 between the union and the client firm, the union was unable to prevent the unilateral imposition of this change.

By 1983, nonunion contractors had made substantial inroads into the market. At the job sites where union and nonunion firms were competing, which represent about 2,800 janitorial jobs, nonunion firms had obtained about 20 percent of the work.

Although both the union and nonunion firms use Mexican immigrant labor forces, important differences exist. The large unionized firms have work forces made up mostly of settled immigrant workers. These workers do not necessarily hold legal immigration papers but have either lived in the United States long enough to move up to this relatively favored place in the job hierarchy or have close friends and relatives who have been able to place them in the unionized jobs. Most of these settled workers have brought their families to California. Nonunion contractors rely to a larger extent on recent immigrants without extensive network contacts to better jobs. Many of these workers are unaccompanied by their Mexican families.

The group of settled immigrants working for the unionized firms has suffered wage depression and displacement in the late 1970s and 1980s because nonunion firms have been able to offer a less costly substitute for their labor—namely, more recent immigrants. As a result, real wages have declined for settled unionized janitors and, due to the loss of contracts, some of these workers have lost their jobs entirely.

Despite this familiar scenario of recent immigrants being used by employers to replace more veteran groups, Local 77 has not settled for an entirely defensive response. Mike Garcia, a bilingual business agent for Local 77, put it this way: "You can't let the contractors say we have to be locked into the lowest bids. The union has power and can use it to get the firms to accept union contractors." Local 77's strategy has three main components: (1) effectively service the rank-and-file members, including immigrants who do not speak English, (2) mount a strategic campaign aimed at contractors' client companies to keep them hiring union workers, and (3) harass the nonunion firms to keep them small and unable to take on the large cleaning contracts.

Garcia would like to avoid the problem that occurred in Los Angeles, where the nonunion contractors grew large enough to take over the "professional" large contracts. He says, "If we can keep any of the nonunion contractors from getting big enough and keep getting the skill to get a big contract, then we are in good shape." The local union monitors the activities of the mid-sized firms closely, taking every opportunity to hurt their business. One tactic is to push for union elections at the nonunion firms, although success (as in Los Angeles) is quite difficult. The union mounted a drive at Collegiate Building Maintenance in 1979, at United Building Maintenance in 1981, at Action Building Maintenance and Service by Medallion in 1982, and at Freitech Building Maintenance in 1985. Elections were won at Action and at Freitech. Garcia feels the elections have kept firms off-balance, and that the constant turnover caused by union drives leads to inferior service and customer dissatisfaction with nonunion companies. For example, Garcia claimed that United turned over most of its workers in 1984 as a result of a union drive that led to customer complaints.

Local 77's strategy is to keep the large accounts. "The strength of the union is in the big accounts. This is the backbone of the union—this gives us the strength and the organizational structure to carry out a harassment campaign against the small contractors to keep them small," Garcia contends. He feels that in Silicon Valley the large companies are particularly sensitive to hostile news stories, picketing, the passing out of leaflets, and rallies. One reason is because many are defense contractors; another is because some face unionizing drives by their non-janitorial employees. Companies like IBM, Amdahl, and National Semiconductor are sensitive to their public images. Garcia does not hesitate to talk to personnel managers and public-relations officials within the client companies of the janitorial contractors in order to make sure they do not shift to nonunion contractors.

Local 77, due in part to the activity of a Latin caucus within the union, has been sensitive to the ethnic and linguistic background of the majority of its members. It has a trilingual newspaper (English, Spanish, and Portuguese); it conducts membership meetings in all three languages; and it emphasizes Latin themes in all its rallies and meetings. Grievances can be handled in Spanish or Portuguese whenever necessary because the union has several bilingual business representatives. Since the nonunion employers know that Local 77 is active among their janitorial work force, wages are kept relatively high as a defensive strategy.

In fairness to Local 399 of Los Angeles, it should be pointed out that the membership of Local 77 has always been predominantly Latin. The rapid switch from black to Latin members, which has caused cultural and language barriers in Los Angeles, did not occur in the Santa Clara Valley local.

In 1984, despite its difficulties, Local 77 still carried out a successful strike against union contractors. In the Santa Clara Valley, the Contractors Association has a joint contract with the union for many of the firms, and most of the independent contractors follow the master contract. In 1984, however, the union and the association had a conflict. First the dispute was over medical and dental coverage, but when the association agreed not to lower employer payments, the disagreement expanded to the issues of back pay and wage increases. This conflict led to an eight-day strike, after which the union was able to obtain its demand.

This union success, however, does not guarantee that nonunion contractors will eventually fail to dislodge the local from its leadership position among janitors in the Santa Clara Valley. The president of J8, the largest nonunion firm in the valley, disagrees with Garcia's account almost entirely. He says that union firms have succeeded in keeping profits high by taking advantage of the new member advancement programs. He charges that these employers have lowered their labor costs and still charge the same rates to their customers—a tactic that results in greater profit margins. Garcia, however, maintains that higher costs of health benefits have canceled out the labor-cost benefits of the two-tier wage system.

Firm J8's president also claims that his firm has grown to the point where it can take on any contract in the valley—at one time, for example, he had almost one hundred janitors at Atari. From his point of view, the union strategy to keep the nonunion firms small has not succeeded. He says that Local 77's "efforts at disruption have failed due to the ineptitude of union management." Garcia realizes that the situation is tenuous and that constant struggle is required to stop deterioration of union strength. If the nonunion firms do erode the base of the local in the large contracts, he admits that the situation could become desperate. As Garcia puts it, "If that happens, the situation could deteriorate in a year or two."

BUSINESS AND UNION LEADERSHIP IN CHANGING TIMES

The areas of greatest union strength for janitors have traditionally been in highly concentrated downtown areas. New York City (with its fifty thousand janitors), San Francisco, and Chicago have been the models. But the decline in the influence of unions that first affected suburban high rises has not been contained there. Downtown Los Angeles, despite its increasing concentration, proves that no union stronghold is safe.

Union leadership must make drastic adaptations if it is to survive in this industry. The ample availability of labor makes it easy for weakly capitalized nonunion firms to attack union contracts, and unions have experienced extreme difficulties in organizing these firms. "Some firms periodically turn over their labor forces, . . . others pay informers . . . to squeal on union activity." Recent immigrants with relatively low expectations are "murder to organize, even with Hispanic organizers."[6] In addition, some union firms take advantage of the situation by not reporting new workers so that unions are denied dues. And the NLRB acts so slowly on elections that entire crews are often turned over by the time an

[6] Dave Stillwell, Local 399. Interview with Richard Mines, 1984.

election is adjudicated. As Lynda McClure of Local 18 says, "The life-blood of unions is organizing." If the new workers cannot be organized, union membership will continue to decline.

Some people in management do not like the present trend because it may exclude those who practice a responsible management style from doing business. The president of Firm J8 states, "I am not against the union; conditions would fall to minimum wage without the union and there [would] be a free-for-all." Jack Egan, vice president of industry giant American Building Maintenance, states:

The industry must try to maintain its high standards and continue to pay fair wages if it is to remain a good industry. We will not be able to continue to recruit good employees . . . without decent wages. In this particular aspect we are on the side of strong unions who seek to provide that fair wage. . . . Sometimes what seems desirable in the short run can be disastrous in the long run. We have a fine industry. We should all work to keep it that way.[7]

In fact, if present trends in the building-maintenance industry continue, the industry could fall into a pattern similar to that in many parts of rural California, where workers are often controlled by labor contractors without respect for minimal labor standards.

AFTERWORD ON THE IMMIGRATION AND NATURALIZATION SERVICE (INS)

Immigration reform may hurt the labor movement in one way and help it in another. The Immigration Reform and Control Act of 1986 may hold the union liable to a fine if it refers undocumented workers to job sites. This policy may harm unionists' ability to build rapport in immigrant communities. On the other hand, as Charley Perkel of Local 77 says, "The law will increase the power of the illegal immigrant in demanding his rights as a worker because employers will no longer be able to blow the whistle on their own workers."

The building-maintenance trade is affected less by the INS than are most other sectors, especially considering that the industry has one of the highest levels of undocumented workers. Two out of three of the most well-established INS practices make it unlikely that janitorial firms will be raided. The targeting of high-wage job sites does not exclude the unionized sector of janitors where many undocumented are present; however, the INS concentrates on sites where many undocumented workers can be found. This criterion excluded most janitorial sites because

[7] Jack Egan, "Contractors Pose Problems—And Offer Solutions," *Building Services Contractor* (Apr. 1985).

few workers are spread throughout the buildings. Also, INS investigators work a 9-to-5 schedule, so they miss most janitors, who work at night or the swing shift. In the interviewed firms, only two large unionized firms were raided. These firms had some of the best labor conditions in the industry.

There is a misunderstanding in both union and management circles about the practices of the INS and possible effects of immigration reform. For example, Charley Perkel in San Jose believes that the Simpson-Mazzoli bill would "put the heat on the nonunion firm." The manager of the unionized Firm J2 concurs, saying "Nonunion companies may be brought to their knees. The law would work for the union companies by forcing the nonunion ones to pay competitive wages." Since the nonunion firms are much more highly dependent on ever-changing networks of recent immigrants, it is not surprising that immigration reform is seen as somewhat of a solution by many individuals, both in unions and in unionized management.

A look at past INS practices shows that they are (1) antiunion, and (2) counterproductive to INS's stated policy of creating high-wage employment for legal and domestic workers. The INS has focused on union firms with high pay scales and mostly legal crews. There are many undocumented among the unionized firms, but these undocumented workers are almost always settled people who have been in the United States for several years, have their families here with them, and probably have assets such as cars and houses. The INS throws these men and women out of the country, but these are the people that normally return the next day. They have the contacts to get back across the border and recover their old job or find another one easily. In effect, no new job openings are freed for domestic or legal workers at all; the opposite has happened. While the unionized firm with mostly legal and domestic workers is being disrupted and harassed, its nonunion competitor, with mostly undocumented workers earning minimum wage, may take advantage of the situation and win a contract from the unionized firm. The INS actions produce the effect opposite to that intended: settled workers and U.S.-born workers are replaced with undocumented workers.

For immigration reform to be successful in the building-maintenance industry, it must start from an understanding that immigrants penetrate the labor market through nonunion and low-wage firms, which underbid unionized firms. The objective of immigration reform is allegedly to improve conditions and wages for domestic and legal workers. But this goal can only be accomplished if the INS reverses its present policies. The INS will have to survey small firms just as much as large ones; work at night;

and most important, concentrate on the most poorly paid immigrants, not the best paid (the better-paying employers on average hire more legal and U.S.-born workers). As these more principled employers expand their operations at the expense of harassed, low-wage firms, more legal, settled immigrants and more domestic workers can be hired.

Technology and Labor-Intensive Agriculture: Competition Between Mexico and the United States

David Runsten and Sandra O. Archibald

A GRICULTURE AND FOOD processing in the United States are increasingly subject to the internationalization of capital and trade. Most areas of the United States have experienced this internationalization in two ways: an increased dependence on export markets, especially for a recurrent surplus production of basic grains, and an increased consumption of both complementary and supplementary imported foods.[1]

Increasing world competition is a direct result of the growth in world trade and industrial development after World War II; the debt crisis in the developing countries and currency realignments have merely exacerbated already existing trends. Agriculture as a world industry has benefited from improvements in transportation, communication, infrastructure, and transfer of technology in a manner similar to many other industries. Moreover, the speed of capital movements and the ability of capital to move to maximize profits have engaged U.S. and Mexican agriculture in an increasingly interconnected set of production and marketing relations.

Labor markets have also become increasingly linked among countries, with large-scale, often unregulated migration occurring across international borders. Agricultural harvests in particular depend on such labor movements, whether it is a migration of Algerian workers to Spain, central Africans to the coast, or Salvadorans to Honduras. The sustained migration of Mexicans to the United States is simply one of the longest-running of these movements, and its cumulative effect has been to in-

---

[1] Complementary products are those not produced in the United States, such as coffee; supplementary products are imports that compete with U.S. production.

crease the viability of seasonal agricultural production throughout the United States.

Although in theory specific countries or agricultural regions have a comparative advantage in the production of certain crops (depending on their factor endowments), nevertheless the *competitive* level of each area in each crop will depend on historical developments such as the creation of infrastructure, learning curves, marketing arrangements, or labor strategies. The realization of *potential* comparative advantage is a process fraught with political and institutional obstacles, but the parameters are clearly changed by the mobility of labor.

Low wages and other factor price differentials are critical to these developments but are not new, just as the shift to take advantage of them at the present time is only possible because of a cumulative historical process. For example, the pronounced trend toward importing supplementary agricultural products into the United States began to accelerate in the mid-1960s,[2] and the current Mexican competitiveness in certain crops is the direct result of a process of development that began earlier in the century (we will analyze this process later).

Since the labor-intensive agriculture of the southwestern United States has employed most Mexican immigrants working in agriculture, we focus here on the crops grown in this area, mainly fruits and vegetables.

California is a focus in our inquiry as a state that has become dependent on exporting. An estimated one-third of the agricultural acreage in California was dedicated to exports in 1984, accounting for more than one-fifth of agricultural income.[3] In addition, California has experienced increased competition from "supplementary" imports into the United States in crops such as garlic, broccoli, grapes, tomatoes, and asparagus.

California has pursued an increasingly industrial agriculture for over one hundred years, so it is not surprising that many of the competitive pressures this system faces, from Mexico and elsewhere, are similar to those challenging other sectors of the U.S. economy. A complex interaction among competition in product markets, shifts in political power, and economic crises in Mexico have contributed to the present shifts in the labor markets and labor processes of California agriculture and to the increase of capital flows into Mexican agriculture.

Both the United States and Mexico face difficult decisions about how to balance migration, trade balances, and investment flows. The process

[2] Susan George, *Feeding the Few* (Washington, n.d.)

[3] California Department of Food and Agriculture, *Exports of Agricultural Commodities Produced in California* (Sacramento, Oct. 1984).

of migration may have developed to the point where it is not easily affected by policy changes, but the dismantling of barriers to the flow of capital and goods between the two countries will have significant effects, and such choices should be made with full awareness of their consequences.

CALIFORNIA'S COMPARATIVE ADVANTAGE

California, producer of over 250 agricultural commodities,[4] has long served as a supplier of specialty crops to less-favorable growing areas of the United States, not only because of good climate and soil, but due to a distinct set of economic factors: large landholdings, access to inexpensive or subsidized irrigation, and use of immigrant hired farm labor.

As early as 1900, over 50 percent of the cropland in California was on farms of one thousand acres or more. In the United States at that time, only 5 percent of the cropland was accounted for by such large farms.[5] Large farms continue to dominate California agriculture, especially in fruits and vegetables. The largest 3.4 percent of California farms, those with annual farm sales of $1 million or more, produce 60 percent of the state's agricultural output and over 70 percent of the fruit and vegetables in the state.[6]

Extensive private irrigation, developed from river runoff, began in the late nineteenth century, followed by federal development of the Imperial Valley in the 1920s; the Central Valley Project beginning in the 1930s; and development of the State Water Project in the 1960s. Today, California has about 9 million acres of irrigated land, or 20 percent of all irrigated farmland in the United States.[7]

While the private runoff irrigation was cheap, the government-built irrigation was subsidized and made artificially cheap. For example, the average water price in the original part of the Central Valley Project is $3.70/acre-foot, and even in the later and much more costly Westlands area the water price is only $9.45/acre-foot.[8] LeVeen and King estimate

[4] *Ibid.*

[5] David Runsten and E. Phillip LeVeen, *Mechanization and Mexican Labor in California Agriculture* Monograph no. 6, Program in U.S.-Mexican Studies (San Diego, 1981), 6.

[6] U.S. Department of Agriculture, Bureau of the Census, *Census of Agriculture, 1987: California* (Washington, May 1989).

[7] Don Villarejo, *Environmental Effects of Living and Working in Agricultural Areas of California: Social and Economic Factors* (Davis, Calif., California Institute for Rural Studies, June 1990), 33; David Hornbeck, *California Patterns: A Geographical and Historical Atlas* (Palo Alto, Calif., 1983), 81.

[8] However, we should note that in general the value of these subsidies have been capitalized into the value of the land. See Ray G. Huffaker and B. Delworth Gardner, "The Dis-

that the actual cost to the Bureau of Reclamation to deliver water to the Westlands was about $97.00/acre-foot in 1985. Of course, California is not the only beneficiary of these subsidies, it is simply the largest.[9]

The final element in the development of California's fruit and vegetable agriculture, and the one that concerns us most here, was the continued importation of immigrant labor to work at seasonal jobs. That is, the key to the successful development of labor-intensive crops was a labor supply of casual workers willing to work seasonally for very low wages, which in recent decades amounted to about 50 to 60 percent of nonagricultural wages.[10]

The history of this management of the agricultural labor market—and the succession of ethnic groups who were employed—has been well documented.[11] What is important to note is that the system of large farms producing labor-intensive crops for large markets rested firmly on the foundation provided by this labor market. If labor costs had been higher, small family farmers utilizing family labor could have competed more successfully with the large farms.[12]

Over time, the advantage that this relatively low-cost labor gave California over other areas was incorporated into the value of the land. As Fuller noted: "Owners who have purchased their land at values already based upon the income received from the employment of cheap labor stand not to make large gains from the continued employment of cheap labor. On the other hand, if, after buying land capitalized on such a basis, real wages, ceteris paribus, commence to rise, the owner stands to suffer more than book losses."[13] Thus the financial structure of California agriculture has been erected on (1) low-cost labor and water, and (2) on money loaned to farmers partly based on the value of the land, which rests on the viability of large-scale production of labor-intensive commodities for distant markets. A loss of comparative advantage for Cali-

---

tribution of Economic Rents Arising from Subsidized Water When Land Is Leased," *American Journal of Agricultural Economics* vol. 68, no. 2 (May 1986).

[9] E. Phillip LeVeen and Laura B. King, *Turning Off the Tap on Federal Water Subsidies. Volume 1: The Central Valley Project* (San Francisco, 1985), table 9.

[10] Runsten and LeVeen, *Mechanization and Mexican Labor in California Agriculture*, 24.

[11] Carey McWilliams, *Factories in the Field* (Salt Lake City, 1971); Varden Fuller, "The Supply of Agricultural Labor as a Factor in the Evolution of Farm Organization in California," Ph.D. diss., University of California, Berkeley, printed in U.S. Congress, Senate, *Hearings of the Committee on Violations of Free Speech and Rights of Labor*, part 54 (Washington, 1940); Cletus E. Daniel, *Bitter Harvest: A History of California Farmworkers, 1870–1941* (Ithaca, N.Y., 1981).

[12] Carey McWilliams, *California: The Great Exception* (New York, 1935).

[13] Fuller, *The Supply of Agricultural Labor*.

fornia caused by changes in these factors of production implies rising costs of labor, water, or other inputs relative to competing regions, with a potential loss of markets and a decline in land values. This schema gives us a historical basis on which to discuss the current problems in California agriculture and perspectives for Mexican-U.S. agricultural and labor relations.

EMERGING CONSTRAINTS ON CALIFORNIA AGRICULTURE

In this section, we briefly discuss the changes that have occurred, and may occur in the future, in the availability and cost of the most important inputs to fruit and vegetable production in California. The degree to which these changes affect California's competitiveness delimits the possibilities of shifting production to Mexico or elsewhere. We begin in some detail with the labor supply.

Immigration and the Agricultural Labor Market

Immigration from Mexico (or anywhere) is a cumulative process. As this process has progressed, it has altered both the context in which the decision to migrate is made in Mexico as well as the jobs available to migrants and the economic structure in the United States. Richard Mines and others have been arguing for some time that migration networks from individual villages develop over time on both sides of the border, and that this strongly influences the pattern of migration and job-seeking.[14]

Thus, there is not only a set of jobs that only migrants will fill,[15] but migrants possess certain characteristics that employers prefer[16]—especially a willingness to work harder at wages lower than U.S.-born workers will accept. This willingness may be due to lower expectations,[17] lower reproduction costs,[18] limited options, or lack of information. It is important to note, however, that all of these factors shift as workers settle in the United States and that this settling in turn alters the conditions

---

[14] Richard Mines, *Tortillas: A Binational Industry* (San Diego, Project on Mexican Immigrants in the California Economy, 1985); Richard Mines and Alain de Janvry, "Migration to the United States and Development: A Case Study," *American Journal of Agricultural Economics* vol. 64, no. 3 (1982), 444–54; Douglas Massey, et al., *Return to Aztlan: The Social Process of International Migration from Western Mexico* (Berkeley, Calif., 1987)

[15] Michael J. Piore, *Birds of Passage* (New York, 1979).

[16] Sheldon Maram, et al., "Hispanic Workers in the Garment and Restaurant Industries in L.A. County," working paper no. 12 (San Diego, Program in U.S.-Mexican Studies, 1983).

[17] Piore, *Birds of Passage.*

[18] Michael Burawoy, "The Functions and Reproduction of Migrant Labor: Comparative Material from Southern Africa and the United States," *American Journal of Sociology* vol. 81, no. 5 (1976).

faced by subsequent immigrants. One result of the maturation of migration is a shift in labor constraints in the United States, which encourages a certain pattern of job creation, labor process design, and technological adoption.

Mexicans are migrating to the United States and settling at an ever-increasing rate. Even if a large percentage of these migrants want to return to Mexico, the labor market situation there, made even worse by the present crisis, will not permit it: the average Mexican is about 15 years old, and a million people per year continue to come onto the job market of an economy that has seen almost no net growth since 1982.

This process of increased settlement probably began in the 1950s and increased as more migrant networks were created and developed.[19] The same is true geographically. While settlements of Mexican immigrants have a long history in certain areas (for example, the Southwest or Chicago), they are more recent in northern California, Washington, Oregon, Idaho, or New Jersey, and in rural areas previously visited only by seasonal (or "circular") migrants.

This dynamic process has several effects. First, it increases the possibility of migration from Mexico because of more contacts and job information, the spreading use of Latino intermediaries for recruitment, and a geographic broadening of labor markets that have been penetrated by immigrant networks.

Second, the maturation and settlement of networks makes it possible for migrants to move into job sectors not available to them when migration was temporary or circular. That is, it creates access to permanent jobs for recent immigrants from long-term sending communities. This may accelerate the exodus from seasonal work, because rather than return to Mexico when laid off, the worker may have the contacts to pursue a job search.

Third, settlement creates new demands for public services, which may or may not be counterbalanced by economic growth.

Fourth, settlement decreases turnover in many jobs, especially those in which wages have risen, because migrants are less likely to leave and return to Mexico. This is a positive result as long as the economy expands to absorb new workers. But if the economy slows or migration accelerates, job openings diminish and competition intensifies in the labor market.

The intensified competition, then, occurs between new migrants and

[19] Richard Mines, *Developing a Community Tradition of Migration: A Field Study in Rural Zacatecas, Mexico, and California Settlement Areas,* Monograph no. 3 (San Diego, Center for U.S.-Mexican Studies, 1981); Massey, et al., *Return to Aztlan.*

older, settled migrants. New migrants may have an advantage because they are initially alone and are willing to work at lower wages than the settled migrants, who face U.S. costs of living and have a family to support. Wages may fall, unions may be undermined, and other attempts to stabilize the labor force and improve working conditions may be eliminated. However, settled immigrants do not move back to Mexico, but rather seek jobs in other sectors of the economy or other regions, depending on the contacts they have.

This same process can occur simply from increased competition in the product market, which is then translated into pressure on the labor market. Of course, the ability of firms to pass on competitive pressures to the labor market depends on the balance of power between capital and labor.

Let us consider the effects of these four factors on labor-intensive agriculture in California.

1. Mexican immigrant farmworkers have become available to many areas of the United States that did not formerly have access to this labor force, which is making possible more intensive farming on irrigated land. For example, Mexican farmworkers have been brought in to work on the large irrigated ranches of southern Idaho;[20] they constitute the bulk of the harvest labor force for Oregon berries in the Willamette Valley, where local teenagers were still an important labor force in the early 1980s; they and the Guatemalans now make up the overwhelming share of the labor force for Florida vegetables and citrus;[21] they have replaced Native American and Texan workers in Washington state, where asparagus, pears, and other crops that compete with California have expanded;[22] and they are increasingly taking the place of blacks and Puerto Ricans in New Jersey nurseries.[23]

Mexican workers also now work in food processing in jobs that are complementary to work performed by the U.S.-born. For example, they constitute an important element of the turkey-processing labor force in southern Utah,[24] they have been substituted for Native Americans in

[20] Idaho Citizens Coalition, *Water, Energy, and Land: Public Resources and Irrigation Development in the Pacific Northwest* (Boise, 1981).

[21] David Griffith, et al., *Farm Labor Supply Study: Second Interim Report to the Office of Policy, U.S. Department of Labor* (Berkeley, Calif., 1990).

[22] Ed Kissam, "Feasibility Study and Project Design for an Enhanced Recruitment Demonstration Project: Washington Apples and Asparagus," report to the Office for Policy, U.S. Department of Labor (Sebastopol, Calif., 1988).

[23] Max Pfeffer, *Farm Labor Recruitment after Immigration Reform: Some Preliminary Findings from Exploratory Research on New Jersey Nurseries* (Berkeley, Calif., 1990).

[24] John Walker, "Stability in Production and the Demand for Mexican Labor: The Case of Turkey Processing in Utah," paper presented at the conference Changing Roles of Mexi-

many fish-processing plants along the Northwest coast,[25] and they play an important role in the shift of meatpacking to rural Midwest non-union plants.[26]

Thus California and Texas, which used most of the contract *bracero* labor in the 1950s and 1960s on a relatively small number of farms, are becoming less unique in their dependence on Mexican immigrant labor. Washington, Idaho, and Oregon used almost no *braceros* after World War II.[27] This also means that California growers may face increasing competition in many fruits and vegetables from other regions of the United States as farmers in these other areas shift from currently low-priced grains and use Mexican labor to grow intensive crops.

The emerging shift in location of fruit and vegetable horticulture in the United States will likely increase demand for farm labor in these new areas as well. While the Southwest continues to concentrate its increasing share of total U.S. production on fewer and larger farms, other areas of the United States are simultaneously increasing production geared for local markets.[28] Direct marketing has grown significantly, even in California.[29]

As the costs of growing and shipping across the country have risen, and as the prices of alternative crops have fallen, local production has become more attractive once again. In addition, this production responds to increased consumer demand for very fresh and fragile produce, which the cross-country system had eliminated in variety changes, green picking, and so forth. To the extent that this system grows, it will do so at the expense of both California and Mexico, countries that are competing for the long-distance and processed markets.

It is not clear, however, that the growth of this system will translate into a lower demand for Mexican laborers, who are increasingly able to be employed wherever labor-intensive production is undertaken.

2. A second consequence of settlement and maturation of migration

---

can Immigration in the U.S. Economy: Sectoral Perspectives (San Diego, Center for U.S.-Mexican Studies, Aug. 1987).

[25] David Runsten, *Mexican Immigrants and Fish Processing in California* (San Diego, Project on Mexican Immigration and the California Economy, 1985).

[26] K. Stanley, "The Role of Immigrant and Refugee Labor in the Restructuring of the Midwestern Meatpacking Industry," paper presented at the U.S. Department of Labor Conference on Migration, Washington, Sept. 1988.

[27] Runsten and LeVeen, *Mechanization and Mexican Labor in California Agriculture*, 56.

[28] Roberta Cook and Ricardo Amon, "Competition in the Fresh Vegetable Industry," in *Competitiveness at Home and Abroad* (Davis, Calif., Agricultural Issues Center, 1988).

[29] Suzanne Vaupel, "Direct Marketing in California," *California Agriculture* vol. 39, nos. 9–10 (Sept.-Oct. 1985).

for agriculture is the tendency for migrants' children to move on to other sectors of the economy. When migrants were circular, their children were raised in Mexico and often took the place of older generations. Such a system continues, for example, in the village of Gomez Farias, Michoacán, which sends a large group to Watsonville, California, to harvest strawberries. While in California, they live principally in a state-operated labor camp that is only open for six months of the year. Since the workers spend six months in Mexico, they own houses in Mexico, their children are raised and schooled in Mexico, and the children aspire to become California agricultural workers like their parents.[30]

With families settled in the United States, however, when the present generation of a network finishes with agricultural work—and many move out of high-stress harvesting tasks at a relatively young age[31]— migrants from newer networks must be found to replace them, because the children will not pursue farm work under current wages and working conditions. We see this trend in many areas of California, Oregon, and Florida, where increasing numbers of recent and undocumented immigrants from southern Mexico and Central America are employed.[32]

Thus while Mexico is still reproducing California's agricultural labor force, albeit in new regions, rural California is back in a position of subsidizing urban development through rural-urban migration, a principal role of rural areas in the development of the United States in this century.[33]

A mitigating factor is the ability of legal farmworkers in California to collect unemployment insurance since 1976. In the 1983 survey by the University of California Employment Development Department, about two-thirds of farmworker households reported receiving unemployment insurance in the previous year, with the proportion as high as 80 percent in some areas.[34] The cost of such a program is borne somewhat by agricultural employers, but there are large transfers from other sectors of the economy that experience less unemployment.[35] However, since farm-

[30] Anna Garcia, personal communication.

[31] Richard Mines and Philip L. Martin, "Foreign Workers in Selected California Crops," *California Agriculture* vol. 37, nos. 3–4 (Mar.-Apr. 1983).

[32] Richard Mines and Ricardo Anzaldua, *New Migrants vs. Old Migrants: Alternative Labor Market Structures in the California Citrus Industry,* Monograph no. 9 (San Diego, Program in U.S.-Mexican Studies, 1982); Griffith, et al., *Farm Labor Supply Study.*

[33] Wyn F. Owen, "The Double Developmental Squeeze on Agriculture," *American Economic Review* vol. 56, no. 1 (Mar. 1966).

[34] Richard Mines and Philip L. Martin, *A Profile of California Farmworkers* (Davis, Calif., Aug. 1985), table III-23.

[35] Martin Brown, A Historical Economic Analysis of the Wage Structure of the California Fruit and Vegetable Canning Industry, Ph.D. diss., University of California, Berkeley, Department of Agricultural and Resource Economics, 1981.

workers average only 22 weeks of employment per year, the maximum of 13 weeks of unemployment benefits that is currently offered is insufficient to compensate for the seasonal nature of their jobs and to make agriculture a viable long-term occupation for most workers.

3. Settlement also affects the rural economy and government services. This is not the place to analyze in depth this long-debated topic. However, it is clear that although some positive benefits to the economy result from migrants' settling in urban areas to work at relatively permanent jobs, and although these benefits may in part make up for the use of social services,[36] the situation is different in rural agricultural areas.

To the extent that families remained in Mexico while farm laborers came to work in rural California, as in the *bracero* program, their return to Mexico after the agricultural season meant that the social costs of health care, education, and other services needed by families would be incurred in Mexico. The increasing settlement of farmworkers in California may benefit local retail business, but it seriously affects government services. Programs such as WIC, subsidized health care, and education are available to all settled farmworkers, while legal workers also have access to unemployment benefits and welfare.

The legalization of over 1 million people under the Special Agricultural Worker (SAW) program of the Immigration Reform and Control Act of 1986 (IRCA) has encouraged farmworkers to settle in the United States by bringing up their families from Mexico. While most family members are unauthorized, and SAWs are not immediately eligible for welfare, over time family reunification programs and similar immigration reforms may lead to a much greater social cost. Thus one of the most significant results of IRCA may be large-scale settlement of farmworker families in California, which, given the labor market dynamics described earlier, may start a new cycle of rural poverty.

If migrants are legally settled, they can collect welfare benefits beyond unemployment insurance. The 1980 Census showed that six San Joaquin Valley communities ranked among the top ten in the nation in the percentage of their populations receiving welfare (SSI and Aid For Families With Dependent Children [AFDC]), with the Visalia Standard Metropolitan Statistical Area (SMSA) having the highest proportion of welfare recipients in the United States at 16 percent.[37] California Department of Social Services data showed increases of over 100 percent in caseloads of

---

[36] Thomas Muller and Thomas Espenshade, *The Fourth Wave* (Washington, 1985).

[37] U.S. Department of Commerce, Bureau of the Census, *Metropolitan Area Fact Book* (Washington, 1984).

AFDC between 1979 and 1984 in nine agricultural counties, a period that ended with serious recession in California agriculture.[38] In the farmworker survey undertaken by the University of California Employment Development Department in 1983, about 11 percent of undocumented households received welfare in the prior year, while over 30 percent of both U.S. citizens and immigrants with varying degrees of legal status received welfare. The most important difference, though, lies in settlement. Of unaccompanied Mexican men, only 3.8 percent received welfare, while 36 percent of settled Mexicans and U.S.-born families received welfare.[39] It is clear that off-season welfare has become significant. This is not surprising when one considers that the year-long unemployment rate in Imperial County in 1989 cycled around 25 percent, and around 15 percent in the San Joaquin Valley.[40]

There is also the issue of increased demand for schooling by settled families. Thomas Muller and Thomas Espenshade found schooling to be the most significant service cost associated with settlement by Mexican families in Los Angeles, because of the population's youth and large size.[41]

This increased use of services can be offset only by increased spending of wages, not by taxes or multiplier effects associated with immigrants' jobs, since these effects existed before settlement. The cost of sustaining the labor force—if not the cost of reproducing it—is thus increasingly borne by rural California communities as settlement increases, and the associated costs of education are all lost to agriculture because U.S.-educated children do not pursue farm work.

While forcing the United States to bear the social costs of this seasonal labor force is perhaps desirable, nevertheless it has created considerable resentment in certain areas of California, especially as county governments have been squeezed by the effects of Proposition 13 and Gann limits, and have found themselves forced to reduce services. In most rural counties, the board of supervisors is controlled by agricultural interests. One result of this control has been an alliance between local police cooperating with the INS to raid bars and neighborhoods after the harvest season,[42] a practice that has become even more prevalent since IRCA eliminated raids at the workplace. There was also considerable support

[38] LeVeen and King, *Turning Off the Tap*, p. 15.
[39] Mines and Martin, *A Profile of California Farmworkers*.
[40] Villarejo, *Environmental Effects of Living and Working in Agricultural Areas of California*.
[41] Muller and Espenshade, *The Fourth Wave*.
[42] *San Francisco Examiner*, 18 Nov. 1984.

for an expanded H-2a (contract labor) program for agriculture under IRCA, which might curtail settlement in rural areas, and agriculture will doubtless pursue even more lenient guestworker programs in the future.

4. Settlement opens up immigrants to the risk of being undermined by newer groups of immigrants.[43] In California agriculture, this undermining effect has operated continuously over the past twenty years and is one of the principal reasons for the loss of union influence. The United Farm Workers, with a U.S.-born leadership, proved unable to come to terms with continued immigration from Mexico, and agricultural employers were able to circumvent their unionized, more settled workers by employing more recent immigrants through farm labor contractors at lower wages.

Martin and his associates estimated that, aided by the passage of the Agricultural Labor Relations Act in 1975, by 1984 the farmworker unions had gained contracts for about one-seventh of California farm jobs, although Wells and West doubted that more than 10 percent of such jobs were ever affected.[44] Regardless of the validity of their claim, at the close of the 1980s the proportion has declined to far less than 1 percent and union organizing has virtually disappeared from the landscape in many areas of the state.

The use of farm labor contractors has risen rapidly in California, more than doubling their share of the agricultural labor force from 1978–88.[45] Farm-labor contractors were found to pay lower than average agricultural wages in every region in California,[46] and the union wage premium over the average increased from about 8 percent in 1976 to 28 percent in 1985.[47] The farm-labor contractor thus provided access to recent migrants at low wages, which became increasingly attractive vis-á-vis the unions. This is not a uniform shift, however, but relates to the need for long-term, stable workers. Nevertheless, the constant influx of new migrants tempts all employers and the result has been that real wages have

[43] This topic was treated at length in Mines ..d Anzaldua, New Migrants vs. Old Migrants on the citrus industry; Mines, "Tortillas: A Binational Industry"; and Richard Mines and Jeff Avina, "Immigrants and Labor Standards: The Case of California Janitors," this volume.

[44] Philip L. Martin, et al., "Farmworker Unions: Status and Wage Impacts," California Agriculture vol. 40, nos. 7–8 (July-Aug. 1986); Miriam J. Wells and Martha S. West, "Regulation of the Farm Labor Market: An Assessment of Farm-Worker Protections under California's Agricultural Labor Relations Act," working paper no. 5 (Davis, Calif., California Institute for Rural Studies, Feb. 1989).

[45] Villarejo, Environmental Effects of Living and Working in Agricultural Areas of California.

[46] Suzanne Vaupel and Philip L. Martin, "Farm Labor Contractors," California Agriculture vol. 40, nos. 3–4 (Mar.-Apr. 1986).

[47] Martin, et al., "Farmworker Unions," 13.

declined faster in agriculture in the 1980s than in other sectors of the California economy.[48]

An alternative example of this undermining effect was the strike at two frozen vegetable plants in Watsonville, California. Led mostly by settled Mexican immigrant women, the workers refused to accept wage and benefit cuts in 1985, which the firms argued were necessary due to increased competition from Mexico and Guatemala. The women argued repeatedly in the press that they would be unable to support their families at the proposed wages. The strike eventually led to the bankruptcy of one firm and a compromise wage level in the other.

In this example, while the firms similarly believed they could lower wages and perhaps eliminate the union given the political climate and labor market conditions, they were driven to this by competition in the product market, as we will see in more detail below. This competition is the direct result of development in Mexico and demonstrates the possible consequences for settled Mexican immigrants in California when production begins to shift to lower wage areas. The firms involved were private processors and at the time were competing directly with Mexican production, unlike the local Green Giant plant, which was able to continue paying high wages to its workers in California while opening a complementary plant in Mexico. Of course the success of that complementary plant eventually led to the elimination of most of the California jobs by Green Giant as well.

The turn of political support against labor organizing has opened the door to a deterioration of labor markets dominated by Mexican immigrants. California agriculture in particular has renewed its effort to recreate an isolated, cheap labor market—at a time when academics are touting the need for agriculture to adopt internal labor markets and adjust to more sophisticated production techniques that use skilled labor.[49] One result of this shift is increasing unemployment of settled immigrants in rural areas. Richard Mines found in the EDD survey that unemployment was the concern most often voiced by farmworkers in California.[50]

Thus, the balance of power between capital and labor in the United States is a crucial element in the nature of the binational labor market. The Watsonville food-processing workers fought back and refused to allow themselves to be undermined by the availability of new immigrants.

[48] California Institute for Rural Studies, "Too Many Farm Workers in California? The Evidence from Wage Trends" (Davis, Calif., Aug. 1990).

[49] John Mamer and Robert W. Glover, "Innovative Approaches Improve Farm Labor," *California Agriculture* vol. 38, nos. 3–4 (Mar.-Apr. 1984).

[50] Mines and Martin, *A Profile of California Farmworkers.*

What they said, in effect, was, "pay us what we need in order to live in the United States, or move production to Mexico." Of course production has continued to shift to Mexico, and workers are in reality powerless to stop this change by themselves. But the argument highlights the dilemma for the United States in considering economic integration with Mexico: will we draw a line in the dust and defend minimum U.S. labor standards (in effect, driving capital over the border), or will we allow U.S. standards to fall toward Mexico's slowly rising standards? Once again, the collective political strength of U.S. labor appears to be a critical factor in the outcome.

Technological Innovation vs. Immigration

Philip Martin argues that just as other U.S. industries have fought labor's attempts to regulate or rationalize them, all the while losing ground to foreign competition,

... so fruit and vegetable farmers are fighting to continue using seasonal alien farmworkers in order to compete with fruits and vegetables other nations are beginning to export in quantity. Cheap labor benefits agriculture in the short run, but it also helps to blind farmers to the technological changes they will have to make in order to compete with foreign producers, who have access to even cheaper labor. . . . Without mechanization, the United States must both accept an isolated, alien-dominated labor force for seasonal handwork and erect trade barriers to keep out produce grown abroad at even lower wages.[51]

California agriculture is already in this predicament. California has been importing foreign seasonal farmworkers for 100 years, and has significant trade barriers in the form of marketing orders and seasonal tariffs. For example, many federal marketing orders, such as the orders for tomatoes or table grapes, contain provisions requiring that all imports comply with the order's quality and packaging requirements.

Evidence suggests that California agriculture will not forgo voluntarily its search for cheaper labor, but will only respond to crisis. The experience surrounding the end of the *bracero* program in 1965 supports this claim. Its termination prompted adoption of the mechanical tomato harvester and the introduction of labor rationalization and stabilization schemes in lettuce, some citrus, and strawberries.[52] The adoption of the tomato harvester in particular so increased California productivity in processing tomatoes that it achieved a virtual monopoly in the United

[51] Philip L. Martin, "Labor-Intensive Agriculture," *Scientific American* vol. 249, no. 4 (Oct. 1983).
[52] Runsten and LeVeen, *Mechanization and Mexican Labor in California Agriculture*.

States as a result. This scenario fits Nathan Rosenberg's theory that inventions are resisted and not adopted until some crisis precipitates dire need, after which the innovation creates a basis for renewed accumulation.[53]

Adoption of this sort of innovation, however, is an extremely costly, complex, and long-term task. In order to adopt the tomato harvester, for example, producers needed not only the machine, but also a tomato that was durable enough to withstand mechanical picking. Plant breeders had been working on such a tomato for 20 years when the change was made. The shift also required new methods of transport and handling, and significant changes in the processing plants.[54]

The rate of mechanization in California slowed during the 1970s and 1980s both because the crops left to mechanize have required the kind of complex changes that tomatoes have needed, and because growers have been reassured by the continued availability of large numbers of Mexican immigrants. For example, there are machines that will harvest lettuce, raisin grapes, or fresh tomatoes, but the labor surplus has minimized interest. No crisis has impelled the industry to change production systems.

In fact, the changes in the labor process that have occurred have often been made to take advantage of the large labor force of young male immigrant workers. For example, some vegetables, such as cauliflower, are now packed in the fields to eliminate the strongly unionized packing-shed workers.[55] This change comes largely at the expense of earlier Mexican immigrants who had settled in California, and helps to explain the high rates of rural unemployment and welfare discussed earlier.

Increased Pressure on Water Supplies

Labor problems are not the only factor affecting the competitiveness of California agriculture, however. Rising costs of water, growing constraints on use of chemical fertilizers and pesticides, and well-known financial constraints contribute to higher production costs. While California agriculture appears to be able to maintain lower wages as a means of remaining competitive, it has been much less successful with water sources.

The key factor in low-cost agricultural water in California has been the maintenance of surplus water in the state. New water projects have become so expensive, however, that it is practically impossible to muster

---

[53] Nathan Rosenberg, *Perspectives on Technology* (Cambridge, Eng., 1976).

[54] Alain de Janvry, E. Phillip LeVeen, and David Runsten, *Mechanization in California Agriculture: The Case of Canning Tomatoes* (Costa Rica, Inter-American Institute for Agricultural Cooperation, 1980).

[55] *Modesto Bee* (Modesto, Calif.), 1 Sept. 1984.

political support for them, given large government deficits and an emphasis on eliminating subsidies. As a result, there is considerable pressure on public agencies to raise the price of water in order to recover operation and maintenance costs, as well as to increase the agreed-upon capital payments from farmers. Many areas, though, cannot farm economically with marginal-cost water prices, especially in the southern San Joaquin Valley. Higher prices will either force this land out of production or into more intensive crops, an option made more difficult by the current over-supplies of many intensive crops (which limit farmers' options). One outcome of increasing competition for water is that current laws will be changed to facilitate the creation of water markets; as a result, it is likely that agricultural land will be taken out of production as the water is sold to enterprises that can take advantage of its higher value.

There are other problems with greater competition for water. Areas dependent on ground water for irrigation face increasingly expensive pumping costs as water tables fall and energy costs rise. This is a more serious problem in areas of the United States such as the Great Plains and Arizona, and is a situation that places on agriculture cost pressures that are only likely to increase. For areas along the coast, groundwater over-drafting has also led to salt incursion from the ocean. This situation is most serious in Baja California, but is also a growing problem in the Watsonville area.

Water pollution, such as at Kesterson Wildlife Refuge, where the drainage water from the Westlands water district was destroying wildlife, has led to examination of groundwater throughout California and a heightened concern that agricultural chemicals are leaching into water tables used for drinking water. Research findings may limit agriculture in certain areas or limit the use of chemicals likely to cause groundwater problems. The inability of the state to provide drainage for irrigation in the southern San Joaquin Valley is reminiscent of the failures of irrigation systems throughout history.

Of course Mexico faces a similar set of irrigation problems, especially ground water overdrafting. How these problems are solved, or not solved, may be an important determinant in future production sharing.

Strategies for Pest Control

High yields in California are attributable in large part to the availability over the last four decades of inexpensive pest control. Use of chemical insecticides and herbicides has come under increasing scrutiny, however, due to the emergence of unexpected externalities, specifically groundwater contamination. Additionally, the evolving resistance of some pests to the pesticides is increasing pest control costs and leading to increased demand for regulations on their use, as well as for more expensive integrated pest-management technology.[56]

California agriculture faces constant efforts by environmental interests to limit pesticide use, symbolized by such laws as plantback restrictions in 1986 (AB-1026), the Environmental Protection Act of 1990 (the Big Green initiative), the Safe Drinking Water and Toxic Enforcement Act of 1986 (Proposition 65), and the Federal Insecticide, Fungicide, and Rodenticide Act as amended in 1988, all of which may lead to the loss of many chemical registrations for particular crops. Such laws doubtless encourage companies to move their operations to Mexico and other areas with less stringent controls. What is unclear is whether the United States and other industrialized countries will continue to be content to look for pesticide residues on imported foods, or whether they will try to develop and enforce corresponding "clean" production practices in developing countries.

One could argue that this practice punishes California vis-à-vis other regions, but the probable result will be to speed up development of integrated pest management techniques and biological control and put California ahead of other areas. Because many biological controls are relatively site-specific, the research being conducted now in California may not be as easily transferable to Mexico as were the rather crude chemical approaches. In this sense, one can see "organic" practices as providing a potentially large competitive advantage for California; creating serious barriers to growing temperate export produce in the tropics; and pointing up the dismal state of research on fruits and vegetables in most developing countries, including Mexico.

Summary

California agriculture's comparative advantage is shifting because the resource endowments are changing: water is becoming relatively more scarce, energy more expensive, chemicals more regulated, land more urbanized. Agriculture is increasingly called on to account for its externalities. The ultimate outcome will be a different agriculture in California, perhaps even more intensive, perhaps with new advantages. Nevertheless, the continued migration of Mexican labor has meant that many growers have been able to move once again into a new labor

[56] S. O. Archibald, "A Dynamic Analysis of Production Externalities: Pesticide Resistance in California Cotton," Ph.D. diss., University of California, Davis, 1984.

cycle, at lowered real wages, and so reproduce the poverty endemic to Southwest U.S. agricultural labor for 100 years.

MEXICAN COMPETITION

The United States is Mexico's most important agricultural trading partner. Nicole Ballenger and Alex McCalla report that about 40 percent of the value of Mexico's agricultural exports and 70 to 80 percent of its agricultural import trade has been with the United States.[57] This trade increasingly involves supplementary products such as fresh and frozen vegetables, which has led to growing competition in product markets between the two countries. This market scenario results in yet another form of interdependence—one that is largely dependent upon capital flows.

Most discussions about U.S.-Mexico fruit and vegetable trade have focused on the market for fresh winter vegetables,[58] in which growing competition between Sinaloa and Florida resulted in efforts by U.S. producers to erect trade barriers as a means of retaining their advantage. When this attempt failed, Florida concentrated on new technologies such as plastic mulch. Maury Bredahl and his colleagues argue that these technologies re-established Florida's advantage.[59]

Here we discuss two commodities, frozen broccoli and frozen strawberries, to illustrate similar lessons about the effects on California agriculture from an increasingly competitive Mexican agriculture and to point out, by example, (1) the means by which California could potentially retain its competitive advantage, and (2) the implications of these strategies for Mexico.

Frozen broccoli exports from Mexico to the United States rose from 14 million pounds in 1978 to over 96 million pounds in 1986.[60] Fresh broccoli exports from Mexico to the United States rose over the same period from 35,000 to 34 million pounds. Over the 1978–1986 period,

[57] Nicole Ballenger and Alex F. McCalla, "Domestic Policy and Trade Interactions: The Case of Mexico," paper presented to the International Trade Research Consortium (Tucson, Ariz., 15 Dec. 1983).

[58] David Mares, "The Evolution of U.S.-Mexican Agricultural Relations: The Changing Roles of the Mexican State and Mexican Agricultural Producers," working paper no. 16 (San Diego, Program in U.S.-Mexican Studies, 1981); Maury E. Bredahl, et al., "Technical Change, Protectionism, and Market Structure: The Case of International Trade in Fresh Winter Vegetables," *Agricultural Experiment Station Technical Bulletin* 249 (Tucson, Ariz., 1983).

[59] Bredahl, et al., "Technical Change, Protectionism, and Market Structure."

[60] This is the first year the U.S. statistics look at broccoli separately. Most, if not all, of the increase in production was still accounted for by Birdseye, which had been exporting since the late 1960s.

Mexican shipments of frozen broccoli rose from about 5 percent of California shipments to over 35 percent.[61] This increase created great concern in the California industry, since broccoli is the most important frozen vegetable in California, and the industry had significant idle capacity.

In contrast to the steady increase in Mexican exports of frozen vegetables is the recent experience in frozen strawberries. Frozen strawberry exports have experienced many peaks and valleys since Mexico held 28 percent of the U.S. market in 1966. In the early 1980s, with the peso overvalued, Mexican exports to the United States fell to below 20 million pounds, or about 15 percent of the market, after having reached 109 million pounds in 1974 and 104 million pounds as recently as 1979.[62]

On the other hand, California's share of the U.S. frozen strawberry market had risen over the 1966–1982 period from 20 percent to 67 percent, or from 60 million pounds to 222 million pounds, in addition to California's complete dominance of the fresh strawberry market.[63] That is, Mexico actually had a larger share of the frozen market in 1966 than California, but by the 1980s produced less than a fifth of California's output. Of course Washington and Oregon also lost out to California, and in that perhaps lies the key to the Mexican problem.

Since both of these products are frozen, both involve California-Mexico competition, and both have interesting links in the labor market (in fact some Mexican strawberry plants are being converted to vegetables), it is worth exploring here some of the reasons for the divergent success of the two industries in recent years and the resulting implications for production sharing between the two regions. We begin by briefly tracing the background of frozen fruits and vegetables in the Bajio.

The Bajio has produced fruits and vegetables for consumption in central Mexico since its settlement by the Spanish in the mid-sixteenth century and the subsequent advent of irrigation. The area principally grew grains, but such exotic crops as strawberries were introduced in Irapuato as early as 1885. The 1950 census, predating any fruit and vegetable processing in the area, reported 12,000 hectares of fruits and vegetables

[61] Kirby Moulton and David Runsten, *The Frozen Vegetable Industry of Mexico* (Berkeley, Calif., 1986).

[62] These figures are inflated by the practice of exporting large quantities of subsidized sugar, a practice that characterized the Mexican trade until the end of the 1970s. The sugar accounted for about 20 percent of the weight of the frozen strawberries, but this amount of sugar was reduced in the 1980s. See David Runsten, "Competition in Strawberries," in *Competitiveness at Home and Abroad* (Davis, Calif., 1988).

[63] Harland Padfield and Helen Thaler, "The U.S. Processed Strawberry Market: An Analysis of Trends and Commodity Characteristics as They Impact on Oregon," *Circular of Information* 695 (Corvallis, Oreg., 1984).

in the state of Guanajuato. By 1981, this acreage had tripled.[64] Certainly, a large part of this growth can be attributed to the influence of agroindustry in the area, but the region continues to respond to demand from the large Mexican cities, as well as to local demand. The agroindustrial fruit and vegetable complex was built on top of an already long-existing production of many of these crops.

The first fruit and vegetable processors in the Bajio were strawberry freezers in Irapuato, established around 1950 to export frozen berries to the United States. A number of these plants were owned and run by North Americans. The growth of this industry occurred in the 1950s and early 1960s, with subsequent rapid growth into the 1970s resulting from increased production in the valley of Zamora to the south in the state of Michoacán.

In the late 1950s and early 1960s, a number of U.S. canneries were established in Guanajuato to produce for the Mexican market behind tariff barriers. These canneries introduced several new crops, such as carrots, asparagus, sweet corn, and green beans. They tended to contract with the largest farmers in the area, and transferred post-war U.S. vegetable production technology through contract control and the provision and specification of inputs.[65]

In 1967, Birdseye located a vegetable freezing plant on a farm north of Celaya. As with the strawberry freezers, because Mexico had no infrastructure for selling frozen foods, the plant was 100 percent for export to the United States. Birdseye also introduced several new crops to the area: broccoli, cauliflower, okra, and zucchini. They similarly pursued contract farming and technological control, with many of the same growers who produced for the canneries.

From the late 1960s until 1978, Birdseye was the only vegetable freezer in the area, except for a small plant that had been set up by a family in Aguascalientes, with close ties to Birdseye. At that point, a group of the largest growers set up their own plant and began to freeze under contract for Birdseye and other buyers in the United States. The success of this venture in the face of an overvalued peso encouraged imitation, especially after the devaluation in 1982 and the crash of internal demand in Mexico. In particular, a Green Giant plant was set up in Irapuato, the Campbell Soup plant was converted to freezing for export, and many of the strawberry freezers moved into vegetables. The industry expanded

[64] Unpublished data from the Secretaria de Agricultura y Recursos Hidráulicos.
[65] Ruth Rama and Raul Vigorito, *El complejo de frutas y legumbres en México* (Mexico City, 1979).

rapidly, averaging a growth rate of about 25 percent between 1979 and 1986.

With the exception of the freezing operations of the transnationals Campbells Soup, Birdseye, and Green Giant, all the other plants are based on integrated operations and owned by large Mexican growers. The farm bases of the plants range from 400 to 3,000 hectares, and the entire frozen vegetable industry can be traced back to contracts with Birdseye.

The frozen broccoli and cauliflower industries have shifted to Mexico because they are the most labor-intensive crops for freezing. As the grower-owned plants came on line in the Bajio, they concentrated on hand-trimming small florets for bulk pack (that is, to be recombined in the United States), a process not even attempted in California, where all such chopping is done by machine. Thus at first Mexico was producing qualitatively different products, and actually complementing California production. However, as the industry expanded, there was increasing movement toward spear trimming and consumer packs, which competed directly with California's industry.

A 1986 study attempted to assess the cost differences between the two regions.[66] This study demonstrated that much of the cost advantage in Mexico lay in the agricultural operations. The costs of growing broccoli in Mexico were about 32 percent of the California cost per acre and 43 percent of the California cost per pound, since yields in Mexico were slightly below those of California. Thus broccoli cost $478 per acre or 6.5 cents per pound in Mexico versus $1,506 per acre or 15.1 cents per pound in California. Interviews with growers in California suggested that many large growers in the central coast area had even higher costs at the time.

The Mexican cost advantage was based on low-cost labor, as one would expect, but broccoli is not a very labor-intensive crop. Equally significant were lower electricity costs for pumping water, lower fertilizer prices, and cheaper land. Of course, Mexican wages were so low at the time that doubling them only added $15.00 per acre to the costs.

While we would expect to find lower costs in Mexico, the key element in the comparison is that yields in Mexico are not much lower in these crops. California broccoli yields reached a peak in 1984 of 11.8 metric tons/hectare, and U.S. yields averaged 10.75 metric tons/hectare in the same year, both higher than the median Bajio yield of 8.2 metric tons/hectare, but not much higher than the best yields by the larger growers

[66] Moulton and Runsten, *The Frozen Vegetable Industry of Mexico.*

in Mexico. Thus while Mexico may have a slight yield disadvantage, it is not significant, and it is overwhelmed by the low labor costs. While broccoli is not the most labor-intensive crop (strawberries require 25 to 30 times the labor input of broccoli), it nevertheless uses 25 to 30 times the labor needed for wheat, for example. The last estimate we have of California labor input comes from the early 1980s, at about 185 person-hours/hectare. A survey in the Bajio in 1983 showed a slightly higher average of 230 person-hours/hectare, but in a similar range.[67] Broccoli is being grown in Mexico and California with very similar technologies.

As a result, Mexican processors were able to buy broccoli for almost 10 cents per pound less than their California competitors, save a few more cents in lower plant labor costs, and get chopped frozen broccoli across the U.S. border, including the 17.5 percent duty, at five to ten cents less per pound than the California free-on-board price.

We find a drastically different story in the strawberry industry. If we make the most generous interpretation of Mexican yields, then from 1977–78 to 1981–82 Michoacán averaged 17.6 metric tons/hectare and Guanajuato 15 metric tons/hectare.[68] In 1982, however, California averaged 61.6 metric tons/hectare.[69] Mexican yields have been flat or possibly declining slightly for 20 years while California yields have shot up due to new varieties and a longer season. The result has been large amounts of frozen strawberries coming out of California and declining prices in the United States because per capita demand has not risen. Real prices to farmers for U.S. strawberries fell 33 percent between 1966 and 1982.[70] Thus even though the Mexican industry enjoys an enormous labor cost advantage and strawberries utilize 5,000 to 6,000 person-hours/hectare, returns have not been good and Mexican strawberries are increasingly marginal to the U.S. market.

While the ills of the Mexican strawberry industry have been variously attributed to control by a small number of U.S. brokers, overcapacity, defective strawberry plants, poor pricing, quality problems, and government intervention,[71] it is apparent that a critical problem is differing technologies. This difficulty is confirmed by the loss of market share to Cali-

[67] Linda Wilcox, "Internationalization of the Labor Process in Agriculture: A Case Study of Agroindustrial Development in Mexico's El Bajio," Ph.D. diss., University of California, Berkeley, Deparment of Agricultural and Resource Economics, 1987.
[68] Union Nacional de Organismos de Productores de Hortalizas y Frutas, "Fresa: Perspectivas de Producción y Comercialización, Programa de Siembra-Exportación," technical report no. 1 (Culiacan, May 1986).
[69] U.S. Department of Agriculture, Agricultural Statistics.
[70] Padfield and Thaler, "The U.S. Processed Strawberry Market."
[71] Ernest Feder, Strawberry Imperialism (The Hague, 1977).

fornia by Oregon and Washington, who also fell increasingly farther behind in yields.[72]

Explaining the difference in Mexico's ability to compete technologically in vegetables versus strawberries is a complex task. Surely the discrepancy has something to do with the involvement in vegetables of the very largest growers in the Bajio. But equally important must be the presence of the transnationals in vegetables, actively transferring technology from the United States.

Whatever one thinks of the appropriateness of that technology for Mexico, it has made Mexican production highly competitive, at least in the short run. In strawberries, on the other hand, the U.S. brokers who supposedly controlled the Mexican industry were not production-oriented but instead were merely financial intermediaries.[73] Mexican producers have been left to their own devices in strawberries, with effectively no agronomic research support from the state.

In the Mexican broccoli industry, there has been an attempt to extend the broccoli season to the entire year. (This is similar to what happened in California strawberries.) In order to accomplish this long season, the transnationals have collected broccoli varieties from all over the world and are engaged in research to improve the summer variety. In fact, one firm sent a student to the University of California, Davis, to pursue this research. As with the strawberry industry, the Mexican-owned firms in the industry have neither the resources nor the personnel to undertake this type of research.

Shifting intensive, high-technology crops from the United States to Mexico is not a simple matter of wage differentials. It requires a process of technology transfer that can be quite time-consuming. The producers in the Bajio who are now competing in export vegetables started growing some of these crops, or similar crops with similar technology, ten to twenty years ago. Mexican asparagus growers who are now exporting to the United States and Europe started with Del Monte in the early 1960s. The entrance of the transnationals reinforced the largest producers, and allowed them to improve their productivity, accumulate capital, and learn the markets, which has in turn made them able to compete with California growers.

Of course a lot of the product ultimately is still channeled through the transnationals, who control certain parts of the market. But interestingly, in frozen vegetables in the Bajio, the transnationals have now been driven to seek new producers and new sources of supply, which has cast them

[72] Padfield and Thaler, "The U.S. Processed Strawberry Market."
[73] Feder, *Strawberry Imperialism.*

into the role of transferring technology to a larger group of smaller growers. This holds out the possibility that the development of the industry
can be made more widely beneficial in Mexico, rather than contributing
to income polarization in agriculture, as it has thus far.

IMPLICATIONS FOR THE BINATIONAL LABOR MARKET

An important question, about which we have much too little information, is whether labor markets in Mexico and the United States that are
using Mexican workers are linked as product markets are. That is, if you
shift production of a commodity from one country to the other, will you
to any degree shift the labor force as well?

There are some industries where this is probably the case; for example,
the Los Angeles shoe industry. The Los Angeles shoe work force is almost
entirely Mexican, most coming already skilled from the principal shoe
towns of Mexico, Guadalajara, and Leon.[74] The Mexican industry has
suffered from very low capacity utilization and exports have been minimal, having risen little during the dismantling of the U.S. shoe industry,
in contrast to Brazil and other countries, where export shoe production
expanded rapidly. One could easily imagine a scenario where a booming
Mexican industry substituting for Los Angeles production would draw
its workers back from the United States as the U.S. plants closed.

However, from surveys of agricultural migrant workers, while most
have worked in agriculture in Mexico, only rarely have they worked in
similar fruit and vegetable crops. Many come directly from rainfed areas
which preclude such experience. The Mixtec migrants from the state of
Oaxaca do work in the tomato industry in Sinaloa, Baja California, San
Diego, and Fresno. But usually once these workers get past San Diego
and learn to operate in the United States, they do not return to working
in the Mexican fields. Thus a shift in the tomato industry from San Diego
to Baja California might move part of the labor force, but a shift from
Fresno to Mexico would not. Working as a migrant laborer in Mexico is
a stage on the road to the United States, and not to be returned to.

There have also been some instances of skilled grape pruners being
taken from California to Mexico by large U.S. firms unable to find skilled
workers in Mexico. These crews were paid at California wage levels,
however, which suggests that wage equalization may be the only way to
induce return migration.

In the frozen vegetable industry, the competition between California
and Mexico is linked via the labor market. Many of the workers in the

[74]David Runsten, *Mexican Immigrants and the California-Mexico Role in the U.S. Shoe
Industry* (San Diego, Program in U.S.-Mexico Studies, Jan. 1986).

California strawberry industry, and a sizeable proportion of the settled immigrants in the Watsonville frozen vegetable factories, come from the Zamora area. However, shifting production to Mexico will not move this labor force back to Mexico. Both the California strawberry industry and the Watsonville frozen vegetable factories are characterized by their use of settled Mexican immigrants.[75] If the competition in Mexico were to shift production away from California, these people would move on to jobs in other sectors of the California economy.

Consider the case of Gomez Farias, discussed above. Although young children from the village do work in the local strawberry fields around Zamora to learn the trade for later work in California, such work in this Mexican village is not considered a desireable career. The village network controls subsidized housing in Watsonville for six months of the year, and they would continue to use this asset to earn the much higher wages available in California, whether strawberries were their source of employment or not. Thus even this group that returns constantly to Mexico would not be induced to work in Mexico without a significant relative rise in Mexican wages.

In summary, while increasing production in Mexico and reducing it in California will increase employment in Mexico, the same people will not be affected, and it is doubtful that migration will decrease, at least in the short run. After all, the shift would occur in *seasonal jobs*. A migrant in California works at a number of different jobs in different crops, some longer than others, with only the most favored having one long-term, well-paying job (in perhaps celery or lettuce). Eliminating a subset of those jobs will create problems in areas that have complementary seasonal job patterns, but it will not eliminate migrants. Indeed, losing these jobs will just exacerbate the long stretches of unemployment already suffered by workers. Also, as we have seen, a large group of immigrants are settled, and they will not return to Mexico: the wage differential is too compelling. Although in the long run migration may fall as workers become discouraged from the long periods of unemployment, migration has created a binational (or transnational) culture that will be difficult to displace.[76]

CONCLUSION

If we look at the broad spectrum of interdependence between the United States and Mexico in labor-intensive agriculture, we see that since

[75] Miriam Wells, "Social Conflict, Commodity Constraints, and Labor Market Structure in Agriculture," *Comparative Studies in Society and History* vol. 23, no. 4 (Oct. 1981).
[76] Massey, et al., *Return to Aztlan.*

World War II such agriculture in the United States has become increasingly dependent on Mexican immigrants, to the point where now over 90
percent of California farmworkers were born in Mexico. At the same
time, bit by bit, capital, technology, and skilled labor have flowed into
Mexican export agriculture, so that this sector is now highly dependent
on research and capital from the U.S. Southwest.

The economic restructuring in Mexico since 1982 has increased these
flows in both directions. As a result, we have a flooded agricultural labor
market in the western United States at a time when moving agricultural
operations down into Mexico is increasingly attractive. Such contradictory forces lead to varying strategies. In particular, certain sectors of California's agriculture and food processing have tried to maintain trade barriers at the same time as they press for a new *bracero* program. The
seemingly inexhaustible supply of labor in Mexico working at US$5.00
per day encourages employers to believe that wages in the United States
should fall toward those in Mexico. The agricultural labor market in the
United States has in fact lowered U.S. workers' wages, suggesting that
U.S. labor's fears of free trade effects in their native labor market are
perhaps warranted.

The consequence of this situation is that new migrants are substituted
for settlers, mechanization and other productivity-enhancing investments
are put off, and the cycle continues to repeat. This strategy has potentially
negative long-run implications for the competitiveness of California agriculture. First, it assumes that barriers against imports from lower-wage
areas that have imitated California technology can be maintained. While
there has been a wave of protectionist sentiment in the United States, it
would appear that most of the winds are blowing in opposing directions:
Mexico's entrance into the General Agreement on Tariffs and Trade
(GATT) and its unilateral lowering of trade barriers; the Caribbean Basin
Initiative; the move on the part of the United States to negotiate a free
trade agreement with Mexico, and perhaps with all of Latin America;
and the continuing movement of U.S. agricultural firms into developing
countries, which transforms these firms into political opponents of U.S.
trade restrictions.

Second, the new technologies coming on line in California, such as
integrated pest management, biological control, biotechnologies, and increased use of microcomputers in production management, all demand
more educated and skilled labor. If the present labor force is replaced by
less-skilled immigrants at lower wages, the adoption of these technologies
will be more difficult, which mitigates against California's long-run ad-

vantage. California growers would lose some of the technological rents from early adoption that they had always enjoyed.

Such a protectionist strategy, while continuing to employ Mexican migrants, would be detrimental to the development of Mexican fruit and vegetable export agriculture. Since these crops occupy relatively little land and provide significant employment, stifling Mexican development in this area is not in anyone's interest. The dilemma in Mexico is rather how to spread the benefits more widely among smaller producers.

An alternative strategy for California growers would be to focus on improving the efficiency of all factors of production, especially water and chemicals. It seems inevitable that California's agricultural industry will have to make such changes, as described above, and making them soon would allow these companies to utilize an increasingly skilled and settled labor force at reasonable wage levels. Such a strategy would improve the situation in rural areas by employing the existing workers for longer periods. Mechanization might continue to increase labor productivity in some crops, but it is likely that future productivity increases will come from other factors. California needs to focus on its technological capabilities and not remain mired in its past reliance on subsidized labor and water. As we saw, a technology-oriented strategy in strawberries, one of the most labor-intensive of all crops, was extremely successful for California growers. These companies have combined a high level of research and development with a steady and skilled labor force.

Where such changes are not possible, production should be allowed to shift gradually to Mexico and similar areas. U.S. agriculture will have to be restructured, to shift low-skill and labor-intensive tasks to developing countries, as Japan did with manufacturing,[77] rather than to continually import new low-wage labor, with its accompanying deleterious effects on other U.S. labor markets. Agricultural land is rather easily shifted into alternative crops, although, as Varden Fuller noted, its real value may fall; the cost of adjustment will weigh more heavily on food processing.[78]

The consequences of this high-road strategy for Mexico are more favorable, insofar as it opens the door to greater production sharing, but it presents a different set of problems. Skill-intensive and science-intensive technologies developed in California may be more difficult than older technologies to transfer to Mexico. This may make it particularly difficult

[77] Terutomo Ozawa, "Japanese Overseas Investment in Its Third Phase: What It Means for Mexico," paper presented at the Conference on United States-Mexico Investment Relations, Stanford, Calif., 24–26 Jan. 1985.

[78] Fuller, "The Supply of Agricultural Labor as a Factor in the Evolution of Farm Organization in California."

to improve the participation of smaller producers. Also, this strategy may just produce an alternative set of trade barriers: food safety standards that effectively exclude the use of the old technology.

Mexico currently depends on foreign corporations to transfer new technology to most of agriculture outside of basic grains. This may occur through the seed and chemical companies, or via the processors and shippers. Only a few of the largest growers are directly in contact with research outside of Mexico.

If Mexico is to expand aggressively its role in producing labor-intensive crops for world markets, this situation must change. The major obstacle appears to have been the belief by many in the government that Mexico should not be engaged in such export production at all. As a result, state-sponsored research has never focused on such crops, and the arena has been ceded to foreign agribusiness. Researchers from the Mexican government have only recently begun to cooperate with the fruit and vegetable producers. Mexican production often suffers from unadapted varieties, poor pest-control strategies, unresearched diseases, and lack of information about microclimatic conditions.

At the very moment when California is discussing "sustainable" agriculture and biological control methods, Mexico is trying to expand its competitive position based on derivative technology. This is a short-run strategy. To take the example of frozen vegetables, what happens if the transnationals move on to Guatemala or South America where wages are even lower? Who will do the research to sustain the Mexican industry? This is exactly the sort of dependence on transnational corporations that Mexico has sought to avoid.

Will a Free Trade Agreement Lead to Wage Convergence? Implications for Mexico and the United States

Clark W. Reynolds

MIGRATION WITHIN and between the United States and Mexico has shaped the labor market interdependence of these two countries. Particular sectors and regions of each nation are experiencing the impact of wage and employment conditions across the border. Families, friends, and entire communities are establishing networks that transcend national boundaries. Amnesty provisions and the desire of families to be together have given an intergenerational dynamic to these linkages as groups of Mexicans move north in response to higher wages; meanwhile, many U.S. retirees and investors have moved south to benefit from lower-cost labor. Such activities, however, are by no means the most important ways in which the labor markets of the two countries interact. In the future labor services will be exchanged far more through trade than migration. Movement toward a North American Free Trade Agreement will make wages and employment in the two countries increasingly interdependent regardless of the treatment of bilateral labor flows.

While the bridging of the two economies' labor markets has a long history, dating back before the forceable acquisition of Mexico's northern territories by the United States, the connections have intensified in the last few years. Mexico's postwar population growth has led to an accelerated increase in the number of job-seekers. The pressures of international competition and domestic shifts toward service sector employment have increased the U.S. demand for labor at Mexican skill levels. In the

The arguments in this chapter are tested empirically in the author's forthcoming volume on the contemporary Mexican economy and the challenge of increased interdependence.

1980s, growth in the United States and Mexican stagnation and peso devaluation enhanced the complementarities of the two economies, as the wage gap between them widened (even when adjusted for differences in productivity). As Mexico worked to restructure its economy by eliminating jobs in inefficient import-substituting industries, imposing budget cutbacks, privatizing public enterprises, and instituting other austerity measures, closer ties to the international market and the United States seemed the only way out.

The debt crisis and subsequent adjustment have severely impaired Mexico's ability to absorb its rapidly growing work force. While employment in the formal sector languished, workers were forced to seek jobs in service occupations, self-employment, and micro-enterprises, many of which offered lower wages and productivity. Those able to cover the rising costs and greater risks of migration sought work in the United States, often clandestinely. Mexico's export sector responded to the falling real wages that resulted from recession and peso devaluation in the 1980s, leading to the growing export of labor services in the form of commodities. *Maquilas* based on the use of lower cost labor for assembly and reexport to the U.S. multiplied.

However, the nature and timing of business cycles also enter into the equation. Today Mexico is beginning to boom while the United States has fallen into a slump. Wages south of the border are recovering, beginning with higher skilled labor and those wages in regions (such as the northern border) more closely connected to the U.S. economy. Faced with the prospects of a slow recovery, the U.S. labor market is softening, weakened by the sustained pressures of international competition and its own shortcomings in education and infrastructure. Real wages, especially for problematic regions, sectors, and occupational skills, are continuing a downward trend that began more than a decade ago. U.S. recession in the 1990s is different from previous downswings. It reflects not only the cyclical underemployment of existing capacity but the need to continue major structural adjustment of the economy and its work force to meet the demands of increased international competition.

Evidence from the research underlying papers in this volume indicates that increased links between Mexico and the United States will facilitate the necessary adjustment process of both countries by stimulating greater efficiency and competitiveness on both sides of the border. But adjustment during a recession is difficult for the United States in the 1990s, just as it was for Mexico in the 1980s. Faced with falling real wages and a growing pool of immigrant job-seekers, not only from Mexico but other developing regions, it is easy for U.S. workers to point the finger, assuming cause and effect even in the absence of conclusive evidence. The problem is felt not only in the border regions but as far afield as Illinois, Colorado, New York, Washington, and the District of Columbia.

The fact of labor market interdependence and the need to restructure the economy along more competitive lines have combined to threaten the historical compromise between labor and capital in the United States (the so-called "social pact") that has been painfully forged over the past century and especially since the 1930s. As the costs of housing, health, education, and consumer durables rise against the backdrop of falling real wages, it seems more difficult for the youth from middle-class households to replicate the material conditions of their parents. For them the American Dream seems at risk. For the new generation of ethnic and racial minorities, hope recedes even further. Yet during the past century migration responded to an earlier dream and helped to make it a reality.

IS THERE A LAW OF ONE PRICE FOR WAGES
IN NORTH AMERICA?

Economic theory argues that when markets are fully competitive and open to international trade, and with exchange rates responsive to the forces of supply and demand, the "law of one price" operates. As a result, all tradable goods and services tend to sell at world market prices (in domestic currency this is expressed in terms of the exchange rate). Additionally, theoretical arguments have been made ever since Ricardo that under strong assumptions about competition and the lack of specialization, economies open to trade experience "factor price equalization," so that wages for the same skill (along with interest rates, and the price of inputs in the production process) will also tend toward equality between countries, net of transaction costs, even without migration. Of course freedom to migrate for labor and capital will speed up the process. But in either case, "the law of one price" will apply to labor markets of similar skills, and wages will tend to converge as markets become more open and competitive, equalizing investment per worker and productivity levels.

If the law of one price applies to the underlying forces of labor market interdependence, what direction may wage convergence be expected to take with closer North American trade and investment relations? There are two possible scenarios. In the positive case, the low-wage economy (for example, Mexico), through growth along the lines of comparative advantage in more labor-intensive activities, will enjoy increases in the marginal product of its labor until wages rise to approach the level of its competitive trading partners (for example, the United States). Meanwhile the high-wage (U.S.) economy will shift production toward more capital and skill-intensive lines of production.

Since the supply of labor in Mexico is relatively small (26 million) compared to U.S. levels (about 125 million), the impact of interdependence would appear to be asymmetrical. U.S. market conditions should have a greater impact on Mexico than vice versa. This argues for upward convergence of Mexican wages, with U.S. wage levels dominating the binational relationship. However Mexico's workers in tradables production and actual or potential migrants (perhaps 8–10 million) compete with the much smaller fraction of the U.S. work force that has lower occupational skills and real wages (about 10 percent or 12 million). In the future Mexico's work force will continue to grow much more rapidly than that of the United States. And as we have mentioned, U.S. wages have already eroded through competition from much wider sources than Mexico, though with NAFTA Mexico is expected to gain market shares from other U.S. suppliers. Hence changes in the supply of Mexican labor or U.S. demand for lower skilled workers on the margin will have a growing impact on real wages in both countries.

Through much of the postwar period, the productivity of labor in North America tended to converge upward, both within Mexico and between it and the United States. Despite the large supply of low-skilled labor in Mexico, real wages in the formal sector in Mexico also tended to rise toward U.S. levels (in relative terms) through the oil boom of the 1970s. Following the crisis of 1982, however, the process reversed and wage levels actually diverged. Now the question is whether the 1990s will restore convergence and whether convergence will once again be upward or whether it will appear to be downward (at least for low skill levels).

In the case of negative convergence, the production of labor-intensive goods and services will tend to shift toward the low-wage economy (Mexico). This will displace labor of similar skills in the higher wage (U.S.) economy, *ceteris paribus*, who will be forced to find employment in occupations with lower productivity (and wages). Without major new investments in capital and technology, wages will tend to converge downward (offset somewhat by lower prices for labor-intensive goods and services). Through most of the 1980s, Mexican output per worker stagnated and real wages fell sharply for all skill levels, raising the real wage gap with the United States and increasing migratory pressures (despite increased cost of job search from peso devaluation).

In the United States real wages for low-skilled domestic labor were also beginning to decline, despite economic recovery and growth in the 1980s, leading to an increasingly dual income structure that favored professionals, skilled labor, and property owners. Such conditions raised fears, especially among labor representatives, that job competition from immigrants would worsen conditions for the U.S. underclass. In such an atmosphere the "Simpson-Rodino" immigration bill (Immigration and Refugee Control Act) was finally passed in 1986.

Attempts at wage equalization can also be made by fiat. Rather than allowing wages to respond to competitive market forces, reflecting the marginal productivity of labor, government policies may decree domestic wage equalization. (Examples include minimum wage legislation, operative in both Mexico and the United States, where national minimums are set at sharply different levels, or the linking of wages between integrating regions—as in the case of the two Germanies, whereby East German wages were decreed to rise above current productivity levels in the direction of West German levels.) Migration barriers are imposed in efforts to maintain gaps between national wage levels and avoid downward convergence, usually by the high-wage market. Collective bargaining can also lead to the fiat establishment of industry-wide or skill-wide wage levels within a given economy.

Ultimately, however, the underlying forces of supply and demand (the availability of workers with given skills [supply], and the amount of investment that determines the productivity of labor [demand]) determine the range within which real wages can fall. Attempts to set wages above that range will lead to underemployment, inflation, loss of competitiveness, balance of payments problems, and devaluation. Attempts to set wages below that range will lead to circumvention of the formal labor market (including undocumented migration and the growth of informal sector employment), deflation, growth in competitiveness, and a revaluation of the exchange rate.

In the U.S.-Mexico situation, attempts to block the pattern of labor market integration increase pressures for capital movements from the United States to Mexico and exacerbate trade pressures between them, both of which will tend to bring about wage convergence. For Mexico this can be growth-enhancing, provided that the U.S. market is kept open to its exports. Convergence between the two countries, whether upward or downward, is beneficial to low-skilled Mexican workers. (Some U.S. and Mexican workers that previously shared the benefits of monopoly or oligopoly prices in the segmented labor markets of protected industries have already experienced falling real wages as a result of increased international openness and competition.) For the United States and Canada, however, only upward convergence is unequivocally acceptable from their social and political points of view. For this to occur, savings, investment, and skill-formation in the north must increase, to permit upward convergence in incomes even while markets are integrated with Mexico.

The distortions from fiat convergence can be ameliorated to some extent if the previously high-wage region sustains the real purchasing power of labor in the previously low-wage region through consumption subsidies paid for by increased taxation and the drawing down of international reserves. This has happened in the two Germanies as enormous fiscal transfers from West Germany (an estimated $100 billion dollars in the past year) have permitted Germans from the East to consume well above their current productivity levels and thereby preventing inflation from seriously eroding the level of real wages. Fiscal transfers from the United States to Puerto Rico (through Social Security and other benefits) have also helped to maintain some degree of wage parity between the two countries. Without such transfers, attempts at fiat wage convergence in the absence of productivity convergence will tend to be offset by price increases, underemployment, and emigration from the lower productivity economy. Where the two have separate trade and currency regimes, the latter will be forced to erode real wages through devaluation.

If the two economies are subject to arbitary real and monetary union by decree (as in Germany), fiat integration will put pressure on the high wage region, tending toward downward convergence in real wages and productivity that can only be offset by fiscal transfers and increased imports, with adverse consequences for the balance of payments. But for Germany and the rest of the European Community, a movement toward functional integration through the progressive liberalization of trade and migration policies and increased monetary cooperation have led to rising real wages at all skill levels. Much of Spain, Portugal, and other parts of southern Europe have experienced upward convergence in productivity and real wages through the increased efficiency and scale-economies of integration.

History has shown that labor productivity and wages can converge or diverge as markets integrate. The outcome will depend on a number of factors in both economies, including the pattern and rate of economic change, growth in the supply of labor, and its skill composition, as well as initial endowments of natural resources, capital, and the structure laws and institutions. Divergence can result (as, for example, between Mexico and the United States in the 1980s) if the lower wage economy is stagnating while the other is growing. Normally, however, increasing integration of markets will lead to some type of convergence. The underlying mechanism that drives convergence is the pattern of labor productivity growth. But the imposition of laws and institutions and the exercise of monopoly and monopsony power (seller and buyer concentration) in labor markets can lead to distortions in productivity and wages even for extended periods of time both within and between countries.

The object of a free trade agreement, such as NAFTA, is to increase the efficiency of production, competitiveness, output, and employment throughout the North American economy so as to incentivate additional investment in plant and equipment, infrastructure, human capital, and research and development. With respect to real wages, the socially acceptable goal must be upward convergence, with increases in productivity and wages for the United States and Canada along with even greater increases for Mexico. To the extent that the law of one price operates in the labor market, at least for labor of given skills, the achievement of upward convergence depends on rapid growth in investment, innovation, and productivity of *all* partners, along with the raising of skill levels (especially in the high-wage regions).

RENT-SEEKING AND THE PROCESS OF LABOR MARKET INTEGRATION

As two labor markets that are initially characterized by very different real wage levels for the same skills respond to the opportunity for greater freedom of trade and investment ties, there will be an opportunity for rent-seeking by those wishing to take advantage of the wage convergence process. (An economic *quasi rent* refers to a return over and above the competitive level, which in this case reflects the spread between cost and price faced by those in the low wage economy who are able to penetrate the high wage market. Such rents exist until prices are pushed down to the new level of marginal cost through competition.)

Migrants will be able to earn rents on the differential between wages at home and abroad, after allowing for the cost of job search—including the risk of migration and other transaction costs such as family disruption and dislocation. Investors will earn rents from shifting production from high- to low-wage locations, again net of transaction costs, at least until the law of one price establishes binational wage parity. While these "market penetration rents" are transitional, they can be very important for substantial periods of time, depending on the speed of labor market equilibration.

In other words, if labor skills of the two countries are in fact identical, so that productivity differences between them only reflect differences in investment per worker, it will be possible for market penetration rents to be earned from investments in response to wage differentials until the forces of competition that such rents engender lead to factor price equalization. Investors in the low-wage economy, with access to markets in the high-wage economy, will be able to reap the "market penetration" rents from adjustment to increased binational competition. Where they take the rents in accounting terms, either within the low-wage economy or through transfer pricing in the high-wage economy, will depend on the respective tax laws and regulations of the two countries. (There is always the danger that some of the rents will reflect the negative social exter-nalities of differential environmental, health, or occupational standards or their enforcement. If so, competitive market penetration rent-seeking will not necessarily lead to a social optimum. Under such circumstances both countries will need to find a mutually satisfactory harmonization of standards and their enforcement.)

In fact, much of the development of international competition in the postwar period has been driven by directly productive market-penetra-tion rent-seeking, focusing on the production of known technology goods and services, in response to differential labor market conditions. Labor market conditions, reflected in terms of "high" and "low" wages in this chapter, refer to much more than the direct payment of labor. They in-clude the entire panoply of labor legislation, union requirements, work rules, health, social security, retirement, job flexibility, and other benefits. Often rents can be earned where nominal wages are equal but labor flexi-bility is much greater in one market than another (this we have seen in the case of the "Third Italy Model" [of central and northeastern Italy], where small enterprises exhibit far greater flexibility in response to changing market conditions and product developments than large firms, even though wages are the same in response to national legislation).

Of course, such market-penetration rents will eventually disappear through competition as the process of adjustment is completed. But as some markets establish a new competitive equilibrium, new ones are al-ways opening up. In the meantime it is expected that unions will form to bargain with capital for a share of such rents. The dynamizing effect on investment of market penetration rent-seeking may be expected to stimu-late economic growth throughout the integrated economy. Although there will be "negative rents" in those sectors that are no longer com-petitive, as a result of falling prices and shifts in comparative advantages, new enterprises will be stimulated. (Negative rents are reflected in falling profits and reduced rent in the wage bill, which is characterized by a decline in wages toward competitive levels.)

Here we are dealing with the dynamics of the *process* of adjustment from a pre-integration equilibrium to a post-integration situation, driven by the force of labor market interdependence. The stimulus to investment from such adjustments, expectations, and feedback mechanisms are likely to be far more substantial in the case of North American integration than conventional comparative static analysis would suggest. The result will be a much greater likelihood of positive than negative convergence, provided there is maximum scope for new enterprise and skill formation both north and south.

CONCLUSIONS

The challenge of a North American Free Trade Agreement is to develop a transnational compact between labor and capital that will incentivate investment and innovation capable of increasing productivity growth while ensuring broad social participation in the gains. This is a difficult balance to achieve. Movements too far in either direction can lead to inefficiency, unemployment, instability, and disinvestment. Cooperation in the management of labor market interdependence, favoring restructuring and growth toward upward rather than downward convergence, will set a precedent for the Americas and the future of global integration.

The next step for policy research in this area is to examine the nature of the two labor markets in much greater detail as an interdependent phenomenon, subject to the changes that will be brought about by NAFTA and those which must come after NAFTA. In both countries regulations affecting wages, hours, and working conditions are highly sophisticated, although they do not yet reflect an awareness of the implications of harmonization (or its absence). Similar adjustment processes in other regions, including EC92, Eastern and Western Europe, and Asia and the Pacific Rim, need to be studied more vigorously for comparative insights.

The changing world economic situation will demand much greater flexibility than past responses to labor market conditions have offered. Enterprises must be able to adjust more rapidly than ever to the evolution of technology, product and process innovation, and the opening and closing of market niches. Buffers for market adjustment must not be created at the expense of the security of workers and their families. And adjustment must not be permitted to skirt the problem of negative environmental externalities, health and occupational hazards, or the improper treatment of any person, including women; ethnic, racial, or other minorities; or children.

The increased supply of labor being brought into the international market through integration raises new questions about labor's share in the gains from growth. It is increasingly important that the profit, interest, or rent components of such gains, which are not directly within the wage bill, become accessible to those providing labor services at all skill levels. This is required not only for reasons of social justice but in order to permit workers to improve their education and technical skills, broaden the scope for scale economies, and increase the rate of accumulation through expanded savings and investment. Funds reflecting social entitlements must become more effective sources of saving for productive investment and not simply private or public transfer payments (including sources of funding of current account deficits of the public sector and public enterprises).

The integration of labor markets in a more interdependent international system gives all a stake in the conditions of each economy. In this regard the fact of U.S.-Mexico labor market interdependence calls for policies that will ensure market flexibility with full employment and social security in the broadest sense. It is evident that upward convergence of wages for Mexico and the United States, for labor of similar skills, depends primarily on U.S. initiatives to restructure its own economy toward increased productivity and competitiveness. While such efforts are already under way, far more needs to be done to reverse the trend in real wages of the U.S. underclass.

A North American Free Trade Agreement will not alone elicit new public policy initiatives and private accumulation in the United States, both of which are needed to accomplish growth with equity. In a world of increasingly tight capital markets, we must pursue policies that will stimulate savings, investment, and skill formation, and thereby permit labor market integration to contribute toward a continent-wide response to the forces of productivity growth.

Index

In this index an "f" after a number indicates a separate reference on the next page, and an "ff" indicates separate references on the next two pages. A continuous discussion over two or more pages is indicated by a span of page numbers, e.g., "pp. 57–58." *Passim* is used for a cluster of references in close but not consecutive sequence.

Library of Congress Cataloging-in-Publication Data

U.S.-Mexico relations : labor market interdependence / edited by Jorge
A Bustamante, Clark W. Reynolds, and Raúl A. Hinojosa Ojeda.
  p.   cm.
  ISBN 0-8047-2020-7 (alk. paper) :
  1. Alien labor, Mexican–United States. 2. Mexicans–Employment–
United States. 3. Mexico–Emigration and Immigration. 4. United
States–Emigration and immigration. I. Bustamante, Jorge A.
II. Reynolds, Clark Winton. III. Hinojosa Ojeda, Raúl A.
IV. Title: U.S.-Mexico relations.
HD8081.M6U15   1992
331.6'272'073–dc20   91-42423
                                                                  CIP

⊗ This book is printed on acid-free paper